D0152769

The Imperfect Union

# The Imperfect Union

## CONSTITUTIONAL STRUCTURES OF GERMAN UNIFICATION

*PETER E. QUINT*

PRINCETON UNIVERSITY PRESS

PRINCETON, NEW JERSEY

KK5096
.Q56
1997

Copyright © 1997 by Princeton University Press
Published by Princeton University Press, 41 William Street, Princeton, New Jersey 08540
In the United Kingdom: Princeton University Press, Chichester, West Sussex
All Rights Reserved

---

Library of Congress Cataloging-in-Publication Data

Quint, Peter E.
The imperfect union : constitutional structures of German unification / Peter E. Quint.
p. cm.
Includes bibliographical references and index.
ISBN 0-691-08656-7 (alk. paper)
1. Germany (West)—Constitutional law. 2. Germany (East)—Constitutional law. 3. Germany—History—Unification, 1990. 4. German reunification question (1949–1990) I. Title.
KK5096.Q56 1996 342.43—dc21 96-39367

---

This book has been composed in Times Roman

The map of Germany in 1945 on page 2 is reprinted from *A History of Modern Germany* by Hajo Holborn. Copyright © 1959 by Hajo Holborn. Reprinted by permission of Alfred A. Knopf Inc.

Princeton University Press books are printed on acid-free paper and meet the guidelines for permanence and durability of the Committee on Production Guidelines for Book Longevity of the Council on Library Resources

Printed in the United States of America
by Princeton Academic Press

10 9 8 7 6 5 4 3 2 1

*TO THE MEMORY OF MY PARENTS*

---

EDWARD DAVID QUINT AND

FRANCES HIGER QUINT

MAR 10 1998

# *CONTENTS*

# PREFACE

THIS BOOK had its origins in a visit to Berlin in early January 1990, a few weeks after the opening of the Berlin Wall. At that point, German unification was still an uncertain prospect, and many East Germans thought that their country would continue on for some time as an independent state under a new democratic constitution. Those weeks were a period of great political excitement in eastern Germany, and it was a kind of civic education to visit highly charged meetings of new democratic organizations like New Forum and the Social Democrats (then known as the SDP), and to travel to Leipzig for one of the great Monday night demonstrations which, in past weeks, had toppled the East German regime.

For a teacher of constitutional law, this visit was also a chance to speak to political figures from across the emerging political spectrum in East Germany—as well as many other members of a newly liberated citizenry—about what they thought a new constitution should look like and what it should contain. The careful attention to difficult constitutional problems that was evident in those conversations made me skeptical of claims, later heard, that citizens of eastern Germany were somehow deficient in democratic or constitutional understanding.

When I returned to Berlin in the middle of March 1990, at the time of the first free East German election, the mood had changed considerably. By then, East German Prime Minister Modrow as well as Soviet President Gorbachev had acknowledged that German unification was inevitable. The results of the election on March 18 confirmed that view. But even so, a working group of the central Round Table was still completing its proposed draft constitution for the GDR. On that visit, I spent a day in an old villa at the edge of East Berlin, while the working group's editorial committee—with a West German advisor—put the finishing touches on parts of the constitutional draft. Again, the level of engagement and analysis was high, but in some ways these quixotic labors on a new GDR Constitution seemed to represent the last flicker of the reform movement of the previous autumn.

I returned to Berlin yet again in summer 1990, as the first State Treaty was about to go into effect. This agreement extended the western Deutsche-Mark to the east and began the official process of unification; the resulting changes were immediately apparent in the western consumer goods that appeared over a weekend in shop windows in downtown East Berlin. But even more profound changes were taking place in the lives of many East German citizens whom I had come to know over the course of these visits.

It was also clear that what had begun as an inquiry into the new constitutionalism of the GDR had turned into a project on the constitutional aspects of German unification. Because of the extraordinary pace of these changes, it seemed best to undertake this project in two stages: initially, an article seeking to analyze the constitutional developments as they appeared immediately after unification itself, to be followed by a broader assessment at a point when most of the constitutional issues seemed generally resolved.

An article representing the first step of this plan was published in the Maryland Law Review in 1991, under the title "The Constitutional Law of German Unification."* That article, accordingly, forms the starting point of the present volume. Yet the present work adds many new developments and new topics that were only vaguely perceived—if perceived at all—at the time of the earlier work. Indeed, even where parts of the earlier text have been included in the present volume, they have often been supplemented or rewritten to reflect what I hope is a deepened understanding of the problems that they addressed.

A large part of the original article was written at the Max Planck Institute for Comparative Public Law and International Law in Heidelberg in the summer of 1990, and I wish to express my gratitude to the directors, fellows, and staff of the institute for their encouragement and hospitality at that time as well as on many other occasions.

A substantial portion of the research and writing of this volume took place during the 1992–93 academic year when I was a fellow of the Wissenschaftskolleg zu Berlin (Institute for Advanced Study Berlin). During that year it was possible to interview individuals who had participated in the central events of German unification, as well as drafters of the new constitutions of the east German states and government officials who were actually carrying out the decisions of the Unification Treaty and related statutes. The Wissenschaftskolleg was unfailing in its support of this project and I wish to express my gratitude to its rector, Professor Wolf Lepenies, as well as to its extraordinary staff. I am also grateful to many of the other fellows of 1992–93 who were particularly interested in unification problems and were a great source of enlightenment on numerous issues: Peter Häberle, Christian Joerges, Wolfgang Schluchter, Hartmut Zwahr, Hans Nutzinger, and Barry Eichengreen. I am also indebted to friends and colleagues who read and commented on portions of the original article or the present manuscript: Mitchell Ash, Winfried Brugger, Mary Edsall, Thomas Giegerich, Peter Häberle, Eckart Klein, Jonathan Marwil, Alexander Reuter, William Reynolds, Paul Schwartz, Edward Tomlinson, Wolfgang Vitzthum, Günter Wilms. I learned much from their valuable comments, but I remain fully responsible for all positions taken here and for any errors of commission or omission.

I also wish to express my gratitude to the University of Maryland School of Law, its excellent library staff, and its deans, Michael J. Kelly and Donald G. Gifford, for their support of this project. Finally, I would like to thank the student research assistants who ably assisted this project over the years: Natalie Coley-Lawrence, Cherylle Corpuz, Joan Gavigan, Helmut Gerlach,

* 50 Maryland Law Review 475.

Nancy Hoffmann, Kristin Klein, Max Lapertosa, Renee Machi, Douglas Nash, Gerk Oberman, and Jonathan Siegel.

For extraordinary secretarial assistance, I am greatly indebted to Marilyn O'Neill of the University of Maryland School of Law, as well as Petra Sonnenberg and Elissa Linke at the Wissenschaftskolleg.

Because of the developing nature of the matters recounted in this volume, it should be noted that the manuscript was completed on September 1, 1995; events occurring thereafter could only be touched upon briefly, if at all.

The Imperfect Union

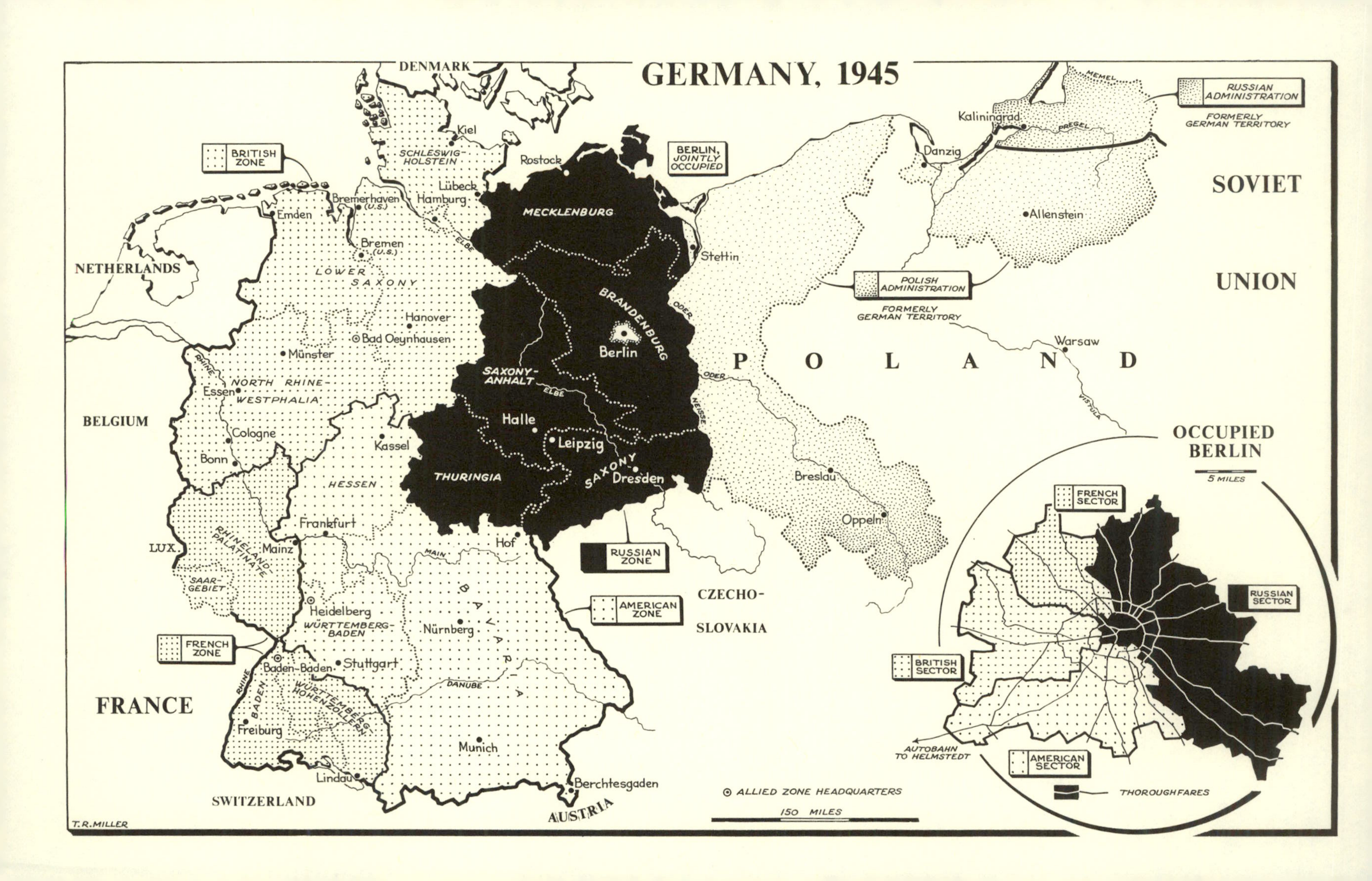
GERMANY, 1945
DENMARK
Kiel
SCHLESWIG-HOLSTEIN
Rostock
BERLIN, JOINTLY OCCUPIED
BRITISH ZONE
Lübeck
Hamburg
Bremerhaven (U.S.)
Emden
MECKLENBURG
ELBE
Bremen (U.S.)
NETHERLANDS
LOWER SAXONY
Stettin
Hanover
Bad Oeynhausen
BRANDENBURG
ODER
Berlin
Münster
RHINE
NORTH RHINE-WESTPHALIA
Essen
SAXONY-ANHALT
BELGIUM
Cologne
Halle
Leipzig
Kassel
Bonn
THURINGIA
SAXONY
Dresden
HESSEN
Frankfurt
Hof
LUX.
Mainz
RHINELAND-PALATINATE
MAIN
SAAR-GEBIET
RUSSIAN ZONE
BAVARIA
AMERICAN ZONE
Heidelberg
WÜRTTEMBERG-BADEN
Nürnberg
FRENCH ZONE
Baden-Baden
Stuttgart
DANUBE
FRANCE
BADEN
WÜRTTEMBERG-HOHENZOLLERN
Freiburg
Munich
Lindau
Berchtesgaden
SWITZERLAND
AUSTRIA
CZECHO-SLOVAKIA
Kaliningrad
MEMEL
PREGEL
RUSSIAN ADMINISTRATION
FORMERLY GERMAN TERRITORY
Danzig
SOVIET UNION
Allenstein
POLISH ADMINISTRATION
FORMERLY GERMAN TERRITORY
Warsaw
POLAND
VISTULA
NEISSE
Breslau
Oppeln
OCCUPIED BERLIN
5 MILES
FRENCH SECTOR
RUSSIAN SECTOR
BRITISH SECTOR
AUTOBAHN TO HELMSTEDT
AMERICAN SECTOR
THOROUGHFARES
ALLIED ZONE HEADQUARTERS
150 MILES
T. R. MILLER

CHAPTER 1

# Introduction

IN THE MIDSUMMER OF 1989 the German Democratic Republic—known as the GDR or East Germany—was an autocratic state led by an entrenched Communist Party, a loyal member of the Warsaw Pact and, in many ways, a haughty counterpart of the Federal Republic of Germany (West Germany), which it confronted with a mixture of hostility and grudging accommodation across the divide created by the Cold War. Over the following year and a half, a dramatic process of change transformed the political system of East Germany and culminated in the GDR's "accession" to the Federal Republic itself. At the same time, the division of Europe, which the division of Germany came to symbolize, had largely ceased to exist. Yet the end of Germany's division evoked its own new and very bitter problems.

Indeed, viewed as a social and economic process, German unification was by no means completed when the GDR acceded to the Federal Republic on October 3, 1990. The two economic systems remained distinctly—even startlingly—different, and the sharp psychic divisions of four decades, which some Germans referred to as the "wall in the head," seemed likely to divide the two regions for years to come. Radically different social structures, as well as quite dissimilar personal histories, continued to divide the citizens of United Germany, and mutual suspicion and distrust perpetuated a high degree of social segregation of the two groups, even in areas like Berlin where they lived in close proximity.

The unification of October 3, therefore, represented primarily an achievement in the realm of politics and law—the culmination of a series of agreements and legislative provisions developed within a highly articulated constitutional framework that was drafted more than forty years ago with such an occurrence in mind. In the rapid events of 1989–90, the legal and constitutional development seemed to be one aspect of the process of unification that—unlike more unruly economic and social phenomena—was subject to a measure of deliberation and rational control.

The constitutional structure that emerged reflected both anxiety and optimism; its drafters sought to diminish baneful legacies of the past while opening opportunities for future social, political, and economic development. Yet like most great constituent acts, it also reflected the weight of political interests and the dominance of some interests over others. Indeed, as the process of unification developed, the main actors in the process adopted an overall strategy for unification that could be seen as growing out of the West German constitutional tradition itself. First, a method of unification was chosen through which eastern Germany would "join" or "accede to" the Federal Republic. The result would not be a new nation, but rather an expansion of the constitutional structures of the Federal Republic itself. This fundamental constitutional decision was accompanied by what often seemed to be an attempt to extend the social, economic, and political structures of the west to the east with as little alteration as possible. Indeed, in some cases, this theoretical construct took extended forms, and it sometimes seemed that the east would not only receive western structures but would also be treated as though it had always belonged to the west—a view that also had roots in western constitutional tradition—with the result that certain past actions in the east would be treated as invalid or would to some extent be punished or undone.

Yet it is a fundamental mistake to view all of the "western" structures that were now being extended to the east as the product of a monolithic western consensus. Indeed, in a number of instances, the prevailing "western" structures reflected a conservative tradition that was itself highly debated in the west. This tradition was most fully represented in the positions of the prevailing coalition partners, the CDU/CSU; in its emphasis on market economics, support of institutions such as the civil service and the army, and resistance to social change in family structures and related matters, this tradition had roots in past decades or centuries. But in the modern Federal Republic, several aspects of this tradition had only narrowly prevailed over less conservative views typically held by the Social Democratic Party (SPD) and some other groups. In a number of cases, therefore, the extension of "western" structures to the east was actually the extension of structures that were vigorously debated—and by no means completely secure—in the west itself.

In the same way, of course, it is also a mistake to consider the "east" as possessing a single set of views and institutions that were being replaced through unification. Although the views and institutions that prevailed until the autumn of 1989 reflected the hard-line positions of the SED —the East German Communist Party—the reform movement of 1989–90 gave rise to a set of democratic views that were quite different from the doctrine of the SED.

Indeed, the ideas of the reform groups of the east were in many ways rather close to the views of the western SPD. To a significant extent, therefore, the attempt to impose aspects of a conservative tradition in the east faced some significant opposition in the west as well. Indeed, in a number of cases, the imposition of "western" ideas on the east reanimated political and ideological struggles that had taken part within West Germany itself over the past decades—this time against the special background of the history of the GDR. Accordingly, one of the main questions arising upon German unification—a question that will be traced in various contexts in the chapters to follow—is the extent to which these traditional ideas have prevailed, and are likely to continue to prevail, against continuing opposition of the western SPD and at least a part of the reform tradition arising in the east. The converse question, of course, is the extent to which the current prevalence of those views in the west itself is unstable and destined eventually to disappear or be modified in both east and west as a result of unification.

Yet the imposition of traditional forms upon unification seems to have occurred primarily in domestic affairs. The effect of unification on foreign affairs reveals a somewhat different picture. The framers of unification feared that the specter of a significantly enlarged Germany in the middle of Europe would evoke old European anxieties. Accordingly, they sought to embed the new united Germany even more deeply in the European political, economic, and military system—with a concurrent further relaxation of German sovereignty. Certainly these goals in foreign affairs could be seen as the outgrowth of constitutional ideas of the Basic Law, which from the beginning of the Federal Republic sought to place Germany in the context of developments toward a united Europe; moreover, from a political perspective, the emphasis on European structures recalled positions supported by Konrad Adenauer at the beginning of the Federal Republic. Yet, this increased emphasis on internationalism seemed inconsistent with certain traditional conservative views that stressed sovereignty and self-assertion in foreign affairs.

As a whole, therefore, the constitutional structures of German unification implicate two sets of developments that seem to exhibit some degree of tension. On the internal questions of unification, the western government sought to impose the ideas and institutions of a relatively conservative western tradition on the east. In the international realm, in contrast, the government attempted to mitigate the traditional conservative idea of strong sovereignty by seeking to dissolve aspects of German sovereignty in wider European institutions.

The framers of unification pursued both of these goals—the internal and the external goals—with great vigor. Particularly the internal goal of reproducing western structures in the east was advanced with a high degree of perfectionism. But theoretical legal and constitutional conceptions—being the product of an inevitable process of simplication—often encounter severe difficulties when confronted with a reality more complex and unpredictable than any conceptual system is likely to accommodate. Thus, the constitutional story of German unification is not only the story of the attempted formation and extension of these structures, but also the story of the problems that they have evoked—problems that have often been increased by the incompatibility of these structures and reality.

One particular deviation of constitutional theory from reality deserves special mention. As one of its basic premises, West German constitutional theory viewed the Federal Republic and the GDR as parts of the same German political community. The psychological internalization of this political and constitutional theory may have contributed significantly to the unifiers' deeply held belief that—being essentially parts of the same "nation," in their view—the two German states could be unified without overwhelming social and economic problems. In this way, the framers of unification profoundly underestimated the social differences that had evolved in forty years of quite extreme separation and disparate development. As a result, the problems that already existed were probably compounded and deepened by the results of this inaccurate perception.

In a number of interesting instances, however, the German governmental system seems to have developed a form of corrective mechanism. The German judiciary—and particularly the Federal Constitutional Court—has frequently employed constitutional doctrines, in a mediating fashion, to mitigate some of the severity of the measures and solutions chosen principally by the western political forces. Thus the courts have also established themselves as major participants in the continuing process of "inner unification."

The following chapters portray the major events of German unification from the constitutional perspective. In this analysis, the "constitution" will be understood in a broad sense—including not only the interpretation of constitutional texts by courts, scholars, and governments, but also extending to important international arrangements that help define the nature of a state, as well as certain central statutes, regulations, and practices that give concrete meaning to the underlying principles of a political system. Of course, even as broadly defined, the constitutional and legal themes form only one aspect of a complex historical process—and in many cases, perhaps, not even the most important aspect at that. Yet in a process like that of German unification, which was viewed by all of its participants as intimately connected with principles of legality and the rule of law, an understanding of the constitutional and legal aspects can be important, indeed perhaps essential, for an understanding of the broader economic, political, and social developments.

The following volume is divided into three parts. Part I traces constitutional developments in eastern Germany—and the development of an eastern constitutional consciousness—from the revolution of 1989 up to the point of unification, and then beyond to the constitutional debates of the new east German states. Part II examines the complex constitutional issues raised by the Unification Treaty and its attempt to re-create western structures in the east—or even to undo the past—in a number of important areas. Part III then shifts to the external aspects of unification and the process through which the western government, while seeking to extend traditional structures within united Germany, simultaneously sought to dissolve a strong German sovereignty externally in the broader structures of the European Union and the Atlantic Alliance.

# PART I

## From Revolution to Accession: Constitutional Change in Eastern Germany

CHAPTER 2

# The Background of German Unification

## Union and Disunion in German History

Unification is one of the great themes of modern German history. Unlike England and France—which had formed unified nation-states in the Middle Ages—Germany came into the nineteenth century as a variegated collection of kingdoms, duchies, city-states, and other principalities, loosely held together in the political league of the Holy Roman Empire. The empire was dissolved in 1806 at Napoleon's order and, following the Congress of Vienna and Napoleon's final defeat in 1815, the "Germanic Confederation" arose in its place. Like the Holy Roman Empire, however, this was more in the nature of a treaty community (*Staatenbund*) than any sort of real political union. But the confederation and the contemporaneous Customs Union were steps in that direction.

In the early nineteenth century—in sharp contrast with twentieth century movements—political progressivism and nationalism were often allied in Germany. A first attempt at an all-German constitution was the Paul's Church Constitution of 1849, drafted under the impetus of the 1848 Revolution. Although this document never went into effect, it exerted a profound influence on later democratic constitutions in Germany. The Paul's Church Constitution reflected the view that basic rights and a measure of popular control could be more readily expected from a unified Germany than from the absolutist monarchs and princes who controlled most of the smaller political subdivisions. Yet when unity did finally come in 1871, it was not the result of progressive or popular movements but rather the product of unification from above, through war and Bismarck's political finesse. The German Empire formed by Bismarck under Prussian control in 1871 excluded Austria, thus reflecting the "small" German solution. Yet the political structure of Bismarck's German Empire extended far to the east—beyond the East Prussian city of Königsberg (now Kaliningrad) in the north, and as far as Silesia in the southeast and the newly annexed provinces of Alsace and Lorraine (including Straßburg) in the west. This broad empire dominated central Europe politically, militarily, and economically from 1871 until 1918.

With the end of World War I, however, the dismemberment of Bismarck's ill-fated empire began. In the Treaty of Versailles, a large section of eastern Germany was detached in order to form part of the newly refounded state of Poland; indeed, the treaty returned to Poland much of the territory that had been seized by Prussia in the Polish "partition" of the late eighteenth century. Part of this formerly German territory constituted the "Polish Corridor," which gave Poland access to the Baltic Sea. Even after World War I, however, substantial territory east of the Oder and Neiße Rivers remained within the German Empire, including not only Silesia and parts of Brandenburg and Pomerania, but also part of East Prussia east of the Polish Corridor.

The end of World War II resulted in further contraction of the territories of Germany. Although Germany and the Soviet Union had signed a nonaggression pact in August of 1939 (a pact that led to the invasion of Poland), German forces attacked the Soviet Union in June 1941. The German armies penetrated deeply and almost entered Moscow, but after the crucial battle of Stalingrad in 1943 they were rolled back beyond their own borders, until the Soviet and western armies met on the Elbe River in the spring of 1945. At the end of the war, therefore, the Red Army occupied much of the eastern part of Germany, and the Soviet Union annexed the northern part of East Prussia, including the territory around Königsberg. At the same time, the Soviet Union also annexed territory in the eastern part of Poland lying on the Russian side of the so-called "Curzon Line."

In order to compensate Poland for this loss, the Soviet Union argued at the Yalta and Potsdam Conferences that all German territory east of a line formed by the Oder and Western Neiße Rivers should be transferred to Poland. At Potsdam the English prime minister and the American president were unwilling to agree that this territory should be permanently transferred to Poland but did provide that it would remain under Polish administration pending a final resolution to be adopted in a peace treaty.[1] The peace conference contemplated at Potsdam was never held, and the territory east of the Oder-Neiße line—which as a practical matter was soon treated as a part of Poland—remained a constant problem of postwar German politics. This shifting of borders was accompanied by the expulsion or flight of millions of German-speaking people toward the west.

While these border adjustments were being made, the victorious Allies, meeting at the Yalta and Potsdam Conferences, divided German territory into zones of occupation—a Russian zone in the east and an American and a British zone in the west. Subsequently, the two western zones were further subdivided, and a portion was placed under control of the French government.[2]

Thus, beginning with the "unified" empire of Bismarck's time extending from Straßburg to Memel, German territory was first substantially contracted at the end of World War I and again at the end of World War II—although part of the latter contraction may have been in theory provisional only. Moreover, the remaining German territory was divided into four occupation zones.

At Potsdam, the Allies contemplated that the four occupation zones would be administered in a cooperative manner and that Germany would eventually coalesce into a single political unit. Although the advent of the Cold War and bitterly hostile relations between the Soviet Union and the west prevented accomplishment of this plan, the western Allies continued to support the principle of German unification. In this sense, however, "unification" was not intended to include any of the territories transferred from Germany at the end of World War I or, most likely, the Oder-Neiße territories placed under Polish administration at Potsdam—although the latter territories did play some role. Rather, the question of German unification referred to the proposed consolidation of the two German states created from the occupation zones at the end of World War II.

## The Legal Status of Germany, 1945–1989

Contrary to the apparent intentions at Yalta and Potsdam, the early political unification of the postwar occupation zones did not occur. Rather, as a result of irreconcilable political differences between east and west—differences that led to an independent western currency reform and the Soviet blockade of Berlin—two separate states were created in the remaining territory of Germany in 1949. The territory of the three western occupation zones coalesced to form the Federal Republic of Germany, under a Basic Law (constitution) adopted in May 1949. Shortly thereafter, the Soviet occupation zone was reestablished as the German Democratic Republic (GDR), also under a constitution adopted in 1949.[3] Although there was some measure of agreement at the outset, these two states came to take quite different views on the central question of the legal status of Germany.

### *The Cold War and the Status of Germany: The View from the West*

As a matter of theory, the framers had originally viewed the West German Basic Law as a temporary or provisional document, pending subsequent unification with the territory in the east. Indeed, the Basic Law looked both to the past and the future. On the one hand, its framers were profoundly concerned to prevent any repetition of the Nazi era and to avoid the weaknesses of the Weimar Constitution that may have impaired the durability of its democratic system; in this respect the framers of the Basic Law directed much of their attention to the problems of the past.[4] On the other hand, the framers looked forward to the time of unification, when the Basic Law might be replaced by a new and perhaps more perfect instrument. In this respect, the Basic Law of 1949 does seem to reflect an almost utopian sense that, with unification and the adoption of a new all-German constitution, Germany might throw off the fetters of the past and again assume its role in the structure of Europe.

Under the prevailing constitutional doctrine, therefore, the West German government was required to work to achieve unification. A number of provisions of the Basic Law could be invoked for this position. The preamble, for example, stated that the "German people remain challenged to achieve the unity and freedom of Germany in free self-determination" and specifically referred to the Basic Law as providing a constitutional order "for a transitional period." Moreover, article 23 contemplated the possibility that "other parts" of Germany would join the Federal Republic, and article 146 provided that the Basic Law would lose its effectiveness when a constitution "chosen by the

German people in a free decision" came into effect. Furthermore, according to article 116, the term "German" was defined to include persons living in the GDR, among others. Although the Basic Law did not purport to be effective outside of the borders of the Federal Republic, all "Germans," including residents of the GDR, could claim rights under the Basic Law as soon as they came within the territory covered by the document.[5]

The constitutional theory that supported the Federal Republic's position on unification may have been subject to conceptual and historical problems, but it was a view that was accepted (in part at least) by the western Allies.[6] According to this view, the "German Reich" never ceased to exist as a single state at the end of World War II. The "Reich" maintained this ghostly existence because, at the end of the war, only the German Army (and not the government) officially surrendered to the Allied forces;[7] moreover, the Allies made clear in the Berlin Declaration of June 1945 that by their occupation they did not intend to annex German territory. According to this theory, the founding of the Federal Republic was not the creation of a new West German state, but rather the "reorganization" of a part of the still-existing "German Reich." Indeed, the Federal Republic was identical with the "German Reich" although—and here the theory rested on a distinction of some metaphysical subtlety—its actual practical power extended only over a part of the territory and population of the "Reich." Since the Federal Republic was the only legitimate, democratically organized state on that former territory, it bore a degree of responsibility for all Germans, including those who resided beyond the reach of the Basic Law. In any event, the Federal Republic was constitutionally required to seek unification with the other parts of that territory.[8]

Under this theory the Federal Republic at first refused to grant any form of recognition to the GDR as a state and, in accordance with the so-called "Hallstein Doctrine" of the mid-1950s, threatened to break diplomatic relations with any third government—other than the Soviet Union—that recognized the GDR.[9] In response, the GDR labored vigorously to achieve the recognition and respect of other nations, particularly those in the west. In the early Cold War period, the governments of the western Allies generally supported the position of the Federal Republic in this dispute.[10]

Meanwhile, in a treaty that took effect in 1955, the western Allies returned to the Federal Republic much of the sovereignty that they had exercised during the occupation.[11] In a related step, the Federal Republic entered NATO, the western military alliance. At approximately the same time, the Soviet Union also returned a degree of sovereignty to the GDR, and the GDR joined the eastern military pact. These events were accompanied by particularly bitter ideological tensions.

### *The Cold War and the Status of Germany: The View from the East*

The views of the Soviet Union and the GDR on the legal status of Germany developed in a somewhat different manner. At the outset, the eastern position resembled that of the west in viewing the two German states as part of a single larger entity, or at least as seeing unification (as contemplated by the Potsdam agreement) as an ultimate goal.[12] During this early period, the east presumably foresaw the possibility of unification under its own political terms—and perhaps also doubted that the GDR could ultimately survive on its own. In a famous note in 1952 Stalin proposed the creation of a unified but neutral German state, a somewhat opaque proposition that was rejected by the western Allies and the West German government of Konrad Adenauer.[13]

In the mid-1950s, however, the Federal Republic became a member of the western military alliance, and the eastern position changed so that the Federal Republic and the GDR were now viewed as two separate, independent states.[14] The new theory of two German states was ultimately reflected in changes in the constitution of East Germany. Although the GDR Constitution of 1949 was originally intended as an all-German constitution, a revised constitution of 1968, as further amended in 1974, deleted all national references and, in unambiguous passages, declared a close, "irrevocable" relationship between the GDR and the Soviet Union.[15]

Thus by the mid-1950s, the governments of the Federal Republic and the GDR maintained inconsistent and irreconcilable positions on the question of the legal status of Germany. The Federal Republic asserted the view that there was a single continuing "German Reich" and that, in some sense, the Federal Republic represented that entire "Reich." In contrast, the GDR maintained that there were now two entirely separate German states. During this period of the deep Cold War, the two German states possessed no formal diplomatic relations and their informal relations were characterized by sharp public attacks and a certain amount of necessary quiet cooperation.[16] Indeed, public hostility was further exacerbated in 1961 when the eastern government closed the border and erected the Berlin Wall which stopped the flow of citizens out of the GDR and suspended normal traffic between east and west. The building of the Wall—which, according to the GDR government was an "anti-fascist protective" measure[17]—was followed by a decisive inward turning of the GDR regime, away from possible accommodation and unification and toward a more exclusive focus on its own internal problems.[18]

## *Ostpolitik and the Basic Treaty*

The period of unrelieved mutual hostility came to an end in the early 1970s when the Social Democratic government of Willy Brandt adopted a new eastern policy (*Ostpolitik*), which included relaxed relations with the countries of the east bloc and seemed to reflect a spirit of accommodation with the regime that apparently had been stabilized by the building of the Wall. In addition to agreements with Poland and the Soviet Union, the Brandt government entered into the "Basic Treaty" with the GDR, with the intention of achieving closer relations and solving certain urgent problems such as those relating to traffic to and from Berlin. This treaty could well have been viewed as a rejection of the theory that the Federal Republic was acting for all of a continuing "German Reich," because it seemed to acknowledge the GDR as a separate political entity. Indeed, the treaty and its ratifying statute were challenged on those grounds in the Constitutional Court of the Federal Republic of Germany.[19]

The Court ultimately upheld the treaty, but interpreted it in a very narrow manner that firmly reasserted the theory of the continuing "German Reich." In so doing, the Court's opinion may have significantly limited the benefits and opportunities for cooperation that the Brandt government hoped would flow from the treaty.[20] Yet even the Constitutional Court seemed to acknowledge the reality of the German Democratic Republic as a separate state and confirmed the legal effectiveness of its constitution.[21] The ultimate effect of the treaty was perhaps best captured in a remark by Egon Bahr, the chief theorist of Brandt's Ostpolitik: "Earlier we had no relationship at all; now at least we have a bad relationship."[22] Yet, notwithstanding the tenuousness of these new contacts, other western countries took the Basic Treaty as a sign that they could now enter into diplomatic relations with the GDR. Consequently, sixty-eight nations including France, Italy, and Great Britain, recognized the GDR in the year following the initialing of the Basic Treaty.[23]

In 1975, thirty-five nations, including both German states, signed the Helsinki Final Act of the Conference on Security and Cooperation in Europe. Because this document confirmed the existing borders of Europe, it was viewed by the East German regime as constituting final international recognition of the legitimacy of the GDR. Yet, in another sense, the Helsinki accord can be viewed as a starting point for the ultimate dissolution of the East German state. By signing the Helsinki Final Act, the regime acknowledged the human rights guarantees that formed an important aspect of the document and, in so doing, strengthened and encouraged the embryonic opposition movement in the GDR.[24]

In 1987 the Federal Republic took a further step toward practical recognition of the East German state when GDR leader Erich Honecker was welcomed effusively by western politicians on an official visit to the Federal Republic. In a contemporaneous attempt at further rapprochement, members of the western Social Democratic Party (SPD) met with members of the eastern SED and drafted a joint document setting forth principles for peaceful cooperation; the Social Democrats hoped that this effort would lead to reform in the GDR.[25]

But these occasional signs of closer cooperation were sporadic and often overlayed with considerable ambivalence. In general, the two states continued to maintain an uneasy relationship of mixed hostility and accommodation until the revolutionary events of autumn 1989 in the GDR.

CHAPTER 3

# Political Revolution in the GDR, 1989–1990

FROM THE beginning days of the Soviet Occupation Zone and the GDR, emigration to the western part of Germany had been a continuing problem for the eastern authorities. The pace of emigration often reflected economic conditions, diminishing during periods of prosperity in the GDR and increasing in times of economic difficulty, although political factors also played a role.

In 1961, during a period of increased emigration, the East German government (with the agreement of the Warsaw Pact leaders) had closed the border of East Germany and built the wall separating East and West Berlin.[1] From that point on, travel to the west was a forbidden dream for most citizens of the GDR. With the exception of the "travel cadre"—a small number of officials and scholars who were viewed as important or reliable enough to be allowed to leave the country for short periods—only those who had reached retirement age were ordinarily allowed to travel because their loss would no longer impair the productive capacity of the nation.[2]

During the tenure of Communist Party chief Erich Honecker (1971–89), the government of the GDR was maintained by physical barriers and by an elaborate system of internal security measures operated primarily by the notorious Ministry for State Security (Stasi). A series of government sponsored organizations—the Pioneers and Free German Youth (FDJ) for children, and the consolidated labor union (FDGB) and the Communist Party itself for adults—sought to encourage a "positive attitude" toward the state.[3] Behind this apparatus lay the power of the Soviet Army which had demonstrated in Czechoslovakia in 1968 that significant liberalization of the existing system would not be tolerated.

In retrospect, it seems clear that the advent of Gorbachev's policies of perestroika and glasnost led to the downfall of the Honecker regime, although the GDR government—unlike some of its east bloc allies—held out to the bitter end against these reforms.[4] The state system could be fatally impaired by a massive outflow of citizens, and the GDR was dependent on its Warsaw Pact neighbors to do their part in keeping the population of the GDR within the boundaries of the east bloc. But under the impact of Gorbachev's reforms, the Warsaw Pact nations—and the Soviet Union itself—no longer remained reliable guarantors of the borders of the GDR, and the power of the regime over its citizens quickly disintegrated.[5]

In 1989, the government of Hungary, which along with Poland had sought most fully to adopt the new Soviet policies, refused to maintain its closed border with Austria.[6] As early as May, part of the wire fence along the Hungarian border had been dismantled, and by the end of August thousands of citizens of the GDR (who generally had been permitted to travel to Hungary and other east bloc countries) had made their way into Austria.[7] During the same period, hundreds of GDR citizens sought refuge in the Federal Republic's embassies in Prague, Budapest, and Warsaw, and in desperation the GDR agreed to permit citizens in the embassy in Prague to travel through the GDR into the Federal Republic in sealed trains.[8] But when refugee trains passed through the main station in Dresden on the evening of October 4, thousands of persons who had come from throughout the GDR stormed the station, desperately seeking to join this flight to the west. For some, this extraordinary scene—making clear to all that a desperate wish to leave the GDR was very widely held—marked the clear beginning of the East German revolution.[9]

In the GDR, meanwhile, there were stirrings of organized political opposition. Although many sought to leave, others were determined to stay and reform the GDR itself. The "decisive breakthrough" came in September with the founding of the first opposition group, New Forum,[10] followed shortly thereafter by other reform groups, Democracy Now[11] and Democratic Awakening. While some groups, such as Democratic Awakening, considered themselves political parties, New Forum sought to constitute itself as a more informal citizens movement (*Bürgerbewegung*), a political form that played an important role in the East German revolution.[12] From the beginning, these new groups called upon the government to give substance to the long-neglected guarantees of free speech and association in the GDR Constitution.

Also in September, regular Monday night demonstrations began to take place in Leipzig after prayer meetings in the Nikolai Church, which had become a center of organized opposition. In the coming months these demonstrations would grow to enormous size—with hundreds of thousands of participants—and would become a central factor in the political life of the GDR.[13] These demonstrations had an immense liberating effect on the thousands who participated. "There were tears in my eyes," reported one demonstrator; "I did not feel left alone; we learned to stand upright. . . . The spell—fear of the Stasi—was broken."[14] Although these demonstrations could possibly have been put down by force, the GDR regime—perhaps sensing its own political weakness—ultimately stayed its hand.[15]

These developments were accompanied by the beginnings of reform in the former "bloc parties"—groups that had been founded in the immediate postwar period and had been permitted to continue in existence as docile adjuncts of the Communist Party (SED) government. These bloc parties included the CDU (Christian Democrats), LDPD (Liberals), NDPD (National Democrats), and the German Farmers Party. Moreover, in October 1989, a new Social Democratic Party (SDP, later SPD) was founded in East Germany, replacing the former SPD that had merged with the Communist Party in the east to form the SED in 1946.

On October 7, in the course of these great changes, the GDR celebrated the fortieth anniversary of its founding. Notwithstanding tight security measures, many citizens of the GDR engaged in protest demonstrations, which were brutally suppressed by police.[16] Arriving at the celebration, Gorbachev warned Honecker that "life will punish those who come too late," and his delegation made clear that the GDR could expect no Soviet military help in repressing reforms.[17]

In the face of the continued departure of thousands of citizens and massive anti-government demonstrations in Leipzig, Erich Honecker was replaced on October 18 as general secretary of the Central Committee of the Communist Party, a post that he had held since 1971.[18] His successor was Egon Krenz, an old-line party functionary who sought to mollify the population by immediately announcing relaxed travel policies for citizens of the GDR. Yet his years of involvement in the GDR system prevented Krenz from understanding that a fundamental political transformation was necessary in place of piecemeal reforms.[19]

On November 4, a huge demonstration of 500,000 people in Berlin seemed to mark a clear turning point in the history of the GDR. Addressing the demonstration, civil rights leaders called for an amendment of the GDR Constitution that would reject the leading role of the Communist Party. Old-line party functionaries like Günter Schabowski and Markus Wolf, who attempted to present themselves as reformers, were subject to deafening catcalls and whistles of disapproval. Artists demanded a new media law that would permit freedom of communication in newspapers and films, and the free-speech guarantees of the GDR Constitution were repeatedly invoked. The venerable author Stefan Heym, introduced as the Nestor of the GDR protest movement, proposed a new democratic socialism—a call that was echoed by the GDR's most famous novelist, Christa Wolf. ("Imagine it is socialism and no one goes away.") Indeed, this meeting was later referred to as a "short, wonderful moment of unity between the left-intellegentsia and the people."[20] But others interpreted the meeting somewhat differently, asserting that it was at this point that the GDR populace took the state power into its hands and finally discredited the SED.[21]

On the evening of November 9, the government of the GDR opened the Wall, precipitating historic scenes of jubilation in Berlin. In an indication of increasing disarray in the east bloc, the GDR apparently took this crucial step without consulting the Soviet Union[22] and, indeed, the precise manner in which this decision was made remains obscure.[23] Shortly thereafter, numerous additional border crossings were opened.

On November 13, Hans Modrow, who had established his reputation as a Communist Party reformer in Dresden, was elected prime minister by the Volkskammer, the East German parliament.[24] Recognizing that fundamental change had become inevitable in the GDR, and that the change would have to come through constitutional amendment, the Volkskammer also established a committee to undertake constitutional reform.

Hans Modrow was an interesting transitional figure.[25] A party functionary since 1960, he possessed a conventional history for a high SED official, including study at an "anti-fascist school" as a prisoner of war in the USSR and further study at the Komsomol School in Moscow. After years as an officer of the Communist Party youth group (FDJ) and as a party official in Berlin, he became head of the "Agitation" section of the party central committee, and in 1973 he became party leader in Dresden.[26] Yet, from an early point, his critical and pessimistic view of economic developments in the GDR—as well as his cooperation with citizens' groups in Dresden in 1989—had given him a reputation as a reformer in the SED.[27]

Modrow's acceptance speech (*Regierungserklärung*) as prime minister in the Volkskammer illustrates his transitional nature. Although the speech emphasized the necessity of economic and political reform, Modrow also clearly declared that the GDR would continue to be a socialist state. Modrow's speech also reaffirmed the GDR's close political and economic ties with the Soviet Union and other countries of the east bloc. Yet, in a passage that seemed to look in a different direction, Modrow announced his government's readiness to enter into a "treaty community" with the Federal Republic.[28]

Modrow is sometimes credited with an important role in preserving peace during the East German revolution, but other aspects of his tenure were deeply problematic. During this period, for example, luxurious villas in the East were sold to party and government officials at bargain prices;[29] and judges and other governmental officials were allowed access to their personnel files with the result that they had an opportunity to remove incriminating information from the dossiers.[30] Moreover, Modrow's own involvement in the falsification of local GDR election returns in May 1989 would later return to haunt him.[31]

The government of the Federal Republic had been carefully observing the dramatic events in the east, and on November 28 Chancellor Kohl proposed a ten-point plan for cooperation between the two German states.[32] Welcoming the proposal for a "treaty community" put forth by Prime Minister Modrow in his acceptance speech, Kohl went further to propose a confederation with unification as the ultimate goal. Before such steps could be taken, however, Kohl insisted on basic reforms in the political and economic system of the GDR.

At the same time a great popular outcry arose in the GDR over revelations of the luxurious villas and hoards of western consumer goods enjoyed by former leading members of the SED and government. These revelations evoked bitterness in a population for whom the propagation of socialist equality had been a constant political theme. The widespread nature of this corruption also confirmed the observation, often noted in the west, that systematic privileges for party functionaries (graduated according to rank) were an important characteristic of a Stalinist political system.[33]

At the beginning of December, reform in the GDR accelerated swiftly. The Volkskammer amended the 1974 constitution to delete the reference to the leading role of the Communist Party. This was the first in a series of constitutional changes that were to characterize the events of 1989–90 as a "legalistic" revolution, transforming society and government through revised legal norms rather than a resort to violence.[34] In a parallel act that rejected Soviet hegemony in foreign affairs, the Volkskammer voted to apologize for the GDR's participation in the invasion of Czechoslovakia in 1968. These changes were also reflected in internal politics. Reformer Gregor Gysi replaced Egon Krenz as leader of the SED,[35] and the CDU and other parties left the "Democratic Bloc," which had faithfully supported the Communist Party for forty years.[36]

On December 7, a "Round Table" composed of seven opposition groups, as well as the SED and the former bloc parties, began its deliberations as an unofficial but extremely influential organ exercising a degree of practical control over the actions of the government.[37] This step was a political necessity: a new GDR government could not be elected immediately, but the existing government created by the SED had been completely discredited. Possessing a temporary legitimacy founded on mass political action, the GDR Round Table followed similar precedents in Hungary, Poland, and Czechoslovakia, where opposition and government groups formed Round Table conferences to undertake political and constitutional reform.[38] The first act of the central Round Table, after setting forth procedures for its agenda, was to establish a committee to draft a proposed new constitution for the GDR. The primacy of this act emphasized the constitutional or legalistic preoccupations of the GDR reformers.

In the middle of December the government announced that the hated Office for National Security (successor to the Stasi) would be dissolved, but the actual process of dissolution was a slow one. On January 15, a demonstration called by the citizens group New Forum turned into a tumultuous scene as thousands of protestors stormed into the central Stasi office in the Normannenstrasse in Berlin. As a result of this event, a citizens committee was formed to keep watch over the central Stasi files and prevent tampering or destruction—a development that paralleled the establishment of citizens committees for the same purpose at other Stasi offices throughout the country.[39]

Although Kohl and Modrow began to hold discussions on a proposed "treaty community," calls for actual unification of the two countries intensified in popular demonstrations in Leipzig and other cities. Yet in December and January there still seemed to be a substantial possibility that the GDR would continue—for some time at least—as an independent country. Accordingly, numerous local groups, often composed of representatives of the reform groups and political parties, began to work on drafts of a new democratic constitution for the GDR to be submitted as proposals to the Round Table's constitutional drafting committee. The most frequently mentioned constitutional reforms included re-creation of the historical states of the GDR, establishment of a constitutional court and actual judicial review, insulation of the independence of the judiciary, and some mixture of private and socialist property.[40]

The tide turned away from a possible continuation of the GDR at the beginning of February, however, when Prime Minister Modrow acknowledged the likelihood and desirability of unification with the Federal Republic.[41] Meeting with Chancellor Kohl in Moscow, Soviet President Gorbachev also conceded the likelihood of unification and seemed not to raise serious objections to such a goal in principle, although a number of specific reservations no doubt remained;[42] the desperate economic and political situation in the GDR had most likely played a role in changing Gorbachev's mind.[43]

In light of a continued stream of emigration and a sharpening economic and social crisis in the GDR, Round Table and government representatives decided that the first free election for the GDR Volkskammer would be moved forward from May 6 to March 18. Moreover, on February 5 Modrow expanded his cabinet to include eight new ministers from the reform parties and the SPD—a so-called "government of national responsibility," which was another unprecedented step in the history of the GDR.[44] In order to keep the new coalition together, Modrow conceded so much effective power to the GDR Round Table that it ceased to be anything like a simple "vetoing organ" and began to exercise central political control.[45] Yet, also at this period, attention began to turn away from the activities of the government and the Round Table to the coming election, in which the parties of the west had already begun to play a massive role with infusions of material support as well as advice and supervision. Although the Round Table sought to discourage this western electoral support, the casualness with which its resolution was ignored marked the Round Table's growing ineffectiveness as the election approached.[46]

In the election of March 18 a surprisingly strong vote for the CDU and its conservative Alliance for Germany made clear that the majority of citizens of the GDR sought unification as soon as possible. A desire to belong to the west and to share in its economic prosperity had been a powerful motivating factor.[47] Following the election, the chair of the eastern CDU, Lothar de Maizière, was elected minister-president of the GDR, a position he was to hold until unification.

De Maizière's career exemplified a personal fate not uncommon in revolutionary times: a sudden rise from relative obscurity to prominence, followed by an almost equally precipitate fall. By the time of the East German revolution in 1989, de Maizière had practiced law in Berlin for a number of years, after physical problems had curtailed a planned career as a musician. At the age of sixteen, de Maizière became a member of the bloc party CDU, perhaps hoping to follow a profession without the necessity of joining the SED. In autumn 1989, after the fall of longtime party leader Gerald Götting—who had been an enthusiastic collaborator with the SED—de Maizière was elected chairman of the eastern CDU.[48] This choice was viewed as an important sign of reform in the previous bloc party.[49] A Lutheran Church official in Brandenburg, de Maizière subsequently became deputy prime minister in the Modrow government, as well as a cabinet member holding primary responsibility for church-state relations. When the CDU—somewhat unexpectedly—emerged as the strongest party in the Volkskammer election of March 18, 1990, de Maizière formed a coalition government and became the first (and only) freely elected minister-president of the GDR.

A quiet man of substantial learning, de Maizière possessed hardness and strength of character to a point, but it was not enough to challenge the massive political power of the western CDU; moreover, his apparent collaboration with the Stasi in the past eventually contributed to ending his political career in unified Germany and may even have weakened his position in the last weeks of his tenure as minister-president of the GDR.

Against the background of the March 18 election, the passage from the Modrow to the de Maizière government marked a crucial moment in the history of the last year of the GDR. The broad goals of the Modrow government had included constructing an independent GDR on the basis of a form of democratic socialism, a goal which probably would have been welcomed with jubilation at an earlier point in the history of the GDR but which—as made clear by the election of March 18, 1990—had no more future in the contemporary eastern Germany. Although Modrow had moved away from such a position in the last weeks of his administration, his steps had been tentative and slow.[50] With the accession of the de Maizière government in the spring of 1990, the GDR turned firmly away from any such solution—and from its prior constitutional documents—and began its rapid swing toward the underlying principles of the West German Basic Law.[51]

Yet, even apart from the official views of the successive GDR governments, the election of March 18 marked a decisive shift in the history of German unification and thinking about the future of eastern Germany. In the early period of the East German revolution—from autumn 1989 to February 1990—the citizens movement seemed to be groping toward a new constitutional understanding that could inform an independent or quasi-independent GDR or contribute to a new or revised constitution for a united Germany. With the election of March 18, and the advent of the de Maizière government led by the CDU, the focus of constitutional and political thought in the east generally moved away from the independent ideas of the citizens movement toward acceptance of the constitutional ideas and structures of the prevailing conservative forces, led by the CDU, in the west.

CHAPTER 4

# Constitutional Reform in the GDR, 1989–1990: Historical Background and the Round Table Draft

THE STIRRING political events of 1989–90 in East Germany were accompanied by a profusion of constitutional and other legal developments, including proposals for an entirely new constitutional document. These changes were played out against the background of the existing GDR Constitution which was amended beyond recognition—but not actually repealed—in the final months of the GDR. This final GDR Constitution was, in turn, the culmination of earlier constitutional developments in eastern Germany.

## THE EARLY CONSTITUTIONS OF EASTERN GERMANY

Something like political life began to re-emerge in the east when the Soviet Union created five Länder or provincial governments in its occupation zone very shortly after the German surrender in 1945. Each of these Länder adopted constitutional documents well before the creation of the GDR in 1949.[1] These documents generally contained liberal rights—guarantees of free speech and equality—as well as social goals such as the protection of "an existence with human dignity for all."[2] The constitutional powers of the state parliaments were very strong, placing the executive government (*Regierung*) in a clearly subordinate position—a factor that some believed unduly impaired the separation of powers. The constitutions were also characterized by numerous provisions directed against national socialism and militarism.[3]

When the GDR was created in 1949, the new government adopted a national constitution. Because at this early point the eastern leaders still believed that they might achieve German unification on favorable terms, the 1949 constitution purported to be a constitution for the entire "German nation." Accordingly, the document contained many provisions that might have been acceptable to the west.[4] Drawn to some extent from the Weimar Constitution of 1919, and reflecting some provisions of the eastern state charters, the GDR Constitution of 1949 originally provided for federalism, guaranteed numerous individual rights, and possessed certain other traits of a liberal western constitution. Moreover, the constitution set forth more elaborate social rights than those contained in the laconic social state clause of the Basic Law.[5] For these reasons the 1949 constitution continued to have some liberal defenders; indeed, during the East German revolution, GDR Prime Minister Lothar de Maizière argued that the 1949 document should be the basis for an interim constitution of the GDR.[6]

Yet this constitution, which after all was adopted under the aegis of the Stalinist GDR leader Walter Ulbricht, also raised ominous problems. The notorious article 6, for example, set forth the ill-defined crime of "boycott-agitation" (*Boykotthetze*) against democratic institutions and organizations. Under this capacious provision, the death penalty and other savage punishments were meted out to political opponents in the early years of the GDR. Moreover, the constitution contained the seeds of the SED bloc system by requiring, or at least strongly encouraging, all significant parties to join the government, thus removing the possibility of an effective opposition.[7] Indeed, in the years after 1949 the constitutional system came increasingly under the sole control of the SED through the abolition of the states, the expansion of executive law-making authority, and other centralizing measures.[8]

By the late 1960s, however, the east had long abandoned the goal of German unification and SED leaders believed that they had made great strides in establishing socialism.[9] Accordingly, in 1968 the GDR adopted a new, more socialist, constitution which was again significantly amended in 1974.[10] The amendments of 1974 comprehensively expunged the remaining national elements in the constitution—elements that might have looked toward a future unification with the west. Indeed, these changes reflected the SED's policy of "demarcation" or "distancing" from the Federal Republic, adopted to combat the perceived threat posed by increased contacts between the two German states following the détente of the early 1970s.[11] Accordingly, the national elements were replaced by emphasis on an even closer relationship with the Soviet Union. Perhaps it was for this reason that the 1974 revision was adopted swiftly by parliament and the executive, without prior presentation to the people for comments and without ratification by plebiscite, both of which had accompanied the adoption of the constitution in 1968.[12]

Although the 1968/74 constitution was adopted long after Stalin's death, it was more clearly Stalinist in its nature than the earlier 1949 constitution adopted in Stalin's lifetime.[13] This constitution represents the final version of "real existing socialism" and was the constitutional document that remained in effect until the revolutionary events of autumn 1989. Certainly, the 1968/74 constitution reflected the reality of government and life in the GDR much more accurately than did the 1949 constitution.[14]

## The 1968/74 Constitution of the GDR

### *Basic Principles*

The two great principles of the GDR Constitution as amended in 1974 were the establishment of Marxism-Leninism and friendship with the Soviet Union. According to the 1974 version, "the German Democratic Republic is a socialist state of workers and farmers. It is the political organization of working people in city and country under the leadership of the working class and its Marxist-Leninist party."[15] Moreover, "the sovereignty of the working people, realized on the basis of democratic centralism, is the basic principle of the structure of the state."[16] Thus, the leading factor in the state was the Communist Party, which governed through the technique of democratic centralism—a doctrine that allowed certain differences of opinion within the leadership circles of the party but required that all leadership decisions be carried out in a uniform manner throughout the government and society, once those decisions were made.[17] Finally, "the economy of the German Democratic Republic is a socialist planned economy."[18]

The second major theme in the 1974 constitution was alliance and close friendship with the Soviet Union, a principle that was immanent in the dependence of the SED leadership on the Soviet Union from the beginning. According to article 6, "the German Democratic Republic is forever and irrevocably bound together with the USSR. The close and brotherly alliance with [the USSR] guarantees the people of the German Democratic Republic further progress on the path of socialism and peace. The German Democratic Republic is an inseparable part of the socialist community of states. . . ."[19] Moreover, "in the interest of preserving peace and the security of the socialist state, the National People's Army [of the GDR] preserves close brotherhood of arms [*enge Waffenbrüderschaft*] with the armies of the Soviet Union and other socialist states."[20] This sort of provision was commonly written into constitutions of east bloc countries in the 1970s, although not all of these provisions were as extreme in their professions of affection for the Soviet Union as the provisions of the 1974 GDR Constitution.[21]

It may well be that these extraordinary provisions of the GDR Constitution represented an acknowledgment of the "basis of the GDR's existence"—i.e., dependence on the Soviet Union—and its general "fragility as a state."[22] In this sense, the GDR's "relinquishment of its sovereignty and its acknowledgment of loyalty, in the text of the constitution, formed the quid pro quo for the Soviet Union's guarantee [of the continued existence of the GDR]."[23] In any case, this constitutional principle of friendship with the Soviet Union and the east bloc seems to have been applied with particular tenacity in everyday life in the GDR: for example, a portion of the oath taken at the *Jugendweihe*—a sort of secular confirmation favored by the GDR state for children reaching the age of fourteen—required the candidate to endorse proletarian internationalism and friendship with the Soviet Union.[24]

### *Property Rules*

The definition of property relationships, and particularly the supremacy of "socialist property," lay close to the heart of the 1968/74 Constitution of the GDR. These provisions reflected the socialist transformation of property relations in eastern Germany that had commenced with the "democratic land reform" and related expropriations of the Soviet occupation period and had continued on through the agricultural collectivization of the 1950s and a final wave of business expropriations in 1972.[25]

In order to carry out the "socialist planned economy," article 10 of the 1968/74 constitution set forth three forms of socialist property: "People's Property," "Collective Property," and property of social organizations of citizens. These forms of property were to be protected and increased by the state.

Of these forms of socialist property, People's Property—state-owned nationalized property—was clearly the most important.[26] According to article 12, People's Property included the basic means of production—for example, minerals, mines, power plants, dams, industries, banks, and insurance companies. Moreover, article 12 prohibited private ownership of these forms of property. As a practical matter, therefore, under the constitution of 1974, there could be no private ownership of industrial organizations and other significant factors of production. Accordingly, article 12 was one of the first constitutional provisions that had to be amended as the GDR began to shift toward a market economy in the months before unification.

In contrast, Collective Property was property of groups of farmers or other working people who were gathered together as collectives.[27] Indeed, much of the agricultural property of the GDR had become Collective Property as a result of a two-step process. First, vast areas of agricultural property were expropriated in the land reform carried out under the Soviet occupation regime between 1945 and 1949, and much of this land was distributed in small allotments (generally less than twenty-five acres) to individual farmers. Subsequently, in a movement that was completed in 1960, the government in effect required individual farmers to form collectives by contributing their property to groups of farmers in the area.[28] Since this property was devoted to the collective and was not owned by the state itself, it was different in form from People's Property. But even so, the use of Collective Property was subject to the directions of the centralized governmental plan.[29]

The third kind of socialist property, property of social organizations of citizens, covered the vast holdings of the SED and the bloc parties as well as property of related "mass organizations" such as the state-run labor union (FDGB).[30] This form of ownership was also to have its own special fate in the efforts to untangle property relations in the period following unification.[31]

### *Basic Rights*

The 1968/74 GDR Constitution contained a full array of basic rights, including what appeared to be traditional defensive rights as well as affirmative rights to social welfare. Yet under socialist legal theory, constitutional rights were primarily intended to further the "harmony of social and individual interests" and create a "socialist personality," and were only to a lesser extent conceived as providing protection of the individual against the state.[32] In any event, many traditional defensive rights were heavily qualified by a requirement that they be exercised "in accordance with the principles of this constitution," or similar formulations.[33] These limiting principles presumably included the doctrines of Marxism-Leninism, the primacy of the Communist

Party, and a rigorous adherence to democratic centralism. In a provision of unintended humor, a right to travel was limited to a right to travel "within the boundaries of the German Democratic Republic."[34]

In contrast with the Basic Law, which contains a general characterization of the Federal Republic of Germany as a "social" state, the 1968/74 Constitution of the GDR set forth a detailed list of "social" rights. These included rights of employment;[35] education and training in a profession or calling;[36] free time and rest (including paid vacation);[37] protection of health, including sickness and accident insurance;[38] care in old age and disability;[39] living space "according to the economic possibilities and local conditions";[40] as well as various special protections for single parents, families with many children, and pregnant women and small children.[41] On the other hand, in accordance with the nature of many socialist constitutions (which typically differed from liberal constitutions in seeking to govern broad aspects of individual life),[42] some of these social rights were accompanied by constitutional duties. The right to work was accompanied by a duty to work;[43] the right to learn an occupation was accompanied by the duty to do so;[44] and every citizen was obligated to engage in service for the defense of the GDR.[45]

Yet, in contrast with the meaninglessness of the defensive rights in the 1974 constitution, the social rights seem to have been generally observed in reality. Particular occupations may not have been very rewarding—and, indeed, the kind of work allocated to some individuals may have been influenced by government pressure—but apparently there was some type of working place for every individual.[46] Apartments may have been small and cramped in many instances, and they may have presented other difficulties, but apparently few if any were homeless in the GDR. Moreover, there was indeed a range of child care facilities available to allow both parents to work—although the psychological effect of these institutions may have raised problems. The dissolution of some of these arrangements after unification formed one of the significant problems faced by former citizens of the GDR. Indeed, these were aspects of the old GDR that even many of the reformers sought to preserve.

### *Governmental Organs*

Under the 1968/74 constitution, the important governmental organs of the GDR were federal because the East German Länder (states) were effectively abolished in the 1950s.[47] Although the "highest organ of state power" was a one-house parliament called the Volkskammer,[48] in reality this body ordinarily accepted measures proposed by the Communist Party without dissent.[49]

The 1968/74 constitution provided for two principal executive organs: the Council of State and the Council of Ministers. The Council of State, which had replaced the office of president of the GDR by amendment to the 1949 constitution, was originally conceived as performing certain functions typically undertaken by a "head of state," as well as certain legislative functions. In contrast, the Council of Ministers was composed of functioning departmental ministers and was referred to in article 76 of the 1974 constitution as the "government" (*Regierung*) of the GDR. During the tenure of SED party leader Walter Ulbricht the Council of State exercised substantial power because Ulbricht was its chairman, but after Ulbricht's fall in 1971, power largely shifted from the Council of State to the Council of Ministers.[50]

*Judiciary*

Although the GDR Constitution proclaimed the independence of the judiciary—a supreme court and lower courts[51]—the constitutional text itself called this independence into question. Indeed, a number of provisions made clear that the Supreme Court was to be responsible to the political organs—the Volkskammer and the Council of State.[52] For example, the Volkskammer chose the judges of the Supreme Court and could remove them at any time.[53] Moreover, provisions relating to the courts emphasized the importance of "socialist legality," a concept that sought to reconcile a degree of legal certainty with a strong role of the Communist Party in the making and interpretation of law.[54]

As an aspect of "democratic centralism," the Supreme Court of the GDR exercised supervisory powers over the lower courts that included the issuance of mandatory special guidelines and went "far beyond the natural radiating force of high court jurisprudence."[55] In any case most accounts agree that, as a practical matter, officials of the SED exercised substantial influence over judicial decisions in cases in which the party took a political interest.[56] Yet in some areas without a strong or direct political component—such as most cases in family law, for example—the GDR judges appeared to view themselves as performing an adjudicatory role, with an important mediating component, that did not differ radically from western models.[57] In any case, the role of the party in influencing the judges in their interpretation of the written law seems to have been a well-understood part of the GDR system. After unification, that role has become a focus of numerous prosecutions of judges for the offense of "perversion of justice."[58]

Through most of the Honecker period, the GDR Constitution of 1968/74 played its role as a flexible tool of the SED hegemony. After the beginnings of perestroika in the Soviet Union, however, the need for constitutional reform—moving toward constitutional structures of the western type—was urged with increasing insistence by a group of younger reformers within the GDR legal establishment. Basically, these efforts yielded little success under the old regime—aside perhaps from some publications evidencing the new tendencies as well as an extremely modest statute creating a mild form of judicial review of administrative decisions.[59] Nonetheless, there was some degree of personal continuity between these young reformers under the old regime, and some supporters of the Round Table draft and other projects for reform in the Modrow and de Maizière periods.[60]

## Proposals for a New GDR Constitution: The Round Table Draft

From the fall of the Honecker regime in late 1989, it seemed clear that the necessary political, economic, and social reforms could not be undertaken on the basis of the GDR Constitution of 1968 as revised in 1974. This constitution was based so completely on discredited Stalinist ideas—particularly the basic concepts of democratic centralism and close alliance with the Soviet Union—that it could not be adequately reformed through amendment. Rather, most believed that an entirely new document was necessary.[61]

### *History of the Round Table Draft*

Because in late 1989 many still thought that the GDR would continue to exist as a separate country for an interim period—perhaps approaching unification through the form of an increasingly closer confederation[62]—the GDR Round Table vigorously pursued its work of preparing a new, democratic constitution of the GDR.[63] Indeed, authorization of a "working group" for constitutional drafting was the Round Table's first substantive act after adopting a general statement of purpose and procedural rules,[64] and reformers hoped that the draft would be the crowning work of the Round Table. Moreover, even if the GDR was not destined to endure, a new constitution could help support the views of the GDR reform groups in negotiations with the Federal Republic over unification.[65] The Round Table contemplated that its draft would be presented for adoption to the new, legitimate Volkskammer after its election, which at that point was set for early May 1990.

Like the Round Table itself, the constitutional working group was composed equally of representatives of the reform movement and representatives of the SED and its allied organizations.[66] It was advised by a few constitutional experts from the GDR who had gained the confidence of the reformers. The working group also invited western advisors who generally came from the left wing of constitutional law teachers in the Federal Republic—a fact that led to harsh criticism from conservative academic circles in the west.[67]

Rejecting the 1949 GDR Constitution as a model, the working group concentrated to some extent on the Basic Law but also reviewed newer constitutions such as those of Spain and Nicaragua.[68] In a highly concentrated process, the working group divided itself into five subgroups to consider various aspects of the constitutional draft. The subgroups met separately and then presented oral or written reports to the plenary session.[69]

Yet notwithstanding the enthusiasm of its participants, the importance of this work waned in February and March 1990 as it became clear that an independent GDR had no long-term future and that unification would take place at an early date. It also became clear that, under the method favored for unification, the West German Basic Law itself—with certain limited amendments only—would become the constitution of the united country.[70] Thus no completely new GDR Constitution was to be adopted; nor would there be a need for a completely new all-German constitution—at least in the first instance.

When the Round Table went out of existence shortly before the GDR election of March 18, 1990, the working group had not yet finished its constitutional draft.[71] Nonetheless, one of the final acts of the Round Table was to charge the working group with the task of finishing the draft and distributing it to the public for discussion.[72] In accordance with this charge, the group continued its work and produced a draft of a proposed new GDR Constitution in April 1990. Its provisions were an interesting mixture, reflecting the underlying structure of the Basic Law but adding a substantial number of social rights and some plebiscitary elements, in accordance with the ideas of the GDR reformers and the western advisors.

Because of these and other novel provisions, the Round Table draft seemed to suggest a new constitutional understanding, departing in a number of ways from that of the Basic Law. In particular the draft seems directed toward breaking down certain political, economic, and social hierarchies and granting more explicit rights to weaker members of society and to the populace at large. Accordingly, from the time of its publication the Round Table draft has remained a central point of debate between contending constitutional views. Indeed, the Round Table draft—although originally intended as a new constitution for the GDR—became a model for many of those who favored the adoption of a new all-German constitution upon unification.[73]

In a moment of high drama, representatives of the Round Table working group presented this constitutional draft to the newly chosen prime minister of the GDR, Lothar de Maizière, in an open session of the Volkskammer shortly after the GDR's first free election. But this ceremonial gesture could not conceal the hard political fact that, given the hegemony of the conservatives in the east as well as the west, there was little possibility of the draft's adoption as a new constitution of the GDR. Indeed, the Volkskammer majority refused even to refer the draft to a committee for consideration.[74] For members of the GDR reform groups, this rejection of the Round Table draft marked a major retreat from the development of a new constitutional consciousness toward a basic acceptance of traditional West German structures.[75]

Yet it is unlikely that the importance of the Round Table draft, as an alternative democratic possibility, will soon fade away. Indeed, the prominence of the Round Table draft in discussions surrounding the adoption of constitutions in the five eastern Länder bears witness to the durability of its constitutional ideas.[76] Under the present governing coalition, significant constitutional reform on the national level has not proved to be a realistic possibility.[77] But if the political constellation so changes that a new federal constitution is seriously considered, the Round Table's extremely interesting draft will certainly play an important role in the accompanying discussion.

*Text of the Round Table Draft*

The Round Table draft is characterized by an expansive catalog of basic rights, including detailed provisions for social rights, and the "direct" application of certain constitutional rights against individuals and groups as well as against the state. The structural provisions of the draft depart to a lesser degree from the fundamental structures of the Basic Law, but the draft does provide significant opportunities for the public to take part in law making through direct popular vote. In an interesting passage, the draft emphasizes the goal of reconciliation with all of the peoples "who were oppressed and persecuted by Germans" during World War II[78]—a frank statement of historical responsibility that is absent in the Basic Law. Moreover, the preamble of the document, written by the GDR's most famous novelist, Christa Wolf, also invokes "the responsibility of all Germans for their history and its consequences."[79] The following are some of the principal characteristics of this interesting document.[80]

"LIBERAL" DEFENSIVE RIGHTS AND ENVIRONMENTAL GUARANTEES

The Round Table draft contains a full complement of traditional rights such as guarantees of equality, free speech, religion, and travel. In some cases these rights reflect similar provisions in the Basic Law and, indeed, in some instances the text incorporates not only the western constitutional provision but also judicial interpretations of the Basic Law set down by the West German Constitutional Court.[81]

Yet some of these "liberal" defensive rights go beyond anything contained in the Basic Law. For example, life imprisonment is prohibited—as well as the death penalty (as in the Basic Law)[82]—and even a foreigner (who, unlike a citizen, might be subject to extradition) cannot be extradited to a place in which he might be threatened by the death penalty.[83] These provisions reflect the view that imprisonment without hope of release, as well as the death penalty itself, are so abhorrent to ideas of human dignity that they cannot be tolerated in a civilized society.

In sharp contrast with prevailing West German doctrine, women have a right to determine whether or not to be pregnant; presumably this is a constitutional right to abortion, although the draft could have been clearer on that point.[84] Indeed, strong guarantees of gender equality form an important theme of the Round Table draft in general: the state is obligated to further the equality of women in the "private law" areas of employment and the family, as well as in the public sphere—an emphasis on the affirmative furthering of gender equality in society that was later to be echoed in the new state constitutions in the east.[85]

In other provisions that protect nontraditional social structures, the draft prohibits discrimination against long-lasting "living communities" (nontraditional family-like groups)[86] as well as prohibiting discrimination on the grounds of sexual orientation.[87]

The strong ecological concerns of the Round Table draft are reflected in a number of important provisions. For example, the state (and all citizens) must protect "the natural environment as the basis of life of present and future generations," and the government's policies must further the "sparing use and recycling of nonrenewable raw materials and the sparing use of energy."[88] Moreover, to further environmental protection, every affected citizen has the right to be heard in the process of planning power plants and other large projects.[89] Similarly, to protect against environmental injury, every individual has the right to the publication of data concerning the environmental conditions in his or her area.[90] Indeed, in a provision that is also frequently echoed in the new state constitutions, all individuals have a more general right to examine data collected with respect to their activities—and can indeed prevent data collection by making an objection, although this right can be limited to some extent by law.[91] The Round Table draft also significantly expands political rights. In contrast with prevailing doctrine under the Basic Law, resident aliens have a right to vote in local elections and to be elected to local office.[92] Moreover, citizens movements (*Bürgerbewegungen*), such as those that came to the fore in the revolutionary events of 1989, are granted special constitutional protection.[93] The citizens movements have a right to introduce their concerns in parliamentary committees—and to have those concerns seriously considered—as well as a qualified right to receive relevant information from the government. If citizens movements take part in national or state elections, their election campaign costs will be reimbursed on the same basis as campaign costs of political parties.[94]

A number of constitutional rights apply directly against individuals and groups, as well as against the state (*Drittwirkung*). These include rights of equality;[95] rights of democracy within associations,[96] political parties[97] and unions;[98] certain rights of free speech within employment relationships;[99] and employees' rights of co-determination in business enterprises that are of particular significance for the community.[100]

On the other hand, some individual rights in the Round Table draft have interesting (and perhaps dubious) limitations. For example, among the limitations of free speech is the requirement that "war propaganda as well as the public declaration of discrimination that injures human dignity is to be prohibited by law."[101] Moreover, "the permissibility of means or methods of research can be limited by law";[102] the context of this provision suggests that it refers to dangerous forms of scientific experimentation, but the statement itself seems considerably broader.

The Round Table draft also strictly qualifies property rights in provisions that retain a very strong social component and sometimes reflect categories and theories of property current under the old GDR. Property for personal use as well as property of collectives is particularly protected; in case of expropriation, only these forms of property are to yield full compensation. Owners of other forms of expropriated property will receive only partial compensation in a "balancing of interests of the community and those involved."[103] Real property may be used only in accordance with an overall property-use plan and—in a clear echo of rules relating to the 1945–49 expropriations in the Soviet occupation zone—the Round Table draft seems to prohibit private property in, or private use of, parcels of agricultural or forest land that exceed 100 hectares (approximately 250 acres). Instead, the draft reserves such extensive holdings for collectives, public institutions, and churches only.[104] Moreover, a property owner may not retain all unearned increments in land values: the local government must be compensated for certain increases in private land values if those increases result from a change in the government land-use plan.[105] Finally, in a complex series of provisions, the Round Table draft provides for the return of some property expropriated by the GDR to its former owners, but does so in a much narrower class of cases than was ultimately provided for in the Unification Treaty.[106]

### "AFFIRMATIVE" SOCIAL RIGHTS

In sharp contrast with the extremely general "social state" provisions of the Basic Law (articles 20, 28 GG), which guarantee social welfare to an undefined degree, the Round Table draft sets forth a detailed catalog of social rights. In including these provisions, the working group reached back beyond the Basic Law to the tradition of the Weimar Constitution, which also contained social guarantees in some detail.[107] More specifically, these provisions were drafted against the background of a comprehensive Social Charter, which set forth a number of detailed social provisions in very strong and unqualified form and was endorsed by the Round Table in its penultimate meeting on March 5, 1990.[108]

The social guarantees of the Round Table draft include a right to social security with respect to sickness, accident, disability, handicap, inability to care for oneself, old age, and unemployment.[109] Moreover, the draft guarantees rights to appropriate living space,[110] and to employment or support in securing employment.[111] In addition to providing equal access to education (including at least a ten-year required public school education), the state is further required to support the creation of day care centers (*Kinderkrippen*) and after-school care for children (*Schulhorte*).[112] Institutions of this sort were universally available in the GDR and made the full employment of women possible—although they have also been criticized on the grounds that separating a child from the family for most waking hours may have had deleterious psychological consequences.

Many of these social guarantees in the Round Table draft are referred to as "rights" of individuals. Yet most are so carefully qualified in the text of the respective provisions that they may actually more closely resemble general state goals—with little chance of actual judicial enforceability except in very clear cases of legislative neglect. Notwithstanding the attacks that have been leveled against the Round Table draft, therefore, these social guarantees do not seem to present "exaggerated promises [awakening] hopes that cannot be fulfilled."[113]

### STRUCTURAL PROVISIONS

The Round Table draft creates a parliamentary system analogous to that of the Federal Republic, with a Volkskammer (a popular assembly) and a Länderkammer representing the states.[114] Unlike the rule in the Federal Republic, the Volkskammer can dissolve itself at any time by a vote of two-thirds of its members.[115] Following the lines of the Basic Law, the Round Table draft provides for a minister-president (chancellor), along with a cabinet and a president, but the office of the president seems to have more real authority than the office of federal president under the Basic Law. Executive powers can be conferred on the cabinet by law, but a statute can state that an executive regulation will be invalid if disapproved by a committee of the Volkskammer.[116] Indeed in a number of respects the Round Table draft accords the parliament a somewhat stronger role—vis-à-vis the executive government (*Regierung*)—than is currently exercised by the Bundestag under the Basic Law; moreover, in the allocation of powers between the federal government and the states, the federal parliament also has a wider competence than the Bundestag.[117] The first of these characteristics may reflect a greater distrust of the executive arising from totalitarian experience. The second may result from lack of experience with a federal system.[118]

### THE ROUND TABLE DRAFT: LESSONS OF THE 1989 REVOLUTION

Certain provisions in the Round Table draft were clearly designed to incorporate the perceived lessons of the 1989 revolution in the GDR and give the population, acting as a whole or acting in loosely formed citizens movements, increased power to affect public decisions. These provisions must also be understood against the background of developments in the Federal Republic where the great power of the political parties has, in the view of many, coalesced to form a "party state" with significantly impaired democratic participation.[119] Some believe that devices of direct democracy could play an important role in mitigating these problems of the "party state."

In addition to the provisions according expanded rights to citizens movements, the Round Table draft seeks to promote direct democracy by granting broad opportunities for law making by popular vote.[120] These plebiscitary provisions, which also had parallels in postwar German state constitutions in east and west, have found wide acceptance in the constitutions of the new eastern states.[121] This strong plebiscitary tradition is also emphasized in concluding sections of the Round Table draft, which require a popular vote (in addition to approval of two-thirds of the Volkskammer) for the adoption of the constitution itself, as well as for the adoption of any possible treaty conditions accompanying the "accession" of the GDR to the Federal Republic under article 23 of the Basic Law. Thus, under the Round Table draft the Unification

Treaty between the two German states would have been presented to the population for approval. A plebiscite would also be necessary for the adoption of a new all-German constitution that might be proposed by a constitutional convention to supersede existing constitutions in east and west.[122]

Finally, a series of special citizens representatives—following the ombudsman tradition of Scandinavia[123]—seeks to break down the perceived distance between citizen and the state. Citizens representatives would give special attention to questions of gender equality, data protection, and prisoners, as well as the problems faced by foreigners.[124]

Thus, at the end of the revolutionary period in the GDR, the loosely formed citizens groups that had led the revolution had also inspired a constitution that could have served as a charter of an independent GDR for a transitional period. It also could have provided ideas for an independent contribution of the GDR to a new all-German constitution. The tradition represented by the Round Table draft—a tradition that has been incorporated to some extent in the constitutions of the new German states—is somewhat different from the tradition of the Basic Law. Although it seeks to maintain liberal individual defensive rights, as does the Basic Law, its emphasis is more explicitly social and plebiscitary than that of the Basic Law. Indeed, where the Basic Law has sometimes tended to preserve social and economic hierarchies, the provisions of the Round Table draft are more egalitarian and seek, in a number of ways, to break down existing hierarchical structures. The political push toward unification doomed the Round Table draft in the spring of 1990. But its basic ideas may be destined to have a longer-lasting influence.

CHAPTER 5

# Constitutional Reform in the GDR, 1989–1990: Amending the Constitution

THE Round Table draft and related attempts to enact a wholly new constitution were not the only constitutional developments in the last year of the GDR. Indeed, beginning in early December 1989, the East German political system moved steadily away from the principles of the old Stalinist document through a series of constitutional amendments and related statutory provisions. Some of these measures were adopted in the Modrow period before the election of March 1990, and other provisions—more clearly directed toward unification—were enacted during the de Maizière regime.

## The Old Volkskammer and the Modrow Government

Even during the period when the eventual adoption of a new GDR Constitution seemed to be a real prospect, most believed that certain constitutional changes were needed so urgently that they should be made by amending the 1968/74 constitution immediately—although that document, resting on Stalinist foundations, was generally agreed to be fundamentally unsalvageable. Because of the urgency of these amendments, it was necessary that they be enacted by the unreformed Volkskammer, even before its replacement by a freely chosen parliament that would be seen as legitimate.

Acting before the election of March 18, 1990, therefore, the old Volkskammer under the government of Hans Modrow adopted four sets of amendments which indicate the areas in which reform was viewed as most urgent in that early period.[1] Although these amendments lacked the full legitimacy of changes enacted by the new Volkskammer after the election of March 18, 1990, they made a more powerful public impression and were in a sense more important. After the election of March 18, it was clear that unification would soon be achieved—on terms basically determined by the conservative coalition in the west—and subsequent amendments were steps leading to that almost certain conclusion. The earlier changes, in contrast, were measures still being undertaken by a more or less autonomous state in the process of groping toward a new and not entirely foreseeable constitutional order.

### *Rejection of Leading Role of the Communist Party*

The first constitutional change was an amendment of enormous symbolic importance: on December 1, 1989, the Volkskammer amended article 1 of the 1974 constitution to abolish the special leadership role of the "working class and its Marxist-Leninist party."[2] Although this provision had first appeared in express terms in the constitution of 1968, it reflected the fundamental structure of the GDR state since its founding in 1949 and, indeed, it was the "core" of that political system.[3] Accordingly, in this brief amendment, adopted even before the Round Table was established, the Volkskammer officially recognized what had actually been determined in the streets over the preceding two months: the overwhelming popular rejection of the former political basis of the GDR and, principally, the rejection of the leadership role of the Communist Party which had manifested itself in numerous aspects of government and life.[4] This amendment abandoned the central Marxist-Leninist tenet that historical laws justify the party's monopoly power and generally opened the way for the recognition of pluralist democratic forms.[5] Given the structure of the Stalinist state—which depended on the party for all significant decisions—this amendment was a revolution in itself.[6]

*Joint Ventures*

A second set of amendments, enacted on January 12, 1990, was impelled by economic imperatives, particularly the urgent need to procure investment from the Federal Republic and other western nations. Western investment in socialist countries often took the form of joint ventures between the government and foreign corporations. Although some of these projects may already have been underway in the GDR by early 1990, they actually violated the constitution of 1974, which prohibited private ownership interests in the basic means of production. The amendment of January 12 removed that prohibition.[7] At the same time, a new section was added to the constitution specifically permitting joint ventures if authorized by law,[8] and shortly thereafter the government issued regulations governing joint ventures.[9]

This was the first amendment enacted after the establishment of the GDR Round Table, and the Volkskammer had apparently not yet understood the practical authority that the new organ was to wield. In a sign of its growing power, the Round Table sharply rebuked the Volkskammer because the amendment had been adopted without presentation to the Round Table and subsequent public discussion.[10]

As a substantive matter, this amendment evoked a bitter political dispute over the percentage of ownership interests that should be allowed to outside investors in joint ventures. Some argued that to permit more than 49 percent ownership by private investors would deliver control of People's Property into the hands of capitalist exploiters; others maintained that outside investors could be attracted only by the prospect of control.

Taking a restrictive position on outside investment, the government's initial regulation ordinarily limited foreign investors to 49 percent of a joint venture. A higher percentage could be permitted, however, if the people's general economic interest and the goal of the undertaking justified it or if the enterprise was "of small or middle size."[11] In a retrospective view, Lothar de Maizière considered it one of the signal failures of the Modrow period that this regulation generally limited outside investment to 49 percent and thus—in his view—seriously discouraged private investors.[12] In any event, the bitterness of this dispute at the time suggests that, even in January 1990, many in the GDR still believed that the country had some future as an independent nation and that this future, which might deviate significantly from that of the Federal Republic, must be carefully charted to avoid undue external control from the west.

Ultimately, of course, this view was not destined to prevail. Nonetheless this dispute over the locus of economic control of the east anticipated serious problems that were to arise after unification. In a practice that has been even more thoroughgoing and universal than that feared by the early opponents of a liberal joint-venture regulation, the system of sale of East German enterprises by the Trust Agency (Treuhand), established in the course of unification, has had the result of shifting effective control of most remaining eastern enterprises to West German or foreign ownership.[13]

### *Structural Changes*

The third set of early constitutional changes was more structural in nature. On February 20, 1990, the GDR Constitution was amended to abolish the "National Front," an amorphous collection of organizations that served as an organ of Communist Party electoral control.[14] Under the 1974 constitution, the National Front and the related bloc-party system assured that "free elections could always be prevented . . . through the practice of using 'unified election lists.' "[15] Thus abolition of the National Front was an important step in preparing the way for free elections in the GDR. The amendment also provided for direct elections to the Volkskammer and guaranteed local voting rights for resident aliens.[16] The number of Volkskammer members was also reduced from 500 to 400.[17]

### *Reform of Labor Unions*

The last set of constitutional changes by the old Volkskammer was intended to transform the nature of labor unions in the GDR. As described in articles 44 and 45 of the 1974 constitution—and also in reality—labor unions in the GDR more closely resembled governmental organs that participated in the planning of the economy than representatives of the work force in an adversary relationship with managers of concerns.[18] Indeed the leader of the FDGB, the East German confederation of labor unions, was one of the most powerful government officials in the GDR.[19]

By a constitutional amendment of March 6, 1990, and an accompanying statute, the Volkskammer sought to change the labor unions into adversary bodies along the lines of the western pattern. Article 44 was replaced by a new provision which contemplated that the unions would represent workers' interests in labor struggles, guaranteed the right to strike, and prohibited lockouts in any form.[20] This provision reflects a phenomenon that is absent in the

United States Constitution but not uncommon in more modern constitutions—the description and regulation of social or economic institutions that are not completely governmental in nature.[21] Indeed the provision prohibiting lockouts could in effect create constitutional rights among "private" parties—in this case, rights of a union against an employing company.[22]

The new constitutional provision prohibiting lockouts was much more favorable to labor unions than analogous provisions of West German law, which indeed guarantee an employer's right to engage in a lockout. Similarly, the GDR amendment and statutory provisions deviated from West German law by doing away with trade union liability in the case of strikes and according more extensive rights of co-determination to workers' councils than were available in West German law. It has been argued that these provisions can be viewed as an attempt by the GDR government "to [signal] the direction in which the law of the [Federal Republic] should be modified in order to reach a common denominator in a future law of a unified Germany."[23] Ultimately, however, in the area of labor law, as in many other areas, the more traditional law of West Germany—in these respects considerably more favorable to employers than the 1990 GDR amendments—came to prevail with little modification.[24]

## Constitutional Legislation during the Modrow Period

In addition to these constitutional amendments, the unreformed Volkskammer under Modrow enacted a number of measures that were closely connected with developing constitutional reform. This legislation was intended to reinforce the development of democratic political life in the GDR. Although in form a product of the Volkskammer, most of these measures were in fact issued by the Round Table—worked out first in drafting committees and then approved by the entire body before being forwarded to the Volkskammer for adoption. In at least one instance in which the government apparently attempted to deviate from the Round Table draft—in a manner favoring continued government control of a news agency—the Round Table reacted with a severe rebuke and ultimately prevailed.[25]

### *Guaranteeing Freedom of Expression*

With the approaching election of March 18, it became particularly important to establish rights of free expression on a solid legal basis, independent of state control. In February 1990, therefore, the Volkskammer issued a regulation protecting freedom of expression and freedom of the media[26] and enacted statutes providing for the free formation of associations and political parties.[27] In early March the Volkskammer also issued a regulation guaranteeing the rights of citizens committees[28] and enacted a statute defining rights of assembly.[29]

In these measures the Round Table and the Volkskammer generally sought to remove rights of expression from the pervasive state control that had existed under the SED. Thus the Regulation Guaranteeing Freedom of Expression and the Media prohibited censorship, sought to achieve diversity of opinion in the mass media, and replaced certain licensing obligations with a registration requirement. The regulation also made clear that radio, television, and the ADN (previously, the government press service) were independent of orders from the government, and workers in the media would not be required to work on material, or take positions, that were inconsistent with their personal views.[30]

Similarly, the Statute on Associations declared that no governmental approval was necessary for the forming of an association.[31] This new statute contrasted sharply with the previous GDR regulation, which in effect limited permissible associations to those acceptable to the SED by stating that associations would be allowed only "when in their character and goals they accord with the principles of the socialist order of society."[32] The previous regulation had also required state approval for the founding of associations or any change in their charters and even for the membership of any GDR citizen in an international association or an association with its headquarters outside the GDR.[33]

In a parallel manner, the new Statute on Political Parties declared that "the formation of parties is free and requires no approval."[34] In sharp contrast with the favored political and economic position of the SED in the past, the new statute insisted on equal opportunity for all parties. It also prohibited political parties from operating businesses not connected with their political activity—a provision directed at the massive property holdings of the SED and the bloc parties.[35] In light of the approaching election, the statute also sought to prohibit parties from accepting economic support from outside the GDR. This provision was widely disregarded, however, and massive assistance was afforded by parties in the Federal Republic to their partners in the GDR. The statute did provide for state subsidies to the parties and partial repayment of the costs of the election campaign.[36]

In a similar manner, the Statute concerning Public Assemblies proclaimed that all citizens have the right to meet in peaceful assemblies without the necessity of governmental approval—in contrast with previous GDR law which required government approval for all outdoor assemblies.[37] Moreover, in reaction to past governmental pressures on individuals to take part in official public assemblies—such as parades on May 1 and October 7, the anniversary of the founding of the GDR—the new law stated that "the principle of voluntariness applies to participation in assemblies."[38]

In late 1989 and early 1990, right-wing movements were making their presence known in the GDR.[39] Accordingly, each of the measures on freedom of organization adopted by the Volkskammer in the Modrow period denied legal protection to organizations that propagated forms of discriminatory speech or expressions of hatred—one of the few points on which the reformers and the old GDR government shared a common point of view.[40] Moreover, on

February 5, 1990, the Volkskammer issued a regulation banning the Republicans—a notorious right-wing party that had had some electoral success in West Germany—from carrying on any activity on the territory of the GDR. The order referred to "increasing activity of right radical and neofascist forces," including recent acts of violence which endanger "the process of comprehensive democratic renewal of society in the GDR." The order also invoked the Volkskammer's "responsibility to our people and the peoples of the world to take care that fascism and war should never again arise from German soil."[41] Later events confirmed that right-wing activity in eastern Germany was not to be taken lightly. Yet, even so, this was an extraordinary bill of attainder that clearly did not accord with the Volkskammer's emphasis on the importance of judicial procedures in related legislation.

### *The GDR Election Law*

Another important structural task undertaken by the Round Table and the Volkskammer was the adoption of an election law for the first democratic election of the GDR, to take place on March 18, 1990.[42] In central provisions, the Election Law paid homage to the origin of the GDR revolution in loose citizens groups. For example, citizens groups—and not only political parties—would be permitted to propose candidates for the election.[43] Moreover, as an almost unique feature among postwar German election laws, the statute omitted any requirement that a party or group receive more than 5 percent of the votes cast in order to enter parliament. Such a provision could have threatened the continued existence of some of the smaller citizens groups or parties. Furthermore, under the statute, coalitions of parties or groups could enter the election as a single combined alliance (*Listenvereinigung*)—another provision presumably intended to further the preservation of small political groups.[44]

A crucial issue, arising in the debates surrounding the Election Law, revealed the tension between the original views of democracy of the Round Table and the rapidly expanding power of the western parties as the election approached. On February 5, 1990, in connection with the Election Law, the "parties and groups represented in the Round Table declare[d]—for the sake of equality of opportunity and a fair election campaign up to March 18, 1990—that they would renounce [the use of] guest speakers from the Federal Republic of Germany and West Berlin."[45] This resolution sought to preserve the election of March 18 as an East German affair, without the possible distortions introduced by the presence of western personnel.

The western parties, however, had already begun to exercise massive influence in the GDR election campaign, and the Round Table's plaintive resolution was ignored. Indeed, on February 12 the eastern CDU—the party that perhaps had the most to gain from western assistance—attacked the Round Table resolution as "a massive invasion of the substantive structure of the election campaign" and thus a massive invasion of the exclusive area of competence of the individual political parties. Indeed, "the political future of our country [i.e., the GDR] and its population can no longer be separated from the activities of political forces in the Federal Republic." Accordingly, the CDU declared that it did not feel itself bound by the "paternalistic demand" set forth in the resolution.[46]

In this revealing episode, the waning influence of the GDR reform groups was pitted in vain against the massive influence of the western parties. The episode foreshadowed a form of unification—a result of the election itself—in which basic decisions were to be made in the west and western structures were to be extended to the east with little immediate opportunity for significant contribution by the reform forces of the east.

The early legislation of the Modrow period on freedom of expression and elections signaled a clear turning away from the repressive tradition of the GDR and represented an attempt to carry into reality previously ignored protections of the GDR Constitution. These provisions responded to demands for the serious implementation of constitutional rights of expression—demands that had been emphasized in the great Berlin demonstration of November 4, 1989. Accordingly, these statutes and regulations—sometimes containing language that may have seemed peculiar to western observers because of its intended impact on specific GDR problems—could be viewed as authentic achievements of the GDR revolution. As was the case with the Round Table draft constitution, these measures suggest an autonomous intention to protect constitutional rights in a manner that arose from the separate experience of the GDR. But, in the end, these perhaps naive strivings toward an independent political system were largely negated by the election results of March 18, 1990, and the developments that were to follow.

## The New Volkskammer and the de Maizière Government

After the election of March 18, 1990, a freely elected Volkskammer replaced the old legislature composed of the SED, other "bloc parties," and representatives of other social groups basically dominated by the SED. The largest group in the new Volkskammer was the CDU which, having abandoned its past as a compliant bloc party, had received strong support from its powerful counterpart in the west. Along with other conservative parties, the CDU formed the "Alliance for Germany," which emerged from the election with slightly less than one-half of the seats in the new Volkskammer.

In a coalition with three small liberal parties, the Alliance for Germany would have had a majority in the Volkskammer and would have been able to form a government. Yet a simple majority would not have been sufficient to carry out the tasks that awaited the new government. Most important, the 1974 GDR Constitution seemed to require a two-thirds vote of the Volkskammer for the changes necessary to achieve unification. Perhaps it might have been possible—as some western commentators urged—to declare the 1974 constitution obsolete as a result of the 1989 revolution and proceed on the basis of majority votes in parliament. Yet, the prevailing political forces clearly decided to pursue change under the forms of the old Stalinist constitution—regardless of its doubtful legitimacy—rather than to take the more revolutionary step of abandoning that constitution altogether.[47] Needing a two-thirds majority in the Volkskammer, therefore, the CDU sought to include the Social Democratic Party (SPD), the second-largest group in the parliament, in the governing coalition. After difficult negotiations, this mélange of political parties formed an uneasy grand coalition—although the SPD was bitterly attacked by some of the GDR reformers for joining a coalition directed toward unification on western terms and thus, in their view, undermining the 1989 revolution.[48] The CDU leader Lothar de Maizière was elected prime minister by the Volkskammer.

Over all, the work of the Volkskammer under de Maizière was extraordinary, producing 164 statutes and 93 regulations (*Beschlüsse*) in 37 sessions between April 5 and October 2, 1990.[49] Although the relations of power between West and East Germany dictated that much of this legislation would pass out of existence upon unification, the basic principles of some statutes were indeed preserved and adopted in the Unification Treaty between the two German states. In some cases, this legislation reflected an independent eastern understanding that differed from views prevailing in the west. In this respect, the work of the Volkskammer under de Maizière has had some lasting effect.[50]

The activity of the DDR Volkskammer under de Maizière was characterized by the overwhelming pressure of work on its members combined with intense and sometimes chaotic public sessions. For many members of parliament it was almost an around-the-clock task—a fact not always fully appreciated by the citizens of the GDR when television cameras, which broadcast Volkskammer meetings in full, caught one of their highly paid representatives napping during a session.[51] The members' occasional unruliness seemed to arise from their deep engagement with the issues being considered,[52] together, perhaps, with their lack of parliamentary experience. Indeed, the new Volkskammer was composed almost entirely of people who—because of their past in the GDR—had no firsthand parliamentary experience of their own and, at the outset, had little clear understanding of how a democratic parliament was conducted. The closest thing to parliamentary experience was possessed by those Protestant ministers in the Volkskammer who had been active in consistorial church government, and that experience had an influence on the Volkskammer as it previously had on the Round Table.[53]

In the crucial opening sessions of April 5 and 12, officers of the Volkskammer were elected and the coalition government was formed. At the same time, the Volkskammer adopted an important declaration recognizing the responsibility of the Germans in the GDR for the actions of the Nazi tyranny and for persecution of Jews in eastern Germany even after 1945, as well as responsibility for East German participation in the invasion of Czechoslovakia in 1968.[54] The resolution acknowledging East German responsibility for Nazi tyranny was important because the SED government of the GDR had denied any continuing responsibility for the actions of the Nazi regime. The resolution on Czechoslovakia may have reflected a historical sense that the GDR revolution—as well as the contemporaneous "velvet revolution" in Czechoslovakia—was part of a process that had antecedents in the Prague Spring of 1968.[55]

One of the major tasks of the new Volkskammer was to create a democratic constitutional system that would approach that of the Basic Law and allow the merger of the two German states. After its rejection of the Round Table draft, the Volkskammer in effect decided to perform this task through the adoption of a series of further amendments of the 1974 constitution. Accordingly, in its first meeting the new Volkskammer revoked the preamble of the constitution with its references to "the revolutionary traditions of the German working class," "the developed socialist society," "the path of socialism and communism," and "this socialist constitution." At the same time, the Volkskammer enacted administrative provisions relating to the Council of Ministers and the Volkskammer itself and also amended the constitution to authorize an office of president of the GDR to replace the traditional socialist organ of the Council of State.[56]

In a somewhat self-contradictory provision, the Volkskammer also amended the GDR Constitution to make clear that members of the new government would not have to refer to the constitution itself in taking the oath of office. This change, which was insisted upon by Prime Minister de Maizière, reflected the profound ambivalence with which the necessity of continuing to work under the old GDR Constitution was viewed.[57]

Indeed the debate on this amendment in the Volkskammer nicely set forth the paradoxical status of the old GDR Constitution during this transitional period.[58] On the one hand, the new Volkskammer and government were chosen pursuant to the provisions of this constitution, and so the document had to retain some formal validity. On the other hand, its fundamental propositions—democratic centralism and the socialist economic structure—had been cast aside in the 1989 revolution, and one member of de Maizière's government even went so far as to declare on the floor of the Volkskammer that he "rejected the content of the present constitution."[59] Another member of the Volkskammer took an intermediate position, affirming the validity of the basic procedural provisions of the constitution, but rejecting other provisions as a "socialist lyric" that had already been abandoned in the Modrow period.[60] Interestingly, the form of oath that was ultimately adopted in this constitutional amendment—containing a pledge of loyalty to the "law and statutes" of the GDR, without a reference to the constitution itself—was drawn from article 72 of the Round Table draft.[61]

On June 17, 1990, the new Volkskammer issued its most sweeping amendment of the old 1968/74 Constitution of the GDR.[62] This amendment sought to alter the basic nature of the constitution by proclaiming a series of new general principles, reflecting the revolution accomplished by the popular upheavals of 1989 and the election of March 18, 1990.[63] The changes also responded to requirements set forth in the first State Treaty, which had been signed by the Federal Republic and the GDR on May 18, 1990.[64] The amendment declared that all constitutional and other legal rules were henceforth to be applied in accordance with these new principles and that any contrary constitutional provisions would be nullified. Through this technique, the drafters sought to change the basic nature of the GDR Constitution in a general way, without having to undertake—in a very short period of time—the detailed work that a full new constitutional draft would require.

Article 1, section 1 of the new general principles proclaimed the GDR a "free, democratic, federal, social and ecologically oriented state based on the rule of law." This provision was similar to a key section of the Basic Law—article 20(1)—except that it added a new ecological orientation. Article 1, section 1 thus implicitly took a position on attempts to include an ecological provision in West German constitutions—a movement that had succeeded with respect to some of the state constitutions but had not yet succeeded with respect to the Basic Law.[65] Article 1, section 2 of the June 17 amendment sought to complement the basic principles of section 1 by declaring that rules "binding individuals or [state organs] to the socialist state and legal order, the principle of democratic centralism, socialist legality, the social legal consciousness, or the views of individual groups of the population or parties, are revoked."[66] In all, the purpose of article 1 was to adopt a basic order resembling that of the Federal Republic and to reject the principles that had guided the constitution and the rest of the legal order up to the 1989 revolution.

The next series of articles in the June 17 amendment sought to support capitalist property and economic relations by guaranteeing private property rights in land and the means of production as well as the freedom of economic activity.[67] Nonetheless, according to article 2, special forms of property would be permissible for government participation in economic affairs, and the use of property should serve the common good and preservation of the natural basis of life. To some extent, the latter provision seems to parallel the statement in article 14(2) of the Basic Law that "property has its obligations,"[68] but the language of the amendment seems, if anything, to qualify property rights to a greater extent than the corresponding language of the Basic Law and also seems to recognize a qualification in favor of environmental protection.[69]

Article 5 of the June 17 amendments amplifies the declaration in article 1 that the GDR is a state based on the rule of law, by strengthening the independence of the judiciary. Indeed, the susceptibility of the judges to political pressure from the Communist Party was one of the characteristics of the old GDR state most criticized by the reformers. Article 5, section 1 is identical to the first sentence of article 19(4) of the Basic Law, which guarantees each individual the possibility of a legal remedy for a violation of rights; this provision, which forms the basis of West German administrative law, secures an extensive system of review of administrative decisions. According to article 5, section 2 of the June 17 amendments, "The judges are independent and subject only to the constitution (in accordance with the provisions of this constitutional amendment) and the law."[70] To make the point absolutely clear, article 5 also provides that the judges are "to that extent subject to no supervision of state or societal organs."[71]

Articles 6 and 7 required the state to protect the environment and to further the right to employment—provisions that elaborated on the general goals of article 1 and reflected an approach to social welfare and environment that went beyond that of the Basic Law.[72] Although the Basic Law contains a very general provision declaring that the Federal Republic is a "social state," there are few provisions that render this guarantee more concrete, and any proposal concerning a right of employment has met strenuous resistance from the prevailing conservative coalition in the Federal Republic.

Finally, articles 8 and 9 make clear that the GDR can confer certain rights of sovereignty on international organs or organs of the Federal Republic and that state treaties and international agreements of the GDR can effect constitutional changes; in both cases approval by two-thirds of the members of the Volkskammer is necessary. The first of these provisions is similar to article 24(1) of the Basic Law; it was necessary in order to authorize those aspects of the State Treaty that conferred substantial authority over economic matters in the GDR on the Bundesbank, an organ of the Federal Republic.[73] The second provision made clear that the State Treaty and the later Unification Treaty could amend the GDR Constitution upon approval of two-thirds of the members of the Volkskammer.[74]

All in all, these provisions, which were criticized for their lack of judicial precision,[75] seemed to be an attempt to form a conceptual bridge to unification by replacing fundamental principles of the GDR Constitution with principles more in accord with those of the Basic Law. Perhaps the use of this imprecise technique best reflected the uncertainty and transitional nature of this period.[76] On the other hand, these technical problems were particularly galling to members of the reform groups, who believed from the beginning that the GDR needed an entirely new constitution instead of amendment of the old constitution and an attempted rapprochement with the Basic Law in the form of an imprecise and insufficient listing of principles.[77]

But interestingly—notwithstanding the reformers' complaints—certain important points of tension with the Basic Law were also evident in these principles. By including specific employment and environmental provisions, and by suggesting increased limitations on property, the Volkskammer seemed to indicate that even the conservatives in the GDR were willing to support certain constitutional changes that had continued to meet the skepticism or opposition of conservative political groups in the Federal Republic. Similar points of tension were also to be suggested by certain provisions of new state constitutions in eastern Germany which go beyond anything that the conservative coalition has been willing to accept in the Basic Law.[78] Thus these constitutional principles of June 17 seemed to suggest—albeit in a manner considerably less pronounced than the Round Table draft—distinct constitutional views in the reformed GDR that differed in some significant respects from those then prevailing under the Basic Law.[79]

CHAPTER 6

# Methods of Unification under the Basic Law

ALTHOUGH the original goal of many GDR reformers was to achieve democracy within an independent East Germany, calls for unification became more insistent—both in the Leipzig demonstrations and elsewhere—in the early months of 1990. Attention, therefore, began to turn to the question of how that goal could be achieved.

There were several possible constitutional methods of unification, and the choice among these techniques would have important implications not only for the relations between the two parts of Germany, but also for the longer-term nature of the united country. Indeed, this choice would determine whether a new constitution would be adopted for Germany upon unification, or whether united Germany would continue on—at least at the outset—under the provisions of the West German Basic Law. More broadly, this choice could reflect the resolution of the fundamental political question of whether unification would generally be an attempt to extend western circumstances as fully as possible to the east or whether, in contrast, unification would involve reconsideration of certain political and social principles in the west as well. In debates about the method of unification, therefore, the main lines were drawn between those who favored retaining the general constitutional understanding of the Basic Law and those who sought a somewhat different constitutional understanding, perhaps reflecting contributions from the experience of the GDR reform movement.

From the beginning, three possible methods of unification seemed to be in prospect.

## CONFEDERATION

In the course of the East German revolution, some political figures proposed a confederation of the two German states—or perhaps an even looser form of "treaty community." Through a technique of this sort, the two states could preserve their individual structures and governments while gradually merging some specified functions. In his inaugural address in November 1989, for example, Hans Modrow, the new minister-president of the GDR, proposed that the two German states form a loose community bound together by a treaty or treaties.[1] Responding to Modrow's initiative, Chancellor Kohl then proposed a confederation in his Ten-Point Plan on November 28.[2] Kohl carefully indicated, however, that this form of partial consolidation would not preclude full unification—called for by the Basic Law—at a later point.[3] Some of the new reform parties in the GDR, particularly Democracy Now, also proposed a confederation,[4] as did an influential article in *Der Spiegel* by two members of the Constitutional Court.[5] Indeed this was also the method favored by significant forces within the GDR Round Table.

The impetus underlying Kohl's proposal, however, differed considerably from that underlying the views of groups like Democracy Now. Kohl's original call for confederation seemed to follow the counsels of caution—a political impulse not to move too quickly for fear of domestic and foreign opposition—and perhaps also uncertainty about the precise nature of the problems ahead. For some of the reform parties, however, confederation was a means of preserving the possibility of developing a form of democratic society different from that of the Federal Republic: more social and egalitarian, less aggressively capitalistic, imbued with more plebiscitary elements—perhaps a type of democratic socialism. In any case, in any of its permutations the idea of confederation would not necessarily have excluded substantial economic support flowing to the GDR from the Federal Republic. With this form of confederation—even if it were to exist only for an interim period—a new GDR constitution would be necessary to replace the Stalinist document of 1968/74, and the original impetus toward constitution drafting in the GDR can be viewed partly in this light. Certainly, the original commencement of work on the Round Table draft rested on this basis.

For all of its attractive possibilities, quasi-unification by confederation had little political support. Kohl abandoned it as soon as he saw that something more permanent was possible. Moreover, the idea of confederation—as well as the reform alliance supporting it—was massively rejected in the election of March 18, 1990, which showed that a substantial majority of GDR voters wanted complete political unification as quickly as possible.[6]

## Article 146 of the Basic Law

A significant degree of German confederation could probably have been achieved by the adoption of a series of treaties under existing provisions of the constitutions of the Federal Republic and the GDR. But actual unification of both German states, as effectively mandated by the election of March 18, required careful examination of the status of unification under both charters.

The 1974 GDR Constitution said nothing about German unification: by the 1970s the GDR and the Soviet government had receded from an earlier position favorable to unification and had adopted the view that the GDR and the Federal Republic were two separate and completely independent states.[7] But even though the constitution did not mention unification in the text, it seemed clear that unification in any foreseeable form would involve dissolution of the GDR—an action that would require amendment of the GDR Constitution by a vote of two-thirds of the Volkskammer.[8]

The requirement of a two-thirds vote in the Volkskammer for this and other constitutional changes leading to unification raised the possibility that a large minority party could seek to exert power by threatening to impede this process. Perhaps as a result, some western experts argued that the democratic revolution of 1989–90 had the effect of rendering the Stalinist constitution of 1968/74 obsolete and therefore no longer valid—except that certain structural provisions could continue on with the force of statutory law only.[9] The result of such a finding might have been that a governing coalition could have put through its program for unification with only a simple majority in the Volkskammer. This argument did not gain wide acceptance, however, and all steps in the GDR leading up to unification were taken on the basis of the existing 1968/74 constitution, as amended in accordance with the procedure of that constitution itself.[10]

In contrast with the GDR Constitution, the Basic Law of the Federal Republic contained important provisions regulating German unification. Indeed, the Basic Law was conceived as a provisional document that foresaw—and, as interpreted by the Constitutional Court, actually required—steps toward eventual unification.[11] Accordingly, in striking contrast with most constitutions of the world, the Basic Law contemplated its own termination, and the constitutional provision governing termination set forth a possible method by which unification could be achieved. Article 146, the termination provision, declared that "this Basic Law will lose its validity on the effective date of a constitution that has been chosen by the German people in a free decision." This provision not only prescribed the method for terminating the effectiveness of the Basic Law, but also could be seen as explaining that German unification was to be accomplished by the adoption of a new constitution by the people of both German states.

In accordance with this provision, therefore, some commentators proposed adoption of a new, all-German constitution that would replace both the GDR Constitution and the Basic Law. Indeed, some even argued that because the intended goals of the Basic Law would be completely achieved by unification, the adoption of a new constitution under article 146 was constitutionally required.[12]

There was little authoritative guidance, however, on how this new constitution was to be adopted. According to the Constitutional Court, a "certain minimal standard of free-democratic guarantees" must be preserved in this process.[13] Perhaps an all-German constitutional convention could propose a draft, or perhaps the draft could be put forward jointly by the West German Bundestag and the GDR Volkskammer—in either case the draft constitution might be ratified by both populations in a plebiscite.[14]

Some commentators argued that upon the adoption of a new, all-German constitution under article 146, *both* the Federal Republic and the GDR would disappear as legal subjects, to be replaced by a new entity: a united "Germany."[15] Most maintained, however, that unification under article 146 would not disturb the continuity of the Federal Republic as the surviving legal subject—primarily because the prevailing doctrine viewed the Federal Republic (but not the GDR) as in some sense identical with the continuing "German Reich."[16]

It was possible that unification through article 146—and particularly the adoption of a new constitution by plebiscite—could cure a democratic "deficit" in the adoption of the Basic Law in 1949.[17] In contrast with the Weimar Constitution and most of the Länder constitutions after World War II, the Basic Law was not proposed by a body that had been directly elected by the people. Rather, the Basic Law was proposed by a "Parliamentary Council" that had been chosen by the legislatures of the Länder.[18] The western Allies originally contemplated that this democratic deficit would be resolved by submitting the proposal of the Parliamentary Council to a popular referendum in each of the Länder.[19] The Parliamentary Council ultimately decided, however, that the Basic Law should be ratified by the legislatures of the Länder rather than the people themselves.[20] On the other hand, it can be argued that the Basic Law has in effect been ratified by usage through its continual observance under democratic forms.[21]

It is indeed arguable that the framers of the Basic Law intended that unification would come about through the adoption of a new constitution under article 146. Moreover, from the point of view of democratic theory, the use of article 146 had another distinct advantage: a new document presumably would be adopted after extensive discussion of constitutional ideas from both the Federal Republic and the GDR, including not only the more or less settled political ideas of the prevailing western coalition but also the new democratic self-understanding arising from the reform movements of eastern Germany.[22]

Accordingly, unification under article 146 might well have opened the process to greater consideration of new constitutional ideas and to more serious consideration of proposals from the new reform movements in the east. Although traditional western views might ultimately have prevailed, the adoption of a new constitution under article 146 for the united Germany could have given the entire process a greater sense of joint and communal effort than it was ultimately destined to achieve. Indeed, a process of broad debate and constitutional communication could have encouraged the east to view the emerging document (even if that document was the Basic Law itself) as something at least partially of its own making—with the result that subsequent problems and crises, which were even then in prospect, might have been somewhat easier to bear.[23] Some also suggested that such a constitutional discussion would help the east in coming to grips with its own baleful past.[24] In any case it seems clear that such a constitutional process would have had profound educational effects, both in the east and in the west. Moreover, the final document would have had the increased legitimacy afforded by adoption by the full population after careful deliberation and debate.[25]

Good arguments were thus available for the use of article 146, and this method had enthusiastic support from sections of the SPD and the GDR reform movement.[26] Yet it was clear after the election of March 18 that this solution also had no practical political chance. Indeed it probably was the democratic advantages of this process—the possibility of a cross-fertilization of ideas from east and west—that assured its demise. The CDU/CSU government in the west (which also largely controlled the conservative coalition in the east) did not want to take the chance that provisions that it considered dubious or even dangerous—for example, expanded social guarantees, such as a right to employment or living space, or increased plebiscitary elements now almost completely absent in the Basic Law—would make their way into a new all-German constitution. Both governments may also have feared that a risk of political and perhaps even economic instability might arise from the time-consuming and contentious process of drafting a new constitution.[27] Consequently, the prevailing conservative coalition sought unification in a manner that would extend the Basic Law in its existing form over the newly united country, with as few changes as possible.

## Article 23 of the Basic Law

The method that was most clearly designed to achieve the conservatives' goals was set forth in article 23 of the Basic Law which, like article 146, did not explicitly regulate unification but nonetheless presented a method for its achievement. The principal function of article 23 was to describe the territorial coverage of the Basic Law—a particularly important provision after the territorial rearrangements following World War II and the division of Germany into occupation zones. According to article 23, the Basic Law would be in effect at the outset in the states of "Baden, Bavaria [and all the original states of the Federal Republic and Berlin.] In other parts of Germany [the Basic Law would] be put into effect after their accession."

This provision raised several interesting points. For example, it assumed that there were "other parts" of "Germany" that could "accede to" (or join) the Federal Republic—the territory of the Basic Law.[28] When these "other parts of Germany" joined the Federal Republic, the Basic Law would be extended to cover them as well. The "joining" parts of Germany would become unified with the Federal Republic, but it is the Federal Republic that would survive; the joining parts, as separate legal subjects, would unquestionably disappear. There was no possibility of arguing, as might have been the case with unification under article 146, that *both* the Federal Republic and the GDR would be replaced by a new legal entity.

Indeed, the relationship between article 23 and article 146 is not entirely clear. Because article 23 speaks of parts "joining" or "acceding to" the Federal Republic, and because article 146 seems to cover the case of general unification, it could be argued that article 23 was only intended to cover the case of relatively small parts of "Germany" joining the Federal Republic. Indeed, the only previous use of article 23 occurred in 1957, when it was invoked to allow the Saarland to accede to the Federal Republic after the voters of the Saar rejected a special "Europeanized" status in a plebiscite.[29] On the other hand, the historical materials may indicate that the Parliamentary Council also viewed article 23 as a possible method for achieving unification of the Federal

Republic with the GDR (or the Soviet occupation zone, as it then was).[30] Indeed, in the Basic Treaty case the Constitutional Court explicitly stated that the GDR was "another part" of Germany that could "accede" to the Federal Republic under article 23, and that this provision had in no way become obsolete.[31]

For many conservatives in the Federal Republic, the use of article 23 was a reassuring solution.[32] Under this section the Basic Law—and forty years of Constitutional Court case law interpreting its provisions—would remain in effect and would be extended to the territory of the GDR. Almost all of the central governmental institutions of the new, united Germany would be the familiar institutions of the Federal Republic, with such alterations and extensions as would be needed to accommodate the additional territory and population. Only a few changes would be necessary in the Basic Law, and they would not touch the fundamental structure of state or society. Rather, these changes would be limited to those necessary to recognize that full unification had been achieved and, in a few cases, to recognize specific historical developments in the former GDR.[33]

The steps necessary for "accession" under article 23 were generally accepted in the West German legal literature.[34] The accession had to be declared by the GDR or by the states or other subdivisions of the GDR. The decision to accede had to be made in accordance with a democratic procedure—either by plebiscite or by the vote of a democratically organized government,[35] although that government need not possess all of the specific democratic attributes of the Federal Republic under the Basic Law. Accordingly, it was necessary for the GDR to amend its 1974 constitution to include sufficient democratic attributes and to remove provisions that hindered unification or prevented economic reform.[36] Moreover, because accession in effect required dissolution of the GDR and revocation of its constitution, a vote to accede to the Federal Republic also required a two-thirds vote of the Volkskammer.[37]

Under article 23, the government of the Federal Republic had no power to reject the accession of "another part of Germany,"[38] although it could examine the method of accession to determine that it was the product of "free will."[39] Thus, although the part of Germany that was joining the Federal Republic must presumably make its decision in a democratic manner, the populace of the Federal Republic had no power through democratic means to reject the accession. This interpretation was consistent with the Constitutional Court's view that the Basic Law requires the government of the Federal Republic to seek unification.[40] Although some argued that a specific statute of the Bundestag was necessary in order to extend the Basic Law over the territory that "acceded,"[41] the Bundestag may have been constitutionally obligated to enact such a statute.[42]

Constitutional arguments of this sort call into question the frequently heard claim that German unification was, in every respect, an example of the doctrine of self-determination. Undoubtedly there was a requirement of self-determination for the GDR, the "part" of Germany that "acceded" to the Federal Republic: its decision had to be made through a democratic process. But because the Federal Republic could not constitutionally reject the GDR's "accession" under article 23, it was evidently required to accept the GDR's accession even if a majority of the western populace or legislature would actually have rejected unification under the relevant circumstances. Because the populace of western Germany was constitutionally required to accept unification, it is doubtful that the process can be regarded as an unalloyed example of self-determination. In any event, however, there is little to suggest that a majority of the West German population actually rejected the principle of unification at the time that it occurred.

In debates over the proper method of unification, the use of article 23 was most sharply rejected by those who favored a form of confederation with a gradual move toward unification. It was also rejected by those who viewed unification under article 146 as an opportunity to pursue significant constitutional reform with the introduction of a new or adjusted constitutional understanding. Some of these groups referred to the use of article 23 as an "Anschluß," a reference to Germany's absorption of Austria in 1938.[43] Employing this vocabulary, the GDR Round Table voted in February 1990 to reject "the Anschluß of the GDR or individual states [of the GDR] with the Federal Republic . . . under article 23."[44]

Yet, notwithstanding these objections, the conservative coalition in Bonn decided in early March 1990 that unification should be accomplished under article 23, even before the GDR election results made the choice of that provision a certainty.[45] Accordingly, in his first major speech in the Volkskammer (*Regierungserklärung*), GDR Prime Minister de Maizière clearly endorsed the use of article 23.[46] Indeed, by that time much of the eastern SPD had also come to favor article 23, and its use was therefore stipulated in the coalition agreement signed by the governing parties, including the SPD.[47] At the same time, however, eastern SPD representatives sought to insist on a unification agreement to regulate the conditions of accession, so that the use of article 23 would not be equivalent to the "capitulation" of the GDR.[48] Yet, notwithstanding such an agreement, many believe that the ultimate choice of unification under article 23—with the wholesale extension of the western Basic Law over the east—had determined much of the structure of unification and many of the social and political developments that were to follow.

## A New Constitution under Article 146 after Accession under Article 23

Even after accession under article 23, however, the possibility of a new all-German constitution under article 146 was not completely foreclosed.[49] Article 146 said nothing about when such a new constitution must be adopted. Although a new constitution could have been the final step in unification in place of accession under article 23, the provisions of article 146 seemed to authorize adoption of a new constitution by vote of an all-German parliament (or by plebiscite, or by a combination of the two) even *after* accession. Indeed it is arguable that the framers of the Basic Law contemplated that unification would be accomplished in two steps: "first the [territorial accession of the east under article 23] and thereafter the working out of a new constitution" under article 146.[50] Consequently, in summer 1990, the West German Länder with SPD governments proposed that within one year after unification the Bundesversammlung—a special organ composed of the members of the Bundestag and an equal number of members chosen by the state legislatures—should elect a constitutional council or convention which would prepare a new constitution modeled on the Basic Law, to be presented to the people for ratification.[51]

Yet, from the outset, the permissibility of using article 146 in this manner was not undisputed. Because article 146 was originally intended as a method of accomplishing German unification, it could have been argued that after unification under article 23 the provisions of article 146 should be deleted from the Basic Law as having no more purpose. Indeed, some suggested that after unification under article 23, the provisions of article 146 would become obsolete and therefore invalid, even if the article remained in the text of the Basic Law.[52]

Perhaps with this problem in mind, the framers of unification made a deliberate decision to retain article 146 as a functioning part of the Basic Law. The Unification Treaty entered into by the Federal Republic and the GDR required the amendment of article 146 in a manner indicating that the provision retains its validity even after unification.[53] This amendment accordingly changed the basic nature of article 146 from a provision contemplating a new constitution in the course of German unification, to a provision providing a broader opportunity for the adoption of a new basic document.[54]

The governing CDU/CSU coalition would almost certainly have preferred to delete article 146 altogether, but it was probably forced to accept this provision by the SPD, Bündnis 90, and the Greens, as a price that it had to pay in order to achieve the two-thirds vote necessary for ratification of the Unification Treaty.[55] Thus those who favored fundamental revisions in the constitutional understanding of the Basic Law—through the inclusion of expanded social rights and plebiscitary elements—preserved at least the theoretical possibility of achieving this end through the use of article 146 at some point in the future.

Neither the original nor the amended version of article 146 sets forth a specific method for adopting a new, all-German constitution. Arguably, therefore, a simple majority in a plebiscite might adopt the new basic document—perhaps following its proposal by a simple majority of a national convention convened for that purpose. As a result some conservative voices in the Federal Republic, including political figures and legal scholars, have tended to view the continued existence of article 146 as a dangerous threat.[56] Indeed, leaders of the CDU have argued that those who favor such a plebiscite seek to create a "different republic" without the necessity of achieving the two-thirds majority required for an ordinary constitutional amendment.[57] In response, others charged conservatives with engaging in a "systematically churned hysteria" and concluded that the conservatives "fear the people and [fear] a broad discussion about the constitution."[58]

Some commentators have denied, however, that article 146 authorizes adoption of a new constitution by a simple majority. According to this argument, article 146 must be read together with article 79(2) of the Basic Law, which requires a two-thirds vote of the Bundestag and the Bundesrat for a constitutional amendment: since adoption of a new constitution is even more sweeping than adoption of a single constitutional amendment, article 146 must be read to require a two-thirds vote at some point in the process. For example, a two-thirds vote of the Bundestag and Bundesrat might be necessary to propose a constitutional amendment for a plebiscite.[59] If article 146 is used to adopt a new constitution by simple majority in the future, this widely debated question will certainly require resolution by the Constitutional Court.[60]

At its core, this dispute over the possible effect of the new article 146 GG reflected a deeper dispute between conservatives, who sought to extend existing structures of the Federal Republic over eastern Germany, and the eastern and western reformers who believed that unification should be an occasion and opportunity for some significant rethinking of constitutional and societal principles. So long as the political constellation remains substantially as it was at the time of unification, however, the same forces that supported the use of article 23 could almost certainly prevent any subsequent use of article 146 to work significant constitutional changes. But if an SPD government were to be formed at some point in the future—perhaps in coalition with the Greens and the remnants of the GDR reform parties—this possibility might again come to the fore.[61]

In the meantime, however, any national constitutional debate evoked by unification seems to have remained within a relatively narrow compass. Indeed, some have complained that in contrast with vigorous constitutional struggles on emergency powers and rearmament in earlier periods, the considerably more important process of unification failed to evoke a serious public debate over constitutional principles in western Germany.[62] This "widespread silence"[63] also contrasts vividly with the enthusiastic popular constitutional discussions that took place in the GDR at the end of 1989 and the beginning of 1990. Although proposals for amendment issued by a Joint Constitutional Commission in 1993 have animated somewhat more interest, real debate on these questions remains largely confined to academic rather than popular circles.[64]

CHAPTER 7

# The State Treaty: Currency and Economic Union

EVEN WITH the choice of article 23 for unification, it seemed clear that the amalgamation of two quite different social, economic, and legal systems could not be accomplished instantaneously. Instead, a process of rapprochement and accommodation was thought to be necessary in which the manifold problems could be faced and to some extent resolved. Because the most exigent problems in mid-1990 were the economic problems that threatened chaos in the GDR, the governing coalition in the west sought to come to grips with these issues. Accordingly, the first official step in the unification process was the signing on May 18, 1990, of a "Treaty concerning the Creation of a Currency, Economic, and Social Union" between the GDR and the Federal Republic—generally known as the first "State Treaty."[1]

With the signing of this agreement—which called for the introduction of the western D-Mark into the GDR on July 1, 1990, as well as the partial merger of the two economic systems—the process of unification had reached a point of no return. Indeed many believe that with the adoption of the first State Treaty—and particularly the sudden introduction of the D-Mark in the east—the major economic structures and problems of German unification were clearly foreordained. For this reason, it could be argued that the first State Treaty was a more important step in German unification than the Unification Treaty itself.

## BACKGROUND OF THE STATE TREATY

The negotiation of an agreement for an economic and currency union became the first concrete step toward German unification, but it was not the result of long and careful deliberation. Rather it was decided upon in an atmosphere of confusion and crisis in which improvisation as well as considerations of political gain played an important role.[2]

First proposed by an SPD financial planner in early 1990,[3] the idea of a currency union was officially endorsed by Chancellor Kohl in a surprise announcement on February 6—at the same time that other high government officials were denying that such a course would be adopted.[4] Although serious economic problems in such a course were foreseen from the beginning, Kohl apparently feared that failure to take immediate steps toward extending the D-Mark to the east would result in a total collapse of authority in the GDR and an increased flow of eastern citizens to the west.[5] Indeed, in an early speech before the Bundestag Kohl acknowledged that he was proceeding in the face of the warnings of economists and that a more gradual path would have been chosen if the political and economic situation had been "normal."[6] In a later speech in the Bundestag, after the signing of the treaty on May 18, Kohl flatly stated that "a delay of the State Treaty—whatever the arguments were—would have meant the collapse of the GDR."[7] It was in this speech that Kohl made an optimistic promise that would later return to haunt him as the economic situation in the east slid into catastrophe in the months after unification. According to Kohl's promise, which was often cited in later months by embittered citizens of the east: "No one [in the GDR] will be worse off than before—and many will be better off [after unification]."[8]

In order for the State Treaty to come into effect, it had to be enacted by both German parliaments.[9] As a historical matter, these votes were bound together with the vote of both parliaments on another important issue of unification—the German recognition of the Oder-Neiße line, separating the territory of eastern Germany from that of Poland. According to Chancellor Kohl, the German confirmation of this border was an essential precondition to the ratification of the State Treaty because otherwise unification would face insurmountable objections from Germany's neighbors and from the victorious Allies of World War II.[10] Accordingly, on June 21, 1990, the Bundestag and the Volkskammer passed a resolution recognizing the Oder-Neiße line as the permanent Polish-German border, and these resolutions were officially communicated to the Polish government. In his speech to the Bundestag on this occasion, Chancellor Kohl attempted to pacify the right wing of his coalition with words of consolation for those expelled from the eastern territories.[11] Thereafter, on June 21 and 22, the Volkskammer and Bundestag, and also the West German Bundesrat, approved the State Treaty.

Although these votes were overwhelmingly favorable, the treaty was not adopted without some objection both to its content and to the process of adoption. Members of the West German SPD sharply criticized the government for negotiating the treaty without adequately consulting parliament and the state governments.[12] Remarks from the East German reform movement on this point were, if anything, even more scathing:

> Government commissions negotiate a state treaty behind locked doors; the parliaments are not consulted. The government . . . then presents the finished draft as a treaty in international law—to which, as everyone knows, [the parliaments] can only say "yes" or "no." . . . Thus the whole German people in free self-determination can only add a couple of grudgingly conceded footnotes to the economic-political [*ordnungspolitischen*] chapters of their future constitution.[13]

Indeed, criticisms of this kind could also be leveled against the government's actions in later stages of the unification proceedings, and lack of public participation was viewed by many as one of the central infirmities of the unification process in general.[14]

The first State Treaty was also sharply criticized on substantive grounds. For example, a minority of SPD representatives rejected the treaty on the ground that it constituted economic shock therapy by introducing a market economy too abruptly—a process that would "heighten the crisis of economic development and could result in dramatic mass unemployment, whose social results would necessarily endanger democracy in both parts of Germany."[15]

Moreover, the first State Treaty—with its extension of the powerful D-Mark to the east, along with social market concepts and the constitutional principles of the Basic Law—was a clear forerunner of the underlying structure of unification under article 23, through which western principles were extended without much adjustment to the east. Accordingly, some eastern criticisms of the treaty were based precisely on that ground. The remnants of those groups that rejected article 23, and sought a melding of constitutional concepts under article 146, protested bitterly against the clear subordination of east to west that was evident in the treaty. Of these opponents, the caucus of Bündis 90/Greens in the Volkskammer was perhaps the most prominent.[16]

Yet even if the signing of the first State Treaty made German unification inevitable, its framers apparently contemplated that its provisions would govern the relations between East and West Germany for a significant interim period. Thus the treaty seemed to presuppose a period in which its requirements could progressively harmonize the economic systems and relations of the two German states. As it happened, however, the astonishing pace of German unification ultimately overtook even its framers, and unification occurred before significant developments could take place under a number of the provisions of the first State Treaty.

## The Provisions of the Treaty

The first State Treaty is in many ways an extraordinary document, for it made clear the depth of the changes to take place in the GDR and the extent to which its economic system and political fate were henceforth to be under the control of the Federal Republic. Indeed, from this point on, "the GDR had a '*state treaty constitution*,' which determined that the organs of the GDR no longer possessed exclusive authority" in economic policy—"one decisive aspect of state sovereignty."[17] The treaty also made clear how important—indeed omnipresent—were the rules and standards of the European Economic Community for the process of unification. As the most pressing problems were economic, it is principally these problems that the State Treaty sought to address. Yet the State Treaty also had more general political implications.[18]

### *Currency Reform and Its Accompanying Problems*

In its economic sections, the treaty was basically intended to accomplish three tasks. First, it introduced the western D-Mark as the official currency of the GDR and provided an exchange rate for GDR Marks.[19] This exchange rate had been the subject of sharp debate and public concern because it would determine how much wealth the citizens of the GDR could salvage from the dissolution of their existing system, and the economic basis on which they would begin their new lives in the Federal Republic. Accordingly, many voices in the GDR called for a one-to-one exchange of GDR Marks for D-Marks—particularly with respect to salaries, pensions, and savings—and Prime Minister de Maizière emphasized this position in his acceptance speech (*Regierungserklärung*) before the Volkskammer.[20] On the other hand, some western observers argued that the ratio should be at least 2 GDR Marks for 1 D-Mark.[21] Indeed the SPD's first plan for a currency union had proposed a 5:1 ratio,[22] and the black market conversion rate at the beginning of 1990 had been at least 7:1.[23]

The State Treaty reached a compromise on this question. Salaries, pensions, rents, and similar recurring payments were to be paid henceforth at the ratio of 1 to 1. On the other hand, ordinary contract payments and other debts were principally to be paid at the rate of 1 D-Mark for 2 GDR Marks.[24] Savings accounts were to be converted at a rate of 1 to 1, up to a maximum of 4,000 GDR Marks for people who were fourteen to fifty-nine years old. For GDR citizens under fourteen the maximum was 2,000, and for citizens over fifty-nine the maximum was 6,000 GDR Marks. Amounts over these maximums were converted at a rate of 1 D-Mark for 2 GDR Marks.[25]

Overall, the average of these sums indicated that the GDR Mark was being exchanged at a rate of 1.8 to 1.[26] According to some, this exchange represented an enormous revaluation of the GDR Mark, which had been exchanged at considerably more than 3 GDR Marks for each D-Mark. Some believe that this revaluation, in itself, had profound deleterious consequences for the eastern German economy because it in effect tripled the price of GDR goods on the world market.[27] The underlying problem, of course, was the desperate condition of the GDR economy which had resulted in part from a long-standing emphasis on the production and subsidization of consumer goods and the accompanying neglect of long-term capital investment.[28] Moreover, economists foresaw that there would be increases in eastern wages, moving toward western levels in the months following unification. The result of revaluation and other factors was to be a unit cost for goods produced in the east that often exceeded west German or other European levels—a development that would clearly spell disaster for the east German economy.

This, of course, was not the way in which the issue of exchange rates was viewed by citizens of the east. Their perspective and their concerns were in many cases, naturally, quite different. The eastern citizens knew that unification would bring the certain elimination of government subsidies that had kept commodity prices low in the GDR. The result would be an increase in prices—now measured in D-Marks. This phenomenon, together with what even then seemed like a likely increase in unemployment, would mean that years of GDR Mark savings could soon be deeply invaded or exhausted. In light of these concerns, the fairness of the exchange rates in the first State Treaty cannot be measured solely according to the market values of the respective currencies outside the GDR.

*The Aspirations of Economic Reform*

The second function of the State Treaty was to introduce a "social market economy" into the GDR—a capitalist economy with a significant social welfare component, similar to that of the Federal Republic. The economic measures were seen as an important complement to the currency union, and the goal of these provisions was the eventual creation of a single economy in the Federal Republic and GDR. Indeed, a number of economists—including West German Finance Minister Waigel[29]—originally believed that reform of the eastern economy should have *preceded* the currency union rather than being attempted at substantially the same moment. According to this view, it was only when the two economies had achieved relatively comparable levels of productivity that a currency union could be introduced without deleterious economic consequences. This position may have been correct, but Chancellor Kohl believed that an even more profound political and economical catastrophe would be caused by a failure to introduce the D-Mark at an early point—certainly at a point well before the east German economic system could be brought up to the level of the west. But, even if there was no time for reforming the eastern economy before the currency union, it was certainly necessary that economic reform accompany that union.[30]

It is perhaps in the area of economic reform that the sweeping changes sought by the State Treaty in the structure and life of the GDR were most notable. According to the treaty, the future economic order of the GDR was to be characterized by "private property, competition, free formation of prices, and in principle fully free movement of labor, capital, goods and services"—although certain forms of public property in the GDR would also be recognized.[31] That these changes would have important constitutional implications for the GDR was clearly recognized. Accordingly, with respect to freedom of contract and similar economic doctrines, as well as other basic principles, the treaty made clear that "contrary rules of the Constitution of the German Democratic Republic concerning the principles of its previously socialist social and governmental order shall no longer be applied."[32] Indeed, the attached Joint Protocol was even more specific:

> Rules that bind individuals or organs of state power (including the legislative and judiciary) to socialist legality, the socialist state and social order, the requirements and goals of central leadership and planning of the economy, the socialist legal consciousness, socialist views, the views of individual groups of the population or parties, or socialist morality or comparable concepts, will no longer be applied.[33]

In these two provisions, therefore, the GDR agreed to change the underlying economic structure of the state and to abandon the fundamental legal doctrines which supported that economic structure. This is an extraordinary instance—but not the only example that we will see in the process of German unification—of a treaty provision mandating certain domestic constitutional requirements.[34] In this respect some have said that after July 1, 1990, the State Treaty was the effective constitution of the GDR.

Moreover, the State Treaty obligated the GDR to take certain concrete steps to further its conversion to a market economy.[35] Among other things the GDR was required to restructure its commercial enterprises in a manner that would "ease the enterprises' swift structural conformity with the new market conditions," with the ultimate goal of creating "a modern economic structure . . . through the development of private initiative."[36] In general, state-owned commercial entities were to be "structured for competition as quickly as possible and, to the extent possible, converted into private property."[37]

In accordance with these provisions of the first State Treaty, the GDR Volkskammer enacted a statute in June 1990 that in effect reconstituted the GDR Trust Agency (Treuhandanstalt), an office established during the Modrow period for the purpose of administering and conserving GDR "People's Property." The new statute transformed the Treuhand into an agency whose principal purpose was no longer to administer that property, but rather to sell the property into private hands.[38] This statute—which was enacted on June 17, the day on which the Volkskammer also adopted general constitutional principles analogous to those of the Basic Law[39]—marked the beginning of the process through which effective control of the principal eastern industries largely passed to the west. The eventual development of this process ignored a provision of the first State Treaty that contemplated the possible distribution of shares (*verbrieftes Anteilsrecht*) of GDR "People's Property" to the citizens of eastern Germany, to compensate them for losses they may have suffered by the conversion of much of their savings into D-Marks at the exchange rate of 2:1.[40]

For the purpose of introducing a market economy, a bewildering array of laws in the GDR was to be annulled, altered, or replaced by statutes of the Federal Republic. The first State Treaty thus commenced the process of extending western law to the east—with some modifications and exceptions—that was to be largely completed in the Unification Treaty. For example, much of the corporation law of the Federal Republic and parts of its antitrust and commercial law were to be adopted in the GDR.[41] Numerous other provisions of GDR law affecting the economy, including substantial provisions of the GDR's Civil Code, were to be repealed or amended.[42] Finally, the GDR agreed to enact statutes that would allow individuals and corporations greater freedom to carry on business in the GDR, as well as legislation that would liberalize commerce in goods, services, capital, and currency exchange with foreign countries.[43]

An additional task of the treaty was to convert the state system of social security in the GDR into a system of comprehensive social insurance, financed by contributions from employers and employees, along the lines of the system prevailing in the Federal Republic.[44] The treaty required that gradual steps be taken to alter the health service of the GDR through the introduction of private physicians and dentists and related private enterprises.[45]

Because it was unlikely that private contributions in the GDR would be able to finance the social security system for an interim period, the treaty contemplated a substantial subsidy from the Federal Republic to the GDR for this purpose.[46]

*The Political Aspects of the Treaty*

Although the most conspicuous aspects of the State Treaty were economic, the agreement also possessed a fundamental—indeed an essential—political component.[47] As noted above, article 2 of the treaty required that the GDR introduce an economic order characterized by private property and declared that contrary rules of the GDR Constitution must be disregarded; similarly, the Joint Protocol explicitly rejected future application of concepts such as "socialist legality." Moreover, the same provisions required the parties to institute a "free, democratic, federal and social basic order, based on the rule of law"—words clearly intended to refer to the fundamental political principles of the Basic Law and to reject the prevailing principles of the GDR Constitution.[48] Thus, "central constitutional principles of the Basic Law" were made applicable to the GDR through the adoption of the State Treaty.[49]

Two other related themes also seem to run throughout the State Treaty. First, the treaty in effect took note of the past control of the judiciary by the executive and by Communist Party authorities and prescribed special measures to ensure the independence of judicial action.[50] In related sections the treaty also attempted to increase the strength, scope, and independence of the legal profession in the GDR.[51]

Moreover, in a number of provisions the treaty required the GDR to take steps to improve the environment.[52] Given the catastrophic absence of environmental control in the GDR, these sections must be viewed as pious exhortations that would have required much more in the way of legal implementation and, above all, economic support before they actually could be put into effect. Yet these provisions may have had some influence on an important amendment of the GDR Constitution that acknowledged basic environmental principles.[53]

To assist the GDR in this transitional period, the State Treaty required that the Federal Republic pay substantial subsidies to the GDR. In the second half of 1990, the Federal Republic was to pay DM 22 billion to balance the GDR budget, DM 750 million for GDR pensions, and DM 2 billion for unemployment compensation in the GDR.[54] As early as July 1990, however, it became clear that these amounts would be seriously insufficient. Even with the required payments, the GDR foresaw a substantial deficit in the 1990 budget, because of unexpected expenses and a rapidly deteriorating economic situation.[55] These early deficits were the forerunners of massive expenditures made and to be made by the federal treasury as part of the process of unification.

## The Aftermath of the State Treaty: Immediate and Long-Term Effects

The most noticeable effect of the State Treaty was the introduction of the West German currency, the Deutsche Mark, into the GDR on July 1, 1990. The immediate result of the currency reform was the sudden appearance of western consumer goods in the GDR. Bananas and other previously exotic fruits appeared in stands on the streets of East Berlin. Over a weekend, shops in the center of East Berlin filled with western clothes, cosmetics, electronics, and running shoes—the insignia of the long-desired consumer society replacing the more sober products of socialist planning. Western banks erected temporary offices on vacant land, and potential customers crowded around parked trailers advertising travel to the Mediterranean and other places now accessible to GDR citizens with D-Marks from the currency reform.

Yet these developments were soon accompanied by difficult problems, and the problems became even more serious in succeeding months. The dominance of western goods in the eastern grocery stores—apparently the result of practices of western food distributors as well as a pent-up demand for western goods—created catastrophic conditions for eastern farmers who found that they could no longer sell their products.[56] Moreover, western goods were sold at very high prices in the east. In Berlin, eastern citizens did their shopping in West Berlin (where the prices were, oddly, lower), but other consumers in eastern Germany farther from the west lacked that opportunity.[57]

More fundamentally, the sudden extension of the D-Mark to the GDR meant that all customers who purchased goods from manufacturers in the GDR would soon be required to pay their bills in hard currency. But for huge customers of the GDR in eastern Europe—the regimes of the east bloc lands—payment was impossible because they had no adequate hard currency reserves. As a result, many businesses in the GDR that had supplied eastern customers faced an uncertain future. Problems flowed in the other direction as well: with western currency in their hands, East German customers and industries no longer wished to purchase what they regarded as inferior east bloc goods. Accordingly, the shock of the currency union had a serious adverse impact on the economies of east bloc states that relied on trade with the GDR.[58]

Yet, for some in the GDR, the currency union also seemed to bring profound psychological benefits. As one eastern political figure noted: "From one day to the next we could [suddenly] feel like people with equal rights, [because we now] held D-Marks in our hands—one of the most stable currencies in the world. Now we were no longer second-class persons when we went on vacations abroad—as we had been earlier."[59]

Whether it was wise to embark on currency reform before accession is a problem that continues to evoke sharp debate. Of course, the implementation of the currency reform on July 1, 1990, together with the entire apparatus of the State Treaty, was thought to be essential in order to avoid a premature accession of the GDR to the Federal Republic, or perhaps a renewed outflow of thousands of GDR citizens to the west. Yet the currency reform did undeniably have the sudden effect of exposing the eastern economy and society to the rigors of capitalism without much preparation; and the exchange rate of 1:1 for wages, set forth in the State Treaty, played its anticipated role in producing extraordinarily high unit costs for east German goods. Indeed, by late summer of 1990, unemployment numbered in the hundreds of thousands because eastern business concerns were unable to compete with their western counterparts.[60]

Accordingly, critics have suggested that, instead of introducing the D-Mark in effect over night, the parties should have accepted the proposal of the European Community for the transitional introduction of a special interim Mark that would have permitted a gradual approach to the value of the D-Mark. Although this would have made it more difficult for GDR citizens to acquire western goods at the outset, it might have created less unemployment during this transitional period.[61]

Whatever the precise causes—which remain a matter of some debate—the currency union and subsequent unification were attended with a loss of almost 50 percent of all jobs in eastern Germany (a decline from well over nine million to five million by mid-1992), as well as a loss of approximately two-thirds of its former industrial output—"a far more dramatic collapse of the East German economy than even the pessimists had expected."[62] Even though the consequences of this dramatic collapse are to some extent covered by various government programs and the massive transfer payments flowing from west to east, the "severity of the depression in East Germany is without parallel in modern economic history. Not even the Great Depression of 1928–1933 was as bad."[63]

In general, many of the reforms called for by the State Treaty, such as the "privatization" of state-owned People's Property, could not be effectively undertaken in the short period between the adoption of that treaty and the ultimate unification of both German states in October 1990. Indeed, unification occurred at an earlier point than was contemplated when the State Treaty was signed, and the two German governments adopted a second state treaty (the Unification Treaty) in late August 1990 for the purpose of regulating the remaining problems in a comprehensive manner.[64] Thus, the State Treaty was an important milestone in the process of unification, particularly with respect to currency reform and underlying constitutional change in the GDR, but it was unable to work effective changes in many of the other important areas that it was intended to cover. Yet by subjecting the weakened and inefficient East German economy to unrestrained western competition, as well as by extending western principles and much of western economic law to the east, the first State Treaty foreshadowed and in many instances preordained the developments that were to come.

CHAPTER 8

# The Final Months of the Volkskammer: Constitutional Problems of Accession and the First All-German Election

AFTER THE signing of the first State Treaty, the GDR Volkskammer entered a period of fevered legislative activity. On the one hand the Volkskammer frantically sought to remake the GDR state in preparation for a unification whose date seemed to be shifting ever nearer. On the other hand, the Volkskammer had to confront the constitutional and political problems raised by the process of unification itself. Finally, as the reality of unification approached, some groups in the Volkskammer attempted to preserve certain aspects of GDR law and society that seemed worth retaining—although in many cases they found that they were too late in this endeavor.[1]

The process of the final months, including the crucial decision on accession, was by no means without its difficulties. On June 17, for example, the German Social Union (DSU)—a small right-wing party in the governing coalition—threw the Volkskammer into uproar and confusion by moving that the GDR immediately join or "accede to" the Federal Republic under article 23 of the Basic Law.[2] The other parties, almost all of which also sought early unification, recognized that this step was premature. Because no Unification Treaty had yet been negotiated, accession would have brought the population of the GDR into unification without the security of any established terms. Moreover, accession before an external settlement among the World War II Allies was completed could have led to chaos. Prime Minister de Maizière feared, for example, that accession on June 17 would have resulted in the instantaneous presence of thousands of Soviet troops on NATO territory—because the GDR would suddenly have become part of the Federal Republic—without any international provision having been made for such a contingency.[3]

The premature initiative of the DSU was buried in committee and thus effectively rejected. On the same day, however, the Volkskammer moved toward unification by approving a series of fundamental constitutional amendments adopting principles of the Basic Law,[4] and also by enacting the statute authorizing and regulating the Treuhand, which contemplated the sale of GDR People's Property into private hands.[5] Perhaps coincidentally, these crucial measures were enacted on the anniversary of the massive GDR uprising of June 1953 which, together with the Prague Spring of 1968, had been an important historical forerunner of the 1989 revolution.

Rejection of the DSU's call for immediate unification, however, did not resolve the difficult issue of when the GDR should accede to the Federal Republic under article 23—a decision which, in constitutional form at least, was confided solely to the GDR itself. Indeed, during the summer of 1990, questions of the timing of accession became curiously involved with another crucial political and constitutional issue—the structuring of the first all-German Bundestag election, which had been set for December 2, 1990.

## The Election Law and the Date of Accession

The questions surrounding the first all-German election were closely related to some of the central issues of unification. The political forces that prevailed in this election would guide the nation through the crucial post-unification period—in which the principles agreed upon in the summer of 1990 would actually be applied, and the long-term political, economic, and social problems of integrating the former GDR into the western system would have to be confronted. This election, moreover, would serve as a plebiscite on the process of unification up to that point, affording West German voters their first opportunity to express a judgment on these issues by ballot.

In the Volkskammer during the summer of 1990, debates over the structuring of the first all-German election came to focus increasingly on the question of whether the GDR should accede to the Federal Republic before or after the December 2 election. At the bottom of this peculiar imbroglio was the most basic of political quarrels—a dispute over future partisan advantage.[6] If the GDR acceded *before* the all-German elections, most observers assumed that the general election law of the Federal Republic would cover the entire country including the former GDR. Under the Federal Election Law, a party that failed to receive 5 percent of the total vote was ordinarily barred from entering the Bundestag.[7] If this rule would require parties to obtain 5 percent of the votes of the entire unified nation—as was thought to be the case if accession occurred before the election—the almost certain result would be the elimination of a number of small but significant parties in the GDR. These would probably include the PDS (the former ruling Communist Party, whose 16 percent showing in the GDR Volkskammer election in March 1990 would not amount to 5 percent of the entire German electorate);[8] the DSU, a conservative party most closely associated with the Christian Social Union (CSU) of Bavaria; and certain small reform parties that led the East German revolution in 1989 but whose electoral alliance "Bündnis 90" had received less than 3 percent of the GDR vote in the Volkskammer election.

On the other hand, an accession that occurred only after the December 2 Bundestag election would apparently allow a separate election law for the GDR with a separate minimum percentage requirement or indeed, as in the

March 18 Volkskammer election, no minimum requirement at all. Under this system, some of the smaller parties in the GDR would probably be represented in the Bundestag at least for one legislative period.[9]

Interestingly, the Christian Democrats, the largest party in the GDR, and particularly their leader Prime Minister Lothar de Maizière, fought strenuously for accession *after* the December 2 election—a move that could have preserved some of the smaller parties.[10] Commentators assumed that this was his (and Chancellor Kohl's) way of paying a political debt by supporting a solution that would preserve the conservative DSU. Moreover, many believed that the continued existence of the PDS might siphon votes from the Social Democrats—another advantage for the conservative coalition.[11] In contrast, the Social Democrats (SPD) argued that accession should occur *before* the election—a move that would presumably eliminate the conservative DSU as well as the threat from the PDS.

The public arguments, however, were conducted on a considerably more elevated plane.[12] Pressing for an early accession, the SPD argued that it was only logical to form a single state before conducting elections for the government of that state;[13] the SPD sought to preserve the heritage of the 1989 opposition parties by suggesting that Bündnis 90 might receive a number of places on the SPD party list. In contrast, de Maizière maintained that a later accession was necessary in order to preserve the smaller parties of the 1989 revolution[14]—although the primary beneficiary would not be those parties but the successor of the SED. Perhaps more convincing was de Maizière's argument that accession—and, indeed, any Volkskammer vote setting a definite future date for accession—should be delayed in order to maintain the GDR's position in negotiations on the Unification Treaty.[15] De Maizière apparently believed that any remaining weight in the GDR's negotiating position rested on its ability to refuse accession on inadequate terms; an early accession, or even an early vote binding the GDR to a future accession, would forfeit this advantage.

These struggles over the election law and the date of accession naturally increased tensions within the fragile GDR coalition. Indeed, the Liberal Party, which also favored the 5 percent clause, left the government in July 1990, accusing de Maizière of delaying the date of accession for the purpose of political gain.[16]

In early August 1990 the Federal Republic and the GDR adopted an election treaty that split the political advantage between the CDU and the Social Democrats.[17] Under the treaty, accession would occur before the first all-German election, and the election would be conducted pursuant to the requirement that a party must ordinarily receive 5 percent of the votes of the all-German electorate in order to enter the Bundestag. But the treaty qualified the draconian 5 percent rule in one important way. Small parties could improve their chances of representation by joining with larger parties for purposes of meeting the 5 percent requirement, but only if the parties thus joining restricted their campaigns to separate Länder. Thus, parties with candidates running in the same state (except Berlin) could not join together for this purpose.

This qualification of the 5 percent rule was significant, but it did not favor all of the small parties equally. For the PDS, for example, the qualification appeared to be useless because the former ruling party of the GDR would certainly be unable to attract any western partner of significance. But for the conservative DSU, an ally of the Bavarian CSU, this provision was a means of political salvation. The political strength of the DSU was concentrated in the former GDR, and the party had no plans to campaign in Bavaria—the only state in which the CSU registered its candidates. Thus the DSU and CSU could easily mount a joint campaign under the election statute. Indeed, the purpose of this provision was so transparent that it was viewed as a special law favoring the DSU and the conservative coalition; accordingly, the provision was attacked as raising "the impression of an unrestrained misuse of power."[18] In contrast, under this provision the PDS would almost certainly fail to meet the 5 percent requirement in an all-German election; it therefore would not have been represented in the Bundestag—a result that was seen as yielding some benefit for the SPD.

Yet the PDS still represented a significant, if minority, position in the former GDR and its exclusion from the Bundestag in this manner raised serious questions. The ultimate effect of the statute on the GDR reform parties was less clear because the western Greens had entered into an alliance with a consolidated group composed of the GDR reform parties and the separate eastern Greens. Yet if this group failed to obtain 5 percent of the total vote, the reform parties of autumn 1989 would also be excluded from the Bundestag. In any case the Greens and other small parties continued to insist that the 5 percent clause—especially in this election—was unconstitutional.

Accordingly, the Greens and the Left List/PDS filed an action in the Constitutional Court, arguing that their rights of equality of political opportunity were infringed by the provisions of the election treaty and the first Election Statute; individual Bundestag candidates of the Greens were also complainants.[19] Argument in this case was heard on an expedited basis, and in late September 1990 in its first major opinion relating to unification—the first in a series that was to extend over years—the Constitutional Court unanimously held the Election Statute unconstitutional as a violation of the equality of opportunity of political parties.[20]

From an early point in its history, the Court had found that constitutional provisions guaranteeing the free formation of political parties and equal electoral rights implied a general requirement that the government treat political parties equally.[21] Although any 5 percent minimum requirement might infringe this principle of equality—because small parties may sometimes receive no representation at all instead of their actual proportionate share—the Court had held that a 5 percent requirement is constitutional in principle as a means of ensuring a stable and functioning parliamentary system.[22] In the

Unification Election case, the Court continued to adhere to this general doctrine but indicated that prior decisions had involved ordinary elections in the Federal Republic and that the constitutionality of any specific 5 percent provision must depend upon the surrounding circumstances.[23] It was the special circumstances of the unification election that made the all-German 5 percent clause unconstitutional.

In this case—in contrast with prior elections in the Federal Republic—the reduction of electoral chances for certain small parties seemed particularly severe. From the point of view of political parties in the GDR, unification represented a sudden expansion of the relevant election territory and population, and these parties were largely unprepared to compete on a broader scale. The disadvantages were particularly acute in the case of the small reform parties which, in contrast with the PDS and the former bloc parties (such as the CDU), had been in existence for a few months only.[24] Under these circumstances, expansion of the election territory would drastically reduce the opportunities available to many parties in the GDR. Indeed, extending the 5 percent clause across the entire united country meant that the new parties of the east would be required to obtain a number of votes equal to more than 23 percent of the voting population of the territory in which they had previously campaigned and were best known. In contrast, the parties of the west would need to receive votes equaling only 6 percent of the previous western electorate.[25] Thus the unequal impact of the all-German 5 percent clause on the eastern and western parties was evident. The government argued that the provision allowing combined party lists would mitigate this unfairness, but the Court noted that, because of its narrow limitations, very few parties would be able to take advantage of this provision. Consequently, this exception worked its own unconstitutional inequality.[26]

This was the Constitutional Court's first major opinion on questions arising from German unification, and it struck a note that was to be followed in later opinions on the subject. In this opinion, as in others, the Constitutional Court appeared to view itself as a mediator of the tensions of unification—with the purpose of settling or mitigating, rather than confirming or exacerbating, sharp differences between east and west (or between other groups) that had arisen in the process. In this case, the traditional parties of the west had won too much, and the heroes of the East German revolution (as well as their opponents, the PDS) were set to vanish from the national political scene. This result would have had the effect of eradicating political groups authentic to the GDR—and particularly those reform groups that had worked out a new alternative constitutional consciousness in the Round Table draft and elsewhere. The established western parties were willing to see these alternative forces disappear, but the loss was apparently too great for the Constitutional Court. Accordingly, its decision preserved these small but important political groups—as well as the PDS—for at least one four-year period of the Bundestag.

In its opinion striking down the first Election Statute, the Court suggested that a constitutionally acceptable alternative would be a statute instituting *separate* minimum requirements, at an equal percentage level, in the two parts of Germany.[27] Because a new statute had to be enacted within a few days if the election was to be held as planned on December 2, the Bundestag almost immediately enacted a second election statute, adopting separate 5 percent clauses for the two parts of Germany, as suggested by the Court.[28]

## The End of the Volkskammer

Meanwhile, after the signing of the Election Treaty in early August, the life of the East German Volkskammer was coming to an end. The final weeks of the Volkskammer in August and September 1990 were characterized by a rush to complete the parliament's last work before unification.[29]

These weeks were also marked by political crisis. In late August, after a period of increasing tension, the SPD resigned from the coalition government. The immediate cause of the split was a clash of views on the financial future of eastern Germany. SPD Finance Minister Walter Romberg announced financial projections for the GDR that were substantially more pessimistic than those of de Maizière and treaty negotiator Günther Krause; and de Maizière responded by dismissing Romberg and another minister.[30]

Yet behind this specific dispute, the approaching parliamentary election heightened the general hostility between the major parties.[31] As part of this process Richard Schröder, a strong supporter of the coalition, was succeeded by Wolfgang Thierse as the leader of the SPD caucus in the Volkskammer, and Thierse brought a more confrontational style to the task. By the time the SPD left the coalition, much of the legislative work was complete.[32] Yet the split sharpened the controversies over the final negotiations on the Unification Treaty, then underway, and the eastern SPD was bolstered in its position by SPD governments in the western Länder, which had recently obtained a majority in the Bundesrat.[33]

On August 23, after much dispute over the date, the Volkskammer voted by a two-thirds majority to accede to the Federal Republic on October 3.[34] In this later period, the Volkskammer also adopted two important statutes that sought to settle accounts with the GDR's political past. The first of these extended to victims of the SED regime the right to "rehabilitation" and a measure of compensation. The second set forth regulations for the preservation and handling of the Stasi files. Both statutes represented deeply held views of the GDR on these incendiary subjects; but the ruling coalition in the Federal Republic had serious reservations on a number of points and these statutes were to be subject to significant modification both before and after unification.[35] The Unification Treaty between the Federal Republic and the GDR was approved by the Volkskammer in September. A majority of the SPD representatives joined in support—although with considerable reservations on the grounds of insufficient social rights in the constitution and lack of clarity about the status of Berlin as the seat of government, among other points.[36]

Finally, on October 2, the Volkskammer had its last meeting. On that final day, the eve of unification, several of the speeches were celebratory in nature, as perhaps befitted the occasion.[37] Speaking for the caucus of Bündnis 90/Greens, however, Jens Reich stuck a somewhat different and distinctly more somber tone. Commenting on the process of unification under article 23 instead of article 146—and the concomitant failure to adopt an all-German constitution—Reich remarked that the Frankfurt Parliament of 1848 "achieved a beautiful, modern constitution, but did not achieve German unity. With us, it is just the other way around!" With respect to the economic problems of many in the former GDR, Reich noted that there will be "millions of destroyed life plans," and he generally refused to praise the work of the Volkskammer, which he characterized as a "mixed record." Finally, Reich referred to the fissure that would mark the future of Germany—a social, regional, political, and spiritual rift, which "our future in Germany will receive as a legacy of the past."[38] To some extent this rift may have been exacerbated by the rapid process of unification under article 23—instead of a more deliberate process under article 146—but fundamentally it arose from forty years of extreme separation and divergent life histories and personal development in quite different social, economic, and political structures.[39]

In a speech on October 3, the day of unification, the Federal President Richard von Weizsäcker expressed confidence that this gap between east and west Germans could be overcome.[40] Chancellor Kohl also emphasized the rapprochement of the two populations, stressing the importance of having "understanding for one another. . . . We must overcome the thought that Germany is still divided into 'this side' and 'that side.'"[41] Because of forty years' separate development, Kohl declared, "we must reach out to each other with understanding and mutual respect. . . . Openness and tolerance will be necessary."[42]

Yet in the years that have followed unification, Jens Reich seems to have been the better prognosticator, as the rifts about which he spoke on October 2, 1990, have shown little sign of being closed. Of these, the economic rift is still the most dramatic, with sharp differences in incomes between the regions accompanied by high levels of unemployment in the east.[43] Yet psychologists and citizens of the east emphasize that these material divisions are accompanied by even more deep-seated rifts in attitudes and psychological structures: the separate development of forty years is not so easily overcome, and many citizens of the east are affected by a profound sense of disorientation in the new social circumstances.[44] Finally, these rifts and the accompanying clashes of interests seem to have led to a progressive "de-unification" of political life, both within the Bundestag and in the ranks of the prevailing CDU. Eastern representatives often do not feel integrated into Bonn's political life,[45] and a palpable reluctance to carry out the governmental move to Berlin has exacerbated this division.[46] Indeed, on important property issues of unification—most notably the extent and nature of compensation for vast lands expropriated under the Soviet occupation—the eastern CDU has joined with other eastern representatives in a hard phalanx against the CDU in the west.[47]

But for present purposes, yet another form of division in political structures bears particular significance. The complex process of drafting the new constitutions of the eastern states has tended to reveal quite different eastern views on what a constitution should contain—and the general attitude that it should represent—than those prevailing in the west. The first part of this volume will conclude with an examination of the re-creation of the eastern states and the revealing process of constitutional drafting that formed an important component and outgrowth of that larger process.

CHAPTER 9

# Reconstitution of the Eastern Länder

ALMOST from the beginning of the East German revolution, it was clear that the former states of the GDR—which had been effectively abolished in 1952—would re-emerge as important factors of political life. During 1990, therefore, preparations were made for the reconstitution of the states, although they were not actually re-created until the moment of German unification. Since that point, the new states have had a rich constitutional development. Indeed, in many respects this development has overshadowed the rather modest constitutional changes of the Basic Law resulting from unification.

## The Five Eastern Länder: Historical Background

When the GDR was founded in the Soviet occupation zone in 1949, it included five states (*Länder*) loosely drawn from the historical subdivisions that composed Bismarck's empire. These five Länder had been created at a very early point in the Soviet occupation, long before the founding of the GDR. Indeed, a number of important measures of the occupation period—such as the vast Soviet land reform—were undertaken, formally at least, as measures of the new Länder.[1]

The original states of the GDR were Mecklenburg, the most northerly of the five; Brandenburg, a part of Prussia that lay west of the Oder-Neiße line (excluding Berlin, which was governed separately); Saxony-Anhalt, composed of Prussian Saxony and the province of Anhalt; Saxony, the largest of the states in population; and Thuringia, located in the southwestern corner of the Soviet zone.[2] Each of these states had its own constitution, and the GDR Constitution of 1949 provided for a Länderkammer, a house of the federal parliament representing the states.[3]

Because some of these states contained former Prussian territory, it seemed evident that the state of Prussia had ceased to exist. Yet to underscore this point—and to quell any doubt about the legality of the new states—the Allied Control Council adopted a statute in 1947 officially abolishing the state of Prussia.[4] In the words of the statute, Prussia "from early days ha[d] been a bearer of militarism and reaction in Germany," and its abolition was viewed as an important step in the democratization of Germany.[5]

The five new states played a political role in the early days of the GDR, but in a centralizing move in 1952 the GDR government effectively abolished the Länder and replaced them with fourteen administrative districts (*Bezirke*). This drastic political act appeared to violate the requirements of the 1949 GDR Constitution and may not have been fully authorized by statute until

1958.[6] In any event, this step was uncannily reminiscent of Hitler's abolition of the states of the Weimar Republic and their replacement by administrative districts. In both cases the central regime sought to consolidate its power by abolishing potential sources of competing authority.[7]

Yet strong regional loyalties persisted in the GDR even after the abolition of the Länder, particularly in the southern states of Thuringia and Saxony. With the revolution of autumn 1989, these loyalties—in many cases stronger than any loyalties that the GDR as a whole had been able to evoke—again came to the fore. Indeed, the great Leipzig demonstrations were marked by the presence of the green and white flag of Saxony (which had been suppressed for forty years), in addition to the flag of the Federal Republic.[8]

After the revolutionary events of autumn 1989—but even before unification became a certainty—it was clear that the historical states of the GDR would be re-created. In reaction to prior centralizing theory, many believed that strong states were necessary in order to resist any renewal of authoritarian tendencies in the central government. Interestingly, a similar view had prevailed among the victorious western Allies in 1948–49 during the drafting of the West German Basic Law. One of the few occasions on which the Allies intervened in this process (after setting down certain basic outlines) was to seek stronger state governments than the West German drafting committee had originally proposed.[9]

The first State Treaty, signed by the GDR and the Federal Republic in May 1990, clearly contemplated that the GDR would again be divided into Länder.[10] Then, in midsummer 1990, the GDR Volkskammer adopted a statute with the force of a constitutional amendment providing for the re-creation of the historical states in the GDR.[11] An accompanying statute also provided that elections would be held on October 14, 1990, for one-house state parliaments.[12] In a provision of great importance for the future, the statutes declared that these parliaments would have the power to adopt state constitutions. Although the state constitutions were to be adopted after accession, much work was already being done in the summer of 1990 on proposals for these constitutions, in some cases with assistance from legal experts from the Federal Republic.[13]

Here as elsewhere, the status of Berlin raised special problems. Until the Allies relinquished their reserved rights, Berlin could not become a state in the full sense, and there was also uncertainty over whether Berlin should remain a separate state or be merged with the state of Brandenburg, which completely surrounds it. The GDR statute provided, however, that East Berlin would receive "state authority," which could be exercised by its city council and magistrate.[14] After unification with West Berlin, the united city could consider whether it would remain an independent state or merge with Brandenburg.[15]

When the GDR's accession to the Federal Republic was first seriously considered in early 1990, the prevailing view seemed to be that, after the re-creation of the Länder, each state would accede to the Federal Republic independently. This method would ensure the continued existence of the individual states in the Federal Republic. Although it was generally contemplated that this step would be taken by all states simultaneously—pursuant to a joint decision or a central resolution of the GDR Volkskammer—there was some anxiety that one or two particularly impatient states would seek to accede prematurely on their own.[16] Perhaps as a result of these fears, it was eventually agreed that accession would be accomplished by the central government of the GDR and not by the individual states, and article 1 of the Unification Treaty clearly reflected this decision. Indeed, under GDR legislation and the Unification Treaty, the eastern states were not re-created until October 3, 1990, the date of the GDR's accession to the Federal Republic. Up to the point of unification, therefore, there were no eastern Länder capable of acceding individually to the Federal Republic, even though planning for the state governments had long been under way.

The existence of the five east German states as new Länder of the Federal Republic was, therefore, guaranteed by the terms of the Unification Treaty and not by separate acts of accession.[17] Some voices have argued that the accession of the GDR as a whole—instead of the individual accession of five eastern states—has contributed to continued feelings of the separateness of the former GDR after unification.[18] But it is questionable whether social, economic, and even psychological consequences can be drawn with any confidence from this rather technical constitutional decision.

## Constitutional Revisions and the New Länder: The Bundesrat and the Financial Constitution

The inclusion of five new eastern Länder in the Federal Republic raised a number of important issues of federalism under the Basic Law, and these constitutional problems in turn reflected questions of political and economic power. Perhaps the most important of these concerned the representation of the five new Länder in the Bundesrat, the second house of the West German parliament.

The Bundesrat represents the states in the federal system, and it is composed of members of the state governments.[19] In contrast with the United States Senate, the representation of the states in the Bundesrat is not equal, but it is not precisely proportional to population either. While the smaller states have no less than three representatives in the Bundesrat, until the Unification Treaty was adopted the largest states had no more than five.[20] Yet the proportional difference in population is much greater. Under this system, for example, the new states of the former GDR would receive a total of nineteen seats in the Bundesrat.[21] On the other hand the West German state of North Rhine-Westphalia, with a population slightly exceeding that of the entire GDR, would have five representatives only.[22]

The existing apportionment of votes in the Bundesrat already imposed considerable disadvantages on the large states, and the accession of the

GDR—with its relatively small states—would seem to exacerbate that apparent unfairness. The Unification Treaty addressed this problem, but undertook only a minor adjustment by adding a clause providing that states with more than seven million inhabitants would be accorded six votes in the Bundesrat.[23] This change increased the representation of North Rhine-Westphalia from five to six votes, but the five new states of the GDR—with approximately the same population—still receive nineteen votes. Nonetheless this step preserved an element of de facto political power among the largest German states.[24]

The re-creation of the East German states suggested another constitutional (and practical) problem that would have existed whether the GDR acceded to the Federal Republic as a single entity or as five separate states. In sharp contrast with the Constitution of the United States, the Basic Law requires that the richer German states in effect make contributions to the poorer states, with the goal of making living standards approximately equal throughout the nation. These contributions are effected through the sharing of revenues between the states and the federal government, coupled with federal distributions to the poorer states, as well as by direct payments from the richer to the poorer states according to a complex statutory scheme enacted pursuant to constitutional requirements.[25] It seems clear that, for the foreseeable future, the five eastern states will be considerably less affluent than the original states of the Federal Republic, but the original states have strongly resisted paying anything close to the daunting amounts that would be necessary to equalize living standards in the two parts of Germany, if indeed such a thing were possible. This difficult constitutional problem was ultimately regulated in article 7 of the Unification Treaty.

## The New Constitutions of the Eastern Länder

On October 14, 1990, less than two weeks after they had been re-created upon unification, the five new Länder of the former GDR held elections for the state parliaments. The conservative CDU received enough votes to form a government, in various coalitions, in four of the five Länder. The exception was Brandenburg in which the SPD formed a coalition with Bündnis 90/Greens and a small liberal party, the FDP. These results, which generally paralleled the balance of power on the federal level, confirmed the political trend that had led to rapid unification in the first instance.

One of the most important tasks of the new states was the adoption of the state constitutions. Yet, although preliminary drafting work had begun in the summer of 1990, the constitutions in the new eastern Länder developed slowly. Delays resulted from hard-fought political struggles in the state legislatures over the underlying nature of the constitution. In these debates a specific east German constitutional consciousness confronted more traditional western views with an immediacy and power that was often lacking in deliberations on the federal level.

Debates over the state constitutions focused largely on a series of provisions that were not contained in the Basic Law but were set forth in the constitutional draft of the GDR Round Table working group.[26] The Round Table draft contained guarantees of social welfare, environmental protection, and other "state goals," as well as provisions allowing the voters to participate in law making through plebiscites. GDR reformers and sections of the SPD argued that such provisions should be included in constitutional amendments or in a new federal constitution adopted under article 146 GG; but it seemed likely from the outset that the prevailing CDU alliance would succeed in resisting many of these changes in the Basic Law itself.

Consequently, theoretical disputes relating to these provisions shifted—at the outset at least—from the national level to the constitutional debates of the five eastern Länder. Interestingly, the developments in the states have differed considerably from the results in the Bundestag. Although four of the five Länder were governed by the CDU or CDU coalitions, all of these constitutions contain substantial provisions for social welfare and other state goals, as well as plebiscitary elements.[27]

To some extent, the inclusion of these provisions in the eastern Länder constitutions seemed to reflect the view that—even though the Stalinist principles of the GDR Constitution have been totally rejected—there were certain aspirations of social welfare in the East German constitutions that should also be recognized in the "social market economy" of Germany under the Basic Law. In light of the desperate ecological situation in the east, constitutional provisions for environmental protection have also had considerable appeal. Moreover, the plebiscitary elements reflected the ideas of direct democracy of the East German revolution.

Yet these constitutional developments in the Länder have also evoked fundamental questions. The inclusion of state goals of social welfare and environmental protection, for example, raise serious doubts about their possible judicial enforceability, as well as arguments that the Länder would not have the competence or resources to fulfill those obligations. A broader question raised by these developments is whether the new state goals and plebiscitary elements represent little more than an elaboration and moderate extension of the principles of the Basic Law or whether these provisions actually imply a shift to another form of constitutionalism or, as some critics have put it, "another republic."

The constitutional developments in the various east German Länder reveal a fascinating diversity while retaining a basic similarity in a number of important themes.

*Constitution of Saxony*

When the constitution of Saxony went into effect on June 6, 1992, it became the first new constitution to be adopted in the eastern Länder.[28] The history of the new Saxon Constitution, which began in the Dresden street demonstrations of 1989, well reflects the tension between conservatives, who sought to limit the document to concepts of the Basic Law, and reform groups which invoked the 1989 revolution to advocate extensive rights and state goals, as well as expanded opportunities for direct democracy.

### BACKGROUND AND HISTORY

Saxony has a tradition that extends back to the first Saxon Constitution of 1831 and the Weimar period constitution of 1920, and the Saxon cities of Leipzig and Dresden were centers of the democratic revolution of 1989.[29] Thus the omens for a liberal constitution in Saxony seemed favorable. Yet the modern constitutional history of Saxony almost began with a serious false step in early 1990, when a group of local SED officials attempted to seize the constitutional initiative. These officials drafted a state constitution that drew heavily upon the 1947 Saxon Constitution of the Soviet occupation period and planned to consolidate power by promulgating this document in a ceremony in the ancient Saxon city of Meißen.[30] To combat these plans of the old regime, an alliance of reformers known as the "Group of 20" hurriedly published a preliminary draft of a liberal constitution at the end of March 1990. Publication of the reformers' draft apparently discouraged any further moves by the SED officials.[31]

The Group of 20 had been formed during a demonstration in Dresden in the unsettled days of early October 1989 when Wolfgang Berghofer, the SED mayor of Dresden, agreed to negotiate with representatives of the demonstrators.[32] Although the Group of 20 was basically chosen by acclamation from the crowd, it endured—with a number of changes in personnel—and developed into a form of opposition Round Table for the city of Dresden.[33]

The constitutional draft of the Group of 20 was preliminary in form—indeed, it had been written literally overnight to counter the plans of the SED. Thereafter, a committee of Saxon reformers met with advisors from the western "partner" state of Baden-Württemberg to produce a more sophisticated charter known as the Gohrisch draft.[34] The eastern participants were chosen by regional Round Tables and reflected a balance among geographical areas and political affiliations. At the beginning of the group's work in April 1990 a substantial degree of cooperation and understanding prevailed among its members; there was no political infighting of the sort that tended to grow up after the influence of the political parties solidified at a somewhat later date.[35] Although the expertise of the western advisors was naturally important, authority over the most significant political decisions seems to have been retained by the Saxon reformers.[36]

After an elaborate process of public hearings and commentary, a revised Gohrisch draft was issued in October 1990 and presented to the new Saxon Parliament (*Landtag*), elected shortly after unification.[37] But the revised Gohrisch draft was not the only proposal that was submitted to the Landtag. During the debates of the mixed commission, Karl Bönninger, one of the eastern academic advisors, became increasingly disenchanted with the tendency of the discussions.[38] Joining with colleagues at the University of Leipzig, Bönninger submitted a separate—more left-wing—draft, which came to be known as the draft of the Leipzig University professors.[39]

After two rounds of public hearings and discussions—in a contentious process that lasted over a year and a half and evoked hundreds of written comments—the Saxon Landtag adopted a constitution based on the revised Gohrisch draft by the requisite two-thirds vote. As the first of the new constitutions, it served as an important model for efforts in other eastern Länder.

### THE TEXT OF THE CONSTITUTION

The Constitution of Saxony sought a middle course between those who favored strict conformity with the Basic Law and those who sought a transformed constitutional document. Yet like the other new charters, the constitution moved away from the Basic Law in important respects. For example, the Saxon Constitution contains a significant list of "state goals"—a form of activist provision that obliges the state to take affirmative measures to achieve particular ends. Thus the constitution includes elaborate provisions for environmental protection, including a specific obligation to further the recycling of raw materials and the sparing use of energy and water, as well as a more general statement on the responsibility toward future generations.[40] The constitution also authorizes "acknowledged environmental groups" to participate in administrative proceedings and to file legal actions in their own names.[41] Something of a novelty in German procedural law, this provision may lend further practical effect to the "state goal" of environmental protection.[42]

Among other "state goals," the constitution contains a general "right" to an existence with human dignity—specifically including rights to employment, appropriate living space, appropriate subsistence support, social security, and education.[43] An important qualifying provision indicates that the state is only obligated to pursue those goals "in accordance with its abilities"; there is no constitutional violation if the state falls short of goals that are beyond its power to achieve.[44]

Although the "state goals" are in some sense "binding" on the Saxon parliament, they are distinct from basic rights and they cannot be made the subject of a constitutional complaint in a court.[45] Yet, even so, these provisions may have some significant judicial impact: the state goals may be considered by the courts in interpreting other provisions of state law, and the state goals must be taken into account by state executive officers in the statutory balancing required by various state or federal programs, such as programs for the building of housing.[46]

The presence of these state goals in the Saxon Constitution is particularly interesting: Saxony was the only eastern state governed by an absolute CDU majority, and the western CDU has generally rejected state goals with great vigor. No doubt the presence of these provisions owes much to the pressure of the SPD, whose votes were necessary for the two-thirds majority required for ratification. Yet, even so, these provisions were basically acceptable to important figures in the CDU leadership in Saxony—a point that may distinguish them from their more traditional western counterparts.[47]

The "defensive" rights of the Saxon Constitution—such as rights of speech, assembly, and choice of profession—are generally drawn from the Basic Law.[48] But some rights go beyond those explicitly stated in the federal document—such as protections against involuntary subjection to experimentation and rights of employee participation in governance of the workplace (codetermination).[49] In addition to general guarantees of equality, specific measures protect the status of the Sorbian and Silesian minorities in Saxony.[50]

In reaction to the GDR past, the Constitution of Saxony contains numerous provisions relating to information and data. Individuals are protected against excessive collection of data concerning their activities and lives, and the executive is required to deliver information to parliament unless competing interests of the executive or a third person intervene.[51] Every affected person has a right to information relating to the natural environment, unless that right is outweighed by particularly important competing interests.[52] As one framer of the Saxon Constitution remarked, the right to environmental data is a result of "our common history in the GDR. Then there was no information about environmental data; rather such data were a state secret and anyone who demanded such data, or used the data as a starting point for politically 'deviating' expressions of opinion, was prosecuted."[53]

The Constitution of Saxony also contains extensive provisions—similar to those set forth in the Round Table draft—for adoption of legislation through direct popular action.[54] These provisions, which were to be echoed in one form or another in all of the new state constitutions, endorsed the claims of popular sovereignty developed in the 1989 East German revolution and indeed can be viewed as "the constitutional consequences of the [Leipzig demonstrators'] slogan 'We are the People.'"[55]

The plebiscitary provisions of the Saxon Constitution contemplate a three-stage procedure.[56] In the first stage (*Volksantrag* or People's Petition), forty thousand qualified voters (approximately 1 percent of the voting population) can present a proposal directly to the legislature (*Landtag*), and the Landtag must consider the proposal and grant a hearing to its proponents. If the proposal is not adopted within six months, the proponents will have at least another six months to launch a "People's Demand" (*Volksbegehren*), which requires the signatures of 450,000 voters, approximately 12 percent of the voting population. If this action is successful, the voters will then have an opportunity to enact the proposal in a plebiscite. Yet the number of voters necessary to trigger a plebiscite is comparatively high—more than twice the number that was required in the Gohrisch draft—and the likelihood that this method will often be used is correspondingly reduced. But even so, it has been argued that because of the long six-month period for gathering signatures—among other features—"here, for the first time in German constitutional history, a rule for popular legislation has been found that has a real possibility of proving itself functional and effective."[57]

The constitution concludes with elaborate sections on education and the relationship between church and state, and some final transitional provisions. The section on religion "pays tribute to the historic role of the churches and religious communities before the [East German revolution] in housing and protecting dissenters and those seeking help."[58] Many of the transitional provisions are focused on the National Socialist or Communist past, promising compensation to individuals for damages incurred under the dictatorships and proclaiming the general intention to abolish the causes of the failures of the past.[59]

Because it was a compromise, the Saxon Constitution was subjected to bitter attack—principally from members of the reform group Bündnis 90/Greens and from the Left List/PDS, who sought greater deviations from underlying views of the Basic Law. Criticizing the unenforceable nature of the state goals as well as asserted inadequacies in provisions for direct democracy, a representative of Bündnis 90/Greens declared that the document did not adequately reflect modern constitutionalism.[60] Invoking similar themes, a representative of the Left List/PDS declared that the constitution deprives "the citizens of Saxony of their identity, rather than giving them a new identity" because the charter reflected "morality and values of the old Federal Republic that are alien to their mentality."[61] In contrast, however, Justice Minister Steffen Heitmann asserted that the "constitutional-political consciousness" of the document was influenced by forty years of the GDR regime and the peaceful revolution of 1989.[62]

### *Constitution of Brandenburg*

The drafting of the Constitution of Brandenburg—the second state constitution to be officially adopted—was attended with extraordinary national controversy.[63] But in its final version it does not deviate as radically from the Constitution of Saxony, and other new state constitutions, as its proponents had hoped or its opponents had feared.

Brandenburg was the only new eastern state with a coalition government led by the SPD, and its constitutional drafts drew substantially from the ideas of the Round Table. Indeed, authorities in Bonn claimed that the results actually violated the Basic Law, and they apparently contemplated challenging the document in the Federal Constitutional Court. Ultimately, however, the SPD was forced to enter into compromises with the CDU which tended to neutralize some of the most distinctive constitutional proposals.[64] But even with these compromises, some supporters asserted that the charter did indeed reflect a new constitutional understanding arising from modern social conditions as well as the East German revolution of 1989.[65] Of all the new state constitutions, therefore, the Constitution of Brandenburg probably resembles most closely the sort of constitutional resolution that GDR reformers and the SPD had hoped to achieve through unification under article 146 GG, instead of accession under article 23.

### BACKGROUND AND HISTORY

Intense constitution-drafting activity took place in Brandenburg before the state was officially formed. As early as April 1990—at about the same time that the Group of 20 issued its draft in Saxony—a "coordinating committee" working with regional Round Tables published a constitutional draft.[66] Numerous written comments were received and a revised draft, issued in September, contributed significantly to later constitutional proposals.[67]

The process of constitution drafting assumed a more official form with the election of the Brandenburg Landtag in October 1990 and the establishment of its constitutional committee. In an apparent attempt to perpetuate the plebiscitary spirit of the 1989 revolution, only one-half of the committee members in Brandenburg were drawn from the parliament itself.[68] The others were outside citizens' representatives who, it was hoped, would strike a balance among various occupations and strata of the population.[69] The initial phase of the committee's work was marked by a spirit of cooperation, and the first draft constitution was approved by representatives of all parties on the committee from the CDU to the PDS.

This consensus, however, was not destined to last. A torrent of national controversy followed publication of the committee's first draft in June 1991, because of what western conservatives considered to be its radical provisions.[70] Indeed, a well-known CDU politician declared that the draft was a model "for another republic."[71] With increased national attention, the previous inter-party cooperation evaporated.

In Brandenburg as in Saxony, therefore, an early consensus—apparently based on the experience of the 1989 revolution—gave way after the incursion of more conservative western constitutional ideas and pressure on the eastern CDU from its partners in Bonn. In this shift, one may perhaps perceive the spirit of article 23 confronting the spirit of article 146. Reflecting developments on the national level, the CDU sought to impose on the constitutions of the new Länder the fundamental concepts of the Basic Law. In contrast, the original views of the eastern consensus sought to modify that traditional structure by including guarantees of social welfare and direct democracy reflecting the experience of the GDR and the revolution of 1989.

The SPD and Bündnis 90 generally supported these new provisions, as did the PDS. But the CDU in Brandenburg was split into two factions by this dispute. On the more conservative side, Ulf Fink—a West Berliner who became chair of the Brandenburg CDU—led the attack against the constitutional draft. But Peter-Michael Diestel, former GDR interior minister under de Maizière, led a significant group of CDU members who favored the proposal.[72] The ultimate struggle focused on the extent to which CDU members would follow Diestel and support the constitutional draft.

After numerous revisions and compromises in an "extraordinarily difficult process," a final draft was approved by an overwhelming majority in the Landtag—including a number of CDU members.[73] The new constitution was then submitted to the voters in a plebiscite. Although the popular vote overwhelmingly supported the constitution (over 94 percent of those voting favored the draft), only about 48 percent of the qualified voters took part in the plebiscite. The constitution was finally approved, therefore, by the vote of somewhat less than half of the qualified electors. Some argue that low participation could impair the charter's legitimacy, and this experience has been invoked—perhaps as a pretext—to justify the omission of constitutional plebiscites in other Länder.

### THE TEXT OF THE CONSTITUTION

The Constitution of Brandenburg elaborates on themes that are found in the other new state constitutions, but following the Round Table draft, it often develops these themes in a more thorough and far-reaching manner. It therefore remained a target of those who favored close adherence to the principles of the Basic Law.[74]

If the Constitution of Brandenburg is based on a new constitutional understanding—as some of its proponents (and opponents) declared—that new understanding could be characterized as an attempt to weaken or dissolve certain governmental and social hierarchies that arguably have persisted under the Basic Law. These include the political hierarchy of the "state" (as represented by the political parties or the "political class") over the people in general, as well as the social hierarchies of men over women, the prosperous over the not so prosperous, and citizens ("Germans" or "Deutsche") over noncitizens ("Ausländer"). Much of the constitution is directed toward dissolving these structures.

An attempt to weaken the power of the political parties or the "political class" is generally found in all of the new state constitutions, but it is probably pursued most thoroughly in Brandenburg. The proportion of the voting population necessary to trigger law making by plebiscite is particularly low;[75] moreover, the constitution may be amended through a plebiscite or by the calling of a constitutional convention with ratification of its proposed draft through a plebiscite.[76]

In addition to rights of political parties, the constitution contains protections for looser citizens movements (*Bürgerbewegungen*) and citizens initiatives (*Bürgerinitiativen*)—provisions that clearly reflect the experience of the East German revolution.[77] As in the Round Table draft, certain citizens groups have special rights to receive official information and to submit proposals that must be considered by state or local governing bodies.[78] Indeed, citizens have broad rights to obtain information from the state—always an important political tool.[79]

Seeking to weaken social hierarchies, the constitution requires affirmative action to achieve the social equality of women: the state is obligated to work toward "the equality of women and men in their occupations, in public life, in education and training, and in the family . . . through effective measures."[80] A related provision declares that men and women "have a claim to equal compensation for equally valuable work," an apparent endorsement of the doctrine of "comparable worth."[81] Furthermore, article 26(4) declares that "work in the home, the raising of children, [and] the domestic care of people in need of such care" are as worthy of respect as work in an occupation, although the provision does not elaborate on the possible legal effects of this declaration.[82]

In a very painful compromise for the SPD, the final constitution omitted an earlier draft provision that obligated the state government to work toward the decriminalization of abortions performed in the first three months of pregnancy.[83] On the other hand, the constitution does contemplate a relaxation of traditional family patterns—which might include traditional patterns of hierarchy—by prohibiting discrimination on the basis of sexual identity and acknowledging the importance of protecting long-lasting "living communities" outside of marriage.[84]

In light of problems of xenophobia that increased after unification, it is noteworthy that the constitution seeks to break down the hierarchy between "Germans" and "foreigners" by providing that citizens of other countries residing in Brandenburg are to receive the same treatment as "Germans within the meaning of the Basic Law" unless the constitution specifically states otherwise.[85] Moreover, these noncitizens residing in Brandenburg shall have the right to vote (and to be elected to office) in local elections, as well as to take part in citizens' initiatives and plebiscites, as soon as such rights are permissible under the Basic Law.[86] This qualification is regrettably necessary because the Constitutional Court has held that it is unconstitutional for the Länder to grant voting rights to persons who are not "Germans" in the sense of the Basic Law.[87]

These sections on noncitizens' rights are complemented by other provisions reflecting a strong international consciousness. The preamble invokes the role of Brandenburg in "a Europe that is becoming united," and another section declares that Brandenburg seeks "to work together with other peoples, in particular with its Polish neighbors."[88] Moreover, the constitution recognizes not only the rights contained in the Basic Law, but also those set forth in various international human rights conventions.[89]

With respect to the mitigation of inequalities based on wealth, the Constitution of Brandenburg contains an extraordinary provision declaring that the state will "further a wide distribution of property, in particular the creation of capital of employees through participation in productive property"—perhaps an attempt to preserve some slight reflections of former socialist ideas in Brandenburg through the furtherance of employee shareholding plans.[90] Additional provisions also seek to bolster the legal position of employees. For example, employees and their unions have a right of co-determination in accordance with statute, and unions have a right of access to places of business.[91] In addition to an employee's right to healthy and humane working conditions, the constitution extends increased protection against dismissal to members of society with special needs or problems—students, pregnant women, single parents, persons with illnesses, handicapped persons, and older employees.[92] Finally, the constitution seeks to protect freedom of speech within the employment relationship except to the extent limited by statute.[93] In a provision intended to assist the weaker party in another important economic relationship, a tenant may be evicted from an apartment only if a substitute apartment has been found.[94] This rule is drawn from statute or practice in the old GDR. But all of these employment and housing provisions—however interesting they may be as models or suggestions for the future—will have little immediate practical effect, because these areas are now almost completely within federal legislative competence under the German Civil Code (BGB) and related statutes.[95]

THE FUTURE OF BRANDENBURG

A significant issue facing the state of Brandenburg is that it could possibly merge with Berlin in the next few years, as suggested—but not required—by article 5 of the Unification Treaty.[96] In April 1995 the governments of Berlin and Brandenburg signed a merger agreement, and the agreement was approved by a two-thirds vote of both state parliaments two months later.[97] The agreement remained subject to ratification by the voters of the two states in plebiscites scheduled for May 1996.[98] Supporters of the merger argued that the economies of both Berlin and Brandenburg would be improved by a unified regional government.

At present the Constitution of Brandenburg stands, along with the Round Table draft, as a possible exemplar of a new constitutional consciousness arising from German unification. Notwithstanding the fact that a number of its provisions may fall outside the competence of the Länder, it represents a document in which some of the more novel aspects of the Round Table draft have found their way into official form and can be employed in the executive and judicial interpretation of legislative measures. Yet the fate of this document in any possible merger of Berlin and Brandenburg remains uncertain: if the merger is finally approved, a joint constitutional committee would begin working on a draft to be drawn from the existing constitutions of the two states.*

## *The Constitution of Saxony-Anhalt*

The Constitution of Saxony-Anhalt was adopted almost simultaneously with the constitutions of Saxony and Brandenburg, but the process of adoption in Saxony-Anhalt had its own disputes and special problems.[99] Most notably, the CDU/FDP government of Saxony-Anhalt strongly advocated the view advanced by some western scholars that state constitutions adopted after the promulgation of the Basic Law in 1949 should not contain their own lists of

* In May 1996, the voters of Brandenburg rejected the merger.

basic rights but rather should rely on the rights contained in the Basic Law.[100] This view, of course, would exclude an independent listing of basic rights from all constitutions of the new eastern Länder. In the end, however, a compromise was struck on this and related points. Accordingly, the Constitution of Saxony-Anhalt—although generally less adventurous than the constitutions of Saxony and Brandenburg—resembles those documents in many important respects.

### BACKGROUND AND HISTORY

The state of Saxony-Anhalt was assembled by the Soviet occupation government (as a "province") after World War II, and it cannot invoke a long political and constitutional history like that of Saxony.[101] From an early point, however, it became clear that the new eastern states would be re-created along the lines of the original Länder of the Soviet occupation zone, and therefore a committee of the central Round Table of Saxony-Anhalt drafted a proposed constitution for the future Land in the summer of 1990.[102] This proposal was roughly contemporaneous with early drafts in Saxony and Brandenburg.

The official work of constitution drafting began in November 1990 with the formation of a constitution committee of the newly elected Landtag of Saxony-Anhalt. The committee met under the direction of Reinhard Höppner, who had achieved distinction as a forceful vice-president of the Volkskammer under de Maizière.[103]

In general, the work of the constitutional committee proceeded smoothly with good cooperation between the representatives of the CDU and the SPD.[104] Indeed, in an interesting twist, the most significant struggle was not within the constitutional committee itself but rather between the committee and the CDU/FDP coalition government. This dispute centered on whether the constitution should contain its own catalog of basic rights, as advocated by the committee, or whether it should only be an organizational statute, with total reliance on the rights listed in the Basic Law—the position strongly favored by the government.[105]

This dispute reflected an interesting tension between east and west because the government was largely composed of conservative western imports. For conservative parties of the west, the existing rights of the Basic Law were relatively safe, and additional rights raised the danger of questionable innovations. The western view also reflected a certain constitutional authoritarianism in its assumption that the Basic Law formed the only true source of constitutional doctrine and that competing or complementary sources of constitutional principle—for example, the constitutional "laboratories" of the states—would violate that unity. This position viewed the drafting of the eastern constitutions principally as a "legal-technical" problem of conformity with the Basic Law and did not acknowledge the political passions and experience that lay behind these eastern constitutional drafts.[106]

In contrast, the members of the parliamentary committee—citizens of the east—sought a document that could reflect the history and experience of the

1989 revolution; they also sought a document that could be the subject of broad discussion among the population and in the schools, and for these purposes they believed that a "full constitution," with its own catalog of basic rights, was essential.[107] In this context, therefore, one may again detect a confrontation between the spirit of article 23—the view that the doctrine of the Basic Law (and little more) should be extended to the east—and the spirit of article 146, which was open to some admixture of additional ideas.

In a compromise, the parliamentary committee agreed to draw its catalog of rights closely from the Basic Law, and indeed the language of the two documents is sometimes very close. Yet the committee also made some significant changes and additions. A proposed draft was issued in September 1991, and hundreds of comments were received from the public.[108] The constitution was finally enacted by a vote of two-thirds of the Landtag in mid-1992, thus concluding a bitter struggle over fundamental constitutional matters that had lasted more than a year. As in Saxony, the document was not submitted to the voters for approval. Omission of a plebiscite was an important factor in votes against the constitution from the ranks of Bündnis 90, the DSU, and the PDS.[109]

## THE TEXT OF THE CONSTITUTION

The Constitution of Saxony-Anhalt contains numerous provisions that reflect the experience of the GDR past. Many regions of the GDR suffered serious environmental damage, but Saxony-Anhalt contains those areas—such as the chemical manufacturing center of Bitterfeld—where the problems were most severe. Accordingly, the constitution of Saxony-Anhalt emphasizes protection of the environment as a particularly important theme throughout the document.[110] In another provision clearly seeking to exorcise the demons of the past, the constitution limits "measures of optical or acoustical spying"—techniques frequently employed by the Stasi.[111]

The Constitution of Saxony-Anhalt is unique among the new state constitutions in that it divides its basic guarantees into three separate sections. Not only is there a sharp distinction between judicially enforceable basic rights and nonenforceable but nonetheless in some sense obligatory state goals. In addition, there is an intermediate category of "institutional guarantees," outlining certain social or governmental institutions—such as marriage, family, schools—that the state is obligated to protect and develop.[112] This tripartite division may reflect a realistic ordering of provisions, and it has been characterized as a "particularly fortunate" device that furthered compromises in the Landtag's work on the constitution.[113] Yet these distinctions have also drawn criticism on the ground that the various forms of protections are not (and perhaps cannot be) clearly distinguished in all cases.[114]

The judicially enforceable basic rights are drawn closely from the Basic Law, with modest alterations or additions.[115] The institutional guarantees generally resemble similar provisions on family, education, and religion in the Basic Law, although there are some differences. For example, there are special protections for the "physical and psychological" development of children, reflecting similar guarantees in the Round Table draft.[116] Moreover, teachers, parents, and children have the right to participate in "structuring the life and work in the school" through representatives—an extensive right of codetermination for schools.[117]

On the other hand, the specific state goals of social welfare are somewhat less extensive than those of Saxony and Brandenburg.[118] Moreover, the jurisdiction of the state constitutional court is restricted in significant ways. The court may strike down a *statute* that "directly" invades constitutional rights, but it is not permitted to review executive or judicial actions. This limitation of jurisdiction may neutralize, to some extent, the victory of the constitutional committee in inserting a catalog of basic rights in the constitution.[119]

Finally, issues of church and state played an important role in the constitutional debates in Saxony-Anhalt. Article 32(1), a section that was disputed with particular vigor, declared that church and state are separate and explicitly affirmed the church's ability to comment on matters of public concern. The significance of this provision can only be understood against the background of the history of the GDR.[120] The position among west German constitutionalists is that church and state are indeed not completely separate, but the view of the Saxony-Anhalt Constitution reflects the less religious society of the east and seeks to avoid the unpleasant associations that religious cooperation with the state could evoke in light of the history of the GDR. The statement of the church's right to comment on public affairs—a provision apparently drawn from the GDR Constitution of 1949—must also be viewed in light of the struggle of the church to maintain its right of expression under the GDR.[121]

The constitutions of Saxony, Brandenburg, and Saxony-Anhalt were adopted as the first wave of eastern state constitutions in 1992. Approximately a year was to follow before the last two constitutions—those of Mecklenburg-Vorpommern and Thuringia—were adopted by the state parliaments in 1993. These final two constitutions are in some ways more modest than their three predecessors and seem to follow the general outlines of the Basic Law somewhat more closely. Perhaps the greater distance from 1989 had further diluted the strength of the ideas of the GDR citizens movement; moreover, the hardening of strong party positions—with the increasing influence of the conservative western CDU over its eastern counterpart—had time in the interim to become even more deeply entrenched.[122]

### *The Constitution of Mecklenburg-Vorpommern*

The Constitution of Mecklenburg-Vorpommern was adopted by the Landtag in May 1993, and it was approved in a plebiscite in 1994. It was unique among the new state constitutions in relying on the Basic Law for most of its constitutional rights—thus basically adopting the resolution that was rejected in Saxony-Anhalt. Mecklenburg-Vorpommern is a small and somewhat remote state, and western experts seem to have influenced the process of constitutional drafting to an unusual degree. Yet, even here, there are important departures from the Basic Law with the inclusion of significant social goals and an emphasis on strong powers of the Landtag vis-à-vis the government and executive offices.

### HISTORY AND BACKGROUND

In early 1990, local round tables of the three administrative regions in Mecklenburg commissioned a working group to draft a proposed state constitution. Completed in mid-1990, this document assumed that Mecklenburg-Vorpommern would remain a state of the GDR.[123] Yet the draft contained many ideas of the 1989 reform movement, and it ultimately had some influence on the final state constitution.[124]

After accession of the GDR to the Federal Republic, the newly elected Landtag of Mecklenburg-Vorpommern established a constitutional drafting commission. As in Brandenburg, not all of the commissioners were members of parliament: the commission also included experts chosen by the four Landtag fractions and by the Greens and an alliance of GDR reform parties.[125]

The commission focused much of its attention on a constitutional draft jointly proposed by the two most active western experts on the commission.[126] The views of these two experts sometimes differed, but where they were in agreement, their position often prevailed. In this way, the outside experts exerted a significant influence on the Constitution of Mecklenburg-Vorpommern.

The commission issued its first draft in April 1992, and 20,000 copies were distributed to the public for discussion in meetings throughout the state.[127] By the summer of 1992, when these meetings took place, massive unemployment had caused considerable bitterness in Mecklenburg-Vorpommern—as in the rest of the former GDR—and much of the public discussion centered around a possible right to employment.[128] These public pressures probably contributed to strengthening the right of employment and other social guarantees as well as plebiscitary elements in the constitution.[129] After some hard parliamentary bargaining, the final draft was adopted by the requisite two-thirds of the Landtag in May 1993—subject to approval by the electorate in a plebiscite in 1994.

### THE TEXT OF THE CONSTITUTION

The important role played by the outside experts in Mecklenburg-Vorpommern was most evident in the area of basic rights. Contrary to the result in Saxony-Anhalt, the constitution adopted the view of some western analysts that new state charters should principally rely on rights of the Basic Law instead of setting forth an independent catalog of rights.[130] Accordingly, article 5(3) of the constitution incorporates the federal basic rights as rights under the state constitution, and the constitution contains few independent basic rights of its own. This resolution can be viewed as a partial bow in the direction of article 23 and the general constitutional decisions of the west.[131] But this technique could also be regretted as reflecting an insufficient independent self-assertion in this eastern state.

Of the few specific basic rights set forth in the constitution itself, perhaps the most notable was a requirement that the state protect the human dignity of "all persons living *or sojourning*" in the state.[132] With an explicit reference to sojourners, the drafters sought to emphasize that noncitizens are entitled to the equal protection of human dignity. This provision was a response to the murder of noncitizens from Turkey in Mölln, in the nearby state of Schleswig-Holstein, while the constitution was being drafted.[133] A provision reacting to the GDR past guarantees equal access to public education "regardless of economic or social position or world view or political opinions."[134] In the GDR, children of working-class families were often favored in education, and persons with disapproved political views were denied access to higher secondary education (*Oberschule*) and therefore to a university education.[135]

A much debated question was whether, as the GDR reform groups proposed, the state constitutional court should be authorized to adjudicate questions relating to basic rights of the Basic Law incorporated by reference in the state constitution.[136] Generally, of course, the Federal Constitutional Court is the prime interpreter of the Basic Law. Yet if the incorporated basic rights are viewed as separate state rights—as well as federal rights—the state constitutional court could engage in its own interpretation of the state right so long as that interpretation did not violate the Basic Law. The result would ordinarily be that the state right could be interpreted to give more protection—but not less protection—than the federal right as interpreted by the Federal Constitutional Court.[137] The Constitution of Mecklenburg-Vorpommern seems to reject this resolution, at least in part, by excluding the incorporated basic rights from the jurisdiction of the state constitutional court in a large proportion of cases.[138]

In contrast with its modest provisions on basic rights, the Constitution of Mecklenburg-Vorpommern contains a catalog of relatively strong state goals, including elaborate environmental provisions that reflect the crucial role of nature and the seacoast in this northern region.[139] State goals of employment and housing were also strengthened as a result of the desperate economic situation following unification.[140] Indeed, one housing provision seems to go beyond a state goal and provide an individual guarantee: the state and local governments will "assure shelter to every person in case of need."[141]

Other important provisions of the Constitution of Mecklenburg-Vorpommern provide for a parliament that is notably strong in comparison with the executive government. Of course, the executive is generally distrusted as a result of the GDR experience, but these provisions also may have arisen from specific early experiences of executive aggrandizement in Mecklenburg-Vorpommern after unification.[142] In any case, these provisions may combat the steady loss of power in state parliaments—vis-à-vis state executives and the administration—that has become common in the West German states over past decades.[143] Accordingly, the constitution proclaims the supremacy of the parliament over the executive and the administration, emphasizes the critical role of the parliamentary opposition, and requires the government to provide information to the parliament or its committees in numerous instances.[144] Indeed, to enhance parliamentary control, the government must provide "timely and complete" information to the Landtag about its proposed statutes and regulations and other plans—including those relating to its participation in the Bundesrat—and its collaboration with the federal government, with other states, and with the European Community.[145]

Although the CDU had originally resisted this procedure, the Constitution of Mecklenburg-Vorpommern was subject to ratification in a plebiscite.[146] But as a result of the experience in Brandenburg—where less than 50 percent of qualified voters participated in a separate plebiscite—the Landtag decided that a vote on the constitution would be combined with the next communal election, scheduled for June 1994. This procedure may have introduced partisan electoral considerations more clearly into the decision. In any case, the PDS launched a vigorous campaign against the constitution, arguing that the state goals of social welfare were not strong enough. In the disastrous economic circumstances of the post-unification period this campaign had some success, and the constitution was approved by the comparatively close margin of 60 percent to 40 percent.[147] Only 65 percent of the qualified electorate of Mecklenburg-Vorpommern took part, and therefore considerably less than 50 percent of the eligible voters cast ballots approving the charter.[148]

### *The Constitution of Thuringia*

The last constitution of the eastern states was adopted by the parliament of Thuringia on October 25, 1993, and was ratified by the voters in a general election in October 1994. Like the Constitution of Mecklenburg-Vorpommern, the Thuringian Constitution is in some ways less adventurous than its predecessors in Brandenburg, Saxony, and Saxony-Anhalt. Yet the document reflects most of the themes that we have seen in the other state constitutions and, indeed, it presents a number of its own special problems.

#### BACKGROUND AND HISTORY

As was also true in Saxony, Thuringia has had a long constitutional history, commencing with local constitutions in Sachsen-Weimar-Eisenach and other constituent principalities in the early decades of the nineteenth century. Thuringia also possessed an important republican constitution during the Weimar period.[149] The early Thuringian principalities had called themselves "free states"—a phrase that is essentially equivalent to "republic"—and the 1993 constitution drew on this history in adopting the name, the "Free State of Thuringia." In so doing, the framers sought to mark a clear break "with an almost sixty-year undemocratic past, of the Nazi period and the SED era."[150]

The official process of constitution drafting in Thuringia commenced in mid-1991 with the creation of a ten-member parliamentary committee, advised by ten outside legal experts. The committee was immediately presented with five fully prepared constitutional drafts, submitted by the five parties of the Landtag: CDU, SPD, FDP, Bündnis 90/Greens, Left List (LL)/PDS.[151] Thereafter, the three most powerful parties apparently worked together to achieve a compromise resolution, leaving the two minor parties—Bündnis 90/Greens and the LL/PDS—effectively outside the process. This exclusion led to disaffection and, ultimately, the two small parties refused to support the final constitutional draft.[152] The constitution was finally adopted by the Landtag in a somewhat raucous meeting on the historic Wartburg in October 1993. On that occasion, two representatives of New Forum, who were refused permission to speak, were ejected or departed in protest, and the representative of the Greens sharply criticized the SPD for joining with the conservative coalition in supporting the draft.[153]

## THE TEXT OF THE CONSTITUTION

At an early point, all parties decided in favor of a "full constitution," rejecting the technique adopted in Mecklenburg-Vorpommern in which many constitutional rights of the Basic Law were incorporated by reference. According to the drafters, a full catalog would allow the basic rights to be given a special accent or emphasis in reaction to experience under the GDR.[154]

The drafters of the Thuringian Constitution showed particular concern for historical investigation of the totalitarian past. For example, certain rights of data protection may be subject to appropriate qualification in light of "the concerns of historical research and the historical working-through [of the past]."[155] Moreover, the constitution declares that "instruction in history [in the public schools] must be directed toward an undistorted presentation of the past."[156] The framers inserted this perhaps naive provision in reaction to the notorious required courses in civics or "citizenship study" (*Staatsbürgerkunde*) in the GDR schools, which "[sought to justify] the SED hegemony and its policies."[157]

The central constitutional guarantee of human dignity goes beyond the text of the Basic Law by explicitly guaranteeing a right of human dignity in dying.[158] This provision was adopted over the opposition of some members of the CDU, who feared that it might be interpreted to authorize euthanasia.[159]

As in other state constitutional debates, the central disputes were between the CDU and the SPD on questions of state goals and plebiscitary elements—with the SPD pushing for broadened goals and more clear obligations and the CDU seeking to limit these provisions. In the end, the constitution contains carefully formulated state goals of social welfare.[160] In an attempt to preserve some social structures of the GDR past, a separate article also indicates that "the state and localities [should] encourage day care establishments for children."[161] This provision was an evident reference to the child care centers (*Kinderkrippen*) of the GDR period which, whatever their ultimate evaluation, allowed parents (particularly mothers) to work.

As is common in German states, the constitution protects a right to education. In Thuringia, a major dispute focused on whether the system would be a "track" system, in which students would attend separate schools according to abilities and career plans, or a "comprehensive" system, in which all students would attend the same schools. The CDU favored the traditional "track" system, which generally prevails in western Germany notwithstanding criticism on the ground that it furthers social elitism. The SPD favored the "comprehensive" system. Ultimately, all systems were acknowledged in the constitution, but the CDU seems to have prevailed because the provision implies that the "track" system will have priority.[162] The CDU prevailed on another question of traditional social structure when it defeated a guarantee for enduring living communities outside marriage.[163]

Environmental provisions were particularly important in Thuringia which, like Mecklenburg-Vorpommern, contains areas of great natural beauty.[164] Moreover, the Thuringian Constitution acknowledges the constitutional status of animals as possessing rights and values in themselves: "Animals are respected as living essences and fellow created beings [*Mitgeschöpfe*]. They are protected from treatment inappropriate to their nature [*nicht artgemäßer Haltung*] and from avoidable suffering."[165] Although this provision goes further than the language of other eastern constitutions,[166] the provision was criticized by some of the Greens on the grounds that, by virtue of its religious flavor, it was unduly anthropocentric and did not grant adequate protection.[167]

Another bitter dispute surrounded the question of whether God should be mentioned in the preamble of the Thuringian Constitution. Only a relatively small proportion of Thuringian citizens (or, indeed, citizens of the eastern states in general) are attached to religious congregations: the old regime's attempts to secularize the society of the GDR had achieved significant success.[168] Yet a carefully formulated "invocation of God" is indeed found in the constitution.[169] In the view of the CDU, the purpose of this provision is to acknowledge that all constitutions must respect some "super-positive source of values"; according to this argument, the provision is not intended to suggest that the great majority of Thuringian citizens who have no religious affiliation are not full participants in the constitutional system.[170] Yet, another way of looking at this result in Thuringia is to see in the decision the pressure of the western CDU on its eastern members to follow traditional views accepted more enthusiastically in the west than in the east.

### *The Constitutions of Berlin*

In its legal and constitutional history—both in the postwar period and in the days leading up to unification—Berlin presented certain unique problems. Because united Berlin contained both of its long-separated eastern and western parts, Berlin became in a sense a new state upon unification. Indeed, unification was accompanied by the dissolution of the reserved rights of the World

War II Allies, which had prevented West Berlin from assuming undisputed status as a state of the Federal Republic.[171]

The constitutional history of postwar Berlin reflected the fate of the divided city. After a temporary constitution of 1946, the city council issued a single charter for the four occupation zones in 1948, but, lacking Allied approval, this document never went into effect. In 1950, after the Federal Republic and the GDR were created, West Berlin was permitted to adopt a revised version of the 1948 document as its own separate "state" constitution, although the Allies resolutely denied that Berlin was actually a state of the Federal Republic. The constitution of 1950, with occasional amendments, remained in effect in West Berlin throughout the Cold War period. Under the GDR, in contrast, East Berlin did not have a separate political status and adopted no separate constitution.[172]

As German unification approached in 1990, the West Berlin parliament and the East Berlin city council, which had been democratically elected in May of that year, worked together to harmonize the two separate legal regimes. But reluctant simply to be merged into West Berlin—indeed, seeking to avoid the one-sided process that was taking place on the federal level under article 23 GG—members of the East Berlin city council sought to create a basis for negotiations on a constitutional compromise. Accordingly, the eastern city council adopted a separate East Berlin Constitution in the "unification summer" of 1990.[173] The council's legal authority to adopt this document was tenuous, and its action was criticized by Prime Minister de Maizière.[174] But eventually, the East Berlin Constitution seems to have been accepted as valid—perhaps as an "artifact of the year 1990."[175]

The East Berlin Constitution was in some respects an extraordinary document, departing from the understanding of the Basic Law at some significant points.[176] For example, the eastern drafters proclaimed a universalist outlook by declaring that public authority flows from "the totality of Germans *and foreigners* residing in Berlin"—ignoring the western constitutional view that the electorate is generally limited to "Germans."[177] The East Berlin Constitution contained detailed social rights such as a "claim for an appropriate dwelling" and protection against eviction, as well as rights to employment or support in gaining employment.[178] Discrimination on the basis of sexual orientation was prohibited, as well as discrimination against "living communities" outside of marriage, and the state was required to further the possibility of employment through the maintenance of various forms of day care institutions.[179] Perhaps most notably, the East Berlin Constitution explicitly guaranteed a right of abortion in early stages of pregnancy—a provision unique in German constitutions.[180]

Of course, it was clear that the constitution of unified Berlin would be based on the existing West Berlin Constitution and that the East Berlin Constitution would have to go out of effect after unification. Yet members of the East Berlin city council, supported by some members of the West Berlin parliament, sought to employ the East Berlin Constitution to preserve some eastern influence over the final joint document. Accordingly, the East Berlin Constitution imposed a restriction on the conditions of its own demise: the eastern constitution would go out of effect at the first meeting of the unified Berlin parliament—but only if the unified parliament acknowledged, in a constitutional provision, that a further, final constitution of Berlin would be drafted and adopted during the first parliamentary term. This final constitution would have to be adopted in a plebiscite and would be based not only on the Berlin constitutions of 1948 and 1950, but also on the East Berlin Constitution of July 1990.[181] In response to these requirements, the West Berlin Constitution—which was to become the constitution of unified Berlin—was amended in September 1990 to include this obligation to adopt a "revised" Berlin constitution in the future.[182]

Also as a result of pressures from East Berlin, the West Berlin Constitution was amended in a number of other respects in October 1990. Provisions were added requiring protection of the environment and "the natural basis of life" and guaranteeing each individual's right to control "personal data."[183] Moreover, another provision accorded the parliamentary opposition equal political rights, a guarantee that reflected "bitter experience" in the SED state.[184]

At the same time, the West Berlin Constitution was amended to provide for a state constitutional court (*Verfassungsgerichtshof*).[185] Such an institution was almost universal in the states of western Germany, but for reasons related to the city's occupation status, a constitutional court had never previously existed in Berlin. The new Berlin court consists of nine judges, four of whom must be members of the professional judiciary. In addition, the statute establishing the court required that not more than six of the nine judges be of the same sex—a unique feature in German rules relating to constitutional courts.

The first all-Berlin parliament was elected at the time of the national elections in December 1990 and, at its first meeting, the parliament adopted the West Berlin Constitution as the constitution of reunified Berlin. Because that constitution had been amended to include the obligation to adopt a further revised constitution of Berlin, the East Berlin Constitution simultaneously went out of effect.[186] Thereafter, the question of planning for the revised Berlin Constitution came to the fore. The SPD and the Greens initially advocated a constitutional convention for this purpose, but the CDU opposed such a potentially wide-ranging body. Eventually the SPD and the CDU—which had formed a coalition government—agreed on a parliamentary commission (Enquete Commission) instead of a convention.

Thereafter, the path of constitutional revision in Berlin was a difficult one, and the Enquete Commission was not even able to begin its work until February 1992. Unlike the original situation in the five new eastern Länder, a western constitution—the Constitution of West Berlin—was already in existence. As a result, those opposing change were not required to yield on issues such as social rights and plebiscitary elements in order to obtain a constitution in the first place.

After some delays, the Enquete Commission issued its final report in May 1994.[187] The commission recommended constitutional changes to strengthen parliament and introduce plebiscitary elements. The commission also proposed new rights and state goals, including those relating to education, protection of the handicapped, access to governmental data, and living communities outside of marriage. The issuance of this report was followed by a further complex process of negotiation to determine which of the proposed provisions would be adopted by the parliament; as coalition partners in Berlin, the CDU and the SPD largely excluded other groups in these negotiations.[188]

After further delays, the new Berlin Constitution was finally approved by a two-thirds vote of parliament in June 1995.[189] Although the commission's proposals for strengthening the parliament were largely rejected, a number of expanded basic rights and state goals were included in the new charter.[190] The constitution also introduced new provisions for direct democracy, although the number of signatures required to trigger a plebiscite was relatively high.[191] All in all, these changes were greater than might have been foreseen at the outset; the CDU's ultimate concurrence in these provisions apparently reflected its view that a new Berlin constitution must be adopted expeditiously, in order to confront the more innovative Constitution of Brandenburg in view of the possible merger of the two states later in the decade.[192]

But even with these significant changes, it may well be that the most important constitutional development in Berlin was the creation of the Berlin Constitutional Court in 1990. In one of its earliest decisions, the new tribunal achieved a sudden prominence and opened up broad new vistas of state court activism in German constitutional law. In this famous decision, the court held that the continued trial of former SED leader Erich Honecker on charges related to shootings at the GDR border violated the Constitution of Berlin.[193] Essentially, the court held that to persist in trying an individual in Honecker's state of health would deprive him of human dignity.

In coming to this decision, the Berlin court went dramatically beyond existing doctrine in a number of respects. According to the court, Honecker's advanced liver cancer would not allow him to live until the end of the trial, and continuation of the trial under those circumstances would violate the guarantee of human dignity by making Honecker into the "mere object" of a proceeding that no longer had a valid purpose. Although the Berlin Constitution did not contain an explicit guarantee of human dignity, the court found that such a value was implicitly protected through other provisions and through the influence of a similar guarantee in the Basic Law.[194] Moreover, the decision was almost universally condemned by western constitutionalists on the ground that it impermissibly entered a federal domain by interfering with the process governed by the Code of Criminal Procedure, a federal statute.[195] Needless to say, the court's judgment caused a public and political sensation. Immediately after the decision, Honecker was released from custody, and he departed for Chile where he continued to reside until his death in May 1994.[196]

In handing down the *Honecker* decision, the Berlin Constitutional Court displayed a remarkable degree of activism, reaching out to create a nontextual guarantee of human dignity and to find—in a most controversial application of that doctrine—that the guarantee required Honecker's release. Perhaps most startling was the court's apparent willingness to disregard the structures of federal law in coming to this conclusion.

Apart from the specific merits of the *Honecker* decision itself, this opinion may suggest a new willingness of state constitutional courts to create an activist jurisprudence that has been largely absent in the states. For our purposes the most interesting question concerns the impact that this decision may have on the new constitutional courts of the eastern Länder.[197] These constitutional courts are still in their early stages, and it is not possible to know whether they will follow a "Berlin model" of activism. But the seriousness with which constitutional drafting was performed in the states, along with the residuum of a special constitutional consciousness arising from the events of 1989 in East Germany, raises a possibility that the creation of these courts may usher in a new era of state court activism. This would be a particularly interesting development in light of various novel constitutional provisions—going beyond those of the Basic Law in many ways—that could to some extent be enforced by those courts. Yet, the overall limits on the constitutional competence of the states, as well as their limited resources, must also be taken into account in contemplating the future of constitutional judicial review in the new eastern Länder.

## Constitutional Development in Eastern Germany—the Past and the Future

At the end of the first part of this volume, we can now review the constitutional development in eastern Germany since World War II. The first constitutions of the Länder in the Soviet Zone, as well as the first GDR Constitution of 1949, shared some liberal traits derived from the Weimar Constitution, but these masked the reality of a developing authoritarian regime, which other provisions of these constitutions in part revealed. The 1968 GDR Constitution—and its 1974 revisions—were more overtly Stalinist in nature, emphasizing the ultimate control of the SED. Moreover, their highly restricted liberal rights were disregarded in practice, although their social promises were more or less realized—at the apparent cost, however, of a deteriorating economic system.

After the East German revolution of 1989, the ideas of the reform groups that had primarily made the revolution were incorporated in the constitutional draft of the GDR Round Table, which in some respects provided an alternative to the Basic Law. It represented an attempt to move toward a less hierarchical society and governmental structure, by increasing the power of women, minorities, and other disadvantaged groups, and by opening up the party state to more general popular participation and a greater measure of popular control. These ideas were apparently rejected, however, in the GDR election of March 1990, which clearly set the course for unification under article 23 GG—a provision that called for the extension of the Basic Law over eastern Germany and, by implication, the extension of other western economic, political, and social structures as well. In effect, the election rejected unification under article 146, which would have opened the possibility of a new German constitution—perhaps deviating in significant ways from the Basic Law in the direction of the Round Table draft and including an admixture of constitutional ideas from the reform circles of the east.

The decision in favor of article 23 was sealed with the signing of the first State Treaty on May 18, 1990, which extended significant economic and legal structures of the west to the GDR. These included not only the all-important western Deutsche Mark, but also western commercial rules and western concepts for the sale of GDR "People's Property" to private investors through the Treuhand.

These developments seemed to reflect the clear dominance of traditional West German concepts in the process of unification. Yet it is important to bear in mind that the more traditional structures of the Basic Law have, in certain instances, prevailed only by rather slim majorities in the west, and are therefore perhaps not entirely stable in the west itself. In any case, even at the time of the first State Treaty, the hints of a somewhat different constitutional consciousness seemed to persist in the east. In a series of constitutional "principles" adopted by the GDR Volkskammer in response to the first State Treaty, a general recognition of the principles of the Basic Law was accompanied by environmental principles and a right of employment that seemed to go beyond the Basic Law—as it then existed—and to look in a somewhat different direction.

In an important decision in autumn 1990, the Federal Constitutional Court began to play a mediating role in German unification by in effect preserving the smaller parties of the east—the reform parties as well as the successor of the SED—for an interim period. Thereafter, the election of December 2, which followed German unification, seemed basically to preserve the political relations that had given rise to the use of article 23 by returning the conservative coalition to power with substantial pluralities in most of eastern Germany. The election was followed by a further deterioration of the economic system in the east, resulting in a catastrophic loss of jobs unparalleled in the history of industrialized countries.

At the same time, the difficult and laborious process of drafting the state constitutions of the new eastern Länder suggested that the ideas of article 23—the uniform extension of concepts of the Basic Law over the east—may not have achieved universal acceptance. Rather, the principles underlying the eastern state constitutions seemed to be as close to the spirit of the Round Table draft as to that of the Basic Law—and perhaps resembled the kind of compromise that could have emerged through the use of article 146 instead of article 23. An important question that remains open is the direction in which the constitutional courts of the new states will interpret these charters.

It is perhaps theoretically impermissible—as one commentator has remarked—for the eastern states to try to reanimate article 146 through the state constitutions, after the use of that article had been rejected at the national political level.[198] But in the text of many of these documents, something like that actually seems to have occurred. Even the most modest of these new state constitutions reflect the lessons of the GDR past and the 1989 revolution, and—with all their similarities to the Basic Law—can still be said to represent a distinctly different, and distinctly eastern, constitutional consciousness. One important question of future constitutional development in Germany is the extent to which the consciousness of the GDR reformers—as embodied in the Round Table draft and, to some extent, in the new charters of the eastern states—may ultimately make its way, through constitutional revision or judicial interpretation, into the constitutional consciousness of the unified nation and the west itself.

PART II

# The Unification Treaty and Beyond

CHAPTER 10

# The Unification Treaty and Amendment of the Basic Law

## HISTORY AND BACKGROUND OF THE TREATY

It had been clear from an early point that German unification would take place under article 23 GG, but it was only as the summer of 1990 approached that the West German leadership realized that unification might occur before year's end—sooner than even the most sanguine westerners had previously imagined. Chancellor Kohl and his cabinet pushed for the earliest possible date, in part out of fear that President Gorbachev's cooperative Soviet regime might topple at any moment. Accordingly, in early summer 1990 the government began to focus on the specific conditions under which unification should take place.

Theoretically, it would have been possible for unification to occur under very general terms, with details of numerous complex problems to be resolved later by the all-German parliament. Such a method had been adopted in 1956, for example, with the accession of the Saar. Some in the west held a preference for this method because it would have given western majorities even greater power after unification. Indeed the simple extension of all laws and institutions of the Federal Republic to the new eastern states might well have been most consonant with the basic theory of article 23, which seemed to contemplate the GDR's "accession" not only to the constitution but also to the legal and social institutions of the Federal Republic.

Yet such a sweeping solution was not acceptable to important figures in the east. In particular, GDR Minister-President Lothar de Maizière sought greater clarity on the terms of unification, and guarantees on some central points, before the GDR actually "acceded" to the Federal Republic.[1] It was therefore clear that the GDR's accession would be accompanied by a second state treaty—a "Unification Treaty"—setting forth the conditions of unification and determining the extent to which western law would be immediately applicable to the former GDR. In this sense, the Unification Treaty represented a softening of the hard-line theory of article 23 because it provided a means—at least theoretically—through which the GDR could participate in forming the basic legal structures of unified Germany.

Negotiations and deliberations over the Unification Treaty occupied the summer months of 1990, and it was signed by representatives of the Federal Republic and the GDR on August 31, 1990.[2] After lively debate, the treaty was approved by the GDR Volkskammer and by the West German Bundestag and Bundesrat. A two-thirds majority was necessary for approval in each body because the Unification Treaty in effect provided for revocation of the GDR Constitution and contained provisions that amended the Basic Law.[3]

The Unification Treaty is the central document of German unification. With its hundreds of pages of detailed attachments, it represents a *tour d'horizon* of German legislation and public life.[4] Accordingly, it sets the basic structures of unification in individual areas as diverse as property claims, abortion, and the future of the eastern universities.

Although the document was adopted after what were in form negotiations between the Federal Republic and the GDR,[5] the parties certainly did not meet on a basis of equality. The Federal Republic would be financing the entire process of unification, and the bankruptcy of the eastern economic and governmental system cast the GDR distinctly in the role of a petitioner. Moreover, the government of East Germany—led by the eastern CDU—was subject to the influence of the western CDU leadership, and GDR Prime Minister de Maizière, notwithstanding his considerable virtues, seemed to lack the strength of personality to hold out against these western pressures. Perhaps most important, the chief GDR negotiator Günther Krause was, to say the very least, favorably disposed to the west. As the chief western negotiator remarked, with perhaps a touch of unintentional irony: "In contrast with [de Maizière], Krause never applied any pressure to preserve something from the old GDR in the new Germany. That made my cooperation with him easier."[6]

In addition to this clear political disparity, the GDR administration hardly possessed the technical competence to draft the detailed provisions necessary for harmonizing the two legal regimes. Instead, this massive work was undertaken by the administrative ministries of the Federal Republic. Thus, in reality, the Unification Treaty—with a few notable exceptions—reflected the general views of the western CDU leadership, with the details worked out by western ministries in Bonn.

Although the western state governments were consulted in this process—and, indeed, were represented at the negotiations[7]—the actual contribution of the states appears to have been minor. Given the swiftness and massive nature of the undertaking, popular participation in the process was minimal as well. Thus, although the process may have been slightly more open than the process of the first State Treaty, the "complexity of reunifying two estranged states took the process out of the public's hands and turned it over to distant bureaucrats."[8]

Moreover, the Unification Treaty was presented to the Bundestag pursuant to the ordinary procedure for approval of treaties, which prohibited any proposals for amendments or deletions. Rather, the members of the Bundestag could only vote to approve or disapprove the document as a whole. Thus, this central document of German unification—a document that among other things involved constitutional amendments, but which in a broader sense could be considered a fundamental constitutional document in itself—was basically the product of the West German executive branches. The democratic deficits in adoption of the Unification Treaty assumed increasing importance when, after unification, some of the treaty's provisions began to reveal severe deficiencies.

## The Text of the Treaty

In drafting the Unification Treaty, the negotiators confronted three basic tasks. First, accession would involve the addition of more than 16 million citizens to the Federal Republic, as well as a new territory of almost 42,000 square miles. These profound changes would require some important modifications of the governmental institutions of the Federal Republic. The addition of five new Länder would require changes in the size and composition of the Bundesrat.[9] Moreover, certain alterations and additions in administrative and judicial institutions would be necessary. An important task of the Unification Treaty, therefore, was to establish the basic structure of those changes.

The second principal task of the Unification Treaty was to determine the substantive law that would apply to the GDR for a transitional period and to specify the length of time that interim adjustments would remain in effect.[10] This task required careful consideration of which measures of the GDR reform movement, or even of the old regime, were to be retained.

Finally, the Unification Treaty looked forward to the future constitutional structure of unified Germany. Although the choice of article 23 indicated that the Basic Law would in general endure, international pressures as well as political and practical exigencies required that the Basic Law itself be amended in a few important respects. Accomplishment of these changes was a third important task of the Unification Treaty. As part of this task, the agreement also made significant recommendations with respect to possible future constitutional change.

### *Structural Provisions*

#### STATE AND FEDERAL POWERS

Although the GDR "acceded" to the Federal Republic as a whole, a central provision of the Unification Treaty made clear that the former territory of the GDR would be divided into five new states of the Federal Republic—Brandenburg, Mecklenburg-Vorpommern, Saxony, Saxony-Anhalt, and Thuringia. This decision was a legacy of the 1989–90 reform period in the GDR, in which the re-creation of the historic states had been a central constitutional aspiration. In addition, a unified Berlin would constitute a separate state, but it was possible that Berlin would be merged with the state of Brandenburg in the future.[11]

The creation of the five new states required some significant practical adjustment because after the effective abolition of the Länder in 1952, the GDR possessed a central government only. After unification, therefore, it was necessary to allocate governmental functions between the re-created eastern states and the central government of the Federal Republic.

This task was accomplished by applying the existing rules on allocation of competence in the Basic Law to the eastern Länder. According to the Unification Treaty, each of the five new states was to be responsible for administrative, judicial, and educational organs that formerly exercised authority within its borders, but only to the extent that those organs exercised powers that fall within the authority of the states under the competence rules of the Basic Law.[12] Under this plan, for example, the lower court systems and the GDR schools and universities were transferred to the states because these organs fall within state authority under the Basic Law. To the extent that former GDR administrative and judicial organs exercised powers that fall within the competence of the federal government under the Basic Law, these organs will be controlled by federal authorities.[13] Thus the GDR military and defense establishment—a matter of federal competence under the Basic Law—passed into the hands of the federal government.

Former property of the GDR regime was allocated between the state and federal governments in a similar manner. If "administrative" property had been used for purposes falling within the competence of the states or localities under the Basic Law, that property went to the relevant state or locality;[14] if the property served purposes principally within the competence of the federal government under the Basic Law, it became federal property—but it must be used to carry out federal administrative tasks within the territory of the former GDR.[15] Thus buildings housing the lower courts, as well as university and school buildings, became property of the states, yet military bases and other property of the Defense Ministry went to the federal government.[16] As with government property, most debts of the GDR were also to be allocated between the federal government and the eastern states, after an interim three-year period in which the federal government and the Treuhand were to bear the main share of interest payments.[17]

After the accession of the GDR to the Federal Republic, the five new Länder were entitled to representation in the Bundesrat, and the formula for representation in the Bundesrat was adjusted slightly by the Unification Treaty.[18] Moreover, article 42 of the Unification Treaty authorized the Volkskammer to choose 144 of its members to represent the territory of the former GDR in the Bundestag from the date of unification until the first all-German federal election on December 2, 1990. This provision raised some constitutional doubts because the 144 eastern members chosen by the Volkskammer may not have been "directly" elected to the Bundestag as required by article 38(1) of the Basic Law. The measure was apparently accepted, however, as fulfilling a practical necessity.

### THE PROBLEM OF THE FEDERAL CAPITAL

After provisions on the re-creation of the states, the second main structural issue of the Unification Treaty concerned the capital of unified Germany and its future seat of government. This question, with its fundamental implications for the future of Berlin, was the subject of bitter debate. Because Berlin is located in the heart of the east, the GDR pressed for explicit acknowledgment of Berlin as both capital and seat of government.[19] Many western voices, on the other hand, favored a lesser role for Berlin, seeking to keep the government in Bonn, the original capital of the Federal Republic. Ultimately, the Unification Treaty temporized on this point, recognizing Berlin as capital but leaving a decision on the seat of government to the future all-German legislature.[20] This resolution was a necessary compromise: the framers feared that a clear resolution of this incendiary issue would risk failure of the Unification Treaty in the Bundestag.[21]

Accordingly, dispute about the future location of the German government continued on in the period immediately following unification. Some argued that Berlin's historical role as German capital favored its claim, while others maintained that the baleful history of Berlin as center of the "Third Reich" required that the seat of government be located elsewhere. For some, the choice of Berlin would be an important source of political and economic support for the five new states of the east, but others pointed out that moving most government offices would add billions of marks to the overwhelming financial burden of unification.[22] Cutting across these arguments were regional rivalries—with roots deep in past centuries—which prompted some representatives to reject the idea that the government should again be located in the former Prussian capital. More recent historical arguments also played a role. Supporters of Berlin invoked a resolution of the Bundestag in 1952 stating that, in case of unification, Berlin would be the capital of Germany.[23]

In a close vote in June 1991, the Bundestag resolved to move the seat of government to Berlin over the coming years.[24] Yet nothwithstanding a burst of euphoria in Berlin, the hard realities of economic and political life after unification also made themselves felt. The enormous cost of moving all government ministries indicated that Berlin would never completely assume Bonn's previous role as sole seat of government; moreover, the national and international importance of retaining some governmental presence in the west was also clear. Accordingly, in its vote of June 1991, the Bundestag also declared that Bonn would continue to be an "administrative center" of the Federal Republic, retaining aspects of government that had a "primarily administrative character."[25] Moreover, while the Bundestag, the chancellor, and the president will move to Berlin, the Bundesrat will probably remain in Bonn.[26]

Yet notwithstanding the Bundestag's vote, which contemplated that the parliament would be sitting in Berlin by 1995, actual plans for the move have progressed very slowly. As a result, the continuing dispute between partisans of Berlin and of Bonn has emerged as a central point of tension between eastern and western Germany. The German government and parliament tend to be composed of a rather permanent group of individuals, and many of the western majority—with houses and comfortable working conditions in Bonn—have resisted the actual move to Berlin with all the bureaucratic and parliamentary skills at their disposal.[27]

According to eastern representatives, in contrast, the move to Berlin is essential for economic recovery in the former GDR as well as for the purpose of bolstering a psychological sense of the parity and equality of eastern citizens. Moreover, greater proximity might lead to improved "inner German" understanding: as Lothar de Maizière suggested, the government might have devised faster solutions if the signs of eastern discontent "were right below its windows."[28] In any case, the political gulf that still separates east from west seems clearly evident in this extraordinarily bitter debate.[29]

### *Law Applicable in Eastern Germany after Unification*

The second central task of the Unification Treaty was to determine the extent to which the law of the Federal Republic would be applicable in eastern Germany and the extent to which former GDR law would continue to apply. A related task was to set forth appropriate modifications of each of these bodies of law, in light of the special problems of unification.

#### THE EXTENSION OF WESTERN STATUTORY LAW

The question of which law should initially apply in the east—the old law of the GDR or the new law of the Federal Republic—seems to implicate the basic theory of article 23. Those who sought a prompt eastern conformity with western structure and practice, as perhaps implied by article 23, would logically seek to apply western law in the east from the outset. In contrast, those seeking a more gradual and differentiated movement of the east toward western norms might seek to continue the effectiveness of eastern law at the outset, with gradually increasing replacement by western rules.

Interestingly, West German Interior Minister Schäuble initially favored the view that GDR law should basically continue on in eastern Germany with certain stated exceptions. This was also originally the view of the GDR government. This position would have had the advantage of not immediately confronting eastern citizens with the complex details of new legal rules, except to the extent required by matters of basic principle. This proposal, however, was rejected by prevailing voices in the CDU leadership—in part on the theory that what purported to be law in the GDR was not really law at all and that this position would unduly perpetuate a state of "GDR injustice."[30] Thus the basic principle of legal harmonization ultimately adopted in the Unification Treaty was consonant with the underlying theory implied by article 23—the extension of western structures to the east—although the detailed provisions of the Unification Treaty qualified or relaxed that principle in many instances.

Accordingly, article 8 of the Unification Treaty declared that the law of the Federal Republic would generally extend to the GDR and East Berlin except to the extent that the Unification Treaty—and particularly attachment I—determined otherwise. Attachment I occupies 240 pages in the version published by the government, and it is clear that although West German law applies in principle to the former GDR, numerous adjustments were made for an interim period.[31]

The status of the law of the former GDR is also complex. The GDR law that would fall within the authority of the Länder under the Basic Law (as well as law that might be federal law under the Basic Law but regulates matters that federal law has not comprehensively regulated) continues on as law of the new eastern Länder—but only if it is consistent with the Basic Law, applicable federal law, European Community law, and the provisions of the Unification Treaty.[32] Moreover, law of the GDR that is specifically mentioned in attachment II (as modified in that attachment) will generally have the status of federal law in eastern Germany if it falls within an area of federal competence under the Basic Law, and if it is consistent with the Basic Law and European Community law.[33]

Thus the underlying principle was as follows: law of the Federal Republic becomes applicable in the former territory of the GDR, except as altered by the provisions of the Unification Treaty, and that federal law invalidates any inconsistent law of the GDR. Law of the GDR that is *not* inconsistent with applicable law of the Federal Republic, however, continues in force as law of the Länder, except that certain GDR law mentioned in attachment II will have the status of federal law within the former GDR (and therefore can presumably override any contrary law of the Länder).[34] Notwithstanding these complex qualifications, however, in basic principle western law prevails.[35]

The general result of this rapid extension of western law, therefore, is that eastern law will retain little lasting effect—even in areas in which some western observers believed that East German solutions were superior. Accordingly, the hopes of some reformers that unification would effect a reciprocal harmonization of law—drawn from the best of western and eastern sources—have not been realized. Instead, even some non-socialist achievements in eastern law have been sacrificed upon unification.

One such area of possible missed opportunities may be seen in the rules on family law. Under the Unification Treaty, West German law generally governs marriage, divorce, and other legal steps relating to the family occurring in eastern Germany after the date of unification.[36] Yet it could be argued that, in imposing this general rule, the Unification Treaty ignored certain enlightened aspects of GDR law and adopted portions of western law that were subject to criticism in the west itself as being in need of reform. For example, family law measures for the equality of women as well as the removal of special rules for illegitimate children seem to have been carried through more completely in the east than in the west.[37] In the weeks before unification, the East German Volkskammer carefully revised the Family Law Code of the GDR,[38] but this attempt to accommodate eastern and western views was largely replaced upon unification by the more traditional provisions of the West German Civil Code. Not surprisingly, serious practical problems have arisen in carrying out a western family law that may not be appropriate for eastern social conditions.[39]

Developments in labor law also illustrate some of the difficulties of this process. Since 1977, the GDR had possessed a comprehensive Labor Code, and this statute was revised pursuant to the first State Treaty for the purpose of incorporating certain provisions borrowed from the Federal Republic.[40] Nonetheless, the GDR statute accorded workers significantly greater rights in some areas than the uncodified labor law of the Federal Republic.[41] In negotiations over the Unification Treaty, the eastern delegation sought to preserve aspects of its Labor Code, but the GDR was largely unsuccessful in this endeavor and West German labor law basically now extends to the east.[42] On the other hand, in an apparent attempt to mollify the east on this point, article 30 of the Unification Treaty seeks to obligate the all-German parliament to adopt a "unified" statute in specified areas of labor law. Whether anything will actually emerge from this provision is, however, far from clear.[43]

The example of labor law illustrates some of the serious problems that can be encountered in abruptly extending a complex legal regime over a different social and economic structure. Difficulties have arisen in the implementation of the West German collective bargaining law in the east because of the general lack of institutions—western-style trade unions, works councils, employers' associations, and labor courts—prevalent in the west, upon which the structure of western collective bargaining law rests.[44] Because of economic problems, it may be some time before these institutions are fully developed and, in the interim, it appears that the structure of eastern collective bargaining is basically also being controlled by trade unions and employers' associations in the west.[45] Moreover, the very complex and variegated western system of social insurance for workers—a structure that was "not uncontested in the Federal Republic" itself—swiftly replaced the uniform system of the east, without the opportunity for discussion of reform.[46] Thus in the area of labor law, a highly complex western system, itself perhaps in need of some reform, was imposed on an eastern society that did not seem prepared for it.

### THE ROLE OF EASTERN JUDICIAL DECISIONS

The extension of western legal rules to the former GDR was not the only issue of eastern law that the Unification Treaty was required to address. A complex topic of comparable importance—indeed, one of the most sensitive issues of unification—was the present treatment of past judicial and administrative actions in the GDR. Yet the parties were not completely prepared to resolve these issues at the time of unification, and they could only be handled in outline in the treaty.

Accordingly, the Unification Treaty set forth general rules relating to the continued validity of GDR judicial decisions. These rules seek to combine the practical necessity of respecting judgments in ordinary cases with a deep suspicion that many decisions may have reflected forms of political oppression. Thus, in principle, decisions of GDR courts issued before accession remain valid. In the course of their enforcement, however, these decisions may be subject to re-examination to ensure that they are consistent with principles of the rule of law.[47] Moreover, the treaty contemplated that subsequent legislation would provide "rehabilitation" and compensation for victims of politically motivated criminal judgments or judicial decisions that were otherwise unconstitutional or violated the rule of law.[48] Similarly, administrative rulings of the GDR remain in effect, unless they are "inconsistent with principles of the rule of law or with this treaty."[49]

### LAW OF THE EUROPEAN COMMUNITY

It was also clear that the legal rules applicable to eastern Germany would not depend on German law alone. In western Europe the law of the European Communities—now the European Union—has assumed a position of central importance that is in many ways comparable with that of national law, and Community law has replaced national law in broad areas of economic and environmental regulation. Accordingly, the Unification Treaty makes clear that treaties of the European Communities will be effective in the former territory of the GDR.[50] Other rules of the European Communities will also apply there except to the extent that the Communities have made exceptions to avoid economic difficulties in the GDR or to accommodate the administrative problems of unification.[51]

### THE HARMONIZATION OF INTERNATIONAL AGREEMENTS

Finally, the drafters of the Unification Treaty also recognized that the Federal Republic and the GDR were subject to numerous international agreements and that it was necessary to resolve the problems that these agreements might pose. The regime for assessing the treaties of the Federal Republic was quite straightforward. Following the general structure of article 23 GG, as reflected in other sections of the Unification Treaty, article 11 of the treaty states that the international agreements of the Federal Republic will remain in effect and will extend to the former GDR, except to the extent set forth in attachment I.[52] If unification appears to require some alteration of a particular treaty of the Federal Republic, the all-German government will resolve the issue through negotiation with the other party to the agreement.

With respect to the treaties of the GDR, however, the situation is considerably more complicated. Under a broad view of the implications of article 23, it might seem reasonable to terminate all or most of the GDR's treaties, in a manner parallel to the eventual termination of most other GDR law. In any event, the Federal Republic was understandably reluctant to assume many obligations of the GDR—including political obligations that might have been entered into under the quite different circumstances of the Cold War. Yet a general abrogation of the GDR's treaties might have violated international law as the Federal Republic was the legal successor of the GDR for some purposes at least. Perhaps most important, the Soviet Union was insistent in the Two Plus Four negotiations that its contracts with the GDR, particularly its contracts for the delivery of various goods, should not be terminated by German unification.[53]

As a result of these countervailing pressures, the Unification Treaty did not take a definitive position on the continuation of the treaties of the GDR. Rather, it adopted a "pragmatic" solution.[54] Under article 12 of the treaty, the federal government was to discuss the possible continuation, adjustment, or termination of each of these agreements with the other party to the agreement, in light of a number of specified factors. These factors include the preservation of international confidence, the interests of the states involved, the treaty obligations of the Federal Republic, the principles "of a free and democratic basic order according to the rule of law," and the observance of the authority of the European Communities.[55] Thus, although in principle the treaties of the Federal Republic will continue on, the treaties of the former GDR were to be carefully re-examined to determine their future validity.[56]

A final point with respect to the renegotiation of these treaties illustrates the extraordinary authority of the European Union and the significant governmental role that it has come to play in Europe. Under the European Community Treaty, the Federal Republic is no longer the legally responsible party for the renegotiation of commercial treaties of the GDR because the Community has received all authority with respect to the foreign commerce of the member states. Thus it is the European Community that must renegotiate commercial treaties of the GDR, to the extent that renegotiation of these treaties is necessary.[57]

## *Constitutional Amendments and Proposals in the Unification Treaty*

### CONSTITUTIONAL AMENDMENTS EFFECTED BY THE UNIFICATION TREATY

By deciding on unification under article 23, the prevailing political forces in effect decided against a major revision of the Basic Law—for the present at least. Yet even the choice of article 23 could not exclude all constitutional change. Unification would bring important structural changes, and it was clear that the Basic Law, although remaining fundamentally intact, would necessarily undergo a few significant alterations. In consequence, chapter II of the Unification Treaty sets forth provisions that expressly amend the Basic Law.[58] Because the Unification Treaty was ratified by the requisite two-thirds vote of both the Bundestag and the Bundesrat, adoption of the treaty itself effected the necessary amendments.

From a theoretical point of view, the most important constitutional amendments were those confirming that the process of German unification was complete with the accession of the GDR and that no additional "German" territory remained outside of the borders of the unified Germany. These amendments, which were insisted upon by the World War II Allies as well as Poland, were intended to obviate any argument that Germany still retained a claim to Polish territories east of the Oder-Neiße line. Accordingly, these amendments were not only contained in the Unification Treaty; they were also required by the Two Plus Four agreement executed by the two German states and the World War II Allies as part of the process of German unification. Thus any attempt to return to the former provisions by subsequent amendment of the Basic Law would violate an agreement that is binding in international law.[59]

Three constitutional amendments were necessary to effect the result sought by the Allies. First, the preamble of the Basic Law, which in its original form declared that unification is something to be achieved in the future, was amended to declare that the "Germans" in all of the German states—including the five eastern Länder—"have achieved the unity and freedom of Germany in free self-determination." Because unity has now been "achieved," there is no further claim that additional territory must be "unified" with Germany as it now exists.[60]

In adopting these quite modest alterations in the preamble, the treaty negotiators ignored or rejected proposals for broader changes emanating from the ranks of the GDR reform movement. For example, the preamble was not amended to include a statement recognizing that the division of Germany was a result of the National Socialist dictatorship—a change that would have put the process of unification in a broader historical context.[61] The Unification Treaty was also sharply criticized for failing to include an explicit declaration along these lines.[62]

The second of the necessary amendments of the Basic Law deleted article 23, which allowed "other parts of Germany" to "accede" to the Federal Republic.[63] If this provision had remained in the Basic Law after the accession of the GDR, it would have suggested that "other parts" of Germany still existed outside of the present territory of the unified country and that those "other parts" could accede to Germany at a later point.

Finally, it was necessary to amend article 146 of the Basic Law which, in its unamended form, foresaw a later date upon which the "German people" would adopt a constitution by a free decision.[64] Although this provision did not specifically state that unification had not yet occurred, the original context of the provision clearly implied that the "German people" adopting the future constitution would include a group that extended beyond the population of the Federal Republic. Thus, this provision also might have suggested that additional territory and population remained to be incorporated into a united Germany in the future. One resolution of this problem would have been to delete article 146 entirely, as the drafters had done with article 23. The conservatives in the Federal Republic would certainly have preferred this result. But the Social Democrats and GDR reform groups sought to retain article 146 and, with it, the possibility of adopting a new, all-German constitution to replace the Basic Law even after accession under article 23. Accordingly, article 146 was amended to read as follows:

> This Basic Law, *which is applicable for the entire German people following the achievement of the unity and freedom of Germany*, will lose its validity on the effective date of a constitution that has been chosen by a free decision of the German people.[65]

This provision makes clear that after unification the Federal Republic includes the entire "German people," but it nonetheless preserves the possibility of a new all-German constitution at some point in the future. The amendment also obviates the argument that article 146 had become obsolete as a result of unification.[66]

Shortly after the signing of the Unification Treaty eight members of the Bundestag filed an action in the Federal Constitutional Court challenging these provisions of the Unification Treaty amending the Basic Law.[67] The petitioners, who sought to further the interests of refugees from territories east of the Oder-Neiße line, believed that these eastern regions should be permitted to "accede" to united Germany in the future. Accordingly, they objected to the amendment deleting article 23 of the Basic Law because that amendment made a future "accession" impossible. Petitioners argued that under the Basic Law any prospective constitutional amendment must be presented to parliament as a separate statute—so that members of parliament can propose changes—rather than as part of a treaty, which must be voted on as a whole without alteration.

In a short opinion, the Constitutional Court rejected this complaint as completely without merit. In so doing, the Court emphasized the broad degree of procedural discretion possessed by the government in undertaking steps toward unification under article 23.[68] Thus, even if full parliamentary consideration is ordinarily required for constitutional amendments, the central constitutional obligation to achieve unification permitted an abbreviated procedure in this instance.

### SUGGESTED AREAS OF FUTURE CONSTITUTIONAL CHANGE

The decision for article 23 was a decision against immediate constitutional reform. Yet, by amending and retaining article 146, the drafters of the Unification Treaty acknowledged the possibility of significant constitutional change in the future. Moreover, article 5 of the Unification Treaty contained "recommendations" that the all-German parliament consider amending the Basic Law within two years in order to deal with certain problems raised by unification.

Two of these recommendations dealt with federalism and the Länder. The first was a recommendation to consider possible changes in the relations between the federal government and the states, in accordance with a resolution of the state governors issued in July 1990; in this resolution the governors had taken the opportunity afforded by the approach of German unification to urge that the authority of the states be increased in comparison with that of the federal government. The second recommendation involved the possibility of a simplified procedure for a future merger of Berlin with the state of Brandenburg.[69]

Even more interesting, however, was the inclusion in article 5 of two further possibilities that reflected proposals of the Social Democrats and reform groups in the GDR in the process of negotiating the treaty. Indeed these provisions formed the remnant of broad proposals of the SPD for constitutional change in the process of unification.[70] First, article 5 recommended that the all-German parliament should review considerations relating to the adoption of "state goals" in the Basic Law. In German constitutional doctrine, state goals often concern matters such as social welfare or environmental protection. Accordingly, this provision urged consideration of amendments long supported by certain sections of the SPD but greeted with reserve or hostility by the more conservative CDU/CSU. Even at the time of the adoption of the treaty, some proposed drafts of new state constitutions contained articles setting forth state goals, and the constitutions adopted in the eastern states in the period following unification contained a proliferation of these provisions.[71]

Second, article 5 recommended that the parliament should consider the question of whether article 146 of the Basic Law should be employed to adopt a new German constitution, perhaps by plebiscite. The conservatives had strongly opposed the use of article 146, and they objected particularly to the adoption of a new constitution by plebiscite. The appearance of these suggestions in the Unification Treaty—guarded as they were—reflected the fact that the votes of the SPD were essential in order to obtain the two-thirds majority necessary to ratify the Unification Treaty.[72] That the SPD could block a two-thirds vote for the Unification Treaty (and thus secure inclusion of these provisions) by no means assured that an affirmative two-thirds majority could be found for any particular constitutional amendment. Perhaps a new constitution could be adopted by a simple majority under article 146,[73] but the calling of a constitutional convention for this purpose seemed most unlikely.

## The Joint Constitutional Commission

Yet even though significant change on the national level seemed unlikely, the all-German parliament had an obligation to consider constitutional amendments in accordance with article 5 of the Unification Treaty. Accordingly, in January 1992, the Bundestag and the Bundesrat formed a joint commission to consider further constitutional changes that might be indicated as a result of unification. The commission was composed of thirty-two members of the Bundestag and thirty-two members of the state governments forming the Bundesrat.[74] In adopting this method, the parliament rejected the SPD's proposal for a constitutional council that would have included not only politicians but also "independent personalities from east and west," including those from the GDR citizens movement.[75]

In the twenty-one months of its existence, the Joint Commission held twenty-six full meetings and nine public hearings, receiving the testimony of numerous expert witnesses from politics and the universities.[76] In addition to its more general deliberations, the commission played a major role in the adoption of constitutional amendments designed to implement the Maastricht Treaty and to increase the authority of the states in matters relating to the European Union.[77] But on proposals for state goals, plebiscitary elements, and other provisions contained in the new state constitutions, its results were modest in the extreme.

In confiding this task of constitutional revision to the all-German legislature, the Unification Treaty may have adopted a method that was preordained to produce few significant results.[78] Indeed, "with the decision in favor of such a body, composed exclusively of active party politicians, constitutional reform was left to the routine business of Bonn"; the result was "that the actors and themes of the old Federal Republic predominate[d]" and that the difference between day-to-day politics and lasting constitutional structures tended to fade away.[79] Although some deplored this result as reflecting an uncritical immobility, traditionalists viewed this parliamentary structure, with its low probability of change, as precisely its most excellent feature.[80]

In any case, everyday politics intruded quite perceptibly into the work of the Joint Commission. At one point, for example, a party whip threatened CDU members with removal from the commission if they voted for a compromise proposal on environmental protection. Although the resolution had been drafted by the commission's co-chair Professor Rupert Scholz, himself a member of the CDU, the formulation had been disapproved by the CDU caucus in the Bundestag. Scholz temporarily withdrew from his position as commission co-chair to protest this interference.[81] Later, the highly respected representative of Bündnis 90, Wolfgang Ullmann, resigned from the commission on the ground that it was no longer undertaking serious work.[82]

Yet the results of the commission's work were not determined by party politics alone. Quite clearly, a certain constitutional consciousness dominated a controlling bloc of the commission, and this was the consciousness of the existing Basic Law as interpreted by the "prevailing doctrine" (*herrschende Lehre*) of the conservative German constitutionalists. This view sought generally to restrict any change in the Basic Law—and particularly any change that might disturb existing social and economic relations. This consciousness furnished a rather sharp contrast to the views of the east German reformers and the SPD, as well as a minority of dissenting western constitutionalists including those who had worked on the Round Table draft. Because a two-thirds vote was necessary to adopt a commission proposal, the result was a stalemate on most issues. In a small number of cases, however, the commission did issue some relatively modest constitutional proposals reflecting some of the ideas of the eastern state constitutions.

### *State Goals of Social Welfare*

The traditional constitutionalists put up perhaps their hardest front on the debate over state goals of social welfare.[83] Opponents of these provisions argued that the founders of the Basic Law rejected the prolific state goals of the Weimar Constitution and—at the end of Nazi dictatorship—chose economic freedom over an economy under the constitutional control of the state. Thus the social goals of the Basic Law are modest, and economic decisions are basically to be made by the legislature.

Moreover, the opponents argued, the insertion of social goals in the Basic Law would have one of two possible deleterious results. Either the social goals would have no practical effect, with the result that the populace—which would take these goals at face value—would be disappointed and lose confidence in the constitutional system; or these goals would actually be enforced by the judiciary, with the result that power would flow from the democratic legislature to the Constitutional Court, and the principle of the separation of powers would be severely impaired.[84]

In contrast, proponents of these provisions argued that social welfare and environmental protection are facts of modern life and that other modern postwar constitutions such as those of Italy and Spain—as well as international conventions to which Germany is a party—do indeed contain state goals of social welfare.[85] But, in the event, the impetus of the eastern state constitutions—as well as the importance of these state goals for the citizens of the east—failed to sway the opponents of these provisions. Accordingly, proposals of the SPD for state goals of housing, employment, and social security received strong majority votes in the commission but not the two-thirds approval necessary for adoption as a recommendation.[86]

*Environmental Protection*

Yet notwithstanding its general rejection of state goals, the Joint Commission did propose a constitutional amendment adding a state goal of environmental protection.[87] Endorsement of this provision marked a crucial step in a long process. Environmental provisions had been proposed both by the SPD and the CDU/CSU in prior years, but none succeeded in obtaining the requisite two-thirds majority in parliament: the CDU/CSU insisted that the constitutional protection should be enforced by the legislature alone, without judicial participation, while the SPD rejected such a dilution of the guarantee.[88]

Discussion in the Joint Commission was marked by that dispute, as well as by differences over whether the provision should be an "anthropocentric" protection of the environment for the benefit of human beings or, in contrast, a protection of nature for its own sake. A last-minute compromise yielded a highly qualified provision, intended to provide a framework in which the values of environmental protection must be weighed against other important values—such as economic values—by the legislature, executive, and courts. The provision may also require a balance between protection of nature for its own sake and for the sake of "future generations" of human beings.[89]

*Ethnic, Cultural, and Linguistic Minorities*

In a provision that evoked vigorous controversy, the Joint Commission also proposed special protections for "ethnic, cultural, and linquistic minorities" similar to those contained in most of the new state constitutions.[90] Analogous provisions were contained in the Paul's Church Constitution of 1849 and the Weimar Constitution of 1919 and are found in the United Nations Covenant on Civil and Political Rights of 1966 and other documents to which the Federal Republic is a signatory.[91] The provision reflected this general trend and took account of the movement of populations in Europe that has followed the end of the Cold War.

The general effect of this proposal would be to discourage undue pressures toward assimilation that might be exerted by the state on minorities in favor of the prevailing majority culture.[92] Because this provision draws no distinction between citizens and "foreigners" living in Germany, its provisions would protect not only groups like Danes or Sorbs who have lived in parts of Germany for centuries, but also national groups that have more recently arrived in the country. In the public discussion, therefore, opponents expressed concern that this provision would further a "multicultural society"—apparently an unwanted goal—and might even result in opening up broader access to German citizenship. Indeed, unpleasant echoes of the past sometimes seemed to surface, as certain CDU members favored protection of traditional groups like Danes and Friesians, but not the gypsy communities of Sinti and Roma and not minorities that might be formed in the future, presumably by immigration.[93]

*Plebiscitary Elements*

On the question of plebiscitary elements, as on the question of prolific state goals, the prevailing view of the traditional constitutionalists was that the framers of the Basic Law had made the correct decision in generally rejecting these devices: here also, it was said that the framers were reacting against the presence of these provisions in the unsatisfactory Weimar Constitution, and even against the use of dictatorial plebiscites by the Nazis.

Under this view, the introduction of plebiscitary elements would weaken parliamentary democracy.[94] Plebiscites would result in unsatisfactory statutes adopted by a straight yes or no vote of the population—instead of the differentiated laws that could be attained through parliamentary compromise reflecting the contributions of various elements, including minorities, represented in the legislature. Indeed, in deciding complicated issues, there was the danger "that the citizens would not be guided by objective criteria, but rather by the subjective [effect that the legislation had on them] or by moods molded by the media. Thus one could fear a de-rationalization of decisions and populism."[95] Moreover, legislation by plebiscite would not be any closer to the people than parliamentary statutes; rather, plebiscites would also be the tool of parties and groups—those that could not prevail in the Bundestag. Finally, the Basic Law requires that the states participate in law making, and this basic principle cannot be changed even by constitutional amendment;[96] accordingly, the introduction of law making by plebiscite, which would involve no direct contribution by the states, might itself be unconstitutional.

A significant proportion of the commission accepted these views, and no proposal on plebiscitary elements received the requisite two-thirds majority.[97] In so acting, the commission rejected the proponents' claim that plebiscites would break the monopoly power of the political parties, thus drawing more people into the political process and actually strengthening parliamentary democracy.[98] The role of direct popular action in contributing to the GDR revolution of 1989 was also discounted, presumably as not having a bearing on the need for change in an already functioning parliamentary democracy.[99]

### *Equality of Men and Women*

The new constitutions of the eastern states extended individual rights beyond the Basic Law in a number of areas. Yet only in one of these areas, did the Joint Constitutional Commission appear to move toward the consciousness reflected in those new state charters. In an almost unanimous vote, the commission recommended that a new sentence be added to article 3(2) of the Basic Law, which provides for the equal rights of men and woman. According to the new provision, "The state furthers the actual achievement of the equal rights of women and men and works toward the removal of existing disadvantages." This amendment may not be as strong as the provisions for affirmative action contained in some of the eastern state constitutions.[100] Yet it does apparently foresee a greater role of the government in achieving equality for women, going beyond a requirement of passive abstention from discrimination.

Why did the Joint Commission appear to follow the eastern constitutions in this specific area? First, this provision may not actually move much beyond what is already required by article 3(2) of the Basic Law as interpreted by the Constitutional Court. Although the present article 3(2) simply states that "men and women have equal rights," the Court has declared that article 3(2) "extends into social reality," and that its goal is "the equalization of the circumstances of life."[101] Under the Court's view of that provision, the government is at least authorized to "equalize existing disadvantages . . . through regulations that provide advantages."[102] Accordingly, it seems that the Constitutional Court was already moving in this direction.

Second, the ambiguity of the proposed constitutional amendment leaves open the possibility of a narrow interpretation. Some commission members argued that the formulation requires equality of opportunity only, and not equality of result.[103] But others maintained that the formulation assures affirmative action and a preference for women when male and female applicants for a position have similar qualifications. Certainly, the portion of the provision calling for the removal of existing disadvantages seems to point in this direction.[104]

On the other hand, stronger formulations such as those found in some of the new state constitutions were rejected on the grounds that "it cannot seriously be considered that the state must or can intervene in all [social] areas," and that any requirement of 50 percent participation of women in employment would constitute an "unjustified" exercise of direction over the economy (*Dirigismus*).[105]

In important respects, the meaning of this provision must await judicial interpretation. For example, the question of whether some sort of affirmative action quotas are permissible remains open.[106] Yet the provision may furnish an opening for the type of constitutional strengthening of social equality that was attempted in some eastern state constitutions but was generally avoided by the Joint Commission. Indeed, more than 90,000 women petitioned the Joint Commission for stronger constitutional protection. It may well be true, as one commentator remarked, that the resulting provision is "less than the women called for, but more than what has ever previously been extended to them by the masculine majority."[107]

### *Other Rights of Nondiscrimination*

In contrast, the Joint Commission rejected a number of expansive basic rights commonly found in the new state constitutions. For example, a prohibition of discrimination on the basis of handicap was rejected on a number of asserted grounds: special responsibility for handicapped persons is already tacitly included in the general social state provision of article 20(1) GG; a special provision would set a precedent for demands by other groups for constitutional recognition; such a provision would "awaken expectations that a constitution would not be able to satisfy."[108]

Moreover, the commission declined to expand the explicit anti-discrimination provisions of article 3(3) GG—prohibiting disparate treatment on the basis of gender, ethnic origin, race, language, religious beliefs, etc.—to prohibit discrimination on the basis of "sexual identity."[109] Opponents argued that the rights of homosexuals were already adequately protected under the equality decisions of the Constitutional Court and that the constitution could be damaged through a process of "atomization."[110] Special constitutional rights for children—adopted in the Constitution of Thuringia and the Round Table draft—were also rejected on similar grounds: opponents argued that the general constitutional protections of free development of the personality and bodily integrity were sufficient to protect children, and that a separate mention of every worthy group in the constitution would give rise to the mistaken impression that "the social problems would thereby be solved." Moreover, granting children's rights might ultimately weaken parental control in favor of direction by the state.[111]

### *Data Protection*

The Joint Commission also failed to recommend any provisions on data protection even though this theme was particularly emphasized in the new state constitutions. Opponents argued that a general right of data protection had already been recognized by the Constitutional Court as an aspect of personality and human dignity and that the Court's requirements were comprehensively reflected in subsequent legislation.[112] A qualified right of access to governmental information—something like the American Freedom of Information Act on a constitutional level—was also rejected. According to opponents, this provision could deeply invade "the core area of the executive" and "impermissibly curtail its independence and its capability to act."[113]

### *Structural Amendments*

The Joint Commission did recommend a number of amendments adjusting government structure and, particularly, increasing the power of the states.[114] Constitutional amendments for this purpose had been proposed by a conference of the governors of the Länder and had been recommended by a commission of the Bundesrat.[115] An important provision expanded the authority of the states by narrowing the circumstances in which the federal government could act in areas of "concurrent authority" and encouraged the Constitutional Court to assure that those limits would be observed.[116] Other provisions limited the intrusiveness of federal "framework legislation" binding the states, and removed central areas of university administration—such as research and teaching—from the "framework" competence of the federation.[117] These proposals for strengthening the powers of the Länder paralleled the increased self-assertion of the states in constitutional amendments relating to the Maastricht Treaty and the European Union.[118] Provisions of this kind—which may have been contemplated by article 5 of the Unification Treaty—have led to fears that the authority of the federal government may be significantly weakened by an expanded European Union, on one side, and increasingly powerful states on the other.[119]

## The Proposed Amendments in Parliament

In a marathon session of the Bundestag in late June 1994, only two of the main proposals of the Joint Constitutional Commission received the necessary two-thirds majority. The parliament approved the amendments for environmental protection and the actual equality of women.[120] Moreover, thanks to the personal intervention of Chancellor Kohl, the CDU caucus reversed its position on constitutional protection for handicapped persons, with the result that this provision was also approved by the Bundestag even though it had failed in the Joint Commission. In contrast, the Bundestag rejected the commission's proposal for the protection of minorities as well as its most important proposals for the expansion of the legislative power of the states.[121] Separate proposals by the SPD for social goals and plebiscitary elements, which had failed in the commission, were also rejected in the Bundestag.

The Bundestag's failure to expand the powers of the Länder enraged some state officials who believed that the CDU leadership had broken its promise on this subject. Accordingly, the fate of all of the constitutional amendments was thrown into doubt as the state leaders in the Bundesrat, in a tactical move, unanimously rejected the Bundestag's entire package.[122] After tense negotiations in late summer 1994, however, two-thirds of the Bundestag accepted a compromise which included some but not all of the advantages for the states that had been proposed by the Joint Commission—as well as the amendments that the Bundestag had previously adopted. Two-thirds of the Bundesrat also approved, and these amendments consequently went into effect.[123]

## The Past and Future of Constitutional Reform in Germany

The decisions of the Joint Constitutional Commission and the Bundestag show that, although the ideas of the Round Table draft found substantial acceptance in the new eastern state constitutions, the changes in the Basic Law directly resulting from unification have been quite modest on an overall view. Indeed, in most respects, the traditional positions of the western constitutionalists seem to have prevailed.

The chief constitutional expert of the CDU/CSU Bundestag caucus interprets this result as a "fundamental confirmation of existing constitutional law. . . . [It makes clear] that the Basic Law has proved itself in the more than forty years of its existence and that, therefore, there is no cause for a total revision of the Basic Law or indeed for the adoption of a new constitution."[124] Not surprisingly, the chief constitutional expert of the SPD Bundestag caucus takes a different view, pointing out that many proposals received a majority vote in the Constitutional Commission, failing only because they did not receive two-thirds: "That a new constitutional consensus could not be found does not mean a positive confirmation of the status quo, or indeed even a constitutional consensus against change: the absence of a recommendation for a change is not a recommendation against change."[125]

So the question of substantial constitutional reform, arising from German unification, remains if anything a question for the future. As some traditionalists have pointed out, the GDR under article 23 "joined" the Federal Republic and, in effect, joined the Basic Law. Under that view, the Basic Law that the GDR joined should remain largely unchanged. Yet, in many areas of politics, economy, and society, the changes effected by German unification may take some time to make themselves fully perceived in the west. In the same way, the impact on the Basic Law of this seismic event may also be slower in coming. As noted in the following chapters, the Constitutional Court has expanded the role of the "social state" provision in recent decisions, and, if this is a continuing trend, it may have the ultimate effect of finding, in the general language of article 20, some of the ideas of the social goals of the Round Table draft and the eastern constitutions. Somewhat less likely, perhaps, is a revival of the possibility of calling a constitutional convention under article 146 to draft a new constitution, to be followed by a plebiscite. Yet this possibility would gain new strength in the event of a coalition government of the SPD and Bündnis 90/Greens. It is in any event clear, from the history of the eastern constitutions as well as the debates and votes in the Joint Constitutional Commission, that some ideas of the Round Table draft have considerable approval—even in certain instances perhaps majority support—in Germany. In that respect, the history of the Joint Constitutional Commission suggests that there will be significant pressure for a continuing reconsideration of these views.[126]

As this chapter has shown, the Unification Treaty set forth the basic legal and structural provisions for the future of the unified Germany. Yet, in its massive compilation of provisions, the treaty also regulated a number of specific constitutional problems that were of particular importance. In many instances, these issues involved sensitive questions of the manner in which the German government should attempt to treat the GDR past and to integrate the two very different societies that had grown up over a separation of more than forty years. Some of these problems—the constitutional issues of property, abortion, and the treatment of the German civil service, universities, and judiciary—had been bitterly debated during the negotiation of the Unification Treaty. Other important issues—prosecution of GDR officials for reprehensible acts under the GDR, "rehabilitation" of victims of the regime, and the handling of the massive legacy of the GDR "Stasi files"—were less fully understood at the time of the negotiation of the treaty, but they quickly came to the fore thereafter. The following chapters of Part II will discuss these sensitive and important problems in turn.

## CHAPTER 11

# The Fate of "Socialist Property": Restitution, Compensation, and the Work of the Treuhand

ONE OF THE most difficult and potentially explosive problems of German unification arose from the millions of acres of property expropriated or placed under state administration under the Soviet occupation and the government of the GDR. The implications of this issue contributed significantly to social tensions and serious economic problems in the period following unification.

In many of its aspects, the legal resolution of this central problem exemplified the systematic extension of western constitutional and legal concepts over the east implied by article 23 GG, as well as the correlative shifting of effective control over eastern concerns to the west. Indeed, in certain rules for the return of expropriated property, the Unification Treaty seemed to treat the GDR as though it had always been a part of the Federal Republic, subject to western constitutional imperatives that had been disregarded for forty years by the eastern regime. To some extent, the property settlement seemed to be part of a western effort to undo the past that was also evident in other aspects of German unification.

Yet western interests by no means prevailed in all aspects of the property settlement on unification. For example, the Unification Treaty seemed to preserve one important aspect of eastern society—the cooperative successors of the vast GDR agricultural collectives—as structures that might continue on in the east and even have some influence in the west. Unification was followed, however, by a tense political struggle in which western interests sought a resolution that could impair the viability of these continuing eastern structures. Indeed, in general, the constitutional and legal rules on property have had the effect of pitting eastern against western citizens in a series of very bitter disputes.

### THE CONSTITUTIONAL BACKGROUND: THE HISTORY OF "SOCIALIST PROPERTY"

Although some real property remained in private hands, the GDR viewed itself as a socialist society and most real property, and all significant business enterprises, eventually came to be held in various forms of "socialist property"—principally state-owned People's Property and the property held by the agricultural and other collectives.[1] In addition some nominally private property was held under comprehensive government administration. Much of this "socialist property" had been expropriated by the Soviet occupation regime before 1949, but the GDR government also undertook its own expropriations in the years that followed.

*Soviet Industrial Expropriations and the Bodenreform*

The first series of expropriations in eastern Germany took place during the Soviet occupation regime, before the founding of the GDR. The Soviet authorities seized the businesses and certain other property of numerous groups and individuals, including persons found to be Nazi Party officials or prominent party members. Through these measures, essentially all large business enterprises of the east were expropriated, in most cases eventually to become state-owned "People's Property."[2]

Moreover, as the first stage of a comprehensive *Bodenreform* or land reform, the authorities of the newly created East German Länder (acting under Soviet inspiration) also expropriated the property of "large landowners." This category included not only the aristocratic Junkers of the east but also any person who owned more than 100 hectares (approximately 250 acres). Although technically measures of the new German states, the expropriations followed a uniform plan of the Soviet military authorities.[3]

More than 7,000 private farms and estates, totaling over 2.5 million hectares, were expropriated under these measures.[4] These expropriations covered vast post-feudal holdings encompassing farmlands, forests, castles, and even whole towns. But they also applied to the lands of smaller farmers whose fields, counted together, just reached the sum of 100 hectares. Many owners were forced to leave their property on a few days' or a few hours' notice, taking only the possessions that they could carry with them. They received no compensation in the east, but those who managed to reach West Germany—the great majority of the large land owners, at least—did receive payments from the West German government under a Statute for the Equalization of Burdens.[5] All in all, the expropriations of the occupation period covered approximately 35 percent of the agricultural land in the Soviet zone.[6]

In a second stage of the land reform—which was also largely completed in the early months of the Soviet occupation—most of the expropriated property was distributed to individual farmers in small plots of seven to nine hectares on the average.[7] Subject to severe restraints on alienation, this property could be inherited but could not be sold or leased. The recipients were agricultural and urban workers, former landless peasants, and a large number of German-speaking persons who had fled from the territories east of the Oder-Neiße line.[8] By the time the process was completed, over one-half million farmers had received more than two million hectares of land.[9]

These measures of land reform reflected the views of Lenin on the relationship between property holding and political power, and they had their parallels in similar actions undertaken in 1945 and 1946 in other countries of eastern Europe under Soviet control.[10] The basic theory in Germany, however, was even more pointed: the Bodenreform statutes emphasized the view that large land holders and monopoly capital were chiefly responsible for the rise of Nazism and that the dissolution of these centers of economic power would assist in preventing the rise of similar movements in the future.[11] Interestingly, a similar view was also held by many in the west, and apparently formed an original impetus for considerably milder measures of land reform (with compensation) in the western Länder.[12] Rather surprisingly, this theoretical aspect of the Bodenreform received very little attention from either side in the bitter debates over the possible return of this property upon German unification.[13]

This expropriation of landed property and distribution to the peasants was, however, not the end of the story. In the decade following the founding of the GDR, the small plots of land reform property were combined along with other private landholdings—often on a mandatory and even forcible basis—into collective farms known as "agricultural production collectives" or LPGs.[14] Although the individual farmers retained formal legal title to their property, effective management and control passed to the collective. By 1960, all private agricultural property had been collectivized in this manner, and the LPGs became the dominant factor in rural life in the GDR.[15]

The Soviet land reform and the later collectivization in the 1950s were events of the first magnitude, and they had a profound effect on the consciousness in the GDR—reflected, for example, in numerous literary works.[16] The importance of these events for the structure of the GDR state was also reflected in central provisions of the East German constitutions.[17]

### *Expropriations under the GDR*

After the cataclysmic events of the Bodenreform and collectivization, the expropriations of the GDR were somewhat less dramatic, although they also had very significant effects. The industrial expropriations of the Soviet occupation period had mainly covered large businesses, leaving numerous medium-sized and small businesses in private hands. These enterprises remained largely private until a final wave of expropriations under Erich Honecker in 1972 placed almost all remaining businesses in the hands of the state. In addition, throughout the existence of the GDR, houses and other property of persons who had fled to the west were either expropriated or placed under a comprehensive form of state administration. Finally, the GDR also undertook programs of expropriation pursuant to statute, usually with minimal compensation, for "defense" and other projects such as the building of the Berlin Wall.

Interestingly, the GDR constitutions of 1949 and 1968/74 both protected private property and seemed to contemplate at least some degree of compensation for governmental takings.[18] Accordingly the 1972 business expropriations, as well as some other important programs of expropriation under the GDR, gave rise to compensation from the GDR government—albeit compensation at a very low rate.

## THE JOINT DECLARATION AND THE UNIFICATION TREATY

As German unification became a real possibility in early 1990, claims for the return of expropriated property—some of it seized decades in the past—were heard with increasing insistence. Most, but not all, of the former owners were now living in the Federal Republic. From the outset, therefore, these claims raised the possibility that control of much industrial and business property in the GDR, as well as much real property, could pass to the west. In any case, the claims generally pitted eastern against western interests.

In its negotiations over unification, the government of the Federal Republic argued strenuously that earlier property rights should be respected and the expropriations undone to the greatest extent possible. Within the western coalition, the FDP—apparently on ideological grounds—pressed most strongly for a return of expropriated property to its original owners.[19] On the other hand, the GDR government sought to preserve aspects of eastern property relations that were of the greatest importance for the lives of eastern citizens—particularly the rights of those who had received Bodenreform property or purchased residences left behind by people fleeing to the west.[20]

The two German governments had sought to include a regulation of property matters in the first State Treaty, but the difficulty of the problems—and the sharpness of the conflicting interests—prevented an early solution. Finally, on June 15, 1990, after very complicated negotiations, the two governments signed a "Joint Declaration on the Regulation of Open Property Questions," intended to resolve these issues. This declaration, in turn, was incorporated into the Unification Treaty.[21]

For the purpose of clarifying the general provisions of the Joint Declaration, the Unification Treaty also set forth two more detailed measures regulating property matters: the "Property Statute" (*Vermögensgesetz*) and the "Investment Statute" (*Investitionsgesetz*).[22] After unification, discussion of property issues focused on these statutes, and in 1991 and again in 1992 they were significantly amended in an effort to accelerate the lagging pace of investment in the former GDR.[23]

The Joint Declaration and these related statutes sought to provide comprehensive treatment of the property problems of eastern Germany. Yet, in perhaps the most basic decision of the Declaration, the expropriations of the Soviet occupation period were treated in a manner that differed sharply from the treatment of subsequent expropriations undertaken by the GDR.

### *The Bodenreform Expropriations under the Joint Declaration*

The first important decision of the Joint Declaration was that the Bodenreform expropriations were to remain permanent. Accordingly, paragraph 1 declares that expropriations "on the basis of occupation law or occupation authority"—that is, the expropriations of 1945–49—are not to be undone, although the all-German parliament may decide on some form of governmental compensation in the future.[24]

This crucial decision not to undo the Soviet Bodenreform seemed to reflect a number of factors. Certainly, the vast amount of property involved—an area comprising about one-third of the agricultural property of the GDR[25]—doubtless played a central role. The GDR government feared substantial social unrest if thousands of farming families, who had exercised some control over collective property, were suddenly to see this property transferred to large land owners from the west. Moreover, GDR legislation in 1990 had reformed the collectives and accorded farmers the right to withdraw their individual property at will; these new arrangements would have been imperiled if the underlying 1945–49 expropriations were undone.[26]

In any case, it is clear that the relevant authorities of the GDR—and also, apparently, the Soviet Union—believed very strongly that the legality of these occupation measures should not be called into question. These views were made clear in a well-known letter from GDR Prime Minister Hans Modrow to President Gorbachev in March 1990—seeking Gorbachev's assistance in preserving existing property relations in the GDR[27]—and also in subsequent statements of the Soviet government and GDR Prime Minister de Maizière.[28] Indeed, immediately following the statement confirming the 1945–49 expropriations, the Joint Declaration notes that the Soviet Union and GDR "see no possibility of revising [*revidieren*] the measures that were taken" during the Soviet occupation period. It might seem extraordinary that the Soviet Union, which was not a party to the Declaration or the Unification Treaty, is specifically mentioned in this provision; but this reference was no doubt intended to suggest that a western concession on this point was essential for the Soviet approval necessary for German unification.[29]

The same section of the Joint Declaration then goes on to record the reluctant acquiescence of the Federal Republic, which "takes note of this [result] in light of the historical development," but declares that, in its view, "a final decision over possible government settlement payments must remain reserved for a future all-German parliament." This statement held out the possibility of some payments to the former owners of Bodenreform land, but did not create an enforceable obligation.[30]

### *Property Expropriated after 1949 by the GDR and Nazi Expropriations 1933–1945*

For property expropriated after 1949—that is, property expropriated by the GDR government—the situation under the Joint Declaration was dramatically different. In contrast with the decision not to return the Bodenreform lands, the Declaration required that property expropriated by the GDR must be returned to the former owners or their heirs. If in some cases the property is not returned, compensation must be paid instead.[31]

This principle reflects a very strong conception of property. The right of recovery extends all the way back to the founding of the GDR in 1949—now more than forty years in the past—and heirs of former owners can pursue these claims even though in many cases they have had no personal contact with the property.

Moreover, this basic principle of restitution is also applicable for the recovery of property confiscated or forcibly sold as a result of racial, political, religious, or ideological discrimination by the Nazi regime from 1933 to 1945 in the territory that later fell within the borders of the GDR.[32] These provisions were included because, unlike the authorities in western Germany, the GDR government refused to accept financial responsibility for oppressive acts of the Nazis: the GDR maintained that the Communists had always opposed the Nazis and therefore should not be responsible for the acts of their opponents. Accordingly, the opportunity for the restitution of this property or compensation arose for the first time after unification.[33]

For the purpose of restitution, the concept of "expropriated property" is not limited to property actually taken by confiscatory decree. Rather it can also include property acquired by the state "as a result of economic coercion."[34] Accordingly, former GDR landowners may recover certain property transferred to the state when permissible rents under GDR law were insufficient to maintain the property.[35] The GDR government had acquired substantial amounts of property in this manner over the years, and a similar device had also been used by the Nazi regime against persecuted groups.[36]

When the Unification Treaty was originally adopted in the summer of 1990, its framers contemplated that property expropriated by the GDR would be returned to the original owner in most cases and that compensation would be substituted in three categories of exceptional situations only. This principle of "restitution over compensation" seemed to reflect the view that compensation can rarely be a fully adequate substitute for return of expropriated property. Thereafter, legal advisors to the CDU took the position that the Basic Law required retention of the principle that the return of property should take precedence over compensation.[37]

Yet the exceptional situations, in which the former owner would be required to accept compensation, were quite important from the outset. Moreover, the first of these exceptions—the exception for property to be used for investment—has been so expanded by later legislation that some believe it may threaten the basic principle that property should generally be returned to the former owners.

### PROPERTY TO BE USED FOR INVESTMENT

In the first of the exceptions, the Unification Treaty provided that a former owner can be denied a return of expropriated property if the property is needed for urgent investment uses that would yield general economic benefits in eastern Germany.[38] Accordingly, the governmental holder of expropriated property (the Treuhand or a municipality) could sell the property to an investor—notwithstanding the claims of a prior owner—if the property is needed for a project that would create or protect jobs, satisfy significant housing needs, or create the necessary infrastructure for such projects.[39] In this way, the economic reconstruction of eastern Germany takes precedence over the property rights of former owners, and the former owner must accept the proceeds of the sale or other compensation.[40]

Although intended to speed investment, the original procedure for these sales was problematic. A local government office had to approve an investor's proposed goals—often a time-consuming process—and an objection by the former owner could cause further delay. As a response to the desperate economic situation following unification, a new law in March 1991 simplified the process of selling expropriated property to those who wished to invest in eastern Germany. In effect, the current manager of the property—the Treuhand or a municipality—would make a final judgment on an investor's plan without the intervention of any other government office. After this accelerated decision, the investor could receive the property and the original owner could be relegated to the proceeds of the sale or compensation.[41] Some commentators claimed that this accelerated process constituted a "second expropriation" of the former owners, and argued that many municipalities managing property were still controlled by former SED cadres that were basically hostile to the expropriated landowners.[42]

The statutory amendments doubtless increased the cases in which the original principle of return of expropriated property was replaced by compensation. Yet even these amendments did not accept the more sweeping argument, advanced by the SPD, that investment would best be furthered if the principle of the return of property were abandoned altogether and all former owners received compensation. Such a proposal evidently went too far for the strong property views held by the governing coalition and generally prevailing in the west.

### IMPOSSIBILITY OF RETURN

In a second exception to the principle of restitution, the Joint Declaration recognized that there are certain cases in which an actual return of the property would be impossible, impractical, or inequitable. In some instances, for example, property has been merged with other property so completely that it cannot be extricated and separately returned. Parcels of expropriated property may have been combined to form the site of a large apartment building, or property may have become an inextricable part of a business enterprise. In these cases, the former owner will receive compensation—to the extent that compensation has not already been paid to a GDR citizen under GDR law.[43]

### "HONEST ACQUISITION" BY THIRD PERSON

Although under the GDR Constitution and laws all industrial property—and indeed almost all businesses—were state-owned People's Property or collective property, many privately owned houses and some other private property did remain. There was the possibility, therefore, that expropriated property could be resold to a private owner, giving rise to a conflict of rights between the original, expropriated owner and the later purchaser. This problem was most likely to arise with respect to expropriated dwellings of persons fleeing to the west, which were sometimes resold to eastern citizens. The eastern negotiators of the Unification Treaty were particularly determined to preserve these interests and, indeed, the treaty resolves this conflict in favor of the later purchaser.[44]

Accordingly, a third exception to the principle of return of expropriated property is made when individuals or certain institutional owners have acquired interests in real property "in an honest manner" (*in redlicher Weise*).[45] In these cases the rights of the innocent third party purchaser are protected, and the purchaser can keep the property. In return, the original owner receives a "socially acceptable exchange"—either real property of comparable value or, if that is not possible, monetary compensation.[46]

The precise meaning of acquisition "in an honest manner," however, raises numerous questions. Certainly, most purchasers in the GDR knew or could easily have discovered that they were purchasing expropriated property. But whether that knowledge—arising in a socialist legal order—should be held against them is another question.[47] Moreover, there is no statutory requirement that a person acquiring in an honest manner must actually have paid value for the property; in any case, the definition of "value" in a nonmarket society can be elusive.

Under the statute, an acquisition is ordinarily "dishonest" (*unredlich*) if it was inconsistent with the prevailing law or administrative practice of the GDR (and the acquirer knew or should have known of the inconsistency), or if the transaction was influenced by corruption or exploitation of a personal position of power, or otherwise the result of coercion or deception.[48] Yet even under this definition there will be difficult questions. For example, persons who sought permission to leave the GDR may have been required to sell their property as a condition of exit; it is not entirely clear whether a purchase in such a context has given rise to an "honest acquisition" under the property rules.[49] Moreover, it may ultimately be necessary to consider the reasonableness of a purchase price as evidence of whether the property was acquired through corruption, coercion, or deception.[50]

There is another highly controversial limitation on the concept of "honest acquisition"—a limitation that was bitterly attacked in eastern Germany. The property rules generally deny the status of "honest acquisition" to any purchase of property occurring after October 18, 1989—the date of the fall of Erich Honecker.[51] The theory of this exclusion is that, with the fall of Honecker, it had become clear that the property regime of the GDR could no longer be relied upon to continue indefinitely; therefore, any purchase of property in those uncertain circumstances should not be considered an "honest acquisition."[52] This rule may also have been intended to invalidate last-minute purchases of property by members of the SED party apparatus. Indeed, in the hectic days of the Modrow government, high party functionaries purchased villas in East Berlin and elsewhere for what reportedly were, by any calculation, bargain prices.[53] Yet in adopting this general rule, the drafters may have swept too broadly because ordinary citizens also used the legislation of the Modrow period to purchase dwellings that they had occupied and maintained for years, and their ability to keep this property could be imperiled by this exception.[54] Indeed, claiming that this provision effects an unconstitutional inequality, the state of Brandenburg announced that it would file a challenge to the provision in the Constitutional Court.[55]

In any case, these rules favoring the "honest" purchaser represent an interesting anomaly in the treatment of property expropriated by the GDR. Unlike the property rules in general, they often favor eastern over western interests. In the typical case in this area, a previous owner now living in the west will be facing an eastern citizen who purchased a house or other property, directly or indirectly, from the government which originally expropriated it. If the eastern citizen can show that the purchase was "honest," the eastern and not the western citizen will prevail. The breadth with which the courts ultimately interpret the phrase "honest acquisition" will help determine the extent to which these provisions will fortify some eastern control over property in eastern Germany.

### *Property Placed under State Administration*

By far the largest number of GDR citizens, however, were not in the fortunate position of the "honest" purchaser of a house or other property. Indeed, many GDR citizens found that their situation had become extremely precarious because they were tenants, rather than owners of real property.

It is important to recall that before the Wall was built in 1961, approximately 2.5 million citizens of the GDR had left for the west. Even after 1961, a significant number left the GDR legally or illegally. Some of the houses and other property left behind by these individuals were eventually expropriated by the state—to be resold in some cases to eastern citizens who became "honest purchasers" under the property rules.

In a large number of cases, however, this property was never actually expropriated by the state. Rather, it was transferred to a state administrative trustee and held in the name of the original owner, with limitations that effectively restricted the owner's use of the property.[56] In a typical case the state administrator then leased the property—often a house—to a citizen of the GDR who paid low, subsidized rates and had the benefit of strong GDR legislation for the protection of tenants.

In a measure that differs sharply from the treatment of property "honestly purchased" by GDR citizens, the Joint Declaration states that this form of administration is to be abolished and the property is to be restored to the original owner:

> Trustee administration, and similar measures involving limitations on control with respect to real property, businesses and other property, are to be abolished. Thus

> those citizens whose property was taken into state administration as a result of flight from the GDR or on other grounds are to recover the authority to control their own property.[57]

This provision raised potentially explosive social problems because many thousands of GDR citizens had lived for years in houses owned by former residents who departed for the west.[58] These tenants faced ejection from their long-term homes by persons who may have long abandoned any hope of recovering their former houses and any real interest in those dwellings. Those who prospered in the west, therefore, frequently recovered the dwellings of those who had remained to face the more difficult circumstances of the GDR.[59]

Particularly difficult issues arise in this area because the GDR state administrator often did little or nothing to keep the houses of departed citizens in reasonable condition. GDR tenants often expended substantial personal efforts and savings on fundamental repairs and maintenance. Without these efforts, many houses could have become completely uninhabitable. To avoid the injustice that might otherwise result, the Property Statute originally provided that the former GDR tenant could recover compensation for certain of these expenditures, although the relevant provision was later deleted.[60] In any case, the tenant of administered property receives nothing equivalent to the full ownership rights accorded to the "honest purchaser" of expropriated property—no matter how extensive the expenditures that the tenant has made on the property over years of residence.[61]

In the period following unification, the massive shift of residential property effected under these and other provisions of the Unification Treaty has led to extraordinary social dislocations. In certain towns in the outskirts of Berlin, for example, more than half of the dwellings are being claimed by former owners or the heirs of former owners, leading to the prospect of homelessness (virtually unknown in the old GDR) and even, apparently, suicides of householders fearing eviction.[62] Often, the claimants are people from the west who do not want to live on the property, but intend to sell it, as real-estate prices in Berlin and its suburbs have increased enormously since unification.[63] Here, as in most other aspects of the property rules, the structure of the Unification Treaty has the effect of pitting east against west in a very clearly perceptible manner.[64]

### *The "Wall Property" and the Problem of Expropriations with Compensation*

One final category of GDR land expropriations has been entirely excluded from the regime of restitution and compensation under the Joint Declaration and the Property Statute. In these important cases, the result was that the former owners were denied not only a return of property but also any compensation upon unification. Perhaps tellingly, this is an area in which the primary recipients of restitution or compensation would be eastern rather than western citizens.

Under the Property Statute, the former owners of expropriated residential property could only receive restitution or compensation if the GDR failed to pay any compensation at all or paid less compensation than normally received by citizens of the GDR.[65] Accordingly, former owners had no remaining rights if the GDR paid them a normal compensation under GDR standards, even though that amount may seem very low in light of the present value of the property.

One class of cases has become particularly important under this provision. For some years, the federal government refused to return property that was expropriated, with normal GDR compensation, under the GDR Defense Statute of 1961 for the building of the Berlin Wall and the clearing of surrounding territory. Most of this "Wall Property" runs through the center of Berlin, and it has now become enormously valuable. Accordingly, some suspected that the administration in Bonn was particularly adamant on this point in order to retain this valuable property, at essentially no cost, for governmental purposes or lucrative resale. The government's reliance on the Defense Statute of 1961, as a normal and permissible form of expropriation under the GDR, drew particularly bitter attack, and some even called it a retroactive endorsement of the Berlin Wall by the West German legal system.[66]

Finally, after years of dispute, the Bundestag in early 1996 enacted a statute that would return much of the "Wall Property" to its former owners, upon payment of one-fourth of its current market value. Owners of certain property retained by the government, or sold by it "in the public interest," may receive compensation equal to 75 percent of market value. Even this legislation, however, has been sharply criticized by some former owners and their supporters as grudging, unsatisfactory, and unjust, and a challenge in the Federal Constitutional Court has been threatened.[67]

## Litigation in the Constitutional Court and the Fate of the Bodenreform Lands

### *The* Bodenreform *Case in the Constitutional Court*

Many of the provisions of the property rules raised problems but, with the possible exception of the section on abortion, the provision denying return of the 1945–49 Bodenreform expropriations was the single most bitterly disputed portion of the Unification Treaty.[68] In the weeks following the signing of the treaty, a constant drumbeat of outraged letters—presenting personal recollections of expropriation as well as prolific legal arguments—appeared in the respected pages of the conservative *Frankfurter Allgemeine Zeitung*, protesting the failure to provide for restitution or compensation for property expropriated during the Soviet occupation.

Indeed, the former owners of Bodenreform land—or their heirs—maintained that the West German Basic Law required the return of these lands to them, and many West German constitutional scholars vigorously supported this view in learned articles and in the press. These arguments set the stage for a notable constitutional confrontation, as former owners of Bodenreform land sought a declaration from the Constitutional Court that this treatment of the 1945–49 expropriations violated the Basic Law.

THE CONSTITUTIONAL ARGUMENTS

Notwithstanding the vigor of their advocates, the constitutional claims of the former landowners faced a formidable difficulty at the outset. Complainants asserted a violation of the Basic Law of the Federal Republic, which guarantees a right of property and requires compensation for a taking by the government.[69] Yet the Basic Law did not go into effect until May 1949—by which time most of the relevant expropriations had taken place.[70] Moreover, even if the Federal Republic was thought to retain some responsibility for the East German territories—as the sole representative of the continuing "Reich"—article 23 of the Basic Law made unmistakably clear that the actual legal effect of the Basic Law was confined to the western Länder until East Germany "joined" the west in 1990.

Thus, both with respect to temporal and geographical coverage, the Basic Law did not apply to the expropriations of the Soviet occupation regime. Accordingly, the central problem faced by the former owners was to establish that the Basic Law somehow required the Federal Republic to undo actions that were not subject to the Basic Law at the time they were carried out.

In attempting to overcome this fundamental difficulty, the complainants could basically assert three sets of arguments. First, it was possible to argue that even if the Basic Law did not originally invalidate the expropriations, there were other reasons that made the expropriations illegal and therefore void at the time they were undertaken. Under this view, the Unification Treaty, with its attempted legal confirmation of those void expropriations, worked a *present* expropriation without compensation in violation of article 14, the property guarantee of the Basic Law.[71]

A number of arguments were advanced to show that the expropriations were void when undertaken. Some suggested that the expropriations were void because they violated property guarantees of the Weimar Constitution of 1919—which, under this argument, were still in effect up to 1949.[72] Others maintained that the expropriations violated rules of international law, such as the Hague Convention of 1907 which enjoined occupying powers to respect the "laws in force" in the occupied country and prohibited expropriations.[73] Still others argued that the Bodenreform expropriations were invalid because they violated general principles of natural law that are binding on all nations.[74] Yet, although vigorously pressed, these arguments posed their own considerable difficulties: few would recognize the Weimar Constitution as having remained in effect; the Hague Convention was of doubtful application to the

Allies' occupation regime; and natural law principles had their own well-known problems.

Accordingly, a second set of arguments maintained that, even if the Bodenreform expropriations were not illegal when undertaken, the principle of the social state—set forth in article 20 of the Basic Law—imposed an affirmative obligation on the government to undo those past actions now. Specifically, complainants argued that the social state provision required the government to take present measures to alleviate a great misfortune that had fallen upon a portion of the community in such a manner. There was indeed some judicial authority for this position: a series of earlier cases decided by the Constitutional Court had imposed related obligations on the federal government to alleviate certain forms of damage incurred in World War II and during the occupation.[75] This argument implied an unusually conservative use of the "social state" clause, looking toward the re-creation of a previously existing status quo rather than the affirmative creation of any sort of present economic or social equality. But it was also perhaps possible to employ concepts of human dignity and the rule of law—also protected by the Basic Law—to achieve a similar result.

Finally, the complainants also urged that exclusion of the 1945–49 expropriations from a general regime of compensation or return of property—applicable to GDR expropriations after 1949 and Nazi expropriations from 1933 to 1945—violated the constitutional guarantees of equality contained in article 3(1) of the Basic Law. This argument did not rely on any claimed invalidity of the expropriations in the past; nor did it claim that the government had any affirmative obligation to return expropriated property to anyone today. Rather, it maintained that if the government did choose to return some expropriated property, it was not permitted to create a substantial inequality by granting redress to some groups and denying it to others.[76]

### AMENDING THE BASIC LAW

The framers of the Unification Treaty were of course well aware of possible constitutional challenges to the resolution of the Bodenreform question, a central provision of the property settlement. Accordingly, they had sought to protect the 1945–49 expropriations against attack by amending the Basic Law specifically for that purpose. The Unification Treaty added a new provision to the Basic Law, stating that the treaty and related regulations would remain permanent "to the extent that they provide that incursions on property [in eastern Germany] are not to be undone."[77] Since it is the 1945–49 expropriations that, in accordance with the Joint Declaration, "are not to be undone," this constitutional amendment declared that those expropriations are permanent.[78]

Under the American constitutional system this amendment—making permanent the nonreturn of the Bodenreform lands—would be the end of the story. Any constitutional amendment adopted under the requisite procedural forms would almost certainly prevail. But the result is not necessarily the same in Germany where the framers of the Basic Law, tragically familiar with the history of the late Weimar and Nazi periods, knew that the destruction of democracy and human rights could take place even under constitutional forms. Accordingly, the Basic Law adopts the view that some principles are so basic to constitutionalism that they are not to be impaired, even through the forms of constitutional amendment. Such purported amendments are invalid.

This view is embodied in article 79(3) GG, which prohibits any amendment of the Basic Law that would adversely affect the principles of articles 1 and 20, the two "cornerstones" of the Basic Law.[79] Article 1 obliges the state to protect human dignity and introduces the general principle of constitutional rights. Article 20 establishes the principles of popular sovereignty and the rule of law and also characterizes the Federal Republic as a "social state." Arguably, the treaty's amendment of the Basic Law to preserve the Soviet expropriations could run afoul of one or more of these principles. In the Constitutional Court, therefore, the complainants argued that article 79(3) GG prohibited the amendments of the Basic Law that were designed to confirm the 1945–49 expropriations.

### THE DECISION OF THE COURT

In a decision of fundamental importance issued in April 1991, the Constitutional Court unanimously upheld the provision of the Unification Treaty which stated that the 1945–49 expropriations were "not to be undone."[80] Although the Court seemed to expand its own power to review the constitutionality of constitutional amendments,[81] the Court concluded that the legislature had not exceeded its authority in giving constitutional endorsement to the decision not to return the Bodenreform lands.

In its decision, the Court first uncompromisingly rejected the view that the Bodenreform expropriations were illegal when undertaken. According to the Court, the expropriations were clearly legal under Soviet occupation law and GDR law, and the West German Basic Law did not apply at the time. Moreover, no rules of international law then recognized in western Germany effectively operated to invalidate the expropriations.[82] By implication, the Court also rejected parallel arguments based on the Weimar Constitution or on natural law. The result was that the Bodenreform expropriations had deprived the former owners of any "legal interest" in the property.[83] The positivistic tone of this part of the Court's opinion was underscored by its remark that "the question of whether someone possesses a specific legal interest can only be answered in light of a concrete legal order."[84] Of course, the "concrete legal order" at the time of the expropriations was the legal order of the Soviet occupation regime.

The Court's opinion becomes considerably more complex, however, when it reaches arguments that the Basic Law requires affirmative governmental action in favor of the former owners. Indeed, the Court indicated that the "social state" clause of the Basic Law might require that the legislature provide some degree of "equalization of burdens" when one part of the population suffers severe and unusual damage. This principle would not require return of the Bodenreform lands, but it might require some degree of compensation to the former owners. Moreover, central aspects of the "social state" principle are protected from impairment by article 79(3) GG.[85]

The core of the Court's decision, however, came in its final passages on the guarantee of equality. First, the Court decided that excluding the 1945–49 expropriations from the provisions contemplating return of property did not violate the fundamental principle of equality. According to the Court, the government had discretion to take special steps—like preservation of the 1945–49 expropriations—that appeared necessary to achieve the constitutionally required goal of unification.[86]

But on the other hand, the Court did indicate that some degree of compensation to the former owners was constitutionally required under the equality principle. Even if the principle did not require actual return of the property, it would be too much of an inequality for the prior owners of the Bodenreform lands to receive nothing at all.[87] Even so, compensation need not be made at full market value: lesser payments might be reasonable in light of the government's other obligations incurred upon unification, such as the cost of economic renewal in the former GDR, and in light of the fact that during the same period of history many people had undergone serious deprivations without compensation.[88] Perhaps the Court was suggesting that if the former Bodenreform owners received too much, that would create a new inequality by virtue of the disparity with those who lost life, health, or freedom without compensation, during the same period.[89]

With this decision, the Constitutional Court sought to settle one of the most important constitutional and political questions arising from unification. In so doing, the Court seemed to employ a mediating technique in which it chose no clear winners or losers but rather sought to create a political structure that embodied a compromise. Thus, the former owners of Bodenreform land did not receive restitution of the property—a resolution that would have interrupted a vast network of property relations and social institutions that had grown up over the past forty years in eastern Germany. On the other hand, the former owners would receive some degree of compensation, and the Court clearly foresaw the possibility that they might use these payments to repurchase a part of their former property.

As the *Election* case of 1990 makes clear,[90] this is not the only mediating decision handed down by the Constitutional Court in the process of unification. Indeed in a number of instances the Court has appeared to place itself in the role of a mediator or compromiser of questions that the political forces may not have adequately resolved. This opinion as well as later decisions show that—especially with respect to those constitutional provisions or legal principles that seemed to pit east against west—this judicial role continues to be a very important one.[91]

### *The Attack on the Court's Decision, and the Future of the Bodenreform Lands*

Notwithstanding its attempt at mediation, the *Bodenreform* decision of the Constitutional Court had deeply disappointed the former large land owners and others who sought to recover expropriated lands in eastern Germany, and the relatively modest amounts of compensation that seemed to be in prospect provided very cold comfort. The correspondence pages of the *Frankfurter Allgemeine Zeitung* contain an extended record of these bitter protests, in which comparisons of the government to "a band of robbers" were not infrequent.[92]

Accordingly, there followed an extraordinary polemical attack on the *Bodenreform* decision of the Constitutional Court, designed to reverse the decision or undermine its authority. The attack focused on claimed factual errors in the Court's opinion. First, the critics argued, the Court decided as it did only because it believed that the Soviet Union would have vetoed unification if the Bodenreform lands had been returned.[93] Proceeding from this position, the critics produced new evidence supposedly revealing that the Soviet Union made no such demand. Rather, the critics maintained, the Soviet Union merely wished to avoid defending its occupation measures in a German court; what the legislature actually did with the Bodenreform property was of no concern to the Soviet negotiators.[94] Thus, the critics concluded, the Court's opinion was based on a false factual foundation and should be retracted. Indeed, in its most extreme form, the argument asserted that the federal government knowingly misrepresented the facts of the Soviet position to the Constitutional Court, in order to retain large amounts of the Bodenreform lands which it could sell to help finance the costs of unification. These arguments were urged in further submissions to the Constitutional Court and in a challenge to the Court's decision that was filed with the European Human Rights Commission.[95] More recently, former Soviet President Mikhail Gorbachev joined the fray by apparently claiming that the Soviet Union had not insisted on the permanence of the Bodenreform expropriations.[96] Gorbachev's claim was supported by some Russian and German sources, but it was strongly denied by others.[97]

Although this attack on the *Bodenreform* decision has little prospect of success in the courts, the arguments may have had a certain political force. In any case, the campaign of the former landowners seemed to have an impact on the federal government, which in 1992 commenced a bitterly disputed program directed—in spite of everything—toward returning portions of the Bodenreform land to the expropriated owners or their heirs.

The disputed program focused on those parcels of former Bodenreform lands that had become state-owned "People's Property" under the GDR. Although most of the Bodenreform lands had become "collective property" by 1960, a farmer's contribution to the collective would be transferred into

People's Property if the farmer left the collective—for the city or for the west—or if he or she died without a suitable heir to work in the collective. By the end of the GDR, approximately one-third of the collectives' property had been transferred into state-owned property through this or other means.[98] Under the GDR, this state-owned property continued to be administered by the collectives as lessees of the state; this arrangement was a virtual necessity because the property was often distributed among parcels belonging to the collectives, and a withdrawal of the property would have seriously impaired their efficiency. On unification, however, this state-owned People's Property did not go to the successor organizations of the collectives—or to the individual small farmers who had originally received it—but was rather transferred to the federal government as owner.[99]

The bitterly disputed question was who should have priority in purchasing this property from the federal government.[100] On this question the lines of dispute were clearly drawn. On the one side were the successor organizations of the LPGs, the former collectives, which argued that these parcels were necessary for their continued efficient production. On the other side were the claims of the former large land owners who argued that they should be entitled to repurchase their former property, perhaps at a favorable price, even though they had no constitutional right to its return under the decision of the Constitutional Court.

Initially, the former owners of the Bodenreform land made significant progress in this dispute as the government in Bonn issued a policy that favored the former owners and seemed to endanger the successor organizations of the collectives. Internal government guidelines adopted in December 1992 gave a clear priority to the former Bodenreform landowners over the claims of the former LPGs with respect to a transitional twelve-year leasing of this agricultural property, leading to its ultimate purchase—although the guidelines also attempted to protect the LPG successor organizations if their very existence was threatened.[101] In a provision clearly designed to exclude and weaken the former collectives, the guidelines also stated that only "natural persons"—that is, individuals—would be eligible to purchase any of the former People's Property.[102]

This important political battle to some extent resembled an old-fashioned class struggle: in many cases it pitted the large land owners or their descendants against persons who had actually worked the land. Yet it was also overlaid with sharp elements of tension between east and west, as the former large land owners now live almost exclusively in the west while those engaged in the LPG successor organizations are eastern citizens. Moreover, the 1992 guidelines reflected political and ideological concerns, as they favored largely conservative private investors over the suspect successors of the former mainstays of socialist agricultural life; they also incorporated the deeply ingrained preference in western Germany for individual rather than cooperative ownership in agriculture.

Due to the nature of their agrarian structure, Brandenburg and Mecklenburg-Vorpommern were the eastern states most closely affected by this dispute. In September 1993 the state of Brandenburg filed an action in the Constitutional Court challenging the government's 1992 program as violating constitutional requirements of equality through its unfavorable treatment of the LPG successor organizations. In response, the federal government informally suspended certain aspects of the 1992 guidelines—thus, in effect, delaying application of the program.[103]

But in any case the government's 1992 program represented only an interim resolution of these questions. A definitive resolution had to await the adoption of a federal statute on compensation, which represented the climax and at least the provisional conclusion of the property settlement upon unification.

### *The Dispute over Compensation and the Enactment of the EALG*

Even apart from the attack of the former landowners, the Court's *Bodenreform* decision left open difficult and troubling questions. No doubt chief among these was the actual level of settlement payments to be received by the former owners—an issue not resolved by the Unification Treaty and discussed only in the most general terms in the Court's opinion. Indeed, it was not only necessary for the legislature to provide settlement payments for the former owners of Bodenreform land; the legislature also had to decide on a standard of compensation for persons whose property had been expropriated by the Nazis or the GDR and who for various reasons—such as "honest acquisition" of the property by a GDR citizen—were not to receive return of the property itself. Moreover, these legislative decisions had to be made against the background of the drastically worsening economic situation in eastern Germany in the period following unification. As might have been expected, the accompanying debate involved a sharp clash of economic interests.

Indeed, the parliamentary negotiations on compensation were extremely difficult. Although the Court's *Bodenreform* decision was issued in April 1991, the government did not even propose a compensation statute until December 1992. By this time, of course, the economic situation seemed desperate and the limitations of the German treasury had become clearly evident.

Accordingly, the government's first proposed statute sought to provide compensation or "settlement payments" without any cost to the federal treasury.[104] Under the proposal, payments to former property owners would generally equal 1.3 times the property's unit worth of 1935—a comparatively small fraction of the present market value of the property.[105] Moreover, a special tax was to be imposed on former owners who received a return of expropriated property under the Unification Treaty. The tax, equaling one-third of the actual value of the returned property, would be used to help finance compensation under the statute.[106]

The proposal for a special tax was bitterly attacked on the ground that the cost of compensation should be shared by all property owners in Germany—not only those who received a return of eastern property.[107] It seemed unjust that, under the plan, some victims of expropriation would be required to compensate other victims. On the other hand, because almost all who had lost their property in the east had basically abandoned hope of its recovery, a receipt of the property upon unification could be viewed as a windfall. In this light, the proposal to use part of the windfall to compensate others may not have been completely unfair. In any case, under these and other constitutional attacks, the government withdrew this first proposal.

After months of deliberation, the government issued a second proposed statute in late November 1993.[108] To meet criticisms of the first plan, the amounts of offered compensation were significantly increased, with different formulas being used depending on the nature and condition of the property.[109] Moreover, there would be no accompanying tax on owners who received a return of their property. Instead, to mitigate the substantial burden on the treasury, compensation would not be paid in the form of immediate cash; rather, the former owners would receive promissory notes that would not be payable until the year 2004 or thereafter. On the other hand, a bonus would be paid if the compensation was used for investment in the eastern states.

One important question, however, was left open in the proposal. The former owners of Bodenreform land maintained that they should receive some of their compensation in the form of real property in eastern Germany held by the federal government. This argument drew objection on the ground that it violated the provision of the Unification Treaty stating that the Bodenreform expropriations were "not to be undone." It was also vigorously opposed by the SPD and political figures from the east, on the ground that such transfers would be a "direct attack on east German interests" and would result in "a concentration of land in the hands of a few."[110]

This issue was addressed in a "compromise" Compensation and Equalization Payments Law (EALG) passed by the Bundestag in May 1994. Instead of "settlement payments," a former owner of Bodenreform land could choose to purchase a portion of the land at a favorable price, although a present lessee of the property (if an individual) would have a prior right of purchase. Moreover, the proportion of land subject to purchase would decline as the previously owned amount increased—for example, the former owner of 1,000 hectares could repurchase only 134 hectares of land at the favorable price. Even with these restrictions, the statute was bitterly attacked by the CDU-led government of Mecklenburg-Vorpommern on the ground that it was part of an attempt to undo the results of the Bodenreform and that the former owners, by being able to purchase about 10 percent of eastern agricultural land, would imperil the successor organizations of the LPGs.[111] In contrast, a voice from the opposing camp implied that the former owners were being "punished," complained about "hatred against the Junkers," and indicated that the authors of the statute had acted from carelessness, envy, or ideological blindness.[112]

Precisely this clash of interests produced severe difficulties for the compensation law in the SPD-led Bundesrat, which rejected the Bundestag's statute in June 1994.[113] Even though the CDU made important concessions in a subsequent conference committee—particularly, improving the position of the former LPGs—the SPD continued to reject the statute because it allowed former owners to purchase Bodenreform property at favorable prices. According to an SPD official, eastern citizens were still treated unfavorably in comparison with the former landowners, and the SPD would not participate in a "program of property accumulation for the 'haves.' "[114] Accordingly, the Bundesrat twice sent this version back to the conference committee for further work.[115]

Finally, in late September 1994, the Bundesrat agreed on a new compromise version of the Compensation and Equalization Payments Law, which continued to allow the former large land owners to repurchase some Bodenreform property at favorable prices.[116] Farmers from east and west, as well as the LPG successor organizations, would also be permitted to purchase specified amounts of previously leased agricultural property at favorable prices, but purchasers who do not intend to farm the land themselves—presumably the case of many former large land owners—may exercise this option only with respect to one-half of the property that they would otherwise receive. Most of the other proposed statutory provisions remained unchanged.[117]

Although the success of the former large land owners in this compromise seems relatively modest, the impact of these provisons on the structure of agriculture in eastern Germany must await actual experience under the statute. It may well be that the restrictions imposed on the purchase of Bodenreform lands, in addition to the relatively low amounts of the settlement payments, will discourage many former landowners from attempting to repurchase agricultural property. In any case, the former landowners have filed another complaint in the Constitutional Court challenging the new statute on these and other grounds.[118] Whatever the result, however, this dispute vividly illustrates the attempt of western political forces to revise the settlement upon unification. The retention of the Bodenreform lands—and the perpetuation of the successors of the LPGs—represented one of the few important areas in the Unification Treaty in which the wishes of the eastern government prevailed. Moreover, the prevalence in eastern Germany of large-scale capitalist cooperatives reflects a kind of economic structure that is less common in the west. Many maintain that these eastern economic structures are more efficient than the small family farms that prevail in parts of western Germany. Accordingly, a success for the eastern cooperatives might have an influence on the structure of agriculture in all of Germany—a contribution from the east, in contrast with the more general process of unification in which institutions have been extended from the west to the east following the pattern of article 23 GG. The final compromise on compensation will play its role in determining whether these eastern structures will remain or whether the possible contribution of the east in this respect will ultimately be overcome through the strength of more traditional western institutions.[119]

## The Privatization of Business Property and the Work of the Treuhand

In addition to the vast amount of real property—agricultural and urban land, houses and commercial buildings—covered by the property settlement, the framers of the Unification Treaty also addressed the fate of thousands of business enterprises operated in the GDR. Indeed it was these enterprises that would determine, in the short run at least, much of the economic future of eastern Germany. In some cases, expropriated eastern enterprises could be returned to their former owners. But in the lion's share of cases, return of the enterprises was excluded for legal or practical reasons. Consequently, one of the major agencies of German unification—the Treuhandanstalt or Trust Agency—was accorded the extraordinary task of determining the future of these enterprises: whether they should be sold to private purchasers, abandoned and closed, or improved and held for future sale. In effect, it was up to the Treuhand to restructure the economy of eastern Germany.

### *Historical Background and the Creation of the Treuhand*

Although most large businesses in eastern Germany were expropriated during the Soviet occupation, the GDR subsequently moved in somewhat slower stages toward its ultimate stage of "real existing socialism." Accordingly, during the early period of the GDR, many small and mid-sized businesses remained in private hands. Indeed private owners of successful companies could still become quite prosperous, although after 1959 the government took steps to acquire a 50 percent share of many private enterprises.[120] Early in the Honecker period, however, the GDR changed course sharply and sought greater conformity with the economic structure of the Soviet Union.[121] A great wave of expropriations in 1972 placed substantially all private businesses under government ownership, where they remained until the events of 1989–90.[122] As the GDR came to an end, therefore, its economy was formed in substantial part by thousands of state-owned enterprises in the form of People's Property.

As unification approached in 1990, it was necessary to determine the fate of these enterprises and to establish an agency to supervise the process. There were differing views on this subject, and a shift in the resolution of these issues reflected the shift toward unification under article 23 that took place in early 1990.

At the time of the East German revolution in 1989–90 it was clear that private property and the market economy would form a significant part of the new order.[123] An amendment of the GDR Constitution in January 1990, which for the first time permitted joint ventures between private investors and state-owned concerns, was a first step in this direction.[124] Yet at the outset it was by no means clear that all ownership interests in the state-owned enterprises should be sold to private entrepreneurs. For example, some GDR reformers proposed that ownership shares of former People's Property be distributed among the citizens of the GDR.[125] Indeed, it could perhaps be argued that such a distribution was legally required because the citizens of the GDR—and not the state—were the true owners of People's Property under the Constitution of the GDR.[126]

With the coming abandonment of the planned economy, GDR reformers also sought to create an agency that would manage the vast enterprises of People's Property in a manner free from direct governmental control. The reform groups of the GDR Round Table, then in substantial control of governmental decision making, feared misuse or appropriation of this property if it remained accessible to the old party apparatus.[127] Accordingly, in an important early move, the GDR Council of Ministers under Modrow issued an order creating a trust agency (*Treuhandanstalt* or *Treuhand*) for the administration of People's Property.[128] At the same time the Council issued a regulation providing for the conversion of state-owned businesses into the capitalist form of stock company (*Aktiengesellschaft*) or GmbH.[129] In this early period, the Treuhand was apparently intended to be more of a general administrator—perhaps working with private joint-venture partners—than a seller or "privatizer" of Peoples Property.[130]

Yet even at this early point, certain fateful decisions had already been made. In creating the Treuhand as a single centralized agency, the government rejected the proposal of some reformers that a separate agency be established in each of the prospective new eastern states. According to this view, separate agencies would have a more intimate understanding of local economic conditions and would be more easily subject to public oversight.[131] Even more important, the decision to enter into a currency and economic union had been made a few weeks earlier, and this decision in effect determined that the principal work of the Treuhand would ultimately be the sale of its own vast properties.[132]

By the time that the de Maizière government came to office and began to plan seriously for unification, these decisions had begun to make themselves felt, and the new attitude was reflected in basic changes in the understanding of the Treuhand. The key step in this process was the signing of the first State Treaty on May 18, 1990—to go into effect on July 1.[133] Under the treaty a "social market economy" was to be introduced in the GDR, although the existence of various forms of property would be allowed. Moreover, state-owned businesses were to be "structured for competition as quickly as possible and transferred into private property as far as possible."[134] In accordance with the State Treaty, the GDR also amended its constitution on June 17, 1990, to adopt legal and economic principles that conformed with those of the Federal Republic, including the principle of private property in land and in the means of production.[135]

On the same day as it adopted the new statement of constitutional principles, the GDR Volkskammer enacted the basic charter of the Treuhand—the Treuhand Law.[136] The statute flatly stated that People's Property was to be "privatized," but it also seemed to contemplate a period of indefinite duration in which state-owned businesses could be developed and rendered efficient in preparation for sale—or, if necessary, dissolved.[137] Moreover, the statute was general in form and accordingly left many basic decisions of policy to the federal executive or the Treuhand itself. The Treuhand Law was carried over in the Unification Treaty with few changes only and basically remained in effect thereafter.

### *The Unification Treaty and the Return of Business Property*

Many of the enterprises controlled by the Treuhand had been expropriated under the GDR, and the framers of the Unification Treaty decided that the general principle of return of property, applicable to other GDR expropriations, should also apply to the expropriated enterprises.[138] Indeed, in the course of the East German revolution—even before the Joint Declaration and the Unification Treaty—the GDR Volkskammer sought to return some businesses nationalized in 1972 to prior owners. A statute of the late Modrow period granted the former private owners (or their heirs) the right to reclaim these enterprises by returning the minimal price paid by the government in 1972.[139]

Yet although the general principle of return of business enterprises was maintained in the Unification Treaty, it was clear that special problems relating to this form of property—some of them legal and technical, some arising from economic factors—required somewhat different treatment. Under the Property Statute accompanying the Unification Treaty, for example, a business enterprise could only be returned to its prior owner if the enterprise remained "comparable" with the business at the time of expropriation—taking into account intervening changes in technology and general economic developments.[140] In contrast with real property, a "business" is a rather fluid entity, and it would make little sense to return a firm that might have the same name but otherwise bore no resemblance to the expropriated enterprise. If the business was "comparable"—and therefore returned to the prior owner—adjustments were to be made for "substantial" changes in the value of the business in the intervening period.[141] The Property Statute contains complicated rules for measuring substantial increases or decreases in value and regulating the problems of joint owners and stockholders and intervening mergers and divisions of businesses, among other issues. In many cases a prior owner can choose compensation instead of return of the enterprise.[142]

The statutory amendments of 1991 and 1992, which were designed to accelerate privatization, also apply to expropriated enterprises. For example, the 1991 amendments basically extend the special rules on investment to expropriated enterprises.[143] Accordingly, a former owner can be excluded by a purchaser with a preferable investment plan, and the former owner would then receive the purchase price or other compensation. Moreover, the 1992 amendments foresee the possibility of setting aside certain geographical areas in which the principle of compensation before restitution of business property shall prevail. In these areas, therefore, restitution of business property could be excluded altogether, and claimants would be entitled to compensation only.[144]

But notwithstanding these important rules for the return of enterprises, it was clear that many GDR concerns would not be returned to their former owners. Most of the larger concerns had been expropriated under the Soviet occupation regime in 1945–49 and thus were excluded from restitution under the Unification Treaty. Other firms had been founded by the state and therefore had no prior owners, while still others would not be returned because they were no longer "comparable" with the enterprises that had been expropriated years in the past. As former People's Property of the GDR, these concerns passed principally to the Federal Republic or to the east German localities under the Unification Treaty.[145]

### *The Work of the Treuhand*

The task of attempting to sell the bulk of the east German businesses accordingly fell to the Treuhand. The agency quickly grew to enormous size, employing thousands of persons in its main office in east Berlin and its fifteen branch offices throughout eastern Germany.[146] Because of the drastically worsening economic situation in the east—to which the Treuhand's economic policies and operational weaknesses may have contributed—the agency's performance became one of the most bitterly debated issues of German unification.

The choice to sell the concerns to private owners—rather than to distribute shares of state-owned businesses to GDR citizens—was, of course, a basic decision extending traditional west German market structures to the east. It was a rejection of any attempt to create new capitalist economic structures, as had in effect happened in the case of the successor organizations of the LPGs. It was a political decision for which the Treuhand probably cannot be held responsible. Yet some charge that, at least in the early periods of its existence, the Treuhand sought to extend market structures with a rigor that seemed even to go beyond the ideas of a social market economy prevailing under the Basic Law—and without the sustained process of governmental participation that characterized an earlier period of economic development in the Federal Republic.[147]

In any case the performance of the Treuhand in its early period was highly problematic. Indeed, the Treuhand got off to a very bumpy start under its new statute enacted at the time of the first State Treaty. In July 1990, in the wake of the currency union called for by the treaty, 5,000 Treuhand concerns became unable to pay their debts and thousands of employees lost their jobs.[148]

Shortly after the passage of the Treuhand Statute in June 1990, Detlev Karsten Rohwedder, long-time official of a West German steel company, was chosen to lead the Treuhand.[149] Rohwedder, whose experience included the revitalization of a failing steel company in the Ruhr, apparently sought to leaven the closing of unprofitable eastern companies (*Stillegung*) with programs of investment intended to save marginal enterprises (*Sanierung*). Yet a rigorous policy of closing supposedly unsalvageable businesses, including some very large concerns, led to a further massive loss of jobs and evoked renewed Monday night demonstrations in the east.[150] Rohwedder believed that the East German industries were worth a combined total of DM 600 billion,[151] but later developments would show that their debts would actually exceed their assets by hundreds of billions of marks.

In April 1991, Detlev Rohwedder was killed by a bullet fired through the window of his house in Dortmund; the terrorist group Red Army Faction took responsibility. In a theater piece that evoked a minor political scandal, the dramatist Rolf Hochhuth seemed to explain this act as an understandable form of revenge for the "brutal economic Darwinism of the Treuhand."[152]

A few days before his assassination, Rohwedder sent a letter to Treuhand employees outlining his goals for the agency.[153] The letter seemed to establish a ranking of goals in which privatization came first, rehabilitation of firms second, and closure of firms third. In the work of the Treuhand, "social, economic, and financial" factors were to be taken into account, and any closures were to be undertaken carefully "in order to gain time for the growth of new [employment opportunities for workers]."[154] This letter seemed to promise a new degree of social concern for employment in the east. According to Lothar de Maizière, it was "such an immense tragedy that Rohwedder was murdered, for he had a vision and a strategy. He had prepared a change of course for the Treuhand."[155]

Rohwedder's successor was Birgit Breuel, former economics minister of Lower Saxony and vice-president of the Treuhand. At the outset of her tenure in spring 1991, the Treuhand seemed to continue a rigorous policy toward the enterprises of the east—valuing projected economic efficiency and the swift sale of businesses above all else, perhaps in conflict with the basic concepts of the Rohwedder letter. By autumn 1992, however, Breuel and the agency seemed to shift toward a somewhat more social view, although by that time the Treuhand's policy was largely animated by political pressure from the Bonn government and the states.[156]

As the primary factor in the eastern economy in the post-unification period, the Treuhand bore the brunt of bitter criticism—justified or not—for the catastrophic economic conditions in the east.[157] At the end of 1992, 4 million of

9 million previously existing jobs had been lost. Of this number 1.5 million former workers were listed as unemployed while others had been accorded early retirement or were engaged in public service jobs or other forms of retraining (with, however, little chance of future employment). A certain number had emigrated to the west or commuted to jobs there. More than 90 percent of women had been employed in the GDR, and unemployment after unification affected women with particular severity.[158]

Certainly, many of these problems stemmed from existing structural factors.[159] GDR economic planners knew in the late 1980s that the country was facing bankruptcy—as a result, among other things, of a policy that concentrated on consumer goods instead of the capital investment necessary to maintain East German enterprises. Accordingly, antiquated plants and deteriorating facilities impaired the competitive abilities of eastern firms in western markets after unification. Moreover, inevitable pressure for parity of wages in the unified country, notwithstanding great differences in productivity between the two regions, tended to push the cost of eastern goods above western levels with disastrous economic consequences. Finally, one of the greatest obstacles to efficient privatization of businesses was the decision to allow former owners of expropriated property to seek actual return of the property. A notice of such a claim—whether relating to the business or to the underlying real property, and whether ultimately successful or not—could substantially delay sale of an enterprise to a private owner.[160]

Yet many argued that the performance of the Treuhand had also contributed significantly to the economic decline. Following the iron rule of market efficiency in its early periods, the Treuhand had ruthlessly closed businesses that could perhaps have been saved, without adequate consideration of the social consequences. Indeed only modest amounts were invested by the Treuhand in redeveloping its enterprises, and the most profitable divisions of large companies—the so-called "filet pieces"—were often extracted and sold to western investors with little concern for the effect on the remainder of the eastern firm.[161] Slowness and inefficiency within the Treuhand led to missed opportunities for privatization, and a number of seriously mistaken decisions were made due to various forms of incompetence—or worse. Indeed, in some cases Treuhand employees may have favored western enterprises in which they had a personal interest: it was suspected that some western managers temporarily working for the Treuhand were "double agents" who, instead of acting for eastern concerns, were really "allied with the western competition."[162] In order to prevent such problems the Treuhand issued a set of "insider rules" in late 1991.[163] Finally, laxity in the Treuhand procedures, as well as the frantic pace of privatization at the outset, sometimes made it possible for deceptive purchasers to loot the assets of private companies or divert subventions paid by the Treuhand, either with or without collusion of corrupt Treuhand employees.[164]

Yet as time went on, the Treuhand came to understand its own problems more thoroughly and became more sophisticated in its techniques of negotiation with potential purchasers. By 1992, for example, the Treuhand frequently insisted on contractual provisions guaranteeing that the purchaser of an enterprise would continue to employ a specified number of workers for a certain number of years, or pay a stated penalty. Moreover, not all privatized businesses were purchased by outside investors. In a popular technique, former managers of GDR enterprises sought to borrow funds from banks and purchase their own enterprises from the Treuhand. But these so-called "management buyouts" often encountered difficulties—among other reasons, because of the lack of experience of the eastern managers in western markets.[165]

All in all, some areas of industry in the east fared better than others. Perhaps the greatest losers were heavy manufacturing industries in which antiquated plant and high labor costs took their greatest toll. Although agriculture may ultimately become one of the profitable eastern sectors, it could only survive at the price of sacrificing two-thirds of its prior work force. In contrast, construction was one of the great success stories, because almost any form of rebuilding of businesses involved construction, as did a number of other great social and political changes (especially in Berlin).

In 1993, the work of the Treuhand, which had evoked deep resentment in the east and substantial unease in the west, came under closer official scrutiny. Initial review by a parliamentary subcommittee, and then by a full standing committee of the Bundestag, had yielded inadequate information.[166] The SPD therefore invoked a constitutional provision that enabled a 25 percent vote in the Bundestag to create a special parliamentary investigating committee.[167] But the Treuhand investigating committee encountered problems because the CDU coalition refused to permit access to important documents, and the SPD filed a complaint in the Constitutional Court to achieve a judicial resolution.[168] Thus the Treuhand's record continued to evoke tension between conservative forces in the west and forces of the SPD and allied reform groups in the east.

Pursuant to its previously announced intention, the Treuhand formally ceased its activities on December 31, 1994. By that date all but one hundred of its thousands of enterprises had been liquidated or sold to private owners. Yet, in reality, essential tasks of the Treuhand were not completed in 1994, and successor agencies will continue to perform these functions for some years to come.[169] For example, approximately thirty thousand privatization contracts contain purchasers' commitments for investment plans and maintenance of employment levels, and these agreements must continue to be monitored. Moreover, the approximately one hundred remaining Treuhand enterprises, as well as large amounts of additional property, must be administered. Therefore, a number of smaller agencies continue to carry on the work of the Treuhand.[170] At the beginning of 1995, the successor organizations had a work force of more than 3,900 employees, a number that will decline gradually over the remainder of the decade. The Treuhand leaves behind debts of DM 275 billion, although the economic costs measured in indirect charges such as payments for unemployment compensation will actually be much higher.[171]

The history of this period seems to illustrate the intractable nature of social and economic structures, which are often impervious to attempts to impose a certain result by law. The government and the Treuhand sought to create western economic conditions in the east—even to reproduce the economic miracle (*Wirtschaftswunder*) of the early Adenauer years. But these efforts have so far evoked the greatest—and, indeed, the central—failure of German unification. From the beginning, some economic experts suggested that better results could have been achieved by seeking a more mixed form of economy in the east—at least for a transitional period—including the sale of some ownership shares to eastern citizens, as well as the establishment of some combined state and private joint enterprises.[172] But in the economic area as elsewhere, the analogy with article 23 GG—the view that western forms should be extended without significant change over the east—has generally prevailed over the view that the combination of two quite different societies could evoke new forms in response to unique problems.

## The Property Settlement in Retrospect

It is difficult to overestimate the enormous conceptual and practical problems raised by the measures outlined in this chapter, many of which represent a sweeping attempt to undo past changes in property relationships extending over the decades since 1949. Inevitably, the ambiguities of the Joint Declaration and related statutes, together with the likelihood of considerable problems of proof in individual cases, will ensure years if not decades of litigation on these property questions. More than one million claims have been filed for the return of property in eastern Germany,[173] and in many areas the understaffed claims offices have been hopelessly clogged.[174] Statutory changes intended to accelerate private investment have eased problems somewhat but, even on the most optimistic assessment, significant difficulties remain.

Moreover, even with the preservation of the 1945–49 expropriations—as well as some other rules like those confirming the rights of "honest purchasers"—the result of these provisions has been a significant shift of effective control of eastern property to the more prosperous fellow citizens of the west. Against the backdrop of some of the other economic problems of unification, the principles of the Joint Declaration may indeed mean substantial social dislocation for significant segments of the eastern population. This effect can be perceived in a number of areas.

First, and perhaps most important, the market strategies reflected in the actions of the Treuhand represent a massive extension of western structures and western personnel to the business enterprises of the east. Purchasers of the surviving companies are mainly from the west and bring with them western personnel at the higher levels. Indeed, the former citizens of the GDR have little or no capital with which to purchase or establish enterprises—although a lack of experience in relevant managing skills also plays a role. Perhaps as time goes on, eastern managers will be trained for the middle levels, but actual eastern ownership—now primarily represented by management buyouts—has yet to establish itself as a significant economic factor. In the meantime in eastern Germany, the employers and supervisors will be mainly from the west and the employees mainly from the east.[175]

Moreover, from the time of the currency union on, large numbers of eastern enterprises have gone out of business or have been closed by the actions of the Treuhand. With them have also disappeared entire social structures—such as day care centers and vacation resorts—that constituted important aspects of life for many citizens of the GDR. Yet one of the most striking results of the importation of western management is that there has been little attempt to preserve these social structures even in the enterprises that have survived. It is evident in such instances that two distinct social systems are confronting each other, and that one system is being replaced by the other. In telling instances of this kind it is most clearly apparent that the two German states indeed formed two quite different societies.

The reclaiming of eastern residential property by western owners is a second aspect of the property rules that extends western control over the east—accompanied by the dismantling of eastern social structures. The principle of restitution before compensation plays a central role—as well as the lifting of state administration over residential property. These principles have resulted in the displacement of entire communities, especially in valuable regions such as those surrounding Berlin. In many of these cases the former owners are prosperous individuals with residences in the west, and it is unlikely that they will actually live in the reclaimed property. Rather, the houses will be sold or leased to those who can pay market prices—most likely, persons coming from the west. These tendencies are mitigated only to some extent by the special rules on "honest acquisition," "tangible easements," and "dacha" occupancy that favor eastern occupiers.

Certainly, some of the most complex and interesting problems are raised by the case of agricultural property in eastern Germany. This was one of the rare instances in which the views of the east prevailed in the negotiations over unification: the Unification Treaty sought to preserve certain eastern structures by specifying that the Bodenreform expropriations were not to be undone. Accordingly it seems possible that farming cooperatives, the successor organizations of the LPGs, will continue on as an alternative to the quite different structure of smaller family farms favored in the west. Indeed, the principal attack on the cooperatives failed when the Constitutional Court held that the Bodenreform lands would not have to be returned. Yet the Court did require a measure of compensation and suggested that the former owners could use these payments to repurchase some of their former property. A compromise Compensation and Equalization Payments Law in 1994 has reduced the advantages accorded to the former owners under prior government policy; but the ultimate result of this process, and its impact on agrarian structures in the east, must await experience under the statute. In any case it seems possible that the cooperatives—one of the few sets of alternative eastern structures retained by the Unification Treaty—may survive challenges from western economic and social forces after unification.

In general, the strong property principles of conservative ideology have played a significant role in the development of these problems. First, these principles prevailed in the basic decision to provide redress for all GDR expropriations. Second, strong property principles were important in the decision to adopt a general principle of return of expropriated property—rather than a general principle of compensation—although the principle of restitution has been qualified by significant exceptions. Overall, the positions adopted in the Joint Declaration and accompanying statutes—notwithstanding the exclusion of the expropriations under the Soviet occupation—can be seen as a qualified victory for strong property principles supported over the years by the conservatives in the Federal Republic.

CHAPTER 12

# The Unification of Abortion Law

ALONG WITH problems of expropriated property, questions about the regulation of abortion evoked some of the most bitter and prolonged disputes in the process of unification. Indeed, the regulation of abortion was one of the few areas in which the GDR insisted to the very end that its own legal and social structures not be entirely abandoned in the Unification Treaty.

From a historical perspective, the struggle over abortion was the continuation of a political debate that had played a prominent role in West Germany long before there was any possibility of unification. Indeed the contemporary dispute—in which the SPD and defenders of women's rights were arrayed against more conservative parties—mirrored similar struggles of the Weimar period.[1] Yet although the debate had its roots deep in the past, it seems that German unification has evoked an important change in the constitutional doctrine on this incendiary subject.

## ABORTION: THE CONSTITUTIONAL BACKGROUND

From an American point of view, the key to an understanding of this issue is the fact that the West German Constitutional Court had taken a constitutional position on abortion that was fundamentally different from that prevailing in the United States. In 1973 in *Roe v. Wade*[2] the American Supreme Court held that a constitutional right of privacy includes a woman's right to an abortion. Under *Roe*, this right was basically unlimited during the first three months of pregnancy; beyond that, up to the point of the fetus's viability (approximately six months), it could be qualified only by measures designed to protect the health of the pregnant woman. In the late 1980s, the Supreme Court eroded the strict rules of *Roe*'s "trimester system,"[3] but in 1992 a sharply divided Court reaffirmed the basic position that a woman has a constitutional right to abortion.[4]

In the 1970s, in contrast, the West German Constitutional Court handed down a decision that was, in theory at least, almost diametrically opposed to the American view.[5] Indeed, the German court held that the state was under a constitutional *duty* to protect the life of the fetus, and consequently the constitution *required* that abortion remain a punishable criminal offense in basic principle. Accordingly, the Court struck down a federal statute—enacted under a coalition led by the Social Democrats—that would have allowed a woman to obtain an abortion without criminal penalty during the first three months of pregnancy as long as she underwent counseling beforehand. The

Court decided that the right to life contained in article 2(2) of the Basic Law extends to fetuses and that the state's duty to protect human dignity, set forth in article 1(1), includes a duty to protect human life. Moreover, the Court decided that, in practice, criminal sanctions were necessary for adequate protection of the fetus. Thus the Court found that the state has an obligation to protect the fetus through a combination of two provisions, articles 2(2) and 1(1) of the Basic Law. Among other things the Court indicated that a different basic resolution of the abortion question would be particularly unfortunate in light of the Nazi government's destruction of "unworthy" life.[6]

The Constitutional Court also found, however, that the right to life was not the only constitutional interest at issue. The Court acknowledged that the pregnant woman also has countervailing constitutional interests, derived from the right to the free development of her personality set forth in article 2(1) of the Basic Law. These rights are presumably similar to those recognized by the Supreme Court in *Roe v. Wade*, particularly in those passages of the *Roe* opinion that refer to a woman's control over her family relationships and her future life.[7] In the view of the West German Constitutional Court, however, those rights of personality are ordinarily outweighed by the state's duty to protect the life of the fetus. Only in particularly exigent circumstances—cases of rape, serious medical problems, congenital defects, or severe social problems for the pregnant woman—could the woman's right of personality prevail.[8]

In sum, therefore, the Constitutional Court found that abortion is constitutionally permissible only when certain circumstances or "indications" are present, and the West German parliament then enacted a statute basically adopting the Court's solution.[9] Of the Court's indications, the most unclear—and the most sharply debated—was the "social indication," allowing an abortion in the case of severe social problems for the pregnant woman. In the Federal Republic the individual states ordinarily administer federal law, and consequently the actual enforcement of the abortion statute was subject to significant variations. In some conservative Länder (notably Bavaria), the social indication could be comparatively difficult to assert, while in some others (particularly those governed by the SPD) it was often easier to establish. Even in the more liberal states, however, the circumstances supporting the claim generally had to be certified by a physician, and the process of obtaining the exception could well be viewed as inherently degrading.[10] Nonetheless, the relatively liberal practice in some Länder was bitterly criticized, and the state of Bavaria filed an action in the Constitutional Court advocating a narrower view of the social exception and seeking greater rigor in its administration.[11]

The view of the GDR with respect to abortion was considerably different from the legal position that had prevailed in the Federal Republic. In contrast with the West German duty of the government to prohibit abortion (with noted exceptions), the GDR in 1972 adopted a statute that ordinarily allowed abortions during the first three months of pregnancy if the abortion was performed by a physician in an obstetrical clinic.[12] Thus while the GDR statute did not go as far as the result in *Roe v. Wade*, it was similar to the liberal West

German law struck down by the Constitutional Court in 1975.[13] By the time of the East German revolution, the ready availability of abortion had become an important aspect of the social structure of the GDR. The ability of a woman to control the size of her family by abortion if necessary—together with the broad provision of day care for children of all ages—constituted important aspects of a system that permitted and indeed required the full employment of women.[14]

## Abortion and the Unification Treaty

In the negotiations over the Unification Treaty, therefore, the drafters were faced with a clash of statutory rules. According to the law of the Federal Republic, an abortion was permissible only if the presence of certain "indications" was established, while under the GDR statute an abortion was generally legal during the first three months of pregnancy without further limitation.

In many such statutory conflicts, the Unification Treaty essentially required that the law of the Federal Republic would replace that of the GDR.[15] In this instance, however, such a resolution would have been difficult or impossible because of the strongly held popular view in the GDR—across a wide spectrum of political groups—that it was essential to retain the more liberal abortion rule as an aspect of eastern social structure that could not be relinquished.[16] Moreover, the western Social Democrats, whose votes were necessary for the requisite two-thirds majority for the Unification Treaty, might well have balked at a resolution that completely extinguished the abortion policy of the GDR.

On the other hand, simply retaining the GDR rule in eastern Germany would have raised its own serious difficulties. Many conservative members of parliament in the Federal Republic might have rejected the Unification Treaty under such conditions. Moreover, accession under article 23 would result in extending the Basic Law—and presumably its interpretation by the Constitutional Court—to the former territory of the GDR, and the Court's jurisprudence seemed to invalidate the GDR statute of 1972, just as it invalidated the West German statute of 1974.

When the drafters of the Unification Treaty addressed these problems, they found themselves confronted by political forces that were even more equally balanced than those relating to issues of expropriated property.[17] Those strongly in favor of retaining the GDR rule—or perhaps even extending it to the west—were the bulk of the population in the GDR and the Social Democrats in the west, led by important women's organizations.[18] On the other hand, conservatives in the east and west could invoke the powerful role of the Constitutional Court in arguing against the retention of the GDR's first-trimester rule.[19]

Because any clear decision of this issue might have imperiled the entire Unification Treaty, the drafters adopted a compromise that postponed an ultimate resolution. Indeed, this compromise—one of the most sensitive in the

Unification Treaty—was not finally reached until the date on which the treaty was signed.[20] Under this provision, the GDR was to retain its previous abortion rule until the end of 1992 at the latest. During the interim, the all-German legislature would have the task of deciding on a new rule for all of Germany.[21]

The nature of this new rule, as sketched in the Unification Treaty, was a masterpiece of ambiguity. According to the treaty, this regulation should "better guarantee the protection of prenatal life and the constitutional resolution of the conflicts [faced by pregnant women] than is the case in both parts of Germany at the present—above all, through legally assured claims of women, particularly claims for counseling and social assistance."[22] The provision went on to require that a comprehensive system of counseling offices be established in the former GDR with the financial assistance of the federal government. These offices must be able to give counseling and (apparently financial) assistance to pregnant women even beyond the point of the birth of the child.[23]

In this compromise, the territory of the GDR retained its former rule for up to two years, but the establishment of the counseling offices during this period was clearly intended to reduce the number of abortions that would take place under the GDR rule. Although the requirement of counseling offices in the first two years was relatively clear, the nature of the ultimate regulation of abortions called for by the Unification Treaty was highly unclear because the provision did not state whether the future abortion statute must continue to make abortions basically illegal. In this way the treaty avoided taking a position on what many believed to be the central question of the abortion debate.[24]

Moreover, this provision raised another basic problem: the two-year compromise of the Unification Treaty—without more—might well have violated articles 1(1) and 2(2) of the Basic Law under the Constitutional Court's abortion decision of 1975. The Unification Treaty, after all, retained for up to two years a GDR statute closely resembling the western statute that had been held unconstitutional in that decision.

In an attempt to deal with this and similar problems, the drafters of the Unification Treaty resorted to a device that they had also used in the case of the Bodenreform lands: they included a general provision that was designed to suspend certain of the provisions of the Basic Law, for an interim period, through an amendment of the Basic Law itself.[25] Accordingly, the Unification Treaty added a new article 143(1) to the Basic Law, which stated as follows:

> For the period up to December 31, 1992 (but not longer), law in [the territory of the former GDR and East Berlin] can deviate from determinations of this Basic Law, so long as and to the extent that, as a result of differing circumstances, full conformity with the order of the Basic Law cannot yet be achieved. [Any such] deviations may not violate article 19(2) and must be consistent with the principles specified in article 79(3).[26]

Presumably the interim regulation on abortion met the basic test of the first sentence of article 143(1) if serious objections among the population constitute the kind of "differing circumstances" that prevent immediate conformity with the Basic Law. But the provisions of article 79(3)—referred to in the second sentence of article 143(1)—seemed to raise more serious problems. As the *Bodenreform* case discussed at length, article 79(3), a central provision of the Basic Law, significantly limits the power of constitutional amendment.[27] Under that provision, no constitutional amendment may "affect" the basic principles contained in article 1 of the Basic Law.[28] Because the West German abortion case rested in part on the guarantee of human dignity contained in article 1(1), it was arguable that principles laid down in article 1 would be "affected" by permitting any regulation of abortion that is less stringent than the system required by the Constitutional Court. As a consequence, it could be argued that no constitutional amendment could change the decision of the Constitutional Court on this point.[29]

Under this view, it would seem that no constitutional amendment could have rendered the GDR abortion statute constitutional within the territory of the Basic Law, even for an interim period. On the other hand, it could be argued that abortion regulations, even if they implicate human dignity to some extent, do not affect that constitutional concept in its essence, and therefore the legislature in enacting constitutional amendments on this subject has substantial discretion in striking an appropriate balance. But in any event this interim provision was not attacked in the Constitutional Court, and so these specific constitutional issues remained unresolved.[30]

## The 1992 Abortion Statute

Notwithstanding its constitutional underpinning, the resolution adopted in the Unification Treaty was in reality no resolution at all because the treaty required the Bundestag to revisit the abortion question before the end of 1992. As was to be expected, the need to adopt a new abortion statute set off a many-sided debate in the German parliament—particularly because the vagueness of the Unification Treaty appeared to allow a broad range of possibilities. Moreover, the contending forces agreed that the vote on abortion would be free from the party and coalition "discipline" that ordinarily maintains a stable majority in a parliamentary system. Accordingly, this vote was more open and uncertain than is generally the case in German politics.

Indeed, from the beginning it was not at all clear that the conservative CDU/CSU would prevail on this issue. The Free Democrats (FDP), a small libertarian party whose votes were essential to the governing coalition, generally supported a liberal position on abortion. Moreover, divisions on this issue ran through the CDU itself: a battle erupted within the party in the summer of 1990 as CDU Bundestag President Rita Süssmuth proposed a "third way" between the three-month abortion period of the GDR and the "indication" exceptions of the Federal Republic.[31] There was a clear prospect that this could be one of the few areas in which German unification actually worked a significant change in the legal status not only in the former GDR, but also in the territory of the old Federal Republic itself.

By September 1991 six separate proposed drafts had been introduced in hearings before a special committee of the German parliament.[32] These drafts ran from conservative proposals to retain the existing western law—with even fewer exceptional circumstances allowing abortion than had been acknowledged by the Constitutional Court—to the proposals of groups on the left to decriminalize abortion completely. Located between these opposing views were proposals of the FDP and the Social Democrats to allow abortion during the first three months of pregnancy, either with or without a requirement of mandatory counseling. Moreover, in mid-1992, as the deadline set by the Unification Treaty began to appear on the horizon, some members of the CDU, led by Bundestag President Rita Süssmuth, entered into negotiations with the SPD and FDP about agreeing on a joint "Group Proposal" (*Gruppenantrag*). This proposal generally resembled the FDP's plan as well as Süssmuth's proposal of 1990 for a "third way."[33]

On June 26, 1992, in a vote of great significance for the question of abortion regulation in Germany, the Bundestag—with votes of the SPD, FDP, PDS, and Bündnis 90/Greens, as well as thirty-two votes of members of the CDU—adopted a modified version of the "Group Proposal." The statute would allow a pregnant woman to make her own decision with respect to abortion in the first twelve weeks of pregnancy, after receiving mandatory counseling.[34] This vote apparently marked the first time that a Bundestag majority had been assembled against the CDU leadership under the prevailing coalition, and it evoked bitter responses from conservative political figures and others. One critic, for example, claimed that the newly enacted statute was based on "Ulbricht legislation"—a reference to the hard-line Communist Party leader of the early years of the GDR—although the legislation in reality resembled the SPD statute of 1974 even more closely than it resembled the GDR legislation of 1972.[35] Subsequently, the modified "group proposal" was approved by the Bundesrat with only one state, Bavaria, opposing the statute.[36]

## The Court's Second Abortion Decision

Yet it was always clear that the ultimate decision on the settlement of the abortion issue after unification would be made by the German Constitutional Court. Shortly after the parliament's vote, 248 conservative members of the Bundestag, as well as the state government of Bavaria, filed an action in the Constitutional Court arguing that the new statute violated articles 1 and 2 of the Basic Law.[37]

As had also been the case in 1975, the Court's pending decision on abortion became the focus of intense speculation and controversy. A speedily issued temporary injunction, suspending operation of the newly adopted statute, suggested that the Court had some doubts about the measure's constitutionality.[38] Among proponents of the statute, considerable indignation was evoked by the news that one of the Court's sitting judges had only recently resigned from an advocacy group that vigorously opposed abortion, and that one of the two experts chosen to write advisory memoranda for the Court remained a member of that organization.[39] Moreover, a second judge of the panel had been a conservative member of the Bundestag in 1975 and, as such, had been one of the complainants challenging the liberal abortion law in the Court's first abortion decision.[40]

In May 1993, the Constitutional Court handed down a wide-ranging opinion finding the new abortion law unconstitutional in significant respects.[41] To this extent it realized the fears of the measure's proponents. Yet, even though the Court reached this general result, it followed a pattern noticeable in other important cases dealing with unification by seeking to strike a middle ground in which interests on both sides would be compromised.[42] This approach is particularly interesting because the Court's first opinion on abortion in 1975 also seemed to compromise interests on both sides, by first requiring criminalization of abortion but then finding rather broad exceptions. The new abortion case therefore represents a compromise between the new statute and the old compromise. The result is that, in a very significant theoretical shift, the Court for the first time moved away from a general requirement of the criminal penalization of abortion. On the other hand, it retained certain important theoretical aspects of the past and also increased the difficulty of securing government funding for abortions.

The court began its opinion by reaffirming its prior view that a fetus is "unborn life" and therefore possesses human dignity which must be protected by the state against dangers from other individuals.[43] Moreover, this protection must be asserted even against the prospective mother and can only be effective if legislation prohibits abortion as a basic matter and imposes a legal duty on the mother to bring the child to term.[44] Indeed, the fetus must also be protected against third persons who might induce a pregnant woman to have an abortion.

On the other hand, the court also followed its 1975 opinion by noting that the interests of the fetus are not the only interests at issue: the pregnant woman has countervailing legal interests of human dignity, bodily integrity, and rights of personality. It is up to the legislature to reconcile these countervailing values, but, in doing so, the legislature must observe a basic minimal protection of the fetus (*Untermaßverbot*).[45]

Accordingly, the court reaffirmed its general view that in situations in which it would be unreasonable for the state to require a woman to bear a child—because of problems of health, or because of rape, diagnosed birth defects, or social and psychological conflicts that are as damaging to the woman as these other problems—the woman's interest would prevail and the abortion will be justifiable. Nonetheless, the constitution obliges the state to work to obviate these problems—for example, by combating problems of resources that might force a woman into a social or psychological conflict and convince her not to have a child.[46] Moreover, the state must take general measures directed toward persuading women not to have abortions, by seeking to imprint the obligation to have a child on the public consciousness through the schools and other public institutions including public and private radio and television.[47]

Yet after reaffirming the basic theoretical principles of its 1975 decision, the Court shifted its ground and adopted a significantly new approach. According to the Court, the parliament had discretion to find that—in the early phases of the pregnancy—more fetuses could be saved if the state works with the pregnant woman and relies on a process of counseling instead of imposing a criminal penalty on the woman's choice.[48] Under this method, the pregnant woman would make the final decision on whether to have an abortion after the process of counseling is completed. According to the Court, the adoption of such a new approach seemed particularly justifiable because the number of abortions since the Court's decision in 1975 has remained high.

Yet in the Court's view, the nature of the counseling undertaken is crucial to the constitutionality of the statute. Accordingly, the process of counseling must be specifically directed toward convincing the pregnant woman to bear the child and, in a long section of the opinion, the Court set forth detailed requirements for the nature and content of this counseling. In general, the goal of the counseling should be to "strengthen the woman's consciousness of responsibility."[49] The woman must be informed that she may decide for an abortion on grounds of social or personal problems only if those problems impose a burden that is equivalent to an injury to her health or problems imposed by a child with a birth defect. Moreover, the Court asserted that third persons and indeed family members "not infrequently" influence the woman "in a criminal manner" to have an abortion, and these persons must also be brought into the process of counseling.[50]

In sum, the result of the counseling was to remain "open" in the sense that the woman's decision would prevail; yet the basic purpose of the counseling must be to direct the woman toward bearing the child. The woman must be told that the child receives special protection under the legal order, and that she may only choose to have an abortion if the prospective burden on her would be very heavy. Any possible "misconceptions" must be corrected by the counselor "in a manner that is understandable by the person seeking counseling."[51] Moreover, the counseling may only be successfully completed if the woman discloses her main reason for considering an abortion.[52] If the counselor believes that the process is not really concluded, the counselor may demand another session. Specifically, if the counselor believes that the woman is accompanied to the session by somebody who is trying to convince her not to bear the child, the counselor may require another session with the woman alone.

An abortion may not follow the counseling session directly, because the woman must have an opportunity to consider what she has heard, and the doctor who undertakes the abortion is not permitted to be the counselor at these sessions. It would be inconsistent with the state's obligation to protect human life if the state merely established or licensed counseling centers and then did nothing more. Instead, the state has an obligation to supervise and inspect the counseling agencies at specific intervals, to determine whether they are carrying out the required counseling process properly.

Yet even when the pregnant woman completes the requisite counseling sessions, she is still to be subject to additional attempts to persuade her not to undertake an abortion. Indeed, in a sort of second step of the counseling process, the physician who is undertaking the abortion must also in effect counsel the woman in a manner that might discourage the abortion. For example, the physician should make clear to a woman "that an abortion destroys human life," because some women can have "incorrect ideas" on this subject.[53] The physician must also determine whether the woman really wants the abortion herself or whether she is under the influence of some third person such as husband, partner, parents, or employer. Knowledge of whether the child is a boy or a girl must ordinarily be withheld from the woman in the early phases of pregnancy, to avoid an impermissible abortion on the basis of the child's gender.[54]

According to the Court, research shows that, to a significant extent, abortions do not have their cause primarily in economic or social problems of need, but rather in disturbed partnership relations or in the rejection of the child—or similar pressure—coming from the child's father or the parents of the pregnant woman.[55] Thus it is also important for the state to impose criminal penalties on those persons in the family of the woman who refuse, "in a reprehensible way," to lend support to the woman and seek to force her to have an abortion.[56]

Even though the legislature may decide not to criminalize an abortion undertaken in the first three months after appropriate counseling, it does not follow that such an abortion can be declared to be "justified" or "not illegal," as set forth in the Bundestag's statute. The abortion could only be found to be "justified" or "not illegal" if the existence of the requisite indications has been determined by a court or by a third person. To allow the woman to make this decision in a way that would result in the abortion being justified would be to allow the woman to be a judge in her own cause.[57]

Thus, although the legislature may decide that a woman will not be subject to criminal penalties for an abortion in the first three months of pregnancy undertaken after such counseling, the abortion still remains "unjustified." As a result, the state cannot constitutionally pay for the abortion out of funds of social insurance. To do so would make the state an accomplice to the act of killing the unborn fetus, when the legality of such an action—that is, the existence of the requisite "indications"—has not been reliably determined by a court or other third person. Yet, on the other hand, various forms of welfare payments are permissible even for such abortions when the woman can show actual financial need for payment for an abortion that, under this rule, would not be subject to criminal penalties.

The result of the opinion, therefore, may be a significant curtailment of public funding of abortions. Under the previous abortion regime all permissible abortions, including those allowed under the expansive social indication, were financed by public or private health insurance like any other permissible measure undertaken by a physician. In contrast, a permissible abortion following a woman's own choice after counseling will be financed from public funds only if the woman can show that she would otherwise be without means to undertake the procedure.[58]

## THE COURT'S DECISION IN RETROSPECT

Although the Court's opinion seemed to be a mediating compromise, the decision was not likely to satisfy any group across the broad spectrum of abortion views. On the one hand, the supporters of restrictive abortion laws were dismayed that the Court, for the first time, allowed a process of counseling to replace a requirement of criminal penalties. This result certainly moved in the direction of the solution favored by the SPD and the FDP in 1974, as well as the prior statutory position of the GDR, which basically foresaw a free choice of abortion by the pregnant woman in the first three months of pregnancy. To this extent, then, some remnant of the legal position brought to unification by the GDR has survived in this area—not only in the Bundestag's statute but also, albeit in somewhat diluted form, in the compromise resolution reached by the Constitutional Court.

Yet the result remains quite far from a full recognition of the position reflected in the 1972 GDR statute or even in the SPD-FDP legislation of 1974. The GDR statute imposed no mandatory counseling while the counseling in the 1974 statute was to be relatively unobtrusive.[59] In contrast, the institution of counseling as foreseen by the Constitutional Court has some extremely onerous features: the pregnant woman is subject to tendentious argumentation against her expressed desire to have an abortion, and she is expected to disclose the basic reason which led her to make that choice. Moreover, the Court requires that even noncriminal abortions after counseling continue to be labeled "not justified" or "illegal" (*rechtswidrig*), with results that are not yet completely foreseeable.[60] One very important result, however, is that general financing under public and private medical insurance plans has been withdrawn from such abortions, and the pregnant woman must apply as a seeker of special state charity for payment when her own financial resources are insufficient.

Although the pregnant woman is thus accorded the final decision on whether to undergo an abortion in the first trimester, the Court is far from enthusiastic about this result. Indeed the Court reaches this conclusion not because it endorses the woman's right of free decision, but rather because it believes that women can be influenced through the process of counseling to undertake fewer abortions than would have been the case under the previous "indications" system.[61]

Moreover, the view of the pregnant woman—and, by implication, the view of women in general—that seems to underlie the Court's opinion is dismaying to say the least. The pregnant woman seeking an abortion is portrayed as a person whose sense of responsibility needs to be "strengthened" and someone who may be subject to "false understandings" with respect to the subject of childbirth and abortion. Indeed, the Court seems to believe that the woman seeking an abortion is someone of weakened or diminished will power: under the Court's view, a woman is "not infrequently" subject to the influence of sinister outside forces—such as husbands, partners, parents, or employers—who have successfully influenced the woman to have an abortion; but her supposedly false decision in this matter may fortunately be corrected by the countervailing influence of the state counselor pushing in the other direction. Although the Court rather defensively asserts that its concept does not treat the woman as an "object" to be manipulated, that is precisely the role that the opinion actually seems to imply.[62]

Certainly this is quite a different view of the role of women than is set forth, for example, in the constitutions of the new east German states, which posit strong and self-reliant individuals taking equal responsibility in all matters of state and society. It is also quite different from the actual self-reliant role played by many women in the GDR, notwithstanding the undoubted discrimination which women faced in that state also.[63] Indeed, the spirit of paternalism that runs through this opinion seems to be precisely the spirit that the more egalitarian constitutions of the new eastern states—particularly that of Brandenburg—seek to combat.[64]

Finally, there is one more particularly striking characteristic of the Court's opinion in the 1993 abortion decision. Even though the entire question was brought to the fore by virtue of German unification and the more liberal abortion legislation of the GDR, there is absolutely no discussion—not even a recognition—of the experience of the GDR with respect to abortion or the role that abortion and the general status of women played in the society of the GDR.[65] With the exception of a brief historical summary at the outset, much of the opinion reads as though German unification had never taken place and the sixteen million individuals of the former GDR, with their own distinct histories and experience, had never become part of the united Germany. Thus, although this decision marks one of the few instances in which the law of the GDR has made a perceptible impact on the law of the united Germany, the Court's opinion seems to be directed toward denying or at least ignoring that influence.

From a purely rhetorical point of view, therefore, the opinion of the Constitutional Court seems to be a reaffirmation of the political principles implied by article 23, the extension of the conservative views prevailing in the west over the society of the east. Yet, in reality, the underlying result of the parliamentary legislation—as modified by the Court's decision—is actually closer to what might have been expected in a new constitution, adopting certain ideas from east and west under article 146. As the Bundestag's basic decision moves away from the criminalization of abortion, it moves toward a new popular consensus on this subject compounded of the majority views from the east in addition to the views of the minority SPD in the west.[66] In the end, therefore, the east kept a remnant of its own position on this matter—a view derived from the old regime but also endorsed in the Round Table's draft constitution. Moreover, unification has been the catalyst to extend at least a watered-down version of that view to the west as well. It is too early to determine the extent to which this kind of alliance—between eastern political forces and the SPD in the west—may be effective in the future on a variety of other important issues.[67]

CHAPTER 13

# The Transformation of Eastern Institutions: The Civil Service, the Universities, and the Justice System

THE "accession" of the GDR to the Federal Republic raised fundamental questions about the future of the civil service in eastern Germany, as well as the related areas of education and the judiciary. The great differences between eastern and western practices in these areas perhaps suggested that western forms should simply be extended to the east, following the analogy of article 23. Yet in light of decades of debate about the traditional civil service in the west, along with sharply increasing dissatisfaction with the western universities, unification also seemed to afford an opportunity for extensive reform in the west as well.

In addition to structural issues, unification posed sensitive questions of the future of eastern personnel. Although the judges, academics, and civil servants of the GDR often occupied positions close to the core of the GDR state, some also formed an intellectual elite that could make important contributions to the united Germany. Many were implicated in the former system, but some shared the alternative democratic understandings of the GDR reform movement, which might enhance diversity within the Federal Republic. For some eastern citizens, the continued presence of former officials could provide reassurance that their entire culture was not being abandoned, to be replaced by that of the west. Yet, for many others, the continued presence of GDR officers would mock the reformers' efforts to sweep away the remnants of the old regime and might leave potentially damaging SED cadres undisturbed. Finally, there was the undoubted fact that there were many more GDR civil servants than were necessary to perform the allotted tasks—and many more than could be supported at western salaries.

In a series of crucial decisions in the Unification Treaty, western structures were extended to the east without significant change—accompanied by the massive, but by no means total, removal of eastern personnel. This resolution also apparently had the effect, for the short term at least, of staving off pressure for change in the west as well.

## Background: The Traditional Civil Service in West Germany

The special nature of the traditional civil service in the Federal Republic of Germany forms the constitutional background for understanding these problems as they arose upon unification. In the German monarchical tradition, the civil service, like the army, was a privileged pillar of the state.[1] But the special privileges—and obligations—of the civil service (*Beamtentum*) did not vanish with the coming of democracy. Rather, the civil service has a special, guaranteed position in the Basic Law derived from the concept of an orderly *Rechtsstaat*—a state based on expert application of general legal rules that had its origin in eighteenth-century absolutism.[2]

The basic idea of the traditional Beamtentum is that the civil servant (*Beamter*) owes a special duty of loyalty and devotion to the state. In this way the modern state steps into the former role of the monarch, who also received a high degree of loyalty from his officials. In return, the state provides the Beamter with life tenure—after successful completion of an initial probationary period—as well as a generous salary and an appropriate pension. Indeed, the salary of the Beamter must correspond to the high social standing of the profession.[3]

A hierarchical structure in the public administration is intended to ensure that decisions affecting citizens are made in accordance with law, but some officials other than administrators, such as teachers in public schools and universities, are also part of the Beamtentum. Moreover, judges are viewed as bearing some resemblance to civil servants—making more or less routine applications of general rules to specific cases in many instances. While, strictly speaking, judges are not part of the Beamtentum, many rules applicable to judges resemble those for civil servants. On the other hand some public workers, of supposedly lower status, are classified as "employees" or "workers" (*Angestellte* or *Arbeiter*) and are not entitled to the privileges of the Beamtentum.

## Extension of the General Principles of the Western Civil Service to the East

In contrast with this highly developed and formalized system of administration, with its own special corps of officials, the public service of the GDR did not provide life tenure and was often under the direct control of party cadres. In carrying out their offices civil servants—like judges—were required to apply the "principles of socialist morality" and "socialist legality."[4] The system of party control was dismantled after the revolutionary events of autumn 1989, but many former administrators and judges, including some who had participated in acts of political oppression, remained in office up to the point of unification and beyond.

It seemed clear, therefore, that fundamental changes in the civil service and judiciary of eastern Germany were inevitable. Specifically, the framers of the Unification Treaty decided that eastern Germany should have the same administrative structure as the west. This view was not challenged in the negotiations over the Unification Treaty, and the treaty explicitly extended the general principles of the Beamtentum to the former GDR.[5]

The Unification Treaty, therefore, distinguishes officers that are "Beamte" from other government employees. In taking this position, the framers rejected proposals to reform or abolish the traditional civil service system, as a part of the process of unification. For example, the German union of public workers proposed that the special class of Beamte should be abolished, to be replaced by a uniform regulation covering all government employees.[6] Proposals for abolition have been advanced over several decades, principally by the Social Democrats, on the ground that the Beamtentum is an undemocratic and retrograde institution that preserves a distinct class of civil officers standing apart from the population. As the Beamtentum is strongly supported by many German conservatives, these proposals have been singularly unsuccessful over the years, and they did not fare any better in the process of unification.[7]

Thus, in this respect also, the framers of unification rejected an opportunity to rethink the contemporary role of traditional western institutions. The necessity of integrating a distinct administrative structure into that of the Federal Republic could perhaps have furnished an occasion for questioning whether the traditional civil service, arising from eighteenth-century absolutism, was an appropriate method of administration in a modern democracy.

## "Abwicklung" and the Constitution: The *Warteschleife* Decision

In extending the traditional western civil service to the east, the drafters of the Unification Treaty were immediately confronted with a very practical problem: the civil service was proportionately much larger in the east than in the west. As a socialist government, the GDR state undertook a broader range of tasks than those performed by the Federal Republic; moreover, the—largely achieved—goal of full employment required the creation of numerous positions that did not fully use the time and skills of the employee and had little economic justification.[8] But henceforth the eastern civil service was to conform to western structures and was not to be used as a method of reducing unemployment. By analogy to the hard discipline of the market in the private sphere, the public service was to be limited to personnel actually required to accomplish certain essential tasks—as was the aspiration, at least, in the west.

The framers of the Unification Treaty sought to achieve this goal through two separate methods. First, the framers recognized that an administrative unit might need to reduce its staff, because it had been too large to begin with or because its tasks had been redefined or reduced. Accordingly, the treaty made it permissible to dismiss a civil servant if there was no longer any "need" (*Bedarf*) for the employee's services.[9]

In addition to the dismissal of individuals on grounds of insufficient "need," the framers of the Unification Treaty also provided a method for the closing or winding up of entire administrative divisions. Upon unification, the various administrative and educational units of the GDR were to be allocated to the eastern states or to the federal government, under the competence rules of the Basic Law.[10] The states or federal government would then have three months to determine which units, or parts of units, would be "carried forward" into the new political structure and which units would be dissolved or "wound up."[11] The word for this process of dissolution—*Abwicklung*—has a peculiar cold and bureaucratic quality, and the word soon became ominous to the huge numbers of eastern citizens whose livelihoods were threatened by this massive process of disassembling the capacious structures of the GDR state.[12] The Unification Treaty provided no criteria for the "carrying forward" or "winding up" of units, but presumably this decision was to rest on whether a given unit would serve a significant function in the new political circumstances.

The Unification Treaty did, however, include rules for employees of a unit that was being "wound up." To mitigate economic hardship, employees of a dissolved unit would receive 70 percent of their salary for a six-month period (nine months, for older employees) while waiting to see if they would be re-employed in some other branch of the Civil Service—an unlikely prospect for most. After this period all salary payments would end, and the employee would only be eligible for unemployment payments according to the ordinary rules.[13] The interim waiting period was colloquially referred to as the "*Warteschleife*" or "holding pattern"—the word used to describe airplanes waiting to land at an airport. Hundreds of thousands of individuals who had been employed in discontinued units were placed in the "Warteschleife" under these provisions.

The vast extent of the resulting unemployment came as a social earthquake in the former GDR, and a number of individuals who found themselves in the "Warteschleife" challenged these rules in the Federal Constitutional Court. Complainants argued that an individual's continued employment should not depend on the fate of a particular administrative unit and that a more differentiated decision, based on the qualities or needs of the individual, was required.[14] Specifically, the claimants contended that the rules violated their rights to the free choice of employment protected by the Basic Law in article 12. The claimants also argued that their prior employment relationship was a form of property and that the new rules, by undoing that relationship, deprived them of property in violation of article 14 of the Basic Law.[15]

Responding to these claims, the federal government argued that the GDR came to an end on October 3, 1990, and that its employment relationships also ended on that date. Any subsequent employment relationship with the Federal Republic arose from the Unification Treaty and could therefore be limited by the treaty itself.[16] Moreover, the Federal Republic was not the legal successor of the GDR and bore no responsibility for its obligations.

In resolving this dispute, the Court focused on article 12 of the Basic Law, which guarantees freedom in the choice of a profession and in the choice of a specific job or position within that profession. Although the state need not create or maintain specific jobs or positions, any incursion by the state into an employment relationship must be measured against the guarantees of article 12.[17] The Court then concluded that the "Warteschleife" regulation did implicate an employee's rights under article 12 GG because it terminated an existing employment relationship. Accordingly, the Court rejected the view that GDR employment relations came to an end upon unification. On the contrary, the Unification Treaty itself provided that the federal government and the Länder would step into the shoes of the GDR as employer in continuing employment relations; "to this extent the Federal Republic is the legal successor of the former GDR."[18]

Yet even though article 12 GG was implicated, the Court went on to find that the "Warteschleife" regulations were generally constitutional. The treaty's invasion of the protected sphere was justified by the need to build a modern and effective administration required for general economic health. If the number of employees was not reduced, the budget would be hopelessly strained, especially in light of the other costs of unification. Achieving this goal was a community interest of subordinating importance.[19]

But the Court's opinion shifted more in the complainants' direction when it approached the question of "proportionality"—the question of whether the "Warteschleife" regulations were more severe than was necessary to achieve their stated goal. In light of economic problems and other factors, the Court concluded that it would only be permissible to dissolve unneeded departments if the individual hardship thus caused could be significantly mitigated. The Court noted that the Unification Treaty itself provided opportunities for reeducation and temporary employment, in addition to the Warteschleife payments, and the Court strongly suggested that these measures were constitutionally required.[20] With respect to handicapped and elderly employees, and single parents, the Court's position was even more exacting. Because these employees will face special difficulties in finding new employment, the state must make special efforts to reintegrate them into the work force and can dismiss them only if they have a well-founded prospect of a new position in the public service.[21] Moreover, pregnant women and mothers of infants enjoy special constitutional protection, and they may not be removed from their positions.[22]

In resolving these issues, the Court seemed to follow a general pattern that it had also followed in the *Bodenreform* case and was to follow in other decisions arising from unification: it sought to strike a mediating compromise and adopt a middle position between contending interests of east and west. On the one hand, the Court generally upheld the rule of the Unification Treaty, rejecting the employees' constitutional complaint and not calling into question the strong political force behind the agreement. On the other hand, the Court construed the treaty in a manner that gave some measure of comfort to the complainants by strengthening its social welfare components. As a result, the decision "made the reorganization of the public service in the former GDR 'more socially tolerable.' Hardships that accompanied the Unification Treaty were mitigated."[23] In drafting its opinion in this manner, the Court significantly strengthened the idea of affirmative governmental obligations of the social state under the Basic Law. A similar tendency, although in quite a different context, seems evident in the *Bodenreform* decision, also. Perhaps these and other recent cases of the Constitutional Court suggest that—even though more concrete aspects of the social state were not included in the Basic Law upon unification, and do not seem likely to be so included in any prospective federal constitutional reform—the Court itself has begun to take on such a task of reconciliation, through its rapid expansion of concrete social state jurisprudence in recent decisions.

## The Individual Review of Eastern Personnel

Even for GDR employees whose agencies were not dissolved in the great wave of "Abwicklung" at the end of 1990, there was no assurance of ultimate acceptance into the all-German civil service or Beamtentum. Although GDR public officials pressed for the swift adoption of the western system, with its numerous material advantages,[24] the government of the Federal Republic was far from willing to take eastern officials into the Beamtentum on an automatic basis.

Two separate but related problems gave rise to these concerns. First, the western government feared that many GDR officials lacked the qualifications necessary to perform at the level of the West German civil service. These doubts were perhaps most acute in the case of judges, whose future tasks required thorough training in the West German legal system, an education that the GDR judges lacked. In the case of professors and academic researchers, moreover, the quality of their scholarly work was often a closed book to western officials, at the outset at least.

Perhaps even more complicated problems arose from the political past. Some administrators, judges, and academic personnel had taken part in acts of political oppression under the old regime or had worked actively for the Ministry for State Security (Stasi). There was general agreement that such officials should not be employed further in the public service.[25]

Yet it was also clear that for practical reasons of personnel it would be impossible to dismiss all GDR officials en masse; many would necessarily have to remain in office to undertake ordinary governmental functions during the process of unification and thereafter. Moreover, such a resolution—which would resemble mass imputations of guilt characteristic of totalitarian regimes—was inconsistent with the precepts of the liberal Rechtsstaat that the GDR was said to be joining. Thus a more differentiated case-by-case determination was necessary.

In order to resolve these questions on an individual basis, the Unification Treaty required that East German civil servants undergo a three-year probationary period before achieving the lifetime status of Beamter.[26] Supervisory officials in the administration would decide whether the applicant met the stringent requirements for lifetime tenure, and special interim rules were provided to take into account the fact that few (if any) applicants from the GDR could have satisfied the specific requirements for education and training contained in West German law.[27]

Each individual would be judged according to the ordinary criteria for the civil service: professional accomplishment and "personal suitability." Moreover, it was also necessary to show a "need" for the individual's specific function in the structure of the new civil service.[28]

In addition to these standard criteria, however, the Unification Treaty contained a special section requiring summary dismissal of employees who had participated in oppressive political acts under the GDR. The difficult and crucial question of how to measure those acts was resolved in an interesting manner. The treaty provided for dismissal if an employee had

> violated the principles of humanity or the rule of law, in particular [if the employee had violated] the human rights that are protected by the International Covenant on Civil and Political Rights of December 19, 1966, or the principles contained in the Universal Declaration of Human Rights of December 10, 1948.[29]

Thus, a candidate's participation in oppressive acts was to be primarily determined under the provisions of these United Nations human rights instruments.[30]

The courts have been interpreting this provision rather narrowly, often requiring a significant violation of the human rights instrument as well as knowledge and consciousness of a violation.[31] Yet members of the public service have been dismissed under this provision. In one case, for example, an official was dismissed because he had rejected citizens' applications to leave the GDR and initiated repressive measures—such as steps leading to the loss of employment—against the applicants. These actions violated article 13 of the Universal Declaration of Human Rights of 1948, which grants each person the right "to leave any country, including his own." The official argued that he had acted in conformity with GDR law, but the court responded that GDR law itself violated the Universal Declaration.[32]

In a second special provision, the Unification Treaty required summary dismissal of any official who had been "active" on behalf of the Ministry for State Security (Stasi), if retaining the employee would be "unreasonable under the circumstances."[33] This provision requires dismissal of many Stasi officials and collaborators, but the requirement of "unreasonableness" could allow retention of some individuals if their collaboration was minor or perhaps very far in the past, or if other mitigating factors prevailed in a case-by-case balancing of the circumstances.[34] In considering this provision, the Federal Labor Court has found that persons who held significant posts in the Stasi will ordinarily be barred from significant employment in the public service, and an individual who was a very high Stasi official will be barred even from a low-level public position.[35] In these decisions, the court emphasized the importance of maintaining public confidence in the civil service and consequently focused to some extent on the damaging public appearance that the retention of these officers could present.[36]

In a highly publicized application of this provision, the rector of the Humboldt University in Berlin, Heinrich Fink, was dismissed on the ground that he had been an "unofficial collaborator" of the Stasi since 1969. This action evoked vigorous student demonstrations on behalf of Fink, who had played a controversial role at the university during the unification period.[37] Although former Stasi officials testified that Fink had not been an "unofficial collaborator," an appeals court rejected their testimony and relied instead on written Stasi files that, in the court's view, implicated Fink.[38] The *Fink* case raised important questions concerning the evidentiary value of the Stasi files, the type or degree of collaboration with the Stasi that should suffice for exclusion from the public service, and the role of federal archival officials (the Gauck Agency) in evaluating the files and characterizing their contents.[39]

In addition to these two forms of summary dismissal, an eastern civil servant could also be dismissed on more general political grounds. Even an official who never cooperated with the Stasi or participated in human rights abuses might be excluded if there were doubts about his or her "loyalty to the constitution"—i.e., to the Basic Law. The quality of "loyalty to the constitution" is essential to the "personal suitability" required of all officials under the federal civil service law.

This loyalty requirement has had a tortured history in western Germany. From the beginning of the Federal Republic, and with particular rigor in the years following 1972, the institution of the public service has been characterized by a strict application of the principle of "loyalty to the constitution." The basic public service law of the Federal Republic—supplemented for a time by a special "Radicals Decree"—requires that applicants be rejected for the public service if they cannot "guarantee that [they] will at all times support the free democratic basic order in the sense of the Basic Law."[40] Although the precise meaning of the phrase "free democratic basic order" is debatable, it refers generally to a political order of the western, liberal-democratic type, respecting the rule of law and individual rights.[41]

This doctrine sometimes excluded members of right-wing parties from the public service, but it was directed principally against members of the West German Communist Party (DKP) and other Communist splinter groups.[42] To justify this doctrine, parallels were sometimes drawn with the Weimar period in which the undemocratic political views of many judges and civil servants may have contributed to the weakening of the republic and the rise of a totalitarian system.

This invocation of the principle of loyalty, which has been compared with aspects of the McCarthy period in the United States, has been the subject of bitter political dispute. Its application was particularly significant in the teaching profession, as almost all teachers and university professors in the Federal

Republic are members of the public service. With the extension of the West German Basic Law to the east under the Unification Treaty, it was clear that this principle of loyalty to the constitution would be extended as well.[43]

Yet this doctrine raised special problems in the context of unification. A stringent application of the loyalty principle could have excluded a high percentage of former GDR civil servants because of the prevalence of former SED members in their ranks.[44] But many believed that a broad exclusion of former GDR officials—and presumably their (at least temporary) replacement by candidates from the west—was an unacceptable method of reconstituting east German political life.[45] The central issue, therefore, was how this requirement would be applied to past membership in the SED—which was common among eastern public officials—and to continuing membership in the PDS, its successor organization.[46]

With respect to membership in the SED, judicial decisions indicated from the beginning that there would be no wholesale dismissal of officials merely on the grounds of former party membership. Rather, civil servants would be dismissed only if they had a special connection or identification with the SED state above and beyond that of party membership alone.[47]

Yet cases in the labor courts have found that this "special connection" may arise from the holding of a significant position in the party. In a case from Saxony, for example, a teacher was dismissed from her position because she had been a long-time SED "party secretary."[48] This position involved writing reports on the political atmosphere within the school and exercising some political supervision over the school principal; the exercise of these functions showed a special identification with the SED and the GDR state. In light of this history, the court doubted that the teacher would support the "free democratic basic order" in a time of crisis.[49] Indeed, the Federal Labor Court has indicated that former long-time party secretaries will generally lose their positions in the public service, unless they can come forward with specific evidence rebutting an inference of their special attachment to the SED state.[50]

In another interesting case, the Berlin government dismissed the assistant principal of a ballet school because she had attended special SED party schools and had worked for almost eight years in the cultural section of the SED Central Committee.[51] In the party schools, the teacher had worked on curricula and literature lists that were used to further the power of the state rather than to assist free inquiry. The court noted that, for the citizens of the GDR, the SED Central Committee was the "essence of political control [*Dirigismus*] and oppression." The court continued: "It seems unbearable that GDR citizens could again encounter people in high positions who had participated during the GDR period—at least according to outward appearances—in spying and oppression of citizens as part of the party's apparatus of power, while a large part of the population, which cannot be reproached [with such conduct], is unemployed."[52]

In some cases it is not the office held, or the general duties of the office, but rather specific actions in office that can lead to dismissal. Thus a historian with an international reputation was dismissed from the Humboldt University largely because he had rudely ejected a student from his class in 1976—apparently for political reasons—and the student was consequently expelled from the university and sent "into the labor force." Moreover, an inadequate apology after unification indicated the professor's insufficient willingness to reform. The Berlin Labor Court upheld the dismissal.[53]

Although these decisions of the labor courts have generally reflected traditional doctrine, the Constitutional Court recently cast doubt on this jurisprudence in an important decision that is likely to reduce the number of GDR officials excluded from office on political grounds.[54] The Court remanded a labor court decision dismissing an East Berlin police official who had a long record of devoted service to the GDR and the SED, including periods as a party secretary. Citing the *Warteschleife* case, the Court emphasized that former GDR officials receive the protections of article 12 of the Basic Law, providing for free choice of employment.[55] Because the negotiators of the Unification Treaty sought to integrate eastern officials into the public service, the treaty provides dismissal for specified activity only in the case of Stasi collaborators and those who violated the principles of humanity. Accordingly, an official cannot be excluded from the public service on the basis of some other single characteristic—for example, a certain level of party activity. Instead, a weighing of individual factors is necessary in each case.

Since the purpose of this weighing is to make a prediction of the employee's "suitability" for the future, the courts must consider the employee's record after unification as well as before. Indeed, the "inner attitude of an individual can change, and it is possible that precisely the experiences and insights that have come to the citizens of the GDR with accession and subsequent developments could have brought about such a change."[56] In this case, the lower court concentrated on the employee's record under the GDR and erroneously ignored his loyal service to the government after unification.

The Court went on to declare that the ordinary collaboration with the SED state required of GDR officials could not, in itself, justify exclusion from the public service. Indeed, the stringent principles developed in the old Federal Republic for the exclusion of radicals from the public service cannot be applied in a "retroactive" manner to eastern officials after unification. Rather, "special circumstances" must be shown for exclusion. These might include actions under the GDR that were "strongly repressive" or "damaging," or the holding of a high office in the public service or full-time party employment—although in such cases an individual balancing of circumstances is still required.[57]

Because the individual balancing must be undertaken by the lower courts in each case, the impact of this decision is not entirely certain. Yet the Court seems to set the requirement of "special circumstances" at a very high level, and it seems likely that the holding of the (usually part-time) position of party secretary will no longer suffice for exclusion. In sum, the decision will probably decrease the number of eastern officials excluded from the public service on political grounds. In this respect, the decision falls squarely into the Court's tradition of seeking inner stability through the mediation of certain eastern and western views and interests after unification.

Notwithstanding the moderating decisions of the Constitutional Court, it is clear that exclusions from the public service have been undertaken vigorously in the eastern states. Hundreds of thousands of public employees were sent into the "Warteschleife"—and unemployment—when the size of the eastern civil service was drastically reduced upon unification. Moreover, although comprehensive figures are not yet available, many thousands have been dismissed as a result of individual examination.[58] Whatever the precise extent of these dismissals, it is clear that the extension of the concepts and rules of the western civil service to the east has resulted in a massive change of personnel in this central aspect of public life.

Moreover, in addition to its impact on the eastern administration in general, the Unification Treaty has had a particular impact on university education and on the legal system—two particularly crucial areas of public endeavor. Under the Basic Law each of these institutions has its own important constitutional role, and each of these areas was almost completely transformed upon unification.[59]

## The Remaking of the East German Universities and the Unification of Scholarship

Because of their special position in intellectual life, the future of the East German universities and research institutes was of particular sensitivity and importance. On the one hand the complete dissolution of GDR institutions could squander or impair a generation of intellectual resources.[60] On the other hand, retention of existing structures could perpetuate incompetence, pockets of totalitarian ideology, and the results of political favoritism.

Yet extension of the western system to the east—the resolution that was basically adopted—involved its own problems. Essentially, the universities of West Germany retained some of the most traditional aspects of the Beamtentum. A strenuous system of "habilitation"—in effect, requiring the completion of two books to qualify a candidate to be a university professor—delays most professorial appointments to the age of forty or more and, it has been argued, tends to dampen creativity in productive early years. The system also tends to exclude women in one way or another; there are few women professors in many areas and almost none in some others.

Social Democratic governments attempted some university reforms in the early 1970s,[61] but the Constitutional Court reinforced traditional structures when it struck down a reform measure in an important decision in 1973.[62] The Court declared that the power of the full professors (*Ordinarien*) to retain control on matters of teaching and research was guaranteed by the rights of academic freedom contained in article 5(3) of the Basic Law. Thus to some extent the constitution itself seemed to require the hierarchical structure of the traditional university.

In recent years, greatly increased enrollment and inadequate funding have placed severe strains on the western universities, and the system was subject to sustained criticism.[63] Yet upon unification it was this system that was extended to the new eastern states without significant change. Indeed, extension of the western system required undoing some educational reforms that had taken place in the structure of the East German universities during the revolutionary period of 1989 and 1990.

### *The "Abwicklung" of the Eastern Faculties*

In order to assist the effort of change, eastern universities typically formed partnerships with western universities in 1990 or 1991, as part of a broader system of cooperation between state governments in east and west. During this early period many western professors visited eastern universities, teaching and advising on difficult problems of structure and personnel. These itinerant "Lufthansa" professors, flying in from their regular duties in the west, often coexisted uneasily with the insecure corps of remaining eastern faculty members.[64]

Indeed, along with difficult problems of securing resources and reforming curricula, the chief question faced by the new state governments and their western advisors was what to do with existing university personnel.[65] Of course, the Unification Treaty contemplated the individual review of civil servants, including university professors, to determine whether they were qualified in accordance with western standards. Yet the process of individual review was expensive and time-consuming, and the results were uncertain. Accordingly, some of the more vigorous reformers wished for a "law-free realm" in which the entire personnel of certain academic departments could simply be swept away.

Of course a department that was to be permanently abolished, such as a department of Marxism-Leninism, could be "wound up" and dissolved under the treaty without difficulty.[66] Yet most of the eastern states sought to extend the concept of "Abwicklung" beyond these clear cases, by attempting to dissolve certain departments that were not intended to be permanently abolished. Instead, these departments were to be swiftly "refounded" after their "dissolution." Some former professors would be retained temporarily on short-term contracts, but they would soon be replaced with a new roster of (generally western) personnel.[67]

Accordingly, in the last days of 1990, four of the new eastern states and Berlin declared that important university departments—including economics, history, law, education, and philosophy—were henceforth dissolved.[68] According to the state governments, these departments were so deeply influenced by the political thought of the old regime, and in general so unlikely to be reformed from within, that the preferred response was total dissolution.[69] Moreover, the Science Council (Wissenschaftsrat)—an influential West German advisory agency overseeing education and research—had recommended sweeping reform, emphasizing the ideologically influenced nature of these departments in the GDR.[70]

This sudden and largely unexpected announcement came as a thunderbolt to the faculties involved, some of which were deeply engaged in attempts at self-reform.[71] Indeed, this upheaval evoked protests and demonstrations by students in Berlin and elsewhere.[72] In Berlin, moreover, faculty members of the Humboldt University filed suit, arguing that the technique of first dissolving a department and then reconstituting it with new personnel was an illegal and unconstitutional attempt to evade the requirement of the individual evaluation of each official in a continuing department.[73]

In June 1991, the Appellate Administrative Court of Berlin agreed that this method of dissolution was illegal and that the "dissolved" departments must remain intact for a transitional period.[74] Drawing on remarks of the Constitutional Court in the *Warteschleife* case, the administrative court found that the dissolution of a department is permissible only when the department is actually unnecessary and therefore slated for permanent abolition. A contrary result would violate the Unification Treaty and unduly invade the constitutional right of choice of employment.[75] Thus the professors of the Humboldt University had a right to remain members of the faculty, pending an individual review of their qualifications and political past.[76]

Notwithstanding the professors' legal victory in Berlin, it appears that most of the other eastern faculties of economics, history, law, education, and philosophy were "dissolved" (*abgewickelt*) and reconstituted with new personnel. Although this procedure had been found illegal in Berlin, that decision applied only to the Humboldt University, and legal challenges were rarely pursued to judgment elsewhere. Perhaps professors of the former GDR doubted that legal action could ultimately prevail against the "Rechtsstaat," and perhaps some thought that more could be accomplished without litigation. In some instances, moreover, claims by professors of dissolved faculties were withdrawn in return for financial settlements.[77]

But even after their "Abwicklung" in midwinter 1990–91, the "dissolved" faculties did not actually suspend operation. Rather, newly appointed "founding deans" from the west decided which former faculty members would be retained on interim short-term contracts, while the principal courses were often taught by visiting professors from the west. Permanent appointments were then made pursuant to the recommendations of an academic "founding commission" under the leadership of the western "founding dean."[78]

Even though all eastern professors underwent quite rigorous review, it apparently made a crucial difference whether an eastern professor had been on a "dissolved" faculty. According to one expert, almost no member of a "dissolved" faculty received a professorial position after unification while, in Saxony at least, perhaps one-third of the other departments ultimately came to be drawn from former GDR professors.[79] It seems to have been an inherent advantage for a professor to apply from inside the faculty, rather than petitioning as an outsider (from a dissolved faculty) seeking readmission. Moreover, preference was sometimes officially extended to inside applicants against outside competition. In sum, the effect of "dissolving" some faculties was "in one blow" to replace eastern with western personnel—and, given the traditional gender structure of western faculties, it was also, in many cases, to replace women with men.[80]

### *Individual Review of Eastern Personnel*

The individual review of eastern professors and other researchers—from the faculties that had not been "dissolved" in December 1990—was a complicated process.[81] Decisions on the three central questions for each professor—professional achievement, past political problems, and programmatic need—were made by a varied array of commissions and committees in the five new Länder. In Mecklenburg-Vorpommern, for example, a separate set of committees was established for the decision of each of these three questions, and other eastern states adopted variations of this basic structure.[82]

In the Humboldt University in Berlin, personnel were reviewed for all three criteria by a single Appointments and Structure Commission for each academic department. A central Personnel Commission was responsible for an overall personnel plan.[83] In addition to these official state commissions, the university itself established a parallel series of personnel and structure commissions for each department (as well as a central commission) which sought an internal "renewal" of the university. But these internal commissions had no legal authority and, in the end, little influence.[84] In all of these cases, work on the commissions could be arduous and subject to extreme pressures of time; a western member of such a commission in Mecklenburg-Vorpommern reports that his commission reviewed almost one hundred applicants in six months.[85]

Notwithstanding the various procedural structures, most decisions on scholarly achievement were in essence made by western experts in accordance with traditional criteria—although some weight may have been given to the numerous disadvantages, from pervasive censorship to a chronic lack of facilities and equipment, under which eastern researchers had to labor.[86] Even if the candidate fully satisfied the criteria of professional achievement and political suitability, however, there was still the question of whether there was a "need" for the individual's work according to the plans of the newly structured university or institute.[87] Moreover, this decision might require choosing among a number of qualified faculty members for the reduced number of positions in a newly streamlined department.[88]

It was also necessary to decide whether eastern faculty members would be given some preference in filling the relatively small number of remaining positions, or whether they would be subject to open competition from western and foreign applicants.[89] It may be the case that the answer to this question significantly determined the number of former GDR professors that ultimately remained on eastern faculties: "[Only through these preferences] could the east German universities prevent the inevitable bloodletting and limit the westernization of their personnel."[90]

In general, this system led to the removal of many former faculty members, particularly in the humanities and social sciences, and in a significant number of cases their replacement by professors from the west. Yet even so, there were complaints—frequently in the pages of the *Frankfurter Allgemeine Zeitung*—that former SED activists were being retained on the faculties nonetheless and therefore that reform was not complete.[91] On some faculties the new western professors (generally with permanent appointments) and the remaining eastern professors (often with limited contracts) viewed each other with mutual suspicion and distrust, and contacts were few.

Overall, there was a striking difference between the very stringent treatment of the GDR faculties and the fate of the professors who had faithfully served the Nazi regime. This contrast can be readily illustrated in the faculties of law. While most of the former GDR law faculties were (perhaps illegally) dissolved—and most of their members permanently removed—almost none of the legal academics of the Nazi period had been required to relinquish their posts in the Federal Republic. Indeed, some of the chief theorists of the Nazi system, who compliantly revised previous legal principles by incorporating racial theories and other Nazi doctrines, subsequently became central figures in the jurisprudence of the Federal Republic.[92] In sum, many "who had participated in shaping the National Socialist legal system returned to their chairs and continued to dominate German legal thinking in the 1950s just as they had in the 1930s and 1940s. Their commentaries on laws, so important in the daily practice of the profession, continued to appear, as if nothing had happened, in new editions prepared by the old authors."[93] Moreover, "the legal academics who were former Nazi supporters were allowed to regain or keep their positions without virtually any proof of political or moral conversion. [Although they ceased propagating Nazi views and some endorsed the new West German order,] hardly any of them ever recanted their pre-1945 views. Even expressions of remorse were almost nonexistent."[94]

### *Research Institutes outside the Universities*

The fate of the eastern universities was not the only issue of academic structure and personnel that had to be settled upon unification. To a significant extent, the GDR regime had separated academic research from university teaching. Although some research was conducted in the universities, research efforts "in their entire spectrum" were focused principally on the gigantic Academy of Sciences, which employed 15,000 scholars and 9,000 other personnel and had a yearly budget of 1.4 billion GDR Marks.[95] To many eastern academics it seemed inconceivable that this centerpiece of East German scholarship could simply disappear upon unification. But to their dismay the Unification Treaty ultimately required that the Academy be dissolved—apparently because it was inconsistent with western academic structures and, perhaps, because it too closely resembled a similar institution in the Soviet Union.[96] Constitutional grounds for this decision—the allocation of authority over research to the individual states, rather than to a central organ such as the Academy—were also asserted.[97]

Under the Unification Treaty, the numerous research institutes that composed the Academy of Sciences were to be temporarily distributed among the respective Länder.[98] At the same time, the West German Science Council was to evaluate these institutes to determine whether individual personnel or even entire units could be accommodated in the research structure of united Germany.[99] Accordingly, some institutes or parts of institutes might continue to exist, and some researchers would continue to be employed, but it was clear that the employment of thousands of other researchers would be terminated.[100]

In a remarkably swift procedure, the Science Council completed its review by autumn 1991, deciding that certain existing positions of the GDR Academy of Sciences should be absorbed into the academic structure of the Federal Republic—in universities or other research institutions.[101] Some eastern observers criticized the speed with which the council made its decisions,[102] but others concluded that the process was, basically, a fair one.

A number of former researchers and employees of the Academy challenged this entire procedure in the Constitutional Court, but the Court rejected their arguments in an opinion similar to its earlier *Warteschleife* decision.[103] Although the plan did indeed restrict the researchers' employment rights, the Court found that the procedure was necessary to achieve the "swift reordering and improvement of research in the new states"—particularly, "the integration of the [Academy's] institutions in the constitutionally preexisting federal order."[104] Requiring a fuller individual evaluation of each researcher, as complainants sought, "would have made a thorough restructuring [in the east] much more difficult if not impossible."[105]

As in the *Warteschleife* case, however, the Court emphasized the social measures that had been taken to mitigate hardships of this plan—particularly the advantages that had been given to former Academy employees in the allocation of remaining positions.[106] The Court's emphasis on social-state concepts in these cases may be a form of tacit recognition that certain ideas from the GDR past, and from the Round Table draft constitution, may play an important role in removing serious barriers to the process of "inner unification"—even though those ideas did not achieve explicit constitutional status in the Unification Treaty.[107]

The underlying concept of the plan for the former Academy was that eastern researchers whose projects survived the Science Council review would be accommodated in the eastern universities or in eastern branches of western research organizations—such as the eminent Max Planck Society with its numerous areas of specialization. But problems soon arose on both fronts. At the outset, western research organizations viewed the prospect of expanding into the east with some reluctance, perhaps fearing a dilution of quality. Eventually, however, the Max Planck Society formulated plans for twenty-nine working groups to be integrated into the universities and founded eight new institutes of its own in eastern Germany.[108] Other new research institutes, such as the eminent Max Delbrück Center for Molecular Medicine in Berlin-Buch, were also founded from certain institutes of the dissolved Academy.[109]

The problem of accommodating former Academy scholars in the universities has been considerably more difficult to resolve. Perhaps because of historic tensions between the GDR universities and the Academy of Sciences,[110] approximately two thousand scholars—whose projects had been approved by the western Science Council—were having difficulty in finding a university position and were being temporarily supported by a federal "scholars integration program" (*Wissenschaftler-Integrationsprogramm* or WIP). The eastern universities had few available openings and, in making faculty appointments, they apparently tended to prefer western scholars instead of seriously considering this pool of eastern talent.[111]

### *The "Academic Landscape" of United Germany*

It is widely acknowledged that German unification came at a time of crisis for the West German universities. By the end of the 1980s, some charged that the western universities had become "mass floodways"[112]—in which thousands of students were taught, often in inadequate facilities, by a small corps of highly trained professors with an inadequate number of academic supporting staff.[113] These conditions contributed to a long period of study for many students and a high dropout rate. Indeed, German unification interrupted discussions that were being undertaken by the influential Science Council, directed toward serious academic reform in the west.[114]

Yet with all of its perceived problems, this was the system that was extended to the east under the Unification Treaty. As some have pointed out, this extension of the western structure followed the pattern of article 23 GG under which unification was achieved, rather than the pattern of article 146, which might have supported a degree of simultaneous reform in east and west.[115] In a manner perhaps analogous to the hasty closing of eastern enterprises by the Treuhand, the "Abwicklung" or westernization of certain eastern faculties interrupted a process of academic self-reform in the east. Moreover, some have suggested that a different process of internal eastern reform could have been useful in creating viable faculties with greater integration of eastern personnel.[116] But others argue powerfully that, due to great structural differences and other factors, the initial extension of the western system to the east was unavoidable—and indeed a necessary precondition for later reform.[117] Yet whether or not this method actually reflected satisfaction with conditions in the west, it may well have suppressed—or at least delayed—moves for western academic reform.

The comprehensive manner in which the traditional educational system of the west was extended to the east has evoked stern criticism. At the beginning of the process in 1990, for example, the Science Council warned against the wholesale extension of the western research system—and called for a self-critical inquiry with the possibility of a restructuring.[118] Then at the end of the process in 1992, the council's chairman bitterly deplored what he viewed as the ultimate failure to carry out reforms of this sort.[119]

In any case, creative new approaches seem to have been few. Perhaps the most notable was the opening of a new "European University" in Frankfurt/Oder, known as the "Viadrina." Located on the German-Polish border, the new university seeks to concentrate on international economics, law, and culture, as an intellectual bridge to the east. Forty percent of the student body will come from outside Germany, including 30 percent from Poland.[120] In addition to this dramatic initiative, some interesting new developments in interdisciplinary research are underway in eastern universities and institutes. Yet these changes seem confined to the east, and the Science Council is resuming its planning for general academic reform where it left off in 1990.[121]

In this process of reform, perhaps something can still be learned from eastern structures. For example, it is often asserted that teaching in the eastern universities was superior to that of the mass universities of the west, and perhaps a renewed emphasis on teaching can take advantage of this experience.[122] Moreover, in the eastern universities, much of the work of teaching, research, and advising was performed by a largely permanent core of mid-level "academic staff members" (*Mittelbau*) in addition to the work performed by professors. A similar group exists in western universities, and it has been suggested that the expansion of this corps could increase the contact of faculty and students and resolve or at least mitigate certain current western problems.[123]

Yet, on the other hand, it may well be that the forces that have preserved the western universities in their basic structure will have hardened after unification, so that little change is now possible. If so, unification may have presented a unique chance but, in the event, a chance that has been irrevocably "missed to build up a new scientific and scholarly landscape shaped by Germans from both the East and from the West."[124]

There is also the final question of how much eastern talent and research potential has been lost in the process of unification. Certainly few continue to support the hasty but much-quoted judgment of a western academic official that scholarship in the GDR was a "desert" or "wasteland."[125] Much work of high quality was carried on in the Academy of Sciences, but thousands of these scholars have lost their positions, and even two thousand researchers positively evaluated by the Science Council face an uncertain future.[126] In the universities, in contrast, a significant number of eastern professors have been appointed or retained in the natural sciences and some other subjects, and eastern personnel remain in the majority in some departments. Yet, even so, many academics with permanent tenure in eastern universities now come from the west. Thus, even at the universities, the overall result has been a significant replacement of eastern by western scholars.[127]

## Review of the Justice System: Judges, Prosecutors, Lawyers

The East German justice system was another institution to be transformed into a copy of the western structure, also principally through the efforts of western personnel. For many participants from the old Federal Republic, this task included not only governmental reform but also the creation of a new eastern legal consciousness. In a patronizing style characteristic of some western reformers, the justice minister of Thuringia remarked:

> Forty years' SED dictatorship has led to a deeper rift than we thought. Even after three years of reunification, a new legal consciousness in the population—a mental image [*Prägung*] of the basis of the rule of law—is still a tender little plant that needs our attention. And that is indeed an extremely difficult undertaking to which we must devote all of our strength.[128]

As in the case of universities, western leaders sought to achieve this goal through a review and exclusion of personnel, as well as by restructuring the institutions themselves.

### *Review of Judges and Prosecutors*

The review of the former GDR judges raised important problems that were to some extent unique. On the one hand, some judges were part of the GDR state in an even more intimate way than many academics and other civil servants; indeed, judges active in political cases were subject to directives from the SED and the Ministry for State Security (Stasi).[129] Yet, on the other hand, the eastern judges could not be easily dismissed en masse. Although many departments of the civil service could simply be dissolved—and the illusion (at least) could be nurtured that much of a generation of scholars could be sent into unemployment or early retirement without undue damage—no such illusion could be maintained with respect to the judiciary. It was absolutely essential to have judges for cases of immediate and pressing importance, such as the proliferating disputes over property questions arising from the Unification Treaty. Although significant assistance was forthcoming from the west, that help would not be enough to carry all or even most of the load.[130] Retention of large numbers of judges from the east would be essential.

But this urgent need raised another serious problem. Unlike the case of at least some scholarship, the skills of the East German judges were only very partially transferable to the new state of affairs. Certainly some techniques of legal reasoning were similar, but even here differences in approach were striking. Most significantly, however, the eastern judges lacked the necessary training and experience in complex areas of western law essential to the performance of the West German judiciary. At the very least, a significant period of re-education would be necessary before the eastern judges could perform at the same level as their experienced western counterparts.

Another specter lurked behind this entire process. Although the exclusion of Nazi officials from public life in the Federal Republic was half-hearted in general, the record of the judiciary was particularly disgraceful. Notwithstanding thousands of death sentences handed down by the special "People's Court" under the Nazis, in procedures lacking any form of due process, few if any Nazi jurists were later convicted of offenses based on these actions, in the West German state. Moreover, many former Nazi judges of the civil and criminal courts served out their full period of judicial office under the Federal Republic.[131] Indeed, of the prior judges taken into the West German judiciary, approximately 70 to 80 percent had been members of the Nazi Party.[132]

In view of this past, some observers pushed for an extremely rigorous exclusion of the former GDR judges from any judicial office in united Germany. That was one approach. According to another view, however, such a program fell into a familiar pattern of favoring right-wing over left-wing deviations in Germany by excluding former Communist judges even more stringently because former Nazi judges had not been excluded.

These, then, were the problems that had to be confronted in assessing the continued role of the eastern judiciary. But notwithstanding these serious difficulties, significant numbers of eastern judges have continued on in their positions, and—with the exception of Berlin, to be discussed below—it does not seem likely that the eastern judiciary will, even at the outset, present a predominantly western face.

### THE PROCEDURE OF REVIEW

The screening procedure for eastern judges was somewhat complex. After completing a comprehensive questionnaire about past activities, a GDR judge was subject to an initial screening by a "judicial appointments committee" (*Richterwahlausschuß*) composed of judges and elected officials.[133] To be successful, the candidate had to be approved by two-thirds of the screening committee as well as by the minister of justice, who was generally represented by a western advisor.[134] A judge who passed this initial screening then entered a five-year probationary period. An analogous procedure was provided for reviewing former GDR prosecutors.

Under the original GDR statute, each screening committee was to be composed of six members of the GDR Volkskammer and four GDR judges.[135] But the presence of GDR judges led to severe problems as it soon became clear that many of these judges themselves had dubious pasts under the GDR and therefore could not be allowed to pass judgment on their colleagues. The need to screen the judges who were to do the screening led to substantial delays and a postponement of the deadline for completion of the work.[136] Indeed, the state of Mecklenburg-Vorpommern abandoned the judicial screening committees altogether, and judges and prosecutors were reviewed by the minister of justice and a parliamentary committee, with the advice of a panel of western experts.[137]

As in the case of the university professors, both personal qualities—including past political activities—and professional qualifications were to be taken into account to determine whether the judge or prosecutor would exercise the office "according to the constitution."[138] Also as in the case of the professors and other civil servants, membership in the SED alone was not enough to exclude a judge or prosecutor from continuation in service; a contrary rule would have swept away almost all judicial personnel—certainly a result that the framers of the Unification Treaty sought to avoid.[139] Yet if a judge had occupied a particularly high judicial office (such as acting as the director of a GDR court) or had fulfilled a noteworthy party function, that in itself was usually grounds for exclusion because such an individual—by virtue of having held an office that was so "close to the state"—would not be likely to secure the confidence of litigants and the public.

In addition to these grounds of "objective" unsuitability[140] there was also the important question of how the judge had actually performed in office. If a judge or prosecutor had participated in numerous political trials designed to suppress opposition views or to punish those attempting to escape from the GDR, that activity would almost certainly mean exclusion from office.[141] Moreover, the screening committees ordinarily excluded judges who had handed down unreasonably severe sentences, imposed unreasonable detention before trial, participated in proceedings in which the forms of due process were manifestly ignored, or cooperated with the Stasi to a greater degree than was ordinarily required of judges.[142]

In making these decisions, the records of cases decided by the judges were available,[143] as well as Stasi files from the Gauck Agency and reports from the West German "Central Registration Office" in Salzgitter, which had attempted to document violations of human rights in the GDR for decades.[144] One very important source, however, was notably impaired: pursuant to an order of the Modrow period, judges and other officials had been permitted to examine their personnel files (*Kaderakten*) and were allowed (indeed required) to extract material that was no longer "relevant."[145] After this process, very little material remained in the files. Later, an attempt was made—how successful is not clear—to request the judges to return the extracted material.

In the five new Länder, most judges and prosecutors continued to try cases after unification until a decision on their future had been made by the screening commissions and the Justice Ministry.[146] In this way, an attempt was made to keep the former GDR courts functioning throughout the unification period. For Berlin, however, a different choice was made. On the date of unification, all of the East Berlin courts were dissolved, and the East Berlin judges were suspended from their offices, pending individual decisions on their futures by the screening committee and the ministry.[147] Until that time, all new and pending litigation in East and West Berlin was tried by the West Berlin judiciary, which faced an enormous case load during this interim period. Indeed, many of these cases involved actions occurring before unification, which had to be tried under the substantive rules of GDR law.

### THE RESULTS OF REVIEW

The use of the individual screening procedure produced relatively lenient results in the five new Länder. In Brandenburg, Saxony, Saxony-Anhalt, and Thuringia, between 41 and 63 percent of applicants seeking to continue on in the judiciary were permitted to remain in office—at least to the extent of entering the five-year probationary period.[148] At 67 percent, the result under the somewhat different procedure in Mecklenburg-Vorpommern was even higher.

Yet a drastic deviation from this pattern came in Berlin, where only 17 percent of the eastern judicial applicants were permitted to resume their work for a probationary period.[149] Various explanations have been advanced for this result. For example, East Berlin probably had more than its proportionate share of the sort of political cases that could disqualify eastern applicants.[150] But the most likely explanation was that Berlin already possessed a seasoned corps of western judges, while the five new Länder had no experienced judges of their own except for the eastern applicants themselves. Thus, Berlin was not in great need of these eastern judges, whereas the need in the new Länder was very great indeed.

The fate of an eastern judge who was accepted for the probationary period was not necessarily an easy one. The natural uncertainties of an eastern official taken into the western system were massively compounded in the case of judges by the necessity of learning—in a very short period—the complex new rules and structures of legal thought of the western system.

It is perhaps unlikely that many eastern judges would have successfully completed the probationary period if it were not for "working groups" (*Arbeitsgemeinschaften*) and other educational programs organized for the courts by the eastern ministries of justice.[151] In Berlin the "working groups" were led by a western judge or other western legal expert. Meeting once a week to review sections of the Civil Code and discuss model cases, they resembled an advanced examination review course for judges. Although the preparation for these sessions was onerous, the working groups gave a sense of support and security to the eastern applicants.[152]

Personal relations between the eastern and western judges varied. In Berlin, relations were generally polite, but some western judges did not disguise their view that no eastern judge was worthy of acceptance in the judiciary. In Brandenburg, on the other hand, a sense of respect for the qualities of the eastern judges developed among western judges from North Rhine-Westphalia who had been transferred there on a temporary basis.[153] Certainly, although the eastern judges lack years of training in the western system, they do have an understanding of the social background and context of litigation arising in the eastern Länder that is not possessed by their western counterparts.[154]

*Rebuilding the Eastern Justice System*

It was necessary to create the justice system of eastern Germany almost completely anew because this system, which was organized on a national basis in the GDR, falls principally within the competence of the states under the Basic Law. In the early months after unification, therefore, it was necessary to establish a ministry of justice in each of the new states, starting with almost nothing.[155] Justice ministers largely imported from the west accomplished this daunting task, with significant reliance on a corps of western personnel.[156] The Unification Treaty also required the conversion of the two-level GDR court system, containing a unified set of trial and appellate courts, into the five parallel court systems of West German law. Accordingly, separate courts were created in each state for civil and criminal matters and for employment, administrative, social security, and tax cases—with trial and appellate courts in each separate system in most instances. Whether it was necessary to introduce this complicated western system so quickly is open to question; certainly many have complained that the complex procedure of western administrative law—also extended to the east—is not at present appropriate for east German circumstances.

It was also clear that, with the great increase in litigation resulting from the change to a capitalist system, the number of former GDR judges and prosecutors continuing in office would be insufficient to handle the new judicial case load. Accordingly, western "partner states" transferred additional judges to the east, either on a temporary or permanent basis. Sometimes, judges who were temporarily transferred were taken by the "pioneer" spirit of the east and have sought a permanent transfer. Moreover, there are a significant number of young, recently graduated jurists, both from the east and the west, who are seeking to pursue judicial careers in the new eastern Länder. The result has been an inexperienced judiciary that has allowed substantial opportunity for younger members. Staffing the differentiated court system newly established in the east—requiring separate judges for administrative, employment, social security, and tax matters—has been a particular challenge.[157]

*Review of Lawyers and Notaries in Eastern Germany*

The GDR had very few practicing lawyers—the necessity for individual representation was thought not to be great in a socialist society in which personal rights were muted and social consensus was stressed.[158] After unification, therefore, many additional lawyers were needed to handle the complex personal and economic problems arising upon the introduction of a market economy and western law. In what seemed to be an equitable act, the Unification Treaty provided that lawyers admitted to practice in the GDR—even those admitted very close to the point of accession—would be able to continue on as qualified members of the German bar.[159]

Yet this provision created a situation that came to infuriate eastern reformers. In the last weeks of the GDR, numerous jurists with questionable political backgrounds moved from offices in the state apparatus into the private practice of law. Thus, some former GDR judges, who knew that they would not be taken into the judiciary after unification because of their past actions or high offices, opened their own practices as private lawyers. Law professors who expected to lose their positions, as well as groups of jurists who had worked for the Stasi, also established their own law firms.[160] Although many in the west did not consider this situation particularly dangerous, eastern reformers and others exerted substantial pressure to bar the possibility of this new haven for persons responsible for injustices of the SED period. Steffen Heitmann, justice minister of Saxony, was particularly active in this connection.[161]

More than a year and a half *after* unification, therefore, the Bundestag enacted a statute requiring the examination and exclusion of certain eastern German lawyers from legal practice.[162] According to this statute, a lawyer's admission to the bar could be annulled if the lawyer's actions under the GDR showed that he or she was "unworthy" of membership in the legal profession. Specifically, "unworthiness" would be shown if the lawyer had violated "the principles of humanity or the rule of law—particularly in connection with activity as an official or unofficial collaborator with the State Security Service [the Stasi]."[163]

The criterion of "unworthiness" has long been employed for exclusion in the existing West German law concerning lawyers. The new statute, therefore, is an attempt to give concrete meaning to this general term in a specific context.[164] Yet the statute also has certain evident peculiarities. First, it applies only to eastern lawyers—those who joined the bar of the GDR and were taken into the western system under the Unification Treaty. Western lawyers are not subject to examination, although some may well have violated principles of humanity or the rule of law by collaborating with the Stasi. Second, the terms "principles of humanity" and "rule of law" are not further defined—not even, as in the Unification Treaty itself, by reference to well-known United Nations documents. Third, the statute apparently has no period of limitation, and actions from the distant past may be taken into account in determining the "unworthiness" of an individual to remain in the legal profession.

Particularly complex problems for the determination of "unworthiness" are posed by the question of collaboration with the Stasi. Many observers claim that it was often necessary for eastern lawyers to have some dealings with the Stasi in order to represent their clients adequately.[165] Accordingly, criteria may have to be developed to distinguish relatively benign contacts with the Stasi—intended to benefit a lawyer's clients—from the sort of damaging contact that should result in exclusion.[166]

Moreover, attempts to exclude individuals from the practice of law raise substantial constitutional problems. In a decision handed down in 1983, the Constitutional Court held that the practice of law is a private calling or occupation protected by article 12 of the Basic Law and, unlike civil servants or judges, lawyers are not part of the state.[167] Moreover, persons of all political views and backgrounds must be able to find lawyers congenial to their views who will represent them adequately.[168] Accordingly, the rule of exclusion ordinarily applicable to members of the public service—failure to guarantee active support of the constitutional system—cannot be applied to exclude lawyers. Indeed, the Court implied that the rules for excluding lawyers from the practice of law must be very narrowly drawn. Although the exclusionary regulation in the 1992 statute is directed toward violations of the principles of humanity and of the rule of law—and does not require anything as affirmative as active support of the constitution—the potential application of these rules to a lawyer who has not committed any criminal offense may raise troubling constitutional doubts.[169]

Indeed, perhaps because of these constitutional doubts, relatively few eastern lawyers have been removed from the bar under the new statute.[170] Although the Federal Supreme Court (BGH) has upheld the 1992 statute against constitutional attack, the court has also emphasized that in each individual case the constitutional interest in free choice of profession, protected by article 12 GG, must play an important role in the judicial balance.[171]

Nonetheless, there have been notable cases of expulsion. In perhaps the most spectacular example, the BGH upheld the exclusion of Wolfgang Schnur, co-founder and former leader of the reform party "Democratic Awakening." As a lawyer in the GDR, Schnur had represented draft resisters and other dissidents from circles related to the Evangelical Church. Schnur was able to gain the close confidence of his clients, but—unknown to them—he was systematically reporting their conversations to the Stasi. The BGH found it particularly damaging that Schnur had violated the obligation of client confidentiality protected under GDR law.[172]

Moreover, for those eastern applicants who are applying to the bar for the first time after unification, the existing statutes on bar admission—which also require that an applicant be "worthy" of admission—have been vigorously applied to review past activities. A GDR state prosecutor was rejected, for example, because, in at least sixty cases, he had prosecuted persons for seeking to leave the GDR.[173] The court noted that these were prosecutions of freedoms that were universally recognized as natural rights; accordingly, the applicant should have had some doubt about whether the GDR legal system was consistent "with higher law, the law of international treaties, and natural law."[174] Yet the judgment of "unworthiness" involves a balancing test and the court indicated that, because most of these judgments lay some years in the past, the applicant might be eligible for the bar in approximately two years' time.[175]

In a similar case, a court in Saxony excluded an applicant for the bar because he had been a long-time "unofficial collaborator" of the Stasi.[176] The applicant had intentionally sought out individuals on whom he was to spy and transmitted information that damaged their personal and professional lives. The court argued that to accept persons with such a history of collaboration would injure the reputation of the eastern bar and give western practitioners an advantage because eastern practitioners might automatically be suspected of Stasi connections. The court also dismissed any constitutional doubts about its ruling by arguing that the interests of society in a "functioning system of justice" outweighed any personal interests of the applicant.[177]

Finally, in an interesting and important case, the BGH found that the holding of judicial office in the GDR, and even the enforcement of GDR statutes on political crimes, would not necessarily exclude a candidate from the bar.[178] Rather, the court is obliged to weigh the individual circumstances and scrutinize the judge's performance in those political cases. In the specific instance, however, the court took a highly disapproving view of the judge's conduct and refused to admit her to the bar. In many prosecutions of citizens who tried to flee the GDR, the judge had imposed excessive sentences and failed to employ mitigating factors that were available. Indeed, these decisions "infringed the defendants' human rights in a serious manner." In sum, the judge had served "the GDR injustice-regime" in a prominent position for many years and "intentionally acted as a part of the apparatus of political repression."[179]

## Reflections on the Exclusion of Officials

In general, the Unification Treaty called for the complete restructuring of the eastern civil service, to correspond with the system that had prevailed in the west, and a similar transformation was effected in the courts and the universities as well. These profound structural changes, undertaken in conformity with the general principles of article 23, were among the most significant results of unification in their direct impact on the citizens of eastern Germany.

Moreover, in the period following unification, many former officials in the eastern civil service, universities, and justice system were subject to removal in programs of great comprehensiveness and efficiency. The necessity for this drastic change of personnel has been widely debated. Some saw the process of political review and removal—particularly in the universities and the educational establishment—as a cynical process directed toward the creation of additional jobs for personnel from the west.[180] Indeed, in some instances the enthusiasm for removal was so great that entire university faculties were "dissolved" (to be immediately "refounded") in a manner that was most likely illegal under the Unification Treaty. On the other hand, many viewed these programs as essential to the creation of a democratic state in which the residue of totalitarian or authoritarian views would be reduced to a minimum.

In any case, however, the vigor of these programs contrasts strikingly with the treatment in the Federal Republic of civil servants, professors, and judges who had previously served the Nazi regime. Although an effort was made during the early occupation period to subject these individuals to "denazification" and similar procedures, many remained in their positions or returned to them after a brief hiatus. Consequently, many individuals prominent in the earlier history of the Federal Republic had had extremely dubious pasts under the Nazi system. Precisely this sad history of the early years of the Federal Republic has led some to argue that the same mistake should not be made again and that particular rigor should be exercised in excluding individuals who had collaborated with the SED regime.

Yet there are some other ways of looking at this problem. Most strikingly, the German political system at the beginning of the Federal Republic failed to take stringent actions against individuals who were viewed as being part of the same community. Indeed, the founders of the Federal Republic may have retained some sympathy for their colleagues who had supported the "Third Reich" because they viewed the "Third Reich" as a perversion of certain conservative principles with which they also generally sympathized.[181] In contrast, now, the dominant political structure of the west can proceed with enthusiasm against people of eastern Germany who are in many ways perceived as belonging to a different social and political community—notwithstanding the constitutionalists' theory that Germany has always remained one nation.

Moreover, the builders of the Federal Republic joined with the former Nazi collaborators to take a very hard position against the West German Communist Party, and allied groups, in the 1950s and thereafter. Whatever the many evils of the SED regime, one may view the enthusiastic application of stringent rules of exclusion to eastern officials as in some ways a continuation of that tradition. Yet, there is also a complicating factor in this view. The generally left-wing collection of groups forming the GDR reform movement has also vigorously advocated the exclusion of persons who collaborated with the SED regime, although the reformers' general point of orientation is considerably different from that of the conservative western groups which take the same position. Thus, in this area as in some others, the conservative CDU and the remnants of the GDR reform movement remain allied in certain aspects of their view of the past.

After all of these legislative and administrative measures of exclusion have been put into effect, the final decision in many cases will be made by the German courts and, in important respects, the courts seem to be exercising a mediating role—mitigating, to some extent, the rigor of programs adopted by the political branches. In the *Warteschleife* case, for example, the Constitutional Court upheld sweeping provisions for the reduction of personnel, but on the other hand sought to lessen the hardships of these measures by imposing constitutional obligations on the government to provide retraining and other programs of assistance. The Court also handed down similar opinions in subsequent cases involving the East German Academy of Sciences and other eastern academic institutes.

In some areas, the lower courts also seem to be playing a similar mediating role. In an important decision, for example, an administrative court in Berlin found that the attempted "dissolution" of a number of crucial faculties at the Humboldt University was illegal under the Unification Treaty and the Basic Law. Other courts have narrowly construed provisions for the exclusion of personnel who have violated principles of humanity, or whose loyalty to the constitution may be questioned because of their past political attachments in the GDR. Indeed, in a decision in 1995, the Constitutional Court seems to have further narrowed the possibility of excluding civil servants because of past activity on behalf of the SED.

In these cases, therefore, the courts seem to be protecting officials of the old regime against what might otherwise be an unduly rigorous application of western standards under the general principles of article 23. These courts may be seeking to further the process of "inner unification" by vindicating the interests of the average GDR citizen or, perhaps, the "median collaborator." This position does not protect the role of officials who deviated drastically from liberal western standards but, on the other hand, it also declines fully to enforce the stringent views of the conservative western anti-Communists and the heroic eastern resisters.

CHAPTER 14

# Undoing the Past: Prosecution of GDR Leaders and Officials

THE CONSTITUTIONAL problems discussed in the preceding three chapters—those concerning property regulations, abortion, and the fate of the civil service—were subjects of sharp debate as the Unification Treaty was being negotiated. Although these issues continued to raise their share of new and unexpected developments, the relevant problems were generally well understood before the date of German unification. In contrast, some other issues of great difficulty and importance were less fully developed during the process of unification and came to the fore as widely debated constitutional and political problems after the merger of the two German states.

Some of these emerging problems seemed to involve a further variation on the prevailing theoretical view of the western constitutionalists—the theory that the Federal Republic represented the continuing German "Reich" and that the GDR was the product of an undemocratic and therefore illegitimate attempt to secede from that continuing "Reich."[1] Unification under article 23 rested on this theoretical view and seemed to imply the extension of western political and even social structures to the east. But in some instances the western leaders even seemed to go farther and to act as though they were seeking to imagine a situation in which the territory of GDR had always been a part of the Federal Republic—in accordance with the theoretical illegitimacy of the GDR's secession from the "Reich"; in those cases the government seemed to be seeking a state of affairs most closely resembling the situation that would now have prevailed if, in accordance with the theory, the GDR had never existed.

The attempt to return property expropriated by the GDR—with all of its problems and inconsistencies—is a primary example of this approach. Moreover, two other extremely important areas, which became the subjects of debate primarily after unification, seemed to reflect attempts to treat the territory of the GDR as though it had always been a part of the Federal Republic in accordance with the constitutionalists' theory.

In the first of these areas, the government sought to prosecute various East German officials and others for acts that arguably did not violate the law of the GDR at the time they were committed but certainly would have violated the law of the Federal Republic if that law had been applicable. These cases include widely publicized prosecutions for shootings at the Berlin Wall and for other oppressive governmental or judicial actions, such as falsifying election results or handing down stern criminal penalties for opposition political activity. Prosecutions of East German intelligence agents for espionage activities directed against the Federal Republic also fall into this category.

The widespread prosecution of these actions—most if not all of which would never have been prosecuted under the GDR—could give rise to the impression that the west was trying to undo the past by applying western law to these acts as though, in accordance with the constitutionalists' theoretical view, the east had always been part of the Federal Republic. Indeed much of the theoretical difficulty of these problems arises from attempts to explain why these cases do not involve the unconstitutional retroactive application of western law to acts that were not subject to that law at the time and place they were undertaken. Yet, in a complexity not uncharacteristic of the ironies of German unification, these prosecutions are not supported only by voices from the west. Indeed, like the exclusion of civil servants, these prosecutions are often supported as vigorously (if not more so) by the remnants of the GDR reform groups and some others in the east as they are by conservative circles in the west.

Second, the government is undertaking a broad plan of "rehabilitation" and compensation for victims of oppressive acts under the GDR regime. This program can be seen as a complement to the prosecution of GDR officials: if the past cannot really be undone, the injustice of past acts will to some extent be mitigated by the compensation of the oppressed as well as the punishment of the oppressors. These statutory plans can also be seen as the more "personal"—and less "proprietary"—analogue of the rules affording restitution or compensation to persons whose property was expropriated under the GDR or the Soviet occupation regime. Yet, as is also the case with compensation for expropriated property, present economic realities greatly limit the scope of these payments. Indeed, in the case of "rehabilitation," compensation for some less easily quantifiable or provable classes of oppression may be completely excluded.

Finally, these and other important developments after unification were played out against the background of an extraordinary event that is most likely without precedent in history—the opening of the vast files of the Ministry for State Security (Stasi) to governmental and individual scrutiny. The opening of these files has had a profound influence on society in eastern Germany by revealing the comprehensive scope of the surveillance and by exposing Stasi informants not only in public life but also in the most intimate circles of friendship and family. The files also provided important information for criminal prosecution of GDR officials and also for assisting claimants under the rehabilitation law. They were also widely employed in the exclusion of individuals from the public service and judiciary based on their activities in the former GDR.

The concluding chapters of Part II will consider these complex issues which generally came to the fore after unification. This chapter will discuss the prosecution of GDR officials, and the following two chapters will discuss the program of rehabilitation and the problems of the Stasi files.

## Prosecutions of GDR Officials and Border Soldiers for Shootings at the Wall

The widespread prosecution of eastern officials for acts that may not have been illegal under the law of the GDR raised some of the most difficult legal issues of the post-unification period.[2] The most sharply debated examples were prosecutions of GDR soldiers who fired on citizens attempting to escape to the west and related prosecutions of high GDR officials for authorizing this use of deadly force. In addition to the formidable complexity of their legal argumentation, these cases raised more general problems of political philosophy that have haunted recent German history—problems of the arguably retroactive application of legal norms against persons who had committed reprehensible acts in the name of the state. In this sense, some comparison of the present cases with the post-World War II prosecutions at Nuremberg seems inevitable.[3]

At their theoretical core, these cases raise the question of whether it is possible—after revolutionary events which sweep away a dictatorship—for the new government to impose criminal punishment for acts that deeply offend a sense of justice but may not actually have been punishable under the dictatorial law of the old regime. Accordingly, these cases may come into conflict with the principle of legal security that rests on a prohibition of retroactive criminal penalties—the principle, generally held fundamental in liberal legal systems, that for criminal punishment an act must have been illegal under law that was applicable at the time the act was performed. This tension—and the disappointments that it evokes in those who seek to settle accounts with the old regime—are well captured in the famous remark of a prominent GDR reformer, Bärbel Bohley, who complained: "We hoped for justice, but what we got was the rule of law."[4] This tension also had to be resolved, in one way or another, by the German legal system after unification.

### *Constitutional Issues*

One radical method of resolving this tension and "avoiding" any problems of retroactivity after unification would simply have been to adopt an extreme version of the West German constitutionalists' theory that the "Reich" never disappeared and that the Federal Republic was the only representative of the continuing "Reich." If, under this view, the Federal Republic was the only legitimate government in the continuing nation, its laws would also have applied in the east from 1949 up to the point of unification.[5] The result would be that the present application of those laws to past actions committed in the east—in disregard of the "invalid" law of the GDR—would be perfectly permissible and not retroactive.

Although such a position was entertained by some scholars after unification,[6] this view has not prevailed. Rather, courts and writers generally acknowledged that the law of the GDR was fully in effect in eastern Germany up to the time of unification. Indeed this position seems required by article 23 GG and by the Basic Treaty of 1972 in which the Federal Republic in effect recognized the general validity of GDR law.[7]

If GDR law is recognized as having been generally valid, the question of retroactivity poses not only a philosophical issue but also an intensely practical problem, because article 103 of the West German Basic Law prohibits the conviction of a person for an act that was not a criminal offense at the time it was committed. Thus the Basic Law itself prohibits retroactive criminal punishment.

Moreover, this command of the Basic Law is reflected in the Unification Treaty, which generally prohibits penalization of actions committed in the GDR unless the acts were punishable under GDR law. Actually the treaty accomplishes this result by requiring that the acts be of a type punishable under *both* the law of the Federal Republic and GDR law and directing that the milder of the two applicable penalties be applied in the particular case.[8] The result, therefore, is that for both constitutional and statutory reasons, the shootings at the Wall (and most other GDR offenses) can be prosecuted only if they were illegal under GDR law at the time the acts were committed.

### *The Interpretation of GDR Law*

If the acts must have been illegal and punishable under GDR law, a central question in assessing criminality is what was the law of the GDR and how is it to be determined? This is an enormously complex question, and its application to the shootings at the Wall yields a profusion of varying approaches and proposed resolutions. Of course, the GDR Criminal Code contained provisions on murder and manslaughter that were not significantly different from those prevailing in the west.[9] These provisions might be employed to penalize the shootings at the Wall in the same way that the ordinary murder and manslaughter provisions of the German Criminal Code were used to prosecute Nazi concentration camp guards.[10]

Yet, notwithstanding these murder and manslaughter provisions, rather sweeping arguments have been made that the shootings at the Wall were *legal* under GDR law. Some theorists, for example, advance the view that it is the law *as applied* that should be crucial for questions of retroactivity, and under the law of the GDR as applied no border guard would have been convicted or even prosecuted for using deadly force.[11] Moreover, under the doctrine of "socialist legality" proclaimed in the GDR Constitution,[12] the GDR Criminal Code may be interpreted to include exceptions for party directives such as authorizations of deadly force to prevent persons from leaving the GDR.

In an even more sweeping view, a West German legal philosopher has argued that since the entire GDR state rested on its ability to keep its citizens from escaping, the entire legal system must be interpreted in light of that basic necessity. Thus, all steps necessary to that end, including the use of deadly force, must be viewed as "legal" under the GDR system, and the kinds of problems raised by shootings at the Wall cannot be handled by criminal prosecutions under the western legal system.[13] Another well-known commentator on German criminal law has advanced a similar argument: under the GDR system, as it actually operated, a person trying to escape from the GDR had no rights and could be shot by border guards without further legal consequences—to assert anything else would be to minimize the perversity of the GDR system; German criminal law has always rested on a positivistic basis and must accept this doctrine as the law of the GDR past without attempting to change it retroactively.[14]

*The Border Law of 1982*

But not all arguments for the legality of using deadly force at the Wall rest on such sweeping premises. More focused arguments against criminalization invoke the GDR Border Law of 1982, a statute that could furnish an exception to the general homicide provisions in these cases. Under the Border Law, the use of a weapon was justified to prevent a felony at the GDR border and, in some cases, an unauthorized attempt to cross the border was a felony under the GDR Criminal Code. A combination of these two provisions could therefore furnish a defense under GDR law to what could otherwise have been homicide in shootings at the Wall.[15] This result might then be further supported through the general doctrine of "socialist legality."

Thus there is a tenable argument that at least some of the shootings at the Wall were legal under GDR statutory law. Moreover, the hard fact is that border guards who shot fleeing citizens were not prosecuted under that legal system—indeed, they were often rewarded. Accordingly, it may be difficult to explain how the Federal Republic can penalize these acts now, without engaging in retroactive punishment.

*Legal Attacks on the Border Statute*

In response to this central problem, scholars supporting the criminalization of the Wall shootings have deployed a number of elaborate arguments. But all of these responses have a common thread—either they disregard a portion of GDR law or they interpret that law in a way in which it was never actually interpreted under the GDR.

Some argue, for example, that the Border Law should be disregarded as a defense, because a statute that allows killing in order to prevent the exercise of the fundamental right of egress violates the *ordre public* of the Federal Republic of Germany. As a result, the statute cannot be accepted by a present German court regardless of its role in the GDR legal system.[16]

This approach, however, is highly problematic. Of course, a nation's courts might reject a foreign cause of action as violating the nation's public policy or *ordre public*: indeed western courts could—and did—refuse to enforce certain

GDR causes of action on this ground. But the use of this doctrine to reject a pre-existing GDR *defense* in a criminal action is clearly to impose a new—western—criminal law on the eastern past in a retroactive manner. Indeed, arguments of this kind involve the covert rejection of the prohibition of retroactivity, without a frank consideration of the values that might be furthered or impaired by such a result.

Occasionally it has also been suggested that if a general category of act—such as manslaughter—was ordinarily punishable under the law of the GDR, unusual defenses or justifications not recognized in the Federal Republic can simply be disregarded.[17] Under this view, the Border Law could be excluded from consideration because it was a defense or justification peculiar to GDR law and not a (primary) element of the offense of homicide.

This form of argument may be an artifact of the complex theoretical structure of the elements of the offense (*Tatbestand*) in German criminal law, which in effect draws a sharp distinction between primary elements of an offense and defenses or justifications, and seems to place defenses in a subordinate position. Yet such an argument ignores the fundamental value at issue in the prohibition of retroactivity—the furtherance of personal security by allowing every person to know beforehand whether certain actions would constitute a crime. This value is equally impaired by the creation of a new offense or the subtraction of an existing defense. Arguments of this sort are rightly rejected by most German authorities.[18]

### *The Creation of an Ideal Law of the GDR*

Most responses to the central problem of retroactivity and the Border Law, however, do not seek to reject a portion of GDR law. Rather, these responses seek to establish an ideal GDR law—a GDR law of the books that is different from the GDR law as it functioned in practice. Because this ideal law is said to have been the actual law of the GDR—and the law in practice was not the actual law—the application of this ideal law now to past events is not, in these arguments, a retroactive application.

To create this ideal GDR law, some arguments interpret written sources of law using methods other than those employed by the courts of the GDR. Other arguments go farther and seek to apply unwritten principles of natural law to alter or override written GDR law—maintaining, nonetheless, that these principles were also in reality part of the law of the GDR.

In both cases, however, these arguments seem to construct a legal regime for the GDR that resembles that of the Federal Republic and to maintain that, on some crucial level of legal reality, that regime always existed in the GDR.[19] Thus the result of these arguments seems to go beyond the basic position, implied by article 23, that the legal structure of the Federal Republic should now be imposed on the GDR. These arguments seem to invoke the deeper theoretical suggestion that in certain ways the former GDR should be treated as though it had always been a part of the Federal Republic—perhaps in tacit accordance with the ideas of single nationhood implied by the constitutionalists' theory of the continuing "Reich" and the identity of the Federal Republic with that "Reich."

The most modest argument for an ideal GDR legal regime invokes a particularly strict interpretation of the permissible sources of GDR law.[20] This argument seeks to draw a clear line between the "formal" GDR law—as set forth in statutes, regulations of the Council of Ministers, and other official sources—and purported GDR law that was not "formal" law, such as party orders or supervisory rules of the Supreme Court. Under this argument, only the "formal" GDR law is worthy of present recognition. Thus, if an act violated a GDR statute and could only be justified under party orders or rules, it could be subject to criminal liability today because it violated the only law that counted then.[21]

There are a number of problems with this argument. First, many pronouncements of the "formal" law do not necessarily give very clear answers in specific cases, and the informal law—the law that was in most cases actually applied—could be viewed as a permissible interpretation of the "formal" law. What would be left as criminally punishable would be a small number of very clear cases in which no plausible interpretation of the "formal" law would yield the result achieved by the informal law. But even more fundamentally, to impose on a system a different conception of the permissible sources of law than the conception actually employed by that system in practice—and to do so in a way that removes a defense to a crime that actually existed under the practice of that system—seems indeed to be another form of retroactive law making. Thus it is difficult to see that the distinction between formal and informal GDR law goes very far toward resolving the problem of retroactive law making.[22]

Most of these arguments for criminalization, however, do not rely on the *subtraction* of sources of law from common GDR practice. Rather, these arguments rely on the *addition* of sources of law that the GDR courts ordinarily would not have recognized. Important arguments focus, for example, on the International Covenant on Civil and Political Rights of 1966, a United Nations agreement that the East German government signed in 1974.[23] Article 12(2) of the Covenant states, in very clear language, that "[e]veryone shall be free to leave any country, including his own." Although article 12 also contains some exceptions to this clear general principle,[24] it is hard to imagine that this provision would have any coverage at all if it did not disapprove the massive denials of the right of egress imposed by the government of the GDR.[25] Accordingly, some argue that use of the Border Law to justify deadly force to prevent egress from the GDR violated article 12 of the Covenant: moreover, since article 12 is a provision in a treaty to which the GDR was a party, that provision might arguably supersede domestic statutes such as the Border Law—even under GDR law itself. If the Border Law were superseded in this manner, the ordinary murder or manslaughter provisions of the GDR

Criminal Code would remain in effect with respect to the shootings at the Wall.

The argument under the 1966 Covenant is problematic, however, because the argument contradicts the GDR's own asserted understanding of the legal status of the treaty. Like many other nations, the GDR held that a treaty had no effect on domestic law until the parliament enacted domestic implementing legislation.[26] In the case of the 1966 Covenant, however, this step was never taken. This omission may have violated international law, but—under an understanding of this problem that is not limited to the former GDR—the internal legal situation was not altered. Accordingly the GDR leadership maintained that the 1966 Covenant, though binding in international law, had no domestic effect.[27]

In sum, the arguments for criminalization based on the 1966 Covenant seem to approach the outer boundaries of the permissible in interpreting the law of the GDR. It is important to bear in mind that, in order to avoid the problem of retroactivity, it is the law of the GDR itself that must have invalidated certain defenses for shootings at the Wall.

### *Arguments Based on Natural Law*

But some arguments, including those accepted by some German courts, have gone even further. These arguments maintain that certain acts so clearly violate natural law or "supra-legal" principles that they cannot be justified in any legal system: any legal rule that purports to justify those acts is invalid. Accordingly, the Border Law, which furnished a legal defense for shootings at the Wall, could be invalidated by these "supra-legal" principles.

Arguments of this sort have a respected provenance in West German jurisprudence. In the early years of the Federal Republic, West German courts declared that measures imposing racial, religious, or ethnic discrimination under the Nazi regime were invalid under these principles.[28] Ideas of natural law had a strong appeal in Germany after World War II, and these ideas seem to be enjoying increased popularity at present also.[29] For example, similar arguments were also advanced in controversies relating to the *Bodenreform* case, although they were not accepted by the Constitutional Court. It is of course to be expected that natural law arguments will appear in cases, such as those involving the Bodenreform and the shootings at the Wall, in which a newer legal system seeks to adjudicate events taking place under an earlier and now discredited regime.[30]

In one sense, natural law arguments of this sort seem to take us outside of the legal system of the GDR entirely—toward an external condemnation, rather like the rejection of a legal rule of the GDR as inconsistent with the West German *ordre public*. So expressed, these natural law arguments purport to invalidate aspects of the GDR system without reliance on any formal or written source of law—even one so rarely applied as the International

Covenant on Civil and Political Rights—and therefore these arguments might be seen to raise the problem of retroactivity in its clearest form.

Yet even in the case of arguments based on natural law, attempts have been made to avoid the charge of retroactivity by finding that such concepts were in reality a part of the law of the GDR and therefore qualified the statutory law of the GDR as well as the law in practice. Since, under these principles, the law of the GDR "actually" penalized certain reprehensible actions, their criminalization today is not retroactive. In such arguments, however, it may not always be clear whether natural law is posited as an internal aspect of GDR law or whether it is asserted as an external value that (perhaps retroactively) overrides GDR law.

### *The Jurisprudence of the Federal Supreme Court*

Indeed, a leading decision of the Federal Supreme Court (BGH) upholds convictions for shootings at the Wall by finding that supra-legal principles were actually part of the law of the GDR.[31] In this case, border guards had fired automatic weapons at a fleeing citizen without first employing non-lethal fire. At the outset of its opinion, the court acknowledged that this act would not have been found illegal under the GDR Border Law as applied in practice in the GDR.[32] Yet the court upheld the manslaughter conviction nonetheless—in substantial part on the ground that employing the Border Law as a defense would violate "superior general principles of law which also were to be observed by the GDR."[33] Consequently the use of the Border Law as a defense was to be rejected.

Drawing on a famous formulation set down by Gustav Radbruch in 1946, which was adopted by courts of the Federal Republic in cases concerning the acts of the Nazi regime, the court found that a purported defense to a criminal charge can be ignored if it expresses a serious and obvious violation of basic principles of justice and humanity generally accepted by all peoples.[34] Although the shootings at the Wall were not comparable with the mass murders of the Nazis, sources such as the 1966 Covenant can assist in determining which basic principles are generally accepted by the worldwide legal community. Moreover, because the GDR was a signatory, the 1966 Covenant can be taken into account in deciding the question of which general principles bound the GDR, even if the treaty may not have actually created a change in the domestic law of the GDR.[35]

After a careful examination, the court found that the practice of employing deadly force to prevent persons from escaping across the Wall violated the right of egress and the right to life set forth in articles 12 and 6 of the Covenant.[36] Moreover, GDR practice imposed a regime of particular hardship because persons on both sides of the border "belonged to one nation," with family relationships and other personal ties.[37] Because the Covenant was violated, the western court could not give the Border Law the expansive application that it had received under the GDR.[38]

Yet, in a very interesting passage the court apparently concluded that to disregard the defense and impose criminal liability would violate article 103 GG as retroactive law making unless the Border Law itself could be properly interpreted to reach the same result—using methods current in the GDR. Accordingly, the court went on to argue that techniques drawn from the GDR Constitution itself could produce a narrow interpretation of the Border Law—an interpretation that was "friendly to human rights" and would not violate the 1966 Covenant. This narrow interpretation would deny a defense to the border guard in the case before the court.[39]

In this argument we see again, very clearly, the construction of an ideal law of the GDR. The court claims that this view was the "correct" interpretation of GDR law even at the time the act was committed; therefore the penalization of the act was "determined" by GDR law and does not violate the prohibition of retroactivity contained in article 103 GG.[40] The defendant border guard in this case did not have a legitimate expectation that the law of the GDR would always continue to be interpreted in a manner violative of human rights.[41]

*An Alternative Approach: The Relevance of Nuremberg*

For all of their earnestness and complexity, opinions of this sort seem to be lacking in candor. The court creates an ideal law of the GDR, through the use of techniques and principles resembling those current in the Federal Republic, solely for the purpose of saying that this hypothetical construct was "really" the law of the GDR and therefore its application today is not retroactive. The elaboration of this construct, which never would have been undertaken under the GDR, serves no other purpose.

It would seem much more direct and honest to say: The law of the GDR as it actually existed was unacceptable and therefore we are applying a new law to these cases.[42] Perhaps under prevailing interpretations of the Unification Treaty and article 103(2) GG that acknowledgment could mean the end of these cases, but these issues nonetheless deserve a more general consideration.[43] The Nuremberg trials, for example, were examples of retroactive law making directed against a reprehensible regime.[44] Yet these proceedings are widely defended as important steps in the history of jurisprudence.[45] The question is whether the factors that made retroactive justice defensible in the Nuremberg trials would also justify retroactive penalization here.

To pursue this point it may be useful to return to the proposition set down by Radbruch in 1946. The requirement of security and non-retroactivity in criminal law—the principle that an individual can only be prosecuted for an act that has been made criminal in a clear and public way before the act was committed—is an extremely important value, but it is not the only value to be respected by a legal system. Although in almost all situations this value is strong enough to prevail, there are some extreme situations in which another value—the importance of imposing sanctions on acts of extraordinary evil—may be even more important. That was the case at Nuremberg. The question of whether specific acts of perceived government criminality in the former GDR could legitimately be subject to criminal penalties might begin by an examination of whether these acts were in various ways comparable with the acts penalized at Nuremberg.

Most observers agree that they are not comparable. The matters that were adjudicated at Nuremberg involved "horrors never before recorded in a court":[46] the crimes of aggressive war were purposeful acts of violence that triggered the deaths of tens of millions of people; the war crimes included massive acts of excessive force in the course of that war; and the crimes against humanity involved the systematic deportation and mass murder of millions of noncombatant civilians from conquered lands as well as Germany itself, solely because of their membership in a racial, ethnic, religious, or other group. Of course, each of the several hundred killings at the GDR border represented an immense tragedy for the family and friends of the victim and was reprehensible from an objective view. Yet this sort of state-sanctioned retaliation for a voluntary act—even an assertion of a human right—in order to protect and prop up a misguided system, seems nonetheless far removed from the destruction of whole societies and cultures through acts of aggressive war and mass genocide adjudicated at Nuremberg.[47]

Some other points of comparison between the GDR cases and the Nuremberg prosecutions have been raised, but they seem in general less central.[48] Some have argued, for example, that retroactive justice was appropriate at Nuremberg to forestall private retribution and to give a memorable lesson in the rule of law to the German elites who had forgotten what an honest trial was like. The trial also served the further educational and historical function of exposing to all, in great and unanswerable detail, precisely what it was that the Nazis had done.[49]

These arguments are only very partially transferable to the situation of the former GDR. In reality there has been little if any private vengeance exacted against functionaries of the previous regime, and the best lessons in the methods of the "Rechtsstaat" will probably be the uneventful and routine functioning of the ordinary courts in the coming months and years. No series of spectacular criminal trials is necessary for this purpose.[50] Perhaps the most persuasive of these analogies in the present circumstances is the general historical and educational function that these trials may perform in exposing precisely what did occur under the GDR. Certainly the very light sentences that have been handed down in many cases of government criminality suggest that it is often this general historical and educational function that is primarily being served.[51]

Yet even in this context, it could be argued that the Nuremberg and GDR cases are actually quite different: in the National Socialist case, the German people were freed from dictatorship not by their own efforts but rather by the efforts of other nations; as a result, it was necessary to teach the lesson of disapproval of dictatorship through the application of criminal law. In the case of the East German revolution, in contrast, the population of the

GDR itself participated in this process of liberation; consequently, there is considerably less need to employ the criminal law to teach the values of democracy.[52]

## Prosecution of GDR Officials for Falsification of Elections and Other Corrupt Acts

When an unjust regime is overthrown, there is often a call for the criminal punishment of the leading political figures.[53] But attempts to impose criminal penalties on the superannuated GDR leadership have yielded a mixed record, and the Soviet officials who often determined GDR policy obviously remain beyond the reach of German courts. Even the three members of the GDR National Defense Council who were convicted for their role in the killings at the border were relatively obscure figures whose names were known to few eastern citizens.

Indeed, attempts to pursue members of the GDR leadership have been attended with notable peculiarities. In some cases, for example, officials were prosecuted for corruption and related actions which may have been the results of unchecked power but seem relatively inconsequential in contrast with the central oppressions of the regime. In such a prosecution Harry Tisch, the head of the state labor union (FDGB), was convicted of diverting some union funds to pay for the vacations of GDR spy chief Erich Mielke and other officials; two more serious corruption charges failed to result in conviction.[54] Tisch was sentenced to an eighteen-month prison term, but he had already served a longer period awaiting trial and was therefore immediately released. Somewhat sheepishly, the presiding judge explained that the court was bound by law and could not necessarily satisfy all moral or political expectations of the east German people.[55]

The case of Stasi chief Erich Mielke was even more bizarre. Indeed, an eminent German commentator called it a proceeding "that is scarcely to be surpassed in absurdity."[56] In 1993 Mielke was convicted of a murder committed in the waning days of the Weimar Republic, more than sixty years earlier. In political unrest in 1931, a demonstrator was killed when police cleared a square in central Berlin; shortly thereafter, two police officers were shot in retaliation. Erich Mielke, then a young Communist tough, was suspected of the crime, but he escaped to the Soviet Union where he remained until his return to eastern Germany after World War II. On Mielke's trial for this offense in 1993, it was ultimately determined that most of a dossier assembled by Nazi officials after 1933, for the purpose of convicting Mielke, could not be used as evidence although the prosecution sought to introduce it.[57] Nonetheless, Mielke was convicted of murder and attempted murder and sentenced to six years in prison.[58] Although the 1931 murder had attracted some notoriety, Mielke certainly would never have been prosecuted after sixty years if he had not been a high official of the GDR.[59]

Another series of prosecutions of high officials arose from the falsification of the results of the GDR local elections of May 7, 1989—an important event in the history of the GDR revolution. These elections took place six months before the opening of the Berlin Wall, and signs of change were already apparent to some. For the first time, members of the civil rights opposition made organized efforts to achieve a significant dissenting vote in the election and to observe the open counting of the ballots.[60] Indeed, in this election, approximately 10 percent of the electorate apparently did cast dissenting votes—a very high number in light of the 98 percent (or higher) tally of approving votes in past GDR elections, but hardly a significant deviation in overall terms.[61]

Nonetheless, this seemingly trivial opposition vote was too high for the central government in Berlin. The results seemed to cast doubt on the carefully nurtured illusion of unanimity in the GDR and perhaps reinforced other signs of social and political dissolution.

As a result, the government took steps to assure that not even this modest percentage of dissenting votes would be fully recorded. Bowing to pressure from the central government in Berlin, local officials in some areas of the GDR reduced the approximately 10 percent negative vote to approximately 2 percent. These actions seemed to violate the general prohibition of election fraud contained in the GDR Criminal Code. The falsification of the May 1989 election results enraged the GDR reformers and remained a continuing sore point throughout the GDR revolution.[62]

Two important figures from the GDR past have been tried for these acts of election falsification. First, the former mayor of Dresden, Wolfgang Berghofer—an SED reformer and an ally of Hans Modrow in Dresden—was sentenced to a fine of DM 36,000 and one year's probation for his role.[63] The court rejected defense counsel's claim that, since all elections in the GDR were fundamentally fraudulent, Berghofer's acts could not really constitute election fraud.[64]

On April 20, 1993, Hans Modrow, former minister-president of the GDR, went on trial for his role in falsifying the results of the May 1989 elections in Dresden.[65] As was to be expected, Modrow's prosecution evoked a sharp reaction. Some argued that in light of his success in maintaining a peaceful transition during the GDR revolution, Modrow should be excused this transgression and not put on trial.[66] Some—including Modrow himself—saw in the trial a further attempt to remove a prominent PDS politician from public life.[67] Others argued that the interest vindicated by the trial—protecting the legitimacy of GDR election results—had never existed in the first place or, in any case, had vanished with the disappearance of the GDR. Modrow and his counsel also maintained that the prosecution was a continuation of political justice against Communists that extended back to the cold war period and the Nazi era.[68]

At the end of May 1993, Modrow was sentenced to a "caution" (*Verwarnung*), the mildest penalty known to the German criminal law.[69] Accepting portions of the defendant's contentions, the presiding judge concluded that Modrow's compliance with the GDR leadership in this instance preserved his ability to work toward reform and "perestroika" in the GDR at a later point. Moreover, the judge noted, the "ritualistic" and "acclamatory" GDR elections did not serve the same democratic function as elections in the west.[70] Finally, any effects of Modrow's actions had been long dissipated in the epochal events of the East German revolution.[71]

This mild judgment, however, was not destined to stand. Reversing the decision of the lower court, the Federal Supreme Court (BGH) found that the special mitigating circumstances required for a mere "caution" were not present. In its judgment, the BGH stressed the nefarious nature of Modrow's actions. The court declared that "it was the goal of [the electoral] manipulation to cover up the real number of opposing votes . . . in order to suppress the extent of the dissenting electorate that had turned against the 'unified list' of the National Front, and also against the repressive control of the SED which that list represented."[72] Accordingly, the BGH remanded the case to the lower court for re-sentencing. Yet even on re-sentencing, Modrow was able to avoid imprisonment; he received a sentence of nine months' probation.[73]

In the context of the Modrow trial, new calls were heard for an amnesty for "offenses related to the division of Germany." Thus Egon Bahr, prominent SPD politician, called for such an amnesty to accelerate "inner unification," noting that offenses similar to those of Modrow had been committed by Gorbachev, Yeltsin, and Shevardnadze, but they were not required to stand before a court.[74]

## Prosecution of GDR Judges for "Perversion of Justice"

The judicial system of the GDR constituted an important factor of political stabilization and repression under the old regime. In addition to numerous cases of ordinary, non-political matters—which were apparently decided according to techniques not much different from those familiar in the west[75]—the courts adjudicated highly sensitive cases criminalizing attempts to flee the GDR as well as speech and political activities that were critical of the existing regime.[76] Political justice was particularly savage in the early years of the GDR when the death penalty was sometimes imposed for the crime of "boycott agitation [*Boykotthetze*] against democratic institutions and organizations." This capacious offense was mandated by article 6 of the 1949 GDR Constitution, but article 6 set forth no definition of the crime, which was apparently available for use against a wide range of real or imagined opposition activity.[77]

This long history of political justice or injustice naturally raised sharp questions of how the participants should be treated after unification. Judges and prosecutors who regularly handled political cases were generally excluded from office, and in some instances they may also be barred from the practice of law.[78] This sort of exclusion is—at least in theory—oriented toward the future, employing evidence of past activities to form a judgment on how a specific individual will carry out the role of a judge, prosecutor, or lawyer in the future.

Yet this form of sanction is not the only possible penalty with which former GDR judges (or prosecutors) may be faced. In a large number of cases, those who participated in the criminal justice system of the GDR may be subject to prosecution for the crime of "perversion of justice" (*Rechtsbeugung*)—an offense which, although unknown in the United States and England, is found in the criminal code of the Federal Republic as well as that of the former GDR.[79]

Thousands of cases of suspected perversion of justice by former GDR judges have been investigated in Berlin alone.[80] Here again, the difficult problem of determining what was the "real" GDR law plays a central role because there can be a conviction for perversion of justice only if the judge deviated significantly from the GDR law applicable to the specific case. Accordingly, cases have been decided by western judges in which certain traits of the law of the Federal Republic are found to be present in the "real" GDR law. The result is that former GDR judges could be convicted for deviating from that posited "real" law by following the actual legal practice of the GDR in the broad interpretation of oppressive statutes or acquiescence in party guidelines handed down under the practice of "socialist legality."[81]

In the case of prosecutions for "perversion of justice," however, an additional requirement is present. The law of the GDR required that a judge disregard the law "knowingly" in order to be guilty of this offense.[82] Although West German law does not include such a clear requirement,[83] it is the East German law which, as the "milder" law, applies to these cases. Accordingly, it may be necessary to undertake difficult inquiries to determine whether a judge "knew" that his or her actions violated the statutory law, perhaps as interpreted by generally applicable supra-legal norms. Attempts to exclude the public from certain types of hearings, or the judge's knowledge that decisions in certain classes of cases were being recorded in the human rights office in Salzgitter, might conceivably be used as evidence for this purpose.[84] On the other hand it has been argued that if the judge was following guidelines or decisions of the GDR Supreme Court, which had a constitutional role in directing the judiciary, the requirement of "knowing" illegality is not present.[85]

Prosecutors have investigated a broad range of cases for possible "perversion of justice." Convictions under the GDR for political offenses, particularly convictions for statements critical of the regime, form a fertile field for these investigations: in these GDR cases, acquittals were rare or nonexistent, and the party and the Stasi took a particular interest in the results. For example, former GDR judges were prosecuted for convicting a couple who—after their application to leave the GDR was denied—placed a New Zealand travel poster on their apartment door with the word "freedom" written on it in lipstick; in another case, a GDR judge was prosecuted for convicting an individual who was denied permission to leave the country and then declared to two

Stasi officials that she felt herself persecuted as the Jews were in the Third Reich and that she enjoyed no human rights.[86] Prosecution for these expressions is clearly offensive to the most rudimentary notions of freedom of speech, but whether the GDR judges can actually be convicted of "perversion of justice" must depend on whether the statements clearly fell beyond the scope of the extremely widely drawn GDR statutes suppressing speech.[87]

The jurisprudence on alleged "perversions of justice" by the former GDR judges may eventually yield a detailed picture of law and practice in the courts of the East German state. At the outset, two separate trends seemed apparent. Some courts sought broad penalization of GDR judges and prosecutors by adopting an expansive interpretation of the eastern offense of "perversion of justice" and rejecting common GDR practice as a source of "law" that could justify eastern judicial actions. In a case in Dresden, for example, a court broadly interpreted the GDR statute on "perversion of justice" to convict prosecutors who had failed to investigate citizens' complaints of fraud in the May 1989 election. The court indicated that the prosecutors' constitutional obligation to preserve socialism—and resulting hierarchical patterns of thought in the prosecutor's office—could not justify these omissions although they could lessen the penalty.[88]

Other decisions, however, took a more respectful view of GDR practice as part of the "law" that the GDR judges and prosecutors were to carry out; in these cases, GDR judges acting consistently with ordinary practice were less likely to have committed "perversion of justice." A Berlin employment judge, for example, was acquitted of "perversion of justice" after she had upheld a worker's dismissal as a "division leader" on the ground that the worker had been expelled from the SED. Although no statute required party membership for such a leadership role, the judge's decision was found permissible "considering the legal understanding that then prevailed in the GDR" and apparent Supreme Court advice to that effect.[89] An exceptional summary procedure employed by the judge was also permissible because Supreme Court guidelines, as generally understood within the GDR legal system, approved the procedure for politically "problematic" cases. In this second type of case, therefore, GDR practice was viewed as part of the law of the GDR, and a judge's action in following that practice was not a "perversion of justice."

In an important opinion, the Federal Supreme Court (BGH) has apparently sided with the second type of decision.[90] The court affirmed the acquittal of the judge in the Berlin labor case, and its opinion showed considerable sympathy for the pressures imposed by the system on the GDR judges. The opinion seemed to accord respect to GDR methods of legal interpretation and allowed judges to follow the constitutional goals of the GDR as well as the informal "standpoints" and "orientation" papers of the GDR Supreme Court—suggesting that decisions following those judicial guidelines would not be "perversions of justice." Yet the BGH also drew upon its own jurisprudence in the border guard cases and stated that some judicial actions were so arbitrary or violative of human rights that they could be punished as "perversions of justice"—a position that could still retain some areas of criminal liability for GDR judges in political cases.[91]

In instances of "show trials," or cases in which procedural rules were grossly ignored, the problems may be in some respects less difficult. In the famous Waldheim trials of 1950, for example, more than three thousand suspected Nazi- or war-criminals, who had been held for years in Soviet internment camps, were convicted in cursory proceedings, ordinarily without defense counsel, and subjected to severe sentences. In twenty-four instances, the death penalty was carried out.[92] The panels that heard these cases were in effect special courts subject to the orders of the SED.[93]

In November 1992, an eighty-six-year-old east German pensioner went on trial on charges of perversion of justice, murder, and deprivation of liberty for his role as judge or prosecutor in the 1950 Waldheim cases.[94] The prosecution argued that, in participating in these decisions, the defendant had violated the GDR Constitution and the code of criminal procedure. The defense attorney responded that, because of the judge's rudimentary legal education, he did not understand that the procedural code was being violated and that, in any event, the Soviet Union was really in control of the proceedings.[95]

In September 1993, the defendant was convicted and sentenced to two years' probation—a considerably milder penalty than the five years' imprisonment sought by the prosecutor.[96] This result seems to be another indication, like the sentences of Berghofer and Modrow, that many of these cases are really being used for purposes of public education, rather than actual punishment of the persons being convicted. But in any case it was expected that additional prosecutions will be brought arising from the Waldheim trials.[97]

## Criminal Prosecution of Former GDR Espionage Agents

The most feared and despised agency of the East German government was the huge Ministry for State Security, more generally known as the Stasi. Most divisions of this agency spied on citizens of the GDR itself, and criminal investigations have been directed against Stasi agents and collaborators for internal spying and related forms of injury.[98]

A special set of problems, however, was presented by the activities of the Stasi's notorious Seventh Division—Hauptverwaltung Aufklärung (HVA)—which conducted external espionage against the Federal Republic and other western countries. These activities raised special issues of retroactivity that were somewhat different from the problems raised by shootings at the Wall or the "perversions of justice" of the GDR judges.

Under West German law, of course, any East German agent who came into the Federal Republic for the purpose of spying was guilty of a crime under western law. The same was true of any West German citizen who had been enlisted to spy for the GDR. Yet, in addition to these groups, a Stasi official who *directed* these spies was also guilty of offenses under West German law, even if the official remained in the east and never actually crossed the border into the west. Of course, these Stasi officials were safe from prosecution under West German law if they remained in the east. When East Germany "acceded" to the Federal Republic in October 1990, however, thousands of former East Germans suddenly became subject to criminal prosecution for espionage activity against West Germany undertaken in the years before unification.

Accordingly, the German government began to prosecute former East German Stasi agents for espionage and related offenses. Yet, from the outset, this development raised questions about whether these prosecutions violated the prohibitions against retroactive law making contained in the Basic Law.

This is not an easy issue to parse. In one sense, the law is not retroactive, because it was in effect at the time that the espionage occurred and, according to the West German statute, the law was applicable even against agents who remained in the east and directed or otherwise participated in spying on the west.[99] This result is derived from the more general doctrine of West German law that activity undertaken in another country may constitute a criminal offense in the Federal Republic if it had a "successful effect" (*Erfolg*)—that is, a desired impact—in the Federal Republic.[100] An espionage official of the GDR who obtained information from agents in the Federal Republic—information that caused damage to the "external" security of the Federal Republic—certainly produced a desired impact or "successful effect" in the west. Accordingly, the GDR official would have violated West German law at the time the acts were performed.[101]

It is important to understand that this is not an unusual doctrine limited to the Federal Republic—rather it is generally accepted as permissible in international law. Indeed, the doctrine has also been employed to give extraterritorial effect to American criminal law. The case of General Noriega—in which the Panamanian dictator was prosecuted in Florida for his involvement in the transportation of drugs into the United States—is only one well-known example of the application of this doctrine.[102]

Because West German law thus criminalized these acts of espionage at the time they were undertaken, the current application of that law to former eastern agents—even those who never came to the west—is technically not retroactive. Viewed realistically, however, the eastern agents knew that the western law could not be enforced against them as long as they stayed in the east. Moreover, they knew that under GDR law and practice, these acts of espionage were not only perfectly legal but also, indeed, highly praiseworthy.

Viewed this way, the sudden extension of western jurisdiction to the east upon unification had a kind of actual retroactive effect: law that the individuals concerned knew could not be enforced against them as a practical matter—or even as a strictly *legal* matter under the GDR regime—was suddenly made applicable to them, in some cases many years after the relevant acts of espionage had taken place. In this respect, it could be argued that the practical effect of these prosecutions violated the constitutional prohibition of retroactive punishment. Moreover, even if not technically retroactive, the prosecutions might violate a more general guarantee of justified reliance derived from the "rule of law" principle protected in the Basic Law.[103] Considerations of this sort impelled a lower court in Berlin to call these prosecutions into question and to certify the issue to the Constitutional Court.[104]

Other constitutional challenges were also advanced. Some argued, for example, that the prosecutions violated constitutional rights of equality because East German agents were being penalized for the same kind of activity that West German agents undertook against the east; yet, of course, the West German agents were not subject to prosecution for espionage against the GDR.[105] This argument was very prominently asserted in the well-known case of Markus Wolf, who was chief of the espionage division of the Stasi for almost thirty-nine years. In his long career, Wolf—who is sometimes thought to have been the model for the Russian master spy Karla in the novels of John le Carré—scored a number of espionage coups against the west. For example, Wolf was successful in placing an agent, Günter Guillaume, in the inner circle of Chancellor Willy Brandt's administration, an action that led ultimately to Brandt's resignation upon Guillaume's exposure.

In May 1993 Markus Wolf went on trial in Düsseldorf for offenses related to espionage. The evidence consisted of representative espionage cases for which Wolf was responsible, including the case of Guillaume.[106] The prosecution's complaint in the court in Düsseldorf charged Wolf with *Landesverrat* (treason) and, in response, Wolf put the question of which country he was supposed to have committed treason against.[107] Yet, from an American view at least, the title of the offense seems to be something of a misnomer. In contrast with the American offense of treason, which requires a state of mind of disloyalty on the part of someone who owes loyalty, issues of loyalty and citizenship play no role in the German offense. Rather this is a typical espionage statute penalizing the transfer of West German "state secrets" to a foreign power in a manner calculated to disadvantage the Federal Republic or bring advantage to the foreign power.[108] Thus this aspect of Wolf's defense, while rhetorically appealing, seemed to miss the point.

Perhaps more weighty was Wolf's plea that he did nothing that was not also done by the western espionage agencies and that to prosecute him would therefore violate constitutional guarantees of equality.[109] This view attracted some adherents, but important counter-arguments also emerged. A formalistic response might simply state that, as a result of unification, the Federal Republic continues to exist while the GDR does not.[110] But a more substantive argument could attempt to distinguish espionage for the Federal Republic from espionage for the GDR by asserting the legitimacy of the Federal Republic and denying the legitimacy of the GDR: the Federal Republic was democratic and the GDR was not; the Federal Republic incorporated the "free democratic basic order" of the Basic Law, and the espionage activities of the GDR sought to impair that free and democratic order.[111] Perhaps these arguments also echo the western constitutionalists' theory that the only legitimate German state was the Federal Republic, as the sole successor of the continuing German "Reich."[112] Some voices further argued that espionage information collected by the GDR was probably transferred to other Warsaw Pact countries, and so the espionage activities could continue to have a deleterious effect on the Federal Republic even after unification.[113]

In light of the argument of inequality, a particular irony of Markus Wolf's prosecution was that Klaus Kinkel, justice minister of the Federal Republic at the time that charges were filed against Wolf, was himself a past chief of the West German espionage agency. Needless to say, Kinkel remained free from any possible prosecution for his espionage activities against the GDR.[114]

In December 1993, Markus Wolf was convicted and sentenced to six years' imprisonment for bribery and "treason" in the case of Guillaume as well as two other cases involving NATO and the West German intelligence service. Indeed, the penalty would have been greater, except that the special circumstances of unification were taken into account, as well as the fact that Wolf and his family had been persecuted and forced into exile during the Nazi period.[115]

Hoping to avoid some of these constitutional and other issues, leading government figures in the west had proposed an amnesty statute for GDR espionage agents shortly before unification. Faced with a storm of protest, however, they withdrew the proposal.[116] After unification, some scholars renewed the call for a legislative amnesty, and the same position was even advanced by a panel of the BGH in an extraordinary *cri de coeur*, citing injustices that it believed were presented by the prosecution of GDR espionage agents.[117] Burned once by popular outrage, however, western political leaders showed little inclination to revisit the problem.

But in a decision in May 1995 that seemed to continue its attempts at mediation between east and west, the Constitutional Court took a substantial step in the direction of what could be considered a judicial amnesty. The Court held that there was a constitutional bar to the prosecution of espionage agents, like Wolf, who were eastern citizens and had conducted their activities from within the GDR.[118] In contrast, the Court did not foreclose the possibility of prosecuting GDR agents whose activities had taken place within the Federal Republic.

In its decision, the Court declined to adopt any of the major arguments that had been advanced in the public debate, although it drew upon aspects of some of those views. Indeed, the Court specifically held that the prosecution of GDR espionage agents did not violate the constitutional guarantee of equality, the prohibition of retroactive law making, or applicable rules of international law.[119]

Instead, the Court reached its decision under the principle of "proportionality," a constitutional emanation of the doctrine of the rule of law. Under this principle, the Court declared, the interest of the Federal Republic in penalizing GDR espionage must be weighed against the reliance interests of those who would never have been prosecuted if German unification had not occurred. In undertaking this balance, the Court indicated, the government's interest in prosecution was weakened by the fact that, unlike most other offenses, espionage is a morally neutral activity that is undertaken by all states. Accordingly, in the case of those who could reasonably rely on non-prosecution because all of their activities took place within the GDR, the state's interest in prosecution was outweighed by the agents' reliance interest. In other instances, however, the result was not so clear. For example, if an eastern citizen had conducted some espionage activities in the Federal Republic, the courts must undertake a balancing of the reliance interest and other relevant factors in the individual case. Moreover, *western* citizens who spied for the GDR remain fully subject to criminal penalties because they never had a justified reliance interest in non-prosecution.[120]

It is clear that this is an important decision, but the reach of its implications remains uncertain. The principle of proportionality that is central to the Court's opinion is a broad principle, capable of considerable flexibility and expansion. Accordingly, this decision opens the possibility that the principle may play a role in other types of prosecutions of GDR criminality—for example, prosecutions for perversion of justice by GDR prosecutors or judges.[121] In any case, the decision has the peculiar result of insulating higher-level GDR Stasi agents from prosecution—because it was they who typically remained in the GDR—while retaining the possibility of prosecuting lower-level agents who undertook the more dangerous work of gathering information in the Federal Republic.

## Debate over a General Amnesty

Calls for an amnesty for GDR espionage agents had been principally based on the specific idea of a violation of equality. Recently, however, there have also been increasing calls for a more general amnesty for the criminal offenses of former GDR officials related to their political or governmental activity—except, perhaps, in the case of serious bodily injury or serious injury to property. Calls for an amnesty of this kind are based on the broader idea that these widespread prosecutions disturb the process of "inner unification" and that their suspension would speed the process of reconciliation.[122] Yet, a "reconciliation" in one direction might lead to bitter dissatisfaction in another, as it is by no means the western conservative parties alone that seem to favor these prosecutions. Indeed, it is the remnants of the GDR reform movement, those who were among the oppressed under the GDR regime, that have most vigorously sought these prosecutions—a position that parallels the reformers' strict views on the exclusion of former Stasi collaborators and SED officials from the public service. One veteran of the GDR reform movement has argued, for example, that an amnesty would impair the crucial process of understanding the GDR system, and the perception that criminals had gone free would increase social tensions in the east.[123] Another prominent member of the former GDR opposition has emphasized the importance of according all GDR victims the opportunity to speak out before a court, and has argued that an amnesty would diminish the recognition accorded to those victims.[124]

In the absence of such an amnesty—which, indeed, does not seem probable—a large number of these prosecutions may well continue in the coming years. There are perhaps three things that can be said about this pattern. First, these criminal cases present a very vivid picture of officials from the west—prosecutors and judges—sitting in judgment over actors from the east. In many cases, moreover, it is likely that they do so without any very deep understanding of the society from which the defendants have emerged. This point was expressly made by Modrow's counsel in the election fraud case. Here, indeed, is a confrontation of strangers very graphically portrayed.

The second point is that when all of these cases are considered together—prosecutions for the shootings at the Wall, the petty corruption of election fraud, espionage by the Stasi, and the routine cruelty of thousands of civil and criminal judicial judgments tending to support the structure of the GDR state—the pattern that emerges is the extensive criminalization of all of the less savory aspects of daily political life in the GDR. Indeed this is a broad criminalization of precisely those institutions that were enlisted to coerce a form of apparent consent to the GDR regime. This was the way the GDR state operated, but the GDR state has disappeared, and it may well be asked what is to be gained now by seeking to apply the criminal law to thousands of cases of low-grade acquiescence.

Third and perhaps most interesting, when these cases do indeed result in convictions, they seem to yield—in most instances at least—the mildest of penalties. Except in the case of convictions at the highest levels, it seems unlikely that many of these convicted "criminals" will actually go to prison. Ultimately, therefore, this immense expenditure of effort seems to serve little more than the function of bringing facts before the public and of labeling the former functionaries of the GDR as criminals. Thus, the ultimate result seems to be rhetorical and political—putting the final public seal of criminality on the actions of the GDR state—rather than actually serving any of the more traditional goals of the criminal law.[125]

CHAPTER 15

# Undoing the Past: "Rehabilitation" and Compensation

## The Background of Rehabilitation

Over the forty-year history of the GDR many individuals suffered bitterly as a result of oppressive judicial decisions and other governmental acts. As a central characteristic of the judicial system, the Communist Party exercised a substantial degree of influence over the courts—particularly over the criminal courts—often ensuring that decisions were made according to certain political criteria. In many instances explicit political pressure was not necessary because the judges in effect knew what was expected of them.

In addition, the East German Criminal Code contained numerous provisions that were employed to penalize broad forms of political activity and expression that could be viewed as critical of the regime. In a crackdown following the Hungarian uprising of 1956, for example, the East German novelist Erich Loest served seven years in prison for writing critical articles, taking critical positions, and being the host of a gathering at which some people said that Walter Ulbricht should be replaced as Communist Party chief.[1] Loest was convicted under section 13(1) of the East German Criminal Code, which made it a crime to "undertake to do away with the constitutional state or social order of the GDR through planned subversion."[2]

Even before the East German penal code was enacted in 1968, article 6 of the 1949 GDR Constitution made it a criminal offense to engage in "boycott-agitation against democratic institutions and organizations." This undefined and capacious provision was broadly employed to punish political action disapproved by the regime.[3] Indeed, in the early days of the GDR, courts sentenced thousands of persons to prison for political offenses, and even death sentences were carried out under this constitutional provision. Persons released from prison after serving sentences under article 6 were then subjected to severe discrimination and disabilities relating to employment, housing, and other aspects of life.[4]

The massive use of political justice in the later years of the GDR must also be viewed against the background of an established practice through which the Federal Republic paid substantial sums to the GDR to secure the freedom of political prisoners. In the period between 1963 and 1987, for example, the Federal Republic spent DM 3.5 billion for the release of approximately 33,700 prisoners—a sum that represented an important component of the budget of the GDR.[5] Some eastern citizens may have been convicted of political offenses precisely for the purpose of providing this source of needed foreign exchange.

## Rehabilitation and Cassation

For these reasons, the GDR was considered by many jurists in the west to be an *Unrechtsstaat*—an "injustice state."[6] Some sort of compensation for the victims of unjust imprisonment and other judicial mistreatment under the GDR was a prominent goal of the GDR reformers, and it was clear that this problem would have to be addressed in the Unification Treaty.[7] But although the general principle of rehabilitation was clear enough, certain complex theoretical and practical problems were not easy to resolve. The early history of "rehabilitation" after 1989 shows a mixture of techniques, and the Unification Treaty—in this case, as in some others—adopted a delaying strategy.

As a general matter, there seemed to be two possible approaches to rehabilitation for the victims of the GDR.[8] These two methods formed a sort of mirror image of two approaches advanced by those favoring the criminal prosecution of officials of the prior regime.

The first approach limited rehabilitation to those who were penalized under the GDR in a manner that actually violated the constitution or other laws of that regime itself. A grant of rehabilitation under this theory might thus require a finding that the GDR had violated its own clear rules. As in the cases considering shootings at the Wall, however, this form of rehabilitation could also involve the construction of an ideal "prior existing law" of the old regime—through the interpretation of statutes and international treaties and the invocation of natural law in a manner quite unlike anything that the courts of the old regime would actually have done. As in the cases of shootings at the Wall, the latter technique could be invoked where the law of the old regime, as actually applied in the past, was designed to achieve a repressive result and was "correctly" applied to achieve that result.

A second possibility, however, would be to ignore the correctness or incorrectness of the result under the law of the GDR—however that law was to be interpreted—and measure the result against the independent concepts of procedural fairness and human rights of the western system. For rehabilitation, this approach posed considerably fewer problems than would the frank application of new legal concepts in the criminal punishment of former officials. The grant of rehabilitation is the grant of a benefit; it is therefore not limited by the prohibition of ex post facto justice—*nullum crimen sine lege*—that is invoked when the officials of the old regime are *penalized* according to legal concepts that were not in force when the relevant acts were committed.[9]

Interestingly, the history of "rehabilitation" of victims of the GDR system shows a shift from the first to the second technique in the course of unification.

Other central questions concerned the types of oppressive action for which rehabilitation should be granted and the nature and extent of compensation that should be granted upon rehabilitation.

*"Cassation" under the Law of the GDR*

Shortly after the fall of the Honecker regime in autumn 1989, persons who had been imprisoned for political offenses in the GDR—some in the distant past—sought reversal of their convictions (and compensation) through the process of "cassation." This device, which was imported from Soviet law, had ordinarily been used in the GDR as a method of exercising centralized party control over the judiciary, by allowing the prosecutor to petition for a change in the judgment even after it had become final.[10] After the fall of the Honecker regime, however, the device of cassation took on the new function of undoing unjust criminal convictions that had been procured by the SED party apparatus.[11] Yet the only permissible grounds for cassation required a showing that the decision being challenged had been incorrect under GDR law—that is, that it rested on a "serious violation" of the GDR Criminal Code or that the penalty was "grossly incorrect."[12]

In an interesting development in early 1990, the Supreme Court (Oberstes Gericht) of the GDR, which seemed anxious to participate in the events of the East German revolution, began to find that its own decisions of more than thirty years before had in fact been incorrect under GDR law.[13] In January 1990, for example, the court granted cassation in the famous cases of Walter Janka and three other SED reformers of the 1950s.[14] Janka and the others had been convicted of "Boykotthetze" under article 6 of the GDR Constitution of 1949 for their attempts to reform the GDR after Khrushchev's dramatic denunciation of Stalin's misdeeds at the Twentieth Party Congress of the Soviet Union.[15] At the heart of the court's decision in 1990 was a finding that the court had been wrong in 1957 when it held that, under the circumstances, a motive to destroy socialism was not an essential element of the offense of "Boykotthetze." According to the court in 1990, the activity for which Janka had been convicted in 1957 was actually the exercise of the right of free expression protected by article 9 of the 1949 GDR Constitution.[16]

Because the cassation statute required a finding that there had been a mistake in the earlier decision—a mistake under GDR law itself—the court created an ideal GDR law of the past that had apparently never existed in fact.[17] The peculiarity of using such a notion of cassation after a political revolution is illustrated by the solemn argument of the government attorney, arguing for reversal of the convictions in 1990, that the defendants in 1956 had not intended to destabilize "the leading role of the working class and its party [the SED]" and did not even want party pluralism, but rather sought "the strengthening of the anti-fascist, democratic bloc, particularly to counterbalance militant nationalistic tendencies in the Federal Republic at that time."[18]

*The Unification Treaty: From Cassation to Rehabilitation*

Until the effective date of the Unification Treaty, the procedure of cassation remained the only method by which victims of GDR injustice could seek reversal of their convictions and a measure of compensation. Furthermore, in its original form, the Unification Treaty only made modest changes in this area. Article 18 of the treaty declared that past judicial decisions of the GDR courts would ordinarily remain in effect but that cassation could be invoked to review GDR criminal convictions. In a significant procedural improvement, an individual convicted under the GDR could file his own petition for cassation, and thus this remedy was no longer dependent upon an official decision.[19]

But the treaty's most important provision in this area was originally expressed as an intention for the future only. Article 17 confirmed the parties' intention to enact a "rehabilitation" statute for the victims of "politically motivated criminal judgments or other judicial decisions that were inconsistent with the constitution or the rule of law." In such a future statute, "rehabilitation of the victims of the SED injustice-regime" would include "appropriate" compensation. Such a pledge was important because many citizens of the former GDR had already served substantial prison sentences for political offenses, and for them a possible reversal of their conviction would afford incomplete relief.[20] Yet a final regulation of this problem was not included in the treaty itself because the views of the two sides diverged: the GDR sought broad coverage and substantial compensation while the negotiators of the Federal Republic, conscious of the soaring costs of unification, sought a more modest resolution.[21]

The leaders of the East German Volkskammer, however, apparently did not want to leave the ultimate decision on rehabilitation to the Bundestag after unification. Less than a week after the Unification Treaty was signed, the GDR Volkskammer—now in its final days—enacted a comprehensive "Rehabilitation Law" seeking to regulate most relevant matters.[22] This statute moved beyond the reversal of decisions that were "incorrect" under GDR law—however construed. Rather, it sought to provide redress for fundamental injustice whether or not it had been in accordance with GDR law. The statute provided "rehabilitation" and compensation for persons who suffered serious deprivations of their "constitutionally guaranteed fundamental and human rights"—including those who were convicted of offenses arising from peaceful expressions of political opposition, as well as those convicted of seeking to leave the GDR or of having contacts with foreign organizations or persons (excluding espionage).[23]

The GDR statute also granted rehabilitation for those who had suffered administrative penalties, or disadvantages in employment, as a result of peaceful political activity—albeit a decision on the amount of compensation was deferred in some of these cases.[24] Moreover, the statute provided rehabilitation for some persons subjected to penalties under the Soviet occupation regime.[25]

This statute was too sweeping for the government of the Federal Republic, whose taxpayers would be paying most of the bills. The chief western negotiator complained that "not even the Ministry of Finance could give anything like an estimate of the cost of such a statute."[26] Accordingly, in an agreement amending and supplementing the Unification Treaty, entered into shortly before unification, the two German states agreed that only the sections of the GDR statute providing rehabilitation for criminal penalties and incarceration in mental hospitals would be carried over into united Germany; in contrast, compensation for administrative discrimination and political discrimination in employment would be deferred.[27] Of course, the treaty's more general requirement that the German parliament enact a comprehensive rehabilitation statute still remained. Yet, because of delays in enacting more comprehensive legislation after unification, thousands of petitions for rehabilitation were decided under the GDR statute as carried over into united Germany in altered form.[28]

## The First Statute for the Correction of SED Injustice

As tensions between east and west increased after unification, the process of enacting a rehabilitation statute in the all-German parliament grew increasingly difficult. Indeed, due to the complexity of the problems, two separate statutes were necessary. The first, regulating rehabilitation and compensation for criminal convictions in eastern Germany, was enacted in 1992. The second statute, providing a measure of compensation for certain discriminations in administrative decisions and employment, was finally approved in spring 1994.

After long and difficult debate, the first federal "Statute for the Correction of SED Injustice" went into effect on October 29, 1992.[29] In its central provisions, the statute provides a framework for undoing criminal convictions for political offenses and certain other offenses and granting compensation for those convictions. The statute also provides a method for undoing politically motivated commitments to psychiatric hospitals, although it had not been judicially established that there was a practice of using psychiatric hospitals for such purposes in the GDR.[30] Overall, the statute was more comprehensive than the provisions carried over in the Unification Treaty and provided a higher level of compensation.

The core of the statute provides that criminal convictions of a German court in eastern Germany, between the date of the German surrender (May 8, 1945) and unification, will be annulled to the extent that those convictions are "inconsistent with the essential principles of a free order [based on] the rule of law."[31] In particular this requirement will be met if the conviction served the purpose of political persecution or if the penalty was grossly disproportionate to the offense.[32]

For greater clarity, the statute specifically lists a number of the most notorious political offenses of the GDR and declares that convictions for these offenses will ordinarily give rise to rehabilitation and compensation. Among others, the listed offenses include:

Boycott agitation [*Boykotthetze*] against democratic institutions and organizations under article 6(2) of the 1949 GDR Constitution—the ill-defined offense under which savage sentences were handed down against political opponents in the early days of the GDR,

Agitation inimical to the state [*Staatsfeindliche Hetze*] under section 106 of the GDR Criminal Code, which penalized any person who attacked or agitated against "the constitutional basis of the socialist state and social order of the GDR,"

Sections 99 and 219 of the GDR Criminal Code, which penalized the transfer of nonsecret information abroad, if that information would damage or disadvantage the interests of the GDR. These provisions were sometimes used to criminalize foreign publications of GDR citizens that were critical of the regime.

In evident recognition of the fact that GDR limitations on egress violated international human rights conventions, the listing also includes convictions for attempting to cross the GDR border or assisting in such an attempt in connection with western groups or government agencies.

In general, the listing was assembled from information provided by victims of GDR justice and from judges in rehabilitation cases under the earlier statute.[33] The listing is helpful in specifying clear cases for rehabilitation, but it is not exclusive, and rehabilitation may also be available for convictions of other political offenses. Of course, other judicial flaws—such as a disproportionate sentence or an oppressive procedure—might also give rise to rehabilitation.[34]

Interestingly, a separate section specifically refers to the Waldheim trials of 1950, in which persons accused of Nazi activities were convicted and sentenced in swift trials without defense counsel and other procedural safeguards.[35] The statute declares that these proceedings were "inconsistent with the essential principles of a free order in accordance with the rule of law." Persons convicted in the Waldheim trials are therefore entitled to rehabilitation and compensation under the statute.[36] This provision reflects earlier judgments by West German courts, as well as a decision in a "cassation" proceeding, that the Waldheim judgments were invalid and would give rise to compensation.[37]

Most interestingly, the statute also ordinarily provides rehabilitation for two sets of crimes under GDR law that are not political offenses in the traditional sense. Rather, these offenses rested on an assumption of the legitimacy of GDR institutions that the all-German parliament appeared unwilling to accord. Thus an individual convicted of failing to perform military service in the GDR could have his conviction annulled under the statute.[38] Moreover, convictions for espionage and similar offenses against the GDR could be annulled if the espionage was carried out for the Federal Republic or one of its allies, or for an organization "devoted to the principles of a free order in accordance with the rule of law."[39]

In these provisions, there may be an echo of the western constitutionalists' view that the GDR—as an entity improperly attempting to "secede" from the continuing "Reich" represented by the Federal Republic—was not a legitimate state and that its basic institutions were unworthy of protection.[40] Indeed, the espionage provision seems to deny the legitimacy of the GDR's interest in protecting its "secrets" and seems to parallel the federal government's position—asserted in prosecutions of GDR espionage agents such as Markus Wolf—that espionage carried out by the GDR was illegitimate and could be criminalized, whereas espionage against the GDR state was legitimate and is properly not criminalized.

Yet the official explanation is somewhat different. According to a committee of the Bundestag, these offenses were included for rehabilitation because they were generally performed by GDR citizens as acts of political resistance to the regime, and their prosecution could therefore be seen as a form of political oppression.[41] Although the listing includes prosecution for failure to perform military service in the GDR, it does not include prosecutions for desertion once in military service—apparently because of a legislative judgment that this offense was not so often committed for political reasons. In cases of desertion from the GDR Army, therefore, the presence of political persecution will have to be proved individually.[42]

Two additional points with respect to the coverage of this statute are worth mentioning. The statute applies to decisions in criminal cases of official German courts in eastern Germany from May 8, 1945 to October 2, 1990. Thus the statute covers not only GDR courts but also any German state courts established during the Soviet occupation period. The statute, however, does not purport to undo decisions of Soviet courts or other actions of the Soviet occupation authorities themselves. This exclusion was apparently made on grounds of international law,[43] and it bears some similarity to the exclusion of the Soviet Bodenreform expropriations from rules requiring a return of property.[44] Yet only the formal annulment of the Soviet judgment is excluded from coverage; another provision grants victims of Soviet occupation courts many of the financial benefits ordinarily afforded under the statute.[45]

A number of tangible results follow from the annulment of a GDR judgment under the statute. If the annulled judgment involved a confiscation of property, for example, the property may be returned under the Property Law and related statutes.[46] Any fines will also be repaid, and the claimant will be reimbursed for any costs of the underlying GDR trial.[47]

Moreover, a "rehabilitated" citizen will be compensated for time spent in prison. Claimants will receive DM 300 for each month of imprisonment, and an additional DM 250 per month of imprisonment will be paid to those who resided in the GDR until November 9, 1989, the day the Berlin Wall was opened.[48] The additional amount represents compensation for the stigmatization to which political convicts who remained in the GDR were often subjected; they confronted a harder fate than those whose freedom was purchased by the Federal Republic or who otherwise succeeded in reaching the west after their imprisonment.[49]

This provision for compensation was one of the statute's most controversial sections. The Bundestag's original bill provided compensation of DM 300 for each month of imprisonment, plus DM 150 per month for those remaining in the GDR until November 1989. Critics argued that these payments were grossly insufficient, noting that persons wrongfully incarcerated in the Federal Republic receive compensation of DM 600 per month of imprisonment. The federal justice minister vainly sought to allay criticism by remarking that the statutory amounts should be considered "symbolic." It was only in response to objections of the Bundesrat that the supplement for persons remaining in the GDR was raised to DM 250 per month. Yet this increase yielded a total monthly amount (DM 550) that was still less than the compensation received for improper imprisonment in the west. A noted western observer has referred to the result as "embarrassing."[50]

Perhaps to allay suspicions on the part of persons seeking rehabilitation, the statute prohibits any former eastern judge from hearing these cases unless the judge has passed all screening processes and has received a new judicial appointment. Even when eastern judges have surmounted this hurdle, not more than one may sit on a three-judge rehabilitation panel.[51] Whatever the justification, however, this regulation certainly furthers the general picture of the western judges passing judgment on the eastern past.

Naturally, decisions under this statute could furnish moral comfort and modest compensation to the persons affected. But, of course, the payments were in no way commensurate with the loss suffered by individuals forced to undergo a long imprisonment.[52]

Moreover, the statute—which was limited to rehabilitation for criminal convictions and commitments to psychiatric hospitals—did not touch the massive claims of administrative discrimination in the GDR or claims of political discrimination in employment. For many citizens of the GDR, this was the form that government oppression ordinarily assumed. These claims of discrimination were reserved for a second rehabilitation statute which was, if anything, even more sharply debated than the first. The basic problems appeared to be the incalculable number of claims that could be forthcoming after forty years of SED rule in the GDR, as well as the continuing financial problems faced by the Federal Republic—problems that rendered a high level of compensation most unlikely.

The long delay in enacting a second rehabilitation law was frustrating to those who had suffered political discrimination in employment under the GDR. Accordingly, one eastern state government began to undertake its own program of rehabilitation. Marianne Birthler, the first education minister of Brandenburg, established a program through which teachers who had been discharged for political reasons could apply for "moral rehabilitation" and reinstatement through a state agency. In some cases reinstatement was granted through this program.[53]

## THE SECOND STATUTE FOR THE CORRECTION OF SED INJUSTICE

In seeking to provide compensation for conviction and unjust imprisonment, the first rehabilitation statute employed concepts that were at least reasonably clear—even if the offered compensation was less than the victims had sought. In contrast, much of the political discrimination experienced by citizens of the GDR came in the form of lower-level administrative or employment decisions, which covered a wide range of possible cases and injuries of greatly varying intensity. Typical cases included, for example, dismissal from employment in retaliation for filing an application to leave the GDR, or exclusion from an advanced high school (*Oberschule*) on political grounds—with the resulting inability to attend university and pursue a professional career.[54] In many of these cases the problems of proof, as well as the difficulties of measuring the ultimate consequences of the claimed discrimination, were daunting. Moreover, it would be impossible to undo the effects of these discriminations, and many asserted that any attempt to provide real compensation for their effects would be quixotic and beyond the resources of the treasury of the Federal Republic.

Yet it was politically necessary that a statutory attempt be made to provide rehabilitation for victims of administrative oppression and discrimination in employment; indeed, such a measure may have been required by the Unification Treaty.[55] But to meet the feared financial problems, the drafters of the second statute sought to provide rehabilitation and compensation only for the most serious cases of injustice in these areas—cases in which continuing effects were perceptible. The result was a statute that seemed to promise few tangible benefits to the politically oppressed of the former GDR and drew bitter attack from eastern reformers on the ground that the Bundestag had failed in its obligations to further inner unification.[56]

The first part of the statute affords rehabilitation for oppressive administrative measures of the former GDR. It provides that administrative measures may be undone if they were "*absolutely* inconsistent with leading principles of a state based on the rule of law, and their consequences directly continue [into the present] in an onerous and unacceptable manner."[57] These measures include acts that "violated the principles of justice, legal security, or proportionality in a serious manner, and furthered political persecution or constituted arbitrary action in the individual case."[58]

This central provision of the statute has drawn bitter attack on a number of grounds. First, the requirement that the administrative acts have been "absolutely" inconsistent with the rule of law seems to require an extraordinarily severe form of injustice before rehabilitation will be triggered and represents a higher hurdle than that set forth in the Unification Treaty.[59]

Moreover, the oppressive acts covered by the statute are defined in a very general manner. Unlike the first rehabilitation law, the statute does not contain a specific listing of representative categories of oppressive acts. This technique will produce uncertainty about which acts should be recognized as "absolutely" inconsistent with the rule of law, and may evoke administrative attempts to narrow the coverage of the statute; in any case, considerable administrative dispute and litigation seem likely.[60]

In order to receive compensation, moreover, there has to be a showing of damage either to health or property, or a disadvantage in employment, and these material consequences must have "directly" continued into the present "in an onerous and unacceptable manner." Again, this strict standard will exclude redress even for cases of obvious injustice where these additional causal factors cannot be proved. In the case of an established injury to health, the claimant will be included under existing West German statutes providing for special health assistance or disability payments, and in the case of loss of property, the claimant may seek return of property or compensation under the general property rules adopted upon unification.[61]

Finally, voices from the GDR reform movement attacked the statute on the ground that it did not separate rehabilitation from compensation.[62] If a claimant could not meet the strict causal and other requirements for receiving compensation, the statute provided no method for obtaining a declaration that the administrative act of the GDR was oppressive and invalid. Such a declaration, which *was* provided for criminal convictions under the first rehabilitation statute, could have assisted the process of "inner" unification.[63]

For disadvantages in employment, however, the Employment Rehabilitation Law sets forth a more complex set of rules. These discriminations occurred not only within the employment relation itself, but in many cases during the process of education, before employment had even begun. Individuals were often prohibited from attending a university—or removed from the university—on political grounds. Indeed, employment discrimination was an inherent aspect of the SED's "restructuring" of eastern society as well as part of its method of retaining power.[64]

To trace the consequences of these discriminations and give some sort of real compensation might well be impossible. Accordingly, this form of rehabilitation is generally limited to cases in which unjust administrative action or detention, or other forms of political persecution, rather clearly led to the interruption or denial of a chosen career.[65] As compensation, the statute grants assistance in re-education or further education in the claimant's area of specialization—in case that is possible—and also provides a small monthly sum for those who can show a special injury to their economic position by virtue of these discriminations.

More generally, however, this problem is addressed through the comprehensive German statutory system relating to pensions and retirement. Perhaps under the dubious theory that the most serious damage generally inflicted by employment discrimination arises upon retirement, the statute attempts to adjust pension payments so that they would resemble the payments that would have been received if the individual had not been subjected to discrimination. Thus, substantial compensation for employment discrimination is deferred until retirement, and limited by the period of time that the claimant receives a pension—a resolution that may ultimately shift the financial burden in this area to the next generation.[66] In contrast, no provision is made for the recovery of a position from which an individual was discriminatorily excluded, or for the payment of any lost wages.

## Rehabilitation and Property

Viewed from the perspective of the GDR reformers and victims of the SED regime, the first and second rehabilitation statutes reveal serious deficiencies. In the first statute, the compensation provided for unjust imprisonment remains below the West German standard. Moreover, the coverage of the second statute is narrow, and its provisions for compensation ultimately quite sparing.

Yet in response to these complaints—however justified they may be from an eastern perspective—some western citizens might raise a countervailing argument. It seems clear that the citizens of the west, whose taxes will largely go to providing compensation upon rehabilitation, bore no responsibility for the imprisonment or other political discriminations suffered by citizens of the east. Western citizens might ask, therefore, why there should be any compensation upon rehabilitation from essentially western sources—or, at least, why citizens of the east should be entitled to complain that these payments are not comprehensive or high enough?

These questions have both a political and a constitutional answer. First, a comprehensive program of rehabilitation and compensation may significantly further the process of "inner unification," a process that will benefit both parts of the united German state. According to the federal justice minister, for example, the process of rehabilitation will "pay tribute to the pain" of those subjected to oppression under the GDR. A review and analysis of those oppressive acts, will "prevent them from being forgotten"—thus according a form of "recognition to the personal fate" of GDR citizens. This process will also have an effect in the west, by heightening western understanding of the life histories of eastern citizens. In sum, the process of "working out the past" will contribute to "building bridges and creating understanding" between east and west.[67]

Similarly, GDR reformers have emphasized that the prosecution of members of the old regime will never be entirely successful. Accordingly, the nature of the rules adopted for rehabilitation will be "a decisive touchstone" for the adequate handling of the juristic past of the GDR.[68] If the western "Rechtsstaat" cannot adequately punish GDR oppressors, at least it can express its understanding by adequately compensating the eastern victims.

In addition to this general political argument, a constitutional argument may also be derived from the decision of the Constitutional Court in the *Bodenreform* case.[69] In this opinion, the Court strongly suggested—although it did not expressly hold—that the social state and rule of law guarantees of article 20 GG require that the state provide some form of equalization payments whenever a group of citizens suffers a particularly grievous misfortune. Indeed, similar ideas lay behind an elaborate system of equalization payments for misfortunes suffered during World War II and the occupation period.[70] Accordingly, it could be argued that some form of equalization payments is also constitutionally due from the German state to former GDR citizens who suffered severe political persecution through imprisonment or discrimination in administrative decisions or in employment.[71] Indeed, in an apparent reflection of this idea, certain payments called for by the rehabilitation laws are referred to as "equalization payments," rather than "compensation."[72]

Indeed, the presence of this common constitutional rationale may suggest some reflections on the contrast between the treatment of rehabilitation and the treatment of the return of property after unification. Under the Unification Treaty, individuals whose property was expropriated under the GDR will recover that property in many cases and, if the property is not returned, they receive compensation.[73] Most of the people receiving property or compensation under these provisions are residents of the west who have had the opportunity to enjoy a prosperous life under politically favorable conditions for decades and who most likely had long ago abandoned any prospect of return of the property. In a large number of cases, moreover, these are not individuals who would find themselves close to the line of subsistence without this property; yet, the Unification Treaty—and the constitutional theory derived from article 20 GG—may require that they be returned to some higher level of prosperity.

In contrast, many of the individuals now seeking rehabilitation had continued to live in the GDR, without the opportunity to accumulate capital and without the relatively pleasant circumstances of the west. Indeed, the persons who are now seeking rehabilitation had been subjected to imprisonment under brutal circumstances or discrimination that in many cases destroyed their opportunity for fulfilling work and a career. Yet, these persons will often receive very little under very narrowly defined tests of eligibility.

Thus, in many cases, the legal structure of German unification seems to favor property claims—generally of westerners—over less tangible personal claims of easterners, even for those who have been wrongly imprisoned under the GDR. Yet this result may well appear paradoxical because the underlying ideas of the social state provision of article 20 would seem to support rehabilitation payments to the relatively disadvantaged at a *higher* level than value received by relatively prosperous westerners for property expropriated decades ago by the GDR or the Soviet occupation regime.

Indeed the disparity between those receiving (at best) modest payments for rehabilitation, in comparison with former landowners receiving restitution or compensation for expropriated property, may well raise significant constitutional questions. The government may seek to justify the differences by invoking the evident difficulties of evaluating such factors as lost life chances in rehabilitation. Yet, whatever the justification, this disparity points out another form of advantage that the unification settlement extends to largely western claimants over many victims of oppression who remained in the east.[74]

## CHAPTER 16

# Confronting the Past: The Stasi Files

BEHIND MANY important issues of German unification loomed the gigantic and mysterious specter of the enormous files of information amassed over four decades by the GDR Ministry for State Security—the Stasi. With a headquarters complex covering many square blocks in Berlin, and numerous branches throughout the country, the Stasi had approximately 100,000 full-time employees out of a total population of approximately 16 million.[1] In addition, the Stasi enlisted hundreds of thousands of "unofficial collaborators" (*inoffizielle Mitarbeiter* or IMs) drawn in secret from the population of the GDR.[2]

This elaborate system of surveillance permeated the society of the GDR. Indeed, as a well-known East German writer remarked, "Hardly ever in the history of a country has a period been so comprehensively and thoroughly documented as these forty years of the GDR through its secret police."[3] But the Stasi was not an information-gathering agency alone: it also undertook covert activities against internal critics and other "enemies" of the regime. Indeed, following the Soviet model, the Stasi served generally as "shield and sword of the party."[4]

The agents of the Stasi recorded their activities in obsessive detail in dossiers that eventually came to occupy approximately 180 kilometers of shelf space in a windowless nine-story concrete building in Berlin, as well as secret locations elsewhere. Of the six million files containing personal data, four million concern citizens of the former GDR, while two million relate to citizens of the old Federal Republic.[5] Because they contained volumes of damaging information, some files were destroyed in the last year of the GDR. Yet, due in large part to the diligence of citizens groups, most Stasi files were preserved from destruction and accompanied the GDR into united Germany, representing an extraordinary storehouse of information as well as a significant problem.

### THE DEBATE OVER THE STASI FILES

The question of what to do with these files, therefore, became a question of great moment as unification approached in 1990. Most agreed that the files should be available to government agencies for certain criminal investigations and the review of former GDR officials for continued employment. More difficult questions, however, concerned the extent to which the files should be available to ordinary citizens and to researchers and the press.

Vigorous arguments were urged on both sides of this issue. Some maintained that the mistakes that were made at the end of the Nazi period should not be repeated, and therefore information about the nature and activities of the GDR regime should be opened to the broadest scrutiny. Such a program would enhance a historical understanding of the GDR as state and society;[6] it would also allow victims of the Stasi to comprehend the reality of their individual pasts and further a sense of self-understanding and liberation:

> The goal is that people who were long oppressed should be able to carry forward the liberation that they dreamed about and struggled for in the streets—through a process of memory and encounter and coming to terms [with the past]. People who were previously oppressed and deprived of autonomy should take possession of their former rulers' knowledge. They should become [active participants in shaping their own understanding] and—in this way—come more to find themselves. They should become more free, for the tasks of tomorrow.[7]

Under this view, destroying the files or keeping them secret would have been equivalent to constructing the new east German society on a kind of lie: the perpetuation of massive deceptions of the past. Opening the files could also hinder former Stasi employees from capitalizing on what would otherwise be their unique (past) access to the files and recollections of what the files contained.[8]

Others, in contrast, feared that a widespread opening of the Stasi files would cause rifts in the society of eastern Germany that would outweigh any benefits gained from such a course. Still others asserted that the files were inherently unreliable and that there was no method of determining the accurate entries from the false—with the result that the Stasi could "continue to carry out its deplorable activity with the legacy of these files."[9] Finally, some argued that the massive invasion of privacy represented by the files would be perpetuated by opening them to any extent—unless accompanied by a comprehensive program of review designed to protect privacy and to weigh the gravity of an individual's acts of collaboration against possible mitigating circumstances.[10]

As a personal matter, the decision to examine one's own Stasi file risked its own serious consequences. A clear understanding of the past could destroy relationships of decades if a friend, relative, or even a spouse had been a Stasi agent.[11] Indeed, even if no close friend was revealed as a Stasi agent, just the act of reading—and for the first time really understanding—how closely everyday activities had been observed and recorded, and seeing the perverse constructions that could be imposed on innocent actions, could lead to a profound shock.[12] The implications of this widespread psychological destabilization, together with other massive personal traumas attendant upon unification, have yet to be fully evaluated.

Yet, in the circumstances of the post-unification period, access to the files could also have benefits for an individual's personal life. For example, the files could yield evidence of political discrimination by the GDR state that could give rise to a claim for rehabilitation and compensation.[13] Moreover, a person wrongly suspected of collaboration with the Stasi might be able to prove his innocence through access to the files.[14] In sum, opening the Stasi files could have important implications for legal actions taken against the oppressors of the GDR regime, and also significant implications for actions to be taken to benefit the oppressed.

After very difficult negotiation and debate, the files were opened to a significant extent, in an action that probably has no parallel in history. The existence and availability of these files was one of the major social and political factors in eastern Germany after unification and profoundly affected a broad range of political and constitutional problems, as well as the relationship between west and east Germany.

The opening of the Stasi files was preceded and followed by prolific revelations of the collaboration of significant GDR figures with the Stasi, including some individuals who had been active in opposition movements. In this way the opening of the files may have impaired the political force of the east by diminishing the power and authority of some of its leading figures. More generally, these revelations of widespread collaboration could be used to label those in the east as second-class citizens who were not fully worthy of democracy—a view quite contrary to the appreciation of the democratic strength of the demonstrators in Leipzig and Dresden, and other portions of the East German populace, at a slightly earlier period.[15]

The contemporary problems and importance of the Stasi files must be understood against the background of the profound role that these files—and the entire question of the dissolution of the Stasi—played during the period of the East German revolution and shortly thereafter.

## The Stasi Files under Modrow and de Maizière

Certainly the extraordinary degree of internal surveillance undertaken by the Stasi was one of the primary characteristics of the GDR. Moreover, through secret ownership of property and enterprises as well as the secret placement of its own officers in important political and economic positions, the Stasi exerted a significant influence on the entire structure of the GDR state.[16] By the time of the revolution in 1989, therefore, the GDR was governed to a significant extent by a secret agency whose activities were outside of the official line of governmental control.

In the revolution of 1989 the activities of the Stasi were a particular focus of political attack, and anxiety arose among the reform groups that the files of the Stasi, which recorded forty years of its misdeeds, might be altered or destroyed. Indeed, "alarmed by black clouds of smoke" rising from the inner courtyards of Stasi complexes, citizens committees began to occupy Stasi offices around the GDR in late 1989, in order to assure that the Stasi records would be preserved.[17]

In the culminating act of this effort, raucous demonstrators burst into the central Stasi headquarters on the Normannenstrasse in Berlin on January 15, 1990. Although the precise origin of this turmoil remains unclear, many now believe that it was intentionally provoked, as a diversionary tactic, by the Stasi itself.[18] In any case, this event led to the creation of a central "Citizens Committee Normannenstrasse," which sought to assure that the Stasi was actually being dissolved and that its records would be preserved.[19]

In addition, the GDR Round Table decided that the Stasi files should be sealed off from access, and the GDR Council of Ministers ordered this measure by a resolution of February 8, 1990.[20] Indeed, dissolution of the Stasi and the preservation of its files were major preoccupations of the GDR Round Table during the Modrow period—amid strong suspicion that the Modrow government was actually working against both goals.[21] During the same period, the Stasi scored a major coup when it convinced the GDR reformers to destroy the files of the Stasi espionage section, as well as a central electronic index of the Stasi files.[22] The reformers later bitterly regretted this astonishing lapse of vigilance.

With the democratic election in March 1990 and the formation of the de Maizière government, the role of the citizens committees—which ultimately rested on the acclaim of the streets—became considerably less secure. In his acceptance speech (*Regierungserklärung*) of April 19, 1990, Minister-President de Maizière praised the "meritorious work" of the citizens committees, but announced that a government commission would henceforth guide the dissolution of the Stasi and the investigation of its activities.[23] Established in May 1990, the government commission contained well-known figures from GDR reform circles such as the author Stefan Heym and the early GDR dissident, Walter Janka.[24] Yet the reformers came to view the new government commission, with its eminent members, as a useless fig leaf.[25] Much of the real work continued to be performed by a somewhat shadowy "state committee" whose structure and personnel had been inherited from the Modrow period. The reformers had reason to believe that this "state committee" was thoroughly infiltrated by the Stasi itself.[26]

Indeed the entire de Maizière period was marked by tension between the GDR reformers and Interior Minister Peter-Michael Diestel over the process of dissolving the Stasi and preserving its records.[27] Diestel had reduced the role of the citizens committees and had proposed the destruction of the Stasi records. For the ostensible purpose of understanding the structure of the intelligence agency, Diestel also worked closely with former Stasi officers—a technique that evoked the deep suspicion of the citizens committees.[28] For his part, Diestel acknowledged that the citizens committees had performed an important service by securing the Stasi records but argued that, with the democratic election of March 18, 1990, legitimate political authority had passed to the parliament and government.[29]

During the same period, the GDR Volkskammer formed its own committee for the purpose of supervising the dissolution of the Stasi. The committee's chairman was Joachim Gauck, a pastor from Rostock and parliamentary representative of Bündnis 90.[30] In the struggles to dissolve the Stasi and preserve its records, the parliamentary committee supported the GDR reformers against the perceived obstructionism of Diestel and the "state committee" inherited from the Modrow period. The choice of Joachim Gauck as chair was a fateful decision. Gauck would later lead the huge agency charged with management of the Stasi files after unification.

The political sensitivity of the issue of Stasi affiliation was so great that the GDR Volkskammer under de Maizière also established a committee to investigate whether any of its members had been informants. The work of the committee resulted in dramatic moments in the Volkskammer, and at least one resignation.[31] Evidence had not yet emerged, however, that de Maizière himself may have been a Stasi collaborator.

## The Unification Treaty and the Stasi Files

Reflecting the difficulty and sensitivity of the problem, debate over the handling of the Stasi files raised serious issues up to the signing of the Unification Treaty and beyond. Fearing the possible misuse of information, the drafters of the treaty wished to grant custody of the Stasi files to the federal archivist, with strict limitations on their use—at least for a transitional period.[32] But on August 24, 1990, the GDR Volkskammer issued quite a different statute.[33] Enacted under the time pressure of approaching unification, the Volkskammer statute "was presumably driven by the desire to regulate a fundamental 'GDR matter' before the accession."[34] The Volkskammer's view was that control of the files should be a state, not a federal, matter and that broad access should be granted to eastern—but not to western—citizens. Accordingly, the GDR statute of August 24 provided that custody of certain files should be divided among the Länder instead of being placed under the central control of the federal archivist. Moreover, in a provision that raised many eyebrows in Bonn, the statute provided that the interests of other nations, presumably including the Soviet Union, should be taken into account in deciding when to deny individual access to the files.[35]

For these and other reasons, the GDR statute encountered the disapproval of the treaty's architect, Wolfgang Schäuble, as well as the GDR negotiator, Günther Krause, and the statute was not included in the Unification Treaty.[36] Rather, the treaty adopted a more limited transitional plan which did, however, concede some authority to the east in this essentially eastern matter.[37] The treaty mandated central control of the Stasi files by an independent federal official—a "special commissioner" to be proposed by the GDR Council of Ministers with approval of the Volkskammer. Moreover, the treaty required that the files be kept in eastern Germany and allowed access to the files for certain specified purposes—although, in general, use or disclosure of the information was permitted only in cases of exigent need. A comprehensive regulation of the Stasi files was to be undertaken by the all-German parliament but—in another concession to the GDR Volkskammer and the citizens committees—the treaty recommended that the parliament take into account the principles of the Volkskammer law of August 24.[38]

This fragile compromise was threatened, however, when shortly after the Unification Treaty was signed, the GDR citizens groups were stung by rumors that the Stasi files were to be moved from eastern Germany to a central archive in the western city of Koblenz. Protesting the feared move, demonstrators again occupied the central Stasi building in the Normannenstrasse; the demonstrators also called for access to their Stasi files.[39]

Whether or not these fears were justified, the demonstrations and related pressures seemed to imperil ratification of the Unification Treaty.[40] Accordingly, on September 18, 1990, the two German states entered into a supplemental agreement that made some concessions to eastern demands. This agreement stated once again—but this time more strongly—that a later parliamentary regulation of the Stasi files would observe the principles of the Volkskammer law of August 24. Although the files would still be centrally controlled, the agreement did provide that special state commissioners could play an important role in advising the central agency on the files. Finally, the agreement made an important concession to the views of the citizens groups in conceding that persons affected by Stasi files should have a right to know what was in those files, as long as the interests of third persons were preserved.[41]

Immediately upon unification, Joachim Gauck, chair of the Volkskammer's special committee on the Stasi, was appointed federal commissioner to take custody of the Stasi files. The agency under his direction, which continues to manage most matters relating to the files, came swiftly to be known as the Gauck Agency.

## Statutory Regulation of the Stasi Files: The Stasi Records Law of 1991

The comprehensive statute called for in the Unification Treaty, and in the last-minute supplemental agreement of September 1990, was finally enacted in December 1991.[42] Known as the Stasi Records Law, it was enacted under pressures of time against the background of urgent demands from eastern delegates whose constituents sought a comprehensive regulation and access to the Stasi files as soon as possible.[43]

The Stasi Records Law reflects an attempt to comply with demands of the GDR citizens groups for broad individual access to the files while also according respect to individual rights of privacy.[44] The statute is also intended to further the historical, political, and judicial "working through" (*Aufarbeitung*) of Stasi activity and the GDR state—including scholarly research as well as the use of Stasi files for criminal prosecutions and for evaluation of individuals for the public service.[45] The statute was supported by the major parties, but in the end it was opposed by Bündnis 90/Greens, including the remnants of the GDR reform movement, because the files were to be administered by a central agency instead of the individual eastern states.[46] The eastern reform groups also objected to provisions allowing the secret services of Germany and its allies broad access to the Stasi files.[47]

The Stasi Records Law perpetuates the role of the agency under commissioner Joachim Gauck as controller of the files.[48] Indeed under the statute, the so-called Gauck Agency has grown into a massive institution, with over three thousand employees, principally engaged in arranging and cataloging the Stasi dossiers and screening documents in preparation for their release to government agencies or individual applicants.[49] As such, it was comparable in size to the Treuhand, the other great federal organ of German unification. Indeed, some maintain that it joined the Treuhand as an agency that perpetuated the control of the west over the east through the systematic weakening of eastern structures and institutions.

At the core of the Stasi Records Law is the right of any individual—whether from the GDR or elsewhere, and whether "victim" or Stasi "perpetrator"—to learn whether information about him exists in the files and, in many cases, to receive access to that information.[50] Yet, for the purpose of determining how much information the individual will receive, the distinction between victim and Stasi perpetrator is a crucial one. If the individual was the "subject" (*Betroffener*) or victim of a Stasi investigation, he or she can read the complete file and receive copies.[51] Thus the applicant can follow the entire history of the Stasi's investigation through files that sometimes encompass hundreds or even thousands of pages and numerous volumes.[52]

The identities of other victims and third persons mentioned in the file are to be rendered anonymous, but the victim has the right to learn the identity of Stasi officials and collaborators who provided information—if the identity of such persons can be clearly determined—as well as the name of any person who filed a written denunciation against the victim to his or her detriment.[53] In contrast, Stasi agents and individuals benefited by the Stasi, such as party officials receiving reports from the agency, have only limited rights to seek the information in their files.[54] The drafters of the statute feared that former agents, with memories refreshed by the files, could use the information to the detriment of their former victims.[55]

Under the statute, victims' names might remain in the files for a limited period only. Commencing on January 1, 1997, victims and third persons may have the right to erase their identities from the files or, if that is not possible, to have the relevant files destroyed; this provision reflects the high status accorded to interests of privacy in the German constitutional system. The files will be preserved, however, if there is a clearly superseding interest of another individual in keeping the files intact or if the files are required for subordinating needs of political or historical research.[56] Historians and researchers have naturally expressed considerable concern about this provision.[57] But an official of the Gauck Agency maintained that provisions favoring political or historical research will provide adequate protection and, in any case, "a mass destruction [of the files] is not to be expected."[58]

Yet access to the files—even files containing personal information—is not limited to the victims. A wide range of public and private organs or groups can also obtain access for specified purposes. In particular, access can be obtained to determine if officials or certain private individuals—such as government ministers, members of the public service, notaries, lawyers, or high corporate officials—have collaborated with the Stasi.[59] Accordingly, this provision furthers the exclusion of former Stasi officials not only from government offices but from some professions and high offices in private industry as well. In most cases, however, this right of access elapses after fifteen years. This resolution apparently reflects a judgment that, after such a period, the relevance of earlier activity may be so tenuous that it no longer outweighs the privacy rights of the individuals concerned.

Personal information in the Stasi files can also be used for the prosecution of certain serious offenses. Indeed, in such cases, personal data in the files may be used against a Stasi victim or a third person, as an exception to the general rule of the statute that personal data in the files may not be used to the detriment of such persons.[60] Finally, in some cases even files containing personal information can be made available to secret intelligence services of Germany and its allies—a point that evoked sharp criticism from Bündnis 90/Greens, which viewed all intelligence services as conspiratorial and undemocratic.[61]

The most bitterly disputed sections of the statute, however, were those concerning the use of Stasi files for political and historical research and publication by the press. On one side, the asserted privacy rights of individuals named in the files favored extensive limits on publication. On the other side, the interest in freedom of the press, including concerns that the files not continue to be the subject of official censorship, militated against such restrictions. On both sides, constitutional concepts of the Basic Law—which seeks to protect both privacy and freedom of the press through an elaborate process of balancing—played an important role.[62] In the final stages of parliamentary consideration, the press conducted a vigorous campaign against what it saw as unduly strict limitations on publication in the statutory draft—such as a requirement that any use of the Stasi files be subject to prior approval by the Gauck Agency.[63] In response, the restrictions on publication were significantly relaxed in the final version.[64]

The result was an elaborate compromise, but one that somewhat favored the press. The press will ordinarily have a right of access to Stasi files that do not contain personal information and files in which personal information has been made anonymous. Material from those files may be freely published.[65] If the files refer to named persons, however, rights of access and publication are available only if the persons consent, or if they are public or political figures or officials who are not themselves Stasi victims or "third persons," or if they were Stasi collaborators or persons favored by the Stasi. In all of these cases, however, the files may not be published if a "subordinating protectable interest" of a named person would be infringed.[66] Although the requirement of a judicial balancing of countervailing interests may raise difficult questions, this provision has one major result: any well-known individual who was an official or unofficial collaborator of the Stasi may ordinarily have his name revealed to the press and legally published.

Moreover, in a significant victory for the press, criminal penalties for improper publication are essentially limited to word-for-word-quotations, and the paraphrasing of a document will not lead to criminal prosecution.[67] This provision, which allows substantial leeway to the press to publish the substance of files that it may have received in any number of ways, was apparently the legislative response to the energetic campaign conducted by the press in the last stages of the legislative process.[68]

## Experience with the Stasi Files: Revelations and Responses

It is clear that the opening of the Stasi files has had a profound effect on the society of eastern Germany. The opening of the files has significant implications for Stasi officials and their collaborators, as well as for the victims of the Stasi.

For Stasi officials and collaborators, the opening of the files can reveal a pattern of deception that may have persisted for years. These disclosures can result in public disgrace. They can also mean exclusion from public or private employment or the legal profession—and even in some cases criminal conviction and punishment.

For the victims, material in the files may yield valuable evidence for a claim for rehabilitation; in some instances it may even furnish the basis for a civil suit against an informant who collaborated with the Stasi.[69] For the first time, moreover, those subject to spying by the Stasi now have the opportunity to understand the full extent of this surveillance and to glimpse the political structures that lay behind it. Ironically the files also present a matchless documentation of the GDR dissident movement itself.[70]

From this massive Stasi archive, published collections of material illustrate the goals and methods of the Stasi in particularly sensitive cases. The Stasi files of poet Reiner Kunze and novelist Erich Loest, both of which were received in mysterious ways before the Stasi archive was officially opened, have proved particularly illuminating. After he had written poems critical of the GDR, Kunze was subjected to elaborate surveillance: his telephone was tapped, his mail opened, and his neighbors enlisted in a minute documentation of his life, which remains recorded in the Stasi files.[71] Some of Kunze's friends were "unofficial collaborators," and they furnished prolific memoranda of personal and political conversations with the poet. Kunze's contacts with other critics of the regime, such as Wolf Biermann and Robert Havemann, were a particular source of fascination to the agency.

In addition to the passive recording of detailed intimate information, the Stasi took active steps to impair Kunze's life and work. The agency sought to prevent Kunze's poems from being published in the Soviet Union and tried to discourage him from accepting membership in a western literary society (and, when he refused to comply, apparently threatened his life). The agency also went to elaborate lengths to steal copies of Kunze's medical records, and enlisted neighbors in a campaign of criticism.[72] Indeed, attempts to discredit Kunze continued even after he left the GDR for the Federal Republic in 1977.[73] Techniques of this sort were commonly employed by the Stasi against persons whom it considered critical of the regime.[74]

An examination of this massive archive can retrospectively cast a new and inevitably more depressing light on even the aspects of the GDR that seemed tolerable. This is certainly the response of some former GDR citizens upon reading their files. For example, the GDR reformer Bärbel Bohley remarked: "One is most shaken by the destruction and breakdown of human feelings. What is rewarded here is treachery, lies, disloyalty, secrecy, haughtiness, arrogance, the lust for power, cravenness, anxiety, and cowardice. . . . For a long time I thought that the GDR could be reformed. Examination of my files finally freed me from these dreams. A state that relies increasingly on the bad qualities of people as the basis of its existence is doomed to extinction."[75]

Problems also came quickly for those who had had some contacts with the Stasi as unofficial informants. Even before the files were officially opened, some prominent eastern politicians were accused of collaboration with the Stasi. As a result of such disclosures, for example, Ibrahim Böhme resigned his position as leader of the eastern SPD. Wolfgang Schnur, the first leader of the reform group Democratic Awakening, met a similar fate.[76] Most notably, Lothar de Maizière, the only freely elected minister-president of the GDR, was accused of collaboration with the Stasi and eventually resigned his position in the hierarchy of the CDU after unification.[77]

After the files were opened, Manfred Stolpe, SPD minister-president of Brandenburg, acknowledged that he had had numerous contacts with the Stasi in his prior role as an official of the Evangelical Church in the GDR. These revelations evoked bitter attacks—but also support from leading political figures. The Gauck Agency eventually issued a report finding that Stolpe, "according to the criteria of [the Stasi]," had been an important "unofficial collaborator" for over twenty years—a conclusion that evoked renewed calls for Stolpe's resignation.[78] But defenders claimed that Stolpe had the task of representing the interests of the church in its relations with the GDR government, a task that necessarily required numerous contacts with the Stasi.[79] In this view, the question was whether Stolpe had become closer to the Stasi than was necessary to perform this function.[80]

The Stolpe case has also come to symbolize tensions between those who sought accommodation with the SED government and the citizens groups who opposed any collaboration.[81] This tension, which has continued on into the post-unification period, has the ironic effect of pitting the eastern reformers against political forces whose social and political goals are otherwise quite similar. In the Stolpe case, the citizens groups are in effect aligned with the conservative forces of the CDU against Stolpe's SPD government in Brandenburg which, in many of its political positions, is rather close to those of the remnants of the GDR reformers.

More recently, revelations of collaboration with the Stasi have impaired the reputations of two of eastern Germany's most important writers. First, it was disclosed that Heiner Müller—perhaps the GDR's most eminent dramatist and a writer whose critical works had sometimes been banned in the GDR—had been an unofficial collaborator.[82] Then Christa Wolf, the GDR's most famous novelist, revealed that for a short period in the late 1950s and early 1960s she had written reports on fellow writers for the Stasi, using the code name Margarete.[83] Even though Wolf was later the subject of intense surveillance by the Stasi, these revelations of complicity seem to have cast a pall over her reputation and career.[84]

## Experience with the Stasi Files: Litigation

In many cases these revelations from the Stasi files were accepted by the named collaborators without resistance. But in some instances, the suspected collaborators have attempted to pursue remedies in court. Although release of information from the Stasi files receives the constitutional protections of speech and press, it must also confront very strong constitutional rights of privacy and personality that can work against disclosure. This tension lay behind disputes over the Stasi Records Law and has persisted in judicial decisions and vigorous public debate.

Indeed, concern about rights of personality has evoked general criticism of procedures employed by the Gauck Agency in releasing information from the files. The agency has transmitted information about individuals to government offices—together with its judgment on whether an individual was a Stasi informant—without any sort of hearing on the question. The Stasi Records Law permits these transmittals, but many fear that the risk of error is nonetheless substantial.[85] These concerns are heightened by the extraordinary credibility that the official opinions of the Gauck Agency, based on the files, are generally accorded; indeed, as a practical matter, the agency has taken on the role of a final tribunal instead of a fallible government agency.[86]

Certain practices of the Gauck office were challenged in litigation arising from the Stolpe affair. In 1992, the Gauck office complied with requests of a parliamentary investigating committee in Brandenburg and delivered detailed reports on "IM Sekretär" (thought to be Stolpe) along with its opinion that "Sekretär" had been an "important" Stasi collaborator. A Berlin administrative court rejected Stolpe's challenge to this action. The court found that the Gauck Agency's opinion did indeed involve an incursion into Stolpe's constitutional right of personality, but it concluded that the statement, in this context, was authorized nonetheless. The court emphasized that the statement was useful in informing the public about the structure and methods of the Stasi and that Stolpe had been a public figure in the GDR. In the report to the parliamentary committee, it would have been difficult to separate statements of "fact" from "opinion."[87]

On the other hand, the court held that Gauck was not authorized to state in a television interview that Stolpe had been an important Stasi collaborator, especially since the parliamentary investigation was not yet concluded. According to the court, that sort of public statement directed to a specific case went beyond what was necessary for the purpose of reporting on the Stasi's structure and methods.[88] The court also disapproved Gauck's public remark that in some Länder—Saxony, for example—the information against Stolpe in the Stasi files would have been sufficient to remove him from office.[89] Such speculation also went beyond Gauck's authorized role.

Rights of personality were also stressed in a case from Halle, in which the citizens group New Forum made available at its office a list of 4,500 persons identified as Stasi informers. An individual on the list sued, and the court ordered that his name no longer be released. Although the plaintiff did have a dossier as a Stasi informant, it was not clear that he had actually undertaken that activity or had even agreed to do so. But even if he was an informant, the court would have issued the injunction: it might be permissible to expose a person's Stasi activity, but only after weighing the individual circumstances and the extent of the activity; that sort of weighing had not been undertaken with respect to the list. The court also found that making the list available violated the intent of the Stasi Records Law.[90]

Finally, two cases involving the GDR author Hermann Kant further illustrate the care with which the German courts are approaching publication of material derived from the Stasi files. Although Kant had been a strong supporter of the GDR regime and the president of the official writer's union, a court in Hamburg enjoined the magazine *Der Spiegel* from calling him a "helper of the Stasi." The available files did not provide adequate support for this conclusion, although a different question might have been posed if *Der Spiegel* had said he was *suspected* of such a role.[91] Thereafter, Kant also won a partial judgment against the GDR opposition poet, Reiner Kunze. In the book documenting his harassment by the Stasi, Kunze published a section of a Stasi file in which Kant was quoted as saying "that it was time to expel Kunze from the GDR." Kant denied that he had ever made that remark, and the court ordered that Kant's denial (along with the supporting testimony of a witness mentioned in the file) be included in further editions of the book.[92]

## Reactions and Proposals for Alteration of the Stasi Records Law

The profound social and personal distress evoked by the opening of the Stasi files has led some well-known figures in Germany to propose that the files be closed or even destroyed. For example, shortly after the opening of the files

Golo Mann, son of the great novelist Thomas Mann and himself an important German historian, indicated that the Stasi records should be destroyed or closed.[93] In contrast, a group of political figures from eastern Germany—some from the 1989 reform movement—issued a manifesto calling for the strengthening and expansion of the work of the Gauck office to enhance the examination of the Stasi files and to further the (at least temporary) exclusion of those who knowingly worked for the Stasi from positions of confidence in such central areas as law, medicine, politics, education, and the church.[94]

At the same time Peter-Michael Diestel, who had played a controversial role in the history of the files as GDR interior minister under de Maizière, re-entered the fray. Diestel defended the "unofficial collaborators" of the Stasi—many of whom, in Diestel's view, acted as "guarantors of internal peace." According to Diestel, the "pitiless witch hunt [arising from the opening of the Stasi files] is completely mistaken." Diestel argued that "unofficial collaborators" of the Stasi should not lose their jobs unless it could be shown that they actually betrayed individuals. Diestel also criticized Gauck's performance as director of the agency, and argued that de Maizière should be fully rehabilitated.[95] At a later point, Diestel regretted that more Stasi documents had not been destroyed and declared that all "politically capable East Germans are being destroyed" by the Stasi debate—a development that necessarily alienated East Germans from democracy.[96]

Indeed it seems likely that there will always be calls for the closing of the Stasi files—sometimes depending upon whose interests are affected at the moment. In November 1993, for example, Chancellor Kohl—apparently stung by information about western politicians that was emerging from the files—suggested that the files should be destroyed.[97] At about the same time, similar views were advanced by important members of the eastern SPD, such as Brandenburg Social Minister Regine Hildebrandt who complained that the files were being accorded undue weight and had been written by people who had an ax to grind.[98] Indeed, civil rights leader and SPD member Friedrich Schorlemmer proclaimed that the files should be consumed in a "fire of joy" at the beginning of 1996.[99]

These surprising proposals encountered a bitter reaction from some members of the former GDR opposition. Steffen Heitmann, justice minister of Saxony, declared that there would be an uprising in eastern Germany if the files were destroyed and indicated that destruction of the files would be a repudiation of the revolution of 1989.[100] Perhaps the most passionate response came from singer and writer Wolf Biermann, hero of the GDR opposition, whose expulsion from the country in 1976 marked an important stage of artistic repression in the GDR.[101] Declaring that the files should not be destroyed just because of the fears of a few western politicians, Biermann emphasized their historical importance and their significance for those who had been spied upon. In his own files, for example, Biermann found stolen or intercepted items such as correspondence of his parents and a forgotten poem he had written in the 1960s; in the file he also discovered that some citizens had resisted the state, and he also had the opportunity to learn about the organization of protests against his expulsion. "In these files are life documents of the victims [such as] private photos; there are also official [judicial] judgments which never reached the hands of the convicted persons, but now will be helpful in the victims' claims for rehabilitation and compensation."[102] All of these items, and much more, would be consumed in Schorlemmer's "fire of joy."

Proposals for the destruction of the Stasi files have apparently led to an increase in the number of citizens submitting applications to see their files. By July 1994 approximately 730,000 persons—most of them eastern citizens—had applied to examine their files, and the Gauck Agency had been able to satisfy about one-half of those requests. The administration of the remaining applications may proceed more quickly as the agency has essentially finished responding to 1.4 million requests from government agencies for Stasi files relating to persons applying for the public service.[103]

Yet these debates have had some parliamentary consequences. Indeed, furor over public release of Stasi files, and particularly over the publication of telephone transcripts of western politicians, led to an amendment of the Stasi Records Law in 1994. The original statute required any person who was in possession of Stasi files to notify the Gauck Agency and, in many cases, to surrender the material to the agency upon demand.[104] Although photocopies and other duplicates were generally included in this requirement, they were not covered by the section imposing a penalty on failure to deliver material to the agency.[105] The statute was therefore amended in summer 1994 to impose a penalty of up to DM 500,000 for a failure to surrender duplicates also.[106] This change may raise serious constitutional problems because it apparently requires surrender of journalists' transcriptions of the files and other copies possessed by journalists, editors, and researchers, whose materials ordinarily receive strong constitutional protection.[107] In another measure that may dampen journalistic investigation of Stasi material, the amendment increased the fees charged for examining and copying the files. This measure has been attacked as an unconstitutional infringement on the government's obligation to provide broad access to the files for journalists and scholars.[108]

## Reflections on the Stasi Files

The decision to preserve and open the Stasi files was one of the most controversial and important decisions made in the course of German unification. On the one side, it could be argued that the present legal use of the files constitutes yet another instrument through which the basic theoretical implications of article 23 GG are carried into reality—that is, another vehicle through which the political system and the general structure of the west has been transferred to the former GDR. Thus, an important use of the files has been to assist in the exclusion of eastern officials from the judiciary and the public service, including the universities. In addition to the use of the files for these official exclusions, the "unofficial" use of Stasi files through publicly discrediting important political and intellectual figures in the east may play a similar role. In this context, the cases of de Maizière and Stolpe, among the politicians, as well as Christa Wolf and Heiner Müller, among artists of the former GDR, are only the most noteworthy. Thus it could be argued that a major use of the files is to continue the disintegration and exclusion of the eastern intellectual elite, whose democratic but often socialist views were displeasing to the SED hierarchy but also do not seem to be particularly congenial to the prevailing doctrines of the Federal Republic.

Although this argument has some force, the problem cannot be resolved so simply. For one thing, it was not predominantly the prevailing figures of conservative politics in the Federal Republic who sought the broad opening and use of the Stasi files. In his negotiations on the Unification Treaty, for example, Interior Minister Wolfgang Schäuble sought stringent limits on the use of the files; indeed, he privately believed that it would not be a bad idea if the files could be destroyed. Rather, it was the citizens committees of the GDR reform movement which insisted that the files be preserved and that individual victims be granted broad access; and it was essentially these groups that achieved that end through demonstrations in January and in September 1990.

Moreover, the descendants of the GDR reform movement continue to be among the firmest supporters of the Gauck Agency and the continued preservation of the files. They also remain among the most vigorous advocates of extensive removal of individuals with Stasi and related affiliations from positions of responsibility in government and elsewhere in public life. In a dramatic expression of this general point of view, Education Minister Marianne Birthler, a veteran of the GDR reform movement and a member of Bündnis 90/Greens, resigned from the government of Manfred Stolpe in Brandenburg because of Stolpe's handling of revelations of his numerous contacts with the Stasi.[109]

Indeed, the position of the reformers themselves seems to involve some contradictions. Certainly, the extension of the old system of the Federal Republic to the east, through implications of article 23, perpetuates political and social structures that are inconsistent in important ways with the ideas of the Round Table constitutional draft, as embodied—to some extent at least—in the new constitutions of the eastern Länder.[110] On the other hand, however, the oppressions documented in the Stasi files obviously represent the residue of a rigid and tyrannical system. The use of the files to undo that past to the extent possible—by excluding persons who had participated in the tyrannical system from present positions of power—seemed to be viewed by the reformers as an essential step in liberation of the individual and society from the residue of past tyrannical hierarchy. This view seems to assume that the future should belong to those whose own reliance on freedom was such that they did not cooperate extensively with the former system; those who did cooperate would, in positions of power today, perpetuate psychological attitudes of obeisance that could inhibit the development of a new free society. But since there are not, by a substantial extent, enough reformers (or other eastern applicants with untainted pasts) to fill the positions vacated by those implicated in the SED regime, the necessary result is that many of these positions will be filled by western applicants and thus the personnel and attitudes of the west may be extended in the east as a result of the use of the Stasi files. But, more important and prior in the views of the reformers, apparently, is the extirpation of the residue of the past.

That is at least one point of view. It has the peculiar effect—seen in other aspects of recent history in the east—of creating an alliance between conservative politicians in the west and the reformers in the east on some questions.[111] The alliance is only an occasional and temporary one, however, for the views of these groups on what should occur in politics and society after the residue of tyrannical politics and "subject personalities" are removed from power in the east are of course quite different.

Moreover, the process of understanding one's personal past, potentially furthered for each Stasi victim who reads his or her file, can be seen as another act of liberation from the (largely unseen, if suspected) tyrannical forces that influenced many lives over decades. This effect is most likely to be revealed in the experiences of countless more or less ordinary citizens whose careers and lives were changed by a forgotten political remark or an unknowingly dangerous friendship. Yet this sort of retroactive self-understanding is also well documented in recent memoirs of more prominent GDR citizens—like the poet Reiner Kunze and novelist Erich Loest—who have gained access to their files and, for the first time, can perceive the extent of the governmental measures taken against them. Moreover an understanding of the way the Stasi operated, and the numerous collaborators that it attracted, may be important as an educational process in creating a stronger open and democratic personality among citizens.[112] For people emerging from societies that had been built on "forgetting" the atrocities of the past, a new beginning could not be appropriately made by perpetuating this fatal habit.

# PART III

# The External Constitution

CHAPTER 17

# The European Context of Unification and the Reserved Rights of the World War II Allies

## The European Context of Unification

For many of those deeply involved in the internal events of 1989–90, German unification may have seemed to be a particularly German affair, depending primarily on actions taken by the governments and the people of the Federal Republic and the GDR. Yet in reality the political conditions of unification required the participation of many nations and, even in the strictest legal sense, the merger of east and west did not depend upon actions taken under German law alone.

In general, Germany's European neighbors had a strong interest in the process of German unification—both as a result of historical memories and through legal relations created by the European Community and other international organizations. Moreover, the historical events that resulted in the division of Germany created rights in the victorious powers of World War II that qualified German sovereignty. The Allies retained a measure of authority to approve or disapprove of plans for unification and to settle the question of a united Germany's eastern border—the debated question of the Oder-Neiße line. Moreover, in the course of the Cold War, both German states had become essential parts of separate and hostile military alliances—NATO and the Warsaw Pact. Unification of the two German states, therefore, would also require adjustments of these relationships.

Indeed the international and constitutional issues of 1989–90 reflected concerns that had been present throughout the history of the West German state. From the beginning, the attitude of the Federal Republic to the world outside its borders had been characterized by two preoccupations. First, the Parliamentary Council in 1948 rejected the possibility that Germany would be permanently divided: accordingly unification was considered a primary goal of the Basic Law and, in a sense, the completion of its original task. On the other hand, the Federal Republic came into being in the international context of occupation and sponsorship by the western Allies. Its early history, therefore, was characterized by sustained attempts to find its own place in a developing west European order. Accordingly, the drafters of the Basic Law also made clear that the Federal Republic was to be part of a larger, united Europe to which Germany might transfer substantial sovereign authority. The conjunction of these two themes was nicely captured in the first sentence of the original preamble, which proclaimed the will of the German people "to protect its national and political unity and to serve world peace as an equal member of a united Europe."[1]

Thus, in a sense, the Basic Law contemplated two forms of unification: the "inner" unification of Germany itself and the "outer" unification of (at least western) Europe, in which Germany was to play a central role. During the course of the Federal Republic, substantial debate focused on the relationship of these two forms of unification. Some believed that the goal of western European integration, which seemed to require a hard line of economic and military defense against the eastern bloc, would interfere with the goal of inner unification; others feared that an undue desire for inner unification might detach the Federal Republic from its western allies and ultimately lead to the dissolution of western European structures. Ultimately, of course, these two forms of unification seemed to have been complementary rather than antagonistic: West Germany's stable integration in western Europe played an important role in the dissolution of the eastern bloc and German unification.

Yet, in the early days of the Federal Republic, the choice between "inner" and "outer" unification seemed particularly stark. It was Konrad Adenauer's basic choice—and by no means an uncontested choice—to pursue western integration first.[2] With singular prescience, Adenauer maintained that this process was not inconsistent with work toward German unification and that integration in the west would ultimately make German unification possible.[3]

In advocating the linkage of German and European integration, although with a somewhat different emphasis, Helmut Kohl was clearly a follower of Adenauer. Indeed, from the beginning of the process in late 1989, Kohl viewed German unification as inextricably linked with accelerated European integration. In his pivotal Ten-Point Plan of November 1989, Kohl declared that "the development of inner German relations remains embedded in the all-European process. . . . The future architecture of Germany must be adapted to the future architecture of all of Europe."[4] And on his return from the fateful meeting of February 1990, where Gorbachev assented to German unification in principle, Kohl noted the leaders' agreement "that the process of unification must remain embedded in a stable European framework," citing Adenauer's remark that "the German question can only be solved under a European roof."[5] Indeed, as the process of German unification accelerated during 1990, Kohl and French President Mitterrand pressed for the "deepening" of European integration that resulted in the Maastricht Accord. This position apparently responded to Kohl's fears that Germany's allies and neighbors would not accept a stronger unified Germany unless it was so embedded in European structures that it could not present an independent political, economic, or military threat. Perhaps Kohl was also animated by the lingering anxiety that—in reality, and not only in the imaginations of its neighbors—an autonomous Germany could indeed present some of these dangers.[6] In harboring such a view, Kohl would also have been a follower of Adenauer.

Viewed from one perspective, however, the position of the federal government on questions relating to the "outer" unification of Europe seemed to remain in some tension with its basic views on "inner" German unification. As earlier chapters have made clear, the process of German unification involved—to a very significant extent—the extension of prevailing western structures to eastern Germany, and those structures often tended to reflect rather conservative aspects of the western tradition. Among the characteristic elements of this conservative tradition might seem to be strong concepts of national sovereignty coupled with the assertion of a strong independent role in foreign affairs. Yet, the extension of conservative ideas *within* Germany seemed to be accompanied by Chancellor Kohl's drive toward the partial dissolution of national sovereignty in external affairs. So an internal insistence on conservative stability and the status quo coexisted with a policy of internationalism and, in many respects, the suppression of strong assertions of sovereignty abroad. But here, also, differing interpretations are possible. For example, a contrasting view—represented more widely in England and France than in Germany—held that the ultimate result of the deepening of European structures would not be to limit German independence, but rather would secure for Germany a leading or even hegemonic role in those expanded structures as well.

The European results of unification resemble the settlement of the Adenauer era in another important respect. Although the period of Cold War hostility was over, the East generally remained excluded from the more permanent aspects of the European unification, for the moment at least. The European security system sought by the Soviet Union—and considered of utmost importance by Eduard Shevardnadze in his memoirs—has not really begun to develop.[7] Moreover, the future role of central and eastern Europe in economic and political arrangements such as NATO and the European Union still remains uncertain.

## The Reserved Rights of the World War II Allies

In light of numerous European and international problems, the constitutional structures of German unification could not be created through internal agreement and "accession" alone. Therefore, at the same time that the Federal Republic and the GDR were negotiating the internal terms of unification in the first State Treaty and the Unification Treaty, the two German states were also negotiating certain external terms of unification with the World War II Allies in the so-called "Two Plus Four" talks. The Two Plus Four process concluded with a treaty among the two German states and the four Allied powers that resolved most remaining issues. Of these, the central problem—the problem that indeed controlled all of the others—was the question of the World War II Allies' reserved powers over German sovereignty and territory. The resolution of this question was a prerequisite in international law for the achievement of German unification.

The reserved rights of the Allies had their origin in actions taken in the last days of World War II. At the end of the war, the Allied armies completely occupied German territory, and any effective government ceased to exist upon the Germans' capitulation in May 1945. At that point, the Allies exercised full sovereignty over German territory. But the seeds of Germany's division were also sown in this period, because the sovereignty of the Allied occupation was not to be exercised in a totally uniform manner. Even before the end of the war, the Allies had agreed at the Yalta Conference that Germany would be temporarily divided into a separate occupation zone for each of the four victorious powers. A Control Commission of the Allied military commanders would exercise "[c]oordinated administration and control."[8]

Although substantial portions of these sovereign rights were eventually returned to the two German governments, the Allies retained certain residual rights up to the point of unification. Because the reserved rights were derived from an authority that pre-existed the founding of the Federal Republic and the GDR, those rights were probably superior to any governmental powers exercised by the two German states.

### *The Occupation and the Establishment of Allied Rights in Germany*

The original Allied rights of occupation were reflected in a declaration of the four victorious powers "regarding the defeat of Germany and the assumption of supreme authority with respect to Germany," issued in Berlin on June 5, 1945.[9] This declaration stated that, as a result of its unconditional surrender, "Germany has become subject to such requirements as may now or hereafter be imposed upon her." Because there was no German government capable of acting effectively under the circumstances, the Allies "hereby assume supreme authority with respect to Germany, including all the powers possessed by the German Government, the High Command and any state, municipal, or local government or authority."[10] The declaration made clear, however, that an annexation of German territory was not intended.[11]

The Berlin Declaration was followed by the Potsdam accord approved by Truman, Stalin, and Attlee on August 2, 1945, after a conference in the outskirts of Berlin.[12] For the succeeding four years of Allied occupation, the Potsdam protocol "was the most important document bearing on the German problem."[13] In the Potsdam accord, the Allies restated their assertions of full governmental power in Germany, noting that:

> [S]upreme authority in Germany is exercised on instructions from their respective Governments, by the Commanders-in-Chief of the armed forces [of the Allied powers], each in his own zone of occupation, and also jointly, in matters affecting Germany as a whole, in their capacity as members of the Control Council.[14]

According to the agreement, one of the purposes of the occupation was to "prepare for the eventual reconstruction of German political life on a democratic basis and for eventual peaceful cooperation in international life by Germany"[15]—and to this end the Allies contemplated the swift re-establishment of local self-government.[16]

At Yalta and Potsdam the Allies did not seem to contemplate the lasting partition of Germany although during the war they had discussed various plans for a permanent division. The use of the word "Germany" in the Potsdam accord seemed to assume the eventual re-establishment of a single country, and, for the purposes of the occupation, Germany was to be "treated as a single economic unit," notwithstanding its division into four separate zones.[17] Indeed, in an important speech, the American secretary of state noted that language in the Potsdam accord "only meant that no central government should be established until some sort of democracy was rooted in the soil of Germany and some sense of local responsibility developed."[18]

Contrary to the original expectations of the Allies, however, hostility and mistrust between the western and Soviet governments continued to harden. In two rancorous meetings of the foreign ministers in 1947, the Allies made little progress toward a peace treaty and failed to agree on such important issues as reparations from current production, border issues, and the centralized or federal nature of a future German government.[19]

As a prelude to the complete separation of west and east, the American and British occupation zones had joined together in late 1946 to create "Bizonia," a joint structure—eventually including administrative and political organs—for the regulation of economic matters.[20] Finally, after steadily worsening relations, the Allied Control Council ceased to function when the Soviet Military Commander and delegation withdrew in March 1948.[21] In June 1948 the Allies proceeded with a currency reform in the western zone, marking the effective division of Germany, and the Soviet blockade of Berlin followed almost immediately thereafter.[22] It was in this context that the initial drafts of the West German Basic Law were written in the summer of 1948.

Accordingly, the separate occupation zones developed in 1949 into two German states, marking one of the fundamental steps in the development of the Cold War. From an early point, the Allies had begun to exercise their occupation rights in a divided manner and, when those rights were partially relinquished, they were relinquished to two separate German states.

## *The Allies' Reserved Rights and the Creation of Two German States*

### RESERVED RIGHTS AND THE ADOPTION OF THE WEST GERMAN BASIC LAW

The western Allies carefully preserved their occupation rights in the process that led to adoption of the Basic Law. In the so-called "Frankfurt Documents," authorizing the convocation of a constituent assembly to draft the Basic Law, the western military governors set forth the general principles necessary for a German Constitution and made clear that they reserved the right to approve the constitution as well as any subsequent amendments.[23] Moreover, the Frankfurt Documents declared that even after a new German government was established, the military governors "reserve to themselves such powers as are necessary to ensure the fulfillment of the basic purpose of the Occupation."[24]

Indeed, the "Military Governors will resume their exercise of their full powers in an emergency threatening security, and if necessary to secure compliance with the constitutions or the occupation statute."[25] When the military governors approved the draft West German Constitution for submission to the states, they were to issue an "Occupation Statute" incorporating broad principles discussed among the military governors and the constituent assembly, so that the people "may understand that they accept the constitution within the framework of this occupation statute."[26]

The Frankfurt Documents evoked an ambivalent response from the governors of the West German Länder—in part because the adoption of a western constitution would confirm the break with the states in the Soviet zone.[27] Indeed, the German drafters decided to call the document a "Basic Law" instead of a "constitution" and succeeded in having it ratified by the state legislatures rather than by a popular vote. Both measures were intended to emphasize the temporary nature of the document and thus mitigate the permanence of the division of Germany.[28]

In their letter approving the Basic Law for submission to the states in May 1949, the western military governors reiterated that its adoption was to be subject to the provisions of the Occupation Statute.[29] The Occupation Statute, in turn, continued to reserve a number of crucial areas to the occupation authorities—including foreign affairs, foreign trade and exchange, disarmament, and reparations.[30] The Allies also reserved the right "to resume, in whole or in part, the exercise of full authority if [the occupation authorities] consider that to do so is essential to security or to preserve democratic government in Germany or in pursuance of the international obligations of their governments."[31] The military governors' letter of approval also qualified certain provisions of the Basic Law and reiterated the Allied position that Berlin could only have observers, not voting members, in the two houses of the West German parliament.[32]

## ALLIED RESERVED RIGHTS AND THE FOUNDING OF THE GDR

The process that led to the founding of the GDR followed a similar pattern. In October 1945, the Soviet military commander Zhukov empowered the provincial and Länder administrations in the Soviet zone to enact laws and exercise other governmental powers, "if they are not contrary to the laws and orders of the Control Council or the orders of the Soviet Military Administration."[33] Although the Länder of the Soviet zone adopted constitutions that were democratic in form,[34] political and economic developments in the eastern zone quickly assumed contours that were quite different from those of the west. In April 1946, for example, the German Communist Party (KPD) and the eastern Social Democratic Party (SPD) merged to form the SED which—as a Stalinist party of the "new type"—rapidly became the controlling force in the east German governments.[35]

In autumn 1949, shortly after the adoption of the first constitution of the GDR, the Soviet Military Administration was converted into the Soviet High

Commission with the function of overseeing the measures of the new government.[36] According to the Soviet "Declaration," the provisional administration of the German Democratic Republic could freely exercise its activity on the basis of the constitution of the German Democratic Republic, "so long as this activity does not violate the Potsdam decisions and the obligations that arise from the joint decisions of the four powers."[37]

### *The "General Treaty" and the Further Release of Sovereign Rights*

The great change in the occupation status of western Germany occurred in 1955 when the "General Treaty" between the western Allies and the Federal Republic came into force.[38] As one of the "Paris Treaties," this agreement was accompanied by a declaration accepting the Federal Republic as a member of NATO. In response to West German rearmament and entry into NATO, the Soviet Union established the Warsaw Pact in May 1955.[39]

The General Treaty declared the end of the occupation regime and lifted the Occupation Statute: as a result, the treaty announced, "[t]he Federal Republic shall have . . . the full authority of a sovereign State over its internal and external affairs."[40] But even though the treaty marked a crucial step in the extension of German sovereignty, the western Allies' relinquishment of authority was not complete. As a result of the international situation—which made unification of Germany impossible—the Allies "retain[ed] the rights and the responsibilities, heretofore exercised or held by them, relating to Berlin and to Germany as a whole, including the reunification of Germany and a peace settlement."[41]

It was this language—reserving rights relating to (a) Berlin, and (b) Germany as a whole, including questions of reunification and a peace settlement—that formed the basis of the occupation rights that the western Allies continued to hold up to the point of German unification. The rights relating to Berlin will be noted below; the rights with respect to "Germany as a whole" were interpreted (at least in the German literature) to include authority over the total geographical structure of the country—particularly the territorial extent of a unified Germany—but *not* to include internal political issues, such as the precise process by which unification would be achieved.[42]

The General Treaty contained two other provisions of lasting importance. In article 3 the Federal Republic pledged that its policy would conform to the principles of the United Nations Charter and to the goals set forth in the Statute of the Council of Europe.[43] The pledge to observe the principles of the United Nations was a continuation of the Allies' attempts to ensure that Germany would not again threaten aggressive war.[44] Of course, a parallel obligation of non-aggression, reflecting aspects of the Nuremberg judgment, was also explicitly written into article 26 of the Basic Law.

In another important provision of the General Treaty, all of the parties—including the Allies—pledged to pursue the goal of a "reunified Germany enjoying a liberal-democratic constitution, like that of the Federal Republic, and integrated within the European Community."[45] A number of German scholars argued that by agreeing to this language, the western Allies pledged *not* to use their reserved rights to deny consent to German unification if the stated conditions had been met. Under this theory, the western Allies in signing the General Treaty greatly limited their own discretion to deny approval for German unification.[46]

Also in 1954—before the final release of the General Treaty but in contemplation of its adoption—the Soviet Union issued a document recognizing the GDR's sovereign rights over "domestic and foreign affairs" and declaring that it would enter into the same relations with the GDR "as with other sovereign nations."[47] On the other hand, the Soviet Union retained those functions that related to the "guaranteeing of security" as well as functions that arose from the obligations growing out of the four-power agreements—including matters affecting Germany as a whole.[48] In this document, the Soviet Union attacked the western Occupation Statute as "one of the main obstacles" to German unification and, in reply, the western Allies denied that the Soviet Union had actually relinquished sovereignty to the GDR.[49]

By 1955, therefore, the Allies' reserved rights had assumed the contours that they would retain until they were finally relinquished pursuant to the Two Plus Four agreement among the Allies and the two German states.[50] Even before their relinquishment, however, some German commentators had raised a number of questions about the Allied reserved rights. Some suggested that these rights were not properly established in the first place. Another view was that occupation rights under international law could not remain in effect after the occupation forces had left. Since Berlin was the only part of Germany that remained theoretically subject to a true occupation, this argument would suggest that by the 1980s the Allies possessed no more occupation rights with respect to the unification of Germany, except for Berlin.[51] Others suggested that even if these rights had been properly established at the outset, their foundation in principles of self-defense had become obsolete and that they had been qualified by other principles and agreements of international law, such as the principle of self-determination and the Helsinki Final Act.[52]

But even though these questions were raised in the German literature, all practical political action of the German states and the four Allied powers proceeded from the premise that the Allied reserved rights were always valid and continued to be so—until their final relinquishment by agreement.

### *The Separate Status of Berlin*

With respect to the Allied reserved rights, as well as in many other areas, the legal status of Berlin raised special problems.[53] From the beginning, the Allies viewed Berlin as the former center of German political and military power and sought to reserve special rights over that area. Indeed, this view animated the western Allies' desire to occupy their own sections of Berlin, even though that city lay deep within the Soviet occupation zone.

Accordingly, when the western Allies began to contemplate the reconstitution of federal political authority in Germany, Berlin was in substantial respects excluded from the new political structure. During the deliberations over the Basic Law in 1948–49, the western Allies objected to the inclusion of West Berlin as a state of the Federal Republic, although they were willing to permit Berlin to send nonvoting observers to the federal parliament.[54] Article 23 of the Basic Law did list greater Berlin as a state of the Federal Republic, but article 144 declared that any state remaining under "limitations" may send (nonvoting) representatives to the German parliament. Accordingly, in their letter to the president of the Parliamentary Council approving the Basic Law, the western military commanders interpreted "the effect of [articles 23 and 144] as constituting acceptance of our previous request that while Berlin may not be accorded voting membership in the Bundestag or Bundesrat *nor be governed by the Federation* she may, nevertheless, designate a small number of representatives to attend the meetings of those legislative bodies."[55] This statement of the military commanders was generally taken as prohibiting the Federal Republic from exercising "governing" power in West Berlin—in order to preserve, in theory at least, the ultimate authority of the continuing occupation regime. Instead, actual political authority in Berlin was to be exercised by its own political organs, pursuant to its own constitution.

Berlin's first postwar constitution was adopted as a provisional document on August 13, 1946, and approved by the Allied Kommandatura, then composed of representatives of all four Allied powers.[56] In late 1948, however, Berlin was effectively divided into two separate parts when Soviet authorities refused to allow citizens of the Soviet zone to participate in Berlin city elections and refused to acknowledge the city assembly so elected.[57] Accordingly, in 1950 West Berlin adopted a new constitution to reflect this separate status. While this constitution was being drafted, the western military commanders made clear that the document would "require the express approval of the Allied Kommandatura before becoming effective."[58] Moreover, in accepting the Berlin constitution, the Allied Kommandatura (now composed of the three western commanders only) set aside provisions proclaiming that Berlin was a state of the Federal Republic of Germany and that the Basic Law and statutes of the Federal Republic were binding on Berlin. The Allied military commanders further required that another section be interpreted so that, during the transitional period, "Berlin [would] possess no characteristics of a twelfth state" of the Federal Republic. The West German Basic Law could prevail over contrary provisions of the Berlin Constitution, but a federal law would only apply if it was separately enacted by the legislature of Berlin.[59] Thus, the Allied view that Berlin remained occupied territory, and not an integral part of the Federal Republic, was maintained.

In subsequent years, the West Berlin government and the Federal Republic sought close relations—perhaps even closer than contemplated by the Allies.[60] The West Berlin legislature adopted federal laws as the law of Berlin and, after some hesitation, the Constitutional Court proclaimed that Berlin was indeed a state of the Federal Republic (although subject to certain Allied reserved rights) and began to exercise judicial review of certain classes of cases arising in Berlin.[61] In reaction to this creeping rapprochement, the Allied commanders in 1967 delivered a sharp note to Berlin officials, rejecting the Constitutional Court's decision in a case that had arisen in Berlin and reiterating their view that "Berlin is not to be regarded as a Land of the Federal Republic and is not to be governed by the Federation."[62] The Allied commanders stated their view that the Constitutional Court "does not have jurisdiction in relation to Berlin" and therefore could not review the constitutionality of actions of Berlin's officials or laws of Berlin—even those laws that incorporated federal legislation.[63]

In the General Treaty, in which the western Allies released a substantial degree of sovereignty to the Federal Republic, they retained rights over Berlin. Although a Four-Power Treaty with respect to Berlin in 1971, adopted in the general context of Chancellor Brandt's new eastern policy, had some effect in mitigating tensions,[64] Berlin remained a special focus of concern. On the western side, the Allies were assiduous in exercising their reserved rights in the city. For the east, the existence of West Berlin remained a continuing threat to the stability and political structure of the GDR: the presence of a major western city so close to the heart of the eastern regime—with increased possibilities of contacts between the divided populations—imperiled the sense of separateness and isolation fostered by the GDR regime after the construction of the Berlin Wall.[65]

In the Four-Power Treaty of 1971 the western powers agreed to a compromise on the status of Berlin, declaring that ties between West Berlin and the Federal Republic would be "maintained and developed," but also acknowledging that West Berlin would "continue not to be a constituent part of the Federal Republic of Germany and not to be governed by it."[66] Although the treaty was an important step in the developing eastern policy, its four-power nature—excluding both of the German states as signatories—emphasized the Allies' intention of retaining their claims with respect to Berlin. Certainly, it would be necessary for the Allies to release their rights with respect to Berlin, as well as those relating to Germany as a whole, if Berlin was to be included within the political structure of the country upon unification.

CHAPTER 18

# The Oder-Neiße Line and the Map of Central Europe

A NUMBER of additional issues affecting the status of Germany in international law were intimately related to the question of Allied reserved rights and to the underlying constitutional theory of unification. Of these, perhaps the most sensitive was the bitterly debated subject of the western border of Poland, the so-called Oder-Neiße line. This issue arose from the history of the last days of World War II, although it had an even more remote background.

During the Weimar period, the map of central Europe looked significantly different than it did after World War II. In addition to the territory that later became the Federal Republic and the GDR, Germany included two substantial areas farther to the east.[1] The first of these was territory adjacent to the present eastern border of Germany, including the province of Silesia and parts of Pomerania and Brandenburg—a region approximately the same size as the GDR. Even farther to the east—and separated from the rest of Germany by the "Polish Corridor" created by the Treaty of Versailles—was a large enclave of German territory bordering on Poland and Lithuania, containing parts of East Prussia and the important city of Königsberg.

At the end of World War II the Soviet Army occupied these eastern territories, and the Soviet Union annexed the northern part of East Prussia including Königsberg, which became Kaliningrad. It also annexed the eastern portion of Poland—the territory lying east of the so-called "Curzon Line"—representing almost one-half of the area of that country as it had existed before World War II; the Soviet annexation of eastern Poland was ratified by the Allies at the Yalta Conference with the understanding that Poland would be compensated for this loss by "substantial accessions of territory in the north and west."[2]

The territory "in the north and west" that was adjacent to Poland was territory in the eastern part of pre-war Germany. At the Potsdam Conference, therefore, the previously German territory east of a line formed by the Oder and the Western Neiße Rivers—comprising Silesia and parts of Pomerania, Brandenburg, and East Prussia—was placed under Polish "administration" pending a final settlement at a future peace conference.[3] Although this declaration was provisional, the understanding at Yalta that Poland would receive territory in compensation for regions annexed by the Soviet Union indicates that the transfer of at least a part of this territory was expected to be final. Indeed, both President Roosevelt and Prime Minister Churchill had proposed at Yalta that significant amounts of German territory be transferred to Poland.[4] No final agreement could be reached on this point, however, because the western Allies were unwilling to extend the German-Polish border as far west as the Western Neiße River, the border sought by the Soviet delegation.[5] The

Potsdam Conference also agreed in principle to the transfer of Königsberg and part of East Prussia to the Soviet Union, and the American president and British prime minister pledged to support this settlement at a future peace conference.[6]

Because of the increasing tensions of the Cold War, which followed almost immediately after the conclusion of hostilities in Europe, the peace conference contemplated at Potsdam was never held.[7] Thus it remained open to German governments to maintain that some or all of the regions placed under Polish "administration" at Potsdam were still German territory and should be returned to Germany at a final peace conference or otherwise.[8] Indeed in the first two decades of the Federal Republic this claim constituted a cornerstone of West German foreign policy.[9] Moreover, this position received significant political support from large groups of "expellees" (*Vertriebene*)—German-speaking persons who were expelled or who fled from the former German territories east of the Oder-Neiße line when these territories were transferred to Polish control at the end of World War II.[10] Nonetheless, by the 1980s it seemed clear to most—including most German politicians—that this was one result of World War II that was not to be undone[11] and, as discussed below, treaties entered into by the West German government in 1970 had apparently conceded the permanence of the Polish and Russian borders.

Yet in a series of bizarre episodes in the course of unification discussions, Chancellor Kohl refused to relinquish unconditionally all claims to the former German territory east of the Oder-Neiße line.[12] Many believed that Kohl was principally seeking to prevent the ranks of the expellees from leaving the CDU en masse for some alternative further to the right.[13] In any case western leaders, among others, were deeply troubled by Kohl's refusal to take an unambiguous position relinquishing these long-lost lands.[14] Perhaps indeed, as some surmised, "Kohl's behavior on Poland . . . revealed the beginning of a new style in foreign policy which was less encumbered by the weight of the past and more inclined to demonstrate and use the weight of German power."[15]

Yet Kohl's argument, oddly, also had a constitutional background.[16] To understand this background and to understand the role that these territories played in the constitutional theory of unification, it is necessary to return to article 23 of the Basic Law, the provision under which the GDR acceded to the Federal Republic.

Article 23—it will be recalled—declared that at the outset the Basic Law was to cover the specified original Länder of the Federal Republic. The provision then went on to state that in "other parts of Germany, [the Basic Law] will be put into effect after their accession." The GDR constituted "another part" of Germany under this provision—as did the Saarland, which acceded to the Federal Republic in 1957.[17] An important question, however, was whether the GDR and the Saarland constituted all of the "other parts" of Germany mentioned in article 23, or whether there were yet other regions that at least theoretically might accede under article 23. Specifically, did the former German territories lying east of the Oder-Neiße line constitute "other parts" of Germany that could accede to the Federal Republic under article 23?

Apparently the prevailing response of the German constitutionalists to this question was yes.[18] Neither article 23 nor any other constitutional provision defines the term "Germany" for the purposes of the Basic Law; it was not entirely clear, therefore, what was to be included within the other parts of Germany. Certainly the concept of "Germany" had some clear limitations; it did not include, for example, parts of the 1871 German Empire that had been ceded to Poland by the Treaty of Versailles in 1919 in a manner clearly recognized by international law. On the other hand, article 116(1) of the Basic Law, in defining the concept "German person," refers to the "territory of the German Empire [Reich] as of December 31, 1937," and a number of authors took the position that "Germany" for the purposes of article 23 also included this territory.[19] The borders of December 31, 1937, encompassed the territory of Germany as it existed after World War I—before the occupation of Austria and the Czech "Sudetenland" in 1938 and other aggressive territorial expansions of the Nazi regime.[20] Under this view, therefore, the "other parts of Germany" referred to in article 23 included the former German territory east of the Oder-Neiße line.

On the other hand, by the 1970s both German governments had recognized the Oder-Neiße line as the western border of Poland. In the Warsaw Declaration of June 1950—followed by the more formal Görlitz Treaty a month later—the provisional government of the GDR recognized the Oder-Neiße line, as described in the Potsdam agreement, as the permanent border between Poland and Germany.[21] In a bitter reaction, a majority of the West German Bundestag (excluding representatives of the Communist Party) condemned the Warsaw Declaration, arguing that the territory in question remained a part of Germany and that, under the Potsdam agreement, Poland only exercised "temporary administration" over that territory. The Bundestag also declared that the "so-called provisional government" of the GDR was in fact acting on behalf of the Soviet Union in "shameful bondage" to a foreign power.[22] The western Allies vigorously rejected the Görlitz agreement as well.[23]

The position of the Federal Republic in 1950 reflected the tensions of the Cold War, but that rather rigid posture was relaxed in the late 1960s. This process of accommodation, which had begun under the Grand Coalition of 1966–69, culminated in the new "eastern policy" (Ostpolitik) adopted by the SPD government of Willy Brandt.[24] In two cornerstones of this policy, the Moscow and Warsaw Treaties of 1970, the government of the Federal Republic recognized the Oder-Neiße line. According to the Moscow Treaty—entered into between the Federal Republic and the Soviet Union—the parties "consider as inviolable, today and in the future, the borders of all states in Europe as they exist on the day of the signing of this Treaty, including the Oder-Neiße line which forms the western border of the People's Republic of Poland."[25] Moreover, under the Warsaw Treaty between the Federal Republic and Poland, the parties declared that the Oder-Neiße line formed the western border of Poland, confirmed the inviolability of existing borders, pledged unrestricted observance of each other's territorial integrity, and declared that they had no present or future claims to each other's territory.[26]

Unqualified as this language may have seemed, however, it was not certain that the Federal Republic possessed the authority to settle this question definitively. Indeed, both the Moscow and Warsaw Treaties made clear that they did not affect earlier international agreements; moreover both treaties were accompanied by a note of the Federal Republic explicitly pointing out that no agreement of the Federal Republic could affect the reserved rights of the four occupation powers. Since the question of the Oder-Neiße line remained open in the Potsdam and other four-power agreements pending a final peace settlement, these provisions (and accompanying notes) suggest that the four occupation powers retained authority to make adjustments of the western Polish border—regardless of anything contained in agreements between the Federal Republic and the Soviet Union and Poland.[27]

Moreover, even without fully relying on the reserved rights of the Allies, some German authors argued that the Oder-Neiße territory could not be effectively relinquished before unification of the Federal Republic and the GDR, even by vote of both German parliaments. Apparently, this was the position originally adopted by Chancellor Kohl.[28] According to this argument, the Federal Republic and the GDR represented only parts of the "entire" German state—the continuing "Reich" of western constitutional theory—and the parts could not act on behalf of the "Reich" in relinquishing its territory. Only the parliament of a united Germany could effectively undertake this task.[29] This position may seem inconsistent with the claims of the Federal Republic that it represented the entire German state in other instances.[30]

In any case, as part of the general settlement upon unification—which would also include relinquishment of the Allies' reserved rights—it was to be expected that these vestigial German claims to long-lost territory would also be definitively relinquished. Certainly the Soviet government would insist on this action. Accordingly, in votes that accompanied the adoption of the first State Treaty, both the West German Bundestag and the East German Volkskammer enacted resolutions confirming the Oder-Neiße line as the western border of Poland.[31]

But even these two resolutions, for all of their moral force, would not have been sufficient to concede this territory definitively under the German constitutionalists' theory. In any case, for its greater security, the government of Poland insisted on a separate treaty confirming the Oder-Neiße line. The World War II Allies strongly supported Poland's position, and the Polish government was invited to present its views at the Two Plus Four discussions. At first, Poland insisted that such a treaty be signed before German unification, but at the Two Plus Four conference in Paris on July 17, 1990—a meeting at which it was obliged to make a number of concessions—the Polish government indicated that it would accept a treaty approved by the all-German parliament after unification.[32] In light of the German constitutional theory of the continuing "Reich," this was in any event the safer course because ratification by the all-German parliament satisfied the requirement of approval by the unified German government.

In any case, when the Polish-German Border Treaty was ultimately ratified in 1991,[33] this persisting problem of World War II was finally resolved as a legal issue—although it had clearly left a legacy of bitterness among some groups in Germany. Although the conservatives generally prevailed in the main issues surrounding unification, this is one area in which they were required to defer to unanimous international opposition. Kohl was correct in referring to the relinquishment of the eastern territories as a price that had to be paid for unification. More positively perhaps, the German agreement—reluctant and delayed as it was—could be viewed as emblematic of the moderation of German national views by the views of the larger European and international community.

CHAPTER 19

# NATO and the Pact System

THE INTERNATIONAL status of Germany was affected not only by events occurring before the establishment of the two German states, but also by international treaties entered into by those states. Indeed, to a significant extent the international role of the two German states was characterized by their membership in two different, and opposing, military and political alliances.

As part of its task of establishing the Federal Republic as an "equal member of a united Europe,"[1] the Basic Law contemplated that the Federal Republic might not only become part of a European political or economic community, but could also join an organization providing for a collective military defense. This authority seems to be derived from article 24(2), which provides that

> the Federal Government can be included in a system of mutual collective security, for the purpose of preserving peace; it will thus agree to the limitation of its sovereign rights for the purpose of establishing and assuring a peaceful and lasting order in Europe and among the peoples of the world.

Yet according to the initial view of the Constitutional Court, authority to join a western military alliance actually flowed from article 24(1)—also employed to authorize participation in the European Community—which simply allows the Federal Republic, acting through a statute, "to transfer sovereign rights to international organizations."[2] It was only after unification, in an important case decided in 1994, that the Court finally held that German membership in NATO was also authorized by article 24(2) GG.[3]

In 1955 the Federal Republic first exercised its authority to join alliances by becoming a member of the North Atlantic Treaty Organization (NATO) after a bruising internal dispute over rearmament.[4] The agreement admitting the Federal Republic to NATO was issued simultaneously with the "General Treaty" in which the western Allies returned a substantial measure of sovereignty to the Federal Republic. Among other things, the General Treaty lifted the Occupation Statute, which had reserved questions of the Federal Republic's foreign policy to the Allies.[5] Thus at the moment in which the Federal Republic regained control over its foreign affairs it also became a member of NATO; through this arrangement, the Allies assured that there would be no period in which Germany would have a truly independent military force. Accordingly, the inclusion of Germany in NATO strengthened the western alliance but did so in a manner that minimized the possible dangers of German rearmament.[6]

The creation of NATO required difficult adjustments of views in a number of countries. Although the alliance could be seen as an outgrowth of the

Marshall Plan of 1947—further strengthening the West European political system through a military pact—it represented a fundamental change in American foreign policy, which previously had sought to avoid "entangling alliances." Similarly, the rearmament of West Germany necessary for its participation in the NATO structure also required substantial changes of views in Great Britain and in France.[7]

The Soviet Union responded to the rearming of the Federal Republic, and its inclusion in NATO, by forming the Warsaw Pact in May 1955, and the GDR became a charter member.[8] By 1955, therefore, the two German states had become parts of a pact system that reflected the division of Europe into two hostile military blocs, perhaps the most visible manifestation of the Cold War.[9] Thus, over the years, the armies of both German states became essential aspects of military planning on both sides of the Cold War. Although both pacts conducted elaborate military exercises, NATO did not actually engage in any military action during the Cold War period. The armies of the Warsaw Pact, in contrast, participated in the invasion of Czechoslovakia in 1968, although this action was directed against supposed internal rather than external "enemies." Similarly, Erich Honecker urged an invasion of Poland in the early 1980s to suppress the nascent Solidarity movement—this time in vain.[10]

By the time that German unification became a real possibility in 1990, however, the Warsaw Pact had lost much of its effectiveness. With the revolutionary changes in the governments of Poland, Hungary, and Czechoslovakia in 1989–90, it seemed most unlikely that forces of those countries would take part in planning significant military exercises with the Soviet Union in the future.[11] Therefore, any remaining obligations of the GDR to the Warsaw Pact were not a serious impediment to unification. Although the GDR's membership in the Warsaw Pact would probably have ended automatically upon its accession to the Federal Republic,[12] the GDR formally withdrew from the pact a few days before unification.[13] Subsequently, of course, the Warsaw Pact dissolved its military alliance and then—even before the dissolution of the Soviet Union—went out of existence completely.[14]

The real problems for unification raised by the vestiges of the pact system surrounded the issue of a united Germany's future membership in NATO. It seemed certain from the outset that the political leadership of the Federal Republic would insist that a united Germany remain a member of NATO.[15] In any case, the American government had made it clear in late 1989, through statements of President Bush and Secretary of State Baker, that continued German membership in NATO was a firm requirement for American approval of German unification.[16] Indeed, "for the west, Germany's continued membership in NATO constituted . . . the cornerstone of the new European order that was to arise parallel to German unification."[17] Moreover, other countries, including some former east bloc nations such as Poland, also strongly advocated that a united Germany remain in NATO.[18] In part at least, these views reflected anxiety over the possible military role that a "neutral"—but not disarmed—Germany might play without the restraint of being embedded in the western security system.

With respect to the NATO Treaty itself, German unification presented few serious problems. Since the GDR was to join the Federal Republic under article 23 of the Basic Law, no additional state would be joining the NATO alliance; rather, an expanded Federal Republic would continue on as a member of the alliance under the principle of "moving treaty boundaries."[19]

For the Soviet Union, on the other hand, this was unquestionably the most difficult problem of German unification.[20] Shevardnadze called it the "question of questions" and Soviet conservatives applied constant pressure on the government to avoid concessions on this—as on the other—issues of unification.[21] Also for many of the reform groups in the GDR, the NATO alliance and the entire bloc system remained deeply problematic. The GDR Round Table, for example, rejected the idea that Germany should remain in NATO and advocated a demilitarized status instead.[22]

The vigorous Soviet opposition to NATO membership for united Germany raised very serious difficulties. The Soviet position was apparently based less on a calculation of international advantages and disadvantages than on domestic political considerations. If a united Germany was to join NATO—with a concomitant withdrawal of Soviet forces from the territory of the former GDR—it might seem that the Soviet participation in the victory in World War II had gone for naught: no more Soviet troops would be occupying Germany, and the territory of the Soviet Union's former ally, the GDR, would henceforth be included in an alliance that the Soviet Union had always seen as directed against itself.[23]

For a substantial period, therefore, the Soviet government refused to agree to NATO membership for a united Germany, implying that it would invoke its reserved rights over Germany as a whole in order to prevent unification if NATO membership for the united Germany was to remain a possibility. Subsequently—apparently as part of a gradual process of retreat from its original view—the Soviet Union suggested that a united Germany could remain a member of both alliances, a proposal that met with unanimous rejection in the west.[24]

From a practical point of view, the problem seemed particularly serious because the Soviet Union had 380,000 troops stationed in the GDR—the largest contingent of Soviet troops outside the Soviet Union.[25] The continued presence of these troops in eastern Germany evoked substantial tensions with the local population. But immediate withdrawal was not a practical possibility: the Soviet Union could not afford the expense of moving the troops, nor could it house them if they returned immediately.

The Soviet government's ultimate acquiescence in NATO membership for a united Germany must be viewed in the context of the groundbreaking "London Declaration" issued by the NATO heads of state and government on July 6, 1990.[26] Resting on earlier indications by NATO leaders that the alliance must undergo important changes in concept and strategy, the Declaration indicated that NATO would be transformed from an alliance confronting the Warsaw Pact into a group that sought to cooperate with the countries of eastern Europe.[27] The signatories emphasized the defensive nature of NATO and urged that the Warsaw Pact join them in reaffirming the peaceful principles of the United Nations Charter and the Helsinki Final Act adopted by the Conference on Security and Cooperation in Europe (CSCE). In other important passages, the Declaration also invited Soviet President Gorbachev to address the NATO Council, requested the Soviet Union and the countries of eastern Europe to "establish regular diplomatic liaisons with NATO," and announced moves designed to reduce the threatening military posture of NATO.[28] At a subsequent press conference, President Bush acknowledged the Soviet Union's fears with respect to NATO and expressed the hope that the London Declaration would allay these fears, with the result that the Soviet Union might accept the concept of a united Germany as a member of NATO.[29]

The London Declaration was issued during the 28th (and final) Party Congress of the Communist Party of the Soviet Union, which took place in July 1990. At this meeting, critical party members bitterly attacked Gorbachev's foreign policy and deplored "the loss of our allies in eastern Europe."[30] In response, Foreign Minister Shevardnadze was able to hail NATO's London Declaration as an important action moving toward stability in Europe.[31] At the conclusion of the meeting, the delegates rejected the critics' challenge and approved Gorbachev's foreign policy. This was a great victory for the president and made further developments in the "new thinking" possible.[32]

The London Declaration and Gorbachev's victory at the Party Congress thus prepared the way for a decisive turn in Soviet policy. On July 15 and 16, 1990—little more than a week after the London Declaration was issued—Chancellor Kohl and President Gorbachev met in Moscow and in the Caucasus Mountains and, at the conclusion of their meetings, announced an agreement through which the Soviet Union would allow a united Germany to enter NATO.[33]

Although the agreement was basically favorable to Germany, it also contained concessions to Soviet concerns. First, and most important, united Germany could choose the alliance to which it would belong, and Chancellor Kohl made clear that that choice would be NATO. On the other hand, Soviet troops would be allowed to remain in eastern Germany during a period of gradual withdrawal that would last from three to four years after unification.[34] The latter agreement, together with related financial arrangements, would greatly ease the overwhelming practical problems of a precipitate Soviet withdrawal.

Moreover, as long as Soviet troops remained in the former GDR during the period of withdrawal, the jurisdiction of NATO would not be extended to this area and no NATO forces could be stationed there. Yet this condition was qualified in two respects. First, the provisions of articles 5 and 6 of the NATO

Treaty—providing for collective defense of any NATO member against attack—would extend to the territory of the former GDR upon unification.[35] Thus, in the event of an attack by a non-NATO member upon this territory, NATO forces presumably *could* intervene in eastern Germany even while Soviet troops remained there. Second, units of the German army that had not become part of NATO—so called "units of territorial defense"—would be permitted to enter eastern Germany immediately after unification and also could be stationed in Berlin.[36] Although Chancellor Kohl's communiqué expressly excluded the "NATO structures" from the former GDR only during the three to four years of the Soviet troop withdrawal, Gorbachev at the same press conference indicated that this territory would remain free of "other foreign troops" even after the Soviet withdrawal, and Kohl subsequently confirmed this point.[37]

As long as Soviet forces remained in eastern Germany, troops of the three western Allies could remain in Berlin.[38] This provision was obviously intended as a sort of quid pro quo: so long as Soviet troops "occupied" a portion of the newly unified and sovereign Germany, they could be balanced by remaining western occupation forces in Berlin. Upon the final Soviet withdrawal, however, these western occupation units would have to leave. (On the other hand, army units of the western Allies would doubtless remain in Germany—outside of the territory of the former GDR—to the extent that they constitute NATO troops stationed there.)

The Kohl-Gorbachev agreement contained two other points clearly intended to quiet Soviet anxieties. In the Vienna negotiations over reduction of conventional forces, the Federal Republic would declare itself ready to reduce its military strength to 370,000 troops within three to four years after the effective date of the first Vienna Treaty. Moreover, the German government would promise not to manufacture, possess, or control atomic, biological, or chemical weapons, and would promise to remain bound by the nuclear nonproliferation treaty.[39]

Given the geopolitical realities of the period—particularly the economic and political weakness of the Soviet Union that was already manifest in 1990—this agreement seems to be balanced and well conceived. It did not force the Russians into an economically damaging immediate troop withdrawal and, to some extent at least, it allayed other Soviet concerns.

Yet the agreement raised a number of questions. Most obviously, for example, the agreement seemed to make dispositions of western Allied troops in Germany—as well as German NATO troops—without consultation with the western Allies. As was the case months earlier when Kohl initiated the unification process with the announcement of his Ten-Point Plan, some irritation was expressed among the western Allies about the unilateral nature of Kohl's actions.[40] More generally, the results of this bilateral meeting preordained the final Two Plus Four settlement, and not all western leaders were pleased with this result. President Bush, for example, was somewhat annoyed by this turn of events[41]—concerned perhaps that this could be a forerunner of other bilateral German-Soviet agreements that might not be so agreeable to the west. In any event, this independent process was likely to be a harbinger of things to come, as a "sovereign" Germany began to make an increasing number of fundamental decisions on its own, albeit within the framework of the western alliance and the European Community.

CHAPTER 20

# The Two Plus Four Treaty and the Legal Status of Germany

THE PRINCIPAL open questions relating to the status of Germany in international law were largely resolved in the Treaty on the Final Settlement with Respect to Germany, signed by the four World War II Allies and the two German states on September 12, 1990, at the conclusion of the Two Plus Four discussions.[1] In these negotiations, the principal parties were the Federal Republic on one side and the Soviet Union on the other—although the United States, through its strong support of unification, was also an important participant.[2] The government of the GDR, in this as in other negotiations, was largely guided by the Federal Republic, and its occasional attempts to assert an independent position were generally futile.[3] The British and French governments would probably have preferred to delay or prevent German unification, but they were ultimately constrained to suppress their disapproval rather than disrupt relations within the western alliance.[4]

## THE NEGOTIATION OF THE TWO PLUS FOUR TREATY

Although some had suggested at the outset that the external questions of unification should be settled by a meeting of the Allies without German participation, the West German government was anxious to avoid a "peace conference" from which Germany would be excluded or appear in a subordinate role.[5] Throughout the process, Chancellor Kohl strongly objected to Germany's being presented as the object of subordination or "discrimination" on the part of the other powers. Moreover, the German government feared that an actual peace conference—which might involve multiple demands for reparations and include the dozens of nations that opposed Germany in World War II—could seriously delay the process of unification.[6] The Soviet Union had at first sought a formal peace treaty, but ultimately decided not to press this point. Indeed, Germany's western allies in NATO and the European Community might have found it embarrassing suddenly to have to sit across the table from Germany again, "as victor and vanquished."[7]

The process of negotiating the Two Plus Four Treaty had begun in February 1990, but by the summer of that year the negotiations faced a number of important deadlines and resulting pressures of time.[8] First, the West German government was adamant that the external issues of unification be resolved along with the internal issues, in time for all-German elections before the end of 1990. The government sharply rejected a procedure, such as that suggested by the Soviet Union, in which the external questions would be "uncoupled" and resolved after internal unification had been achieved. Second, because the Two Plus Four agreement was to be embedded in the larger structure of the Conference on Security and Cooperation in Europe (CSCE), the signed agreement would have to be ready for presentation at the CSCE summit in November 1990.[9] Third, and more generally, the Kohl government was anxious to conclude the agreement while President Gorbachev was still in office; in light of internal and external Soviet problems in the summer of 1990, the duration of his tenure seemed highly uncertain. Accordingly, the Two Plus Four Treaty was completed in a hectic flurry of activity in late summer 1990 after the meeting between Kohl and Gorbachev in the Caucasus had provided the ultimate key.[10]

This important treaty—which can be viewed as the legal conclusion of World War II in Europe—effectively settled the issues of German sovereignty, the Oder-Neiße line, and the membership of a united Germany in NATO. In the agreement, the Federal Republic obtained Allied—principally Soviet—agreement to its position on the remaining issues of German legal status. The Allies would completely relinquish their remaining reserved rights over Berlin and Germany as a whole, thus basically according Germany the same sovereignty as any other western European nation. Moreover, this united Germany would be permitted to be a member of NATO and, as a result, Soviet forces would completely withdraw from the former territory of the GDR over a period of years.

In return for these crucial concessions, the Soviet Union received effective confirmation of the Oder-Neiße line, as well as agreement on a number of other important points. Indeed, the Two Plus Four Treaty (as well as its predecessor, the Kohl-Gorbachev declaration) can be viewed as an attempt to allay Soviet fears through a carefully devised series of concessions—some of them actually protecting the security of the Soviet Union, and others serving as face-saving devices for the Soviet government. The structure of the agreement, which emphasized provisions designed for the security of the Soviet Union and Poland, seemed clearly designed to have this rhetorical force.

Yet if the treaty was designed to emphasize points favorable to the Soviet Union, it was obvious that the agreement embodied significant Soviet concessions, measured by the positions that it had asserted earlier in 1990.[11] Indeed, the final agreement reflected the drastic erosion of Soviet power that had taken place during 1990. In early 1990, the Soviet Union was still counted as a great power, and some in the Soviet Union still retained the view that the Soviet government could dictate the terms of unification.[12] But during 1990 a deepening economic crisis progressively weakened the Soviet position; indeed, in May 1990 the Soviet government's solvency became dependent on loans advanced by West German banks and guaranteed by the government of the

Federal Republic—a development that naturally played its role in the respective power relationships in the treaty negotiations.[13] By the end of the year, the German government was sending tons of food and other provisions to the Soviet Union to allay widespread suffering.[14]

## The Two Plus Four Treaty: Structure and Content

In the preamble of the Two Plus Four Treaty, the signatories noted that Europe has lived in peace since 1945 and that recent changes in Europe have allowed the division of the continent to be overcome.[15] In a tone reminiscent of the Basic Law,[16] the preamble also invoked the principles of the United Nations and the Helsinki Final Act. In a passage that reflected NATO's London Declaration of July 1990, the signatories also declared that they were ready to cease viewing each other as opponents and to work toward a relationship of trust and cooperation. In light of these factors—and because of German unification on a democratic and peaceful basis—"the rights and responsibilities of the Four Powers relating to Berlin and to Germany as a whole" have lost their previous function.

After this general introduction, the treaty itself began with a resolution of those issues that were most important to the security of the Soviet Union, particularly the issue of the Oder-Neiße line. Article 1 declared that united Germany will consist of the territories of the Federal Republic, the German Democratic Republic, and Berlin, that these borders are final, and that confirmation of the permanence of these borders is essential for peace in Europe. Moreover, "united Germany has no territorial claims whatsoever against other states and shall not assert any in the future,"[17] and united Germany and Poland will confirm their present border in a treaty binding under international law.[18]

To make this point even more clearly, the Two Plus Four agreement went on to require that the constitution of a united Germany exclude any provision that would be contrary to these principles.[19] Specifically, this section required amendment or deletion of the preamble of the Basic Law (foreseeing future unification), article 23 (allowing "accession" of "other parts of Germany"), and article 146 (also foreseeing future steps for unification). At the time this agreement was signed, the Unification Treaty had already required deletion of article 23 and amendment of the preamble and article 146 in an appropriate manner, but it was clear that these provisions had been inserted in the Unification Treaty to comply with the wishes of the Allies.[20] In any case, the signing of the Two Plus Four Treaty required united Germany to retain the principle of these changes permanently. Any future amendment seeking to revert to the previous provisions of the Basic Law would be a violation of a treaty obligation binding in international law.[21]

Thus, in these interesting provisions, the two German states agreed that when they became united, their joint constitution would conform to certain principles. Yet this was not the only section of the treaty in which the Allies sought assurance that the constitution of a united Germany would contain specified provisions. In article 2, the German states declared that "only peace will emanate from German soil," and noted that "[a]ccording to the constitution of the united Germany, acts tending to and undertaken with the intent to disturb the peaceful relations between nations, especially to prepare for aggressive war, are unconstitutional and a punishable offence." This is almost a word-for-word quotation of article 26(1) of the Basic Law, and article 2 of the treaty accordingly ensures that this provision will remain in any future German constitution. In article 2 the two German states also declared that a united Germany will not use weapons except in accordance with its own constitution and the Charter of the United Nations; of course, article 2(4) of the UN Charter imposes very strict limitations on any nation's employment of "the threat or use of force."[22] Thus, even though a united Germany has theoretically become "sovereign," the signatory Allied powers have extraordinary rights under international law to ensure that the provision referred to in article 2 of the treaty remain in the constitution of the new united Germany and that this provision be observed.[23]

Article 3 of the treaty contained additional important measures of security for the Soviet Union. Article 3, section 1 declared that a united Germany would continue to renounce the manufacture, possession, and control of nuclear, biological, and chemical weapons[24] and that the rights and duties of the Treaty on the Non-Proliferation of Nuclear Weapons would also apply to united Germany.[25] This provision represented a concession on the part of Germany; the Kohl government had originally resisted provisions of this kind on the ground that they treated Germany unequally and discriminatorily in comparison with the other states in the Two Plus Four negotiations.[26] On the other hand, the Soviet Union had originally proposed an even stricter provision prohibiting weapons based on "new physical principles" (in addition to nuclear, biological, and chemical weapons) and also banning the stationing on German soil of any prohibited weapons in addition to banning German manufacture, possession, or control of those weapons.[27]

In another significant provision, the Two Plus Four Treaty noted that in the Vienna negotiations on conventional forces in Europe, the Federal Republic had declared its commitment to reduce its forces to a maximum of 370,000 troops.[28] The result of this provision was that the unified Germany would make a 40 percent reduction in troop strength because the previous West German Army (Bundeswehr) totaled 495,000 troops and the People's Army (NVA) of the GDR, which was to be merged with the Bundeswehr under the Unification Treaty, had a strength of 170,000.[29] In the negotiations Kohl pointed out that this was the greatest reduction of conventional forces that a modern state has undertaken in recent years.[30]

This was a crucial provision for the Soviet Union, which saw the reduction of German troops as important in rendering Germany's continued membership in NATO palatable.[31] Indeed, the limitation of German troops played a significant role in ultimately persuading the Soviet Union to agree to the continued membership of Germany in NATO.[32]

The limitation of German forces reflected a principle already adopted in the Kohl-Gorbachev agreement of July 1990,[33] and articles 4, 5, and 6 of the Two Plus Four Treaty essentially developed certain other provisions of that agreement. Article 4 contemplated that a united Germany would enter into a treaty with the Soviet Union relating to the withdrawal of Soviet troops from the territory of the GDR and Berlin. Instead of the more general three- to four-year period for withdrawal of Soviet troops mentioned in the Kohl-Gorbachev discussions, the Two Plus Four Treaty required that Soviet troops be withdrawn by the end of 1994. The withdrawal of Soviet troops was coupled with the concomitant reduction of the size of the German armed forces contemplated in article 3, section 2.[34]

Articles 5 and 6 regulate the complicated subject of the presence of western forces in former GDR territory—before and after the ultimate departure of Soviet troops. These provisions add considerable detail to the general statement in Kohl's communiqué of July 16 that, as long as Soviet troops remain in the territory of the GDR, the "NATO structures would not be extended to this part of Germany."[35] Article 5, section 1 of the treaty made clear, as did Kohl's communiqué, that until all Soviet troops are withdrawn (no later than 1994), only German units of territorial defense—which are not integrated into the NATO structure—could be stationed in eastern Germany. Moreover, during this period, other nations could not station forces in this territory and could not undertake other military activities there.

As the Kohl communiqué indicated, French, British, and American occupation troops could remain stationed in Berlin as long as Soviet troops remained in eastern Germany. The number of troops of the western Allies could not exceed the amount present when the Two Plus Four Treaty was signed, and no new categories of weapons could be introduced into Berlin by the foreign troops.[36] These provisions gave a certain leeway to the German government: there was no requirement that during this period French, British, and American troops *must* remain in Berlin; rather, they were permitted to do so "upon German request," pursuant to agreement between the united German government and the western Allies. This provision underscored the new German "sovereignty" in Berlin: up to the point of unification, Berlin was the only place in Germany where Allied troops had remained under reserved rights of occupation, but after unification, Allied troops could remain there only pursuant to agreement with the German government. Accordingly, Germany entered into agreements providing for the continued stationing of western Allied forces in Berlin during this interim period.[37]

Article 5, section 3 sought to spell out the possible military role of eastern Germany after the withdrawal of Soviet troops—a subject not specified in Kohl's communiqué, although referred to in general terms by Gorbachev and Kohl in their press conference on July 16.[38] In some ways, this was one of the most far-reaching provisions of the Two Plus Four agreement. According to article 5, section 3, German troops, including German troops integrated in NATO, could be stationed in former GDR territory after the withdrawal of Soviet troops, but foreign troops may never be stationed in that territory, nor may they be "deployed" there. Thus after the departure of Soviet troops only German NATO forces, but not NATO forces of other nations, may be stationed or deployed in eastern Germany. Accordingly, one part of unified Germany—the territory of the former GDR—will remain under permanent limitations with respect to the presence of foreign armed forces.

This resolution of the military status of eastern Germany was a modification of a crucial early suggestion of German Foreign Minister Hans-Dietrich Genscher, advanced in January 1990, that eastern Germany forever remain free of NATO forces. The purpose of Genscher's proposal was to help make German membership in NATO palatable to the Soviet Union by assuring that after unification NATO forces would not move closer to the borders of the Soviet Union than they had been before unification.[39] But "as a result of western—particularly American—influence," the final agreement did not make as much of a concession to the Soviet Union on this point as Genscher had originally proposed.[40]

Article 5, section 3 also reveals the great sensitivity of the Soviet government with respect to the stationing of nuclear weapons in the former territory of the GDR: foreign nuclear weapons and carriers for nuclear weapons may not be stationed or deployed there.[41] Moreover, German NATO troops stationed in that territory may not possess carriers for nuclear weapons. Of course, under article 3, united Germany will not possess its own nuclear weapons; therefore German nuclear weapons are not expressly excluded.

A significant dispute arose on the question of weapons carriers because certain conventional weapons systems can also be used as nuclear weapons carriers, and NATO apparently believed that German NATO forces should eventually be free to use those conventional systems in eastern Germany.[42] This problem was resolved by a provision stating that the German NATO forces may possess conventional weapons systems that *could* be used for nonconventional (nuclear) purposes in eastern Germany, so long as the systems are armed solely with conventional weapons and only designated for such use.[43]

Yet, by the very nature of the NATO structure, the provisions of the Two Plus Four Treaty with respect to eastern Germany might not necessarily prevail in all foreseeable instances. Cutting across all of the limitations of the Two Plus Four agreement are the provisions of articles 5 and 6 of the NATO Treaty, which allow (and require) members of the alliance to come to the defense of NATO territory invaded by other states. In accordance with the agreement reached by Kohl and Gorbachev in the Caucasus, article 6 of the Two Plus Four agreement permits united Germany to belong to "alliances, with all the rights and responsibilities arising therefrom."[44] It seems clear, therefore, that the Two Plus Four Treaty itself recognizes that the obligations of NATO—the alliance to which united Germany belongs—will take precedence over other sections of the Two Plus Four Treaty. That result would apply, at least, to those NATO obligations existing at the time of the signing of the Two Plus Four Treaty. Presumably, therefore, if there was an attack on former GDR territory, articles 5 and 6 of the NATO Treaty would allow German and other NATO forces to come onto that territory to repel the attack—before or after the departure of the Soviet troops stationed there—notwithstanding any contrary provisions in the Two Plus Four agreement.[45]

Not all of the concessions to the Soviet Union (and perhaps to the other Allies) were contained in the actual Two Plus Four Treaty. GDR Prime Minister de Maizière and West German Foreign Minister Genscher supplied the Allies with a separate letter containing additional points.[46] The first section of the letter sought to provide the Soviet Union with additional support for the decision of the Unification Treaty relating to the Soviet Bodenreform of 1945–49.[47] Accordingly, the letter noted that the two German states had agreed that expropriations on the basis of occupation measures from 1945 to 1949 were not to be undone, and that the Federal Republic would not enact any legal rules inconsistent with that principle, but that the all-German parliament might provide for compensation.

It is difficult to assess the effect of this representation incorporated in a letter rather than in the text of the treaty.[48] Viewed at its strongest, however, this statement could bind a united Germany to the observance of the Joint Declaration's position on the 1945–49 expropriations, through an obligation enforceable by the signatories of the Two Plus Four agreement (including the Soviet Union or its successor, Russia) in international law.

In a second point in the letter, the signatories declared that war memorials and graves on German soil—presumably those of the Allies, principally the Soviet Union—are protected under German law.[49] In an extremely interesting third point, the signatories declared that "the free democratic basic order" would be protected by the constitution of a united Germany and that, on this basis, it would be possible to ban political parties "which, by reason of their aims or the behavior of their adherents, seek to impair or abolish the free democratic basic order as well as associations which are directed against the constitutional order or the concept of international understanding."[50] This language tracks provisions of article 21(2) and article 9(2) of the Basic Law, providing for the prohibition of "unconstitutional" political parties and associations. In their long and controversial history, these and related doctrines of the Basic Law have been directed principally against the left—particularly the Communist Party and related groups—and only to a lesser extent against movements of the right.[51] The Soviet Union's apparent insistence on this provision, at a time when it was still governed by a Communist Party, was therefore somewhat ironic.[52] But in any case the provision seemed intended principally to combat the danger of new right-wing movements in a united Germany and, indeed, the letter goes on to state specifically that those constitutional provisions cover "parties and associations with National Socialist aims."[53]

In light of articles 1 through 6 of the Two Plus Four Treaty—and also in light of the points in the letter of de Maizière and Genscher—the four Allied powers then declared that they "hereby terminate their rights and responsibilities relating to Berlin and to Germany as a whole"; all related four-power agreements, decisions, practices, and institutions were also dissolved.[54] Consequently, "the united Germany shall have . . . full sovereignty over its internal and external affairs."[55] Unification would therefore be accompanied by the achievement of practical sovereignty by the unified country.

At the insistence of the Soviet Union, the Two Plus Four agreement took the form of a treaty, and it was therefore necessary that the text be ratified by the legislatures of the participating states. From the German side, ratification would come from a united Germany—an action that could take place only after unification. Moreover, ratification by the four Allied powers required legislative procedures that would also extend beyond the point of the GDR's "accession" on October 3, 1990. In order to confer practical sovereignty on a united Germany at the time of unification, therefore, the four Allies declared that they would "suspend" all of their reserved rights from the date of unification until the final ratification of the treaty, and the Allies signed a document effecting the suspension in New York on October 1, 1990.[56]

Although the Two Plus Four Treaty was generally greeted with satisfaction in Germany, for some voices the agreement did not go far enough. For example Wolfgang Ullmann, a well-known representative of the reform movement, declared that in some respects the Two Plus Four agreement was "no more than an unimaginative compromise on the basis of the status quo" because it did not impose adequate limits on the exercise of military power by Germany.[57] For Ullmann, therefore, the Two Plus Four agreement did not make sufficient progress in the direction of a new internationalist constitutional understanding. In any case, the Two Plus Four agreement could have regulated the bitterly contested subject of the use of German military forces outside of the NATO territories—but it did not do so. Instead, these issues, which were sharply raised by the proposed actions of a "sovereign" Germany after unification, had to be debated within the framework provided by the Basic Law in the post-unification period.

Indeed, although the Two Plus Four agreement could be viewed as a "peace treaty" ending World War II in Europe, in many respects it was little more than a framework in which subsequent issues of the role of united Germany in Europe could be debated and resolved. In the period immediately following unification, three sets of these issues came to the fore. First, the Two Plus Four Treaty contemplated that united Germany would enter into certain additional agreements with its former World War II enemies and victims, such as Poland and the Soviet Union, and—sometimes after very difficult negotiations—these agreements were adopted. Second, unified Germany, free of the tutelage of the Allied powers, would be called upon to make more substantial contributions to the military efforts of NATO and other international organizations. Whether this activity—not regulated by the Two Plus Four agreement—was consistent with the underlying limitations of the Basic Law was an unresolved and sharply debated question. Finally, the imperatives of German unification led to acceleration of proposals for the "deepening" of the European Community. The terms and conditions of these changes, which were set forth in the Maastricht accord of 1992, also raised issues of German "sovereignty" under the Basic Law. The next three chapters—which conclude this volume—will examine each of these complex problems in turn.

CHAPTER 21

# Sequels and Consequences of the Two Plus Four Treaty: Germany and the Structure of Central Europe

THE Two Plus Four Treaty recognized that the final European settlement would not be brought to a close by the terms of that treaty alone. Rather, the negotiators contemplated that unified Germany would also enter into important agreements with Poland and the Soviet Union—accords that would complete the task of the Two Plus Four agreement in revising the political structure created at Yalta and Potsdam and establishing agreed borders and stable relations. Similarly, Germany also entered into treaties with other eastern European countries, particularly Czechoslovakia, a nation that had suffered grievously from the aggressions of the Nazi regime. Although these agreements transformed the political structure of central Europe at the end of the Cold War—or, at least, legally confirmed that transformation—they also revealed that certain long-standing tensions had not been completely resolved.

## THE GERMAN-POLISH TREATIES

Against a background of decades of mistrust, the relations between West Germany and Poland during the negotiation of the Two Plus Four Treaty were particularly difficult—indeed, the Polish government was obliged to make concessions on provisions that it thought important for its future security.[1] In this light, the negotiation of treaties between Poland and Germany in 1990 and 1991 presented an opportunity to establish more friendly relations. This goal was only partially achieved. The treaties contained general pledges of cooperation in a wide array of areas, but there were also evident assertions of German power, and some passages reflected strong assertions of concepts of German "ethnicity" in securing benefits for the "German minority" in Poland.

### *The Border Treaty*

On November 14, 1990, the foreign ministers of Germany and Poland signed the Border Treaty called for by article 1 of the Two Plus Four agreement, for the purpose of permanently confirming the Oder-Neiße line.[2] The preamble of the treaty invoked the UN Charter and the Helsinki accord and declared the parties' intention to create a peaceful European order "in which borders will no longer divide," and to "further a policy of lasting understanding and reconciliation" between the two peoples. In a rather extraordinary provision, however, the preamble referred to World War II and noted the sufferings of "numerous Germans and Poles" who lost their homes through "expulsion or emigration"—without making any distinction between the moral claims of the two groups and without acknowledging that Germans were only expelled after Germany had invaded Poland and carried out a five-year occupation of unparalled brutality, marked by systematic destruction and genocide.[3]

After that questionable beginning, the treaty went on to confirm the existing border between Germany and Poland. Adopting the boundary agreed upon by the GDR and Poland in the Görlitz Treaty,[4] and also invoking Willy Brandt's Warsaw Treaty of 1970, the parties declared the inviolability of the Oder-Neiße line—now and in the future—and pledged that neither party would raise any territorial claim against the other.[5] At the request of the Kohl government, however, ratification of the Border Treaty by the German and the Polish parliaments was to await the signing of a Friendship Treaty between the two states.[6] Under political pressure from groups of "expellees," Kohl sought to include treaty guarantees for the "German minority" in Poland as a quid pro quo for renunciation of the Oder-Neiße lands.

### *The Friendship Treaty*

The Polish-German Treaty of Good Neighborliness and Friendly Cooperation was signed on June 17, 1991, many months after signature of the Border Treaty, and the two treaties were ratified together in autumn 1991.[7] Negotiations over the Friendship Treaty had been very difficult, and much of the delay resulted from debates over the demands of "expellee" groups for special rights for members of the "German minority" living in Poland.[8]

A review of the Friendship Treaty shows an earnest attempt at rapprochement but also makes clear that relations between the two countries remain delicate. Seeking to "close out the sad chapters of the past" (preamble), the parties pledge general cooperation in a wide range of areas such as finance, culture, education, transportation, and environmental control. Invoking the CSCE Charter of Paris for a New Europe, as well as other international conventions, the parties pledge not to use force against each other, and they agree to work toward a reduction of armaments.[9] The Federal Republic will help work toward economic development in Poland and will further Poland's affiliation with the European Community to the extent possible.[10] According to article 8, the Federal Republic takes a favorable view of Poland's full membership in the European Community, as soon as necessary conditions have been met.

On the other hand a detailed set of provisions protects the "German minority" in Poland, thus seeking to settle what had been a very important issue in Germany for more than two decades.[11] These provisions, as well as similar provisions on language teaching and preservation of cultural objects and historical places, may have the effect of sustaining this minority as a distinct cultural group.[12] In any event, the significant benefits—including financial payments—extended to members of the "German minority" by so-called "home associations" have tended to create "a *de facto* two-class society in Poland."[13]

A Joint Letter accompanying the agreement indicated that some sensitive points, raised by German "expellee" groups as demands in the course of negotiations, had not yet been resolved:[14] at present, the Polish government "sees no possibility" of erecting German-language street signs in areas of "German minorities" in Poland, but it will re-examine this question in the future; it is currently difficult for former "expellees" or other German citizens to settle in Poland, but the prospect of EC membership for Poland, contemplated in the treaty, might make this process increasingly easier. Finally, the Joint Letter expressly excludes questions of citizenship and property ownership from coverage under the treaty. Accordingly, those "expellees" who sought restitution or compensation for property seized at the end of World War II receive nothing under the agreement.

Yet, on the whole, Germany seems to have prevailed on the issues actually covered by the German-Polish treaties, a result that no doubt reflects its stronger political and economic position. Of course, the German government agreed to accept the existing Oder-Neiße border, but that concession was a foregone conclusion because it was demanded by the World War II Allies as a condition of German unification. Beyond that, Germany made few concessions: it is obliged to support the progress of Poland toward membership in the European Community, but that obligation is highly qualified. On the other hand, the Polish government agreed to significant protections of German-speaking minorities in Poland, which had been an important goal of foreign policy in the Federal Republic for decades.

In a sense these agreements could be seen as creating a bridge between Germany and eastern Europe, and, indeed, the two treaties did have an effect on opinion in Poland, reducing public "perceptions of a German threat."[15] Addressing the Bundestag in April 1995, Polish Foreign Minister Bartoszewski declared that "in our eyes in Poland" the treaties "form the end of a tragically burdened period in the mutual relations of Germany and Poland [and are] an optimistic proclamation of a new structure in the framework of the common European order."[16] In an indication of these new relations, German and Polish troops have been engaging in joint maneuvers in the framework of NATO's "Partnership for Peace." Certainly such an action would have "seemed unthinkable only a short time ago."[17]

## The German-Soviet Treaties

The accords with Poland were intended to resolve specific issues for unified Germany, but the treaties with the Soviet Union lay at the heart of German foreign policy for the post-unification period. These agreements included detailed provisions for the withdrawal of Soviet forces from eastern Germany as well as the broad structural provisions of the Soviet-German Partnership Treaty. In these accords, Germany promised billions of marks to the Soviet government, in financial and other material aid. These payments were perhaps implied compensation for Soviet acquiescence in unification, but in 1990–91 they were also intended to ward off the fall of the liberal government in the Soviet Union—an event that could have evoked a return of east-west hostility or a state of chaos that could also have endangered Germany and the rest of Europe.

### *Treaties on the Withdrawal of Soviet Troops*

Article 4 of the Two Plus Four Treaty required the withdrawal of Soviet troops from the territory of the former GDR by the end of 1994 and called for a bilateral treaty to regulate matters related to the withdrawal. The military relationship between the Soviet Union and the GDR had been truly remarkable: the Soviet Army's "Western Group," stationed in the GDR, was larger than the East German Army itself, and it was so autonomous that the GDR government did not even have precise information on the number of Soviet personnel on its territory. Nor did the GDR government know exactly how much of its land was being occupied by Soviet forces, although the amount apparently totaled almost 2 percent of the GDR's territory.[18]

The German-Soviet Treaty with respect to the gradual withdrawal of Soviet troops was signed on October 12, 1990.[19] In addition to detailed provisions on the withdrawal of forces, the treaty contained regulations covering the hundreds of thousands of Soviet personnel during the period of withdrawal. In general, the treaty obliged the Soviet forces to respect German law and sovereignty, in contrast with the virtual legal autonomy that they had previously enjoyed.[20] But in a final display of occupier's bravado in March 1991, Soviet forces secretly flew the ailing Erich Honecker to the USSR from a Soviet military hospital in eastern Germany.[21] This action ignored German law and seemed a clear violation of the troop withdrawal treaty which had been signed, but not yet ratified, by the Soviet Union at the time.

In addition, the two nations signed a "Treaty on Transitional Measures," which provided that the Federal Republic would defray substantial costs for Soviet troops temporarily remaining in Germany as well as for their return transportation.[22] To resolve a drastic housing shortage in the Soviet Union, the German government also agreed to finance the construction of housing for the returning Soviet troops. These payments were to total DM 12 billion, together with an additional DM 3 billion five-year interest-free loan.[23]

In accordance with these provisions, the Soviet forces finally departed from eastern Germany in summer 1994, some months before the December deadline of the Two Plus Four Treaty. The troops left behind vast tracts of abandoned military land and an environmental catastrophe of undetermined proportions, resulting from fuel and other pollutants that had been poured into the soil over four decades. At the same time—also in accordance with the Two Plus Four agreement—the forces of the western Allies departed from Berlin, although of course a separate contingent of NATO troops will remain in the western part of Germany.[24]

*The German-Soviet Partnership Treaty*

At the core of the process of Soviet-German rapprochement was the comprehensive Treaty on Good Neighborliness, Partnership, and Cooperation, which was signed on November 9, 1990.[25] Chancellor Kohl had proposed such an agreement to the Soviet ambassador as early as April 1990, intending that it would be an important part of the unification process intimately related to the Two Plus Four agreement.[26] Indeed, in seeking to bolster Soviet fortunes, the Moscow government considered the Partnership Treaty more important than the Two Plus Four agreement itself.[27] Foreign Minister Shevardnadze declared that the treaty placed the Soviet Union and Germany "on a qualitatively new level of relations and cooperation."[28]

The Soviet-German Treaty contained a number of general provisions pledging cooperation in such areas as economy, research and technology, environmental protection, and transportation. Like the agreement with Poland, the Soviet treaty provides protections for the "German minority" in the Soviet Union.[29] The treaty also provides for the return of objects of art that were wrongfully seized in World War II—a provision that evoked controversy in the Soviet parliament before ratification and continued to attract considerable debate thereafter.[30]

The treaty also contained reciprocal guarantees of national borders and an agreement to refrain from the use of force in mutual relations. Indeed, the treaty went substantially beyond these fairly common provisions and declared that if one of the parties is attacked by a third state, "the other party will not furnish the attacker any military help or other assistance."[31] Even though the treaty expressly preserves earlier international obligations such as NATO, and even though the main western allies apparently made no protest, "the non-aggression clause raised concerns in some Western capitals that it could lead to a weakening of Germany's commitment to Western defense."[32]

Negotiations on the Partnership Treaty had been difficult. The Soviet Union had advocated broad provisions for mutual security as part of its general goal of providing a new security structure in Europe. The Federal Republic, in contrast, sought more modest security provisions and attempted to gain more comprehensive protections for the "German minority" in the Soviet Union.[33] Finally, a German-Soviet Economic Treaty, signed on the same day as the partnership agreement, gave added concreteness to German promises of economic cooperation.[34] Under this and other agreements, Germany offered the Soviet Union up to forty billion dollars of aid and credits, amounting to approximately 3 percent of the gross national product of Germany—a commitment that is "comparable to the U.S. commitment to the Marshall Plan," although the Marshall Plan grants did not involve commercial credits.[35]

According to some, this complex network of agreements—entered into by the two nations in the context of German unification—could represent a return to the collaboration between Germany and Russia that, in the late nineteenth century under Bismarck, assisted in securing the peace of Europe.[36] Indeed, before unification, a "legacy of confidence . . . had been built up between Germans and Russians over two decades of détente."[37] In contrast, others feared that the Treaty of Rapallo might turn out to be the more appropriate comparison.[38] This pessimistic analogy evoked fears of joint Russian-German adventures that were independent of the western European nations.[39] Yet decades of a foreign policy directed toward embedding Germany in western Europe—a policy even more fully developed by Chancellor Kohl upon German unification—made fears of this kind seem considerably overdrawn.

## The German-Czech Treaty

In addition to the treaties with the Soviet Union and Poland, the Federal Republic of Germany has negotiated a complicated friendship treaty with Czechoslovakia.

The Treaty on Good Neighborliness and Friendly Cooperation with Czechoslovakia was initialed by Foreign Ministers Genscher and Dienstbier on October 7, 1991, but the agreement was not actually signed until February 27, 1992; indeed, even before the treaty was initialed, negotiations had lasted for a year and a half.[40] In effect, the agreement replaced the German-Czech Treaty of 1973, entered into as part of Chancellor Brandt's eastern policy, but it recalled issues from an even more remote past.

Relations between West Germany and Czechoslovakia had been generally difficult in the postwar period, particularly because of Hitler's forcible absorption of Czechoslovakia in 1938 and 1939 and the extraordinary brutality of the occupation that followed. These fateful events had been preceded by the four-power Munich Agreement, which provided that the western "Sudeten" territories of Czechoslovakia would be transferred to Germany.[41] Although this measure marked the high tide of west European "appeasement" of Nazi Germany, it did not satisfy Hitler who soon occupied the entire country.

Immediately after World War II, the restored Czechoslovakian government of President Beneš retaliated for past injuries by expelling approximately three million German-speaking citizens of Czechoslovakia—the so-called "Sudeten Germans"—into western Germany and seizing their property.[42] Many of the "Sudeten Germans" living in the Federal Republic nourished lasting resentments arising from these events, and—like the "expellees" from the Oder-Neiße territories of Poland—represented a powerful political force in the Federal Republic of Germany.

The first step toward a rapprochement was taken in 1973 when, as a part of Willy Brandt's eastern policy, Czechoslovakia and the Federal Republic signed a treaty pledging that they would settle their differences by peaceful means in accordance with the UN Charter.[43] An issue of importance for the German representation of the "Sudeten Germans"—and also perhaps for the underlying property questions—was whether the Munich Treaty had been void from the beginning, as the Czech government argued, or whether it was initially valid but later became ineffective, as maintained by the Federal Republic.[44] In an ambiguous response to this problem, the 1973 treaty acknowledged that the Munich accord had been "forced upon the Czechoslovak Republic . . . through the threat of violence" but also employed language suggesting that the accord was invalid only with respect to subjects covered in the 1973 agreement.[45]

The 1973 treaty expressly left undisturbed questions of citizenship and matters relating to legal acts performed under the Nazi occupation—including, presumably, property transfers—except those that violated human rights. It did, however, expressly confirm the existing border between the two nations, thus confirming the return of the "Sudeten" lands to Czechoslovakia.[46]

The German-Czech Friendship Treaty of 1992 was framed against the background of this difficult history. Like the Polish Treaty, it did not resolve all issues, and its provisions suggested the persistence of serious problems between the two nations. In a manner reminiscent of the Polish Treaty, the preamble seemed intended to place German and Czech wartime and postwar actions on an equal level of immorality—with a reference to "the numerous victims exacted by dictatorship, war, *and expulsion*" and a pledge to "end the use of force, injustice, and *the repayment of injustice by new unjust acts*."[47] This explicit acknowledgment of unjust "expulsion" led to a popular outcry in Czechoslovakia and severe difficulties in parliament.[48]

On the tortured question of the Munich accord, the 1992 treaty perpetuated the ambiguous resolution of 1973.[49] In contrast, Czechoslovakia has entered into treaties with Italy, France, and Russia that contained provisions stipulating that the Munich accord had been void from the beginning.[50]

The power of the "Sudeten homeland associations" is reflected in provisions on the rights and protection of minorities. The "German" minority in Czechoslovakia as well as the "Czech" and "Slovak" minorities in Germany have broad rights to develop their "identities," but only the "German" minority is explicitly declared to be "free from all attempts to be assimilated against its will."[51] A somewhat ominous provision supports efforts by the "joint historians commission" and the "independent German-Czechoslovakian school book conference" to contribute toward "a joint understanding of German-Czechoslovakian history—particularly of this century."[52]

In another parallel with the Poland Treaty, the German government agreed to support Czechoslovakian efforts to qualify for full membership in the European Community, and a joint letter of the foreign ministers noted that the prospect of Community membership "will create an increasing possibility that citizens of the Federal Republic will be able to settle in Czechoslovakia."[53] Thus the approach toward EC membership will create increasing opportunities for "Sudeten Germans" to purchase property in their former regions.[54]

On the other hand, the 1992 treaty did not address the subject of the actual return of property or compensation for the expelled "Sudeten Germans," and the foreign ministers' letter explicitly noted that this subject was excluded from the agreement.[55] The Czech government had apparently proposed that Bonn relinquish the "Sudeten" claims in return for Prague's renunciation of any claim for World War II reparations. The Federal Republic rejected this proposal, however, fearing that the German government itself would then become the focus of claims of the "Sudeten Germans."[56]

The Federal Republic delayed signing the treaty out of deference to the "Sudeten Germans," and the SPD leadership criticized Kohl for bowing to the influence of "interest groups" and thus interfering with the creation of confidence between the two nations.[57] In contrast, a representative of the "Sudeten Germans" argued that the Czech government's sale of property claimed by that group represented a breach of the Friendship Treaty even before the treaty was signed.[58] The German-Czech Treaty, as well as a treaty between Germany and Hungary, was approved by the Bundestag on May 20, 1992.[59]

In the period following the signing of the Friendship Treaty, relations between the two governments have not notably improved.[60] Certainly, contacts on the individual level have greatly increased and investment flowed into Czechoslovakia from the Federal Republic; but relations between the two governments continue to be deeply disturbed by claims of the "homeland associations" of "Sudeten Germans" for property lost during the postwar expulsions of fifty years ago—claims that are supported particularly by the Bavarian CSU, a member of the ruling conservative coalition.[61] In response, the Czech prime minister, Václav Klaus, has declared: "We cannot resolve everything that we have inherited from the past . . . and this includes [the measures that were taken] in the days immediately following World War II. It is unacceptable that these constants [of our political life] are being called into question. . . . [We] cannot bring the world back to February 24, 1948."[62]

## The Dissolution of the Soviet Union and Czechoslovakia and the Status of International Accords

The status of the Two Plus Four Treaty and other agreements was called into question in a fundamental way by the dissolution of the Soviet Union at the end of 1991. Although the Bonn government had hoped for its survival, the Soviet Union was effectively dissolved on December 3 by a joint declaration of the presidents of Russia, Ukraine, and Belarus, joined later by the president of Kazakhstan. The Soviet Union then formally ceased to exist upon the resignation of President Mikhail Gorbachev on December 25, 1991.

With respect to treaty relationships between Germany and Russia—the largest of the former Soviet republics—the situation was generally clarified by the declaration of President Boris Yeltsin that the Russian Federation represents a continuation of the Soviet Union and is therefore "partially identical" with the Soviet Union. Accordingly, Russia continued in the United Nations General Assembly and Security Council seats of the Soviet Union, without the necessity of any additional legal act. Moreover, Russia continued to have rights and duties of the Soviet Union under treaties to which the Soviet Union was a party. On December 26, 1991, German President Richard von Weizsäcker sent a letter to Russian president Boris Yeltsin, acknowledging this legal status.[63]

With respect to the other republics of the former Soviet Union, the situation was somewhat more complicated. Most of these republics were recognized by member states of the European Community after they were found to satisfy a series of special criteria set forth by the EC ministers at a special meeting in December 1991.[64] Although these states do not consider themselves "identical" with the Soviet Union, most of them have signed the agreement forming the Commonwealth of the Independent States, and this argeement contains a pledge that the signatory parties "undertake to discharge the international obligations incumbent on them under treaties and agreements entered into by the former Union of Soviet Socialist Republics."[65]

Similar questions with respect to the German-Czech Treaty were raised by the dissolution of Czechoslovakia into the Czech and Slovak Republics, on January 1, 1993. The dissolution agreement, however, made clear that each of the new republics succeeded to existing treaty relations of Czechoslovakia.[66]

The history of the treaties in this chapter—and particularly the German treaties with Poland and Czechoslovakia—makes clear that even after unification it is probably not correct to speak of "normal" relations between Germany and some of its eastern neighbors. Indeed, sensitive issues of this kind have characterized much of postwar European relations and partly explain continued moves to mitigate the strength of German sovereignty—and possible hegemony in Europe—by its inclusion in military and economic structures of alliance. Yet Germany has only gone so far in seeking to allay these sensitivities. Notwithstanding some efforts at conciliation, the history of these treaties also reveals strong insistence by Germany on the assertion of its own perceived "national interest," particularly in seeking to advance the rights and claims of "German minorities" in eastern European lands and "expellees" from these territories now residing in the Federal Republic.

CHAPTER 22

# United Germany and the Western Security System: The Future Role of German Armed Forces

A CENTRAL premise of German unification, both inside and outside the Federal Republic, was that the unified country would remain imbedded in NATO and the western security system. Even though it had now become a "sovereign" nation, the Federal Republic would continue to adapt its military stance to the joint decision making of the western alliance, under the predominant influence of the United States. Through this limitation, the increased strength of Germany would be made palatable to its neighbors, and any external dangers of internal nationalist excess would also be restrained.

Yet this foreign policy structure, first supported by Adenauer and enthusiastically endorsed by Kohl, had one crucial lacuna in light of present problems: Adenauer's structure presupposed a monolithic "east" against which the Federal Republic and the entire west had to be defended. The structure made no provision for struggles within a more or less friendly east, in which Germany might conceivably find itself inclined or impelled to intervene.

This shift in the basic context of action presented three sets of problems. First, it called into question the very structure and basis of NATO itself and evoked uncertainty about the future of the European security system. Second, it opened unexpected possibilities for unilateral diplomatic initiatives in unfamiliar contexts on the part of a German government that lacked experience as a truly independent actor. Finally, the new context paradoxically increased the likelihood of European hostilities and raised the issue of Germany's constitutional role in international efforts to quell these dangerous localized struggles.

## UNIFIED GERMANY AND THE FUTURE OF NATO

The end of the Cold War, accompanied by the termination of the Warsaw Pact and the dissolution of the Soviet Union itself, transformed the role of NATO in the European political structure. For decades NATO was a central factor in the western confrontation of eastern Europe, but now it had become the only effective European security system, and east European nations and former Soviet republics were clamoring for membership. Many of these states have joined the North Atlantic Co-operation Council founded by NATO in December 1991,[1] and some have also joined NATO's Partnership for Peace. For most of these nations, however, full membership in NATO may not be imminent. Notwithstanding an American position favoring early admission, and general NATO resolutions along those lines, some resistance may remain in the alliance against extending the defense umbrella eastward.[2] Even so, discussion of the possibility has led to considerable edginess in the Russian government, which foresees the possibility of its own future diplomatic and military isolation.

Yet these developments, while apparently marking a bloodless "victory" for NATO itself, actually called the entire military alliance into serious question. Indeed, "it is difficult to exaggerate the conceptual challenge to NATO's existence that has been caused" by these events.[3] The importance of NATO as a military alliance has declined because the perceived threat against which it was directed has ceased to exist, and a number of NATO member states are undertaking a significant reduction of forces in Europe.[4] Moreover, a new type of European civil conflict seemed to be arising—as exemplified by the war in the former Yugoslavia—and it is not clear that NATO is equipped to handle these new conflicts.[5] Some suggested that NATO could "remain as present reassurance" but probably would "[decline] in a genteel way as circumstances permit."[6]

Another challenge to NATO arose from the fear of European governments that, with the end of the Cold War, the United States would substantially withdraw its troops from Europe.[7] Accordingly, the French and German governments sought to establish a joint military force—the "Eurocorps"—presumably to remain outside of the NATO structure.[8] Similar proposals focused on the troops of the Western European Union (WEU), an organization that is loosely connected with the structures of the European Community—to which the United States is not a party. Indeed, an annex to the Maastricht Treaty indicates that the WEU forces should be viewed as a significant component of the movement toward European political union.[9] Yet some voices within Germany view these moves with skepticism, and argue that an independent European force could not replace NATO and therefore serves little independent function.[10] In any case, the future of such an independent European force—within the Western European Union or otherwise—remains at present uncertain.[11]

Debates about the future American role in an Atlantic Alliance have significant implications for the position of Germany within the alliance. If the United States remains a strong factor, the role of Germany and of any other individual European state would remain secondary. Without American participation, however, the possibility that a unified Germany could dominate the alliance assumes somewhat greater reality.

In the course of German unification, the Conference on Security and Cooperation in Europe (CSCE) was sometimes advanced as a possible European security system.[12] In the Two Plus Four negotiations, for example, President Gorbachev seemed to view the organization as the possible beginning of an all-European security system that could eventually replace NATO and the

Warsaw Pact. The Soviet Union was a member of the CSCE, and it therefore represented a more favorable choice for Gorbachev than NATO, from which the Soviet Union was excluded.

It seems most unlikely, however, that the CSCE—or OSCE, as it is now known—will be strengthened in the near future to take the place of NATO in a European security structure. Indeed, this organization was not originally established as anything resembling a security system. Founded as a product of détente in the early 1970s, the Conference scored its greatest success as a human rights organization with adoption of the Helsinki Final Act in 1975.[13]

Development of the CSCE into an all-European security system would of course be consistent with article 24(2) of the Basic Law, which allows the Federal Republic to join "a system of mutual collective security" for the purpose of ensuring "a peaceful and lasting order in Europe and among the peoples of the world." Indeed, membership in such an organization could satisfy the general aspirations of article 24 more fully than membership in an alliance such as NATO, which currently covers only a part of Europe. Yet, under present circumstances at least, such a development remains elusive.

Indeed the relative remoteness of such a goal was emphasized immediately after German unification when, on November 21, 1990, the CSCE adopted the Charter of Paris for a New Europe.[14] This agreement was a direct outgrowth of the process begun in Helsinki, and it perpetuated the basic principles of the 1975 Final Act. The Charter also recognized the new situation created by the unification of Germany and the end of the Cold War, declaring that it was "a time of profound change and historic expectations," that the "era of confrontation and division of Europe has ended," and that "[o]urs is a time for fulfilling the hopes and expectations our peoples have cherished for decades."[15] Specifically, the signatories noted "with great satisfaction" the signing of the Two Plus Four agreement and declared that the "establishment of the national unity of Germany is an important contribution to a just and lasting order of peace for a united, democratic Europe aware of its responsibility for stability, peace and co-operation."[16]

But notwithstanding this brave rhetoric of late 1990, the reality was that the Charter of Paris did not go much beyond the general aspirations of the Helsinki accord. Nor did it show substantial progress in creating an independent administrative structure. The agreement established a secretariat of the organization in Prague, and offices in Vienna and Warsaw. Significantly, however, it did not establish enforcement mechanisms for its provisions and fell far short of the creation of a new security system to replace NATO and the Warsaw Pact, as sought by the Soviet Union.[17]

In this light it seems clear that NATO, with all of its present problems and potential weaknesses, will remain the only viable European security system for the foreseeable future. Yet it is also important to understand that there are no legal restrictions that would prevent Germany's withdrawal from NATO if it should decide to do so. Article 24 of the Basic Law authorizes Germany to transfer governmental powers to "international organizations" and to participate in organizations for "collective security," but it is doubtful that this provision is mandatory. Moreover, article 6 of the Two Plus Four Treaty acknowledges the "right" of Germany "to belong to alliances." Although this provision was drafted in contemplation of Germany's choice to remain in NATO, the provision itself does not mention NATO and does not require that Germany belong to this or, indeed, any other alliance.[18]

## The Recognition of Croatia

Predominant among the anxieties raised among some in Europe by German unification was a fear that the unified country might return to a traditional assertiveness and a quest for hegemony in foreign policy.

Indeed, Germany's first independent foreign policy move since unification seems to have been impelled by a form of nationalistic impatience, and it casts a troubling light on the role of Germany in independent policy making. In any case, this unilateral act seems to have contributed to disastrous consequences.

In the dissolution of Yugoslavia in 1990–91, the two northernmost constituent republics, Slovenia and Croatia, voted to secede from the unified state. The United States and Great Britain viewed these moves cautiously, preferring not to recognize the new republics until a general political settlement had been reached in the area.[19]

The mood in the German government, however, was quite different. Some in the government asserted that Germany, having recently been reunited through an exercise of "self-determination," was morally bound to support self-determination in other nations.[20] Accordingly, the German government announced its intention to recognize Slovenia and Croatia, and was even "prepared to break asunder the principle of a common European foreign policy" by proceeding unilaterally if other EC members did not agree.[21] The uncompromising nature of this position, and the peremptory tone with which it was asserted, seemed disturbing to say the least. Indeed, "[i]t appears that for [Foreign Minister] Hans-Dietrich Genscher, the recognition of Croatia . . . became the litmus test of German diplomatic muscle after 1989."[22] Moreover, the government's position seemed to ignore the problems raised by the presence of a large Serbian minority within secessionist Croatia, which made the concept of "self-determination" particularly difficult to apply with confidence in this context. Indeed, at the same time, the German government refused to recognize the secessionist state in Macedonia. It seems likely, therefore, that in reality the government was acting "not out of principle but out of self-interest."[23] To some, these moves seemed to suggest attempts to establish a German sphere of influence in southern Europe—including Slovenia and Croatia—that evoked painful memories of similar sturctures in earlier periods. These charges were vigorously rejected by German officials.

According to some informed observers, it was the German push for recognition of Croatia that triggered a civil war in Bosnia that has had no parallel in

Europe since World War II.[24] Indeed, precisely this danger had been made clear to Foreign Minister Genscher in a letter from UN Secretary-General Pérez de Cuéllar warning that recognition of Croatia would bring about "the most terrible war" in Bosnia-Herzegovina. This letter, however, "was dismissed by Genscher who was clearly determined to go ahead . . . regardless of the cost to Bosnia."[25]

There can be no excuse or mitigation for the atrocities committed in this war particularly by Serbian forces—whose policies of "ethnic cleansing" chillingly recall the actions of the Nazis—but the sad history of recent years does clearly suggest that the more cautious policies of other western allies might have avoided at least part of the disaster in Bosnia. In any case serious questions are raised by the spectacle of united Germany bullying its European neighbors to follow a policy that seemed to reflect its own diplomatic self-interest and evoked recollections of old Balkan alliances of World War I and the Nazi period.[26]

## Unified Germany and the Use of Armed Force outside the NATO Territory

The most important security issue of constitutional status raised in the years immediately following unification concerned the constitutional limits on the use of German armed forces outside of the NATO territory. The answer to this question had implications for the structure of NATO itself, but it also seemed to have broader implications for the role of unified Germany as a "sovereign" actor in foreign affairs. The constitutional debate on this issue rested on theories drawn from the history of the armed forces in western Germany.

The original decision to establish armed forces in the Federal Republic of Germany had been made in the context of the Paris Treaties of 1955, through which the Federal Republic received a substantial measure of sovereignty from the western Allies and also agreed to join NATO.[27] At that time few contemplated that these forces could be used for any purpose other than the defense of the territory of West Germany or other western nations pursuant to the NATO Treaty. These assumptions, with some modifications, seem to have been enshrined in a series of amendments of the Basic Law in 1968, which authorized use of the armed forces for "defense" and other specifically described tasks, such as protecting against imminent dangers to the "free democratic basic order."

This quite limited view of the constitutional role of the military was reflected in the position, adopted by successive German governments since the early 1980s, that the Basic Law prohibited German armed forces from participating in action outside of the NATO territory.[28] This view received a severe test immediately after unification when the government argued that German troops could not constitutionally participate in the Persian Gulf War of 1991, which was outside of the NATO territory, although Germany was permitted to supply financial assistance and equipment and to send a small contingent of soldiers to Turkey, a NATO ally.[29]

In the wake of the Gulf War, some Allied officials criticized Germany's failure to provide troops for this venture, as they had criticized similar assertions of constitutional disabilities in the past.[30] Accordingly, the German government felt that it was under international pressure to change its policy, and this crisis—as well as succeeding crises after unification—rekindled the constitutional debate over the use of the military outside of the NATO territory.

In the course of these debates, the three principal political parties took quite different positions on the constitutional status of the use of German armed forces.[31] The CDU/CSU argued that the Basic Law already permitted an expanded use of the armed forces, but it supported a constitutional amendment to make that proposition clear. In contrast, the SPD maintained that troops could be used outside of the NATO area for peace-keeping purposes only, and it advocated a constitutional amendment to confirm that view. Taking a middle position, the FDP supported an amendment that would allow expanded use of the armed forces when approved by a special super-marjority of the Bundestag.[32]

Behind the constitutional arguments lay important political issues: on the one side, the government claimed that without military participation in UN and NATO ventures, a unified and "sovereign" Germany would lose its role as a reliable ally; on the other side, some feared that such claims could cover a dangerous revival of militarism in Germany. Accordingly, an underlying question was whether these military measures would represent the further dissolution of German sovereignty in European institutions, or whether they would mark the reassertion of an old militaristic tradition that could eventually—if tolerated or encouraged—lead to dangerous unilateral actions in the future.

In light of the sharp differences among the political parties, it was impossible to assemble the requisite two-thirds votes in parliament to adopt a constitutional amendment on military actions outside the NATO area: the parties could not reach agreement on whether to authorize UN peace-keeping operations only, as the SPD basically proposed, or whether UN combat missions, or even WEU missions, should be allowed.[33] In three extremely important instances, therefore, the government sent military forces outside of the NATO territory without securing a constitutional amendment that would have specifically authorized such a course.

Each of these cases followed a similar pattern. First, an external agency—NATO or the UN—requested German participation in a military action. The CDU/CSU favored the action, but the SPD denied that there was authority for the action without a constitutional amendment. The coalition proceeded nonetheless—sometimes over the doubts or objections of the FDP—and the SPD filed an action in the Constitutional Court.

*Monitoring the Embargo in the Adriatic*

The first two of these problems arose in connection with the continuing conflict in Yugoslavia. For the purpose "of establishing peace and stability" in the region, the UN Security Council ordered an embargo of weapons and trade against Serbia and Montenegro—the remaining components of the former Yugoslavia.[34] On July 10, 1992, NATO and the WEU agreed to "monitor compliance" with the UN embargo, and shortly thereafter the German government announced its decision to provide ships and aircraft in the Adriatic area, as part of this effort. The SPD Bundestag caucus, as well as individual SPD members of parliament, filed an action in the Constitutional Court arguing that this use of German military forces was unconstitutional.[35]

*Enforcement of Prohibition of Flights over Bosnia-Herzegovina (AWACS)*

While the Constitutional Court action was pending, the UN Security Council issued a prohibition of air flights over Bosnia-Herzegovina, to inhibit supplies from reaching military units of Bosnian Serbs there and to stop the bombing of civilians.[36] Shortly thereafter, NATO agreed to enforce the resolution through AWACS reconnaissance aircraft which would detect violations, and also by jet fighter planes which would intercept the violators. It was understood that German fighter planes would not participate in these measures, but German forces comprised more than 30 percent of the integrated AWACS teams made up of personnel from NATO member states.[37] It was possible, though not intended, that AWACS surveillance aircraft could be involved in hostilities.

In April 1993, the federal government decided to permit German forces to participate in the AWACS flights. This decision was made over the protest of the FDP—a partner in the governing coalition—which filed a challenge in the Constitutional Court. The SPD also extended its constitutional complaint over the embargo, to challenge these new measures as well. Shortly thereafter, the Constitutional Court denied the complainants' motion for a preliminary injunction.[38] Accordingly, as arguments were being filed on the merits in the Constitutional Court, the AWACS flights commenced with German participation.[39]

*Humanitarian Efforts in Somalia*

At the same time, similar issues were arising in a different context. In April 1993, the UN secretary-general formally requested that German troops participate in humanitarian measures then underway in Somalia, and the government agreed to send troops to a pacified area to support the distribution of humanitarian supplies.[40] Thereafter, the Bundestag adopted an advisory "sense of the house" resolution (*Entschließungsantrag*) supporting this measure.[41] The SPD parliamentary caucus extended its pending constitutional complaint to cover these new plans and, after twenty-two UN troops from Pakistan were killed in Somalia in June 1993, the SPD caucus moved in the Constitutional Court for a preliminary injunction.[42]

Yet there was substantial uncertainty about what the role of the German troops could be in Somalia,[43] and when the first German forces were actually dispatched, the nature of the proposed mission had indeed changed. Instead of supporting the distribution of supplies, the German forces were now to provide logistic support for a UN brigade from India.[44] In light of this change, and also because of the evident danger in which the troops could be placed, the Constitutional Court issued a very cautious preliminary decision in the Somalia case. The Court denied a preliminary injunction, but it did so only on the condition that the Bundestag approve the venture through a formal resolution.[45] In response to this decision, the Bundestag proceeded to issue the necessary approval.[46]

### *The Constitutional Arguments*

It was against this factual and procedural background that these cases were argued and decided in the Constitutional Court. Although many factors entered into the debate, most constitutional arguments centered on the meaning of one provision of the Basic Law—article 87a(2) GG, which imposed some limitations on the use of German military force. According to the complainants, this provision reflected the view that—in light of twentieth-century history—the use of German armed force should be limited by substantial constitutional restraints, in addition to the general prohibitions on waging or planning aggressive war contained in article 26 GG.[47]

Article 87a(2) tersely states: "Apart from *defense*, the armed forces may only be *deployed* [*eingesetzt*] to the extent that the Basic Law expressly permits."[48] Even though this provision is very short, its language raises a host of issues that have been vigorously debated in recent years. Behind a number of linguistic perplexities lay profound disagreements over the permissible constitutional role of German military force, a question that had become even more pressing after unification.

The first set of arguments focused on the meaning of the word "defense" in article 87a. Even article 87a acknowledged that German troops could be employed for purposes of "defense," but what, precisely, did that mean? Did this term refer to the defense of German territory only, or did it extend to encompass—as many thought—"defense" of the territory of other signatories of the NATO Treaty? Or did it even go farther to envision "defense" of United Nations policy, or of the "free world" and its ideals—or, indeed, to include any action that was not in violation of international law?[49] These broad interpretations would allow German military action outside of the NATO territory—and perhaps even outside the confines of any international system—on the theory that these uses of force involved "defense."

A second question surrounded the use of the word "deploy"—*einsetzen*. What exactly constitutes the type of "deployment" that is limited by 87a? Does the term "deployment" cover the sending of troops into actual or likely hostilities only, or does a "deployment" also include participation in more general peace-keeping activities or the provision of technical or other assistance by military forces?[50]

Finally, in recent years, some authors have argued that article 87a, notwithstanding the apparent sweep of its language, was intended to impose limitations on the *internal* use of the armed forces only.[51] Under this view, article 87a was intended to restrict the use of military force against demonstrations, disturbances, and riots, and did not limit external use of the armed forces at all. This argument was based on a historical analysis of the context of the section's adoption and the fact that discussion of possible external use of the Bundeswehr played no role in the legislative history. But opponents of this view countered that, in light of German aggression in World War II, it would be "hardly comprehensible" if the framers of article 87a had intended to limit internal use of forces only.[52] In any case, this was the most sweeping of the arguments surrounding article 87a: its adoption would allow any use of the Bundeswehr outside of Germany—as part of an international effort or not—so long as the prohibition of aggressive war was not violated.

### *The Decision of the Constitutional Court*

In one of the most important decisions of the post-unification period, the Constitutional Court issued a consolidated opinion in these cases on July 12, 1994.[53] In its decision the Court sought a middle way between the narrowest and broadest assertions of the constitutional use of military force—thus reaching a mediating resolution that bore some resemblance to its decisions in important cases relating to the "internal" problems of German unification.

In principle, the Court upheld the constitutionality of the use of German forces in the Adriatic, AWACS, and Somalia enterprises, but its opinion also had the effect of emphasizing that these ventures were deeply embedded in military actions of international organizations—the UN, the WEU, and NATO. Thus the ability of German forces to aid in activities of the international system was affirmed, but the Court refrained from approving—in this case at least—any independent military adventures. The Court also required that any military actions—even within the framework of an international organization—must be approved by a specific vote of the German parliament.

The Court reached this result by declining to focus its primary attention on article 87a GG at all. Rather, the Court rested its decision on article 24(2) of the Basic Law, which allows the federal government to join "*a system of mutual collective security*, for the preservation of peace" and, in so doing, to limit its sovereign rights in order to "create and secure a peaceful and lasting order in Europe and among the peoples of the earth."[54]

In the first step of this argument, the Court found that the UN and NATO are systems of "mutual collective security" under article 24(2) GG; moreover, the participation of German forces in the military activities of these organizations was contemplated by the treaties that established these systems.[55] Yet with respect to the NATO Treaty, a succeeding step of the argument raised significant problems because the treaty does not explicitly authorize military actions that are not undertaken to defend NATO territory—such as the deployments at issue in the embargo and AWACS cases. In an elaborate discussion, however, the Court found that the NATO Treaty covered these actions nonetheless. After the end of the Cold War the NATO nations are seeking a new security structure in Europe—the Court declared—but they are attempting to do so within the framework of existing treaties and, in any event, they have not manifested the requisite will to enter into new international agreements. Therefore a new NATO Treaty, with new parliamentary approval, was *not* constitutionally required under article 59 GG—the provision of the Basic Law that sets forth the general procedure for entering into treaties.[56] The Court also found that no new approval was required under article 59(2) for participation in humanitarian efforts of the United Nations in Somalia.[57]

Having found that article 24(2) GG authorized these German military actions, the Court then held that article 87a did not operate to limit this authorization. Article 24(2) had been in the Basic Law from the beginning and article 87a, when it was added in 1968, was not intended to limit authorization of the use of troops already set forth in the Basic Law. Accordingly, it was not necessary for the Court—in this case—to resolve tortured questions of the meaning of "defense" or "deployment" in article 87a or whether article 87a limited internal use of forces only.[58]

Yet after rejecting substantive limits on the troop deployments in these cases, the Court went on to impose one additional procedural restriction: the Court found that any deployment of "armed troops" required previous approval of the Bundestag as a general rule.[59] Although the Basic Law does not expressly impose this requirement, the Court found that it was implied by the history and text of constitutional measures authorizing the armed forces as well as by "German constitutional tradition since 1918." Thus the army is not to be under the executive alone, but rather should be considered a "'parliamentary army' [embedded] in the democratic constitutional order under the rule of law."[60] The requirement of legislative approval applies even when German forces are to be deployed pursuant to the NATO Treaty or a UN Security Council resolution. The requirement may indeed be suspended in case of emergency, but even then the Bundestag must consider the matter immediately and can order the withdrawal of troops so dispatched.[61]

Yet, notwithstanding this complex argument, it is not entirely clear whether this requirement will have a substantial practical effect. In most instances, the government will probably control a solid majority of the Bundestag, and any executive decision to commit forces would almost certainly be supported by the parliament as well. Accordingly, although the Court indeed found that the Adriatic embargo and AWACS enterprises had not received adequate parliamentary approval, the Bundestag speedily met in a special session and voted the necessary authorization.[62] It would only be in rather rare instances of real dispute on the merits of a military venture within a ruling coalition, or when the coalition is governing by a narrow and uncertain margin, that the requirement of parliamentary approval would make any real difference.[63]

It is clear that unification and the end of the Cold War have ushered in a period of uncertainty in German foreign policy. Reliable verities, such as the function and role of NATO, have been called into question, and Germany—as a "sovereign" actor—may be inclined to make independent foreign policy decisions for which it may not be readily prepared. Finally, these developments have increased the possibility that Germany may feel itself called upon to contribute forces to international ventures outside of the NATO territories. In an important decision on this issue, the Constitutional Court has reversed a long-held understanding and has given constitutional approval to Germany's participation in these actions—if parliament agrees—so long as they are undertaken within the framework of the United Nations, NATO, or other international organizations under article 24(2) GG. In essence this constitutional change can be viewed as supporting the further and deeper involvement of Germany in the European structure, a move that will further channel and restrict its freedom of independent action. Yet, on the other hand, the removal of supposed constitutional limitations on the use of German armed forces could possibly also clear the way—through decisions in the future—for unilateral military ventures on the part of the unified and "sovereign" Federal Republic.

CHAPTER 23

# The Unification of Germany and the Unification of Europe: European Community and European Union

FOR THE purpose of "embedding" or dissolving German sovereignty in European structures, the most important institution was not NATO—as important as the alliance may have been—but rather the economic and political organization of the European Community or European Union. Indeed, much of Germany's future in Europe, as well as much of the future of European unification, lies within this institution. Accordingly, the decisions of the Union play an increasingly crucial role in German law, and the German constitution itself—both in its text and its interpretative doctrine—has come to recognize the special role of the European institutions.

The European Community or Communities, which include most of the countries of western Europe, were originally created through the adoption of three treaties: the European Coal and Steel Agreement (1951), the European Atomic Energy Agreement (Euratom) (1957), and, by far the most important, the Treaty Establishing the European Economic Community (EEC) (1957).[1] The origins and development of the European Community parallel, in the area of economics, some of the goals and intentions of NATO in the realm of security.[2] The European Coal and Steel Community, the EC's predecessor, grew out of European cooperation on Marshall Plan aid and was intended, at least in part, as a bulwark against the east bloc as well as a defense against any residual threat from an economically resurgent Germany.[3]

In the following years, however, the European Community came to assume an independent economic role that went far beyond its function as a possible instrument of the Cold War. Indeed, the Community became a central factor in the economic and legal life of Europe. A significant portion of the internal law of the member states, extending far beyond direct economic regulation into areas such as environmental control, is determined by treaty, legislation, or judicial interpretation of the EEC. Indeed, it has been estimated that, with the completion of the single European market, approximately 80 percent of legislation affecting markets would be issued by the EC rather than the member states.[4]

In its founding and subsequent development, the EC was also intended to serve a central political goal. The founders believed that economic integration, coupled with eventual steps toward political union, was the only way to prevent the national rivalries that could lead to European war.[5]

## The European Community in the Process of German Unification

The Federal Republic was a founding member of the European Economic Community. Its membership is consistent with the Basic Law and indeed strongly encouraged by that document. According to the preamble, the German people are "animated by the will . . . to serve world peace as an equal member of a united Europe," and article 24(1) authorizes the federal government to transfer "sovereign rights to international organizations." These provisions reflect the outward-looking aspects of the Basic Law and formed the constitutional basis for the Federal Republic's accession to the European Community in 1957.[6]

Yet the outward-looking aspects of the Basic Law, notwithstanding their important position, were also subject to significant limitations. The Constitutional Court has held, for example, that article 24(1) does not allow the Federal Republic to negate central constitutional requirements of the Basic Law by grants of sovereignty to international organizations. Thus no such grant could impair the fundamental preservation of Basic Rights. It was also clear that the constitutional imperative of German unification could not be discarded for the purpose of furthering European integration.[7]

Indeed, the western constitutionalists' views of the continuing German "Reich"—as well as the goal of unification with East Germany—were incorporated into the Federal Republic's relationship with the Community and, from the beginning, the EC recognized the special legal status of Germany. In negotiations over the EEC Treaty, for example, the leader of the West German delegation made clear that in the event of German unification, the treaty would be open to re-examination.[8] Although this remark was not made part of the treaty, it did not encounter contradiction and therefore may have been tacitly accepted by the other delegations, with the result that it may have had a measure of binding legal effect. In 1990, therefore, some argued that the Federal Republic (or perhaps any other member state) could have required renegotiation of the treaty upon German unification.[9] But, in any case, no member state sought to make use of this possibility.[10]

The constitutional goal of "internal" unification with East Germany was also recognized by the EC in other ways. Under the Constitutional Court's theory of the continuing German "Reich," the GDR could not be considered a separate country; accordingly, the Federal Republic always treated trade with the GDR as domestic trade—to have done otherwise might have compromised the underlying constitutional view. Yet EEC rules would ordinarily have compelled the Federal Republic to create a customs frontier that would have imposed the Common Customs Tariff and other restrictions on trade with the GDR. To avoid that result, a "protocol on internal German trade" was made an integral part of the EEC Treaty in 1957.[11] Under the protocol, the Federal Republic could continue to treat intra-German trade as domestic trade. The ordinary EEC rules on trade with non-EEC countries would thus not apply to goods traveling between the GDR and the Federal Republic, although such rules would apply to goods traveling between the GDR and other EEC countries. In this way the GDR has always received some benefits of the EEC and, even before unification, was often referred to as a quasi member of the Community.

In the early months of 1990, as German unification became increasingly probable, attention turned to the problems of incorporating the territory of the GDR into the structure of the European Community. Some issues turned on the constitutional method of unification that would be chosen. If German unification had proceeded through an interim period of cooperation in a form of confederation or "treaty community"—as originally suggested by Kohl and Modrow—the GDR might have petitioned for associate status in the EEC under article 238 of the EEC Treaty. The GDR might even have sought full independent membership under article 237—a complex process requiring unanimous approval of the European Council, a majority vote of the European Parliament, and approval of a related agreement or treaty by each member state.

Because the GDR "acceded" to the Federal Republic under article 23, however, this complicated process was not necessary. Upon accession, the GDR became part of the existing Federal Republic and lost its independent legal status. Moreover, under the doctrine of "moving treaty boundaries," the EEC Treaty applied to new territory incorporated into the boundaries of a member state, without any requirement that the treaty be amended. After accession, therefore, the Federal Republic—now including the territory of the former GDR—remained a party to the treaty.[12] Because the treaty was not amended, however, the Federal Republic had to remain content for the moment with its existing number of votes on the Council and representatives in the European Parliament, and the existing number of judges on the European Court—even though its population increased substantially upon unification.[13] Thereafter, at a summit of member states in December 1992, the number of German representatives in the European Parliament was increased to accord official status to eighteen representatives from eastern Germany who had been named as observers following unification.[14]

Because the GDR became part of the Federal Republic upon accession, it would seem to follow that EEC law would immediately apply in the former GDR to the same extent as it applied in the rest of the Federal Republic.[15] Here as elsewhere, however, some of the hardest problems were not constitutional or legal, but economic. It was clear that the economy of the GDR was not strong enough for immediate application of all aspects of EEC law. Enterprises in the east could not withstand unrestricted competition from other EEC countries and were not equipped to comply with all applicable EEC environmental and product quality standards. Rather, it was necessary to devise a series of special measures for an interim period.[16]

In order to accomplish a smooth transition that would take these serious problems into account, the process of German unification was marked by close cooperation with the relevant Community institutions.[17] Accordingly, the first State Treaty contained a number of provisions specifically acknowledging the authoritative role of the law of the European Communities.[18] In this cooperative spirit, the Economic Community allowed most goods from the GDR to have free access (without tariff barriers) to the countries of the EEC, even before unification. Thus "a de facto customs union . . . existed between the Community and the German Democratic Republic since 1 August 1990."[19]

These measures, however, did not resolve the necessity of excepting the former GDR from the rigor of certain rules of the Economic Community. In order to deal with these problems adequately in light of the accelerated pace of German unification, the Council authorized the European Commission to recommend certain exceptions for this purpose. Pursuant to this authorization, the Commission proposed measures dealing particularly with agriculture, transportation policy, energy, environment, and the law relating to food and protection of workers.[20] The government of the Federal Republic, in turn, issued regulations adopting these proposed exceptions as internal German law.[21]

In December 1990 the Council accepted these proposed rules and they accordingly became part of Community law.[22] These regulations generally excluded east German manufacturers and agricultural producers from EC regulations—particularly from regulations relating to environmental protection—for an interim period, but obliged the federal government to take measures to assure that the nonconforming goods be sold only within the territory of the former GDR.[23] In light of continuing economic uncertainties in the five eastern Länder, additional EEC measures were considered possible, but this transitional period was in general concluded by the end of 1992.[24]

The practical impact of the EC on German unification did not come in the form of economic regulation only. Indeed, as a region in need of economic assistance, eastern Germany was entitled to substantial subsidies from the Community. Although Chancellor Kohl was originally prepared to forgo these subsidies—to placate southern EC member states which feared the diversion of funds they otherwise could receive—the EC rejected this act of self-denial.[25] Accordingly, eastern Germany received approximately DM 6 billion from the European Community between 1991 and 1993. In its next five-year plan, commencing in 1994, the EC classified eastern Germany as a "Goal 1 territory"—an underdeveloped territory—in need of assistance.[26]

## German Unification, Maastricht, and the Future of the European Union

Yet the importance of the European Community for German unification was not limited to the EC's previous role as an economic lawgiver for the member states and a provider of financial support for eastern Germany. Perhaps an even more important aspect lay in its function in Chancellor Kohl's Adenauer-like vision of a united Germany whose power was restrained and modified by being embedded in a Europe that was moving closer to its own unification. This vision accorded a central role to the European Community, which would ultimately involve a substantial merger of the German national economy with the larger economy of Europe, as well as the transfer of much national political power to European institutions.

From an early point in the course of German unification, the government of the Federal Republic believed that—in order to render unification palatable to the European and western allies, and perhaps to restrain possible nationalistic tendencies within Germany itself—unification must be accompanied by a substantial further "deepening" of the European Community, which would develop toward a form of political confederation. Steps in the direction of an economic "deepening" had already been taken in the 1980s, with the adoption of the Single European Act. But at an early point in 1990 Chancellor Kohl and French President Mitterrand pushed for the creation of a single European currency supervised by a single European bank, as well as considerably more pervasive powers of monetary and financial regulation within the Community.[27] These developments were also accompanied by the skepticism of some voices—particularly in England and France—which proclaimed that these plans would not limit Germany's power by setting it within the larger European context, but would rather establish a structure through which the German economy and political system would dominate the European Community in the long run. Certainly, even before the 1990s West Germany clearly possessed the strongest economy in the Community and also exercised a predominant role in the Community's monetary policy.[28]

These objections were brushed aside, however, and the Community adopted important changes that would "deepen" the European structure. The changes were also to require significant constitutional amendments within the Federal Republic itself. These provisions represent an important movement toward a more political function of the EC—a "politicization"[29] that seemed to parallel a similar development toward the political in NATO.

### *The Adoption of the Maastricht Treaty*

In 1987 a complex of economic and political factors had led the European Community to amend its governing documents in the Single European Act for the purpose of abolishing most remaining internal trade restraints and creating a single European market.[30] But many recognized that the goal of a true single market could not be accomplished as long as the free flow of capital was impeded by differing currency regimes. Accordingly, in a process dramatically accelerated by Kohl and Mitterrand during the period of German unification, the nations of the Community signed the pathbreaking Maastricht Treaty in February 1992. The agreement created a new European Union which was to include—but would also move beyond—the existing Community structures.

The central provisions of the Maastricht accord were economic and monetary, providing for a central European bank and a single European currency and monetary policy by 1999. Economic provisions accord the European Union power, for example, to police the deficits of the member states.[31] The agreement contained a number of somewhat more modest political provisions as well. It sought to further democracy, often said to be lacking in the EC structure, by strengthening the European Parliament to some extent, and it also created an overall Union citizenship, which was to provide local electoral rights for EU citizens residing in other member states.[32] Moreover, the accord contained provisions on European security and foreign policy and contemplated cooperative efforts with respect to the justice system and other internal matters.[33]

Because of the almost revolutionary changes foreseen by the treaty—particularly the replacement of national currencies by a European monetary unit—the path toward ratification was by no means easy. The first clear sign of trouble came with the rejection of the treaty in a plebiscite in Denmark in June 1992.[34] The treaty was then narrowly approved in a plebiscite in France—hardly a ringing affirmation, however, in a country traditionally friendly to Europe. Finally, a rebellion of conservative members of parliament in England delayed ratification and almost caused the fall of the Conservative government.

In contrast, however, the German Bundestag approved the treaty in December 1992 by the overwhelming vote of 543 to 17, with 8 abstentions,[35] and the Bundesrat also voted its approval. But along with its ratification, the Bundestag adopted a resolution expressing some important qualifications.[36] The resolution urged progress toward a European political union, but it recognized popular anxiety over the prospective replacement of the Deutsche Mark by a European currency. Accordingly, it insisted that the treaty's criteria for monetary stability be strictly observed when the European currency is ultimately introduced in the treaty's "third stage" (no later than 1999), and it declared that commencement of the third stage would require a separate vote of approval by the German parliament. Whether or not this separate vote would have any legally binding effect, Chancellor Kohl stated that the government would observe this wish of the Bundestag.[37]

In a meeting in December 1992 in Edinburgh, the EC agreed that Denmark would not have to participate in the European central bank or the European currency union and that Denmark would be exempt from the defense policies of the European Union.[38] In light of these concessions, Danish voters approved the Maastricht accord by a clear majority in May 1993.[39]

*Amending the Basic Law in Response to the Maastricht Treaty*

It was at least arguable that the Maastricht accord went beyond what was contemplated or permitted by the Basic Law and that significant constitutional amendments would therefore be necessary. Moreover, the German Länder saw an opportunity to employ their power in the Bundesrat to achieve a greater independent role in the European Union[40]—a goal they had also pursued in negotiations over the Single European Act. In response to these concerns, therefore, parliament adopted a series of constitutional amendments in December 1992. Interestingly, these were the first amendments to emerge from the Joint Commission that had been established under the Unification Treaty to propose constitutional changes related to unification.[41] Some of these amendments may reflect a changing constitutional consciousness that could have important implications for the future.[42]

The central constitutional question raised by the Maastricht accord was whether the German government had the authority to transfer powers of sovereignty to a "European Union" such as that envisioned in the treaty. Of course, article 24(1) of the Basic Law does authorize the transfer of sovereign rights to "international organizations" (*zwischenstaatliche Einrichtungen*), and this provision may well have authorized German participation in the Maastricht Treaty without any constitutional change.[43] But some argued that the European Union, with its autonomous power over a projected European currency, was itself something like a state or that it was, in any event, an entity that went beyond the type of "international organization" contemplated by article 24.[44] Probably not very much is to be gained through conceptualistic debates over the difference between an "international organization" and a "state-like entity." Rather, the essential question is whether the political decision of 1948–49 to allow the transfer of powers of sovereignty to an international entity is broad enough to permit the transfer of *these* powers in this way. Given the extraordinary openness and flux of political forms in that period, it is difficult to find much significant limitation in article 24(1).

Yet, perhaps to be on the safe side, the government decided that a constitutional amendment to permit this transfer of power was advisable. Accordingly, in the central constitutional amendment evoked by the Maastricht Treaty, the parliament added a new article 23 authorizing the transfer of sovereign rights to a "European Union."[45] In this provision, moreover, the parliament included institutional restrictions on the kind of "European Union" to which sovereign rights could be transferred. According to the new article 23, such a European Union must be characterized by democratic, social, and federal principles, as well as the principle of the rule of law. Although the restrictions mirrored provisions that were already in the Maastricht Treaty, the listing of these characteristics evoked at least some theoretical problems.

Of these requirements, the specification of "democracy" raised the most serious contemporary issues.[46] Although the European Community is certainly "republican" in the Madisonian sense—because it traces its legitimation (indirectly) back to the people—its basic legislative organ is the Council of Ministers, composed of executive officers of the member states who are themselves indirectly elected in most cases. Moreover, many substantive rules are made by the Commission, an appointed rather than an elected body, and the European Parliament is still far from being a comprehensive legislative organ.[47] Consequently, some argue that the European institutions remain too far removed from the people to meet the constitutional requirement of democracy. Perhaps this limitation requires that the authority of the European Parliament be significantly expanded.[48]

Article 23 also states that the European Union must be bound by the principle of "subsidiarity," and the same requirement is contained in the Maastricht accord itself. This vague and conceptually difficult principle is intended to preserve the authority of the member states by according to the European Union—in certain areas—only the power that cannot be exercised in an adequate manner on the national level.[49] This entire attempt to restrict the power of a central organ through a definitional "parchment barrier" seems deeply problematic; certainly, relevant American experience during the twentieth century is far from encouraging.[50] Yet the attempt certainly responds to a widespread belief in Europe that the Community has unnecessarily extended its authority into matters of primarily local concern.[51]

Article 23 also requires that the European Union guarantee basic rights in a manner substantially comparable with the protections of the Basic Law. In this provision, the Basic Law explicitly incorporates a concept that has been developed by the Constitutional Court in a series of important cases referred to as its "Solange" decisions.[52] In the first of these cases, the Court held that it would examine decisions of the European Court of Justice for their constitutionality under the Basic Law and would continue to do so "so long as" (*solange*) the European Court was not bound by a catalog of human rights guarantees.[53] After some years, however, the Constitutional Court changed its view and held that it would no longer review the constitutionality of European decisions. In light of the expanding protection of human rights on the European level, the Court concluded that the European Court of Justice now protects a series of constitutional rights that are comparable with those of the Basic Law.[54] In accordance with this position, the Maastricht Treaty explicitly requires the Union to "respect fundamental rights, as guaranteed by the [European Human Rights Convention] and as they result from the constitutional traditions common to the Member States, as general principles of Community law."[55]

Article 23 of the Basic Law also requires that any German statute transferring sovereign rights to the European Union must be approved by the Bundesrat. Moreover, any EU treaty alteration that would have the effect of amending or extending the Basic Law must comply with the provisions for amending the Basic Law set forth in article 79 GG—including a two-thirds vote of approval in the Bundestag and the Bundesrat and limitation by the substantive restrictions on amendment set forth in article 79(3).[56] It is likely that some, but not all, future changes in the EU treaty would require approval by these special two-thirds majorities.[57]

Once these powers have been transferred to the European Union, however, it seemed clear that their exercise by the Union would represent a further shift of authority away from the German parliament and the states to the federal executive, which participates in the European Council of Ministers. To redress this asserted imbalance, the states sought to increase their participation in the European process by significantly strengthening the role of the Bundesrat, the representative of the states. Some may speculate that this interesting development could mark the beginning of a movement toward a Europe of regions,[58] in which sub-national political units and the European Union might be as strong as the traditional nation states and eventually might even exceed the traditional nation states in importance.

Accordingly, article 23(4) authorizes the Bundesrat to participate in federal decisions on European measures to the extent that the states would have had authority to undertake analogous measures within Germany—or to the extent that the Bundesrat would have been authorized to participate if the decision were being made solely under German law. Even where the measure falls within the exclusive province of the federal government, the government must take into account the views of the Bundesrat. Moreover, when the institutions or powers of the states are *principally* affected, the federal government must take the wishes of the Bundesrat into account in an authoritative manner.[59] The use of the word "authoritative" (*maßgeblich*) implies that the Bundesrat will ordinarily have the last word on such matters.[60]

Most interestingly, the federal government is required to relinquish much of its actual authority in European affairs when a proposed European measure principally touches the *exclusive* legislative authority of the German states. In such a case, the rights of Germany as a member state are to be transferred to a representative of the Länder, chosen by the Bundesrat, and that representative will conduct the negotiations for Germany with the relevant European institutions. On the other hand, however, this officer must act with the participation and coordination (*Abstimmung*) of the federal government.[61] Accordingly, only practice will show how truly independent the representatives of the states can be under these circumstances. Yet, at least one commentator has referred to this as the "decisive" provision of the new article 23 and has speculated that the division of foreign policy competence that it portends may ultimately weaken the authority of Germany within the European Union.[62]

Article 88 of the Basic Law accords constitutional status to the German central bank—the Bundesbank—and this institution has long symbolized monetary stability and the strength of the Deutsche Mark. The Maastricht Treaty touched a sensitive nerve, therefore, when it provided that monetary authority would be transferred from the central banks of the member states (including the Bundesbank) to a European central bank by 1999. In accordance with this provision, parliament amended article 88 GG to permit the transfer of monetary authority to the European central bank, but—reflecting popular sensitivity on this issue—it also imposed strict limitations on the nature of the European bank to which authority could be transferred. Designed to assure that only a strong and stable European currency would replace the Deutsche Mark, article 88 requires that the European central bank be "independent . . . and dedicated to the primary goal of assuring the stability of prices." Indeed, the contemplated European bank has "been patterned on the Bundesbank," and the constitutional requirements for the European bank have been drawn from statutory principles currently applicable to the Bundesbank.[63]

A final constitutional amendment required by the Maastricht Treaty may signal at least a partial change in a particularly troubling aspect of German constitutional theory under the Basic Law. The concept of German citizenship under the Basic Law rests primarily on the principle of *jus sanguinis*—the view that citizenship is principally dependent on "ethnicity."[64] Indeed, this concept was reinforced in recent cases in which the Constitutional Court struck down state statutes granting voting rights in local elections to "non-Germans" (non-citizens) who were longtime residents of the locality.[65] In contrast, the Maastricht Treaty creates a European citizenship and requires that each member state extend voting rights in local elections to citizens of other member states residing there. Accordingly, an addition to article 28(1) GG relaxes the principal of *jus sanguinis* by permitting citizens of other EC member states to vote (and be elected) in German local elections in accordance with the law of the European Community.[66]

In sum, the constitutional amendments that have resulted from the Maastricht Treaty effect significant shifts in certain aspects of doctrine under the Basic Law. First and most important, the amendments represent a further transfer of German sovereignty to broader European structures, in accordance with Kohl's general strategy for German foreign policy during and after unification. Second, the amendments relax the traditional hegemony of the central government in foreign affairs and accord the states (through the Bundesrat) an independent role in relations with the European Union; this change could portend a further strengthening of the states as regions in the future structure of Europe. Third, the exclusionary principle of *jus sanguinis*—a traditional principle of "ethnic" hegemony whose presence in the Basic Law seems to ignore a crucial lesson that should have been learned from the racialist horrors of the "Third Reich"—has been loosened, in a small way at least, to extend local electoral rights to nationals of other EU member states residing in Germany.

## The Constitutional Challenge to the Maastricht Accord

The adoption of these constitutional amendments, however, was not the end of the story. Urging a number of arguments, a former German EC official as well as certain members of the Greens filed complaints in the federal Constitutional Court, arguing that German approval of the Maastricht Treaty would be unconstitutional. In response to these claims, the Constitutional Court contemplated issuing a temporary injunction against adoption of the treaty and was apparently dissuaded from doing so only because President von Weizsäcker agreed to delay filing the final documents of ratification.[67] Although approved by the Bundesrat and Bundestag, therefore, the final ratification of the treaty had to await a decision of the Constitutional Court. When the Court issued its favorable decision, Germany became the last of the EU member states to ratify the Maastricht Treaty.[68]

The constitutional attack on the Maastricht Treaty and the European Union reflected two sets of concerns. First, some feared that the extensive powers transferred to the European Union would be removed from democratic control—because of the weakness of the European Parliament, the strength of the unelected community bureaucracy in Brussels, and the indirect election of members of the all-important Council of Ministers.

But a second aspect of the challenge raised even deeper and more unsettling issues. Reflecting nationalistic premises, these arguments advanced the view that the German people must constitutionally be represented by a "German" state and that the Maastricht Treaty gave too much *Staatlichkeit*—state authority—away to an international system in which the German people would not necessarily be in control. Indeed, because these changes had been accomplished by constitutional amendment, the argument went even further to assert that article 79(3) GG preserves this core of inherent "German statehood" even against a constitutional amendment. In this view, therefore, the total rejection of the Basic Law and the adoption of a new constitutional system (perhaps by plebiscite) would be necessary for adoption of the Maastricht accord.[69] This challenge represented a frontal attack on the attempts of Chancellor Kohl to transfer substantial aspects of German sovereignty to the broader structures of the European Union.

The case—with its importance and drama—was argued for two days in the Constitutional Court. When the decision came, the Court focused its opinion on the question of whether the Maastricht accord violated democratic norms.[70] Yet, even so, it found a way to intimate some of its views on the question of "statehood" as well.

In handing down this decision, the Court seemed to follow a pattern of compromise familiar in other recent cases that have arisen out of German unification. It upheld the treaty in principle, but it also intimated some substantial—and even somewhat surprising—limits on what the government might do under the treaty. In this way, the Court in effect endorsed Kohl's attempts to embed the enlarged Federal Republic in Europe, but it also gave a measure of comfort to those who asserted that there were some limitations on this process. Indeed, given the skepticism shown in the ratification process in Denmark, France, and elsewhere, the Court's scarcely veiled warnings against further "deepening" of the EU in the near future may have done little more than recognize a situation that already existed on the political level.[71]

The Court began its opinion with a general discussion of the constitutional principle of democracy in the context of the European Union.[72] The Court noted that the Basic Law contemplates European integration, and therefore the danger that German interests could be outvoted did not in itself make a European Union unconstitutional.[73] On the other hand, the Basic Law requires that an appropriate degree of democratic and popular legitimation be maintained in the construction of the Union.[74] Indeed, democracy presupposes the presence of certain "pre-legal" factors, such as a free exchange of views "among contending social forces, interests and ideas" and a public opinion that "forms the political will." The resulting political process must be "intelligible and open to view," and the citizens must be able to communicate with the government in their own language.[75] The requirements that the Court is imposing for democracy in the European Union in this broad passage are not entirely clear: if the Court is implying that democracy to some extent requires unity of language, that restriction in itself could impose very substantial limits on a European Union.

The Court went on to note that, at present, the European Parliament plays a relatively modest role, and therefore the Union's democratic legitimation cannot rely on the acts of that parliament. Rather the Union's democracy must principally arise from a linkage with the democratic parliaments of the member states.[76] But if democratic legitimacy is to come principally from the national parliaments, instead of from the Union itself, the authority of the Union must be subject to significant limits. Indeed, the member states must retain "their own sufficiently important areas of competence, in which each 'state-people' [*Staatsvolk*] . . . can develop and express itself—in order to give legal meaning to [those things] that bind it together spiritually, socially, and politically."[77] In sum, in order to satisfy the constitutional requirement of democracy, significant governmental authority must remain with the German Bundestag.[78]

Accordingly, the decision to participate in the European Union must be made by the Bundestag, and any transfer of sovereign rights by the Bundestag must be made with sufficient clarity. A transfer of rights in unclear language would be equivalent to a general grant of authority to the Union and would go beyond the constitutional limits of democracy.[79] Moreover, any Union measures that exceed the powers granted by the Bundestag would not be binding in Germany, and German officials would be constitutionally prohibited from applying them. Indeed, the Constitutional Court remains the final judge of whether measures of the Union exceed the Bundestag's authorization.[80]

The Court then concluded that the European Union created by the Maastricht Treaty did indeed satisfy the requirements of democracy. It found that the Union was not itself a new state; rather, it was an "integrated system of states" (*Staatenverbund*) in which the independence and sovereignty of the member states continue to be recognized. The Federal Republic retains power to withdraw from the treaty and, in any case, the Bundestag can exert significant influence on the Union's affairs, through the special rules of article 23 GG in addition to the usual methods of parliamentary control of the government.[81]

The Court also found that the treaty satisfied the requirement that German governmental authority be transferred with sufficient certainty and clarity.[82] Under the treaty the Union only receives "limited individual grants of power" from the member states,[83] and it depends on the member states for its funds. The Union has no authority to determine its own competence or to raise funds on the basis of its own determination of what is necessary to achieve its goals. If the European organs were to assert such authority, those measures would exceed the limits of the Union Treaty—as approved by the Bundestag—and therefore would not be legally binding in Germany. Indeed, German officials would necessarily refuse to enforce such measures.[84]

Moreover, the contemplated development toward a currency union does not represent an undue alienation of democratic authority: this process requires independent actions of member states, and the creation of a central European bank must respect the member states' constitutional requirements. Indeed, the Bundestag's demand that it approve Germany's entry into the "third stage" of the currency union apparently will be respected.[85]

The measures to be taken after entry into the currency union are also set forth with adequate clarity: the European central bank is dedicated to independence and price stability, and the treaty contains regulations designed to protect those qualities. Indeed, the concept of a currency union devoted to stability is the basis of the Bundestag's grant of power: if the currency union failed to develop in accordance with that principle, the fundamental conception of the treaty would have been abandoned.[86]

In the Court's view, therefore, the treaty allows "adequate tasks and authorities of substantial political weight" to remain with the Bundestag. It limits the Union's dynamic development and reaches an adequate compromise between the authority of the Union and that of the German parliament.[87] The treaty does contain a statement of general goals, but this statement does not constitute a grant of authority to the Union. The goals may assist in interpreting specific grants of authority, but if they were used expansively to change the treaty, such an interpretation would have "no binding effect for Germany."[88]

Moreover, the Union's "limited authority" is further restricted by the principle of subsidiarity. In considering a proposed measure, the European lawmaker must decide whether its purpose could be adequately achieved on the national—rather than the European—level. This principle, which preserves the authority and "national identity" of the member states, must be monitored by the European court.[89] Similarly, the principle of proportionality, set forth in the Union Treaty, is intended "to preserve the national identity of the member states, and . . . their parliaments, against over-reaching by European regulations."[90]

In general, the Court recognizes that the democracy of the European Union has not been developed in accordance with the extension of the Union's authority. Because of the present democratic deficits in the Union, the principle of democracy requires the continuation of a substantial independent role for the member states and their parliaments. At this point, therefore, the Court's insistence on the principle of democracy in effect also requires an insistence on the principle of independent "stateness" (*Staatlichkeit*) of the individual member states. For now, the principle of democracy yields a strong principle of individual statehood. In its interpretation of the democracy principle, therefore, the Court effectively imposes constitutional limitations on the present extent of Union activities. Whether that principle will be altered, in case democracy within the Union is substantially increased, remains still to be determined.

In understanding the broader implications of the *Maastricht* case it may be useful to view that opinion in light of the Court's recent *Bundeswehr* decision.[91] In an important sense, both the *Maastricht* case and the *Bundeswehr* decision deal with constitutional issues of state "sovereignty." Indeed, in both decisions, the Constitutional Court in effect contrasts what might be viewed as the imperatives of individual state sovereignty against the drive to dissolve aspects of this sovereignty in a larger international structure.

In both of these cases, the Court indicates that these contrasting values remain in a perhaps unstable tension. In the *Bundeswehr* case, the Court allows a more extensive assertion of German "sovereignty"—achieved in the Two Plus Four agreement—by relaxing constitutional restrictions that had been supposed by many to exist on the use of German armed forces. Yet, even so, the Court's decision seems very carefully drawn—at present going only so far as to allow the use of forces within the restraining confines of some international system, whether it be the United Nations or NATO.

Conversely, in the *Maastricht* decision, the Court allows the further dissolution of German sovereignty in the more extensive competence and authority of the European Union. Yet in doing so, it reserves for at least the immediate future the constitutional necessity of significant German "statehood"—although the decision is reached under the rubric of democracy and article 38 GG.

In reaching these decisions, the Court—as in the internal cases dealing with German unification—seems to be serving a mediating or balancing function. In those internal cases, the courts seemed to mitigate some of the hard-line positions of the western conservative tradition—to some extent in favor of less well represented eastern interests. In the external cases, in contrast, the Court seems at least as interested in preserving traditional elements of German "sovereignty" and statehood, against arguments that they should be restricted (as in the *Bundeswehr* case) or more fully dissolved into a developing European Union. Accordingly, where internal peace or "inner unification" may be threatened, the Court reaches a balance by loosening some aspects of the Unification Treaty or of the prevailing conservative tradition in their application to the east. But in the *Maastricht* decision, where the Court may believe that the government is moving too quickly toward internationalism, the Court raises a warning hand, to protect what it views as core aspects of traditional state "sovereignty."

CHAPTER 24

# Conclusion

THE CONSTITUTIONAL problems of German unification, which began to assume tangible form in late 1989, have occupied the attentions and energies of participants and observers for more than five years and will probably continue to do so for years to come. Yet at this point, in the autumn of 1995, many of the constitutional issues have been resolved in principle, and it is possible to review these extraordinary developments with some degree of perspective.

The problems that seemed most pressing at the outset—in late 1989 and early 1990—concerned the transformation of the constitutional system of the GDR into a democratic regime that could be merged with that of the Federal Republic. The events of this early period were played out against the background of the 1968/74 Constitution of the GDR, which clearly revealed the hard-line characteristics of the East German state. Under this document, the dominance of the Communist Party was implemented through the technique of democratic centralism, and the entire state was sustained through an extraordinary servile relationship with the Soviet Union. Traditional constitutional rights were highly qualified and, in any event, not observed in practice—although economic rights played a more significant role.

As the East German revolution gathered momentum, the central constitutional task was to move away from the Stalinist constitution of the past toward a liberal document that would be consistent with basic western principles. Under the reformist SED government of Hans Modrow, therefore, the GDR Constitution was amended to abolish the leading role of the Communist Party and to dissolve institutions of democratic centralism such as the "National Front." Another amendment moved tentatively toward market capitalism by relaxing strict ideas of socialist property and allowing joint ventures with foreign investors.

After the first free election in the GDR, more sweeping constitutional amendments under the government of Lothar de Maizière formed part of the constitutional preparation for unification; in particular, the GDR Volkskammer adopted a series of bridging amendments that incorporated the fundamental principles of the Basic Law. These changes were required by the first State Treaty between the GDR and the Federal Republic—an agreement that also extended the western Deutsche Mark to the east and confirmed the government's choice of "accession" under article 23 GG, rather than merger of the two states through the adoption of a new constitution under article 146.

Although the East German Round Table sought to prepare a new constitution for an independent and democratic GDR, these plans were overtaken by the movement toward unification. Nonetheless this draft charter—reflecting a constitutional consciousness that was somewhat more egalitarian and plebiscitary than that of the Basic Law—attracted substantial attention and influenced numerous aspects of the constitutions adopted by the five new Länder after unification. But, on the federal level, a parliamentary Joint Commission that was established to consider amending the Basic Law generally rejected these innovations. Ultimately, rather modest constitutional amendments on environmental protection, affirmative action for women, and protection of the handicapped were adopted.

The Unification Treaty that was signed in the summer of 1990 represented an extraordinary triumph of legal expertise. Yet critics found that it was impaired by some deficits of democratic legitimacy, as most of its detailed provisions were drafted by western governmental agencies and the contributions of the parliaments and the public were correspondingly reduced. In general, the treaty extended western law to the east, although elaborate attachments introduced some qualifications in this process.

Moreover, the document reflected deeper constitutional problems that quickly came to the surface after the euphoria of the unification period. Dramatic rifts between east and west were evident, for example, in constitutional questions relating to property. In principle, the treaty returned property expropriated by the GDR to its prior (now largely western) owners at the expense of many eastern residents and tenants; in contrast, land expropriated in the Bodenreform of the Soviet occupation period was excluded from restitution under the Unification Treaty. Although this resolution was upheld by the Constitutional Court, parliamentary consideration of compensation and related matters led to a bitter struggle between the former large landowners (or their heirs)—now generally living in the west—and the eastern successor organizations of the former GDR agricultural collectives. With respect to the ownership of industrial and other enterprises, the western government—acting through the Treuhand—rejected an interim regime of mixed business forms and pursued a relentless policy of the sale of eastern concerns into western hands. The result was a massive shift of control of eastern enterprises to the west.

The Unification Treaty struck a temporizing compromise between eastern and western constitutional views of abortion, and these disputes also continued on in the post-unification period. But in other instances the treaty seemed to impose western solutions of problems on the eastern past—although some eastern reformers also supported these measures which often penalized former collaborators with the GDR regime. Accordingly, broad regulations excluded individuals from the public service on political grounds or because of affiliation with the Stasi; and eastern institutions such as the civil service, the judiciary, and the universities were almost completely transformed to accord with western structures. Similarly, there were numerous prosecutions of former GDR officials for shootings at the Wall, oppressive judicial decisions, and other offenses, in cases that raised complex constitutional issues of retroactive justice. But even when there were convictions in these cases, the generally light penalties suggested that the actual goal was affirming the criminal nature of the GDR regime, rather than punishment in the more traditional sense. At the same time, millions of Deutsche Marks were awarded for "rehabilitation" of those who had been oppressed in the GDR, although victims complained that this compensation was grudging and insufficient. All of these contentious issues were played out against the background of the massive specter of the files of the East German secret police (Stasi), which occupied a central position in East German life and society after unification.

But while the conservative coalition in Bonn was seeking to extend traditional western structures to the east, it was asserting a somewhat different position in the external aspects of unification. On these foreign policy issues, the government of Chancellor Kohl—following the general outlines of Konrad Adenauer's views—turned away from vigorous assertions of German "statehood" and, in contrast, sought to dissolve aspects of German sovereignty in wider European structures.

In a crucial foreign policy measure, the Allied powers released their reserved rights over Germany in the Two Plus Four agreement which accompanied German unification. In return for that measure, and for the Soviet Union's agreement that united Germany be permitted to remain in NATO, Germany relinquished any residual claim to territory east of the Oder-Neiße line, agreed to significant restrictions on the size of its armed forces, and confirmed its renunciation of atomic, biological, and chemical weapons. Moreover, the Federal Republic furnished substantial financial support to the Soviet Union, and the two powers entered into a comprehensive friendship agreement.

Notwithstanding the continuation of delicate relations—arising from memories of the Nazi period and its aftermath—Germany also entered into friendship treaties with its neighbors Poland and (the former) Czechoslovakia, as well as other members of the former east bloc. Moreover, Chancellor Kohl strongly supported the "deepening" of the European Union through the merging of aspects of national sovereignty—particularly control over economics and currency—in wider European structures. In entering into the Maastricht agreement, which provided for a European currency by the end of the decade, Kohl pursued an aspect of these aims although he had sought even stronger joint European institutions. The prevailing coalition in Bonn also maintained that it had a constitutional basis for employing German armed forces outside of the NATO territory, albeit within the larger institutional structures of NATO and the United Nations. The Constitutional Court generally supported the government in this view.

But even in internal affairs, where the conservative coalition was generally able to extend many of its favored structures to the east, a number of qualifications were necessary. Many of these prevailing "western" views were not universally accepted in the west itself—indeed, many of these views had only been adopted in the west over substantial minority opposition, primarily from the SPD. Accordingly, in disputes between east and west, the western SPD often supported prevailing eastern positions on constitutional and legal issues. Moreover, the SPD's political authority became substantially stronger after it achieved majority status in the Bundesrat in the midst of the unification process in 1990. Therefore, on certain aspects of legislative action relating to constitutional issues, the influence of the SPD allied with eastern Länder in the Bundesrat formed a very powerful counterweight to the position of the western government. This alliance was important, for example, in complex negotiations on the property compensation law (EALG), in which the SPD and some eastern state governments achieved a result that may preserve the cooperative successors of the GDR collectives against challenges from the former large land owners now generally living in the west. The western SPD (and the FDP) also combined with eastern representatives to preserve important aspects of the GDR's three-month decriminalization of abortion, thus marking a significant change in abortion law in the west as well.

Moreover, in the period following unification, segments of the German judiciary have played a somewhat similar role. The Federal Constitutional Court has sought to act as a powerful mediating organ, seeking an adjustment between competing interests and, particularly, mitigating the strength of western views when they seem to have overborne eastern interests too completely. Among other things, the Court supported the interests of the smaller GDR political parties against a western decision to eliminate them from parliament; required heightened measures of social welfare for eastern public officials rendered jobless through the "Abwicklung" or dissolution of their overstaffed agencies; acted to narrow the exclusion of individuals from the public service on political grounds; and invalidated the criminal prosecutions of many eastern intelligence agents for "treason" and related offenses. In some instances, the Federal Supreme Court (BGH) and other important German tribunals have acted in a similar manner.

Conversely, the Constitutional Court has occasionally intervened to mediate in favor of more traditional forces—most notably by holding that the former owners of property expropriated under the Soviet occupation regime are constitutionally entitled to a measure of compensation. In the abortion case of 1993, the Court upheld the statute providing for three months' decriminalization, but sought to defer to more traditional views by imposing strict requirements of tendentious counseling in favor of childbirth and removing certain abortions from public benefit payments.

In sum, it appears that unification has accelerated the Court's emergence as an organ of government that sees social integration as one of its most important tasks, particularly in the face of the major social cataclysms brought about by a unification that the Court's doctrine itself seemed to require. How the judiciary and the Constitutional Court in particular will pursue these goals into the future can only be the subject of speculation. But it may be important to focus attention on the possibility that the Court may seek to promote social integration by further implementing certain social welfare ideas, which found elaborate expression in the eastern Round Table draft and the eastern state constitutions, through an expansive interpretation of its own jurisprudence on the "social state" provision of the Basic Law.

# NOTES

CHAPTER 2
THE BACKGROUND OF GERMAN UNIFICATION

1. The map at the outset of this volume illustrates these changes.

2. Although France was not represented at Yalta or Potsdam, the French government acceded to relevant portions of the agreements. See 5 BVerfGE 85, 114 (1956). The borders of the occupation zones were first outlined in agreements signed by the three Allies in late 1944. See von Goetze, Die Rechte der Alliierten auf Mitwirkung bei der deutschen Einigung, 1990 NJW 2161, 2162.

3. The Soviet Union had contemplated forming a separate East German state during the Berlin blockade of 1948—or even earlier—but apparently delayed taking this step for tactical reasons. See J. P. Nettl, The Eastern Zone and Soviet Policy in Germany 1945–50, at 109–11(1951); Wolfgang Leonhard, Das kurze Leben der DDR 45–59 (1990).

4. Cf. Friedrich, The Political Theory of the New Democratic Constitutions, in Arnold J. Zurcher (ed.), Constitutions and Constitutional Trends since World War II, at 14–15 (1951): postwar constitutions of Western Europe were products of "negative revolutions"; they were not "the result of any positive enthusiasm for the wonderful future; they [flowed] rather from the negative distaste for a dismal past."

5. See 36 BVerfGE 1, 30–31 (1973).

6. See, e.g., 77 BVerfGE 137, 158–59 (1987).

7. Cf., e.g., Otto Kimminich, Die Eigentumsgarantie im Prozeß der Wiedervereinigung 10 (1990).

8. For important judicial statements of this theory, see 77 BVerfGE 137; 36 BVerfGE at 15–17; 5 BVerfGE at 126–27; see also 6 BVerfGE 309, 336–37, 363–64 (1957) (Concordat case). For general discussions of the constitutional status of the two German states, see Piotrowicz, The Status of Germany in International Law: *Deutschland über Deutschland*?, 38 International and Comparative Law Quarterly 609 (1989); Simma, Legal Aspects of East-West German Relations, 9 Maryland Journal of International Law & Trade 97 (1985); McCurdy, German Reunification: Historical and Legal Roots of Germany's Rapid Progress towards Unity, 22 New York University Journal of International Law & Politics 253, 257–67 (1990).

Yet at least one very distinguished voice rejected the view that the "German Reich" survived the end of the war. The eminent legal philosopher Hans Kelsen argued that by "abolishing the last Government of Germany the victorious powers have destroyed the existence of Germany as a sovereign state. . . . Germany has ceased to exist as a state in the sense of international law." Kelsen, The Legal Status of Germany according to the Declaration of Berlin, 39 American Journal of International Law 518, 519 (1945); see also Kelsen, The International Legal Status of Germany to Be Established Immediately upon Termination of the War, 38 American Journal of International Law 689 (1944). Kelsen's view, however, was largely ignored in the constitutional law of postwar Germany.

9. See Stephen F. Szabo, The Diplomacy of German Unification 7 (1992); David Childs, The GDR: Moscow's German Ally 299–300 (1988). The Soviet Union was

presumably excepted from the Hallstein Doctrine because of its special role as an occupation power.

10. See, e.g., Statement by the Foreign Ministers of the United States, the United Kingdom, and France, September 28, 1955, Dept. of State Bulletin, Oct. 10, 1955, at 559–60 (the "three governments do not recognize the East German regime nor the existence of a state in the Soviet zone"); see also Childs at 299–300.

The judicial systems of the western Allies, however, took a somewhat more variegated position on the acts of the East German government. Invoking a foreign secretary's certificate, for example, a British court found that certain acts of the GDR were entitled to respect on the ground that the GDR was a functioning unit of the Soviet government, which was recognized by Great Britain. Carl Zeiss Stiftung v. Rayner & Keeler Ltd., [1967] 1 A.C. 853. The American courts generally refused to give effect to the actions of the East German government (until it was recognized by the United States in 1974), but certain measures were nonetheless found to be valid on the ground that the GDR was a "de facto" government. See Upright v. Mercury Business Machines Co., 13 A.D.2d 36, 213 N.Y.S. 2d 417 (App. Div. N.Y. 1961); cf. Carl Zeiss Stiftung v. V.E.B. Carl Zeiss, Jena, 293 F.Supp. 892, 900–901 (S.D.N.Y. 1968), *modified* 433 F.2d 686 (2d Cir. 1970).

11. See Ch. 17.

12. See, e.g., Simma, 9 Maryland Journal of International Law & Trade at 98–100.

13. Henry Ashby Turner Jr., Germany from Partition to Reunification 126 (1992); Hermann Weber, DDR: Grundriß der Geschichte 72 (1991). For new information on this incident gained from recently opened Soviet files, see FAZ, Nov. 24, 1993, at 37 col. 3.

14. See, e.g., Piotrowicz, 38 International & Comparative Law Quarterly at 620–21.

15. Rauschning, Deutschlands aktuelle Verfassungslage, 1990 DVBl 393, 394. See Ch. 4. Indeed, the new view was so thoroughly propagated that the text of the GDR national anthem, written by poet and East German government minister Johannes R. Becher, was banned in the GDR itself—principally because of its nationalistic last line: "Germany united fatherland!" See Richard Schröder, Deutschland schwierig Vaterland 11–12 (1993).

16. For the extravagant propaganda campaigns conducted by both sides during this era, see Dieter Vorsteher (ed.), Deutschland im Kalten Krieg 1945–1963 (1992), Catalogue of an Exhibition of the German Historical Museum (Berlin), Aug. 28 to Nov. 24, 1992.

17. Hartmut Zwahr, Ende einer Selbstzerstörung: Leipzig und die Revolution in der DDR 11 (1993).

18. See A. James McAdams, East Germany and Detente: Building Authority after the Wall 9–38 (1985).

19. See 36 BVerfGE 1 (1973); Simma, 9 Maryland Journal of International Law & Trade at 105–8.

The Constitutional Court is a special judicial organ created in the Basic Law principally for the purpose of deciding constitutional questions. See arts. 92–94 GG. In the four decades of its existence, the Court has come to occupy a role in the political life of the Federal Republic that is not unlike that of the Supreme Court in the United States, although there are also many important differences between the two courts in jurisdiction, procedure, and composition. For example, the German Court is divided into two "Senates," each with eight members, and jurisdiction over constitutional questions is divided between the two bodies. See generally Donald P. Kommers, Judicial Politics in

West Germany: A Study of the Federal Constitutional Court (1976); see also Quint, Free Speech and Private Law in German Constitutional Theory, 48 Maryland Law Review 247, 248–49 & n. 4 (1989). The Federal Constitutional Court should not be confused with another important German court, the Federal Supreme Court (Bundesgerichtshof or BGH), which is the chief German court for civil and criminal matters.

20. See Simma, 9 Maryland Journal of International Law & Trade at 115. In his memoirs former Chancellor Brandt referred to the "astonishing argumentation" of parts of the Court's opinion. See Willy Brandt, Erinnerungen 233 (1989).

21. See 36 BVerfGE at 22, 29; 3 Ingo von Münch (ed.), Grundgesetz-Kommentar, art. 146, No. 3 (1983). See also McCurdy, 22 New York University Journal of International Law & Politics at 267–71: "Overall, the treaty's text did a great deal more to bolster the GDR's claims to sovereignty and independence than it did to further the Basic Law's reunification commandment."

22. See Bender, Wege zu einer Nachkriegsgeschichte Deutschlands, in Wolfgang Hardtwig & Heinrich A. Winkler (eds.), Deutsche Entfremdung 76 (1994).

23. See McAdams, East Germany and Detente, at 138–39. Both East and West Germany joined the United Nations in 1973, and the United States recognized the GDR in 1974.

Brandt and his advisors viewed the Ostpolitik as a program that would not only further peace but would also eventually bring the GDR closer to the western system. See Szabo at 7–8. After the collapse of the GDR, however, Brandt's policy has been subject to increased retrospective attack as an unnecessary accommodation that prolonged the life of a regime that had been stabilized by the building of the Wall. In contrast, others argue that Bonn's eastern policy did indeed begin the historical process that led to the dissolution of the GDR. For some current views of the Ostpolitik, see McAdams, Revisiting the *Ostpolitik* in the 1990s, German Politics and Society (No. 30) 49 (1993).

24. Moreover, the GDR's adherence to the Helsinki Final Act—which appeared to guarantee a citizen's right of egress from his or her own country—resulted in a significant increase of applications to leave the country. See Anne Worst, Das Ende eines Geheimdienstes 15 (1991).

25. See, e.g., FAZ, Nov. 19, 1993, at 10 col. 1 (correspondence); FAZ, Nov. 30, 1993, at 10 col. 1 (correspondence); Friedrich Schorlemmer, Bis alle Mauern fallen 115 (1993).

## Chapter 3
## Political Revolution in the GDR, 1989–1990

1. See Hermann Weber, Geschichte der DDR 321–26 (1985). By 1961, more than 2.6 million residents of the GDR had emigrated to the west. Id. at 325.

2. See Konrad H. Jarausch, The Rush to German Unity 18 (1994). After 1984, East German travel restrictions were liberalized to some extent. See Wolfgang Schäuble, Der Vertrag: Wie ich über die deutsche Einheit verhandelte 266–67 (1991). But these changes increased direct experience with western living standards and may actually have furthered discontent in the east.

3. See, e.g., Böhme, Jugendbande oder der mißbrauchte Idealismus, Kursbuch 111, Feb. 1993, at 13; Simon, Ich und sie, id. at 25; Geißler, Kampfreserve der Partei, id. at 35.

4. See Hacker, Das unaufhaltsame Ende der DDR, FAZ, Sept. 26, 1990, at 14 col.

1; cf. Timothy Garton Ash, The Uses of Adversity: Essays on the Fate of Central Europe 251 (1990); Hermann Weber, Aufbau und Fall einer Diktatur 161–64 (1991). Although the GDR government maintained a hard line, there was some admiration for Gorbachev's policies in minority circles in the SED and even in the Stasi. See Jürgen Kuczynski, Schwierige Jahre—mit einem besseren Ende? Tagebuchblätter 1987 bis 1989 (1990); Ariane Riecker et al. (eds.), Stasi intim: Gespräche mit ehemaligen MfS-Angehörigen 40, 49, 216 (1990) (hereafter, Stasi intim).

5. See Kaiser, Germany's Unification, 70 Foreign Affairs (No. 1) 179, 182–84 (1990–91). These events were foreshadowed by a joint declaration, signed by Gorbachev and West German Chancellor Helmut Kohl in June 1989, which referred to a universal right of political self-determination—a right that presumably applied to the peoples of eastern Europe including the GDR. Id. at 183.

6. For useful summaries of the events described here, see, e.g., Micha Wimmer et al. (eds.), "Wir sind das Volk!": Die DDR im Aufbruch (1990) (hereafter, Wir sind das Volk); Neues Forum Leipzig, Jetzt oder nie—Demokratie: Leipziger Herbst '89, at 313–42 (1990). See also Benno Zanetti, Der Weg zur deutschen Einheit (1991); Timothy Garton Ash, The Magic Lantern 61–77 (1990). For a theoretical analysis, see Hirschman, Exit, Voice, and the Fate of the German Democratic Republic, 45 World Politics 173 (1993); for a comprehensive account, see Elizabeth Pond, Beyond the Wall: Germany's Road to Unification (1993).

7. Hungary then officially opened the Austrian border in September. See Jarausch at 15–16. See also Quaritsch, Eigenarten und Rechtsfragen der DDR-Revolution, 1992 VerwArch 314, 327–28; Elster, Constitutionalism in Eastern Europe: An Introduction, 58 University of Chicago Law Review 447, 454–55 (1991).

8. By requiring that the trains first return to the GDR, the regime sought to treat this mass flight as a face-saving "expulsion." See Jarausch at 21; see also Richard Kiessler & Frank Elbe, Ein runder Tisch mit scharfen Ecken: Der diplomatische Weg zur deutschen Einheit 28–44 (1993).

9. See generally Hans Modrow, Aufbruch und Ende 13–14 (1991). For vivid descriptions of other tense scenes along the trains' planned route, see Friedrich Schorlemmer, Bis alle Mauern fallen 95–96 (1993); Pond at 98.

10. Barrios, Von der Revolution zum Beitritt: Die Entwicklung eines gesamtdeutschen Wahl- und Parteiensystems, in Ulrike Liebert & Wolfgang Merkel (eds.), Die Politik zur deutschen Einheit 139 (1991) (hereafter, Die Politik zur deutschen Einheit). For the founding proclamation of New Forum and other early statements of the group, see Jens Reich, Rückkehr nach Europa: Zur neuen Lage der deutschen Nation 184–95 (1991). See also Hartmut Zwahr, Ende einer Selbstzerstörung: Leipzig und die Revolution in der DDR 32–35 & n. 30 (1993).

11. See Wir sind das Volk at 35–37. Democracy Now had roots, extending back to the mid 1980s, in small opposition movements that had grown up within the Evangelical Church. See Bernhard Maleck, Wolfgang Ullmann: "Ich werde nicht schweigen" 66–73 (1991).

12. See Rainer Eppelmann, Wendewege 5–6 (1992); Barrios in Die Politik zur deutschen Einheit at 140; see generally Jarausch at 39–44.

13. For a firsthand account of the Leipzig demonstrations, see Reiner Tetzner, Leipziger Ring (1990); see also Neues Forum Leipzig, Jetzt oder nie—Demokratie. For what will almost certainly become the classic account, see Zwahr, Ende einer Selbstzerstörung.

14. Zwahr, Ende einer Selbstzerstörung, at 25.

Unless otherwise indicated, all translations in this book are those of the author.

15. A significant turning point was reached at the great Leipzig demonstration of October 9. After having employed violent tactics against demonstrators in Berlin two days earlier, the East German Communist Party leader, Erich Honecker, was apparently prepared to dissolve the huge Leipzig demonstration by force of arms. Such a resolution—resembling that imposed by the Chinese government in Tiananmen Square earlier in 1989—could have had incalculable consequences. Cf. John Borneman, After the Wall: East Meets West in the New Berlin 21–22 (1991).

Troop carriers and ambulances filled the streets near the parade route, and demonstrators were gripped by fear as they prepared to march. Zwahr, Wir sind das Volk! Leipzig am 9. Oktober 1989, in Rainer Eckert et al. (eds.), Wendezeiten—Zeitenwände 95 (1991); see also Zwahr, Ende einer Selbstzerstörung, at 79–102; Pond at 111–20. But in ways that are not yet entirely understood, the apparent intention to employ violence was reversed—or orders were not carried out by the local officials in Leipzig. Indeed, "the communist rulers themselves may well have suffered self-doubt and a loss of nerve and were in the end unable or unwilling to perpetrate yet another *Schrecklichkeit.*" Hirschman, 45 World Politics at 196. In any case, according to one observer, after these unfulfilled threats "something broke on this evening deep within [the state], and so at last the whole thing collapsed like a house of cards." Zwahr, Ende einer Selbstzerstörung, at 100.

16. Zwahr, Ende einer Selbstzerstörung, at 61–70; see also Stasi intim at 88–100.

17. See Hacker, FAZ, Sept. 26, 1990, at 14 col. 1; Wolfgang Leonhard, Das kurze Leben der DDR 212 (1990). Indeed, President Gorbachev had ordered Soviet troops to stay in their quarters during these demonstrations, and in summer 1989 high Soviet Army officers in the GDR had already indicated that they would not intervene in civil strife in East Germany. See Smyser, U.S.S.R.-Germany: A Link Restored, 1991 Foreign Policy (No. 84) 125, 127; Quaritsch, 1992 VerwArch at 326.

18. On November 7 the entire government of the GDR resigned, followed on November 8 by the resignation of members of the Politburo of the SED. See Pond at 131.

19. Weber, Aufbau und Fall, at 170, 176–77. For a devastating portrait of Krenz, see Biermann, Wer war Krenz?, in Hubertus Knabe (ed.), Aufbruch in eine andere DDR 29 (1990): "It is the spiritually impoverished and lying optimism, it is the monotonous strength-through-joy cheerfulness that has laughed down at us for decades from this ravaged [Communist Party youth group] face."

20. Wolfgang Thierse, Mit eigener Stimme sprechen 53 (1992); see also Stefan Heym, Filz: Gedanken über das neueste Deutschland 97 (1992): "that memorable meeting in the Alexanderplatz where a few authors and actresses suddenly formed a spiritual bond with the masses and something perceptibly stirred in the people."

21. See Wolfgang Ullmann, Verfassung und Parlament 58–60, 163–64, 199 (1992). See also Reich, Rückkehr nach Europa, at 196–97: "It marked the end [of the GDR], but it could also have been a wonderful beginning. [It was] a kind of swan song. It was the best that the GDR had produced—a final show of political fireworks."

Speeches of the November 4 demonstration were reproduced on three tape cassettes, under the title "Berlin Alexanderplatz 4.11 '89," distributed by Litera, VEB Deutsche Schallplatten Berlin-DDR.

22. Schäuble, Der Vertrag, at 17.

23. See, e.g., Margarita Mathiopoulos, Das Ende der Bonner Republik 198–99

(1993). For the initial confusion about what the Politburo's directive actually meant, and a vivid description of the scene at the Wall on the night of November 9, see Pond at 1–4; see also Pond at 132–34.

24. Mathiopoulos, Das Ende der Bonner Republik, at 197–200; Jarausch at 63–65.

25. See generally Modrow, Aufbruch und Ende; Günter Gaus, Deutsche Zwischentöne: Gesprächs-Porträts aus der DDR 115–40 (1990); Uwe Thaysen, Der Runde Tisch. Oder: Wo blieb das Volk? 163–72 (1990); 5 Dietmar Keller (ed.), Nachdenken über Deutschland 45–75, 149–50 (1991).

26. Keller at 149–50.

27. But the true GDR reformers in Dresden, who had had their difficulties with Modrow and his administration, viewed Modrow's liberal reputation with considerable skepticism. Interview with Steffen Heitmann, Justice Minister of Saxony, Dresden, Nov. 6, 1992.

28. See Erklärung von Ministerpräsident Hans Modrow vor der Volkskammer am 17. November 1989, reprinted in Ingo von Münch (ed.), Dokumente der Wiedervereinigung Deutschlands 33–57 (1991) (hereafter, Dokumente—Wiedervereinigung). For development of Modrow's ideas on the "treaty community," see Modrow at 170–83 (appendix 4).

29. See Anne Worst, Das Ende eines Geheimdienstes 160–69 (1991); Gesetz über den Verkauf volkseigener Gebäude, of March 7, 1990, GBl DDR I 157.

30. See Verordnung zur Arbeit mit Personalunterlagen, of Feb. 22, 1990, GBl DDR I 84; Inga Markovits, Imperfect Justice: An East-West German Diary 141–42 (1995); see also Mathiopoulos, Das Ende der Bonner Republik, at 204.

31. See Ch. 14.

32. For Kohl's plan, see Dokumente—Wiedervereinigung at 57–66. See also Horst Teltschik, 329 Tage: Innenansichten der Einigung 48–62 (1991); Hans-Dietrich Genscher, Erinnerungen 669–75, 683–87 (1995). Western governments complained that they had not been consulted before this important plan was announced, but the Kohl government maintained that consultations had been adequate. See, e.g., Teltschik at 61; Ralf Dahrendorf, Betrachtungen über die Revolution in Europa 157–58 (1992); Pond at 138; Kiessler & Elbe at 49–55.

33. Pond at 140; Weber, Aufbau und Fall, at 177; see also Wolfgang Leonhard, Die Revolution entläßt ihre Kinder (1990). But compare Stern, Freedom and Its Discontents, 72 Foreign Affairs (No. 4) 108, 113 (1993): "As the Communist regime crumbled, East Germans, left in their crowded, drab, decaying dwellings, saw pictures of how the *nomenklatura* had lived in insulated comfort. . . . Had they really not noticed that the much-touted egalitarianism of the first German socialist state had been traduced daily, visibly and invisibly? The apparatchiks had their own Volvos, their children had privileged access to education, and all of them could shop in the Intershops, where Western goods could be bought for Western currency."

34. See, e.g., Quaritsch, 1992 VerwArch at 316–19. See generally Ch. 5.

35. See Barrios in Die Politik zur deutschen Einheit at 141.

36. See Thaysen at 120–30. At a special party congress in early December the SED sought to assert its own status as a reformed party by changing its name to SED-PDS (Party of Democratic Socialism). Cf. Jarausch at 84–85. Thereafter, the initials SED were dropped entirely, and the party became simply the PDS. See Thaysen at 118–20 (discussing reform measures within the SED); McCurdy, 22 New York University Journal of International Law & Politics at 253 n. 4.

37. Helmut Herles & Ewald Rose (eds.), Vom Runden Tisch zum Parlament 23–26 (1990). For historical background of the Round Table, see Thaysen at 25–39; Maleck at 71–73.

Membership in the Round Table was divided equally between the reform groups and the SED and its allies; the SED's significant level of representation may have furthered its acceptance of the Round Table's decisions. See Quaritsch, 1992 VerwArch at 318.

38. See, e.g., Elster, 58 University of Chicago Law Review at 449, 455–58; Rapaczynski, Constitutional Politics in Poland: A Report on the Constitutional Committee of the Polish Parliament, 58 University of Chicago Law Review 595, 598–601 (1991).

In addition to the national Round Table, numerous round tables were created at the local level to maintain negotiations between reformers and the SED leadership in various districts and in specific institutions of the GDR. See, e.g., Interview with Erich Iltgen, President of Saxon Parliament, Dresden, Jan. 18, 1993 (Round Table in Bezirk Dresden); Gläser, Die Akademie der Wissenschaften nach der Wende: erst reformiert, dann ignoriert und schließlich aufgelöst, APuZ, Dec. 11, 1992, at 37, 40 (Round Table in Academy of Sciences). These local round tables often perpetuated dialogues between reformers and local SED leaders that had grown out of the street demonstrations of late 1989. Zwahr, Ende einer Selbstzerstörung, at 76.

39. David Gill & Ulrich Schröter, Das Ministerium für Staatssicherheit: Anatomie des Mielke-Imperiums 183–91 (1993). See Ch. 16.

40. For a contemporary report on the constitutional discussions of that period, see Quint, Building New Institutions in East Germany, The Sun (Baltimore), Jan. 21, 1990, at E1 col. 2.

41. See, e.g., Schäuble, Der Einigungsvertrag—Vollendung der Einheit Deutschlands in Freiheit, 1990 ZG 289, 291; Modrow at 115–26, 184–88 (appendixes 5–6).

42. Kuppe, Modrow in Bonn, 1990 DA 337; Helmut Kohl, Die deutsche Einheit: Reden und Gespräche 150 (1992). Gorbachev's willingness to concede this point encountered some sharp criticism in the USSR. Yuli A. Kvitsinsky, Vor dem Sturm: Erinnerungen eines Diplomaten 18 (1993).

43. See Teltschik at 137–44.

44. Modrow at 79–85; Christa Luft, Zwischen WEnde und Ende 151–59 (1992).

45. Thaysen at 82; see generally id. at 76–98. Indeed, certain GDR statutes of the period delegated a degree of governmental authority to the organizations of the Round Table. See Gesetz über Parteien und andere politische Vereinigungen—Parteiengesetz, of Feb. 21, 1990, GBl DDR I 66 § 18 (1) (certain subsidies to GDR parties will be determined by Council of Ministers "in collaboration with the parties and groups of the Round Table").

46. See Ch. 5. Similarly, in the face of the coming election, Chancellor Kohl had little further interest in negotiations with the Modrow government. A visit to Bonn by Modrow and his coalition leaders, for the purpose of seeking interim financial assistance, encountered a frigid and even humiliating response. See generally Teltschik at 144–45; Schäuble, Der Vertrag, at 29–30; Mathiopoulos, Das Ende der Bonner Republik, at 201–2, 207–9; Modrow at 130–36; Luft at 160–74.

Even in its waning days, however, the Modrow government undertook substantial legislative activity—in effect under the direction of the Round Table. During this final period, such statutes as the Election Law, the Statute on Political Parties, and the Statute on Associations were enacted. See Ch. 5.

47. See Bertram, The German Question, 69 Foreign Affairs (No. 2) 45, 47–48 (1990); see generally McCurdy, 22 New York University Journal of International Law & Politics at 285–95 (discussion of factors favoring swift unification).

48. Mathiopoulos, Das Ende der Bonner Republik, at 170–72; Zwahr, Ende einer Selbstzerstörung, at 54 & nn. 8–9. On de Maizière, see generally, e.g., Gaus, Deutsche Zwischentöne, at 35–55; Margarita Mathiopoulos, Rendezvous mit der DDR 230–62 (1994).

49. Thierse, Mit eigener Stimme, at 30.

50. See, e.g., Roesler, Die Treuhandanstalt: Wirtschaftsimperium oder Politikinstrument?, in Rudiger Liedtke (ed.), Die Treuhand und die zweite Enteignung der Ostdeutschen 19–22 (1993).

51. This shift was clearly apparent, for example, in de Maizière's acceptance speech before the Volkskammer. See Regierungserklärung des Ministerpräsidenten der DDR, Lothar de Maizière, Apr. 19, 1990, reprinted in Dokumente—Wiedervereinigung at 190.

In de Maizière's acceptance speech, numerous references to a western style "social market economy" contrasted sharply with the aspirations for "democratic socialism" in the speeches of former Minister-President Modrow. Yet, although de Maizière clearly contemplated unification as a goal, a number of passages suggested that he believed the process would be a protracted one. In his speech, de Maizière also expressed views that deviated somewhat from those of the western government in Bonn; for example, de Maizière proposed the gradual dissolution of eastern and western military pacts in favor of a European security system. See Dokumente—Wiedervereinigung at 211.

For the hidden role of western advisors in the drafting of de Maizière's acceptance speech, as well as a generally approving western evaluation of the outcome, see Teltschik at 197–203.

## Chapter 4
## Constitutional Reform in the GDR, 1989–1990: Historical Background and the Round Table Draft

1. See Erich Fischer & Werner Künzel (eds.), Verfassungen deutscher Länder und Staaten 274–335 (1989); Andrea Zieger & Gottfried Zieger, Die Verfassungsentwicklung in der sowjetischen Besatzungszone Deutschlands/DDR von 1945 bis Sommer 1952 (1990).

2. See, e.g., Verf. Thür. (1946) art. 56.

3. Although the state constitutions showed some variations, they apparently all rested on a single draft issued by the SED in 1946. See Hans von Mangoldt, Die Verfassungen der neuen Bundesländer 19–20 (1993). These constitutions lapsed when the states of the GDR were abolished in the 1950s, and there was little enthusiasm for their revival when the eastern states were re-created in 1990. See Ch. 9.

4. See David Childs, The GDR: Moscow's German Ally 118 (1988). The Soviet Union's "all-German perspective" during this early period may also have reflected its pessimism about the GDR's chances for long-term survival. See Manfred Uschner, Die Ostpolitik der SPD 45 (1991).

5. See, e.g., Verf. DDR (1949) art. 15 (right to employment); art. 16 (right to paid vacation and to social insurance); Abendroth, Zwiespältiges Verfassungsrecht in Deutschland, 76 AöR 1, 9 (1950).

6. Günter Gaus, Deutsche Zwischentöne: Gesprächs-Porträts aus der DDR 38 (1990).

7. Verf. DDR (1949) art. 92; see Abendroth, 76 AöR at 14–17.

8. See Childs at 119–20.

Other provisions of the 1949 constitution suggested socialist economic themes that were more fully developed at a later stage of the GDR. Article 21 provided for a governmental economic plan, and article 25 required that certain important enterprises be transferred into publicly owned "People's Property."

Following the pattern of the eastern state constitutions, the anti-fascist concerns of the GDR found a very prominent place in the 1949 constitution. According to article 24, "the businesses of war criminals and active National Socialists are expropriated"; the same section also confirmed the sweeping land reform expropriations of the Soviet occupation period. In provisions evoking the issues of the Nuremberg trials, article 135 exempted measures taken against Nazism, fascism, and militarism from the prohibition of retroactive law making, and article 144 declared that constitutional rights cannot undo measures taken "to overcome National Socialism and militarism and to compensate for injustices of which they are guilty." For a provision in the Basic Law intended to have a similar effect, see art. 139 GG.

9. Childs at 77.

10. The final 1974 revisions reflected the views of the government of Erich Honecker, which had replaced that of Ulbricht in 1971.

11. See A. James McAdams, East Germany and Detente: Building Authority after the Wall 128–47 (1985).

12. Müller-Römer, Zur Verfassung der DDR, in Die neue Verfassung der DDR 15, 21–26 (1974) (hereafter, Müller-Römer).

13. The GDR was not the only Warsaw Pact country in which "the constitutions . . . became somewhat less liberal as the Stalinist terror relaxed." This trend was apparently a general one in eastern Europe. See Rapaczynski, Constitutional Politics in Poland: A Report on the Constitutional Committee of the Polish Parliament, 58 University of Chicago Law Review 595, 596 (1991).

14. See Martin McCauley, The German Democratic Republic since 1945, at 143 (1983).

15. Verf. DDR (1974) art. 1.

16. Id. art. 47(2).

17. On "democratic centralism," see, e.g., Weber, Die Geschichte der DDR—Versuch einer vorläufigen Bilanz, in Klaus-Dietmar Henke (ed.), Wann bricht schon mal ein Staat zusammen! Die Debatte über die Stasi-Akten auf dem 39. Historikertag 1992, at 28–29 (1993).

18. Verf. DDR (1974) art. 9(3).

19. Id. art. 6(2).

20. Id. art. 7(2). See generally Zieger, Die Verfassungsänderung in der DDR vom 7.10.1974, 1975 NJW 143. The principle of friendship with the Soviet Union, emphasized in the 1974 constitution, was reinforced in an extraordinary Treaty of Friendship, Cooperation and Mutual Assistance, adopted by the GDR and the Soviet Union in 1975. McAdams, Detente, at 150–51.

21. See, e.g., Rapaczynski, 58 University of Chicago Law Review at 596–97 n. 5; Müller-Römer at 37.

22. See Quaritsch, Eigenarten und Rechtsfragen der DDR-Revolution, 1992 VerwArch 314, 327.

23. Id. In a conversation with Erich Honecker in 1970, for example, Soviet General Secretary Leonid Brezhnev flatly declared that without the Soviet Union the GDR would no longer exist. Id. at 325–26 (citing Peter Przybylski, Tatort Politbüro—Die Akte Honecker 280–85 [1991]).

24. See FAZ, May 11, 1993, at 11 col. 2 (correspondence). On the Jugendweihe, see generally FAZ, Apr. 13, 1994, at 14 col. 2.

25. See Ch. 11.

26. See Müller-Römer at 41; Elling, Privatization in Germany: A Model for Legal and Functional Analysis, 25 Vanderbilt Journal of Transnational Law 581, 601 (1992).

27. See Verf. DDR (1974) art. 13.

28. See Ch. 11. See also Hermann Weber, Geschichte der DDR 314–18 (1985); Verf. DDR (1974) art. 46 (agricultural production collectives). Although the collective held the right to use the property, the legal title remained in the individual owner. Siegfried Mampel, Die sozialistische Verfassung der Deutschen Demokratischen Republik 361 (1982). There were also numerous collectives of workers engaged in the handworking trades.

29. Mampel, Die sozialistische Verfassung, at 361.

30. Id. at 362–63.

31. See Ch. 11. The GDR Constitution of 1968/74 also protected "personal property," held for the purpose of "satisfying the material and cultural needs of the citizens," and it acknowledged the existence of other "private property." Verf. DDR arts. 11, 12; see generally Herwig Roggemann, Die DDR-Verfassungen: Einführung in das Verfassungsrecht der DDR 257–60 (1989). Especially after the final wave of business expropriations in 1972, however, private property played a distinctly subordinate role in the economic and legal structure of the GDR.

32. Brunner, Das Staatsrecht der Deutschen Demokratischen Republik, in Josef Isensee & Paul Kirchhof (eds.), Handbuch des Staatsrechts der Bundesrepublik Deutschland 385, 433 (1987) (hereafter, Handbuch des Staatsrechts). See also Hohmann, Etappen des verfassungsrechtlichen Diskurses und der Verfassungsgesetzgebung nach der revolutionären Wende in der DDR, in Bernd Guggenberger & Tine Stein (eds.), Die Verfassungsdiskussion im Jahr der deutschen Einheit 91 (1991) (hereafter, Verfassungsdiskussion): basic rights in the GDR Constitution have only "semantic parallels" with those of the western type.

33. See, e.g., Verf. DDR (1974) art. 27(1) (right to free expression of opinion "in accordance with the principles of this constitution"); art. 28(1) (right of assembly "in the framework of the principles and goals of the constitution"); art. 29 (right of association "in conformity with the principles and goals of the constitution"); see also id. art. 39(2) (churches and religious communities "order their affairs and exercise their activity in conformity with the constitution and the laws").

34. Verf. DDR (1974) art. 32. In a parallel provision, article 11 of the West German Basic Law grants a right of travel within the territory of the Federal Republic only—although the reality in west and east differed considerably. See, e.g., Klaus Lüderssen, Der Staat geht unter—das Unrecht bleibt? Regierungskriminalität in der ehemaligen DDR 30–31 (1992). Both provisions were apparently derived from an analogous section in the Weimar Constitution. See WRV art. 111.

35. See Verf. DDR (1974) art. 24(1),(3).

36. Id. art. 25(1),(4).

37. Id. art. 34.

38. Id. art. 35.

39. Id. art. 36.

40. Id. art. 37(1).

41. Id. art. 38(2)-(3).

42. See generally Markovits, Law or Order—Constitutionalism and Legality in Eastern Europe, 34 Stanford Law Review 513, 517–18 (1982).

43. See Verf. DDR (1974) art. 24(2). Some early state constitutions in West Germany contained similar obligations. See, e.g., Verf. Hessen (1946) art. 28(2). A possible forerunner, article 163 of the Weimar Constitution, imposed a qualified ethical duty on citizens to use their capacities for the common good.

44. Verf. DDR (1974) art. 25(4).

45. Id. art. 23(1).

46. Indeed, for many in the GDR, social life was largely defined by the "collective" at the workplace—an aspect of social structure that made widespread unemployment after unification particularly difficult to bear. See Hans Joachim Maaz, Das gestürzte Volk oder die verunglückte Einheit 44–49 (1991).

47. See Ch. 9. The GDR Constitution did, however, make provision for local government. See Verf. DDR (1974) arts. 81–85.

48. Verf. DDR (1974) art. 48.

49. See Roggemann, DDR-Verfassungen, at 218–19, 230–31; Günter Grass & Regine Hildebrandt, Schaden begrenzen oder auf die Füße treten: Ein Gespräch 20 (1993) (remarks of Regine Hildebrandt); Wolfgang Leonhard, Das kurze Leben der DDR 220 (1990): the old Volkskammer was "a decorative body of yes-men."

50. See generally Brunner in Handbuch des Staatsrechts at 385, 416–21; Zieger, 1975 NJW at 149–50.

The constitution also emphasized the role of labor unions as part of the structure of the state. Verf. DDR (1974) arts. 44–45. Indeed, the central organization of the unions (FDGB) was authorized to propose statutes in the Volkskammer. Id. art. 65(1).

51. Verf. DDR (1974) art. 96(1); see also id. art. 92.

52. See, e.g., id. arts. 93(3), 74(1), 49(3).

53. See id. art. 50.

54. See id. arts. 90(1), 97. For discussions of "socialist legality" and ideological debates in the GDR concerning this concept, see Mampel, Die sozialistische Verfassung, at 568–72; Roggemann, DDR-Verfassungen, at 155–58; Brunner in Handbuch des Staatsrechts at 405–7.

55. Brunner in Handbuch des Staatsrechts at 430; Verf. DDR (1974) art. 93. For a fascinating description of how the Supreme Court's supervision was sometimes exercised by oral instructions in certain particularly sensitive cases, see Inga Markovits, Imperfect Justice: An East-West German Diary 25–28 (1995).

56. Indeed, more than 80 percent of all the GDR judges (and more than 90 percent of the prosecutors) were members of the SED. See Roggemann, DDR-Verfassungen, at 298.

57. Markovits, Imperfect Justice, at 8–12.

58. See Ch. 14.

59. Gesetz über die Zuständigkeit und das Verfahren der Gerichte zur Nachprüfung von Verwaltungsentscheidungen, of Dec. 14, 1988, GBl DDR I 327. Cf. Markovits, Imperfect Justice, at 176–77.

60. See Hohmann in Verfassungsdiskussion at 88–90.

61. See, e.g., id. at 90; Schlink, Deutsch-deutsche Verfassungsentwicklungen im Jahre 1990, in Verfassungsdiskussion at 21.

62. Templin, Der Verfassungsentwurf des Runden Tisches. Hintergründe und Entstehungsbedingungen, in Verfassungsdiskussion at 352.

63. See Ch. 3; Round Table Declaration of December 7, 1989, reprinted in Arbeitsgruppe "Neue Verfassung der DDR" des Runden Tisches, Verfassungsentwurf für die DDR 75 (1990) (hereafter, RT-Entwurf).

64. See Helmut Herles & Ewald Rose (eds.), Vom Runden Tisch zum Parlament 24 (1990).

65. Schlink in Verfassungsdiskussion at 21.

66. Templin in Verfassungsdiskussion at 350.

67. The working group was also advised by Helmut Simon, a retired justice of the Federal Constitutional Court.

68. Templin in Verfassungsdiskussion at 352.

69. See Klaus Michael Rogner, Der Verfassungsentwurf des Zentralen Runden Tisches der DDR 45–47 (1993).

70. See Ch. 6.

71. The time available for drafting had been sharply curtailed when the GDR elections were advanced from May 6 to March 18 in order to forestall a feared political and economic breakdown in the GDR. See Ch. 3.

72. RT-Entwurf at 75. Several speakers at the Round Table's last meeting viewed adoption of a new GDR Constitution as a means of preserving the country's independence, so that the GDR would go into unification talks as an autonomous entity—with its own values—and not be simply absorbed into the structure of the Federal Republic. See Uwe Thaysen, Der Runde Tisch. Oder: Wo blieb das Volk? 146–47 (1990).

73. For commentary on the Round Table draft by one of the West German advisors, see Preuß, Der Entwurf der Arbeitsgruppe "Neue Verfassung der DDR" des Runden Tisches für eine Verfassung der Deutschen Demokratischen Republik, 1990 KJ 222; Preuß, Auf der Suche nach der Zivilgesellschaft, in Verfassungsdiskussion at 357; see also Preuß, Zu einem neuen Verfassungsverständnis, in Verfassungsdiskussion at 60–62. For a bitter attack on the Round Table draft on the grounds that it represents the "constitutional ideas of a green-red [presumably, Greens and SPD] coalition," see Roellecke, Dritter Weg zum zweiten Fall. Der Verfassungsentwurf des Runden Tisches würde zum Scheitern des Staates führen, in Verfassungsdiskussion at 369. See also, e.g., Isensee, Mit blauem Auge davongekommen—das Grundgesetz, 1993 NJW 2583, 2584–85.

A common charge leveled against the Round Table draft was that it contained proposals that the western academic advisors had for years attempted to insert in the Basic Law, largely without success. Critics also maintained that the draft was not a true product of the Round Table because it was completed and issued by the working group after the Round Table's dissolution—albeit in accordance with its charge. Interview with Lothar de Maizière, Berlin, Dec. 4, 1992; see generally Thaysen at 143–49. Quite different views, however, came from the ranks of the GDR reformers. See, e.g., Bernhard Maleck, Wolfgang Ullmann: "Ich werde nicht schweigen" 82 (1991)(Round Table draft was an "authentic document" reflecting the views of the reform citizens movements and the parties of the old Volkskammer concerning the reformation of the GDR); Friedrich Schorlemmer, Bis alle Mauern fallen 93 (1993): "All in all, the essence [*Extrakt*] of our independently developed experiment in democracy can be found in the constitutional draft of the Round Table."

74. See Fischer, Verfassungsgeschichte der DDR 1990, 1990 KJ 413; Mampel, Das Ende der sozialistischen Verfassung der DDR, 1990 DA 1377, 1385–86;

Häberle, Der Entwurf der Arbeitsgruppe "Neue Verfassung der DDR" des Runden Tisches (1990), 39 JöR 319, 325–27 (1990). This brusque rejection seemed inconsistent with language in the coalition agreement of the GDR's new government which stated that the Round Table draft (along with the GDR Constitution of 1949) would be "taken into account" in any constitutional developments. See Ingo von Münch (ed.), Dokumente der Wiedervereinigung Deutschlands 169 (1991) (hereafter, Dokumente—Wiedervereinigung).

75. One prominent reformer noted: "For me and my friends, one of the most painful experiences of the last half year was that a parliamentary majority decided upon total self-expropriation by not even allowing this product of a self-achieved democracy to be discussed in a committee of the Volkskammer. Was this on outside orders, or in anticipatory obedience?" Friedrich Schorlemmer, Versöhnung in der Wahrheit 102 (1992); see also Schorlemmer, Mauern fallen, at 93.

76. See Ch. 9.

77. See Ch. 10.

78. RT-Entwurf art. 41(1).

79. For discussion, see Schorlemmer, Mauern fallen, at 92–93.

80. For a detailed analysis of the Round Table draft, see Häberle, 39 JöR 319; see also Rogner.

81. See, e.g., Häberle, 39 JöR at 333.

82. See RT-Entwurf art. 12(5).

83. Id. art. 7(2).

84. Id. art. 4(3); Richard Schröder, Deutschland schwierig Vaterland 74–75 (1993). For discussion of the constitutional problems of abortion in the context of German unification, see Ch. 12.

85. RT-Entwurf art. 3(2). This provision reflects the concern of the Round Table itself in pursuing gender equality—as evidenced by detailed principles "for equalization of women and men" adopted in the Round Table's penultimate session on March 5, 1990. See Herles & Rose at 263–78. At this session, the Round Table declared that pursuit of an active gender equalization policy "is to be anchored in the Constitution of the GDR and in other laws." Id. at 275. For the subordinate role of women in the society of the GDR, notwithstanding the high representation of women in the work force, see Rita Süssmuth & Helga Schubert, Bezahlen die Frauen die Wiedervereinigung? (1992).

Perhaps in response to the Round Table draft and the eastern state constitutions, an affirmative action provision for gender equality was subsequently added to the Basic Law. See Ch. 10.

86. RT-Entwurf art. 22(2).

87. Id. art. 1(2).

88. Id. art. 33(1).

89. Id. art. 21(4).

90. Id. art. 33(3).

91. Id. art. 8(2).

92. Id. art. 21(2),(3). In 1990, the Federal Constitutional Court held that the right to vote in local elections could not constitutionally be extended to individuals who were not "Germans" (Deutsche) under article 116 of the Basic Law. 83 BVerfGE 37. This decision can be seen as a regrettable endorsement of an "ethnic" view of citizenship, although it is possible in some instances for persons belonging to another "ethnic" group to become "Germans" by naturalization.

More recently, the Basic Law has been amended to grant voting rights in local elections to citizens of member states of the European Union residing in Germany. This amendment was necessary in order to conform with obligations arising under the Maastricht Treaty. See Ch. 23.

93. RT-Entwurf art. 35. In general, the citizens movements are referred to as "bearers of free societal structuring, criticism, and control." Id. art. 35(1). This phrase seems to reflect the view that organized members of society should exercise some supervision of the government—the actual experience of the GDR Round Table in 1989/90.

94. Id. arts. 35(2), 37(3).

95. Id. art. 1(2).

96. Id. art. 36(2).

97. Id. art. 37(2).

98. Id. art. 39(3).

99. Id. art. 15(1).

100. Id. art. 28.

101. Id. art. 15(3).

102. Id. art. 19(2).

103. Id. art. 29.

104. Id. art. 32(1). For a discussion of the 1945–49 expropriations in the Soviet occupation zone, see Ch. 11.

105. Id. art. 32(2). This provision seems to echo article 155 of the Weimar Constitution, which declared that an "increase in value of land, arising without the investment of labor or capital in the property, is to be made available for use by the community."

106. RT-Entwurf art. 131. In essence, the Round Table draft confirms the 1945–49 expropriations and generally requires return of property or compensation only for those post-1949 expropriations that violated GDR law at the time they were undertaken. For the treatment of these issues in the Unification Treaty, see Ch. 11.

107. See Schlink in Verfassungsdiskussion at 21–22. Of course, these guarantees also reflect provisions of the old GDR constitutions.

108. Herles & Rose at 238–62; Thaysen at 140.

109. RT-Entwurf art. 23(2).

110. Id. art. 25.

111. Id. art. 27(1).

112. Id. art. 24.

113. See Schneider, Deutschland in neuer Verfassung, in Michael Müller & Wolfgang Thierse (eds.), Deutsche Ansichten: Die Republik im Übergang 235 (1992); see also Zielke, Das Recht auf Arbeit in der Verfassung, 1992 RdA 185, 191.

114. Of course, the draft also provides for the re-creation of the states in the GDR. RT-Entwurf art. 129.

115. Id. art. 55(3). In light of German history, the Basic Law contains a number of provisions that seek to preserve governmental and parliamentary stability, and the circumstances under which the Bundestag can in effect dissolve itself are sharply debated. See 62 BVerfGE 1 (1983).

116. RT-Entwurf art. 94(2). Thus the Round Table draft expressly permits a form of "legislative veto" found unconstitutional in the United States. See INS v. Chadha, 462 U.S. 919 (1983).

117. Schlink in Verfassungsdiskussion at 25–26.

118. Id. The Round Table draft also creates a court to decide constitutional matters and prohibits any amendment of the constitution that would impair certain basic princi-

ples. RT-Entwurf arts. 109–12; 100. In both provisions the draft resembles the Basic Law although it differs in some details.

119. See, e.g., Hildegard Hamm-Brücher, Wider die Selbstgerechtigkeit 107–24 (1991).

120. RT-Entwurf art. 98. See Häberle, 39 JöR at 345–46; Schwartz, Constitutional Change and Constitutional Legitimation: The Example of German Unification, 31 Houston Law Review 1027, 1065–68 (1994).

121. See Ch. 9.

122. See RT-Entwurf arts. 135, 132(2), 136; Häberle, 39 JöR at 344–45. See also Ch. 6.

123. Häberle, 39 JöR at 345.

124. See RT-Entwurf arts. 62, 65, 81(2).

## Chapter 5
## Constitutional Reform in the GDR, 1989–1990: Amending the Constitution

1. For a comprehensive discussion of the 1989–90 amendments of the GDR Constitution, see Mampel, Das Ende der sozialistischen Verfassung der DDR, 1990 DA 1377. See also Hohmann, Etappen des verfassungsrechtlichen Diskurses und der Verfassungsgesetzgebung nach der revolutionären Wende in der DDR, in Bernd Guggenberger & Tine Stein (eds.), Die Verfassungsdiskussion im Jahr der deutschen Einheit 91–96 (1991) (hereafter, Verfassungsdiskussion).

2. Gesetz zur Änderung der Verfassung der DDR, of Dec. 1, 1989, GBl DDR I 265. At the same time, the Volkskammer declined to alter language in article 1 proclaiming that the GDR is "a socialist state of workers and farmers." See Mampel, 1990 DA at 1379. This language, which had been added in the 1974 revision, was drawn directly from the 1936 constitution of the Soviet Union. See Zieger, Die Verfassungsänderung in der DDR vom 7.10.1974, 1975 NJW 143, 147. Abandonment of this phrase was apparently too much for the old Volkskammer.

3. See Hohmann in Verfassungsdiskussion at 92. The special leadership role of the Communist Party had been acknowledged as a fundamental principle by German Communist Party leaders as far back as 1944 in their exile in the Soviet Union. FAZ, Nov. 14, 1992, at 4 col. 1.

4. Calls for the amendment of article 1, and abolition of the leading role of the SED, had been heard in the Leipzig demonstrations in November 1989, and citizens in Berlin had gathered signatures on petitions directed against the SED's leadership role. Hartmut Zwahr, Ende einer Selbstzerstörung: Leipzig und die Revolution in der DDR 132 (1993); Günter Grass & Regine Hildebrandt, Schaden begrenzen oder auf die Füße treten: Ein Gespräch 18 (1993) (remarks of Regine Hildebrandt). By December 1 the absolute necessity of such an amendment was clear; the Volkskammer deliberations on the amendment "lasted all of fifteen minutes." Elizabeth Pond, Beyond the Wall: Germany's Road to Unification 11 (1993).

5. Cf. Herwig Roggemann, Die DDR-Verfassungen: Einführung in das Verfassungsrecht der DDR 193–94 (1989) (special role of party in Marxist-Leninist theory).

6. Abolition of the leading role of the Communist Party was also an initial step in constitutional reform in other countries of the east bloc. On November 28, 1989, for example, the Czechoslovak Communist Party pledged to relinquish its monopoly of power, New York Times, Nov. 29, 1989, at A1 col. 6, and on January 15, 1990,

Bulgaria became the last of the Soviet Union's European allies to abolish the party's monopoly by deleting the relevant provision from its constitution. New York Times, Jan. 16, 1990, at A1 col. 2. And, finally, on March 13, 1990, the parliament of the Soviet Union repealed article 6 of its constitution, the provision that had guaranteed the party's political monopoly. New York Times, Mar. 14, 1990, at A1 col. 6.

7. Gesetz zur Änderung und Ergänzung der Verfassung der DDR, of Jan. 12, 1990, GBl DDR I 15. According to article 12(1) of the 1968/74 GDR Constitution, "the minerals of the earth, mines, power plants, dams, large bodies of water, the natural resources of the continental shelf, industrial concerns, banks, [and] insurance companies . . . are People's Property. Private property therein is not permitted." The amendment of January 12, 1990, removed the last sentence and added the statement, "Deviations from this [rule] are permitted if authorized by statute."

8. See Verf. DDR art. 14a. This section also sought to preserve employees' rights of co-determination in concerns with foreign participation in ownership.

9. Verordnung über die Gründung und Tätigkeit von Unternehmen mit ausländischer Beteiligung in der DDR, of Jan. 25, 1990, GBl DDR I 16; see generally Roggemann, Rechtsgrundlagen für Auslandsinvestitionen in der DDR, 1990 NJW 671.

Among other things, these regulations required the approval of a government economic committee for the founding of any joint venture. Approval could be denied on the basis of environmental concerns or if there was a danger that the foreign participant would dominate the concern to the disadvantage of the GDR participants and the GDR economy. The joint venture was required to establish a special fund "to assure the social and cultural rights of the workers."

10. Helmut Herles & Ewald Rose (eds.), Vom Runden Tisch zum Parlament 71 (1990).

11. GBl DDR 1990 I 16.

12. Interview with Lothar de Maizière, Berlin, Dec. 4, 1992. But, for a different view, see Christa Luft, Zwischen WEnde und Ende 120–21 (1992). Indeed, some argue that the practical effect of these measures was minimal because other characteristics of the GDR system of property—reflected in regulations accompanying the amendments—made it difficult for entities of the GDR to enter into joint ventures with foreign investors in any case. See Turner & Pflicke, DDR-Recht im Umbruch, 1990 NJW 1637, 1639.

13. See Ch. 11.

14. Article 3, providing for the "National Front," was repealed. Gesetz zur Änderung und Ergänzung der Verfassung der DDR, of Feb. 20, 1990, § 1, GBl DDR I 59. For interesting references to the National Front in the Federal Constitutional Court's first major opinion on issues arising from unification, see Ch. 8. On the National Front, see generally Eckart Klein & Sighart Lörler, Überlegungen zur Verfassungsreform in der DDR 44–45 (1989).

15. Hohmann in Verfassungsdiskussion at 94.

16. Gesetz zur Änderung und Ergänzung der Verfassung der DDR, of Feb. 20, 1990, §§ 2, 3, GBl DDR I 59 (amending Verf. DDR [1974] art. 22).

17. Id. § 3 (amending Verf. DDR [1974] art. 54). In addition, article 23 was amended to grant a right of civil alternative service instead of an exclusive requirement of military service. Gesetz zur Änderung der Verfassung der DDR, of Feb. 20, 1990, GBl DDR I 60.

18. See Weiss, The Transition of Labor Law and Industrial Relations: The Case of

German Unification—A Preliminary Perspective, 13 Comparative Labor Law Journal 1, 1–2 (1991): "The link between Party and trade union was so close that it was difficult to draw a line of demarcation. . . . [Agreements relating to labor] were not conceived as compromise in collective conflicts, but rather as a sort of additional legislation"; see also Markovits, Law or Order—Constitutionalism and Legality in Eastern Europe, 34 Stanford Law Review 513, 590–95 (1982) (noting, however, that in recent years unions sometimes represented individual workers in disputes about specific employment decisions). For the diverging historical development of trade unions in eastern and western Germany, see Hermann Weber, Aufbau und Fall einer Diktatur 39–43 (1991).

19. Harry Tisch, the last leader of the FDGB, was the first East German official to go on trial for corrupt acts while in office. See Ch. 14.

20. Gesetz zur Änderung der Verfassung der DDR, of Mar. 6, 1990, GBl DDR I 109.

21. See also, e.g., art. 9(3) GG.

22. A statute accompanying the constitutional amendment set forth details of the new type of labor union in the GDR. Gesetz über die Rechte der Gewerkschaften in der DDR, of Mar. 6, 1990, GBl DDR I 110. A vestige of the older system remained in the unions' continued authority to propose legislation in the Volkskammer. Id. § 10(1); cf. Verf. DDR (1974) arts. 45(2), 65(1). Moreover, the right to strike was qualified by provisions allowing strikes only after unsuccessful attempts at mediation and authorizing the government to suspend strikes "on the basis of the general good." GBl DDR 1990 I 110 § 18(1).

The Round Table draft also includes a provision on labor unions. See RT-Entwurf art. 39. It possesses some similarities to the March 6 amendment but is much more detailed. Particularly interesting in the Round Table draft is an explicit guarantee of members' free speech within the union. See id. art. 39(3).

23. See Weiss, 13 Comparative Labor Law Journal at 5.

24. Id. at 5–7. See generally Ch. 10.

25. See Herles & Rose at 91.

26. Beschluß der Volkskammer über die Gewährleistung der Meinungs-, Informations- und Medienfreiheit, of Feb. 5, 1990, GBl DDR I 39.

27. Gesetz über Vereinigungen—Vereinigungsgesetz—of Feb. 21, 1990, GBl DDR I 75 (associations); Gesetz über Parteien und andere politische Vereinigungen—Parteiengesetz—of Feb. 21, 1990, GBl DDR I 66 (political parties).

28. Verordnung über die Tätigkeit von Bürgerkomitees und Bürgerinitiativen, of Mar. 1, 1990, GBl DDR I 112.

29. Gesetz über Versammlungen—Versammlungsgesetz—of Mar. 7, 1990, GBl DDR I 145. In a number of these measures, the Volkskammer invoked relevant provisions of the 1974 GDR Constitution as well as international covenants signed by the GDR—particularly the International Covenant on Civil and Political Rights of 1966.

30. See GBl DDR 1990 I 39 §§ 5, 7, 9, 11.

31. GBl DDR 1990 I 75 § 2(1).

32. Verordnung über die Gründung und Tätigkeit von Vereinigungen, of Nov. 6, 1975, § 1(2), GBl DDR I 723.

33. Id. §§ 2, 6–9, 11.

34. GBl DDR 1990 I 66 § 3(1).

35. Id. § 15. In the short period before the March 18 election, this rule was disregarded by the SED and the bloc parties. But the statute was later amended to require the

parties to render an accounting and relinquish all property not acquired in accordance with the rule of law. See Ch. 11.

36. GBl DDR 1990 I 66 §§ 17(3), 18, 19.

In the Regulation concerning Citizens Committees, these groups were accorded certain rights of access to governmental information and access to the process of governmental decisionmaking—provisions that anticipated similar rights of citizens committees in the Round Table draft constitution. See GBl DDR 1990 I 112 §§ 4–6.

37. See Verordnung über die Durchführung von Veranstaltungen (Veranstaltungsverordnung—VAVO), of June 30, 1980, § 3(1), GBl DDR I 235.

Because the SED regime was likely to approve only those public meetings which it or allied groups had sponsored, this provision in effect criminalized any outdoor assembly or demonstration by alternative or opposition groups. Indeed, the Leipzig demonstrations were illegal under this provision of GDR law. In contrast, the great demonstration of November 4, 1989, in the Alexanderplatz in Berlin received a government permit. Most likely, this was the first example of an approved opposition demonstration in the history of the GDR.

38. GBl DDR 1990 I 145 § 1(2).

In all of these new provisions, the Volkskammer sought to assure that possible disputes would be decided by the courts rather than by the executive itself, as had generally been the case in the past. For example, any government decision relating to assemblies was subject to judicial review, and the court could adjudicate the entire matter—instead of being limited, as under previous GDR law, to determining whether or not procedural mistakes had been made. Id. § 10. Even the previous—quite modest—degree of judicial review for procedural regularity had only been achieved in the last years of the GDR after decades of official resistance to judicial review of any kind. Cf. Inga Markovits, Imperfect Justice: An East-West German Diary 171–77 (1995).

I am indebted to Frank Andree, of the Berlin bar, for an enlightening discussion of the process of drafting the statutes concerning associations, political parties, and assemblies. Interview with Frank Andree, Berlin, Dec. 12, 1992.

39. See, e.g., Herles & Rose at 36.

40. Thus the new measures on political parties, associations, and citizens committees contained identical provisions prohibiting certain extremist associations: "The founding and activity of [groups] which pursue fascist, militaristic, antihumanistic goals and make known or disseminate racial or religious hatred or hatred based on nationality; or which discriminate against persons and groups on the basis of their nationality, political affiliation, gender, sexual orientation, or physical or mental handicap; or which seek to achieve their goals by force or through the threat of force, are prohibited." The law relating to assemblies contained a somewhat different formulation.

These provisions were presumably patterned on West German models, as well as article 6(5) of the 1968/74 GDR Constitution, but the forms of discrimination excluded from protection extend beyond those previously disapproved in the Federal Republic or the GDR. For example, the prohibition of groups that discriminate on the basis of sexual orientation or handicap represented a new step in this area.

41. Beschluß der Volkskammer der Deutschen Demokratischen Republik zu Aktivitäten der Partei Die Republikaner auf dem Territorium der DDR, of Feb. 5, 1990, GBl DDR I 40.

42. Gesetz über die Wahlen zur Volkskammer der DDR am 18. März 1990, of

Feb. 20, 1990, GBl DDR I 60 (hereafter, Election Law); see Herles & Rose at 58–59, 70, 82, 87–88, 106–7, 146–48, 184–86. The leaders of the Round Table Committee for the Election Law were Lothar de Maizière and Wolfgang Ullmann, a prominent GDR reformer. Herles & Rose at 30.

43. Election Law § 8(1). The Round Table particularly insisted upon this provision. See Herles & Rose 58–59, 87–88.

44. Election Law § 5(3). The Election Law also excluded radical parties, in a provision paralleling that of the political party and association statutes. Id. § 8(2).

45. Herles & Rose at 107.

46. Id. at 147–48.

47. See, e.g., Wolfgang Schäuble, Der Vertrag: Wie ich über die deutsche Einheit verhandelte 82 (1991). Similar decisions were made in other countries of the former east bloc during the same period. Perhaps, in a situation in which the locus of constitutional legitimacy was difficult to ascertain, the new forces preferred the stability of a dubious document that had been in effect for years, so long as it could be reinterpreted or revised in a democratic manner.

48. For commentary from the GDR reform movement, see, e.g., Friedrich Schorlemmer, Bis alle Mauern fallen 87 (1993): "Thus the grand coalition became a part of the self-surrender [*Selbstaufgabe*] of the Germans in the GDR." The Coalition Agreement of the GDR governing parties is reprinted in Ingo von Münch (ed.), Dokumente der Wiedervereinigung Deutschlands 163–90 (1991) (hereafter, Dokumente—Wiedervereinigung).

49. Sabine Bergmann-Pohl, Abschied ohne Tränen: Rückblick auf das Jahr der Einheit 169 (1991).

50. Among the legislation that survived, in whole or in basic principle, as part of the framework of united Germany was a statute comprehensively regulating the Treuhand, the agency designed to conserve and ultimately sell the former People's Property of the GDR; a general statute regulating the preservation and use of the files of the GDR secret police (Stasi); and a statute setting forth the basic structure of local government in the eastern Länder. Interview with Steffen Reiche, Potsdam and Berlin, Nov. 25, 1992. Among the statutes that ultimately disappeared, however, were such important regulations of social life as reformed provisions relating to family law as well as comprehensive labor legislation, among other subjects. See Ch. 10.

51. Cf. Bergmann-Pohl at 132–35.

52. Interview with Reinhard Höppner (vice-president of GDR Volkskammer during the de Maizière period), Magdeburg, Jan. 11, 1993.

53. Interview with Lothar de Maizière, Berlin, Dec. 4, 1992. The general sense of disorder in the Volkskammer was increased by demonstrations, on behalf of disgruntled groups such as farmers and students, which took place before every session following the signing of the State Treaty. Interview with Reinhard Höppner, Jan. 11, 1993.

54. Bergmann-Pohl at 64; Erklärung der DDR-Volkskammer: Bekenntnis zu Verantwortung und Mitschuld für Vergangenheit und Zukunft, April 12, 1990, reprinted in Herles & Rose at 393–96. Complete transcripts of the April 5 and April 12 sessions are reprinted in Herles & Rose at 343–446. The Volkskammer declaration also acknowledged that the invasion of Czechoslovakia violated article 8(2) of the 1968 GDR Constitution which stated that the GDR would "never undertake a war of conquest or employ its armed forces against the freedom of another people."

55. For the relationship between the Prague Spring and the East German revolution

of 1989, see, e.g., Zwahr, Den Maulkorb festgezurrt: Auch die DDR hatte ihr 68er Erlebnis—der Prager Frühling weckte die Hoffnung auf Wandel, Die Zeit, June 11, 1993, at 14.

56. For these amendments, see Gesetz zur Änderung und Ergänzung der Verfassung der DDR, of Apr. 5, 1990, GBl DDR I 221.

The newly created office of president of the GDR was, however, never filled or even officially established by statute. Instead, the Presidium of the Volkskammer—a group composed of the president and vice-presidents of the Volkskammer and some other members—performed the functions of the Council of State under the GDR Constitution, and the president of the Volkskammer filled the ceremonial role of head of state. See Bergmann-Pohl at 37–38; see also Interview with Reinhard Höppner, Jan. 11, 1993. The Council of State, which was abolished by this amendment, had itself been created to replace the original office of president of the GDR, set forth in the 1949 GDR Constitution.

57. Gesetz zur Änderung und Ergänzung der Verfassung der DDR, of Apr. 12, 1990, GBl DDR I 229. For the background of this provision, see Bergmann-Pohl at 59–60.

58. See Herles & Rose at 431–38.

59. Id. at 421 (remarks of prospective Interior Minister Peter-Michael Diestel).

60. Id. at 434 (remarks of Richard Schröder, chair of the SPD caucus).

61. GBl DDR 1990 I 229.

62. Gesetz zur Änderung und Ergänzung der Verfassung der DDR (Verfassungsgrundsätze), of June 17, 1990, GBl DDR I 299. Previously the Volkskammer had adopted another constitutional amendment, which deleted certain prior provisions relating to local government. See Mampel, 1990 DA at 1387.

63. In May 1990, after the Volkskammer's rejection of the Round Table draft but before the sweeping amendments of June 17, the justice minister of the de Maizière government convened a commission of constitutional experts drawn from the Federal Republic and GDR governments and from the universities. This group was charged with the task of drafting a proposal for a new interim constitution based on the GDR Constitution of 1949. The commission apparently finished its work in the extraordinarily short period of time allotted to it, but the results were ignored by the GDR government, which chose to issue the constitutional amendments of June 17 instead. The commission's draft was never published. See generally Fischer, Verfassungsgeschichte der DDR 1990, 1990 KJ 413, 419–21; Schlink, Deutsch-deutsche Verfassungsentwicklungen im Jahre 1990, in Verfassungsdiskussion at 27–29.

Some members of this special commission reacted bitterly to the rejection of its work (see Fischer, id.), but Lothar de Maizière argued that the commission had substantially departed from its mandate to produce a draft based on the 1949 document. Interview with Lothar de Maizière, Dec. 4, 1992. In any case, this episode marked the end of efforts to draft a new constitution of the GDR: "the energy and will to form an independent constitution were exhausted." Schlink in Verfassungsdiskussion at 28.

64. Stern, Der Staatsvertrag im völkerrechtlichen und verfassungsrechtlichen Kontext, in 1 Klaus Stern & Bruno Schmidt-Bleibtreu (eds.), Verträge und Rechtsakte zur Deutschen Einheit 25 (1990). See Ch. 7.

65. See Häberle, Verfassungspolitik für die Freiheit und Einheit Deutschlands, 1990 JZ 358, 363; Mampel, 1990 DA at 1388. Subsequently, the German parliament adopted a highly qualified environmental guarantee as article 20a of the Basic Law. See Ch. 10.

66. A provision similar to that of article 1(2)—rejecting various principles such as socialist legality and the socialist legal consciousness in the GDR—was already contained in a protocol to the State Treaty. See Ch. 7. The reference to "views of individual groups of the population or parties," a phrase also contained in the protocol, is evidently a reference to provisions in the GDR Constitution referring to the working class and the SED.

Article 1(3) of the June 17 amendment introduced the principle of judicial review into the GDR but left the details to future regulation by statute.

67. Under the 1968/74 GDR Constitution, private property interests in the principal means of production had been totally prohibited until the constitutional amendment of January 12, 1990. See Ch. 4.

68. See Mampel, 1990 DA at 1389.

69. Article 3 of the amendment goes on to set forth a right to enter into contracts and economic activity in general. Article 4 grants rights to form labor unions and employers' associations, a provision that to some extent complements the March 6 constitutional amendment changing the nature of labor unions.

70. This provision is a close adaptation of a portion of article 97(1) of the Basic Law, which states that "the judges are independent and subject only to the law."

71. Indeed article 5 also states that "leadership of the jurisprudence of lower courts by higher courts is not permissible"—a provision that seems to promote "independence" of the judiciary to an extraordinary degree. This section was doubtless a reaction to the system through which the Supreme Court of the GDR set forth mandatory guidelines—sometimes written and sometimes in oral form—that were intended to direct the lower courts as an aspect of democratic centralism. See Ch. 4; Verf. DDR (1974) art. 93; see also Markovits, Imperfect Justice, at 25–28.

72. See Hohmann in Verfassungsdiskussion at 100. Similar provisions were contained in the Round Table draft and, subsequently, in the new constitutions of the eastern Länder. See Chs. 4 & 9.

73. Fischer, 1990 KJ at 423. See Ch. 7.

74. This provision was useful because the June 17 amendments were adopted after the State Treaty was signed, but before that treaty had been ratified by the Volkskammer. For critical commentary on the provision, see id. at 423; Mampel, 1990 DA at 1389–90. See generally Schlink in Verfassungsdiskussion at 28–29.

75. For a particularly bitter criticism, see Fischer, 1990 KJ at 421–24.

76. Schlink in Verfassungsdiskussion at 31.

77. Wolfgang Ullmann, Verfassung und Parlament 64–70, 82–87 (1992).

78. See Ch. 9.

79. On July 5, 1990, the Volkskammer adopted additional constitutional amendments relating to the subject of judges and state prosecutors, one of the areas of greatest abuse under the old regime. Verfassungsgesetz zur Änderung und Ergänzung des Gerichtsverfassungsgesetzes, of July 5, 1990, GBl DDR I 634; Verfassungsgesetz zur Änderung und Ergänzung des Gesetzes über die Staatsanwaltschaft der DDR, of July 5, 1990, GBl DDR I 635. These constitutional changes, which were accompanied by detailed statutory amendments, sought to create a professional and independent judiciary and prosecutorial force in place of organs previously subject to political control. The changes gave greater specificity to the general principles relating to the judiciary previously adopted in the June 17 amendments and, like those amendments, were designed to implement the provisions of the first State Treaty. See Ch. 7.

Later in July, the Volkskammer amended the constitution to provide for the prospective re-creation of the five GDR states that had been effectively abolished in the 1950s. See GBl DDR 1990 I 955. Because the re-creation of the East German Länder is an important topic in its own right, this amendment will be discussed in detail in Chapter 9. Finally, in July the Volkskammer adopted an amendment allowing the establishment of private schools, which had not been permitted under the constitution of 1968/74. Verfassungsgesetz über Schulen in freier Trägerschaft, of July 22, 1990, GBl DDR I 1036.

## Chapter 6
## Methods of Unification under the Basic Law

1. See Ingo von Münch (ed.), Dokumente der Wiedervereinigung Deutschlands 56 (1991) (hereafter, Dokumente—Wiedervereinigung); Hans Modrow, Aufbruch und Ende 40 (1991).

2. Dokumente—Wiedervereinigung at 63. See Ch. 3.

3. Dokumente—Wiedervereinigung at 63. Ironically, the idea of confederation had been first suggested (under quite different terms) by GDR leader Walter Ulbricht in January 1957, and it was repeated by Soviet and GDR officials thereafter. See Martin McCauley, The German Democratic Republic since 1945, at 87 (1983).

4. See, e.g., Micha Wimmer et al. (eds.), Wir sind das Volk: Die DDR im Aufbruch 224 (1990) (confederation as interim step in unification plan); Konrad H. Jarausch, The Rush to German Unity 88 (1994). Some prominent members of the SPD also favored this method.

5. Böckenförde & Grimm, Nachdenken über Deutschland, Der Spiegel, 10/1990, at 72–77. For other proposals along these lines, see Rosemarie Will, Der verfassungs- und völkerrechtliche Weg zur deutschen Einheit. Eine Stellungnahme, in Bernd Guggenberger & Tine Stein (ed.), Die Verfassungsdiskussion im Jahr der deutschen Einheit 201 (1991) (hereafter, Verfassungsdiskussion).

6. See, e.g., Starck, Deutschland auf dem Wege zur staatlichen Einheit, 1990 JZ 349, 352.

7. See Ch. 2. The GDR Constitution of 1949, which was designed as an all-German constitution, sometimes employed the all-inclusive terms "Germany" or "German people." See, e.g., Verf. DDR (1949) art. 1(1) ("Germany is an indivisible democratic republic"); art. 51(1) ("The Volkskammer consists of representatives of the German people"). The 1968 Constitution of the GDR also contained references to "Germany" or "the German nation"; see, e.g., Verf. DDR (1968) preamble, arts. 1, 3; but these references were removed in the 1974 amendments. See Ch. 4.

8. The 1968/74 GDR Constitution could be amended by a two-thirds vote of the Volkskammer, so long as the measure explicitly stated that it was intended to amend or add to the constitution. See Verf. DDR (1974) arts. 63(2), 106. Under the GDR Constitution of 1949, as well as under the Weimar Constitution, it had also been possible to adopt amendments by plebiscite. Verf. DDR (1949) art. 83(3); WRV art. 76.

9. See Isensee, Staatseinheit und Verfassungskontinuität, 49 VVDStRL 39, 43 n. 9 (1990).

10. See Mampel, Das Ende der sozialistischen Verfassung der DDR, 1990 DA 1377, 1382; Stern, Der Staatsvertrag im völkerrechtlichen und verfassungsrechtlichen Kontext, in 1 Klaus Stern & Bruno Schmidt-Bleibtreu (eds.), Verträge und Rechtsakte zur Deutschen Einheit 24–25 (1990) (hereafter, Verträge und Rechtsakte). See gener-

ally Helmut Herles & Ewald Rose (eds.), Vom Runden Tisch zum Parlament 431–38 (1990).

11. See Ch. 2.

12. See Storost, Das Ende der Übergangszeit. Erinnerung an die verfassunggebende Gewalt, in Verfassungsdiskussion at 172–85.

13. 5 BVerfGE 85, 132 (1956).

14. See, e.g., 3 Ingo von Münch (ed.), Grundgesetz-Kommentar art. 146, No. 5 (1983) (hereafter, GG-Kommentar).

15. See Möschel, DDR-Wege aus der Krise, 1990 JZ 306, 310.

16. See, e.g., Frowein, Die Verfassungslage Deutschlands im Rahmen des Völkerrechts, 49 VVDStRL 7, 25–26 (1990); Isensee, 49 VVDStRL at 47–48. See generally Ch. 2.

17. See, e.g., Simon, Markierungen auf dem Weg zu einer neuen gesamtdeutschen Verfassung, in Verfassungsdiskussion at 145.

18. Accordingly, the Parliamentary Council included "only a narrowly drawn leadership elite of the political parties. . . . That the Parliamentary Council represented the German people in its full extent was accordingly an obviously untenable fiction." Mußgnug, Zustandekommen des Grundgesetzes und Entstehen der Bundesrepublik Deutschland, in 1 Josef Isensee & Paul Kirchhof (eds.), Handbuch des Staatsrechts der Bundesrepublik Deutschland 219, 254 (1987) (hereafter, Handbuch des Staatsrechts). See also Storost in Verfassungsdiskussion at 176–77.

19. See Frankfurt Documents, July 1, 1948, reprinted in 1 Ingo von Münch (ed.), Dokumente des geteilten Deutschland 88–89 (1976).

20. This decision was consistent with the Basic Law's general hostility to plebiscites. See 3 GG-Kommentar, art. 144, No. 12. Perhaps ratification by plebiscite might also have suggested that the Basic Law would possess a permanence inconsistent with the document's intended "provisional" status. See also Friedrich, Rebuilding the German Constitution (Part II), 43 American Political Science Review 704, 718 (1949): "The German politicians were afraid that such a referendum would provide too golden an opportunity to Communist and Fascist elements."

21. Cf. also Mußgnug in 1 Handbuch des Staatsrechts at 255–56 (arguing that the constitution received popular legitimation in the first Bundestag election because most citizens voted for parties supporting the Basic Law).

22. Cf. Häberle, Verfassungspolitik für die Freiheit und Einheit Deutschlands, 1990 JZ 358, 360 (emphasizing the importance of the new "constitutional culture" that had arisen in late 1989 in the GDR).

23. See Grimm, Zwischen Anschluß und Neukonstitution. Wie aus dem Grundgesetz eine Verfassung für das geeinte Deutschland werden kann, in Verfassungsdiskussion at 126–27. See also Schneider, Deutschland in neuer Verfassung, in Michael Müller & Wolfgang Thierse (eds.), Deutsche Ansichten: Die Republik im Übergang 232 (1992) (hereafter, Deutsche Ansichten).

24. Hohmann, Verfassungsstreit um Einigung. Ein Beitrag zur gesamtdeutschen Verfassungsdiskussion, in Verfassungsdiskussion at 210.

25. See, e.g., Jürgen Habermas, Die nachholende Revolution 216–18 (1990). See generally Quint, Constitution-Making by Treaty in German Unification: A Comment on Arato, Elster, Preuss, and Richards, 14 Cardozo Law Review 691 (1993).

26. See, e.g., Ulrich Albrecht, Die Abwicklung der DDR 52–53 (1992).

27. See Wolfgang Schäuble, Der Vertrag: Wie ich über die deutsche Einheit verhandelte 55–56, 65–66 (1991).

28. The Basic Law was not the first German constitution to contain such a provision. The Constitution of the North German Confederation (1867) and the Weimar Constitution both contained sections contemplating the possible accession of additional territory. See Frowein, 49 VVDStRL at 14.

29. For historical background on the problem of the Saar, see 4 BVerfGE 157 (1955) (Saar Statute case). See also Rudolf Dolzer, The Path to German Unity: The Constitutional, Legal and International Framework 17–18 (American Institute for Contemporary German Studies, German Issues No. 8, 1990); Leicht, Einheit durch Beitritt. Eine neue Verfassung kann nur schlechter werden, in Verfassungsdiskussion at 195–200. Arguing before the Constitutional Court in the *Basic Treaty* case (see Ch. 2), the Brandt government asserted that article 23 of the Basic Law was intended *solely* for the accession of the Saarland, but this view was rejected by the Court. Otto Kimminich, Die Eigentumsgarantie im Prozeß der Wiedervereinigung 20 (1990); Stern in 1 Verträge und Rechtsakte at 33.

30. See Binne, Forum: Verfassungsrechtliche Überlegungen zu einem "Beitritt" der DDR nach Art. 23 GG, 1990 JuS 446, 448.

31. 36 BVerfGE 1, 29 (1973). The "other parts of Germany" referred to in article 23 might theoretically also have included territories east of the Oder-Neiße line transferred to Polish administration after World War II. To avoid revanchist claims that these Polish territories could still "accede" to Germany sometime in the future, article 23 was deleted from the Basic Law upon unification. See Chs. 10 & 18.

32. See, e.g., McCurdy, German Reunification: Historical and Legal Roots of Germany's Rapid Progress towards Unity, 22 New York University Journal of International Law & Politics 253, 262 n. 48 (1990) (conservatives favored accession under article 23 because it would retain the "tested" West German system).

33. See Ch. 10.

34. See generally Binne, 1990 JuS 446; Heintschel von Heinegg, Der Beitritt "anderer Teile Deutschlands" zur Bundesrepublik nach Art. 23 Satz 2 GG, 1990 DÖV 425.

35. See, e.g., Degenhart, Verfassungsfragen der deutschen Einheit, 1990 DVBl 973, 974.

36. For a discussion of this process, see Ch. 5.

37. See supra. In the *Basic Treaty* case, the Constitutional Court noted that "'other parts of Germany' have . . . found their statehood in the German Democratic Republic," and therefore these "other parts" can declare their "accession" to the Federal Republic only through a process consistent with the Constitution of the GDR. 36 BVerfGE 1, 29 (1973). In this way the Constitutional Court, while not actually recognizing the GDR as a separate state, did acknowledge the effective validity of the GDR Constitution.

38. See Stern in 1 Verträge und Rechtsakte at 36.

39. Theodor Maunz, Günter Dürig et al., Grundgesetz Kommentar art. 23, No. 44.

40. See Ch. 2.

41. Maunz & Dürig, art. 23, No. 43.

42. Id. art. 23, No. 44; Rauschning, Deutschlands aktuelle Verfassungslage, 1990 DVBl 393, 401.

It is not clear whether the entire West German legal system would have been extended to the GDR immediately upon accession if no special provision were made for this purpose. Article 23 declared that the Basic Law would be extended to the acceding territory but it said nothing about the rest of the legal system. One could argue, however, that the remainder of the legal system would be extended by implication. An intermediate position might be that remaining GDR law would continue in effect as a form of state law in all of the Länder constituting the GDR, but would be superseded to the extent inconsistent with federal law. As a practical matter, however, these questions were subject to comprehensive regulation in the Unification Treaty. See Ch. 10.

43. See, e.g., Friedrich Schorlemmer, Bis alle Mauern fallen 93 (1993): With the Round Table draft, the reform groups wanted to bring something of their own into unification, but "the Anschluß-train already had a full head of steam." See also Habermas, Die nachholende Revolution, at 205: "The triumphant chancellor lets the little honest minister-president know the conditions under which he will purchase the GDR. . . . [H]e sets the course for Anschluß under article 23 GG."

At the time of the March 18 elections, a much cited campaign poster referred to article 23 and added "Kein Anschluß unter dieser Nummer." This was the phrase commonly used by telephone operators to say that a caller had reached a non-working number, but the phrase could also be understood as declaring "no accession (or Anschluß) under this provision."

44. See Herles & Rose at 168. On the day that the Round Table voted to reject use of article 23 (and to seek a demilitarized status for Germany) Horst Teltschik, an important advisor to Chancellor Kohl, remarked in his diary: "This decision [of the Round Table] demonstrates yet again that reasonable discussions with the GDR will only be possible after the [GDR] election." Horst Teltschik, 329 Tage: Innenansichten der Einigung 152–53 (1991). The great gulf between the GDR Round Table and the western conservatives is clearly apparent in this laconic comment.

45. Teltschik at 168.

46. See Dokumente—Wiedervereinigung at 195; see also Teltschik at 202.

47. See Dokumente—Wiedervereinigung at 163; Wolfgang Thierse, Mit eigener Stimme sprechen 39–40 (1992).

48. Thierse, Mit eigener Stimme, at 40.

49. See, e.g., Grimm in Verfassungsdiskussion at 129; see also Hohmann in Verfassungsdiskussion at 209–10.

50. See Schneider in Deutsche Ansichten at 230.

51. FAZ, July 26, 1990, at 2 col. 2; see art. 54(3) GG. Indeed, as early as April 1990, members of the eastern SPD were advancing a similar view. See Thierse, Mit eigener Stimme, at 40; see also Schäuble, Der Vertrag, at 63–65.

52. See Degenhart, 1990 DVBl at 976 (suggesting that the GDR, having chosen to accede under article 23, accepted the Basic Law and could not seek to replace it under article 146). See also Badura, Deutschlands aktuelle Verfassungslage, 115 AöR 314, 318–20 (1990).

53. See Ch. 10.

54. See generally Stern, Der verfassungsändernde Charakter des Einigungsvertrages, 1990 DtZ 289, 293. The retention and amendment of article 146 should be considered together with other provisions of the Unification Treaty recommending that parliament examine the possibility of constitutional reform. Id. See also Ch. 10.

55. See Isensee, Mit blauem Auge davongekommen—das Grundgesetz, 1993 NJW 2583, 2584.

56. See FAZ, Sept. 24, 1990, at 1 col. 5; Isensee, Selbstpreisgabe des Grundgesetzes?, FAZ, Aug. 28, 1990, at 10 col. 1.

57. See, e.g., FAZ, Sept. 24, 1990, at 5 col. 1 (CDU official fears that right of employment and right to a dwelling might be introduced through Bundestag vote and plebiscite under article 146). For a contrasting view, see, e.g., Göhring, Einigungsvertrag

und Mietrecht, 1990 DtZ 317, 318 (arguing that a right to a dwelling should be introduced into a new all-German constitution).

58. Seifert, Klassenkampf von rechts oder Modernisierung des Grundgesetzes, in Verfassungsdiskussion at 234–35.

59. See, e.g., Stern, 1990 DtZ at 293–94.

60. A related question is whether a new constitution adopted under article 146 GG would be limited by the restrictions of article 79(3) GG, which prohibits amendment of the Basic Law in a manner that would impair fundamental principles of human dignity, democracy, and the rule of law. For a discussion of this issue, see Storost in Verfassungsdiskussion at 181.

61. A very pessimistic view of the possibilities of constitutional reform under article 146 was reflected in the ultimate fate of a group known as the "Curatorium for a Democratically Constituted Federation of German States." The Curatorium was founded in September 1990 by civil rights organizations, the Greens, Bündnis 90, and others, for the purpose of drafting a new constitution that would be based on the Round Table draft and the Basic Law and would be proposed for adoption by plebiscite. See FR, Sept. 18, 1990, at 1 col. 2. After substantial efforts, the Curatorium published an elaborate draft along these lines in 1991. See Bernd Guggenberger et al. (eds.), Eine Verfassung für Deutschland: Manifest, Text, Plädoyers (1991). Having produced its constitutional draft, but seeing little apparent likelihood of the adoption of a new constitution by plebiscite in the near future, the Curatorium formally disbanded itself at a meeting in Berlin on May 22, 1993.

A considerably more modest proposal for the use of article 146 was that the democratic deficit in the original adoption of the Basic Law be removed, after accession under article 23, by adopting the Basic Law itself under article 146 through parliamentary decision followed by a plebiscite. See Frowein, Das Grundgesetz behalten—per Volksentscheid, Die Zeit, July 6, 1990, at 9 col. 1; see also Mahrenholz, Das Volk muß "Ja" sagen können. Jede Verfassung braucht die ausdrückliche Zustimmung der Staatsbürger, in Verfassungsdiskussion at 220–23.

62. Simon in Verfassungsdiskussion at 140–41.

63. Id. at 140.

64. See Isensee, 1993 NJW at 2583. See generally Ch. 10.

## Chapter 7
## The State Treaty: Currency and Economic Union

1. Vertrag über die Schaffung einer Währungs-, Wirtschafts- und Sozialunion zwischen der Bundesrepublik Deutschland und der Deutschen Demokratischen Republik, of May 18, 1990, BGBl II 537. The treaty was accompanied by a "Joint Protocol concerning Principles" as well as nine Attachments. The treaty and its accompanying documents are reprinted with extensive commentary in 1 Klaus Stern & Bruno Schmidt-Bleibtreu, Verträge und Rechtsakte zur Deutschen Einheit (1990) (hereafter, Verträge und Rechtsakte). See also Schmidt-Bleibtreu, Der Vertrag über die Schaffung einer Währungs-, Wirtschafts- und Sozialunion zwischen der Bundesrepublik Deutschland und der Deutschen Demokratischen Republik, 1990 DtZ 138. A statute of the Federal Republic that approved the State Treaty also contained extensive provisions amending existing economic, financial, and commercial legislation of the Federal Republic, for the purpose of carrying out the treaty's provisions. See 1 Verträge und Rechtsakte at 239–317.

For an English version of the State Treaty and related documents, with commentary, see 29 I.L.M. 1108 (1990).

2. See generally Jan Priewe & Rudolf Hickel, Der Preis der Einheit 81–87 (1991).

3. Peter Christ & Ralf Neubauer, Kolonie im eigenen Land 68 (1991).

4. See id. at 74–75. Indeed, in making this decision Kohl did not even consult his cabinet, although he obtained the agreement of the other two coalition leaders. Thereafter, negotiations on the first State Treaty between the Federal Republic and the Modrow government began on February 20. See Volkskammer der Deutschen Demokratischen Republik, 10. Wahlperiode, Stenografische Niederschrift, May 21, 1990, at 211 (Remarks of Walter Romberg, GDR Finance Minister) (hereafter, Volkskammer Protocol).

5. Horst Teltschik, 329 Tage: Innenansichten der Einigung 125–26, 129–33, 192, 237 (1991); Helmut Kohl, Die deutsche Einheit: Reden und Gespräche 158–60 (1992). Ominous threats of massive migrations to the west were common during the Modrow period. In February 1990, demonstrators in Leipzig declared, "If the D-Mark comes here, we will stay; if it does not come, we will go to it." Christ & Neubauer at 66–67.

The Kohl government may also have believed that swift currency union, and related measures, would have the effect of accelerating full unification at a time when the international situation remained favorable. Christ & Neubauer at 100. Indeed, the announcement was made three days before a crucial meeting in Moscow at which President Gorbachev agreed in principle to German unification; perhaps Kohl in his swift announcement of the currency union sought to present Gorbachev with a fait accompli before the Moscow meeting, as an indication of the inevitability of the process.

In any case, the announcement of the proposed currency union was immensely popular in the GDR, and thus yielded significant political gains for Kohl and his newly formed "Alliance for Germany." Busch, Die deutsch-deutsche Währungsunion: Politisches Votum trotz ökonomischer Bedenken, in Ulrike Liebert & Wolfgang Merkel (eds.), Die Politik zur deutschen Einheit 197–99 (1991) (hereafter, Die Politik zur deutschen Einheit). See also Wilhelm Hankel, Die sieben Todsünden der Vereinigung 27 (1993).

6. Kohl at 159–60; cf. Busch in Die Politik zur deutschen Einheit at 196.

7. Kohl at 178.

8. Id. This promise was repeated in a later televised address on July 1, the day on which the currency union became effective. Priewe & Hickel at 86. For wry commentary on this speech, see Stefan Heym, Filz: Gedanken über das neueste Deutschland 54 (1992): "I heard . . . the beautiful round sentences ('no one will, no one should') which, in the chest tones of conviction, came out of your mouth, Dr. K., and I thought to myself, let his words [find their way] into God's right ear. But God was, as could be expected, deaf in that ear." For a somewhat blunter statement along the same lines, see Hans-Joachim Maaz, Das gestürzte Volk oder die verunglückte Einheit 117 (1991): "The beautiful and campaign-like promise: No one will be worse off! has turned out to be humbug."

9. Moreover, because the treaty effected constitutional changes in the GDR, a two-thirds vote was necessary in the Volkskammer. See Ch. 6.

10. FR, June 22, 1990, at 4 col. 1. According to Kohl: "No one should deceive himself: we stand today before a very clear decision. Either we confirm the existing border, or we throw away today and for now our chance for German unity." Kohl at 182 (Bundestag speech of June 21, 1990). Kohl's certainty on this point most likely reflected the severe international criticism that he had received when he failed to take

an unambiguous position on the finality of the Oder-Neiße line in public statements at an earlier point in the process of unification. See generally Ch. 18.

11. See FR, June 22, 1990, at 1 col. 1. Kohl referred to the "unspeakable pain and injustice" inflicted by the Germans during World War II, but he also stated that a "great injustice" was done to Germans driven from their homes in the eastern territories. FR, June 22, 1990, at 4 col. 1.

The passage of the resolution on the Polish border seems to have been attended with considerably fewer problems in the GDR Volkskammer than in the Bundestag. For an enthusiastic account of this moment in the Volkskammer, emphasizing reconciliation with enemies and victims of the past, see Sabine Bergmann-Pohl, Abschied ohne Tränen: Rückblick auf das Jahr der Einheit 70–71 (1991).

12. See FR, June 23, 1990, at 1 col. 4; FR, June 22, 1990, at 4 col. 5.

13. Jens Reich, Rückkehr nach Europa: Zur neuen Lage der deutschen Nation 221 (1991). See also Wolfgang Ullmann, Verfassung und Parlament 84–85 (1992): The State Treaty and related changes were adopted in "a process that reduces the legislative power to the mere notary of the executive."

14. See Ch. 6.

15. FR, June 22, 1990, at 4 col. 5. For a similar view, see Reich, Rückkehr nach Europa, at 227. As discussed below, these predictions of mass unemployment were fully borne out in reality.

16. See, e.g., Reich, Rückkehr nach Europa, at 220–26. Indeed, the GDR Round Table and the leading GDR reform groups had opposed a swift currency union from the very beginning, fearing a loss of autonomy to the west. The group Democracy Now, for example, feared that if "the western Mark marches in, the process of democratic renewal [in the GDR] will be cut short." Christ & Neubauer at 76–77.

17. Hohmann, Etappen des verfassungsrechtlichen Diskurses und der Verfassungsgesetzgebung nach der revolutionären Wende in der DDR, in Bernd Guggenberger & Tine Stein (eds.), Die Verfassungsdiskussion im Jahr der deutschen Einheit 101 (1991) (hereafter, Verfassungsdiskussion). This loss of fiscal sovereignty was an important focal point of the Volkskammer debate on the treaty. See, e.g., Volkskammer Protocol, May 21, 1990, at 211 (Walter Romberg, GDR Finance Minister); 217–18 (Richard Schröder, SPD).

18. See Kriele, Die politische Bedeutung des Staatsvertrages, 1990 DtZ 188.

19. In general, currency reform was placed under the control of the German Federal Bank (Bundesbank), a West German governmental organ with its own independent status under the Basic Law. See art. 88 GG; see also Gesetz über die Deutsche Bundesbank, of July 26, 1957, BGBl I 745. Under the treaty, therefore, the Bundesbank assumed a major role in the fate of the GDR. See, e.g., State Treaty, attachment I, arts. 12–14.

20. See Ingo von Münch (ed.), Dokumente der Wiedervereinigung Deutschlands 195, 198 (1991).

21. This ratio was proposed, for example, by the Bundesbank. See FAZ, Mar. 21, 1991, at 1 col. 2. See also Christ & Neubauer at 80–81.

22. Priewe & Hickel at 83.

23. See Gerlinde Sinn & Hans-Werner Sinn, Jumpstart: The Economic Unification of Germany 52 (1992); Christ & Neubauer at 65. Yet notwithstanding the sharp differential on the black market, Sinn & Sinn argue—presumably because of highly subsidized prices in the GDR—that the "quality-adjusted purchasing-power parity between the two currencies was, in fact, very close to 1:1." Sinn & Sinn at 53.

24. State Treaty art. 10(5).

25. Id. attachment I, art. 6(1). This system may reflect the view that the youngest are least in need of a favorable rate of exchange for savings—perhaps in part because they will come of age in a different economic system—whereas the oldest, whose savings represent their life's work, are most in need of this form of support.

26. Sinn & Sinn at 51 n. 2. This was the government's assessment; other calculations put the ratio at 1.6 to 1. Id.

27. See, e.g., Priewe & Hickel at 79. Yet, because "the [domestic] purchasing powers of the two currencies were approximately equal," Sinn & Sinn argue that the less than 1:1 conversion rate for savings meant "a substantial real conversion loss for the people of the GDR"—indeed, a loss of "almost one-third of their total financial wealth." Sinn & Sinn at 69–70.

28. This policy, through which lower prices were in effect exchanged for loyalty to the state, had begun in earnest with the accession of Erich Honecker to power in 1971. Christ & Neubauer at 36–38. Other significant factors in the decline of the GDR economy were the wasteful subsidization of certain technical industries—such as the development of computer microchips—largely for purposes of international prestige at the expense of other portions of the economy (id. at 43–44), as well as the formation in the 1970s of huge government monopolies (*Kombinate*), resulting in further centralization and inefficiency. Id. at 44–48. Indeed, as early as 1988 some state planners perceived that the GDR was facing bankruptcy, but these warnings were ignored by Honecker and the GDR leadership. Id. at 58–63. See also Konrad H. Jarausch, The Rush to German Unity 97–101 (1994), for an enlightening historical resume of these problems.

29. Priewe & Hickel at 83–84.

30. For a history and analysis of proposals for economic reform that would have preceded the currency union, see Priewe & Hickel at 77, 87–92; see generally Christ & Neubauer 68–74, 98–106. Priewe & Hickel conclude that it would have been politically impossible to equalize the economies before the currency union and that such a plan might not even have produced economic benefits. They thus direct their criticism not at a swift currency union as such, but rather at the government's failure to understand the great economic dislocations that this union would cause and to take adequate countervailing measures. See also Hankel at 40–41; Christ & Neubauer 100–101, 103–4.

31. State Treaty art. 1(3); see also Joint Protocol, part A, § II (principles of economic union under treaty).

32. State Treaty art. 2(2).

33. Joint Protocol, part A, § I(2).

34. Accordingly, after the signing of the State Treaty but before its effective date, the GDR amended its constitution to remove the concept of "socialist legality" and related principles. This change was accomplished in the fundamental constitutional amendment of June 17, 1990. See Ch. 5. Moreover, this amendment made clear that the adoption of a treaty by a two-thirds majority would have the effect of amending the constitution to the extent that amendments were required by the treaty. Thus the adoption of the State Treaty by a vote of two-thirds of the Volkskammer actually accomplished whatever constitutional changes were required by its terms.

35. See generally State Treaty art. 11; id. attachment IX.

36. Id. art. 14.

37. Joint Protocol, part A, § II(7). Moreover, the treaty required that real property in the GDR be legally available for purchase by anyone—in contrast with the GDR coalition agreement which sought to limit full ownership rights in property to GDR citizens for a ten-year period. See State Treaty, attachment IX; Christ & Neubauer at 91–92. This treaty provision was bitterly attacked by GDR reformers on the ground that it

would open a huge field for property speculation in which eastern citizens themselves would be hopelessly at a disadvantage. Cf. Volkskammer Protocol, May 21, 1990, at 225–26 (remarks of Jens Reich, Bündnis 90/Greens). In any event this provision, as many others, pitilessly revealed the one-sided nature of the power relationship between the two German states. See generally Christ & Neubauer at 92.

Throughout this economic conversion, the legal requirements of the European Communities were also to be taken into account. See, e.g., State Treaty art. 11(3) (general economic policy should be oriented to goals of the EC); art. 13(3) (in foreign commerce, the authority of the EC is to be observed); art. 15(1) (central role of the EC in agricultural economy requires adoption of a system conforming to that of the EC).

38. Gesetz zur Privatisierung und Reorganisation des volkseigenen Vermögens (Treuhandgesetz), of June 17, 1990, GBl DDR I 300. See Ch. 11.

39. See Ch. 5.

40. State Treaty art. 10(6). For critical commentary on this provision, see Volkskammer Protocol, May 21, 1990, at 225 (remarks of Jens Reich, Bündnis 90/ Greens). A similar provision was contained in the Unification Treaty, but it was also ineffective. The process of sale therefore tacitly rejected the argument that GDR "People's Property" actually belonged to the citizens of eastern Germany and, therefore, that they had a constitutional claim to shares of the property.

41. State Treaty, attachment II, art. III.

42. Id. attachment III, art. II. In the first decades of its existence, the GDR had continued to use the historic German Civil Code of 1900 (BGB). In 1975, however, the GDR adopted its own Civil Code, and the BGB went out of effect in East Germany. The adoption of the new eastern Civil Code in 1975 may have some parallels with the constitutional changes of 1974 in the GDR—which were intended to recognize its development into the stage of "real existing socialism." In any case, the relevant provisions of the first State Treaty marked the beginning of the return of eastern Germany to the BGB.

43. Id. attachment IV, art. I.

44. Id. arts. 18–25; id. attachment IV, art. II. The treaty also sought to conform the general structure of labor-management relations to that prevailing in the Federal Republic. See id. art. 17.

45. Id. art. 22(2).

46. See id. arts. 25, 28(1).

47. See generally Kriele, 1990 DtZ 188.

48. See State Treaty art. 2(1); Joint Protocol, part A, § I(1). Similarly, the preamble of the State Treaty specifically referred to the "peaceful and democratic revolution" of autumn 1989 in the GDR.

49. See Schmidt-Bleibtreu, 1990 DtZ at 140. As noted above, the fundamental amendment of June 17, 1990, changing the principles of the GDR Constitution, was adopted in response to these treaty requirements. See Ch. 5.

50. See, e.g., State Treaty, attachment III, art. II, § 21 (requiring the GDR to adopt laws strengthening judicial independence and the rights of the accused, and extending judicial review of administrative action); Joint Protocol, part B, art. I (concepts such as "socialist legality" should no longer be applied). These themes were also emphasized in amendments of the GDR Constitution enacted under the de Maizière government. See Ch. 5.

51. State Treaty, attachment III, art. II, § 21(h).

52. See, e.g., id. art. 16.

53. See Ch. 5.

54. State Treaty art. 28(1).

55. FR, July 31, 1990, at 1 col. 1.

56. See, e.g., Richard Schröder, Deutschland schwierig Vaterland 71–72 (1993); Priewe & Hickel at 80. This phenomenon extended substantially across the entire range of consumer goods and reflected "the large difference in quality between East and West German goods," as well as the power of West German advertising and "a simple desire for goods that were once almost unobtainable." Sinn & Sinn at 77. More recently, however, the eastern preference for western goods seems to have abated. Id. at 77–78.

57. Bergmann-Pohl at 148–49.

58. Ulrich Albrecht, Die Abwicklung der DDR 35, 95–96 (1992). Some experts, however, tend to discount the changes in the eastern European market as an important factor in the collapse of the East German economy. Sinn & Sinn at 37–39.

59. Bergmann-Pohl at 150. For the situation before the currency union, see, e.g., Reich, Rückkehr nach Europa, at 67: "To be a second-class German with strictly rationed and unfavorable currency exchange stamps, to be shoved into a back corner or bundled off into the broom closet when the West-Mark Mitsubishi owner appeared—that frustrating experience was the lot of many." See also Eppelmann, Die Schwierigkeiten des Zusammenwachsens, in Wolfgang Hardtwig & Heinrich A. Winkler (eds.), Deutsche Entfremdung: Zum Befinden in Ost und West 83–84 (1994). Indeed one West German writer, viewing the eastern currency as another form of restraint, noted that the Wall was not the only thing that had fenced GDR citizens off from foreign lands: so long as eastern citizens had the inconvertible GDR Mark, they remained "monetarily in restraint—in a currency prison." Hankel at 26. This general point was also noted in the Volkskammer debate on the State Treaty; see remarks of Richard Schröder (SPD) in Volkskammer Protocol, May 21, 1990, at 217: "The currency policy of the old GDR was objectively degrading."

60. Moreover, in the early months of 1991 the economic situation in the east declined further, and the president of the Bundesbank declared that the "overly hasty introduction" of the D-Mark into the GDR, through the State Treaty, had been a "catastrophe." FAZ, Mar. 21, 1991, at 1 col. 2. See also Sinn & Sinn at 62–65.

61. FAZ, May 25, 1992, at 5 col. 1 (remarks of Oskar Lafontaine).

62. Sinn & Sinn at 29.

63. Id. As a result, western transfer payments to eastern Germany have averaged DM 150 billion per year. See also Stern, Freedom and Its Discontents, 72 Foreign Affairs (No. 4) 108, 121 (1993): "In March 1993 the Bonn parliament finally approved a solidarity pact that has brought some predictability into the economic picture. It provides for new taxes to fund specified payments to the new *Länder*. Approximately seven percent of GNP will be transferred to the East over the next decade—roughly one trillion Deutsche marks."

64. See generally Ch. 10. Article 40(1) of the Unification Treaty provided that the obligations of the first State Treaty would ordinarily remain in effect unless they were inconsistent with the Unification Treaty or otherwise obsolete.

## Chapter 8
## The Final Months of the Volkskammer: Constitutional Problems of Accession and the First All-German Election

1. See Günter Grass & Regine Hildebrandt, Schaden begrenzen oder auf die Füße treten: Ein Gespräch 26 (1993) (remarks of Regine Hildebrandt).

2. See Sabine Bergmann-Pohl, Abschied ohne Tränen: Rückblick auf das Jahr der Einheit 150–53 (1991).

3. Interview with Lothar de Maizière, Berlin, Dec. 4, 1992.

4. See Ch. 5.

5. See Chs. 7 & 11.

6. See, e.g., Peter H. Merkl, German Unification in the European Context 147–49 (1993).

7. Bundeswahlgesetz, in the version of Sept. 1, 1975, BGBl I 2325 (as amended) § 6(6). A party could also achieve representation if it received the highest vote in three electoral districts, but such local strength has rarely been shown by a party that failed to receive 5 percent of the total national vote. In the election of 1994, however, the PDS did enter the Bundestag in this manner.

The German electoral system is particularly complex because it requires two votes from each voter—a first ballot for a representative from a specified district and a second ballot for a political party only. As a practical matter, it is the proportionate vote on the second (party) ballot that determines each party's representation in the Bundestag, and this ballot is also used to determine whether the 5 percent requirement has been met. See generally Donald P. Kommers, The Constitutional Jurisprudence of the Federal Republic of Germany 185–86 (1989). For historical background, see John Ford Golay, The Founding of the Federal Republic of Germany 138–58 (1958).

8. Because the sixteen million inhabitants of the GDR must be compared with more than sixty million in the Federal Republic before unification, a significant number of votes in the GDR could still fall below 5 percent of the total combined vote in an all-German election.

9. On these points, see generally Wolfgang Schäuble, Der Vertrag: Wie ich über die deutsche Einheit verhandelte 84–90 (1991). For Schäuble's discussion of the entire election imbroglio, see id. at 79–97.

10. See FR, July 25, 1990, at 3 col. 3; id. at 1 col. 1.

11. FR, July 25, 1990, at 1 col. 1.

12. Cf. Merkl, European Context, at 147.

13. FR, July 9, 1990, at 1 col. 4. FDP leaders also took the position that the GDR should accede before the election. Id.

14. FR, July 25, 1990, at 1 col. 1; see also Schäuble, Der Vertrag, at 126–27.

15. FAZ, July 21, 1990, at 1 col. 2. In fact, it has been argued that this consideration, rather than the quest for electoral advantage, was de Maizière's principal reason for seeking to delay the date of the GDR's accession. Barrios, Von der Revolution zum Beitritt: Die Entwicklung eines gesamtdeutschen Wahl- und Parteiensystems, in Ulrike Liebert & Wolfgang Merkel (eds.), Die Politik zur deutschen Einheit 153 (1991) (hereafter, Die Politik zur deutschen Einheit).

16. See Schäuble, Der Vertrag, at 85, 89–90, 148–49; Barrios in Die Politik zur deutschen Einheit at 150.

17. BGBl 1990 II 822. The treaty, along with an accompanying statute, is reprinted in 2 Klaus Stern & Bruno Schmidt-Bleibtreu, Verträge und Rechtsakte zur Deutschen Einheit 191–206 (1990) (hereafter, Verträge und Rechtsakte).

18. FAZ, Aug. 3, 1990, at 2 col. 5 (quoting Rhein-Neckar-Zeitung).

19. The Left List/PDS was a western counterpart of the eastern PDS. See FAZ, Aug. 16, 1990, at 3 col. 3. The complainants were joined in the Constitutional Court action by the Republicans, a far right-wing group that had experienced some success in local elections in the Federal Republic in recent years. The Republicans also believed

that their chances would be impaired by the imposition of a national 5 percent requirement. Because the Republicans had been banned in the GDR from February until August 1990, they did not take part in the March 18 Volkskammer election and their electoral strength in the GDR was unknown. See Ch. 5.

Although the GDR reform groups that formed Bündnis 90 were not parties to the action, they were allowed to participate in oral argument before the Constitutional Court. See 82 BVerfGE 322, 334–35 (1990).

20. 82 BVerfGE 322 (1990).

21. See arts. 21(1), 38(1) GG.

22. See, e.g., 6 BVerfGE 84 (1957) (Bavarian Party case); for an edited English version of this opinion, see Kommers, Constitutional Jurisprudence, at 187–89.

23. 82 BVerfGE at 337–39.

24. The Court emphasized that, under the 1968/74 GDR Constitution, associations were only permitted to exist if they conformed to the "principles of the socialist order of society," and political parties could only be formed within the "National Front" of the GDR. 82 BVerfGE at 340–42. The National Front, which was abolished in one of the early amendments of the GDR Constitution in 1990, was an organization designed to further electoral control by the SED. See Ch. 5.

25. 82 BVerfGE at 340.

26. Id. at 342–45. The Court went on to prohibit any temporary joint lists among parties for a particular election only. In contrast, it approved the actual consolidation of parties for permanent common action. Id. at 345–47, 349–50.

27. Id. at 348–49.

28. BGBl 1990 I 2141, reprinted in 2 Verträge und Rechtsakte at 207–8. The Greens voted against the new statute on the ground that any 5 percent clause was an unfair and unnecessary impairment of the democratic principle. For another decision of the Constitutional Court, based on principles of equality, that resulted in placing two small West German parties (including the right-wing NPD) on the December 2 ballot, see 82 BVerfGE 353 (1990).

In the election of December 2, 1990, a strong vote for the CDU/CSU seemed to indicate general approval of the results of unification up to that point. The SPD was a somewhat distant second in both east and west. The western Greens received less than 5 percent of the vote in West Germany, thus losing their representation in the Bundestag, but the eastern Greens (allied with the reform parties of Bündnis 90) obtained more than 5 percent of the eastern vote and entered the parliament. See FAZ, Dec. 4, 1990, at 2 col. 4. The PDS was also represented because its vote exceeded 5 percent of the electorate of the former GDR, although it did not approach 5 percent of the unified country; yet, denied the status of an official "fraction" by the parliamentary leadership, its later path in the Bundestag was not smooth. See 84 BVerfGE 304 (1991); cf. 84 BVerfGE 290 (1991). The DSU, which was dependent on its alliance with the CSU, fell below the 5 percent mark in eastern Germany and was not represented in the Bundestag.

Although the Bundestag election of December 1990 was conducted with separate electoral regimes for east and west, the election of October 1994 returned to a system that extended the 5 percent provision across the entire nation. Thus, the PDS and the small reform parties of the former GDR had in effect gained a four-year grace period in which to establish themselves as factors on the national scene.

In the 1994 election both groups entered the Bundestag. Although the PDS fell short of 5 percent of the total vote, it achieved representation by receiving the highest vote in four Bundestag districts in East Berlin. Bündnis 90 and the Greens merged into a combined party on the national level, and the new party easily exceeded the 5 percent minimum requirement. See Peter Pulzer, German Politics 1945–1995, at 180–81, 187 (1995).

29. See, e.g., Schäuble, Der Vertrag, at 196–97.

30. See id. at 187–89; Wolfgang Thierse, Mit eigener Stimme sprechen 65–66 (1992). Romberg's pessimism evoked a harsh response, but experience seems to have shown that Romberg's views were, in the end, more accurate than those of his opponents. Interview with Steffen Reiche, Potsdam and Berlin, Nov. 25, 1992.

31. Interview with Reinhard Höppner, Magdeburg, Jan. 11, 1993.

32. Interview with Lothar de Maizière, Berlin, Dec. 4, 1992.

33. See, e.g., Schäuble, Der Vertrag, at 91, 188–89, 192; Thierse, Mit eigener Stimme, at 61.

34. GBl DDR 1990 I 1324, reprinted in Ingo von Münch (ed.), Dokumente der Wiedervereinigung Deutschlands 326 (1991). Interestingly—notwithstanding de Maizière's earlier fears on the subject—the GDR voted to declare its accession to the Federal Republic a few days before the Unification Treaty was actually signed. Accompanying its declaration of accession, therefore, the Volkskammer also stated its understanding that the Unification Treaty would be finished by the date of accession and that the Two Plus Four negotiations and preparations for the creation of the eastern Länder would have reached a sufficiently advanced stage by that time. Id.

35. See Chs. 15 & 16.

36. See Thierse, Mit eigener Stimme, at 58–71.

37. See generally Bergmann-Pohl at 168–79.

38. Jens Reich, Rückkehr nach Europa: Zur neuen Lage der deutschen Nation 271–74 (1991).

39. See, e.g., Konrad H. Jarausch, The Rush to German Unity 160–62 (1994).

40. Weizsäcker declared that the "constitutional patriotism" of the west could be united with the "human solidarity" of the east into a "powerful whole." Richard von Weizsäcker, Von Deutschland nach Europa 212 (1993).

41. Helmut Kohl, Die deutsche Einheit: Reden und Gespräche 221 (1992) (radio and television address of Oct. 2, 1990).

42. Id. at 225 (parliamentary policy statement of the first all-German government, Oct. 4, 1990). Kohl also suggested that the historical burden of the Holocaust would play a role in unification of the populations: "As we bear this historical burden together, we also show ourselves that we are worthy of freedom together." Id. at 224.

43. See Ch. 7. These economic divisions have been exacerbated by other phenomena directly related to unification, such as thousands of property claims by western citizens for houses and other dwellings occupied by citizens of the east. Cf. Thierse, Wahrnehmungen zum deutschen Befinden in Ost und West, in Wolfgang Hardtwig & Heinrich A. Winkler (eds.), Deutsche Entfremdung: Zum Befinden in Ost und West 18–20 (1994) (hereafter, Deutsche Entfremdung). See generally Ch. 11.

44. See generally Hans Joachim Maaz, Das gestürzte Volk oder die verunglückte Einheit (1991). See also Merseburger, Von der doppelten Vergangenheit, in Deutsche Entfremdung at 129: "The tabula rasa of social values, which [came] unavoidably with accession under article 23, brought not only the total collapse of all previous authority; it led also to the breakdown of the entire previous system of orientation"; Thierse in Deutsche Entfremdung at 19–20: "What happens to the social experiences [of GDR citizens], which were experiences of a society of scarcity . . . [of] a community of need?

How can they be useful in an open society?"; Eppelmann, Die Schwierigkeiten des Zusammenwachsens, in Deutsche Entfremdung at 95–96: "You begin again at the age of 46 as an apprentice or as a pupil or student. . . . For there is no area of my life that remained on October 4, 1990, as it was up until October 3." See generally Jarausch at 194–96.

45. Cf., e.g., Thierse in Deutsche Entfremdung at 24–25.

46. See Ch. 10.

47. See FAZ, Apr. 22, 1994, at 5 col. 1. See generally Ch. 11. For a period, eastern CDU representatives in parliament formed a separate group within the party caucus, as a protest against "the West German dominance in the policies of the [CDU/CSU] in general and with respect to the unification policies in particular." See generally FAZ, June 6, 1992, at 1 col. 5. Moreover, in a similar move, Peter-Michael Diestel (a former CDU party official in Brandenburg) joined with Gregor Gysi—at the time, the leader of the PDS—to found the "Committees for Justice," a movement designed to represent and advance the interests of eastern Germany. Although this movement has faded somewhat from the public consciousness, its appearance was seen as a reaction to the failure of the governing parties adequately to represent eastern interests.

## Chapter 9
## Reconstitution of the Eastern Länder

1. See Ch. 11.

2. See, e.g., Bastuck, Unity, Law, and Freedom: Legal Aspects of the Process and Results of German Unification, 25 International Lawyer 251, 258 (1991). For the state borders, see the map of Germany, 1945, at the outset of this volume. Although the historical units composing the German states remained largely intact under the Weimar Constitution, the Soviet occupation made some significant changes, such as creating the new state of Saxony-Anhalt from part of Saxony and the previously existing state of Anhalt. See Blaschke, Alte Länder—Neue Länder: Zur territorialen Neugliederung der DDR, APuZ, June 29, 1990, at 42.

3. See Verf. DDR (1949) arts. 71–80, 109–16; Erich Fischer & Werner Künzel, Verfassungen deutscher Länder und Staaten 274–335 (1989).

4. See Lucius D. Clay, Decision in Germany 144 (1950).

5. Control Council Law No. 46 (Feb. 25, 1947), reprinted in 1 Ingo von Münch (ed.), Dokumente des geteilten Deutschland 54–55 (1976) (hereafter, Dokumente); Harold James, A German Identity 162 (1994).

6. Czybulka, Zur Entwicklung des Föderalismus in der DDR und in Deutschland (mit einem Seitenblick auf Europa), 1990 ZRP 269, 270. Indeed, some argue that the five states of the GDR were never properly abolished, although they were not recognized in the 1968/74 GDR Constitution.

7. For the historical context of this action in the GDR—a general strengthening of the principle of "democratic centralism" and implementation of the Soviet cadre principle—see Hermann Weber, Geschichte der DDR 219–31 (1985). Abolition of the Länder may also have been a response to the obstruction of policies of the central GDR government by remaining non-SED officials in the governments of the Länder. See Peter H. Merkl, The Origin of the West German Republic 17 (1963). For Hitler's conversion of the states into administrative districts of the central government, see Gordon A. Craig, Germany 1866–1945, at 582–83 (1978); Hajo Holborn, A History of Modern Germany: 1840–1945, at 730 (1982).

8. Moreover, the green-and-white flags appeared throughout Saxony in the early months of 1990. Interview with Steffen Heitmann, Justice Minister of Saxony, Dresden, Nov. 6, 1992.

9. See, e.g., Stammen & Maier, Der Prozeß der Verfassunggebung, in Josef Becker et al. (eds.), Vorgeschichte der Bundesrepublik Deutschland 410–13 (1979); Merkl, Origin, at 119–25; see also Clay at 421–22, 424–25, 431–34.

10. Czybulka, 1990 ZRP at 270. The preamble and other provisions of the State Treaty required that the GDR be a "federal" state. See generally Ch. 7.

11. See Verfassungsgesetz zur Bildung von Ländern in der DDR—Ländereinführungsgesetz—of July 22, 1990, GBl DDR I 955 (hereafter, Law for the Establishment of the Länder); FAZ, July 23, 1990, at 1 col. 2. The statute set forth each state's boundaries but contemplated that border localities might petition—through plebiscites and votes of local councils—to be transferred to an adjoining state.

12. Gesetz über die Wahlen zu Landtagen in der Deutschen Demokratischen Republik, of July 22, 1990, GBl DDR I 960. In the elections for state legislatures, a 5 percent minimum vote for any party would be required for entry into the legislature, with the exception of parties representing the Sorbian minority in the east. This was the first time that a 5 percent requirement had been adopted in the GDR.

13. See, e.g., FAZ, Aug. 28, 1990, at 12 col. 2; see Lapp, Fünf neue Länder—Das Ende der DDR, 1990 DA 1315, 1317. Notwithstanding this early work, the first new state constitution, that of Saxony, was not adopted until June 1992.

14. Law for the Establishment of the Länder § 1(2). Even after accession on October 3, 1990, separate East and West Berlin governments continued to exist until a single local government was elected at the time of the national elections in December. The impact of this dual arrangement on constitutional development in Berlin is discussed below.

15. See Vertrag zwischen der Bundesrepublik Deutschland und der Deutschen Demokratischen Republik über die Herstellung der Einheit Deutschlands—Einigungsvertrag—of Aug. 31, 1990, BGBl II 889 art. 5 (hereafter, Unification Treaty).

16. On the other hand, a renegade state's attempt to accede individually might well have been invalid. Such a move would have violated the GDR Constitution and contravened the principle of nonintervention recognized by the Basic Treaty of 1972. See Tomuschat, Wege zur deutschen Einheit, 49 VVDStRL 70, 76–77 (1990).

17. See Unification Treaty art. 1(1).

18. See FAZ, June 6, 1992, at 1 col. 5.

19. The Bundesrat is an important governmental organ because it has the power to reject certain legislation of the Bundestag. In many cases this authority can be overruled by a contrary vote of the Bundestag—although, even here, the views of the Bundesrat are accorded substantial weight. See art. 77 GG. But in certain matters closely affecting the states, a negative vote of the Bundesrat will absolutely prevent enactment of the legislation. See, e.g., art. 109(3),(4) GG (certain matters affecting state budgets).

As a practical matter, the role of the Bundesrat is particularly prominent when the opposition parties in the Bundestag control a majority of votes in the Bundesrat. Such a situation developed in 1990, during negotiations over the Unification Treaty, when the opposition SPD came to power in Lower Saxony and thereby became the controlling party in the Bundesrat. See Wolfgang Schäuble, Der Vertrag: Wie ich über die deutsche Einheit verhandelte 91 (1991).

20. According to article 51(2) GG (in its original form), "each state has at least three votes [in the Bundesrat], states with more than two million inhabitants have four, states

with more than six million inhabitants have five votes." The votes of each state cannot be split but must all be cast for the same position on a particular question. Art. 51(3) GG.

21. The smallest of the new states was Mecklenburg-Vorpommern, and the largest was Saxony. See Rauschning, Deutschlands aktuelle Verfassungslage, 1990 DVBl 393, 399. Four of these five states had between 2 and 6 million inhabitants, and each therefore received four votes in the Bundesrat. The fifth state, Mecklenburg-Vorpommern, had slightly less than 2 million inhabitants and therefore received only three Bundesrat votes.

22. Id. at 399–400.

23. Unification Treaty art. 4(3). This change required an amendment of article 51(2) of the Basic Law. See generally Ch. 10.

24. Before unification, the four largest states of the Federal Republic, voting together, possessed more than one-third of the votes in the Bundesrat and therefore could block the adoption of any amendment of the Basic Law. The provision of the Unification Treaty increasing the seats allocated to states with more than seven million inhabitants was apparently intended to preserve this veto power of the largest states, even after expansion of the Bundesrat by the representatives of the five new Länder and Berlin.

Some have urged that unification should be followed by a complete redrawing of state boundaries, in the west as well as the east. If so, a complete revision of the states' representation in the Bundesrat would certainly also be required. Cf., e.g., Schneider, Die Zukunft des Grundgesetzes. Bedarf die Verfassung einer Bestätigung?, in Bernd Guggenberger & Tine Stein (eds.), Die Verfassungsdiskussion im Jahr der deutschen Einheit 134 (1991) (hereafter, Verfassungsdiskussion); Schneider, Deutschland in neuer Verfassung, in Michael Müller & Wolfgang Thierse (eds.), Deutsche Ansichten: Die Republik im Übergang 233 (1992) (hereafter, Deutsche Ansichten).

25. See arts. 106–7 GG; Dam, The American Fiscal Constitution, 44 University of Chicago Law Review 271, 294–98 (1977).

26. See Ch. 4.

27. Such provisions are not strictly limited to the constitutions of the eastern Länder. Some constitutions of the west German states, especially those early constitutions in the former American zone, contain similar provisions. Yet overall, the provisions of the western state constitutions are not so far-reaching as those in the new eastern constitutions.

28. "The peaceful revolution started in October 1989 in Saxony, and in Saxony it achieved its first completion." Hans von Mangoldt, Die Verfassungen der neuen Bundesländer 9 (1993).

29. See generally Tautz, Die Entstehung einer Verfassung im Freistaat Sachsen, in I Klaus Stern (ed.), Deutsche Wiedervereinigung: Die Rechtseinheit 25 (1991) (hereafter, Deutsche Wiedervereinigung).

30. Id. at 28; Bönninger, Verfassungsdiskussion im Lande Sachsen, 1991 LKV 9, 10; Interview mit Staatsminister Arnold Vaatz, in Der Sächsische Landtag, Von der Wende zum Parlament 47 (1991); Heitmann, Entstehung und Grundgedanken der Verfassung des Freistaates Sachsen, in Peter Caesar et al., Die Entwicklung der Rechtsstaatlichkeit in den neuen Bundesländern 12 (1992).

31. Heitmann in Caesar et al. at 12–13. See Verfassung des Landes Sachsen (Textentwurf der "Gruppe der 20"), reprinted in 39 JöR 427 (1990).

32. These demonstrations included the storming of the Dresden railway station on

October 4 and continued through the fortieth birthday celebrations of the GDR on October 6–8. See Ch. 3. For the origins of the Group of 20, see Hartmut Zwahr, Ende einer Selbstzerstörung: Leipzig und die Revolution in der DDR 57, 76–77 (1993); Elizabeth Pond, Beyond the Wall: Germany's Road to Unification 108–9 (1993).

33. Interview with Steffen Heitmann, Nov. 6, 1992.

34. Verfassung des Landes Sachsen: Gohrischer Entwurf (August 1990). The so-called "mixed commission" that drafted the document in the resort town of Gohrisch was part of a larger pattern of cooperation between Saxony and Baden-Württemberg. See Tautz in I Deutsche Wiedervereinigung at 29. Indeed each of the new eastern Länder had one or more western "partner" states that lent assistance in rebuilding the state governments and restructuring public institutions.

35. Interview with Steffen Heitmann, Nov. 6, 1992.

36. Id. The draft of the Group of 20 was taken as an initial basis for the Gohrisch draft and, to some extent, the personnel of the two drafting groups was the same. Bönninger, 1991 LKV at 9. Yet the more cautious Gohrisch draft omitted certain bold provisions endorsed by the Group of 20—such as the categorical rejection of a secret service for the state of Saxony. Some argue that it was precisely in these omitted provisions that "one feels the breath of the revolutionary citizens movement of autumn 1989." Id. at 9–10.

37. Verfassung des Freistaats Sachsen; Gohrischer Entwurf—Überarbeitete Fassung (1990).

38. An important figure in the legal history of the GDR, Bönninger had encountered difficulties of his own with the SED leadership. See Inga Markovits, Imperfect Justice: An East-West German Diary 107–10, 200–204 (1995).

39. For Bönninger's own analysis of the professors' draft, see Bönninger, 1991 LKV at 11–12. See also von Mangoldt at 22–23; Feddersen, Die Verfassunggebung in den neuen Ländern: Grundrechte, Staatsziele, Plebiszite, 1992 DÖV 989, 994.

40. Verf. Sachs. art. 10; see also id. art. 1. These ecological provisions, which are reflected to some extent in all of the new eastern state constitutions, echo and develop an environmental provision that was included in the basic constitutional principles adopted under the de Maizière government in June 1990. See Ch. 5.

Although the Basic Law contained no environmental guarantee when the new state constitutions were drafted, it was later amended to include such a provision. See art. 20a GG; see generally Ch. 10. Echoing the new eastern constitutions, this provision also refers to a responsibility for future generations.

41. Verf. Sachs. art. 10(2). For a similar provision, see Verf. Br. art. 39(8); cf. RT-Entwurf 33(3).

42. Cf. Kutscha, Soziale Grundrechte und Staatszielbestimmungen in den neuen Landesverfassungen, 1993 ZRP 339, 342.

43. Verf. Sachs. art. 7. This provision has been criticized for mixing the distinct terms "rights" and "state goals."

44. Id. art. 13.

45. Heitmann in Caesar et al. at 22; Hinds, Die neue Verfassung des Freistaates Sachsen—Berechtigte oder unberechtigte Kritik an der Verfassungsgebung, 1993 ZRP 149, 151; see generally Schneider in Deutsche Ansichten at 236.

46. See Kutscha, 1993 ZRP at 342; Degenhart, Grundzüge der neuen sächsischen Verfassung, 1993 LKV 33, 35–36. Yet the constitution provides little guidance for establishing priorities in cases in which various state goals—for example, goals of ecology and the promotion of housing—may conflict. Id. On provisions for "state

goals" in the state constitutional drafts, see generally Vitzthum, Auf der Suche nach einer sozio-ökonomischen Identität?, 1991 VBlBW 404.

47. See, e.g., Iltgen, Rede zur Vorstellung der Sächsischen Verfassung am 27. Mai 1992, reprinted in Sächsischer Landtag (ed.), Verfassung des Freistaates Sachsen 10–12 (1992) (hereafter, Sächs. Verf. Broschüre).

48. See Verf. Sachs. arts. 14–38.

49. Id. arts. 16, 26.

50. Id. arts. 2(4), 5(1), 6.

For enforcement of the "defensive" and other constitutional rights—but not the "state goals"—the constitution provides for a constitutional court with broad power to hear citizens' constitutional complaints. Id. art. 81. Cf. Degenhart, 1993 LKV at 36. Following the pattern of the Basic Law, the court is also authorized to hear inter-branch disputes and certain "abstract" challenges of the constitutionality of legislation. The Constitutional Court of Saxony was established and its initial members were chosen in 1993.

51. See Verf. Sachs. arts. 33, 57; 50, 51, 54(4). For similar provisions in other eastern constitutions, see, e.g., Verf. Sachs.-Anh. arts 6(1), 63; 6(2), 53(3)–(4); 61, 62; Verf. Thür. art. 6. See also Höppner, Fragen und Anworten zur Verfassung, in Landeszentrale für politische Bildung Sachsen-Anhalt, Die Verfassung des Landes Sachsen-Anhalt 30 (1992): "We come . . . out of a history in which protection of [private] data was trodden underfoot and kilometer-long mountains of personal files were set up for the purpose of controlling individuals. That . . . must never happen again."

52. Verf. Sachs. art. 34; see also, e.g., Verf. Meckl.-Vorp. art. 6 (3).

53. Iltgen in Sächs. Verf. Broschüre at 10. Cf. Friedrich Schorlemmer, Versöhnung in der Wahrheit 22–23 (1992).

54. Verf. Sachs. arts. 71–73, 74(3).

55. Hinds, 1993 ZRP at 151; cf. Thierse, Wahrnehmungen zum deutschen Befinden in Ost und West, in Wolfgang Hardtwig & Heinrich A. Winkler (eds.), Deutsche Entfremdung: Zum Befinden in Ost und West 17 (1994).

56. In contrast, some state constitutions of the western Länder set forth a more modest two-stage system. See Hinds, 1993 ZRP at 151; Degenhart, 1993 LKV at 38. See also Verf. Thür. arts. 68, 82.

57. Schneider in Deutsche Ansichten at 240. See also von Mangoldt at 59: These provisions "afford a real chance for dialogue between the parliament and the proponents of the People's Petition."

58. Iltgen in Sächs. Verf. Broschüre at 15.

59. See Verf. Sachs. arts. 116–17; see also id. arts. 118–19. The preamble also refers to the past, mentioning the "National Socialist and Communist rule of force" as well as the peaceful revolution of 1989. See generally Andrea Franke, Zur Verfassung des Freistaates Sachsen, in III Deutsche Wiedervereinigung at 59.

60. Sächs. Verf. Broschüre at 74–76 (remarks of Cornelia Matzke).

61. Id. at 72–73 (remarks of Klaus Bartl).

62. FAZ, May 27, 1992, at 1 col. 2.

63. Brandenburg was actually the first state to have a constitution adopted by the Landtag, but it followed Saxony in final adoption because the constitution was subject to approval in a plebiscite in June 1992. See FAZ, May 27, 1992, at 1 col. 2.

64. The SPD sought to achieve the required two-thirds approval in the Landtag without having to rely on the votes of the PDS. Moreover, for the charter to be truly legitimate, SPD leaders believed that it had to receive some support from all political

groups, including the CDU. Interview with Steffen Reiche, Chair of Brandenburg SPD, Potsdam and Berlin, Nov. 25, 1992.

65. See, e.g., Hans-Dieter Schütt, Peter-Michael Diestel: "Rebellion tut gut" 13–14 (1992): the Brandenburg Constitution reflects "another political understanding" than that of the old Federal Republic. See also interview with Steffen Reiche, Nov. 25, 1992.

66. Entwurf einer Verfassung für das Land Brandenburg, Apr. 22, 1990, reprinted in 39 JöR 387 (1990). See Dietrich Franke, Der Entwurf der brandenburgischen Landesverfassung, in III Deutsche Wiedervereinigung at 3. This draft was clearly a transitional document: it acknowledged important institutions of the still-existing GDR, such as agricultural collectives, public ownership of important industries, and property relations arising from the Soviet land reform.

67. II. überarbeiteter Entwurf der Verfassung für das Land Brandenburg, Sept. 1990. See Sachs, Zur Verfassung des Landes Brandenburg, 1993 LKV 241, 242. This draft was issued by federal representatives who exercised a sort of pre-unification state authority in the administrative regions that later formed the state of Brandenburg.

68. See Sachs, 1993 LKV at 241. A similar pattern was followed in the constitutional drafting committee of Mecklenburg-Vorpommern, as will be discussed below.

69. Interview with Steffen Reiche, Nov. 25, 1992.

70. See Sachs, 1993 LKV at 242: some reactions were "extreme on the positive as well as on the negative" side.

71. See Feddersen, 1992 DÖV at 993.

72. Diestel later split with the CDU leadership and became a co-founder of the Committees for Justice. See Ch. 8.

In my understanding of the history of the Brandenburg Constitution, I was greatly assisted by conversations with Dr. Dietrich Franke, then of the Brandenburg Ministry of Justice.

73. Dietrich Franke in III Deutsche Wiedervereinigung at 10–11. In this process, the original constitutional committee first submitted a revised draft to the Landtag. Then, under the guidance of an internal parliamentary committee, the draft underwent three more sets of revisions and hard-fought compromises. Id.

74. See, e.g., FAZ, Apr. 22, 1992, at 5 col. 1 (remarks of Ulf Fink and Rupert Scholz).

75. See Christian Starck, Die Verfassungen der neuen deutschen Länder 27–28 (1994). Signatures of 20,000 residents of Brandenburg are sufficient to require the legislature to consider a matter, and signatures of 80,000 registered voters—about 4 percent of the total—are sufficient to force a plebiscite if the legislature does not enact the measure. But considerably higher percentages are necessary if the measure seeks dissolution of the parliament. See Verf. Br. arts. 76–78.

76. Verf. Br. arts. 78(3), 115. Ulf Fink, the leader of the CDU forces opposing the constitution, particularly criticized the plebiscitary provisions, which could "open the door to radicals of the left and of the right." See FAZ, Apr. 15, 1992, at 4 col. 5.

77. Verf. Br. arts. 20, 21. See Ch. 3.

78. Verf. Br. art. 21(3); see RT-Entwurf art. 35(2). The new constitutions of Mecklenburg-Vorpommern and Thuringia contain somewhat more modest provisions protecting citizens groups.

79. See Verf. Br. arts. 21(4), 39(7); see also id. arts. 56(2)–(3), 71, 94.

80. Id. art 12(3). For similar provisions in other eastern constitutions, see Verf. Sachs. art. 8; Verf. Sachs.-Anh. art. 34; Verf. Meckl.-Vorp. art. 13; see also Verf. Thür.

art. 2(2). Since the adoption of the Brandenburg Constitution, a provision on affirmative action for women has also been added to article 3(2) of the Basic Law. See Ch. 10.

81. Verf. Br. art. 48(3). This doctrine requires equalizing the compensation of men and women in different occupations if it is shown that certain work ordinarily performed by women (at lower wages) is of social value equal to that of occupations often performed by men (at higher wages). This state constitutional provision is probably inapplicable to ordinary employment relations because most civil law, including employment law, falls within federal competence.

82. For a similar provision, see Verf. Sachs. art. 22(2).

83. Interview with Steffen Reiche, Nov. 25, 1992. In 1975 the Constitutional Court held that decriminalization of first-trimester abortions violated the Basic Law. But the Court changed its mind somewhat on this issue in a decision handed down after the adoption of the Constitution of Brandenburg. See Ch. 12.

84. Verf. Br. arts. 12(2), 26(2). It has been argued, however, that the Basic Law's special protection of marriage and the family (art. 6 GG), could invalidate any state constitutional provision granting equal status to other forms of "living communities." See Dietlein, Der Schutz nichtehelicher Lebensgemeinschaften in den Verfassungen und Verfassungsentwürfen der neuen Länder, 1993 DtZ 136. For a contrary view, see Sacksofsky, Landesverfassungen und Grundgesetz—am Beispiel der Verfassungen der neuen Bundesländer, 1993 NVwZ 235, 237.

Numerous provisions protecting handicapped persons are directed against the exclusion of another disadvantaged group. Discrimination on the basis of handicap is prohibited, and the government must work toward equality of living conditions for handicapped persons. Verf. Br. art. 12(2), (4). Families with handicapped members receive special support, and persons with handicaps receive special consideration in higher education, sports, and employment. Id. arts. 26(l), 29(3), 35, 48(4). See also id. art. 45(3). For similar provisions, see, e.g., Verf. Sachs. 7(2); Verf. Sachs.-Anh. art. 38. Since the adoption of the Brandenburg Constitution, article 3(3) of the Basic Law has been amended to prohibit discrimination on the basis of handicap. See Ch. 10.

85. Verf. Br. art. 3(3).

86. Id. art. 22(1)–(2).

87. 83 BVerfGE 37 (1990); 83 BVerfGE 60 (1990). In accordance with the Maastricht Treaty, however, article 28(1) of the Basic Law has recently been amended to grant local electoral rights to citizens of other European Union member states residing in Germany. See Ch. 23.

88. Verf. Br. art. 2(1). In an early example of these collaborative efforts, the state of Brandenburg has established a "European University" (Viadrina) in Frankfurt/Oder on the Polish border. It is contemplated that approximately 30 percent of the students will be citizens of Poland. See Ch. 13.

For similar but less extensive provisions seeking to further international cooperation, see Verf. Meckl.-Vorp. preamble, art. 11.

89. Verf. Br. art. 2(3).

90. Id. art. 41(3). The constitution also contains comprehensive rights or state goals of social welfare. Id. arts. 45, 47, 48; cf. Schneider in Deutsche Ansichten at 235–36. But perhaps as a counterpoint, an explicit provision proclaims a broad right "to the free development of economic initiative" within limits similar to those in the Basic Law. Verf. Br. art. 42(1).

91. Id. arts. 50, 51.

92. Id. art. 48(3)–(4); cf. RT-Entwurf art. 27(5). Interestingly, in a case arising from mass dismissals of eastern workers upon unification, the Constitutional Court insisted—as an aspect of constitutional provisions relating to employment—that protection be granted to disadvantaged people falling into a similar set of categories. 84 BVerfGE 133 (1991). See Ch. 13.

93. Verf. Br. art. 19(1).

94. Id. art. 47(2); cf. RT-Entwurf art. 25(1).

95. The constitution also endorses social equality by seeking to improve access to university studies for working people and others who have not followed the traditional paths of university preparation. Adult education is also encouraged. Id. arts. 32(3), 33. Some similar provisions were in the Brandenburg Constitution of 1947.

96. The Basic Law was amended to facilitate this merger. See art. 118a GG; Rohn & Sannwald, Die Ergebnisse der Gemeinsamen Verfassungskommission, 1994 ZRP 65, 70.

97. See FAZ, June 23, 1995, at 1 col. 2.

98. See FAZ, Apr. 3, 1995, at 1 col. 2; FAZ, Apr. 24, 1995, at 4 col. 1.

99. See generally Kilian, Die neue Verfassung des Landes Sachsen-Anhalt, 1993 LKV 73.

100. Under this view, only those state constitutions adopted in the Länder before 1949 properly contain their own catalogs of basic rights.

101. von Bose, Der Stand der Verfassungsberatungen in Sachsen-Anhalt, in III Deutsche Wiedervereinigung at 79; Kilian, 1993 LKV at 74.

102. See Arbeitsgruppe Landtag, Unterarbeitsgruppe Verfassung, Entwurf, Verfassung Sachsen-Anhalt, June 29, 1990, reprinted at 39 JöR 455 (1990).

103. Höppner later became minister-president of Saxony-Anhalt in a minority coalition of the SPD and Bündnis 90/Greens.

104. See Starck, Verfassunggebung in den neuen Ländern, 1992 ZG 1, 7: "All in all, there prevailed a pleasant atmosphere, like a seminar." See also von Bose in III Deutsche Wiedervereinigung at 80; Interview with Reinhard Höppner, Magdeburg, Jan. 11, 1993.

The committee considered three draft constitutions submitted by the political parties, including a revised version of the draft of the Saxony-Anhalt Round Table, submitted by Bündnis 90/Greens. See Starck, 1992 ZG at 5–6.

105. Interview with Reinhard Höppner, Jan. 11, 1993; cf. Höppner, Fragen und Antworten zur Verfassung, in Landeszentrale für politische Bildung Sachsen-Anhalt, Die Verfassung des Landes Sachsen-Anhalt 28 (1992) (hereafter, Fragen und Antworten).

106. See, e.g., III Deutsche Wiedervereinigung at 76–77 (remarks of Andrea Franke).

107. Interview with Reinhard Höppner, Jan. 11, 1993.

108. Feddersen, 1992 DÖV at 995; Höppner, Fragen und Antworten, at 29.

109. See FAZ, July 16, 1992, at 4 col. 4.

110. See, e.g., Verf. Sachs.-Anh. preamble; arts. 2(1), 6(2), 18(2), 27(1), 35, 39(2), 99. Moreover, environmental protection is considered so important that the freedom of research may possibly be limited in order to protect "the natural basis of life." Id. art. 10(3). For a similar provision, see Verf. Meckl.-Vorp. art. 7(2).

111. Verf. Sachs.-Anh. art. 17(4).

112. Id. art. 3.

113. See Kilian, 1993 LKV at 78.

114. See, e.g., III Deutsche Wiedervereinigung 91–93 (remarks of von Bose and Isensee).

115. Verf. Sachs.-Anh. arts. 4–23. See generally Feddersen, 1992 DÖV at 995; von Münch, Die Zeit, Mar. 20, 1992, at 56.

116. Verf. Sachs.-Anh. art. 24(2)–(4); RT-Entwurf art. 22(4)–(5). Indeed the protection of children was a special concern of the Round Table itself: a position paper of the Round Table declared that "the civil, political, economic, social and cultural basic rights of children and young people are to be set forth in the future constitution." Helmut Herles & Ewald Rose (eds.), Vom Runden Tisch zum Parlament 279 (1990).

117. Verf. Sachs.-Anh. art. 29(2). For a comparable provision, see Verf. Sachs. art. 104(1).

118. Verf. Sachs.-Anh. arts. 39, 40 (employment, appropriate living space, abolition of homelessness). Among the other state goals, see, e.g., id. art. 36(3) (state should further "cultural activities of all citizens" by supporting public museums, theaters, etc.)

119. Verf. Sachs.-Anh. art. 75(6). For a defense of this more limited jurisdiction, see Starck, 1992 ZG at 19–20. But the constitution authorizes the legislature to add to the court's jurisdiction, and a future statute could someday fill this jurisdictional lacuna. Verf. Sachs.-Anh. art. 75(8).

120. Interview with Reinhard Höppner, Jan. 11, 1993.

121. Id.; see also Herles & Rose at 332–33; Verf. DDR (1949) art. 41(2). Cf. Richard Schröder, Deutschland schwierig Vaterland 143 (1993).

122. Cf. Häberle, Fast blühten tausend Blumen, Thüringer Allgemeine, Nov. 20, 1993, at 3 col. 1.

123. See Entwurf, Verfassung für das Land Mecklenburg-Vorpommern: erarbeitet im Auftrag der Bezirksverwaltungsbehörden Schwerin, Rostock, Neubrandenburg (July 1990), reprinted in 39 JöR 399 (1990).

124. See Hölscheidt & von Wiese, Grundrechte und Staaatsziele im Verfassungsentwurf für Mecklenburg-Vorpommern, 1992 LKV 393.

125. The Greens and the reform parties had been excluded from the Landtag because they entered the election separately and none achieved the requisite 5 percent vote—although their combined total exceeded 10 percent. They were represented on the constitutional commission because of their significant combined support. Interview with Professor Rolf Eggert, Member of Landtag of Mecklenburg-Vorpommern (SPD), Schwerin, June 14, 1993. Additional members of the commission were chosen to present the views reflected in the 1990 draft of the regional round tables and in another early draft. See generally Starck, 1992 ZG at 8.

126. These experts were Professors Christian Starck of Göttingen (chosen by the CDU) and Albert von Mutius of Kiel (chosen by the SPD). See generally Starck, 1992 ZG at 8.

127. See Zwischenbericht der Kommission für die Erarbeitung einer Landesverfassung (Verfassungskommission), Landtag Mecklenburg-Vorpommern, Drucksache 1/2000 (1992) (hereafter, Zwischenbericht). This draft contained two separate proposals for plebiscitary elements—one representing the views of Professor von Mutius, the other setting forth the views of Professor Starck. See Feddersen, 1992 DÖV at 992.

128. Interview with Heiko Braß, Verwaltung/Landtag Mecklenburg-Vorpommern, Schwerin, June 14, 1993; see also Hölscheidt & von Wiese, 1992 LKV at 398.

129. Interview with Heiko Braß, June 14, 1993.

130. This was the view of Professor Starck. See 1992 ZG at 22–23. This technique is employed, for example, in article 3 of the constitution of the western state of Lower Saxony. One commentator probably represented the views of many western academics when he remarked that this method adopted in Mecklenburg-Vorpommern was "the wisest and least problematic resolution." Feddersen, 1992 DÖV at 997.

131. Indeed, the original justice minister of Mecklenburg-Vorpommern, who came from the west, presented a proposed constitution that contained no basic rights at all and would therefore have relied completely on the federal basic rights. Interview with Professor Rolf Eggert, June 14, 1993.

132. Verf. Meckl.-Vorp. art. 5(2).

133. In a related provision, article 15(4) declares that a goal of the state school system is to develop a sense of "community with other individuals and peoples."

134. Verf. Meckl.-Vorp. art. 8; see also id. art. 15(3),(5); Verf. Br. art. 29(3).

135. In other specific provisions, the constitution also guarantees certain rights of personal data, rights of art, scholarship, research, and religion, and the right of petition. See id. arts. 6–7, 9–10; see also id. art. 37.

136. See Zwischenbericht at 48; cf. Hölscheidt & von Wiese, 1992 LKV at 395.

137. See generally art. 142 GG; Sacksofsky, 1993 NVwZ at 236–38; see also Sachs, Die Landesverfassung im Rahmen der bundesstaatlichen Rechts- und Verfassungsordnung, 1993 ThürVBl 121; 36 BVerfGE 342 (1974).

138. Article 53(7) excludes the incorporated basic rights from the court's authority to hear constitutional complaints against exercises of "public power" and expressly states that the court's jurisdiction under that section extends only "so far as there is no jurisdiction of the Federal Constitutional Court." Yet article 53(6) may allow the state constitutional court to review violations of incorporated federal rights to the extent that they are directly violated by state *statute*.

139. See Verf. Meckl.-Vorp. art. 12. The drafters deliberately included a phrase requiring the state to protect "the natural basis of present and future life"—instead of "present and future *human* life"—in order to avoid an anthropocentric emphasis in this environmental provision. See Hölscheidt & von Wiese, 1992 LKV at 396. See also preamble, arts. 6(3), 7(2), 15(4). Article 12(2) may create an enforceable right of access to places of natural beauty; Kutscha, 1993 ZRP at 342 n. 36; and another notable provision, which may be difficult to put into effect because of its sweeping nature, seeks to avoid "invasions of nature or of the countryside." Verf. Meckl.-Vorp. art. 12(4). See Wedemeyer, Das Verfahren der Verfassungsgebung in Mecklenburg-Vorpommern, in III Deutsche Wiedervereinigung at 41.

140. Verf. Meckl.-Vorp. art. 17.

141. Id. art. 17(3); for similar provisions, see Verf. Sachs.-Anh. art. 40(2); Verf. Thür. art. 16.

142. Interview with Professor Rolf Eggert, June 14, 1993. A number of these provisions were drawn from the new constitution of the neighboring (western) state of Schleswig-Holstein, which was adopted in June 1990.

143. Cf. Dehnhard, Verfassungsrevision in Berlin, 1991 LKV 177, 178; Wedemeyer in III Deutsche Wiedervereinigung at 42.

144. Verf. Meckl.-Vorp. arts. 20(1), 26, 34–35, 38(1), 40. For similar provisions in other new eastern constitutions, see, e.g., Verf. Br. art. 55(2); Verf. Sachs.-Anh. art. 48; Sacksofsky, 1993 NVwZ at 236.

145. Verf. Meckl.-Vorp. art. 39(1). But this obligation may not infringe the executive's ability to function, or invade its independent responsibilities. Id. art. 39(2).

146. Interview with Professor Rolf Eggert, June 14, 1993.

147. Indeed, in the major cities of Rostock and Schwerin, the constitution was narrowly defeated. FAZ, June 14, 1994, at 5 col. 1.

148. Id.

149. See Rommelfanger, Die Verfassung des Freistaats Thüringen des Jahres 1993, 1993 ThürVBl 145, 146–48.

150. CDU Fraktion im Thüringer Landtag, Verfassung des Freistaates Thüringen 68 (1993) (remarks of Jörg Schwäblein) (hereafter, CDU Verfassungs-Broschüre). Among the eastern Länder, Saxony is also known as a "free state"—as is Bavaria in the west.

151. Some earlier constitutional drafts in 1989–90 did not substantially influence the final product, although the draft of a group under the direction of Professor Gerhard Riege (Jena) drew some approving attention in the west. See, e.g., 39 JöR 468 (1990); Interview with Professor Peter Häberle, Thüringer Allgemeine, Nov. 20, 1993, at 3 col. 1.

152. Interview with Marie-Luise Franzen, Bündnis 90/Greens, Erfurt, Jan. 5, 1994. In this section I have drawn from this interview, as well as from an interview on the same day with Harald Stauch (CDU), chair of the Constitutional Committee of the Thuringian Landtag, and Ulrich Rommelfanger, CDU official in the offices of the Thuringian Landtag. I have also drawn from Dr. Rommelfanger's comprehensive two-part article on the Thuringian Constitution, Die Verfassung des Freistaats Thüringen des Jahres 1993, 1993 ThürVB1 145; 173.

153. See Thüringer Landtag, Plenarprotokoll, 1/95, Oct. 25, 1993, at 7267–90.

154. See, e.g., Thüringer Landtag, Plenarprotokoll, 1/95, Oct. 25, 1993, at 7278 (remarks of Andreas Kneipert, FDP).

155. Verf. Thür. art. 6(3).

156. Id. art. 22(2).

157. CDU Verfassungs-Broschüre at 65 (remarks of Jörg Schwäblein).

158. Verf. Thür. art. 1(1).

159. For comparable provisions, see Verf. Br. art. 8(1); RT-Entwurf art. 4(1).

160. Verf. Thür. arts. 15, 36.

161. Id. art. 19(3). For a similar provision, see Verf. Meckl.-Vorp. art. 14(2).

162. Verf. Thür. art. 24(1).

163. Cf. id. art. 17. The CDU was also able to impose stringent requirements for the use of plebiscites. See id. art. 82; Starck, Verfassungen, at 27. In the view of Bündnis 90/Greens, this provision did not provide an effective form of plebiscitary democracy, which could loosen the control of the established parties between parliamentary elections. See Thüringer Landtag, Plenarprotokoll, 1/94, Oct. 22, 1993, at 7177 (remarks of Olaf Möller, Bündnis 90/Greens). The SPD also viewed the provision as inadequate. Thüringer Landtag, Plenarprotokoll, 1/95, Oct. 25, 1993, at 7276 (remarks of Dr. Gerd Schuchardt, SPD). See also Verf. Thür. art. 68.

164. See, e.g., Verf. Thür. arts. 31–33.

165. Id. art. 32.

166. See, e.g., Verf. Br. art. 39(3).

167. The religious tone of the word "fellow-created beings" (*Mitgeschöpfe*), which is derived from the federal Animal Protection Statute, was also subjected to criticism in the federal Joint Constitutional Commission—in debate on the question of whether a similar guarantee should be added to the Basic Law. Ultimately, the commission did not recommend such a provision. See Ch. 10.

168. Interview with Reinhard Höppner, Jan. 11, 1993; Kilian, 1993 LKV at 76. See Pond at 94.

169. According to the preamble, ". . . the people of the Free State of Thuringia issue this constitution in free self-determination and also in [their] responsibility before God." A similar provision is contained in the preamble of the Constitution of Saxony-Anhalt.

170. A CDU leader also views this provision as part of a "conscious rejection of past totalitarianism and collectivism." CDU Verfassungs-Broschüre at 63 (remarks of Jörg Schwäblein).

In contrast, the Constitution of Mecklenburg-Vorpommern does not contain a reference to God, even though the draft preamble was proposed by church authorities in the state. Instead, the preamble declares that the constitution is issued "with consciousness of the limits of human actions." See Hölscheidt & von Wiese, 1992 LKV at 394.

A proposal was made in the Joint Constitutional Commission to remove the reference to God from the preamble of the Basic Law, but this proposal drew little support. See Ch. 10.

171. See Ch. 17.

172. See Finkelnburg, Verfassungsfragen des wiedervereinigten Berlin, 1991 LKV 6–7.

173. Die Verfassung von Berlin (Ost) vom 23. Juli 1990, reprinted in Ingo von Münch (ed.), Dokumente der Wiedervereinigung Deutschlands 291 (1991).

174. See Ehrhart Körting (with Klaus Finkelnburg et al.), Das Parlamentarische Tagebuch der Einheit Berlins 9–19 (1992).

175. Interview with Renate Künast, Chair of Constitutional Enquete-Commission of Berlin Parliament, Berlin, May 25, 1993. I have drawn from this interview at a number of points in this section. See also Finkelnburg, 1991 LKV at 8.

176. The East Berlin constitution drafters generally came from the circles of the central Round Table and sought to preserve a GDR identity reflecting aspects of the eastern reform movement. When the constitution was adopted in July 1990, the East Berlin CDU had not yet fallen under the influence of its quite conservative sister party in West Berlin, and there were few conservative pressure groups in East Berlin to oppose these views. In my understanding of the history of the East Berlin Constitution, I was assisted by a discussion with Hans-Jürgen Will, Humboldt University Berlin, one of the drafters of the constitution. Interview with Hans-Jürgen Will, Berlin, July 15, 1993.

177. Verf. Berlin (Ost) art. 2(1); see Finkelnburg, 1991 LKV at 8. Notwithstanding this sweeping pronouncement, however, "non-Germans" received voting rights in the local district councils, but not in the city council. Verf. Berlin (Ost) arts. 26(2), 54(2).

178. Verf. Berlin (Ost) arts. 15(3), 20. These rights were accompanied by restrictions on private property—such as the state's right to receive some compensation from landowners if government planning decisions increased land values, id. art. 15(5); see RT-Entwurf art. 32(2), as well as the requirement that the city council must approve any sale of real property that is large enough to be of significance for the city. Verf. Berlin (Ost) art. 81(2).

179. Verf. Berlin (Ost) arts. 6(2), 17(1)–(2).

180. Id. art. 7(4). See generally Ch. 12.

181. Verf. Berlin (Ost) art. 88(4).

182. See Verf. Berlin (1990) art. 88(2).

183. Id. arts. 21a, 21b.

184. Finkelnburg, 1991 LKV at 8. See Verf. Berlin (1990) art. 25(3).

185. Id. art. 72.

186. Pursuant to the Unification Treaty, both East and West Berlin governments had continued to function separately even after unification, until a single Berlin city government was elected at the time of the national elections on December 2, 1990. See Unification Treaty art. 16.

187. 2. Bericht (Schlußbericht) der Enquete-Kommission "Verfassungs- und Parlamentsreform," Abgeordnetenhaus von Berlin, Drucksache 12/4376.

188. See FAZ, Apr. 4, 1995, at 5 col. 1; Interview with Renate Künast, Berlin, Mar. 16, 1995.

189. See Abgeordnetenhaus von Berlin, Beschlußempfehlung, June 6, 1995, Drucksache 12/5637; Verfassung von Berlin, 1995 GVBl Berlin 779. The constitution was ratified by the voters in a plebiscite in October 1995. FAZ, Oct. 24, 1995, at 5 col. 5.

190. See Verf. Berlin (1995) art. 10(2) (no discrimination on the basis of "sexual identity"); art. 10(3) (affirmative action for women); art. 11 (protection for handicapped persons); art. 12(2) (no discrimination against "long-lasting living communities"); art. 12(7) (protections for child care and single parents); art. 20 (right to education; state support of cultural life); art. 31(2) ("Animals are to be respected as living creatures and to be protected against avoidable suffering"). See FAZ, June 10, 1995, at 6 col. 1; FAZ, June 16, 1995, at 14 col. 2.

191. Verf. Berlin (1995) arts. 61–63.

192. FAZ, June 16, 1995, at 14 col. 2. See discussion above.

193. Berlin Constitutional Court, Judgment of Jan. 12, 1993, 1993 NJW 515. See Uwe Wesel, Der Honecker-Prozeß: Ein Staat vor Gericht (1994).

194. Interestingly, the East Berlin Constitution, which went out of effect after the election of December 1990, contained an explicit guarantee of human dignity. Verf. Berlin (Ost) art. 6(1). In any case, article 6 of the 1995 Constitution of Berlin repairs this lacuna by including a protection of human dignity in language identical to that of the Basic Law.

195. See, e.g., Starck, Der Honecker-Beschluß des Berliner VerfGH, 1993 JZ 231; Wassermann, Zum Ausgang des Strafverfahrens gegen Honecker, 1993 RuP 14.

196. In a later case, in contrast, the Constitutional Court of Berlin rejected the petition of former Stasi director Erich Mielke, who sought to be released from prison on grounds of ill health. The eighty-six-year old Mielke had been convicted of a murder that had occurred in 1931 and was awaiting trial on other charges. See FAZ, Dec. 13, 1993, at 4 col. 4. See Ch. 14.

197. See, e.g., Hesse, Verfassungsrechtsprechung im geschichtlichen Wandel, 1995 JZ 265, 269.

198. See Sachs, 1993 ThürVBl at 121.

## Chapter 10
## The Unification Treaty and Amendment of the Basic Law

1. Wolfgang Schäuble, Der Vertrag: Wie ich über die deutsche Einheit verhandelte 37–38 (1991); see also Schäuble, Der Einigungsvertrag in seiner praktischen Bewährung, 1992 DA 233, 234–35.

2. Vertrag zwischen der Bundesrepublik Deutschland und der Deutschen Demokratischen Republik über die Herstellung der Einheit Deutschlands—Einigungsvertrag—of Aug. 31, 1990, BGBl II 889 (hereafter, Unification Treaty). See also Vereinbarung zur Durchführung und Auslegung des Einigungsvertrages, of Sept. 18, 1990, BGBl II 1239. For a detailed memoir of the drafting of the Unification Treaty by its chief author,

the former West German interior minister, see Schäuble, Der Vertrag. See also Schäuble, Der Einigungsvertrag—Vollendung der Einheit Deutschlands in Freiheit, 1990 ZG 289; Schäuble, 1992 DA 233.

3. The Basic Law may be amended, with the approval of two-thirds of each house of the German parliament. Art. 79(1)–(2) GG. No amendment, however, may impair basic principles of democratic political organization and human dignity. Art. 79(3) GG. See Ch. 11. The Unification Treaty received more than 90 percent of the votes in the Bundestag and 100 percent of the Bundesrat. It received almost 80 percent of the votes in the GDR Volkskammer. Schäuble, 1992 DA at 236.

4. Bastuck, Unity, Law, and Freedom: Legal Aspects of the Process and Results of German Unification, 25 International Lawyer 251, 257–58 (1991).

5. For a chronology of the negotiations, see Konrad H. Jarausch, The Rush to German Unity 170–74 (1994).

6. Schäuble, Der Vertrag, at 141. For a considerably less sympathetic assessment, see Wolfgang Thierse, Mit eigener Stimme sprechen 65 (1992): "Indeed it was not easy for Mr. Krause to fulfill the double task of representing the interests of GDR citizens and, at the same time, securing for himself a ministerial office in Bonn." Krause became transportation minister in the all-German government after unification, but he resigned in 1993 after questions were raised about possible financial improprieties.

7. A representative of the European Community also attended each session of the negotiations. Schäuble, 1992 DA at 234.

8. Jarausch at 176. See also Schneider, Die bundesstaatliche Ordnung im vereinigten Deutschland, 1991 NJW 2448, 2452: ". . . [T]he process of 'unification' before October 3, 1990 was intentionally organized as a techno-bureaucratic transaction for experts, in which neither the Länder nor their parliaments—nor indeed the population of both German states—had any share worth mentioning."

9. See Ch. 9.

10. Of course, the process of legal adjustment and "harmonization" had already begun under the provisions of the first State Treaty. See Ch. 7.

11. Unification Treaty arts. 1, 5. See generally Ch. 9.

12. Unification Treaty art. 13. See arts. 70–75 GG.

13. Unification Treaty art. 13(2).

14. A similar method had been used to allocate former property of the "Reich" among organs of the federal government and the states at the outset of the Federal Republic. See art. 134(2) GG.

15. Unification Treaty art. 21.

16. Of the GDR government property *not* used for administrative purposes, one-half was to go to the GDR Länder (divided proportionately according to population), and one-half was to go to the federal government for the fulfillment of public tasks in eastern Germany. An exception to this provision was People's Property used (or intended to be used) for public housing; such property went to the local communities, for gradual privatization. Id. art. 22(4).

To the extent that any public property had been used primarily by the former Ministry for State Security (Stasi), however, that property went directly to the state Trust Agency or Treuhand (see Ch. 11), unless after October 1, 1989 the property had been devoted to some social or public purpose. Unification Treaty, arts. 21(1), 22(1). Reformers charged that this provision was misused by former members of the Stasi to retain or derive economic advantage from former property of the Ministry for State Security. See Anne Worst, Das Ende eines Geheimdienstes 180–82 (1991).

17. Unification Treaty art. 23; see also id. art. 24.

Other important structural provisions set forth rules relating to the merger of the state-owned railroads in east and west, and the merger of the two post offices. Id. arts. 26, 27.

18. Id. art. 4(3). See Ch. 9.

19. See, e.g., Thierse, Mit eigener Stimme, at 66–67.

20. Unification Treaty art. 2(1).

21. See Schäuble, Der Vertrag, at 131–34, 170, 172–73.

22. In the Bundestag debate, the German finance minister suggested that the additional cost would be DM 30–40 billion or perhaps more. See, Helmut Herles (ed.), Die Hauptstadt Debatte 42 (1991) (hereafter, Hauptstadt Debatte).

23. Wolfgang Ullmann, Verfassung und Parlament 196 (1992); see also Sabine Bergmann-Pohl, Abschied ohne Tränen: Rückblick auf das Jahr der Einheit 199 (1991).

24. The Bundestag vote was 337 to 320. See Hauptstadt Debatte at 288.

25. Id. at XVIII. Later in 1991 the federal cabinet decided that eight ministries—including Defense, Health, and Agriculture—would retain their primary offices in Bonn. See Winters, Berlin-Umzug und deutsche Einheit, 1994 DA 113, 114. Even the ministries that are moving to Berlin will maintain secondary offices in Bonn.

26. Hauptstadt Debatte at XVIII. Some predict, however, that the Bundesrat will also ultimately decide to move to Berlin. See Scholz, Das Berlin/Bonn-Gesetz, 1995 NVwZ 35, 37; see also FAZ, Aug. 16, 1995, at 6 col. 3.

27. See, e.g., Winters, 1994 DA at 113: "In Bonn, those have triumphed who stand for West German immobility, unchecked concern for their own property, triviality, and the attempt not to accept and seize the challenges and favorable opportunities of reunification. Rather they continue to act as though nothing had happened other than the 'Anschluß' of rather desolated territories in the east, experienced as an unpleasant burden."

28. Interview with Lothar de Maizière, Berlin, Dec. 4, 1992.

29. Increasingly acrimonious parliamentary wranglings on the subject have been likened to a "medieval religious war," and the exasperation of eastern representatives over the delay was bluntly expressed by one member of Bündnis 90 who remarked, "No argument was too stupid, no trick too foul for the purpose of prolonging the *dolce vita* [in Bonn] on the Rhine." FAZ, Jan. 21, 1994, at 1 col. 2.

In 1994, the German parliament enacted a Berlin-Bonn Law, which officially determined the allocation of government ministries between the two cities. BGBl 1994 I 918; for commentary, see Scholz, 1995 NVwZ 35. While Berlin remains the "federal capital," the statute accords Bonn the honorific title of "federal city." Although the statute contains no deadline for the move to Berlin, an accompanying resolution contemplated that the Bundestag would begin its work in Berlin by summer 2000, at the latest. FAZ, Mar. 19, 1994, at 1 col. 2. In this respect among others, the real function of the new statute might be—as one commentator suggested—to "make forgotten" substantial parts of the original Berlin-Bonn Resolution of June 1991, with its four-year timetable. Winters, 1994 DA at 116.

30. See generally Schäuble, Der Vertrag, at 150–56. Among other things, this somewhat opaque view ignored the democratic revision of important aspects of GDR law undertaken in mid-1990 by the freely elected Volkskammer under de Maizière. Of course, the first State Treaty also effected broad reforms in GDR law. See Ch. 7; see also Drobnig, Anwendung und Auslegung von DDR-Recht heute, 1994 DtZ 86, 87–88.

31. For the background of this immense work of legal drafting, see Schäuble, Der Vertrag, at 151–53. See generally Bastuck, 25 International Lawyer at 257–58.

32. Unification Treaty art. 9(1).

33. Id. art. 9(2),(4).

34. On these provisions, see generally Schäuble, 1990 ZG at 298–99.

35. In addition to those areas, listed in attachment II to the Unification Treaty, in which GDR law continues on after unification, eastern law also continues to apply to many contracts and other transactions entered into in the east before unification. Even in these instances, however, eastern law will frequently be interpreted and applied in accordance with West German legal principles. See Drobnig, 1994 DtZ at 88.

36. In order to protect settled expectations, however, all actions taken under eastern family law *before* the date of unification will retain their validity. Frank, Germany: Family Law after Reunification, 30 Journal of Family Law 335, 337–38 (1991–92); see also art. 234(4) EGBGB. Moreover, in some instances where reliance on the continuing effect of eastern law is particularly important—as in the case of rules applicable to property rights arising during marriage—the previous GDR rules will also have some continuing validity. Thus persons married in the GDR may choose to continue to be governed by the GDR's community property system instead of the different rules of western law. Frank, 30 Journal of Family Law at 341–43; Brunner, Was bleibt übrig vom DDR-Recht nach der Wiedervereinigung?, 1991 JuS 353, 356; see also Grandke, Familienrecht in der ehemaligen DDR nach dem Einigungsvertrag, 1990 DtZ 321, 323–24; Wolf, Das Familienrecht der DDR und der Einigungsvertrag, 1995 DtZ 386, 390.

37. See generally Grandke, 1990 DtZ at 323–24; see also Brunner, 1991 JuS at 356; Westen, Der Stand des Zivilrechts in der DDR und seine Reformbedürftigkeit, 1990 DtZ 1, 5–6.

38. Gesetz zur Änderung des Familiengesetzbuchs der DDR (Erstes Familienrechtsänderungsgesetz), of July 20, 1990, GBl DDR I 1038. See Eberhardt, Änderung des Familiengesetzbuchs der DDR, 1990 NJ 401.

39. See Irwin, Bringing Justice to the Wild East, 79 American Bar Association Journal 58 (April 1993). See also FAZ, Sept. 8, 1993, at 3 col. 1 (view of justice minister of Saxony that it would have been preferable to adopt the simpler provisions of GDR family law in the east and west).

40. Gesetz zur Änderung und Ergänzung des Arbeitsgesetzbuches, of 22 June 1990, GBl DDR I 371; see State Treaty art. 17; id. attachment II(IV); Joint Protocol (B)(IV); Weiss, The Transition of Labor Law and Industrial Relations: The Case of German Unification—A Preliminary Perspective, 13 Comparative Labor Law Journal 1, 6 (1991); Brunner, 1991 JuS at 357.

41. Weiss, 13 Comparative Labor Law Journal at 6.

42. See id. at 6–7.

43. See Pfeiffer & Birkenfeld-Pfeiffer, Arbeitsrecht nach dem Einigungsvertrag, 1990 DtZ 325, 326.

44. Weiss, 13 Comparative Labor Law Journal at 7–12; see also Maydell, Labor and Social Security Aspects of German Unification, at 5–7 (unpublished manuscript, on file with author); cf. Pfeiffer & Birkenfeld-Pfeiffer, 1990 DtZ at 330.

45. See Weiss, 13 Comparative Labor Law Journal at 7–12.

46. Maydell at 6.

47. Unification Treaty art. 18(1); see also id. art. 18(2); id. attachment I, ch. III(A), para. III (14)(d).

48. Id. art. 17. The Unification Treaty also provided a right of convicted criminal defendants in the GDR to seek review of judicial decisions. Id. art. 18(2). The issues

of "rehabilitation" and compensation for victims of oppression under the GDR have posed some of the most difficult legislative problems following unification. See Ch. 15.

49. Unification Treaty art. 19.

50. Id. art. 10(1).

51. Id. art. 10(2). The complex relationship between German unification and the European Union is discussed in Ch. 23.

52. The treaties listed in attachment I, which were not to be extended to the territory of the former GDR, were principally related to the stationing of NATO troops in Germany. See Unification Treaty, attachment I, ch. I, para. I. Under the Two Plus Four Treaty, foreign NATO troops are not to be stationed in eastern Germany. See Ch. 20.

53. See Horst Teltschik, 329 Tage: Innenansichten der Einigung 180, 198, 201–2 (1991).

54. Hailbronner, Das vereinte Deutschland in der Europäischen Gemeinschaft, 1991 DtZ 321, 327.

55. Unification Treaty art. 12(1).

56. For the background of these provisions in the "state succession" doctrines of international law, see, e.g., Doehring, Die Anwendung der Regeln der völkerrechtlichen Sukzession nach der Wiedervereinigung der beiden deutschen Staaten, in Rudolf Wildenmann (ed.), Nation und Demokratie 11–19 (1991). See also Note, Taking Reichs Seriously: German Unification and the Law of State Succession, 104 Harvard Law Review 588 (1990).

As a result of the Unification Treaty provision, many of the international agreements of the former GDR have been canceled after negotiation. Bernhardt, Unification of Germany, in 2 Rudolf Bernhardt (ed.), Encyclopedia of Public International Law 592 (1995).

57. Hailbronner, 1991 DtZ at 327–28. But article 29 of the Unification Treaty specifically states that existing economic agreements between the GDR and east bloc countries are worthy of international confidence—one of the factors listed in article 12 of the Unification Treaty. Accordingly, these agreements were presumably subject to extension in accordance with market principles. Id.

58. See generally Stern, Der verfassungsändernde Charakter des Einigungsvertrages, 1990 DtZ 289.

59. See Ch. 20. The problem of the Oder-Neiße line is discussed in Ch. 18.

60. In its amended form, the preamble states in full:

> With consciousness of their responsibility before God and human beings, and animated by the will to serve world peace as an equal member of a united Europe, the German people have adopted this Basic Law by virtue of their constitution-giving power.
>
> The Germans in the states of Baden-Württemberg, Bavaria, Berlin, *Brandenburg*, Bremen, Hamburg, Hessen, *Mecklenburg-Vorpommern*, Lower Saxony, North Rhine-Westphalia, Rhineland-Palatinate, Saarland, *Saxony*, *Saxony-Anhalt*, Schleswig-Holstein and *Thuringia* have achieved the unity and freedom of Germany in free self-determination. Thus this Basic Law is effective for the entire German people.

Unification Treaty art. 4(1) (emphasis added, indicating new German states).

The retention of the word "Germans" in this and other provisions of the Basic Law reflects the "cultural and ethnic" nature of the basic idea of German citizenship, in contrast with the prevailing view of the United States (and some other nations) that citizenship, and participation in the political community, are related basically to long-term presence within the territorial boundaries of the country rather than ethnic qualifications. See generally Hailbronner, Citizenship and Nationhood in Germany, in William Rogers Brubaker (ed.), Immigration and the Politics of Citizenship in Europe and North America 67 (1989); Quint, Constitution-Making by Treaty in German Unification: A Comment on Arato, Elster, Preuss, and Richards, 44 Cardozo Law Review 691 (1993).

61. See generally Rita Süssmuth & Konrad Weiss, Neuland: Dialog in Deutschland 12–14 (1991); Ullmann, Verfassung und Parlament, at 139. Such a revision could have drawn on a resolution of the GDR Volkskammer acknowledging responsibility for the National Socialist past. See Ch. 5. The Round Table draft also contained such a declaration. See RT-Entwurf art. 41(1); cf. also Verf. Sachs. preamble, art. 116; Verf. Thür. preamble.

62. See Thierse, Mit eigener Stimme, at 67.

In additional criticism, GDR reformer Wolfgang Ullmann—a theologian—deplored the retention of a reference to God in the preamble of the Basic Law. Ullmann noted that many citizens of Germany, including the overwhelming majority of citizens in the former GDR, have no religious affiliation; "but a constitutional text must speak a language that is common to all citizens. As a result, a religious declaration in a constitution should be as little permissible as those ideologically freighted statements which made such an unpleasant impression in the GDR Constitution of 1968." Ullmann, Das Recht und die Grundrechte in der neuen Demokratie, in Bernd Guggenberger & Tine Stein (eds.), Die Verfassungsdiskussion im Jahr der deutschen Einheit 409 (1991). A similar issue marked constitutional debates in Saxony-Anhalt and Thuringia. See Ch. 9.

63. Unification Treaty art. 4(2).

64. See Ch. 6.

65. Unification Treaty art. 4(6). The language added by the amendment is in italics.

66. Whether a new constitution could be adopted under article 146 by a simple majority in a plebiscite, or whether some form of two-thirds approval would be required, continues to be the subject of debate. See Ch. 6.

Additional constitutional amendments were required to adjust matters of finance. Article 7 of the Unification Treaty set forth rules for revenue sharing by the former GDR Länder as well as provisions granting special support for those Länder. Basically, this provision mitigated or deferred the western states' obligation to share certain revenues with the eastern Länder, on an interim basis. Another section amended article 135a of the Basic Law in a manner that made clear that the Federal Republic would not be required to pay obligations incurred by the government of the GDR. Unification Treaty art. 4 (4); see Ch. 11.

Other constitutional amendments effected by the Unification Treaty are closely related to the reconstitution of the Länder and the constitutional problems of expropriated property and abortion. Consequently, these amendments are discussed in the context of those specific issues. See Ch. 9 (Länder); Ch. 11 (expropriated property); Ch. 12 (abortion).

67. 82 BVerfGE 316 (1990).

68. Id. at 321. See generally Schäuble, 1992 DA at 235–36.

69. See generally Ch. 9.

70. Cf. Jarausch at 169.

71. See Ch. 9.

72. See generally Schäuble, Der Vertrag, at 173–75.

73. See Ch. 6.

74. See Bericht der Gemeinsamen Verfassungskommission, Nov. 5, 1993, Bundestag Drucksache 12/6000, at 5–7 (hereafter, Joint Commission Report).

75. Vogel, Die Reform des Grundgesetzes nach der deutschen Einheit, 1994 DVB1 497, 498.

76. Joint Commission Report at 11.

77. See Ch. 23. The commission played a marginal role in a constitutional amendment narrowing the right of asylum in Germany. See Joint Commission Report at 63–64.

78. See Grimm, Verfassungsreform in falscher Hand? Zum Stand der Diskussion um das Grundgesetz, 1992 Merkur 1059.

79. Id. at 1060. On the distinction between day-to-day politics and constitutional politics, see Ackerman, Constitutional Politics/Constitutional Law, 99 Yale Law Journal 453 (1989).

80. See Isensee, Mit blauem Auge davongekommen—das Grundgesetz, 1993 NJW 2583, 2584.

81. See Joint Commission Report at 8; Vogel, 1994 DVBl at 499.

82. According to Ullmann, the commission's inactivity left unremedied "a serious democratic deficit in the German unification process." See Press Release of Bündnis 90/Greens, No. 100/1993, May 7, 1993.

83. See generally Joint Commission Report at 75–82.

84. Id. at 80–82; Badura, Die Staatsaufgaben nach dem Grundgesetz und die Reformfrage, 1992 ThürVBl 73.

85. See, e.g., Lübbe Wolff, Staatsziele und soziale Grundrechte, in Gemeinsame Verfassungskommission, Stenographischer Bericht, 2. Öffentliche Anhörung, June 16, 1992, at 100–101.

86. Joint Commission Report at 77.

87. The commission proposed that the following provision be added to the Basic Law as article 20a: "In its responsibility for future generations, the state protects the natural basis of life, [acting] within the framework of the constitutional order, through legislation and, in accordance with statutory law and justice, through the executive and judiciary." For commentary, see Vogel, 1994 DVBl at 498–500; Schneider, Das Grundgesetz—auf Grund gesetzt?, 1994 NJW 558.

88. See Meyer-Teschendorf, Verfassungsmäßiger Schutz der natürlichen Lebensgrundlagen, 1994 ZRP 73, 75. A state goal of environmental protection had also been urged by a federal advisory commission in 1983 and by a Bundesrat commission in 1992. Id. at 74; see Bericht der Kommission Verfassungsreform des Bundesrates 58–60 (1992).

89. See Joint Commission Report at 65–68.

After detailed discussion, the Joint Commission rejected a constitutional amendment that would have provided a separate "state goal" for the protection of animals. The commission received 170,000 citizens' communications on this subject—a number second only to those received on the issue of plebiscitary elements in the constitution. Id. at 68–71. A state goal of animal protection is contained in the constitutions of Brandenburg and Thuringia. Verf. Br. art. 39(3); Verf. Thür. art. 32. See Ch. 9.

90. See Verf. Sachs. arts. 5–6; Verf. Sachs.-Anh. art. 37; Verf. Meckl.-Vorp. art. 18. See also Verf. Br. art. 25. The constitution of the western state of Schleswig-Holstein, a state that includes a significant population of Danish-speaking people, also contains such a provision. See Verf. Schles.-Holst. art. 5.

The Joint Commission proposed a provision declaring that: "The state respects the identity of ethnic, cultural, and linguistic minorities." An additional sentence obliging the state actively to support ethnic groups and "national minorities of German nationality" did not achieve the requisite two-thirds majority. See Joint Commission Report at 71–75.

91. Joint Commission Report at 72–73; Rohn & Sannwald, Die Ergebnisse der Gemeinsamen Verfassungskommission, 1994 ZRP 65, 72 & n. 108. In addition, a number of treaties between the Federal Republic and eastern European states, executed after the end of the Cold War, contained reciprocal guarantees for rights of minorities in each nation. See Ch. 21.

92. See Rohn & Sannwald, 1994 ZRP at 72; Vogel, 1994 DVBl at 501.

93. See Vogel, 1994 DVBl at 501.

94. This and most of the following arguments of the opponents are set forth in the Joint Commission Report at 85–86.

95. Id. at 85. See also Jahn, Empfehlungen der Gemeinsamen Verfassungskommission zur Änderung und Ergänzung des Grundgesetzes, 1994 DVBl 177, 185, invoking "the danger of the de-rationalizing and emotionalizing of the political process of decision."

96. See arts. 20, 79(3) GG.

97. Joint Commission Report at 84. The commission received more than 266,000 communications on plebiscites—by far the most that it received on any subject. The Commission Report acknowledged that the issue had received new impetus through the inclusion of such provisions in the constitutions of the new Länder. Id. at 83.

98. See Vogel, 1994 DVBl at 505.

99. Joint Commission Report at 86. In another decision maintaining the status quo in parliamentary democracy, the commission rejected changes that were designed to bolster the role of the parliament against the executive, such as those found in some of the new state constitutions. See, e.g., Schneider, 1994 NJW at 560–61. See generally Ch. 9.

100. See Verf. Br. art. 12(3); Verf. Sachs.-Anh. art. 34.

101. 85 BVerfGE 191, 207 (1992). See Vogel, 1994 DVBl at 500; Jahn, 1994 DVBl at 183.

102. 85 BVerfGE at 207; see also 74 BVerfGE 163, 178–82 (1987).

103. See, e.g., Jahn, 1994 DVBl at 183.

104. This language may be particularly useful in reversing the existing view of some lower courts that any favoring of women for the purpose of undoing past disadvantages is itself unconstitutional. Cf. Zapfe, Gleichberechtigung durch die Verfassung?, APuZ, Dec. 24, 1993, at 11–15. On the other hand conservative voices have argued that some forms of affirmative action for women would violate "fundamental structures of our constitution" and might even exceed the limits on permissible constitutional amendment contained in article 79(3) GG. Brohm, Soziale Grundrechte und Staatszielbestimmungen in der Verfassung, 1994 JZ 213, 220. It also appears that affirmative action provisions may be subject to some limitations under the law of the European Community. See European Court of Justice, Judgment of Oct. 17, 1995 (Kalanke v. Freie Hansestadt Bremen), Case C-450/93; FAZ, Oct. 18, 1995, at 1 col. 2.

105. See Joint Commission Report at 50–51.

106. See Rohn & Sannwald, 1994 ZRP at 71.

107. Faerber-Husemann, Keine Quote—aber immerhin Präzisierung, Das Parlament, Jan. 14, 1994, at 11 col. 4.

108. Joint Commission Report at 53. Some opponents also argued that protection for handicapped persons was a "societal rather than a constitutional problem." Jahn, 1994 DVBl at 183. But see Verf. Br. art. 12(4); Verf. Sachs. art. 7(2); Verf. Sachs.-

Anh. art. 38; see also Verf. Berlin (1995) art. 11. Although this provision received a majority in the commission, it did not receive the required two-thirds vote. But the provision was ultimately approved in the Bundestag after the special intervention of Chancellor Kohl. See below.

109. Joint Commission Report at 54. Such a provision is contained in the Constitution of Brandenburg as well as the Round Table draft. See Verf. Br. art. 12(2); RT-Entwurf art. 1(2); see also Verf. Berlin (1995) art. 10(2). This proposal was also favored by a majority of the commission but did not receive the requisite two-thirds vote.

110. Joint Commission Report at 54. Similarly, the commission declined to extend constitutional protection to "long-lasting living communities" outside of marriage. Id. at 56–58.

111. Id. at 59–60; Jahn, 1994 DVBl at 183. Finally, the commission also rejected a proposal from an eastern representative that the constitution contain a general state goal favoring "humanity and concern for the public good." Joint Commission Report at 82–83.

112. A right of data protection—the so-called right of "informational self-determination"—was acknowledged by the Constitutional Court in the famous 1983 Census case. See 65 BVerfGE 1 (1983).

113. See Joint Commission Report at 60–63. The commission also rejected proposals for a special ombudsman for data protection. Id.

114. Id. at 30–48. See Rohn & Sannwald, 1994 ZRP at 68–70.

115. See Vogel, 1994 DVBl at 501–3; Bericht der Kommission Verfassungsreform des Bundesrates at 7–34. Moreover, article 5 of the Unification Treaty had specifically charged the parliament with considering this proposal.

116. Joint Commission Report at 30–31, 33–34. See Rohn & Sannwald, 1994 ZRP at 68–69.

117. Joint Commission Report at 31, 35. See Rohn & Sannwald, 1994 ZRP at 69.

118. See Ch. 23. See also Isensee, 1993 NJW at 2586. Other significant proposals of the commission simplified the procedure for redrawing state borders in general, and more specifically with respect to Berlin and Brandenburg. See Ch. 9.

119. See FAZ, Apr. 22, 1994, at 3 col. 3; FAZ, May 2, 1994, at 9 col. 1.

120. FAZ, July 1, 1994, at 1 col. 2; see also FAZ, July 5, 1994, at 4 col. 1; id. at 12 col. 2.

121. Some less important provisions on state borders and state competence were, however, approved.

122. FAZ, Aug. 27, 1994, at 1 col. 2; see also FAZ, July 9, 1994, at 4 col. 6.

123. FAZ, Sept. 7, 1994, at 2 col. 4; FAZ, Sept. 24, 1994, at 1 col. 2. See BGBl 1994 I 3146; Sannwald, Die Reform des Grundgesetzes, 1994 NJW 3313.

124. Jahn, 1994 DVBl at 186.

125. Vogel, 1994 DVBl at 498.

126. See, e.g., FAZ, Sept. 7, 1994, at 2 col. 4.

## Chapter 11
## The Fate of "Socialist Property": Restitution, Compensation, and the Work of the Treuhand

1. Verf. DDR (1974) arts. 10, 12, 13. This system was basically drawn from the model of the Soviet Union. See Herwig Roggemann, Die DDR-Verfassungen: Einführung in das Verfassungsrecht der DDR 257 (1989). For an analysis of the forms of socialist property, see Ch. 4.

2. See, e.g., Soviet Military Administration (SMAD) Befehl Nr. 124, of Oct. 30, 1945; SMAD Befehl Nr. 126, of Oct. 31, 1945; reprinted in Gesamtdeutsches Institut—Bundesanstalt für Gesamtdeutsche Aufgaben (ed.), Bestimmungen der DDR zu Eigentumsfragen und Enteignungen 50–53 (1971). Some of this property was used to furnish Soviet war reparations agreed to at Yalta and Potsdam. See Elling, Privatization in Germany: A Model for Legal and Functional Analysis, 25 Vanderbilt Journal of Transnational Law 581, 590–92 (1992).

3. The expropriations were mandated by the five new eastern states and subsequently approved by an order of the Soviet Military Administration. See SMAD Befehl Nr. 110, of Oct. 22, 1945; Weber & Wilhelm, Die Enteignungen unter sowjetischer Besatzungsherrschaft und ihre Behandlung im Einigungsvertrag, 1991 BB (Beilage 3) 12, 13; Wolfgang Leonhard, Die Revolution entläßt ihre Kinder 506–8 (1990); and see generally id. at 503–13.

4. See Joachim von Kruse (ed.), Weißbuch über die "Demokratische Bodenreform" in der Sowjetischen Besatzungszone Deutschlands 135 (1988) (hereafter, Weißbuch). More than 4,000 smaller holdings (totaling almost 124,000 hectares) were also expropriated. Id.

5. Lastenausgleichsgesetz, of Aug. 14, 1952, BGBl I 446.

6. Martin McCauley, The German Democratic Republic since 1945, at 22–24 (1983).

7. Id. Recipients were required to pay the value of one year's harvest, but this amount could be spread over a period of years. Otto Kimminich, Die Eigentumsgarantie im Prozeß der Wiedervereinigung 59 (1990). The complex task of dividing the property was undertaken by local commissions. See Verordnung über die Bodenreform in der Provinz Sachsen, of Sept. 3, 1945, reprinted in Weißbuch at 110–14.

8. See Weißbuch at 136.

9. Id.

10. Leonhard, Die Revolution, at 507. Indeed, a similar program of land reform took place in Hungary in 1945, two years before the Communists came to power. See Klingsberg, Judicial Review and Hungary's Transition from Communism to Democracy: The Constitutional Court, the Continuity of Law, and the Redefinition of Property Rights, 1992 Brigham Young University Law Review 41, 105 n. 158, citing Gati, From Liberation to Revolution, in P. Sugar et al. (eds.), A History of Hungary 370 (1990).

The Soviet Bodenreform also had counterparts in other German occupation measures, such as school reform, designed to further socialization in the eastern zone.

11. See, e.g., Verordnung über die Bodenreform in der Provinz Sachsen, of Sept. 3, 1945, art. 1, reprinted in Weißbuch at 110.

12. Cf. Friedrich, Military Government and Democratization: A Central Issue of American Foreign Policy, in Carl J. Friedrich et al., American Experiences in Military Government in World War II, at 14 (1948); 46 BVerfGE 268, 269–70, 288–89 (1977).

On the western land reform, see generally Lucius D. Clay, Decision in Germany 18, 268–69 (1950); Kimminich at 51; Weber, Die Entschädigung in der westdeutschen Bodenreform, 1953 DÖV 353. See also Verf. Hessen (1946) arts. 42, 39(4).

13. For an exception, see Wolfgang Ullmann, Verfassung und Parlament 22–23 (1992): "As a member of the [Modrow] government, I had to consider how we would handle the matters that had resulted from [World War II]. I was of the opinion that one consideration must be that certain things would not be undone. For me, one of these things had always been the Bodenreform and the expropriation of groups in society that had contributed very significantly to the seizure of power by Hitler and the preparation

of World War II." But for a different historical view, see Richard Schröder, Deutschland schwierig Vaterland 67 (1993).

14. Indeed, in some cases, farmers were imprisoned for refusing to join an LPG. See, e.g., FR, Feb. 25, 1993, at 12 col. 1.

15. See McCauley at 98. Although intended to consolidate socialism in the GDR, these measures of collectivization actually led to a decline in agricultural production as well as increased emigration. A. James McAdams, East Germany and Detente: Building Authority after the Wall 23 (1985). Thus the effect of collectivization in 1960 may have contributed to the crisis that led to the building of the Berlin Wall in 1961.

16. Well-known East German authors wrote generally approving accounts of these developments. See, e.g., Helmut Sakowski, Wege übers Land: Ein Lesebuch (1984); Erwin Strittmatter, Ole Bienkopp (1963). In contrast, dramatist Heiner Müller's ironic and distanced portrayal of both events led to prohibition of his work and a notable artistic scandal. See Heiner Müller, Die Umsiedlerin oder das Leben auf dem Lande (1975); Heiner Müller, Krieg ohne Schlacht: Leben in zwei Diktaturen 160–87 (1992). Writing from western exile, the great novelist Uwe Johnson sketched a bitter portrait of collectivization, including the suicide of a farmer forced into an LPG. See Uwe Johnson, Das dritte Buch über Achim (1961). For later recollections of the Bodenreform by another well-known GDR author, see Erich Loest, Durch die Erde ein Riß: Ein Lebenslauf 105–9 (1990).

17. Each state constitution in the Soviet zone expressly guaranteed property rights derived from the land reform. See, e.g., Verf. Thür. (1946) art. 57(2); Verf. Sachs. (1947) art. 78(1). The 1949 Constitution of the GDR also confirmed the results of the Bodenreform and the expropriation of businesses of war criminals and active National Socialists. See Verf. DDR (1949) arts. 24(2)–(6), 144(2). Adopted after the completion of agricultural collectivization, the 1968/74 Constitution of the GDR recognized that transformation in central passages. See Verf. DDR (1974) arts. 10, 13 (collective property); art. 46 (role of the LPGs).

As an interesting modern pendant to this constitutional development, the 1990 Round Table draft of a new democratic constitution for the GDR also included a provision preserving the results of the Bodenreform. See RT-Entwurf art. 131(1). Indeed the draft prohibited private ownership of land in excess of 100 hectares. Id. art. 32(1). See Ch. 4.

18. The 1949 constitution protected property subject to "the social duties in favor of the community," allowed expropriations "only for the good of the community on the basis of a statute," and required compensation, "as long as the law does not determine otherwise." Verf. DDR (1949) arts. 22–23; see also id. art. 27 (socialization of property); cf. WRV art. 153.

The 1968/74 constitution guaranteed "personal property," but the use of property "may not contradict the interests of the community." Verf. DDR (1974) art. 11. The term "personal property" basically referred to "property in consumer goods purchased from income from work"—a considerably narrower concept than "personal property" in the Anglo-American sense. See Roggemann, DDR-Verfassungen, at 258. Article 16 of the constitution stated that expropriations could only be undertaken "in return for appropriate compensation."

19. See Wolfgang Schäuble, Der Vertrag: Wie ich über die deutsche Einheit verhandelte 254–55 (1991).

20. Schröder, Deutschland schwierig Vaterland, at 62–70.

21. Unification Treaty art. 41(1); id. attachment III. The Federal Republic also

agreed not to make any future legal change that would contradict the Joint Declaration. Id. art. 41(3).

22. See Gesetz zur Regelung offener Vermögensfragen, printed in Unification Treaty, attachment II, ch. III(B), para. I(5) (hereafter, Property Statute); Gesetz über besondere Investitionen in der Deutschen Demokratischen Republik, printed in Unification Treaty, attachment II, ch. III(B), para. I(4) (hereafter, Investment Statute).

23. See Gesetz zur Beseitigung von Hemmnissen bei der Privatisierung von Unternehmen und zur Förderung von Investitionen, of Mar. 22, 1991, BGBl I 766; Zweites Vermögensrechtsänderungsgesetz, of July 14, 1992, BGBl I 1257. At the time of the 1992 amendments, the Investment Statute was repealed and replaced by the Investment Preference Statute (Investitionsvorranggesetz). See BGBl 1992 I 1257 art. 6. Thereafter, the revised Property Statute was reprinted in a compilation of Aug. 3, 1992. See BGBl 1992 I 1446. Citations of the Property Statute will refer to this compilation unless otherwise noted.

24. Unification Treaty, attachment III § 1. The provisions preserving the 1945–49 expropriations were confirmed in a letter from the foreign ministers of the GDR and the Federal Republic to the four Allied powers, as part of the matters concluded in the Two Plus Four discussions. See Ch. 20. Accordingly, these provisions may now also have the force of a treaty in international law.

25. Der Spiegel, 25/1990, at 29.

26. According to the new GDR legislation, the collectives were to be transformed into closed corporations or cooperatives recognized under West German law; as part of this process, farmers could withdraw their individual lands if they wished. FAZ, Nov. 11, 1991, at 17 col. 1; see Landwirtschaftsanpassungsgesetz, of June 29, 1990, GBl DDR I 642.

27. See FAZ, Mar. 8, 1990, at 2 col. 1; cf. Ullmann, Verfassung und Parlament, at 23. At the same time Modrow sent a similar letter to Chancellor Kohl. See also Fieberg & Reichenbach, Zum Problem der offenen Vermögensfragen, 1991 NJW 321, 322 (quoting Soviet responses to Modrow letter).

28. In his inaugural address, for example, de Maizière flatly declared in the name of the government that the "results of the Land Reform in the territory of the GDR are not open to negotiation [*stehen nicht zur Disposition*]." Regierungserklärung des Ministerpräsidenten der DDR, Lothar de Maizière, Apr. 19, 1990, reprinted in Ingo von Münch (ed.), Dokumente der Wiedervereinigung Deutschlands 203 (1991) (hereafter, Dokumente—Wiedervereinigung).

29. The view that the Soviet Union insisted on the permanence of the 1945–49 expropriations is now being contested in a revisionist argument on the Bodenreform problem, discussed below.

30. Indeed even the term "settlement payments" (*Ausgleichsleistungen*) seemed to contemplate something less than full compensation. See Papier, Verfassungsrechtliche Probleme der Eigentumsregelung im Einigungsvertrag, 1991 NJW 193, 197.

For a different decision on restitution of landed property after the French Revolution, see Vitzthum, Das Bodenreform-Urteil des Bundesverfassungsgerichts: Analyse und Kritik, in II(1) Klaus Stern (ed.), Deutsche Wiedervereinigung: Die Rechtseinheit 3–4 (1992) (hereafter, Deutsche Wiedervereinigung).

31. Unification Treaty, attachment III § 3. For useful commentary on these problems, see Wolfram Försterling, Recht der offenen Vermögensfragen (1993); see also Gruson & Thoma, Investments in the Territory of the Former German Democratic Republic, 14 Fordham International Law Journal 540 (1990–91).

32. Property Statute § 1(6); see Elling, 25 Vanderbilt Journal of Transnational Law at 588–90. Claimants of property confiscated by the Nazis take precedence over later holders of the same property who may have been subject to expropriation under the GDR. Property Statute § 3(2).

33. In contrast, after World War II the American military government had sought to return property seized by the Nazi government to its original owners. See Clay at 311.

Other post-Communist governments in eastern Europe have taken different views on which expropriations of earlier periods will be undone. In the Czech Republic, for example, original (Czechoslovakian) legislation only prescribed restitution for property expropriated after the beginning of the Communist regime in 1948. More recently, a statute has also provided return of property expropriated from Jews during the Nazi occupation (1938–45) but does not accord similar treatment for property expropriated from the "Sudeten Germans" expelled from Czechoslovakia after World War II. See Wall Street Journal, July 15, 1994, at 1 col. 1; 3 East European Constitutional Review, Spring 1994, at 8. See also Ch. 21.

34. Unification Treaty, attachment III § 4.

35. See Property Statute § 1(2); Bertrams, Das Gesetz zur Regelung offener Vermögensfragen, 1994 DVB1 374, 378–79; cf. Property Statute § 9(1).

36. Interview with Lothar de Maizière, Berlin, Dec. 4, 1992.

37. FAZ, Jan. 30, 1992, at 3 col. 3. See also FAZ, Jan. 23, 1992, at 4 col. 1.

38. See Unification Treaty art. 41(2).

39. Investment Preference Statute §§ 1–3.

40. Id. §§ 16–17.

41. The former owner could also propose an investment plan, and that plan could be given precedence if it was "equal or nearly equal" to the plans of the other investors. Id. § 7(1).

42. See FAZ, Apr. 2, 1991, at 8 col. 4; FAZ, Mar. 20, 1991, at 1 col. 5.

Even after the 1991 amendments, the pace of investment remained disappointing, and in 1992 the Bundestag adopted yet another statute directed toward accelerating investment in expropriated property. Zweites Vermögensrechtsänderungsgesetz, of July 14, 1992, BGBl I 1257. See generally, Schmidt-Räntsch, Das Zweite Vermögensrechtsänderungsgesetz, 1992 DtZ 314; Elling, 25 Vanderbilt Journal of Transnational Law at 615–18. Among other things, this statute further simplified applicable procedures and severely limited the period of time in which a former property owner could contest the investor's proposal. See Schmidt-Räntsch, 1992 DtZ at 316.

43. Unification Treaty, attachment III § 3(a); Property Statute § 4(1). The same principle is applicable when the property has been devoted to public use, or when a substantial expenditure has been made to adapt property for a particular function and it is in the public interest that this function continue. See generally Property Statute § 5.

44. See Schröder, Deutschland schwierig Vaterland, at 64–66, 69.

45. Unification Treaty, attachment III § 3(b); Property Statute § 4(2). For commentary, see Göhring, Zum Begriff der Redlichkeit im Vermögensgesetz, 1991 DtZ 401; Bertrams, 1994 DVBl at 381–82.

46. Unification Treaty, attachment III § 3(b); Property Statute § 9(2). But since there is apparently little if any substitute property available, the original owners will ordinarily receive compensation. See Schröder, Deutschland schwierig Vaterland, at 70.

47. See Fieberg & Reichenbach, 1991 NJW at 327.

48. Property Statute § 4(3). As defined in this section, the concept of "dishonesty" is different from the concept of bad faith (absence of "guter Glaube") in the German

Civil Code—a concept which, like the analogous concept in Anglo-American law, primarily involves knowledge that the property belongs to a third person. See Othmar Jauernig (ed.), Bürgerliches Gesetzbuch 1027–31 (1984) (section 932 of Civil Code and related commentary); Fieberg & Reichenbach, 1991 NJW at 327–28. But it is not entirely clear that the definition in the Property Statute is intended to be an exhaustive definition of "dishonesty." See, e.g., Horst, Zum Begriff der Redlichkeit im Vermögensgesetz—Erwiderung auf Göhring, 1992 DtZ 43.

49. Compare Försterling at 219, with Bertrams, 1994 DVBl at 382.

50. See Bertrams, 1994 DVBl at 382. For influential decisions on these matters, see BGH, Judgment of Apr. 3, 1992, 1992 NJW 1757 (provisions of the Property Law on acquisition "in an honest manner" supersede rules in the GDR Civil Code and the BGB); BVerwG, Judgment of Jan. 20, 1994, 1994 DtZ 223 (upholding the constitutionality of excluding restitution in cases of acquisition of property "in an honest manner").

51. Property Statute § 4(2).

52. See 94 BVerwGE 279, 285–86 (1993); Bertrams, 1994 DVBl at 381–82.

53. Der Spiegel, 41/1990, at 54–55. Sales of state-owned villas, "dachas," and other houses were made possible by a statute enacted in March 1990 at the very end of the Modrow period. Gesetz über den Verkauf volkseigener Gebäude, of Mar. 7, 1990, GBl DDR I 157; see Försterling at 219.

54. Försterling at 220. In the 1992 statutory amendments, some post-October 18 expropriations were returned to the status of "honest acquisition," but the cutoff date was in principle retained. Id. at 223–24; see Property Statute § 4(2)(a)–(c). This resolution has been upheld against constitutional attack by the Supreme Administrative Court. 94 BVerwGE 279 (1993).

For another provision of the property rules directed against oppressive acts of SED officials, see Unification Treaty, attachment III § 8 (no claim for recovery of property that was obtained by a person engaged in "dishonest machinations," such as "misuse of power, extortion or fraud"). See also Property Statute § 1(3); Bertrams, 1994 DVBl at 379. Cf. Unification Treaty, attachment III § 9 (GDR to provide relief for property forfeitures undertaken in criminal cases in a manner contrary to the rule of law).

55. FAZ, Aug. 1, 1994, at 4 col. 2.

56. See, e.g., Gerlinde Sinn & Hans-Werner Sinn, Jumpstart: The Economic Unification of Germany 88 (1992).

57. Unification Treaty, attachment III § 2; Property Statute §§ 1(4), 11–15. In this case, also, the claimant has the option of choosing compensation instead of return of the property. Id. § 11(1).

58. "On the eastern side, the fear dominated that one would lose the house that, under the difficult circumstances of the GDR, had been purchased, built, or even just rented, but cared for and preserved as if it had been owned. One must bear in mind the psychology of dwellings in the GDR. In an inhospitable society the apartment is exalted into a place of [retreat or withdrawal]. . . . [B]ehind the apartment door you walk into a microcosm that has been established with much expense, sometimes with somewhat too much expense. . . . In the confusion of the upheaval [of unification], anxiety about the loss of a house or apartment was particularly severe." Schröder, Deutschland schwierig Vaterland, at 62–63.

59. Although the Unification Treaty and subsequent legislation provided interim protection for these tenants, significant aspects of that protection have now come to an

end. Tenants under GDR leases were generally protected until the end of 1995, but thereafter eviction is possible if the landlord can show a personal need for use of the property. FAZ, Jan. 25, 1995, at 15 col. 3. See generally Unification Treaty, attachment III § 5; Property Statute §§ 16, 17. See also Göhring, Einigungsvertrag und Mietrecht, 1990 DtZ 317, 318–19 (discussing landlords' rights of eviction under applicable sections of Civil Code as modified by Unification Treaty).

For eastern tenants generally, the Unification Treaty and subsequent statutes provide measures of rent control, coupled with government subventions to landlords. Aspects of this program have been upheld in the Constitutional Court against claims asserting violations of property rights. 91 BVerfGE 294 (1994).

60. Property Statute (1990 version) § 19.

61. The current tenants of a one- or two-family house also have a right of first refusal (*Vorkaufsrecht*) if the property is sold. Property Statute § 20(1). Yet in those areas of eastern Germany where land values have soared after unification, this right may be illusory because the eastern tenants would not be able to pay the purchase price in any event. The tenant of a one-family house being reclaimed by a prior owner can also request the state administrator to offer the prior owner an equivalent piece of property in the same area as a substitute. If the prior owner accepts the substitute property, the original property can be sold to the tenant. Id. § 21.

62. See New York Times, June 5, 1992, at A3 col. 1 (towns of Zepernick and Kleinmachnow in the outskirts of Berlin); cf. Rolf Hochhuth, Wessis im Weimar: Szenen aus einem besetzten Land 149–71 (1993).

63. New York Times, June 5, 1992, at A3 col. 1. See also the somber remarks of Steffen Heitmann, justice minister of Saxony: "Entire sections of east German cities are changing owners and, therefore, populations. Eighty percent of returned property is being immediately sold by the heirs. But the east Germans—the tenants—lack the financial means to participate in the bidding." FAZ, Sept. 2, 1994, at 13 col. 1.

64. In a further complexity of socialist law, many in the GDR occupied an intermediate status between property owner and tenant. In some cases, for example, the ownership of a house was separate from the ownership of the underlying land, which typically remained state-owned People's Property. See Stürner, Sachenrechtsbereinigung zwischen Restitution, Bestandsschutz und Rechtssicherheit, 1993 JZ 1074. If the eastern citizen had gone through the legal formality of acquiring a "concrete easement" (*dingliches Nutzungsrecht*) in the house, those rights could receive protection as an "honest acquisition" after unification. Property Law § 4(2). Moreover, important legislation in 1994 now allows those easement owners—and certain other occupiers who have made substantial investments in their houses—to acquire the underlying real property at one-half of current market value or to obtain a long-term leasehold interest (Erbbaurecht) at one-half of the normal yearly payment. See Gesetz zur Sachenrechtsbereinigung im Beitrittsgebiet, of Sept. 21, 1994, BGBl I 2457; Dirk Brouër, Herbert Trimbach et al., Offene Vermögensfragen—ein Ratgeber 116–72 (1995); Leutheusser-Schnarrenberger, Bewältigung der rechtlichen Probleme der Wiedervereinigung, 1994 DtZ 290, 295–96.

Furthermore, because vacation travel outside the country was limited, many GDR citizens maintained a small vacation house, known as a "dacha," in addition to their primary residence. Dachas were often located on People's Property and were occupied under a form of long-term lease (*Mietvertrag*, *Pachtvertrag*, or *Überlassungsvertrag*). After unification, the underlying real property often reverted to its prior owner.

But because of the importance of the dachas in the life of eastern Germany, the 1994 legislation allows the lessees to remain as tenants for a significant period—for 10 or more years in many instances and for life in the case of elderly persons. Gesetz zur Anpassung schuldrechtlicher Nutzungsverhältnisse an Grundstücken im Beitrittsgebiet, of Sept. 21, 1994, BGBl I 2538; Brouër, Trimbach et al. at 173–207; Leutheusser-Schnarrenberger, 1994 DtZ at 296–97.

In this legislation, parliament sought to preserve the rights of the underlying (often western) property owners while also protecting the expectation interests of the eastern lessees. Yet the permissible rents will gradually rise toward market value, and many eastern occupiers may find the financial burden of a dacha difficult to sustain—especially in expensive areas such as those surrounding Berlin. At the other end of the spectrum, some of the underlying property owners argue that the 1994 statutes unduly infringe their rights, and they have challenged the legislation in the Constitutional Court. Neubauer, Die Vertreibung findet nicht statt, Die Zeit, Mar. 24, 1995, at 11 col. 1.

65. Property Statute § 1(1). See Bertrams, 1994 DVBl at 378.

66. See Hochhuth, Wessis in Weimar, at 130–31: "So now we know it: Honecker says, the Wall was necessary, / the [Justice] Minister in Bonn concludes: Yes sir, for defense." See also id. at 107–47.

In a rather different approach, the Senate of Berlin argued that, in light of the city's four-power occupation status, the GDR had no legal authority to apply its Defense Statute in Berlin. Under this view, there was no legal basis for the expropriation of the "Wall Property." See FAZ, Jan. 26, 1994, at 2 col. 1. This argument, however, met with little success in the courts. See FAZ, Feb. 28, 1996, at 10 col. 4.

67. FAZ, Feb. 10, 1996, at 1 col. 2.

In a survey of the fate of "socialist" property, one additional form of holding deserves mention. As the leading force in the GDR, the SED accumulated vast amounts of property—some estimates range as high as DM 1.8 billion in value. These holdings were classified as "property of societal organizations of citizens" under article 10 of the 1968/74 GDR Constitution. See Ch. 4.

It was clear that the PDS, the SED's successor organization, would not be permitted to retain these vast holdings after unification. Indeed, under the Statute on Parties enacted by the GDR Volkskammer in 1990, as amended and carried forward in the Unification Treaty, the PDS was permitted to retain only that property that was "demonstrably" obtained in a manner consistent with the rule of law. See Unification Treaty, attachment II, ch. II(A), para. III(1)(d). Cf. Ch. 5. After years of litigation and dispute, the PDS and a government commission concluded an agreement under which the PDS retained its headquarters in Berlin, and a small amount of additional property, and relinquished all other property claims. To the extent that the property so relinquished is not returned to former owners, it will be used for public purposes in eastern Germany. See FAZ, June 19, 1995, at 5 col. 2.

68. Perhaps not coincidentally, the abortion and the 1945–49 property rules were the principal areas in which concerns of the east had to some extent prevailed in the treaty negotiations.

69. Art. 14 GG.

70. See Badura, Der Verfassungsauftrag der Eigentumsgarantie im wiedervereinigten Deutschland, 1990 DVBl 1256, 1261.

71. See, e.g., Kimminich at 84.

72. See WRV art. 153; Scholz, Die Welt, Oct. 30, 1990; cf. Kimminich at 43–44; 6 BGHZ 270, 274 (1952). But see 2 BVerfGE 237, 248–53 (1953).

73. See, e.g., Scholz, Die Welt, Oct. 30, 1990. For skepticism about this argument, see, e.g., II(1) Deutsche Wiedervereinigung at 34 (remarks of Rudolf Bernhardt); Heslop & Roberto, Property Rights in the Unified Germany: A Constitutional, Comparative, and International Legal Analysis, 11 Boston University International Law Journal 243, 267–70 (1993).

74. See Weber & Wilhelm, 1991 BB (Beilage 3) at 17; Badura, 1990 DVB1 at 1261–62; Ernst Forsthoff, Ist die Bodenreform in der Deutschen Demokratischen Republik im Falle der Wiedervereinigung als rechtswirksam anzuerkennen? (1954). But see 2 BVerfGE at 253–54; 41 BVerfGE 126, 157 (1976).

75. See, e.g., 27 BVerfGE 253, 283 (1969); 41 BVerfGE at 153–54.

76. See, e.g., Maurer, Die Eigentumsregelung im Einigungsvertrag, 1992 JZ 183, 190–91.

77. Unification Treaty art. 4(5); art. 143(3) GG.

78. The Unification Treaty also amended article 135a of the Basic Law to negate any obligation of the government—under article 14 GG—to pay compensation for the 1945–49 expropriations or to pay other debts of the GDR. Unification Treaty art. 4(4). See Matthias Herdegen, Die Verfassungsänderungen im Einigungsvertrag 15–17 (1991).

79. See 30 BVerfGE 1, 39 (1970) (dissenting opinion).

80. 84 BVerfGE 90 (1991). Academic commentary on the Court's decision was almost all sharply critical. For a sampling, see Leisner, Verfassungswidriges Verfassungsrecht, 1992 DÖV 432; Maurer, 1992 JZ 183; Vitzthum in II(1) Deutsche Wiedervereinigung at 3. For an earlier decision, denying a preliminary injunction in this case, see 1990 EuGRZ 556.

81. In an earlier decision, the Court had given a very narrow construction to the constitutional limitations on constitutional amendment. See 30 BVerfGE 1 (1970) (Klass case).

82. Even if the former owners had some claim against the Soviet Union under international law, those claims were impossible to enforce and "worthless as a practical matter"; therefore the Federal Republic could relinquish these claims in a general settlement directed toward unification. 84 BVerfGE at 124–25.

83. Id. at 122.

84. Id.

85. Id. at 125–26.

86. See id. at 127–28. Indeed, at oral argument in the Constitutional Court, Lothar de Maizière and others asserted that unification could not have been achieved without this provision in the Unification Treaty.

87. Id. at 129. Because the constitution had only been amended to prevent actual return of the property, and not to limit equality of compensation, this final point was decided directly under the equality provision of article 3 GG, rather than under article 79(3). Cf. 84 BVerfGE at 128. The Court also appeared to suggest that a similar result might be required under the "social state" and rule of law principles of the Basic Law. Id. at 126.

88. 84 BVerfGE at 130–31. See generally II(1) Deutsche Wiedervereinigung at 34 (remarks of Rudolf Bernhardt); 41 BVerfGE 126, 153–54; Vitzthum in II(1) Deutsche Wiedervereinigung at 22–23.

89. See Ch. 15. See also Heitmann, Aktuelle Probleme des Vermögensrechts aus der Perspektive eines neuen Bundeslandes, 1995 NJW 299, 301.

90. See Ch. 8.

91. Questions about the status of expropriated property have also arisen in other countries of the former eastern bloc. In Hungary, for example, the Constitutional Court upheld a plan through which the former owners may receive vouchers in lieu of restitution; rights under the statute are not limited to the former landowners, but will also accrue to a deceased landowner's spouse or heirs. In this decision, the Hungarian court reversed its prior view that compensation for expropriated property might involve a form of constitutionally invalid discrimination against persons who had not been property owners. See Klingsberg, Safeguarding the Transition, 2 East European Constitutional Review, Spring 1993, at 44; Paczolay, Judicial Review of the Compensation Law in Hungary, 13 Michigan Journal of International Law 806 (1992). Similarly, Czechoslovakia (and its successor republics) established a broad program of return of expropriated property, although claimants must be citizens of the country. In Poland, however, parliament has had greater difficulty in enacting a comprehensive property settlement. See The Sun (Baltimore), June 12, 1995, at 1A col. 4.

92. Cf., e.g., FAZ, May 31, 1994, at 12 col. 3; id. at col. 1.

93. See, e.g., Höch, Die Forderungen der DDR und der Sowjetunion als sachliche Gründe für den Restitutionsausschluß, 1995 DtZ 76. Certainly, the Soviet Union's assumed position was important in the Court's justification of different treatment for the Bodenreform lands in comparison with property expropriated by the GDR. Yet the GDR also insisted on nonreturn of the Bodenreform lands, and it is far from clear that the Court would have decided any differently if it believed that only the GDR—and not the Soviet Union—had asserted this view. Id.

94. See, e.g., FAZ, May 4, 1995, at 5 col. 1. This complex argument rested in part on inferences drawn from preliminary Soviet drafts of the Two Plus Four agreement, which was being negotiated in the summer of 1990, as well as on certain remarks of Soviet negotiators.

95. See generally Wasmuth, Zum besatzungshoheitlichen Charakter der Berliner Liste 3, 1993 VIZ 186, 188.

In April 1993, a three-judge screening panel of the Constitutional Court rejected the former owners' renewed petition on the ground that it lacked sufficient chance of success. 1993 DtZ 275. The panel found insufficient evidence to change the Court's view of the Soviet Union's demands; therefore it was not necessary to discuss whether, if that view were changed, the constitutional result would actually be affected.

96. See Der Spiegel, 36/1994, at 27–31.

97. See, e.g., FAZ, Sept. 12, 1994, at 6 col. 4 (letter of Yuli Kvitsinsky, former Soviet ambassador to the Federal Republic); see also FAZ, Aug. 27, 1994, at 1 col. 2; FAZ, Aug. 30, 1994, at 1 col. 3; id. at 6 cols. 4 & 5.

98. Interview with Joachim Domeratzky, Brandenburg Agricultural Ministry, Potsdam, Aug. 16, 1994. In addition to the transfer of collective property into People's Property, certain large estates (so-called *Volksgüter* or "People's Estates") had been transferred directly into People's Property at the time of the Bodenreform.

99. Because the small farmers had received Bodenreform lands subject to significant restrictions, the reversion of the property to the GDR state upon failure of the conditions was not viewed as an "expropriation" under the Property Statute. Therefore a farmer who had abandoned the property under the GDR had no claim for its recovery upon unification. Cf. Bertrams, 1994 DVBl at 378.

100. The administrator of the property was the BVVG, a subsidiary of the Treuhand.

101. See Materialien: Verwertung bisheriger volkseigener land- und forstwirtschaftlicher Flächen—Bericht des Bundesfinanzministeriums, 1993 VIZ 345.

102. See FAZ, Dec. 9, 1992, at 15 col. 3; Der Tagesspiegel (Berlin), Dec. 9, 1992, at 25 col. 3.

103. Interview with Joachim Domeratzky, Aug. 16, 1994.

104. For contemporary discussion, see FAZ, Dec. 2, 1992, at 1 col. 2; FAZ, Feb. 26, 1993, at 1 col. 2.

105. Any compensation previously paid by the West German government under a program for "equalization of burdens" would be subtracted from this amount. Moreover, particularly high amounts of compensation would be reduced according to a progressive formula—so that the highest amount of compensation receivable would be DM 950,000, for property valued at more than DM 10 million. The draft relied on data from 1935 because that was the time of the last uniform property valuation in Germany.

106. The plan would thus reduce the disparity between those former owners who recovered their property (thereby receiving 100 percent of current market value) and those required to accept compensation at a substantially lesser amount. Most single-family houses were exempt from the tax, and payment of the tax could be extended over a substantial period.

107. See FAZ, Mar. 8, 1993, at 1 col. 5; FAZ, Sept. 16, 1993, at 1 col. 2.

108. See FAZ, Nov. 24, 1993, at 1 col. 2; FAZ, Dec. 4, 1993, at 10 col. 2. See also Zimmermann, Wiedergutmachung zwischen materieller Gerechtigkeit und politischem Kompromiß, 1994 DtZ 359.

109. But to counterbalance the increased rates of compensation, the progressive rates of reduction for high amounts of compensation were also substantially increased. Zimmermann, 1994 DtZ at 359.

110. FAZ, Nov. 4, 1993, at 6 col. 2; see also FAZ, Oct. 28, 1993, at 2 col. 1. Return of property was apparently also opposed by the federal finance minister, who viewed these extensive federal lands as an important resource for financing unification.

111. See FAZ, May 18, 1994, at 4 col. 2; FAZ, May 20, 1994, at 5 col. 3; FAZ, May 21, 1994, at 2 col. 2.

112. FAZ, May 24, 1994, at 10 col. 3 (correspondence).

113. FAZ, June 11, 1994, at 1 col. 2.

114. FAZ, July 1, 1994, at 2 col. 5.

115. FAZ, July 9, 1994, at 4 col. 4. Cf. art. 77 GG.

116. Entschädigungs- und Ausgleichsleistungsgesetz, of Sept. 27, 1994, BGBl I 2624 (hereafter, EALG).

117. FAZ, Sept. 24, 1994, at 2 col. 4. See generally Schmidt-Preuß, Das Entschädigungs- und Ausgleichsleistungsgesetz, 1994 NJW 3249.

A particularly interesting section of the statute denies settlement payments to former owners who violated the principles of humanity or the rule of law or who gave significant assistance to the Nazi or Communist regimes. EALG art. II § 1(4). In part, therefore, this provision might test the extent to which certain former owners were indeed "Nazi activists," as claimed by the Soviet Union with respect to some expropriations of the occupation period. See Brouër, Trimbach et al. at 104–5.

118. It has been argued, for example, that the statute's progressive reduction of payments for large property claims exacerbates an unconstitutional inequality between those who recover property and those who receive settlement payments instead. See

generally Wasmuth, Die Willkür des Entschädigungs- und Ausgleichsleistungsgesetzes, 1995 VIZ 74.

119. The future of the LPG successor organizations is also imperiled by the continued existence of billions of marks of debts stemming from the GDR past. Under the socialist economy these debts were apparently employed as a tool of central planning, but the Unification Treaty converted them into obligations under the western Civil Code (at the rate of one Deutsche Mark to two GDR Marks), and they were acquired at bargain rates by western banks. See Der Spiegel, 10/1994, at 55–66. The LPG successor organizations—as well as numerous local governments, which are also subject to these debts—are hoping for a measure of relief from the federal government or from the Constitutional Court. FAZ, July 1, 1995, at 14 col. 1.

It should be noted that the LPG successor organizations—notwithstanding their apparent economic successes—have come under sharp criticism on the ground that they are often controlled by individuals and groups who led the collectives under the GDR; it is also alleged that some of these controlling groups have used unfair devices to diminish the residual share received by other members of the former collectives. See, e.g., Der Spiegel, 24/1995, at 132–43. Accordingly, the critics refer to the leaders of the new cooperatives as "red junkers" or "the red barons" of eastern agriculture. See, e.g., FAZ, Sept. 9, 1994, at 10 col. 3; see also Süddeutsche Zeitung, Feb. 5, 1994 (correspondence): "the old SED/PDS agro-apparatchiks will govern what happens on the land—just as before."

120. Elling, 25 Vanderbilt Journal of Transnational Law at 594.

121. See, e.g., Zieger, Die Verfassungsänderung in der DDR vom 7.10.1974, 1975 NJW 143, 148.

122. These final expropriations were part of a process of "delimitation" (*Abgrenzung*), through which the GDR sought to differentiate itself decisively from the Federal Republic and thus ward off political threats posed by increased contacts between the two German states in the détente of the early 1970s. A. James McAdams, East Germany and Detente 133 (1985). During the same period, the GDR pursued further economic concentration by forming huge business combines (*Kombinate*) and greatly increasing the size of the agricultural collectives.

123. See, e.g., Helmut Herles & Ewald Rose (eds.), Vom Runden Tisch zum Parlament 37–44 (1990).

124. See Ch. 5.

125. See, e.g., Birgit Breuel (ed.), Treuhand intern 29(1993) (hereafter, Treuhand intern). Cf. Hochhuth, Wessis in Weimar, at 30.

126. The first State Treaty and the Unification Treaty contemplated that interests in People's Property might be distributed to eastern citizens as compensation for losses from the 2:1 conversion of certain bank deposits under the State Treaty. See State Treaty art. 10(6); Unification Treaty art. 25(6); see also Gesetz zur Privatisierung und Reorganisation des volkseigenen Vermögens (Treuhandgesetz), of June 17, 1990, GBl DDR I 300, preamble; Sinn & Sinn at 84. See also Ch. 7.

127. Peter Christ & Ralf Neubauer, Kolonie im eigenen Land 116–17 (1991).

128. Beschluß zur Gründung der Anstalt zur treuhänderischen Verwaltung des Volkseigentums (Treuhandanstalt), of Mar. 1, 1990, GBl DDR I 107. Two weeks later, at the very end of the Modrow period, the Council of Ministers issued a more detailed charter (Statut) of the Treuhand. Statut der Anstalt zur treuhänderischen Verwaltung des Volkseigentums (Treuhandanstalt), of Mar. 15, 1990, GBl DDR I 167.

129. Verordnung zur Umwandlung von volkseigenen Kombinaten, Betrieben und Einrichtungen in Kapitalgesellschaften, of Mar. 1, 1990, GBl DDR I 107.

130. Christ & Neubauer at 119; Statut, 1990 GBl DDR I 167. See also Roesler, Die Treuhandanstalt: Wirtschaftsimperium oder Politikinstrument? in Rüdiger Liedtke (ed.), Die Treuhand und die zweite Enteignung der Ostdeutschen 19–22 (1993) (hereafter, Die zweite Enteignung); cf. Hochhuth, Wessis in Weimar, at 11 (citing Stefan Heym). Accordingly, the Treuhand's main work in the early period of its existence—until the end of June 1990—was to supervise the conversion of state enterprises into a corporate form recognized by western law. Treuhand intern at 30–32.

131. Cf. Dieter Kampe, Wer uns kennenlernt, gewinnt uns lieb: Nachruf auf die Treuhand 148–49 (1993) (quoting Klaus von Dohnanyi).

132. Some significant problems also resulted from decisions of this early period. Prime Minister Modrow installed many former functionaries of the planned economy in the Treuhand, and this move may have complicated the ultimate transformation to a market economy. Martin Flug, Treuhand-Poker: Die Mechanismen des Ausverkaufs 18 (1992); but see Roesler in Die zweite Enteignung at 29.

133. See Ch. 7.

134. Joint Protocol to State Treaty, art. A(II)(7); see also id. at art. A(II)(1),(3); State Treaty art. 14, attachment IX.

135. See Ch. 5.

136. Gesetz zur Privatisierung und Reorganisation des volkseigenen Vermögens (Treuhandgesetz), of June 17, 1990, GBl DDR I 300 (hereafter, Treuhand Law); cf. Unification Treaty art. 25.

137. See Treuhand Law §§ 1, 2, 8, 9. In a gesture toward decentralization, the statute provided that subsidiary corporations were to be created between the Treuhand and the operating concerns. Id. §§ 7–10. These subsidiaries, however, were never established. See Roesler in Die zweite Enteignung at 41.

138. See generally Unification Treaty, attachment III.

139. Gesetz über die Gründung und Tätigkeit privater Unternehmen und über Unternehmensbeteiligungen, of Mar. 7, 1990, GBl DDR I 141 §§ 17–19. These sections were later superseded and repealed by the Property Statute. See Property Statute (1990 version) § 39(10).

This was an early step toward privatization, but the results were not always encouraging. Some owners found, for example, that businesses expropriated in 1972 had suffered severely from poor management and insufficient investment in the intervening years. Accordingly, what some owners received from the GDR government in 1990 was a failing enterprise that could not compete against its western counterparts. Perhaps one solution was to enter into a joint venture with a western firm, but that was to risk losing control of the enterprise itself. See, e.g., New York Times, Feb. 14, 1991, at D1 col. 3.

140. Property Statute § 6(1).

141. Id. § 6(1)–(4); see also Unification Treaty, attachment III, § 7.

142. See Property Statute § 6(7).

143. See Property Statute (1991 version) § 3a(1)(2); Investment Preference Law § 1.

144. Investment Preference Law § 18; Försterling at 185–90.

145. See Unification Treaty art. 25; Treuhand Law § 1(1).

146. The Treuhand originally received approximately 8,500 east German enterprises, but the number increased to 12,500 as some huge conglomerates were divided

into smaller units. Rudolf Hickel & Jan Priewe, Nach dem Fehlstart: Ökonomische Perspektiven der deutschen Einigung 51 (1994). In addition, subsidiaries of the Treuhand supervised the sale of thousands of non-industrial concerns such as restaurants, hotels, and retail stores.

147. Flug at 51–53.

148. Roesler in Die zweite Enteignung at 35–37. See Ch. 7.

149. Rohwedder succeeded the first president, Rainer Maria Gohlke, who was apparently overwhelmed by the problems confronting the agency. Roesler in Die zweite Enteignung at 40–41.

150. Among the businesses closed during this early period were a huge automobile manufacturer in Thuringia and the GDR airline, Interflug. See id. at 43–44.

151. Sinn & Sinn at 84 n. 10.

152. See Hochhuth, Wessis in Weimar, at 11–31; Hochhuth, "Wer so etwas tut wie Rohwedder . . .," in Die zweite Enteignung at 136–43. In a eulogy in Berlin, however, Federal President Richard von Weizsäcker presented a considerably different view of Rohwedder and his leadership of the Treuhand: "[H]e strove to prevent people from being materially or spiritually crushed. He was a convinced advocate of the market economy, but he intervened vehemently when all too clever privatization arrangements conflicted with his view of the public good and the social obligations of a humane economic policy." Abschied von Detlev Rohwedder, in Richard von Weizsäcker, Von Deutschland nach Europa 215 (1991). For yet another view of Rohwedder, see Kampe at 114–17.

153. Rohwedder, An alle Mitarbeiterinnen und Mitarbeiter der Treuhandanstalt, reprinted in Die zweite Enteignung at 54–56.

154. Id. at 55, 56.

155. See Kampe at 116.

156. Cf., e.g., Breuel, Grenzenlos überfordert, Die Zeit, Nov. 13, 1992, at 30; Kampe at 120, 156–57. In this phase of its activity, the Treuhand sought to save an "industrial core" of enterprises, in the face of the imminent danger of "extensive deindustrialization" in many eastern areas. Hickel & Priewe at 61–62.

157. See, e.g., Günter Grass, Gegen die verstreichende Zeit 152 (1991): "A centralistic monster called the Treuhand—whose bureaucratic structure could have been thought up by [GDR economic czar] Mr. Mittag and company—bestows or denies almost like fate itself, as it shatters already damaged lives with one stroke of a pen."

158. See, e.g., Hildebrandt, "Wir werden ein Volk von Rentnern sein," in Die zweite Enteignung at 76–77 (after unification, less than 50 percent of women in eastern Germany were employed).

159. See Ch. 7.

160. In some cases, sales of businesses were made without the underlying real property—which went to the prior owner—with the property owner and the business then entering into long-term arrangements for the leasing of the property.

161. Kampe at 129, 144–47.

162. Priewe, Die Treuhand und die Bonner Politik, in Die zweite Enteignung at 95. It was also charged that west German firms bought east German enterprises from the Treuhand, perhaps at bargain prices, and then closed those enterprises to eliminate competition for their own products. On other occasions, western firms acquired customer lists and other secret information of competing eastern firms by posing as possible purchasers. See, e.g., Hildebrandt, in Die zweite Enteignung at 74–75; Kampe at 132–33; Hickel & Priewe at 72.

163. Flug at 214–19.

164. See Neubauer, Preis der Eile, Die Zeit, July 2, 1993, at 19 col. 1.

165. See Flug at 103.

166. Kampe at 166–68; Hickel & Priewe at 76.

167. See art. 44 GG; Cloes, Neuer Stellenwert der Parlamentarischen Kontrolle der Treuhandanstalt, 1994 DtZ 239.

168. Cloes, 1994 DtZ at 241.

169. See FAZ, Dec. 29, 1994, at 10 col. 1; FAZ, Apr. 20, 1994, at 17 col. 1; id. at col. 4; Stapper & Rödder, Das Gesetz zur abschließenden Erfüllung der verbliebenen Aufgaben der Treuhandanstalt, 1994 NJW 2673.

170. In addition to two existing agencies that administer agricultural and non-agricultural real property (BVVG and TLG), new agencies were established to operate and privatize the remaining concerns (BMG), manage existing contracts (BVS), and handle the Treuhand's informations system and service functions (Disos). FAZ, Dec. 29, 1994, at 10 col. 1.

171. FAZ, Dec. 29, 1994, at 10 col. 1; cf. Priewe in Die zweite Enteignung at 95–96.

172. See, for example, the views of five West German experts in a report submitted to the federal government in early 1990. Sachverständigenrat zur Begutachtung der gesamtwirtschaftlichen Entwicklung. Zur Unterstützung der Wirtschaftsreform in der DDR: Voraussetzungen und Möglichkeiten. Sondergutachten vom 20. Januar 1990, quoted in Roesler in Die zweite Enteignung at 26–27. See also Sinn & Sinn at 124–39. A system of privatization that involves distributing ownership shares of state-owned enterprises to the population seems to have worked relatively well in the former Czechoslovakia. Id. at 125, 129–31.

173. See, e.g., Wolfgang Graf Vitzthum & Wolfgang März, Restitutionsausschluß 18 (1995).

174. By May 1995, almost five years after unification, only approximately one-half of the open property questions had been resolved. FAZ, May 6, 1995, at 4 col. 3.

175. See Jens Reich, Rückkehr nach Europa: Zur neuen Lage der deutschen Nation 224 (1991): "We [the eastern Germans] will become a people of minor employees, without property—that has been clear to me for a long time." See also Joost, Über die Bedeutung von Selbst- und Fremdbildern für die innerdeutsche Verständigung, in Karl Otto Hondrich et al., Arbeitgeber West—Arbeitnehmer Ost: Vereinigung im Konflikt 45 (1993).

## Chapter 12
## The Unification of Abortion Law

1. See, e.g., Note, German Abortion Law: The Unwanted Child of Reunification, 13 Loyola Los Angeles International & Comparative Law Journal 643, 655 (1991) (unsuccessful abortion reform measures proposed by SPD justice minister in 1922).

2. 410 U.S. 113 (1973).

3. See Webster v. Reproductive Health Servs., 492 U.S. 490 (1989).

4. Planned Parenthood of Southeastern Pennsylvania v. Casey, 112 S. Ct. 2791 (1992).

5. 39 BVerfGE 1 (1975); see Donald P. Kommers, The Constitutional Jurisprudence of the Federal Republic of Germany 348–59 (1989). For comparative discussions of the German and American cases, see Mary Ann Glendon, Abortion and Divorce in Western Law 25–39 (1987); Kommers, Abortion and Constitution: United

States and West Germany, 25 American Journal of Comparative Law 255 (1977); Brugger, Abtreibung—ein Grundrecht oder ein Verbrechen?: Ein Vergleich der Urteile des United States Supreme Court und des BVerfG, 1986 NJW 896. Apparently, the German court was familiar with *Roe v. Wade* and consciously rejected its teachings. Kommers, The Constitutional Law of Abortion in Germany: Should Americans Pay Attention?, 10 Journal of Contemporary Health Law and Policy 1, 6 (1994).

6. See 39 BVerfGE at 36–37, 66–68.

7. 410 U.S. at 153.

8. See 39 BVerfGE at 48–51.

9. See §§ 218, 218a, 218b, 219 StGB a.F. Under the statute, certain "indications" could be invoked only at relatively early stages of the pregnancy. In the case of violations, the statute more frequently imposed penalties on the physician than on the woman obtaining the abortion. See generally Eser, Reform of German Abortion Law: First Experiences, 34 American Journal of Comparative Law 369, 374–80 (1986). This abortion statute was upheld by the European Commission of Human Rights against charges that it unduly invaded the "right to respect for private life" guaranteed by article 8(1) of the European Convention on Human Rights. See Brüggemann & Scheuten v. The Federal Republic of Germany, 10 European Commission of Human Rights, Decisions & Reports 100 (1978).

10. See, e.g., Eser, 34 American Journal of Comparative Law at 382 (procedure to be followed by pregnant woman seeking abortion).

11. See Starck, Der verfassungsrechtliche Schutz des ungeborenen menschlichen Lebens, 1993 JZ 816, 818; Wilms, Rechtsprobleme des Schwangerschaftsabbruchs im vereinten Deutschland, 1990 ZRP 470, 472.

The action brought by the state of Bavaria also challenged aspects of a statute providing that the costs of a legal abortion would be paid by national social insurance. The Constitutional Court had previously rejected challenges by individuals against these financing provisions (or their enforcement) on grounds of justiciability—see 78 BVerfGE 320 (1988); 67 BVerfGE 26 (1984)—but this defense was not necessarily available in an action brought by a state. The action filed by the state of Bavaria was ultimately consolidated with later actions filed against the 1992 Abortion Statute, discussed below.

12. Gesetz über die Unterbrechung der Schwangerschaft, of Mar. 9, 1972, GBl DDR I 89. The preamble of the statute invoked the provision of the GDR Constitution that affirmed the principle of gender equality. See Wilms, 1990 ZRP at 473; Verf. DDR (1968) art. 20(2). The GDR abortion statute of 1972 followed the enactment of similar measures liberalizing the law of abortion in the Soviet Union and eastern Europe in the 1950s. See Note, 13 Loyola Los Angeles International & Comparative Law Journal at 671–72. Previously, an abortion was only permissible in the GDR if a commission determined that a medical or social "indication" was present. Grandke, Anmerkungen zum Urteil des BVerfG zu § 218 StGB, 1993 NJ 347. For historical background of the GDR statute, see Note, Abortion Law Reform: The Nexus between Abortion and the Role of Women in the German Democratic Republic and the Federal Republic of Germany, 10 Dickinson Journal of International Law 137, 147–48 (1991).

13. Interestingly some members of the East German CDU, ordinarily a compliant bloc party, voted against the liberalized abortion statute of 1972. This vote marked one of the very few instances in the history of the GDR—until the revolutionary days of 1989—when a legislative measure was enacted by anything less than a unanimous vote

of the Volkskammer. See Herwig Roggemann, Die DDR-Verfassungen: Einführung in das Verfassungsrecht der DDR 230 (1989).

14. No doubt reflecting this institution, two East German constitutional drafts of 1990—the Round Table draft and the Constitution of East Berlin—set forth a woman's right to abortion. RT-Entwurf art. 4(3); Verf. Berlin (Ost) art. 7(4); see Chs. 4 & 9.

In the United States, also, constitutional decisions establishing a woman's right to an abortion have led to the growth of important social structures. See Planned Parenthood of Southeastern Pennsylvania v. Casey, 112 S.Ct. 2791, 2809, 2812 (1992) (opinion of Justices O'Connor, Kennedy, and Souter): "The ability of women to participate equally in the economic and social life of the Nation has been facilitated by their ability to control their reproductive lives. . . . An entire generation has come of age free to assume *Roe's* concept of liberty in defining the capacity of women to act in society, and to make reproductive decisions. . . ."

15. See Ch. 10.

16. Cf., e.g., Wolfgang Schäuble, Der Vertrag: Wie ich über die deutsche Einheit verhandelte 231–32 (1991).

17. On the tense negotiations over the abortion regulation in the treaty, see generally id. at 229–51.

18. See generally Frommel, Strategien gegen die Demontage der Reform der §§ 218ff. StGB in der Bundesrepublik, 1990 ZRP 351 (arguing that the GDR rule could be extended to all of Germany).

19. See Schäuble, Der Vertrag, at 234.

20. Id. at 251–52.

21. Unification Treaty art. 31(4).

22. Id.

23. But see Grandke, 1993 NJ at 347: "It is one of the peculiarities of the Unification Treaty that improvement in social assistance is demanded, while at the same time in the attachments to the treaty the assistance system of the GDR is largely dismantled without replacement."

24. The treaty was somewhat more successful in resolving a related issue that had been subject to contentious discussion. For most of the period of negotiations, the drafters assumed that during the two-year interim period, the GDR's more liberal abortion rule would apply to residents of the former territory of the GDR only, and the stricter western rule would continue to apply to western residents even if they obtained an abortion in the territory of the former GDR. See FR, July 20, 1990, at 1 col. 1. This provision was intended to discourage travel by women from the west to the east for the purpose of obtaining an abortion.

In tense last-minute negotiations, however, the drafters of the Unification Treaty abandoned this residency requirement and provided that an abortion obtained in the east by a western resident would be measured by the more liberal rule of the GDR. The conservatives' abandonment of the residency requirement was part of a compromise in which the permissible period for retention of the separate GDR abortion regulation was reduced from five to two years. See Note, 13 Loyola Los Angeles International & Comparative Law Journal at 674–75; Schäuble, Der Vertrag, at 229–51.

25. It was not entirely clear that a constitutional amendment was needed to accomplish this result. Some commentators argue that article 23 GG actually contemplated the possibility of a gradual, incremental introduction of the Basic Law into the territory that is acceding to the Federal Republic under that provision—with the result that

article 23 itself could allow some deviations from the Basic Law for an interim period. See, e.g., 2 Ingo von Münch (ed.), Grundgesetz-Kommentar art. 23, No. 27 (1983). When the Saarland acceded to the Federal Republic, for example, certain provisions of the Basic Law were introduced into that territory in an incremental manner. See Rauschning, Deutschlands aktuelle Verfassungslage, 1990 DVBl 393, 401; Stern, Der Staatsvertrag im völkerrechtlichen und verfassungsrechtlichen Kontext, in 1 Klaus Stern & Bruno Schmidt-Bleibtreu (eds.), Verträge und Rechtsakte zur Deutschen Einheit 37–38 (1990).

26. Unification Treaty art. 4(5). As set forth in the Unification Treaty, new article 143 of the Basic Law contains a second section, which allows noncompliance with the Basic Law for a five-year period—to December 31, 1995—in the case of certain structural provisions such as those relating to federalism, administration, the judiciary, and the financial system.

27. See Ch. 11.

28. Article 19(2) GG, also referred to in the second sentence of article 143(1), provides that a statute may not disturb a basic right "in its essential content." This provision probably does not add significantly to the impact of article 79(3) in the present context.

29. Indeed, this would presumably be the case whether or not article 79(3) were specifically mentioned in article 143(1). See, e.g., Stern, Der verfassungsändernde Charakter des Einigungsvertrages, 1990 DtZ 289, 290–91.

30. See Kommers, 10 Journal of Contemporary Health Law & Policy at 11–12. Indeed, no case in the Constitutional Court has passed upon the status of the Court's abortion jurisprudence under the limitations on amendment of article 79(3) GG, and cases interpreting the scope of article 79(3) in general remain extremely rare. The Court's most recent analysis of the provision is contained in its *Bodenreform* judgment. See Ch. 11.

31. While the Unification Treaty was being negotiated, Süssmuth proposed a treaty provision that would grant a woman freedom to choose an abortion after first undergoing compulsory counseling; concurrently, both counseling and opportunities for social assistance would be improved. See FR, July 31, 1990, at 10 col. 1 (text of Süssmuth proposal); FR, July 30, 1990, at 4 col. 2. In a refined version of her plan, issued in March 1991, Süssmuth proposed that an abortion would not be punishable in the first three months of pregnancy, if the pregnant woman had received mandatory counseling and certified that, in her "best conscience," the abortion is necessary. The woman would thus decide whether the requisite social or psychological "situation of necessity" was present. FAZ, Mar. 9, 1991, at 4 col. 2.

32. See, e.g., Eser, Das neue Schwangerschaftsabbruchsstrafrecht auf dem Prüfstand, 1992 NJW 2913, 2914; see also FAZ, Sept. 27, 1991, at 1 col. 2; id. at 3 col. 1.

33. See Eser, 1992 NJW at 2914 & n. 19. See also Fromme, Erlaubtes Unrecht?, FAZ, May 22, 1992, at 1 col. 5; FAZ, May 22, 1992, at 4 col. 3; Der Spiegel, 22/1992, at 21–23.

34. The vote in the Bundestag was 355 to 283, with 16 abstentions. See Eser, 1993 NJW at 2914. This rather healthy majority contrasted significantly with the much narrower victory of the SPD's abortion reform statute in 1974. Cf. Kommers, 10 Journal of Contemporary Health Law & Policy at 4. On the Bundestag vote and the proposals that were at issue, see FAZ, June 27, 1992, at 1 col. 2; FAZ, June 26, 1992, at 1 col. 2.

35. FAZ, July 1, 1992, at 11 col. 5 (correspondence). Moreover, the GDR's abortion statute of 1972 was actually enacted during the Honecker period, a year after the fall of party leader Ulbricht.

36. Three eastern German states with governments led by the CDU—Berlin, Saxony, and Saxony-Anhalt—voted in favor of the statute. Three states with CDU coalitions—Baden-Württemberg, Mecklenburg-Vorpommern, and Thuringia—abstained. See FAZ, July 11, 1992, at 1 col. 2.

37. See Eser, 1992 NJW at 2915; see generally FAZ, June 27, 1992, at 1 col. 2. Under the Basic Law, it is possible for a statute to be challenged in the Constitutional Court by a state government or by one-third of the members of the Bundestag. See art. 93(1)(2) GG.

38. 86 BVerfGE 390 (1992).

39. The judge in question refused to recuse himself, and the full panel of the Court upheld his decision. See 88 BVerfGE 17 (1992); Kommers, 10 Journal of Contemporary Health Law & Policy at 16.

40. Cf. Jonas & Gorby, West German Abortion Decision: A Contrast to *Roe v. Wade*, 9 John Marshall Journal of Practice & Procedure 605, 607 (1976).

41. 88 BVerfGE 203.

42. This pattern was evident, for example, in the *Election* and *Bodenreform* decisions (see Chs. 8 & 11) as well as the so-called *Warteschleife* decision to be discussed in Chapter 13. See also Hermes & Walther, Schwangerschaftsabbruch zwischen Recht und Unrecht, 1993 NJW 2337, 2347; cf. Neuman, *Casey* in the Mirror: Abortion, Abuse and the Right to Protection in the United States and Germany, 43 American Journal of Comparative Law 273, 290–91 (1995).

43. During pregnancy, the unborn child is an "individual indivisible life, already determined in its genetic identity and therefore in its uniqueness." 88 BVerfGE at 251–52.

44. Id. at 252–53.

45. For discussion of the concept of "minimal protection" (*Untermaßverbot*), see Starck, 1993 JZ at 817.

46. 88 BVerfGE at 255–61.

47. Id. at 261. The question of whether such an obligation might conflict with the guarantees of freedom of expression receives no extended discussion in the Court's opinion.

48. Id. at 264–69.

49. Id. at 270.

50. Id. at 271.

51. Id. at 284.

52. Id. at 284–85.

53. Id. at 290–91.

54. Id. at 291.

55. Id. at 297.

56. Id. at 298.

57. Id. at 274–76.

58. The Court's decision on the question of public funding was not unanimous. In a separate opinion, two judges disagreed with the majority and argued that a first-trimester abortion after counseling should be considered justified and legal; therefore, ordinary health insurance payments for such abortions could not be properly denied. 88

BVerfGE at 338–58. Another judge—the justice who refused to recuse himself—argued that the legislature had discretion to provide social insurance payments for abortions after counseling but was not constitutionally required to do so. Id. at 359–66.

59. Cf. Eser, 1992 NJW at 2917–18.

60. Cf. Kommers, 10 Journal of Contemporary Health Law & Policy at 18–19; Schulz, Verschlungene Wege des Lebensschutzes. Zum zweiten Abtreibungsurteil des BVerfG, 1994 StV 38, 44–45. The elaborate dogmatic structure of German criminal law permits subtle distinctions of this sort between legality and nonpunishable illegality. Yet, even so, the manner in which the distinction was made in the 1993 abortion case apparently remains unique. Schulz, 1994 StV at 44–45.

61. See Hermes & Walther, 1993 NJW at 2338.

62. Cf. id. at 2343: the Court's decision "does not take the woman seriously as a responsibly acting person." See also id. at 2346; Grandke, 1993 NJ at 348.

63. For notable literary examples, cf. Christoph Hein, Drachenblut (1982); Christa Wolf, Nachdenken über Christa T. (1968).

64. See Ch. 9.

65. See Grandke, 1993 NJ at 348.

66. On this subject, moreover, the libertarian FDP moved away from its conservative coalition partners to join the SPD.

67. As a result of its decision in the 1993 abortion case, the Constitutional Court suspended the Bundestag's 1992 statute and imposed its own interim abortion regulation. 88 BVerfGE at 209–13. Thereafter, the parliament attempted to enact its own statute within the Court's constitutional framework, but it found this process very difficult because of bitter disputes between the CDU and the SPD on a number of issues. Disagreements focused on the nature of the required counseling, the criminal penalties to be imposed on third persons, and the source of funding for abortions for women in financial need.

In a very close vote in late May 1994, the Bundestag approved a statute proposed by the governing CDU coalition. See FAZ, May 27, 1994, at 1 col. 2; FAZ, May 26, 1994, at 1 col. 2. But this CDU measure encountered insuperable difficulties in the SPD-controlled Bundesrat, and that body sent the statute to a conference committee of both houses for review. Failing to reach an agreement, the committee suspended its work in September 1994, in light of the approaching national elections. FAZ, Sept. 8, 1994, at 1 col. 2; id. at 14 col. 2.

After the election of 1994 the new Bundestag resumed negotiations. See generally FAZ, Feb. 11, 1995, at 1 col. 2; FAZ, Feb. 27, 1995, at 1 col. 5; FAZ, May 2, 1995, at 4 col. 1. Finally, in June 1995—almost five years after unification—the Bundestag adopted a compromise statute that was supported by all three major parties, including the CDU. FAZ, June 30, 1995, at 1 col. 2. Closely following the guidelines of the Court's opinion, the statute removed criminal penalties for any abortion undertaken in the first twelve weeks of pregnancy if the pregnant woman undergoes a program of counseling directed toward convincing her to bear the child. Although some minor concessions were made to the CDU in ancillary provisions, the conservative *Frankfurter Allgemeine Zeitung* declared that "in essence" the statute contained precisely the measure "that the SPD and FDP have long sought to implement and that the [CDU] has fought against for twenty years." FAZ, June 30, 1995, at 1 col. 5. Another critic complained that the CDU's support of the statute represented a fundamental break in its history and predicted that a consideration of euthanasia would be next on the nation's agenda. FAZ, July 4, 1995, at 6 col. 2 (correspondence). But, at the other end of the spectrum, a representative of the PDS declared that although the law improved the position of some women in western Germany, it worsened their position in the east and that, once again, "control over women" was being exercised in a "patriarchal society." FAZ, June 30, 1995, at 1 col. 2 (quoting FAZ summary of argument).

## Chapter 13
## The Transformation of Eastern Institutions: The Civil Service, the Universities, and the Justice System

1. Cf. Fritz K. Ringer, The Decline of the German Mandarins: The German Academic Community, 1890–1933, at 16–18, 22–23 (1990).

2. See art. 33 GG. Indeed, in the Parliamentary Council which drafted the Basic Law in 1948–49, as in earlier constitutional assemblies, a significant number of representatives were civil servants. See Peter H. Merkl, The Origin of the West German Republic 131–32 (1963). The Weimar Constitution also granted special protection to the Beamtentum. See WRV art. 129.

3. In the Basic Law, these rights are derived from an expansive interpretation of article 33(5), which states that the "law of the public service is to be regulated in a manner that takes into account the traditional principles of the professional civil service."

4. See Krüger, Die Wiedereinführung des Berufsbeamtentums nach Maßgabe des Einigungsvertrages, 1992 ThürVBl 193, 193–97. On "socialist legality," see Ch. 4.

5. Krüger, 1992 ThürVBl at 193. The task of carrying out public functions was to be conferred on Beamten "as quickly as possible," in accordance with a special set of interim rules. Unification Treaty art. 20; see also id. attachment I, ch. XIX (A); Denkschrift zum Einigungsvertrag, Bundestag Drucksache 11/7760 at 364–65; Goerlich, Hergebrachte Grundsätze und Beitrittsbeamtentum, 1991 JZ 75.

6. Krüger, 1992 ThürVBl at 193. Because of the special protection of the Beamtentum in article 33 of the Basic Law, this proposal would have required a constitutional amendment. Id.

7. See Nicksch, Die Einführung des Berufsbeamtentums im Gebiet der früheren DDR nach dem Einigungsvertrag, 1990 DtZ 340, 341–42.

8. Indeed, the GDR civil service was approximately three times the size of the civil service of North Rhine-Westphalia, a western state with approximately the population of the GDR. See Wolfgang Schäuble, Der Vertrag: Wie ich über die deutsche Einheit verhandelte 199 (1991).

9. Unification Treaty, attachment I, ch. XIX (A), para. III (1)(4)(2).

10. See Ch. 10.

11. Unification Treaty art. 13; Protokoll zu art. 13.

12. The word *Abwicklung* had been employed in Nazi terminology, as a "Germanized" equivalent of the word "liquidation" in company law, and was also used by the Nazis in connection with the "aryanization" of property owned by Jews. Mechthild Küpper, Die Humboldt-Universität: Einheitsschmerzen zwischen Abwicklung und Selbstreform 24 (1993); cf. Wolf Lepenies, Folgen einer unerhörten Begebenheit 45 (1992). After the Nazi period, the word *Abwicklung* was used in the Basic Law to refer to the dissolution of former administrative units of the "Reich." See art. 130(1) GG.

13. Unification Treaty, attachment I, ch. XIX (A), para. III (1)(2)–(3). Indeed, after a certain period, unemployment payments would also cease, and the former employee would be relegated to "social assistance"—a considerably more stringent regime.

14. See, e.g., 84 BVerfGE 133, 139 (1991). See generally Hammer, "Warteschleife" statt Rationalisierungsschutz—die Tarifautonomie des öffentlichen Dienstes im Einigungsprozeß, in Monika Wulf-Mathies (ed.), "Warteschleife" und Einigungsvertrag 17–45 (1992).

15. See Däubler, Verfassungsrechtliche Einwände gegen die sog. "Warteschleife" (Dokumentation der im Auftrage vom DGB und ÖTV abgegebenen Stellungnahmen), in Wulf-Mathies at 49–101. See also 84 BVerfGE at 138–41.

16. 84 BVerfGE at 141–42.

17. Id. at 146–47.

18. Id. at 147.

19. Id. at 151–52.

20. Id. at 153–54.

21. Id. at 154–55.

22. Id. at 155–57. See art. 6(4) GG.

23. Däubler, Die sogennante Warteschleife auf dem verfassungsrechtlichen Prüfstand, 1991 NJ 233, 236.

24. See, e.g., Püttner, Der öffentliche Dienst im geeinten Deutschland, 1992 DVBl 204, 205.

25. Similar questions had arisen at the outset of the Federal Republic, with respect to members of the public service under the "Third Reich"—many of whom were denied jobs or pensions as a result of denazification proceedings or otherwise. In important early decisions, the Constitutional Court held that these civil servants had lost their tenure rights because the Nazi government transformed the public service into an organ serving the Nazi Party and its leader. This transformation was inconsistent with traditional ideas of neutral service to an abstract state, upon which the principles of life tenure depended. See 6 BVerfGE 132 (1957) (Gestapo case); 3 BVerfGE 58 (1953) (Civil Servant case); see generally Baade, Social Science Evidence and the Federal Constitutional Court of West Germany, 23 Journal of Politics 421 (1961). On the other hand, the government of the Federal Republic provided a measure of pension support or employment for most of these former public employees (see Baade, 23 Journal of Politics at 433–34; art. 131 GG); and a statute enacted in 1951, providing a preference in hiring for unemployed civil servants, led to the re-employment of many officials removed under denazification. See John D. Montgomery, Forced to Be Free: The Artificial Revolution in Germany and Japan 80–81 (1957).

26. Unification Treaty, attachment I, ch. XIX(A), para. III(3)(b). This probationary period could be reduced in some cases, but not to less than two years.

27. See Nicksch, 1990 DtZ at 343.

28. Unification Treaty, attachment I, ch. XIX(A), para. III (1)(4)(2).

29. Id. attachment I, ch. XIX(A), para. III(1)(5)(1).

30. Adopted by the UN General Assembly, these two documents contain guarantees of fair procedures and prohibitions against political discrimination and invasions of privacy—all of which might apply against actions of GDR administrators or judges. The GDR signed the 1966 Covenant in 1974, but its leaders maintained that the agreement was binding in international law only and had no internal effect. Mampel, Das Ende der sozialistischen Verfassung der DDR, 1990 DA 1377, 1379–80. See also Ch. 14.

This section of the Unification Treaty was based on provisions of earlier West German statutes that excluded compensation payments to refugees and former prisoners if they had violated the principles of humanity and the rule of law. See BAG, Judgment of Jan. 20, 1994, 1994 NJ 430, 431.

31. Korinth, Zur Konsolidierung des Arbeitsrechts im Beitrittsgebiet, 1993 NJ 532, 535. See also BAG, Judgment of Jan. 20, 1994, 1994 NJ 430.

32. Employment Court Berlin, Judgment of Oct. 22, 1991, 1992 NJ 133.

33. Unification Treaty, attachment I, ch. XIX(A), para. III(1)(5)(2). The requirement of "unreasonableness" is also applicable to exclusions for past violations of human rights.

34. See Stapelfeld, Zum aktuellen Stand der Rechtsprechung und zur Praxis des Sonderkündigungsrechtes im Einigungsvertrag wegen Tätigkeit für MfS/AfNS, 1995 DtZ 186, 187–88. Some statutes of the new eastern states, however, purport to go further and exclude all Stasi collaborators from the public service, without any determination of "unreasonableness." See Hillermeier, Stasi-Mitarbeiter im öffentlichen Dienst, 1995 LKV 141.

35. See 70 BAGE 309 (1992) (former mid-level Stasi officials dismissed from employment as telephone-system technicians in Post Office Department); 70 BAGE 323 (1992) (former Stasi colonel who was head of section in counterintelligence division dismissed from employment as guard in Berlin Museum). On the other hand, a former Stasi employee was permitted to retain his job as cook in a city-operated social hall. BAG, Judgment of Jan. 28, 1993, 1993 NJ 379.

36. For sharp criticism of this technique, see Schlink, Vergangenheit als Zumutung, in Rolf Grawert et al. (eds.), Offene Staatlichkeit: Festschrift für Ernst-Wolfgang Böckenförde zum 65. Geburtstag 341 (1995).

37. Fink generally supported student activists in seeking "self-renewal" of the Humboldt University instead of reform directed from the west. Some maintained that Fink was too lenient toward former supporters of the SED regime. On Fink, see generally Bernhard Maleck, Heinrich Fink: "Sich der Verantwortung stellen" (1992); Küpper at 49–63.

38. Tagesspiegel (Berlin), Dec. 17, 1992, at 1 col. 5.

39. For general discussions of the evidentiary use of the files, see FAZ, June 10, 1992, at 14 col. 2; Lansnicker & Schwirtzek, Der Beweiswert von Stasi-Unterlagen im Arbeitsgerichtsprozeß, 1994 DtZ 162; Kunze, Nochmals: Der Beweiswert von Stasi-Unterlagen im Arbeitsgerichtsprozeß, 1994 DtZ 399. See also Ch. 16.

40. Bundesbeamtengesetz, in the version of Feb. 27, 1985, BGBl I 479 (as amended) § 7; see also Beamtenrechtsrahmengesetz, in the version of Feb. 27, 1985, BGBl I 462 (as amended) § 35.

In 1972 during a period of alarm over "radical" political activity, Federal Chancellor Willy Brandt and the governors of the states issued a "Radicals Decree" which contemplated particularly strict enforcement of the loyalty requirement. See Hans Koschnick (ed.), Der Abschied vom Extremistenbeschluss 84 (1979). The Decree has been generally abandoned in recent years, but the underlying statutory principles of loyalty for the public service remain in effect in all German jurisdictions.

41. See 2 BVerfGE 1, 12–13 (1952).

42. The Constitutional Court has found that these statutory and administrative rules reflect a *constitutional* requirement of loyalty applicable to members of the public service. See art. 33(5) GG; 39 BVerfGE 334 (1975).

43. See Unification Treaty, attachment I, ch. XIX (A), para. III (1)(4)(1). In the case of judges, a resolution of the reformed GDR Volkskammer under de Maizière

specifically imposed a requirement of "loyalty to the free, democratic, federal, social and ecologically oriented state under the rule of law [*Rechtsstaat*]." This provision remained in effect under the Unification Treaty. See Beschluß der Volkskammer der DDR zum Richtergesetz—Ordnung über die Bildung und Arbeitsweise der Richterwahlausschüsse—of July 22, 1990, § 5(2), GBl DDR I 904; Unification Treaty, attachment I, ch. III(A), para. III(8)(o).

44. Although party membership is only one element in the ultimate judgment of loyalty (see 39 BVerfGE at 353–55, 359–60), activity as a member of the Communist Party was generally a central factor in cases of exclusion in the west.

45. Thus, West German Interior Minister Schäuble stated at the time of unification: "Even if most of the two million persons active in the public administration of the GDR have been members of the SED, they must have a fair chance to 'find themselves' again in the process of German unification. They too belong to a unified Germany, and we do not want to exclude a chance for a better future, even for them." Debate in German Bundestag, quoted in Nicksch, 1990 DtZ at 343. This view, however, was far from universal in the west. See, e.g., FAZ, Nov. 23, 1990, at 15 col. 1 (letter from West Berlin judge suggesting that East German judges—because of their education, almost universal SED membership, and required cooperation with the Stasi—most likely cannot "guarantee that they will at all times support the free democratic basic order in the meaning of the Basic Law").

46. Up to this point it does not appear that individuals are being excluded from the public service for active membership in the PDS, which asserts that it is a reformed and democratic party. Indeed, recent electoral successes, which may portend the party's movement further into the mainstream, make such a development even more unlikely.

Yet occasional arguments are heard from conservative governments of western Länder that the PDS should be classified as "inimical to the constitution" (*verfassungsfeindlich*)—a step that could give rise to strong inferences against the loyalty of PDS members applying for positions in the civil service. See FAZ, Dec. 15, 1990, at 5 col. 3; see also FAZ, Dec. 17, 1990, at 4 col. 4; FAZ, Mar. 15, 1991, at 2 col. 5. Moreover, the federal Interior Ministry has recently reported that it sees "unmistakable indications that the [PDS] does not accept the free democratic basic order . . . but rather seeks to overcome it." FAZ, July 7, 1995, at 1 col. 2.

47. See generally, e.g., BAG, Judgment of Mar. 18, 1993, 1994 DtZ 42. This approach generally followed earlier doctrine in the old Federal Republic, which required "active" membership in a constitutionally suspect political party—rather than membership alone—for exclusion from the public service.

48. LAG Chemnitz, Judgment of Dec. 9, 1992, 2 Sa 144/92. Copy on file with author.

49. According to the court, loyalty to the constitution was particularly important because of a teacher's position as a model for young people, who are greatly susceptible to influence. Moreover, a teacher who was closely identified with the SED state would be viewed with mistrust if she purported to reject those views today. Accordingly, she would fail in the teacher's obligation to gain the confidence of students.

For similar reasons, an individual who had joined the East German Army voluntarily and remained an officer for twenty-five years was dismissed from his position as a metalworking teacher in a vocational school. LAG Chemnitz, Judgment of Nov. 25, 1992, 1993 NJ 236. The soldier had been obliged to submit reports on other soldiers and on the contacts of eastern citizens with people from the west. He had also exercised significant functions in the SED. Altogether, this pattern indicated a special identification with the SED state.

On the other hand, a physics and mathematics teacher who had been a cadre advisor within a local government council was not dismissed. The post of advisor had not required submitting political judgments or any other acts characteristic of special identification with the SED state. LAG Chemnitz, Judgment of Oct. 28, 1992, 1993 NJ 236. Similarly, exercising the functions of "Goodwill Pioneer Leader," a type of teaching position with minor party duties, did not in itself justify exclusion from the public service. BAG, Judgment of Nov. 4, 1993, 1994 NJ 330.

50. BAG, Judgment of Oct. 13, 1994, 1995 NJ 161; BAG, Judgment of Apr. 28, 1994, 1994 NJ 483.

51. LAG Berlin, Judgment of July 23, 1992, 1993 NJ 42; affirmed, BAG, Judgment of May 27, 1993, 1993 NJ 525.

52. LAG Berlin, 1993 NJ at 44.

53. Tagesspiegel (Berlin), May 15, 1993, at 15 col. 1.

In some instances political criteria for exclusion have been very stringently applied. In Mecklenburg-Vorpommern, for example, the state culture minister accepted a commission's recommendation that Professor Horst Klinkmann, a world-renowned medical researcher, be removed from his academic post at the University of Rostock. Although Klinkmann's qualifications are universally recognized, he was dismissed on the grounds of his "mistaken behavior" under the SED regime: he belonged to a leading SED group in Rostock and he appeared before the Ninth Party Meeting of the SED in 1976 to deliver an address recommending more basic research in medicine. As a result of these and related activities, the reviewing commission found that he was part of the SED party apparatus. Klinkmann has challenged this decision. See FAZ, June 23, 1992, at 34 col. 3; Maier & Wenske, Personelle "Erneuerung" der Hochschulen in Mecklenburg-Vorpommern, in Hilde Schramm (ed.), Hochschule im Umbruch 32 (1993) (hereafter, Hochschule im Umbruch).

54. BVerfG, Judgment of Feb. 21, 1995, 1995 NJ 307.

55. Moreover public officials are covered by article 33(2) GG, granting equal access of citizens to the public service, and the Unification Treaty must be interpreted in light of these guarantees. 1995 NJ at 307–8.

56. 1995 NJ at 308.

57. Id. at 308–9.

58. See, e.g., FAZ, Sept. 10, 1991, at 4 col. 2.

59. The question of excluding functionaries of the old regime from significant positions in public life has also raised bitter debate in other countries of the former eastern bloc. In Czechoslovakia, for example, a sweeping "lustration" statute excluded individuals from many private and public offices and the judiciary, for a five-year period, if they had collaborated with the secret police, had held significant government office, or had been a member of certain groups connected with the old regime. No particular degree of involvement in a listed organization was necessary—apparently, bare membership would suffice—and the applicant had the burden of providing a certificate of non-membership in the listed groups. Many former opposition figures, including President Havel himself, criticized this statute. See generally, Cepl, Ritual Sacrifices, 1 East European Constitutional Review, Spring 1992, at 24; Laber, Witch Hunt in Prague, New York Review of Books, Apr. 23, 1992, at 5. In late 1992, the Czechoslovak Constitutional Court struck down the provision that covered persons

who had collaborated with the secret police. To a large extent, however, the program continued in effect in the new Czech and Slovak Republics. See Schwartz, Lustration in Eastern Europe, 1 Parker School Journal of East European Law 141 (1994).

In Poland, in contrast, an attempt at "lustration" led to the fall of a government when secret police files produced in parliament turned out to be ludicrously inaccurate. See Osiatynski, Agent Walesa?, 1 East European Constitutional Review, Summer 1992, at 28; Rzeplinski, A Lesser Evil?, 1 East European Constitutional Review, Fall 1992, at 33. Subsequent efforts to enact such a statute have not been successful.

Most recently, the Hungarian parliament enacted a lustration law in 1994. Under the statute, three-judge commissions will examine the records of members of parliament, certain other holders of public office (including prosecutors and judges), and officials of the media, to determine if they were members of the Hungarian Nazi Party, participants in certain paramilitary units, or collaborators with the secret police. If such a finding is made, the official may voluntarily leave office and the commission's report will remain secret for thirty years. Otherwise, the report may be published—apparently the only sanction under the statute. See Constitution Watch—Hungary, 3 East European Constitutional Review, Spring 1994, at 10.

60. See, e.g., Friedrich Schorlemmer, Versöhnung in der Wahrheit 133 (1992).

61. For an overview, see Kadritzke, Wissenschaft und Hochschulreform in der alten Bundesrepublik, in Hochschule im Umbruch at 51–59.

62. 35 BVerfGE 79.

63. See, e.g., Kadritzke in Hochschule im Umbruch at 56–59.

64. See generally Claussen, Reflektionen eines "Lufthansa"—oder "Spagat"—Professors, in Bernhard Muszynski (ed.), Wissenschaftstransfer in Deutschland: Erfahrungen und Perspektiven 95 (1993) (hereafter, Wissenschaftstransfer). Teaching duties were performed by western professors principally in those eastern academic departments that were dissoved in 1990, as described below.

65. These problems were faced by the state governments because education generally falls within their authority under the Basic Law—although each state's regulations must remain within the outlines of a federal "framework" law. See art. 75(1a) GG.

66. Yet even in these cases, there were attempts to convert departments of Marxism-Leninism into departments of political science, with the hope that they would somehow survive. See KreisG Gera-Stadt, Judgment of May 23, 1991, 1991 LKV 274.

Certain other GDR university departments, which were unknown in the west and seemed influenced by Marxist-Leninist thought, were also permanently dissolved. See, e.g., Geyer & Koop, Berufsverbleib Leipziger Kulturwissenschaftler, hochschule ost, 6/1993, at 28 (*Diplomstudiengang Kulturwissenschaft*).

67. See, e.g., Pasternack, Gründer-Zeit in Leipzig: Miszellen, in Wissenschaftstransfer at 273. Although some former professors might be re-employed permanently—they could apply along with all other candidates—chances for most would not be bright.

68. See, e.g., FAZ, Dec. 27, 1990, at 8 col. 2 (Berlin). These steps were taken precipitately in order to meet a deadline of January 2, 1991, prescribed by the Unification Treaty. In general, however, the eastern state of Mecklenburg-Vorpommern did not engage in this form of "Abwicklung."

69. The state of Berlin, for example, defended this step in the following manner: "[L]egal scholarship that was oriented to the principle of socialist legality must change completely under the conditions of the democratic rule of law. [Law professors] who taught the judges and prosecutors of the former GDR, and who were bound by Marxist-

Leninist legal theory, are not in a position to teach [the typical courses] of the Federal Republic. In the department of economics, [instruction] was exclusively oriented toward Marxist-Leninist political economy. . . . Similarly, the one-sided perspective of Marxist-Leninist history must be fundamentally corrected. Here, too, personnel must be replaced from the ground up. Finally . . . an educational theory that was oriented on the model of the socialist personality is not an appropriate basis for the future training of teachers." VG Berlin, Judgment of Feb. 20, 1991, 1991 LKV 173, 175–76 (court's summary of decision of Berlin government).

70. Krull, Neue Strukturen für Wissenschaft und Forschung, APuZ, Dec. 11, 1992, at 15, 22. On the Science Council, see generally id. at 18; see also id. at 24.

71. See, e.g., Nolte, Staats- und Europarecht in Leipzig, in Wissenschaftstransfer at 241–43.

72. See FAZ, Jan. 3, 1991, at 2 col. 2; Middell, Ostdeutsche Hochschulen zwischen Abwicklung und Integration in die gesamtdeutsche Wissenschaftslandschaft—Einige Erfahrungen und Vermutungen eines Leipziger Historikers, in Wissenschaftstransfer at 15–16; Wilsdorf & Mühler, Die Ab- und Aufwicklung des Bereichs Soziologie an der Leipziger Universität, in id. at 292–93. For contemporary academic criticism of this technique of dissolution, see Konzen, Die "Abwicklung" und der Rechtsstaat, FAZ, Feb. 12, 1991, at 10 col. 1; Battis, Correspondence, FAZ, Dec. 27, 1990, at 6 col. 2; for a contrary view, see Meier, Lieber abwickeln, FAZ, Dec. 21, 1990, at 33 col. 1.

73. Similar legal challenges were filed in Erfurt and elsewhere, but the litigation in Berlin was by far the most important. Cf. Pasternack in Wissenschaftstransfer at 273 & n. 5; FAZ, Aug. 17, 1991, at 4 col. 4 (faculty of education in Erfurt-Mühlhausen).

74. OVG Berlin, Judgment of June 6, 1991, 1991 LKV 269, reversing, in part, VG Berlin, Judgment of Feb. 20, 1991, 1991 LKV 173.

75. OVG Berlin, 1991 LKV at 272; see 84 BVerfGE 133, 150–51 (1991).

76. Yet even after this legal victory, the eastern members of the Humboldt faculty were relegated to second-class status, as legislation in Berlin excluded them from rights of faculty self-governance usually guaranteed under West German law. Berlin officials maintained that these rights could only be exercised by professors who had been appointed to faculty status under western procedures. See FAZ, July 18, 1991, at 4 col. 2; Inga Markovits, Imperfect Justice: An East-West German Diary 195–98 (1995). Some Humboldt professors filed a complaint in the Constitutional Court against this subordinate status, arguing that the constitutional freedom of scholarship (art. 5[3] GG) guarantees the right of *all* university professors to participate in faculty governance. The complaint, however, was dismissed on procedural grounds. Indeed, relevant legislation of other new eastern states also relegated remaining eastern professors to second-class status, on an interim basis.

77. Kiel, "Personelle Erneuerung" an ostdeutschen Hochschulen. Versuch einer ganzheitlichen Betrachtung, hochschule ost, 1/1994, at 63–64.

78. See generally FAZ, Apr. 4, 1992, at 43 col. 2. Cf. Nolte in Wissenschaftstransfer at 247. The administrative styles of the western "founding deans" differed widely. One notorious example was a "colonial officer" who declared to an eminent eastern professor "You are a nothing"; but another—quite different—type of dean possessed an "internalized democratic understanding of his office." See Pasternack in Wissenschaftstransfer at 274–79. See also Nolte in id. at 245–47.

79. Schluchter, Die Hochschulen in Ostdeutschland vor und nach der Einigung, APuZ, June 24, 1994, at 12, 20–21. Final statistics for this process, however, are not yet available. Id at 21.

80. Id.

81. See generally Hüfner, Start in eine ungewisse Zukunft, FAZ, Nov. 19, 1992, at 12 col. 1.

82. In Mecklenburg-Vorpommern, decisions on scholarly competence were made by sixteen separate Transition Commissions (Überleitungskommissionen), each composed of three professors—generally from the west—together with a student and a mid-level university researcher. These commissions largely relied on evaluations of the candidates' work written by western professors. The political past of the faculty members was reviewed by Disciplinary Commissions (*Ehrenkommissionen*), whose members were chosen by the universities and the state parliament. The decisions of these commissions were not final but were presented as recommendations to the state minister of culture. Finally, a third set of commissions passed upon the ultimate issue of "need"—deciding which of the professors who had passed the first two inquiries would actually fit into the new (and generally greatly reduced) personnel plan of the universities. See Maier & Wenske in Hochschule im Umbruch at 31–35.

For the structure of commissions reviewing candidates in other states, see Schramm, Hochschulgesetzgebung in den neuen Bundesländern und Ost-Berlin, in Hochschule im Umbruch at 97–98 (Thuringia); Kehler, Hochschulerneuerungsgesetz von Sachsen-Anhalt, in Hochschule im Umbruch at 115–18 (Saxony-Anhalt); Borchardt & Sändig, Hochschulgesetz in Brandenburg, in Hochschule im Umbruch at 106–8 (Brandenburg); Interview with Hans Joachim Meyer, hochschule ost, 6/1993, at 50–58 (Saxony).

83. See FAZ, June 4, 1993, at 14 col. 2.

84. See Küpper at 81–87; for a personal memoir of the process at the Humboldt University, see Markovits, Imperfect Justice, at 110–13, 128–38, 192–93.

85. Hüfner, FAZ, Nov. 19, 1992, at 12 col. 1.

86. See generally Krull, APuZ, Dec. 11, 1992, at 25; Gläser, Die Akademie der Wissenschaften nach der Wende: erst reformiert, dann ignoriert und schließlich aufgelöst, APuZ, Dec. 11, 1992, at 37–38.

87. See Unification Treaty, attachment I, ch. XIX(A), para. III (1)(4)(2). It should be noted that the question of "need" was ordinarily not a question of how many positions in a particular area would be useful for students or for scholarship, but rather the question of how many positions in the area could be supported with available financing. See Interview with Hans Joachim Meyer, hochschule ost, 6/1993, at 57.

88. The same system applied to middle-level researchers and assistants in the university. At the Humboldt University, for example, approximately 2,000 former mid-level university personnel had to compete for approximately 1,250 positions. See Jahnke & Otto, Stellen- und Personalabbau an den Hochschulen 1989 bis 1993—Zwischenbilanz 1992, in Hochschule im Umbruch at 417.

89. In Mecklenburg-Vorpommern, for example, all faculty members who had passed the review for "personal suitability" and scholarly competence were insulated from outside competition in applying for available positions. In Saxony, in contrast, many candidates who had satisfied the first two inquiries were then required to compete for positions with applicants from the Federal Republic and abroad—although others were directly appointed without outside competition in a special "shortened procedure." Even in Mecklenburg-Vorpommern, however, there were no qualified internal candidates for approximately 30 percent of the positions, and these were then opened to outside candidates. See Hüfner, FAZ, Nov. 19, 1992, at 12 col. 1.

90. Schluchter, APuZ, June 24, 1994, at 21.

91. See, e.g., FAZ, June 4, 1993, at 14 col. 2 (Humboldt University will retain two "former leading ideologues and high party functionaries" as professors in the social sciences department until 1997); see also FAZ, May 15, 1993, at 12 col. 2; FAZ, Apr. 14, 1993, at 14 col. 2; Schluchter, APuZ, June 24, 1994, at 21 n. 41.

92. A particularly striking example was that of Karl Larenz who, in many contributions to the legal doctrine of the Nazi regime, recast civil law principles to justify diminished rights for persons not of "German blood." See Bernd Rüthers, Das Ungerechte an der Gerechtigkeit: Defizite eines Begriffs 88–106 (1993). Yet in the Federal Republic, Larenz was accepted as a leading figure—perhaps the leading figure—in the interpretation of the German Civil Code.

Similar careers were also plentiful in public law. Theodor Maunz and Ernst Forsthoff, for example, were central apologists for the Nazi state, but they enjoyed eminent careers in the universities of the Federal Republic, wrote influential treatises on the Basic Law, and left their mark on generations of postwar students. Indeed, Maunz was forced to resign political office when "his past caught up with him," but even then his academic career was not threatened. See Reimann, National Socialist Jurisprudence and Academic Continuity: A Comment on Professor Kaufmann's Article, 9 Cardozo Law Review 1651, 1653 (1988); see also Kaufmann, National Socialism and German Jurisprudence from 1933 to 1945, 9 Cardozo Law Review 1629 (1988). Indeed, for a period of twenty-five years before his death in 1993, Maunz apparently contributed hundreds of unsigned articles to a right-wing extremist newspaper in Germany. See Stolleis, Eckstein des Anstoßes, FAZ, Dec. 21, 1993, at 27 col. 1.

93. Ingo Müller, Hitler's Justice: The Courts of the Third Reich 237 (1991).

94. Reimann, 9 Cardozo Law Review at 1654.

95. Schluchter, Der Um- und Neubau der Hochschulen in Ostdeutschland. Ein Erfahrungsbericht am Beispiel der Universität Leipzig, hochschule ost, 8/1993, at 29, 33. See 85 BVerfGE 360, 363 (1992): "[The Academy's] areas of research were mathematics and information science, physics, chemistry, biological sciences, medicine, geology, and astronomy as well as social sciences. The Academy consisted of 50 to 60 institutes, as well as service facilities, workshops, construction units, printshops, and publishing companies. It was equipped with observatories, freshwater research stations, a research station on the Antarctic continent, and two research ships." See also Mayntz, Die außeruniversitäre Forschung im Prozeß der deutschen Einigung, 20 Leviathan 64, 65 (1992).

96. For the institutional background of the decision to dissolve the Academy—in which West German officials sought to preserve the existing western system by extending it to the east—see Mayntz, 20 Leviathan 64; see also Mitchell Ash, Higher Education and Science Policy in and for the New German States (Paper presented at the American Institute for Contemporary German Studies, Feb. 25, 1992) at 5–6 (hereafter, Ash [1992]) (copy on file with author). For another interesting sketch of this history, focusing on democratization and reform in the Academy of Sciences in 1989–90, see Gläser, APuZ, Dec. 11, 1992, at 37–46. See also Macrakis, *Wissenschaft* and Political Unification in the New Germany, in Kurt-Jürgen Maass (ed.), From Two to One: U.S. Scholars Witness the First Year of German Unification 72 (1992) (hereafter, From Two to One).

97. Mayntz, 20 Leviathan at 73; Simon, Die Quintessenz, APuZ, Dec. 11, 1992, at 29.

98. Unification Treaty art. 38 (2). The Academy's function as "Gelehrtensozietät"—an honorary society of eminent scholars—was also to be separated from

the active research institutes and its future was to be decided under state law. Eventually, this function was assumed by a newly founded Berlin-Brandenburg Academy of Sciences, composed of approximately two hundred members, which sponsors a small number of important scholarly projects. See FAZ, June 26, 1992, at 8 col. 3.

99. Unification Treaty art. 38(1). Certain other research institutions of the GDR, such as the Agricultural Academy and the Construction Academy (*Bauakademie*), were to be reviewed by the Science Council in a similar manner. Id. art. 38(4).

100. Cf. id. art. 38(3).

101. FAZ, Sept. 17, 1991, at 7 col. 1.

102. See Macrakis in From Two to One at 78–79.

103. 85 BVerfGE 360 (1992).

104. Id. at 372–75. The Court also noted that "[r]esponsibility for and financing of the research assignments must be embedded in existing [western] structures." Id.

105. Id. at 376.

106. Id. at 379–82; see 84 BVerfGE 133 (1991). As in the *Warteschleife* decision, the Court did find the regulation unconstitutional to the extent that it failed to provide special consideration for pregnant women and mothers of infants. 85 BVerfGE at 372. The regulation was also unconstitutional in providing less than one month's notice of termination of employment. Id. at 378–79.

107. In a later decision, the Court also upheld the dissolution of two other research institutions of the GDR—the Construction Academy and the Agricultural Academy. 86 BVerfGE 81 (1992). The fact that the Construction Academy had been in the process of implementing its own internal review of personnel did not indicate that it should receive more lenient treatment than the Academy of Sciences. Id. at 87–88. Indeed, at the time of the Unification Treaty many of the institutions of the GDR were undertaking or planning internal measures of self-reform, but most of these measures were swept away by the provisions of the treaty.

108. Neuweiler, Das gesamtdeutsche Haus für Forschung und Lehre, APuZ, June 24, 1994, at 7. See also, e.g., Globig, MPG gründet Institut für Wissenschaftsgeschichte, hochschule ost, 8/1993, at 57. More recently, the Max Planck Society announced plans for a total of fifteen to twenty institutes to be founded in eastern Germany by the end of the decade. FAZ, Dec. 6, 1994, at 4 col. 6.

109. FAZ, Dec. 9, 1992, at N3 col. 1. Another successful new institute is the Environment Center in Halle and Leipzig. Neuweiler, APuZ, June 24, 1994, at 9.

110. See Schluchter, APuZ, June 24, 1994, at 15.

111. See, e.g., Simon, Verschleudert und verschludert, Die Zeit (overseas ed.), Apr. 14, 1995, at 17 col. 2.

To ease the way of former members of the Academy of Sciences into further academic employment, the WIP program finances continued work of scholars favorably evaluated by the Science Council. For example, a younger scholar from the Academy might receive a WIP position as a professor's assistant at an eastern university, while seeking to write the "habilitation" necessary for qualification as a university professor.

In addition, a number of small institutes—so-called *Forschungsschwerpunkte*—have been founded to employ eastern researchers in areas such as linguistics and literary research. In at least one case, however, an institute has fallen prey to what might seem to be an inherent structural problem: in the summer of 1993, a "Forschungsschwerpunkt" for research on contemporary history, located in Potsdam, was bitterly accused of giving academic shelter to those who had cooperated too much with the GDR regime, and thus also perhaps distorting the writing of that history. The main attackers were other eastern historians who were less favored during the period of the GDR and who feared that their disfavored status was being perpetuated after unification. For representative contributions to this debate, see Mitter & Wolle, Inquisitoren auf der Faultierfarm, FAZ, Sept. 9, 1993, at 37 col. 1; Kocka, Auch Wissenschaftler können lernen, FAZ, Aug. 25, 1993, at 31 col. 3.

112. Zimmer, Einstürzende Mittelbauten, Die Zeit, Nov. 27, 1992, at 41.

113. Id.

114. See Neuweiler, APuZ, June 24, 1994, at 3.

115. Cf. Schluchter, hochschule ost, 8/1993, at 29.

116. Cf., e.g., Middell in Wissenschaftstransfer at 20–21. And see Roggemann, Die Justiz auf dem Prüfstand der Justiz, in Im Namen des Volkes? Über die Justiz im Staat der SED (Wissenschaftlicher Begleitband zur Ausstellung des Bundesministeriums der Justiz) 297 n. 20 (1994) (hereafter, Im Namen des Volkes): Western academic administrators "must ask themselves why pluralistic democracy in Germany—always cited in this context—could not take the academic risk of allowing a series of capable and politically not clearly intolerable [scholars] from the socialist past to take part in the new all-German contests in teaching and university discourse."

117. Schluchter, APuZ, June 24, 1994, at 21; Schluchter, hochschule ost, 8/1993, at 34.

118. Krull, APuZ, Dec. 11., 1992, at 16.

119. Simon, APuZ, Dec. 11, 1992, at 34–36.

120. FAZ, June 26, 1992, at 14 col. 2; hochschule ost, 8/1993, at 64–66. Establishment of the Viadrina by the state of Brandenburg is consistent with the state's constitutional obligation to further friendship with Germany's neighbors, particularly Poland. Verf. Br. art. 2(1). See Ch. 9.

121. Neuweiler, APuZ, June 24, 1994, at 5–7.

122. Cf. id. at 6; but see Schluchter, APuZ, June 24, 1994, at 17.

123. See Zimmer, Die Zeit, Nov. 27, 1992, at 41; see also Schmidt & Werner, (K)eine Chance für den Mittelbau, in Hochschule im Umbruch at 418. Yet, instead of extending this idea to the west, the effect of unification has been largely to destroy this permanent corps of mid-level academics in the east—by greatly reducing its numbers and by filling its ranks with temporary personnel in accordance with the West German model. See Zimmer, Die Zeit, Nov. 27, 1992, at 41.

124. Macrakis in From Two to One at 72.

125. Cf. Ash (1992) at 5. See also Lepenies at 40: "The question . . . of whether there was anything at all worth keeping in GDR scholarship was answered in the west with a swift and relieved 'No'—and only later corrected to a hesitant 'Maybe.'"

126. By 1993, it was estimated that only one-third of the persons who had been active in GDR research in 1989 retained a research position; in the humanities and social sciences, the figure was as low as one out of four. Kocka, Auch Wissenschaftler können lernen, FAZ, Aug. 25, 1993, at 31 col. 3.

127. German unification also meant a fundamental transformation of the public school system in the east, with its own profound psychological impact. A uniform eastern school system, supervised by Margot Honecker and designed to create a "socialist personality" (see Verf. DDR [1974] art. 25), was replaced by a two- or three-track system characteristic of western Germany. The close relationship between the schools and the SED youth groups was naturally abolished, and the notorious courses in Marxist indoctrination ("citizenship study" or *Staatsbürgerkunde*) were replaced by offerings more consonant with the "free democratic basic order."

Perhaps more than most other professional groups, public school teachers were deeply embedded in the structure of the SED state, and a large number—thousands, for example, in Saxony—were dismissed after unification. Yet thousands of GDR teachers remain, the vast majority of whom had in various ways actively supported the former system in their messages in the classroom. In essence from one day to the next these teachers totally reversed what they were teaching—an effect that may well have a profound influence on this generation of students in eastern Germany. See, e.g., Rudolph, Vielfalt statt Einheitlichkeit. Zur Umgestaltung des Bildungssystems in den östlichen Bundesländern, in Gert-Joachim Glaeßner (ed.), Der lange Weg zur Einheit 275–92 (1993); Küpper at 38.

128. Jentsch, Der Aufbau des Rechtswesens in Thüringen, 1993 NJW 2513. See also Rainer Faupel, Der Neuaufbau der Justiz in Brandenburg 5 (1992), remarking on the "depth of the rift that had to be done away with in minds, economy, work-life and, finally, also in the justice system—and which could not be diminished by false optimism." The first five hundred days after unification were only long enough to "lay the foundation" for overcoming that rift. Id.

129. See, for example, the remarks of a former Stasi interrogator in political cases: "The judge had no other choice. . . . I don't think that any investigation that came to the point of a prosecution could have failed in court. It was all well arranged so that no failure could occur. . . . If [the judge] had done anything wrong, that would have been her last trial. At least in this kind of case. From then on she would have heard cases of rabbit theft. . . . Indeed, it was a concert: the court was just the one who performed it." Gilbert Furian, Der Richter und sein Lenker: Politische Justiz in der DDR 146–48 (1992). This view was echoed by a former judge of the GDR's highest court: "The judges who acted in political cases . . . were transmitters of the will of the Stasi." Id. at 22. See also Grasemann, Die justitielle Aufarbeitung des Stasi-Erbes: Grenzen und Probleme, in Klaus-Dietmar Henke (ed.), Wann bricht schon mal ein Staat zusammen! Die Debatte über die Stasi-Akten auf dem 39. Historikertag 1992, at 66–67 (1993) (hereafter, Wann bricht).

130. Cf. Faupel at 23.

131. See Roggemann, Richterwahl und Rechtspflege in den Ländern der früheren DDR, 1991 NJW 456, 461, 463. For a famous literary treatment of this general problem, see Rolf Hochhuth, Juristen (1979).

132. Majer, Die Überprüfung von Richtern und Staatsanwälten in der ehemaligen DDR, 1991 ZRP 171.

133. Unification Treaty, attachment I, ch. III (A), para. III (8)(o); see Majer, 1991 ZRP at 173–75. The screening committees were originally authorized by GDR legislation of the de Maizière period, which required that judges be reviewed for their integrity, capability, and "loyalty to the free, democratic, federal, social, and ecologically oriented state under the rule of law." Richtergesetz (der DDR), of July 5, 1990, GBl DDR I 637; Beschluß der Volkskammer der Deutschen Demokratischen Republik zum Richtergesetz—Ordnung über die Bildung und Arbeitsweise der Richterwahlausschüsse, of July 22, 1990, GBl DDR I 904 § 5 (2).

134. Majer, 1991 ZRP at 175. The western advisor also ordinarily served as chair of the screening committee. Id. at 177.

135. GBl DDR 1990 I 637 § 12(1). After unification and the creation of the new Länder, members of the state parliaments (or local legislative bodies) were substituted for the Volkskammer representatives on the committees. Unification Treaty, attach-

ment I, ch. III(A), para. III (8)(o). Screening of the judges in Berlin was undertaken by the state's existing judicial screening committee.

136. See FAZ, Feb. 18, 1991, at 5 col. 4; FAZ, Feb. 9, 1991, at 4 col. 3.

137. FAZ, June 6, 1991, at 4 col. 5. A complaint has been filed in the Constitutional Court seeking a judgment that the use of this procedure, which deviates from the Unification Treaty, violates federal law. On this issue, see generally Fastenrath, Die Bindungswirkung des Einigungsvertrages am Beispiel der Richterüberprüfung in Mecklenburg-Vorpommern, 1991 DtZ 429.

138. Limbach, Der Aufbau des Rechtswesens in den östlichen Bezirken Berlins, 1993 NJW 2499, 2500.

139. Cf. Roggemann, 1991 NJW at 461.

140. Cf. Limbach, 1993 NJW at 2500.

141. Those political offenses had generally been tried by separate senates or panels of the GDR courts. See, e.g., Roggemann, 1991 NJW at 464.

142. See generally Limbach, 1993 NJW at 2500; Bräutigam, Der Aufbau des Rechtswesens in Brandenburg, 1993 NJW 2501, 2502–3; Heitmann, Der Aufbau des Rechtswesens in Sachsen, 1993 NJW 2507, 2508; Remmers, Der Aufbau des Rechtswesens in Sachsen-Anhalt, 1993 NJW 2511, 2512; Jentsch, 1993 NJW at 2514.

143. See, e.g., Faupel at 23: "Of decisive importance was the time-consuming evaluation of thousands of decisions, from the courts' collection of judgments, which gave the most comprehensive overview of [the candidates'] earlier activity."

144. See Heiner Sauer & Hans-Otto Plumeyer, Der Salzgitter Report (1991).

145. Verordnung zur Arbeit mit Personalunterlagen, of Feb. 22, 1990, GBl DDR I 84; see Markovits, Imperfect Justice, at 141–42; FAZ, Feb. 9, 1991, at 4 col. 3; FAZ, Nov. 8, 1990, at 14 col. 2; cf. Wann bricht at 110 (remarks of Isolde Stark).

146. See Unification Treaty, attachment I, ch. III(A), para. III (8)(o); FAZ, Nov. 8, 1990, at 14 col. 2; FR, Oct. 29, 1990, at 4 col. 1; FR, Oct. 12, 1990, at 8 col. 1. In at least some of the new Länder, however, the presiding judges of the GDR courts were informally forced from office in early 1990 and replaced by judges from the west.

147. See Unification Treaty, attachment I, ch. III(A), para. IV; Roggemann, 1991 NJW at 459; Limbach, 1993 NJW 2499; Majer, 1991 ZRP at 176. For a vivid description of the anxiety and anger that this decision caused among the East Berlin judges, see Markovits, Imperfect Justice, at 4–6.

148. The figures are: Brandenburg, 55 percent; Saxony, 63 percent; Saxony-Anhalt, 41 percent; Thuringia, 56 percent. See Roggemann in Im Namen des Volkes at 297 n. 21.

149. Id.

150. Interview with Detlef Borrmann, Undersecretary, Berlin Justice Administration, Berlin, Apr. 8, 1993.

151. See, e.g., Remmers, 1993 NJW at 2513 (Saxony-Anhalt); Jentsch, 1993 NJW at 2515 (Thuringia).

152. Interview with a former eastern judge. See also Interview with Malte Kupas, Brandenburg Ministry of Justice, June 28, 1993.

153. Markovits, Imperfect Justice, at 159–65; see also Interview with Malte Kupas, June 28, 1993. Cf. Fromme, Der öffentlichen Hand unbequem, FAZ, May 27, 1995 (Bilder und Zeiten) at 2 col. 1.

154. Cf. Jentsch, 1993 NJW at 2515.

155. When the Brandenburg justice minister took office in November 1990, for

example, he found eight employees—five of them lawyers. By April 1992, the number had grown to 151. See Faupel at 13–15.

156. There were some exceptions. For example, the influential justice minister of Saxony, Steffen Heitmann, was a native of eastern Germany.

157. See, e.g., Kramer, Der mühsame Übergang zum Rechtsstaat, 1994 NJ 19.

It was also necessary to reorganize the prison system in the east and review its personnel for Stasi connections and past violations of human rights. Moreover, the "catastrophic condition" of the land records offices, "which had been neglected for forty years," had to be put in order if outside investment, which would require stable property relations, was to be encouraged in the east. Jentsch, 1993 NJW at 2515; see also Faupel at 61 (remarking on the "desolate" condition of land records offices).

158. Before the east German revolution, the GDR had approximately 600 lawyers—in contrast with approximately 15,000 practicing lawyers in North Rhine-Westphalia, a West German state with a population of comparable size. Faupel at 35.

159. Unification Treaty, attachment I, ch. III (A), para. II(2). Moreover, GDR legislation of 1990 opened the practice of law to individual practitioners and reformed the profession to conform with West German patterns. Verordnung über die Tätigkeit und die Zulassung von Rechtsanwälten mit eigener Praxis, of Feb. 22, 1990, GBl DDR I 147; Rechtsanwaltsgesetz, of Sept. 13, 1990, GBl DDR I 1504.

160. Interview with Detlef Borrmann, Apr. 8, 1993; see also Schaich, Zum Gesetz zur Prüfung von Rechtsanwaltszulassungen, Notarbestellungen und Berufungen ehrenamtlicher Richter, 1992 DtZ 321.

161. See Kleine-Cosack, "Selbstreinigung" der Anwaltschaft?, 1991 NJ 331; Interview with Detlef Borrmann, Apr. 8, 1993. Federal Justice Minister Klaus Kinkel also declared that the bar should not become the refuge of "former Stasi officers, and pitiless judges and prosecutors." See Faupel at 39–40.

162. Gesetz zur Prüfung von Rechtsanwaltszulassungen, Notarbestellungen und Berufungen ehrenamtlicher Richter, of July 24, 1992, BGBl I 1386 (hereafter, Lawyers' Review Statute). Even before the statute was enacted, the justice minister of Saxony-Anhalt—in a highly controversial move—had requested lawyers to sign a declaration denying past collaboration with the Stasi. Kleine-Cosack, 1991 NJ at 331. A number of justice authorities also had caused "significant uneasiness" by requesting eastern lawyers to complete questionnaires about their pasts. Stellungnahme des Deutschen Anwaltvereins zur Überprüfung von Rechtsanwälten in den neuen Bundesländern, 1992 DtZ 79, 80.

163. Lawyers' Review Statute § 1. The Justice Ministry's original draft required that, for exclusion, a lawyer must have violated the principles of humanity or the rule of law "in a significant manner." Although this phrase was eliminated in the final version, the limitation may nonetheless remain understood. Busse, Die Anwaltschaft im geeinten Deutschland, 1993 NJW 2009, 2011 & n. 37.

164. Cf. Kleine-Cosack, Anwaltliche Berufsverbote auf dem Prüfstand, 1994 NJ 246, 247.

165. Schaich, 1992 DtZ at 322; Kleine-Cosack, 1991 NJ at 334.

166. Schaich, 1992 DtZ at 322; Kleine-Cosack, 1991 NJ at 334. Thus in recent decisions the Federal Supreme Court (BGH) has particularly condemned those Stasi contacts that involved the disclosure of confidential information in a manner that converted the lawyer into a "henchman" of the government. BGH, Judgment of Feb. 21, 1994, 1994 NJ 283, 284. See also BGH, Judgment of July 11, 1994, 1994 NJ 598, 599.

The evaluation of contacts with the Stasi is likely to remain an important factor in the future of the east German bar. The justice minister of Thuringia estimates that at least 10 percent of all GDR lawyers and bar applicants had collaborated with the Stasi. See Jentsch, 1993 NJW at 2515.

167. 63 BVerfGE 266.

168. Cf. Kleine-Cosack, 1991 NJ at 331–32; Faupel at 42.

169. Some also argued that the 1992 statute violates the Unification Treaty because the treaty's framers intentionally omitted post-unification review of lawyers already admitted to the bar. Kleine-Cosack, 1994 NJ at 246–47. But this argument has been rejected by the Federal Supreme Court on the ground that the Unification Treaty, as a form of federal law, can be altered by a subsequent statute. BGH, Judgment of Feb. 21, 1994, 1994 NJ 283.

170. Busse, 1993 NJW at 2012 & n. 42. Up to July 1994, for example, only three lawyers in Berlin had been expelled from the bar under the 1992 statute. FAZ, July 16, 1994, at 4 col. 2.

171. BGH, Judgment of Feb. 21, 1994, 1994 NJ 283, 284.

172. BGH, Judgment of July 11, 1994, 1994 NJ 598; FAZ, July 16, 1994, at 4 col. 2. The facts of the Schnur case were particularly egregious: "Everything that his clients revealed to him in confidence was reported to the Stasi, comprehensively and in minute detail. On some days he dictated more than ten such reports. [These reports and those of his Stasi contact officer] filled 21 volumes with 5,937 pages. . . . In August 1987, a client . . . trusted [him] with two letters, to be sent to the UN and Amnesty International in case of [the client's] arrest. He promised to hold the letters for safekeeping, but instead he included them as attachments in his report to the [Stasi]. . . . If he resumed his activity as a lawyer, it would rightly be met with incomprehension among the populace and create the impression that the public's justified interest in legal counseling by reliable lawyers was not being taken seriously." 1994 NJ at 598–99. See also Klier, Aktion "Störenfried," in Hans Joachim Schädlich (ed.), Aktenkundig 91 (1992). As a result of his Stasi activity, Schnur has been charged with the crime of "political denunciation" (*politische Verdächtigung*). See, e.g., FAZ, Feb. 21, 1996, at 4 col. 5.

In a number of subsequent cases the BGH has also upheld expulsions from the bar on grounds of a lawyer's previous Stasi activity. See BGH, Judgment of Oct. 24, 1994, 1995 NJ 276; BGH, Judgment of Nov. 21, 1994, 1995 NJ 330; BGH, Judgment of Jan. 9, 1995, 1995 NJ 388 (notary); but see BGH, Judgment of July 11, 1994, 1995 NJ 108. In a decision announced in late December 1995, however, the Constitutional Court declared that the BGH was following an unduly rigid practice of bar expulsion in cases of this kind and indicated that it would approve expulsion only where there had been significant injury or potential injury to third persons. See FAZ, Dec. 29, 1995, at 1 col. 2.

173. EGH Berlin, Judgment of Sept. 7, 1992, 1993 DtZ 318. In one typical case, the prosecutor had obtained a sentence of one and a half years' imprisonment against a person who had carried a placard reading "Please let me out at last, Mr. Honecker!"

174. Id. at 319.

175. Employing a similar technique, the court in a later case declined to exclude a judge (and court director) from the practice of law because her oppressive decisions were few and far in the past. EGH Berlin, Judgment of Dec. 2, 1992, 1993 NJ 238. Although she was a member of the SED (as were all court directors), she "had not persistently suppressed the free rights of citizens or fought against the democratic basic order in an unconstitutional manner."

176. SächsBerGH, Judgment of Sept. 30, 1992, 1993 NJ 237.

177. Id. at 238. This judgment was later affirmed by the Federal Supreme Court which indicated, however, that by 1995 enough time might have elapsed to permit a different result. BGH, Judgment of March 14, 1994, 1994 NJ 284. Cf. also BGH, Judgment of Oct. 24, 1994, 1995 NJ 165; BGH, Judgment of June 19, 1995, 1996 NJ 52.

178. BGH, Judgment of Nov. 21, 1994, 1995 NJ 332.

179. Id. at 332–33. Cf. also BGH, Judgment of Jan. 20, 1995, 1995 NJ 390.

180. See, e.g., Kuczynski, Kahlschlagsanierung, hochschule ost, 6/1993, at 41–42; Schwartz, 1 Parker School Journal of East European Law at 148.

181. Cf. Harold James, A German Identity 145, 151–52 (1994).

## Chapter 14
## Undoing the Past: Prosecution of GDR Leaders and Officials

1. See Ch. 2.

2. Indeed, in confronting its Communist past, "no country has concentrated so much on the criminal law as has Germany." Schlink, Rechtsstaat und revolutionäre Gerechtigkeit, 1994 NJ 433.

Most important prosecutions of GDR officials were concentrated in Berlin because the centralized government of the GDR was located there. But Berlin alone could not sustain the burden of prosecuting these cases, and therefore other German states contributed personnel to a special "Working Group on (GDR) Governmental Criminality," established in Berlin. See Weber, Praktische Probleme der strafrechtlichen Verfolgung staatlichen Unrechts in der ehemaligen DDR, in Ernst-Joachim Lampe (ed.), II Deutsche Wiedervereingigung (Strafrecht) 40–41 (1993); Uwe Wesel, Ein Staat vor Gericht: Der Honecker-Prozeß 46–47 (1994). The task of this working group was immense. By September 1994, it had commenced investigations in approximately 3,000 cases and had completed 1,450 of these investigations; actual prosecutions had been opened in 100 cases. FAZ, Oct. 1, 1994, at 6 col. 4. More recently, the working group has been converted into an official section of the Berlin prosecutor's office.

3. See generally Klein, Die Bedeutung der Nürnberger Prozesse für die Bewältigung des SED-Unrechts, 1992 ZRP 208.

4. Roggemann, Zur Strafbarkeit der Mauerschützen, 1993 DtZ 10, 11 n. 7 (quoting Die Zeit, 14/1992, at 44).

5. Indeed, such a position had been supported by the Federal Supreme Court (BGH) in some decisions in the early years of the Federal Republic. Küpper & Wilms, Die Verfolgung von Straftaten des SED-Regimes, 1992 ZRP 91.

6. Id.

7. See 36 BVerfGE 1 (1973) (Basic Treaty case); see also 77 BVerfGE 137 (1987).

8. Unification Treaty arts. 8, 9; § 2 StGB; art. 315(1) EGStGB, in the version set forth in Unification Treaty, attachment I, ch. III (C), para. II(1)(b). See Klaus Lüderssen, Der Staat geht unter—das Unrecht bleibt? Regierungskriminalität in der ehemaligen DDR 71 (1992).

9. § 112 StGB-DDR (murder); § 113 StGB-DDR (manslaughter); see Roggemann, 1993 DtZ at 14.

10. Many acts of oppression under the Nazis were prosecuted in the Federal Republic on the ground that those acts were illegal even under the laws that existed during the period of the "Third Reich."

11. Indeed, such officers were "praised and rewarded" in the GDR. Schlink, 1994 NJ at 434.

12. Verf. DDR (1974) arts. 90, 97. See Ch. 4.

13. Pawlik, Das Strafrecht gerät an seine Grenzen, FAZ, Mar. 31, 1992, at 36 col. 3.

14. Jakobs, Vergangenheitsbewältigung durch Strafrecht? Zur Leistungsfähigkeit des Strafrechts nach einem politischen Umbruch, in Josef Isensee (ed.), Vergangenheitsbewältigung durch Recht 51–54 (1992) (hereafter, Vergangenheitsbewältigung durch Recht); see also Isensee, Nachwort: Der deutsche Rechtsstaat vor seinem unrechtsstaatlichen Erbe, in id. at 105–7. For criticism of Jakobs's position, see Lüderssen at 35–37; see also Bernd Rüthers, Das Ungerechte an der Gerechtigkeit 141–45 (1993).

15. Grenzgesetz, of Mar. 25, 1982, § 27, GBl DDR I 197; § 213 StGB-DDR ("Ungesetzlicher Grenzübertritt"). See 39 BGHSt 1, 10–14 (1992). Before the statute of 1982, administrative regulations and less formal rules purported to authorize use of force at the border. See Roggemann, 1993 DtZ at 15 nn. 54–56.

16. Küpper & Wilms, 1992 ZRP at 93; Wassermann, Zur Aufarbeitung des SED-Unrechts, APuZ, Jan. 22, 1993, at 3, 7. For a contrary view, see 39 BGHSt 1, 15 (1992).

17. See Woesner, Deutsch-deutsche Strafrechtskonflikte, 1976 ZRP 248; Schröder, Zur Strafbarkeit von Tötungen im staatlichen Auftrag, 1992 JZ 990, 991.

18. See, e.g., 39 BGHSt at 27–28.

19. Cf. Isensee in Vergangenheitsbewältigung durch Recht at 106.

20. See, e.g., Lüderssen at 32–35.

21. See id. For similar views, see Herwig Roggemann, Systemunrecht und Strafrecht 57–59 (1993); Klein, 1992 ZRP at 213.

22. Indeed, in an important decision the Federal Supreme Court has clearly recognized aspects of the informal GDR law by giving weight to supervisory "guidelines" and "orientation" positions set down by the GDR's highest court. 40 BGHSt 30, 40–41 (1993); see also 40 BGHSt 272 (1994).

23. 999 U.N.T.S. 171. See Ch. 13.

24. Under article 12(3), the right of egress may be subject to restrictions that "are necessary to protect national security, public order (*ordre public*), public health or morals or the rights and freedoms of others, and are consistent with the other rights recognized in the present Covenant."

25. But see Robert Alexy, Mauerschützen: Zum Verhältnis von Recht, Moral und Strafbarkeit 17–20 (1993); Lüderssen at 151.

26. Verf. DDR (1974) art. 51. See also International Covenant on Civil and Political Rights art. 2(2).

27. See 39 BGHSt 1, 16–17 (1992). See also Roggemann, 1993 DtZ at 17–18; Alexy, Mauerschützen, at 16–17. Indeed, taking a similar position, the United States Senate has declared that the Covenant's substantive provisions are not "self-executing" within the United States. 138 Congressional Record S4781 (1991); cf. also Sei Fujii v. State, 38 Cal. 2d 718, 242 P.2d 617 (Sup. Ct. Cal. 1952).

The GDR also took the position—certainly with little justification—that its practice was in compliance with the substantive provisions of the treaty. 39 BGHSt at 18.

28. See, e.g., 2 BGHSt 234 (1952). See also 3 BVerfGE 225, 232–33 (1953); 6 BVerfGE 132, 198 (1957); 23 BVerfGE 98 (1968); Alexy, Mauerschützen, at 5–6.

29. See, e.g., Hruschka, Die Todesschüsse an der Berliner Mauer vor Gericht, 1992

JZ 665; see also Wassermann, APuZ, Jan. 22, 1993, at 7–8 (orders to use deadly force at Wall violate "universal, fundamental human rights").

30. Indeed, natural law arguments are enjoying a general revival in the former countries of the east bloc. See, e.g., Symposium, Truth and Justice: The Question of Accountability for Stalinist Crimes in Eastern Europe and the Soviet Union, 9 New York Law School Journal of Human Rights 599, 614 (1992) (remarks of Vojtech Cepl): "[I]n stable times, the positivists prevail. . . . But in times of change, the natural lawyers come from the grave, and press for change. And I think this is exactly the situation which we are facing in Eastern Europe."

31. 39 BGHSt 1 (1992).

32. Id. at 14. In another preliminary ruling, the court found that the Anglo-American "act of state doctrine"—which protects some governmental actions from challenge in the courts of another state—was not applicable in this case. Id. at 5–6. Moreover, the defendants were not entitled to official immunity from criminal prosecution, such as that extended in the 1980s to Erich Honecker as head of state of the GDR. Id. at 6; see 33 BGHSt 97 (1984).

33. 39 BGHSt at 15.

34. Id. at 15–16. See Radbruch, Gesetzliches Unrecht und übergesetzliches Recht, 1946 Süddeutsche Juristen-Zeitung 105; 3 BVerfGE at 232–33; 6 BVerfGE at 198; see also Hart, Positivism and the Separation of Law and Morals, 71 Harvard Law Review 593, 615–21 (1958); Alexy, Mauerschützen, at 3–7; Limbach, Vergangenheitsbewältigung durch die Justiz, 1993 DtZ 66, 68.

35. 39 BGHSt at 16–17.

36. Id. at 17–21. GDR practice did not fall within the exceptions in article 12(3) for "national security" and public order because these provisions were directed toward unusual cases rather than a general denial of egress such as that imposed by the GDR. Id. at 19.

37. Id. at 20.

38. Id. at 22–23.

39. Id. at 23–26. In reaching this result, the court engaged in a major reconstruction of the constitutional law of the GDR, apparently ignoring important aspects of that system's constitutional theory. The court noted that article 89 of the GDR Constitution declared that law must not violate constitutional commands and that, under article 30, rights of "personality and freedom" could "be limited only to the extent that this is legally permissible and absolutely necessary." Finding that article 30 contained a right to life not explicitly set forth in the text, the court concluded that the GDR Constitution prohibited the taking of life unless, under the "principle of proportionality," it was absolutely necessary to do so.

The court then proceeded to apply the "principle of proportionality"—one of the central principles of West German constitutional law—to the East German statute, and concluded that the GDR Border Law should be interpreted so as not to provide a defense for a guard who used potentially lethal automatic fire against someone peacefully trying to climb over the Wall.

40. Id. at 26–30.

41. Id. at 29–30.

The BGH has reaffirmed the principles of this decision in numerous later cases. In 1994, for example, the court upheld the conviction of a GDR border guard who, in 1969, shot and killed a fleeing citizen who had crossed the border into the west. The court found that the act violated GDR law because prevailing GDR rules prohibited firing into the west, and any verbal orders to the contrary should be disregarded. The court also found that any applicable statute of limitations was suspended because the GDR government had violated the rule of law by refusing to prosecute such border offenses on political grounds. Consequently, a statute of the Federal Republic, enacted in 1993, purporting to revive these offenses if the statute of limitations had expired, was only declaratory of the legal situation that already existed. The court did, however, overturn the defendant's penalty of five and a half years' imprisonment. 40 BGHSt 48 (1994).

For other border guard cases, see 39 BGHSt 168 (1993); 39 BGHSt 199 (1993); 39 BGHSt 353 (1993); 40 BGHSt 113 (1994); 40 BGHSt 241 (1994); BGH, Judgment of Feb. 7, 1995, 1995 NJW 1437. For a recent opinion containing an elaborate answer to critics of the court's jurisprudence in these cases, see BGH, Judgment of Mar. 20, 1995, 1995 NJW 2728.

42. Cf. Hart, 71 Harvard Law Review at 619–21; but see Fuller, Positivism and Fidelity to Law—A Reply to Professor Hart, 71 Harvard Law Review 630, 649 (1958).

43. Theoretically, however, it might be possible to amend the Basic Law for the purpose of limiting the coverage of article 103(2) GG. Cf. Schlink, 1994 NJ at 437. Indeed, even in its present form, article 103(2) might not bar the application of new rules in extraordinary circumstances. See 51 VVDStRL at 132–34 (remarks of Robert Alexy).

44. The retroactive nature of the Nuremberg trials seems reasonably clear, notwithstanding efforts to prove the contrary. See Luban, The Legacies of Nuremberg, 54 Social Research 779 (1987); cf. Harris, Justice Jackson at Nuremberg, 1986 International Lawyer 867, 882.

45. Indeed, article 15 of the 1966 Covenant on Civil and Political Rights reflects the Nuremberg principles by allowing penalization of an act that "was criminal according to the general principles of law recognized by the community of nations," even if it was permitted by relevant national law. A similar provision is contained in article 7(2) of the European Convention for the Protection of Human Rights and Fundamental Freedoms, but the Federal Republic filed a reservation to this section, noting the prohibition on retroactivity contained in article 103 GG. See Isensee in Vergangenheitsbewältigung durch Recht at 107; 39 BGHSt at 27. For similar provisions in early East German constitutions, see Ch. 4.

46. Wechsler, The Issues of the Nuremberg Trial, 62 Political Science Quarterly 11, 14 (1947); see also Gellhorn, *Ohne Mich*: Why I shall never return to Germany, Granta, Winter 1992, at 203: "Every day in that courtroom [at Nuremberg] was a soul-sickening history lesson. . . . The detail and the scale as pieced together from innumerable witnesses and innumerable documents truly disturbed the balance of one's mind."

47. On the other hand, respected German jurists have argued that, even though the shootings at the Wall cannot be compared with Nazi terror, they are sufficiently reprehensible to justify disregarding defenses provided under GDR law. Limbach, 1993 DtZ at 68–69. See also Alexy, Mauerschützen, at 29–30.

One additional point might also be considered. The government of the GDR sometimes concealed shootings at the Wall, and prohibited the use of deadly force when important international meetings were taking place in Berlin. Cf. Reiner Kunze, Die wunderbaren Jahre 16 (1978). Perhaps these evasive actions betrayed an underlying sense of guilt; if so, the impropriety of retroactive law making may be lessened—because the GDR government evidently "knew" that it was doing something wrong. Yet this principle applies more readily to the GDR leaders than to the soldiers who actually pulled the trigger. See generally Fricke, Honecker unter Anklage, 1992 DA 1009, 1010; Reich, A la lanterne? Über den Strafanspruch des Volkes, Kursbuch 111, Feb. 1993, at 3, 6–7.

Interestingly, some GDR judges questioned whether the offense of "illegal egress" was consistent with UN and other international norms. The SED regime sought to quell those doubts by circulating an elaborate response to judges and prosecutors. See Limbach, 1993 DtZ at 69.

48. A formalistic argument notes that the Allies created a legal basis for international criminal law by establishing the Nuremberg tribunal, while the German legal system is bound by the Basic Law and the Unification Treaty, which provide no comparable basis for international criminal law. Lüderssen at 115–18. This argument, however, does not touch the underlying theoretical issues. Cf. also art. 25 GG.

49. See Judith N. Shklar, Legalism: Law, Morals, and Political Trials 155–70 (1964).

50. Indeed, as the Honecker case suggests, great "state trials" may actually work against such a goal. Nonetheless, some respected legal voices in Germany have argued that the prosecution of GDR criminality is important in order to strengthen the German "legal culture." Starck, Der Rechtsstaat und die Aufarbeitung der vor-rechtsstaatlichen Vergangenheit, 51 VVDStRL 9, 42 (1992); Limbach, 1993 DtZ at 70–71.

51. Yet there is also the risk that ordinary criminal trials—with their focus on specific legal rather than general historical questions—may in the end actually distort history. Cf. Symposium, 9 New York Law School Journal of Human Rights at 636 (remarks of Andras Sajo).

52. Cf. Jakobs in Vergangenheitsbewältigung durch Recht at 64.

The guards who actually pulled the trigger were not the only GDR officials to be charged with offenses relating to the border regime. In September 1993, a court in Berlin handed down the first convictions of high GDR officials for their role in killings at the East German border. LG Berlin, Judgment of Sept. 16, 1993, 1994 NJ 210; see FAZ, Sept. 17, 1993, at 1 col. 2; see also Winters, Ein Sieg der Gerechtigkeit, 1993 DA 1121. In this judgment, however, the most important actors were missing: Erich Honecker had been released as a result of a decision by the Constitutional Court of Berlin and was residing in Chile (see Ch. 9); the case of former Prime Minister Willi Stoph had been severed on grounds of ill health; and Erich Mielke, feared head of the Stasi, was temporarily excused in light of his concurrent trial on murder charges. See Kleinschmid, Der Prozeß gegen Erich Honecker und andere, 1993 DA 3.

Yet three members of the GDR hierarchy—Heinz Keßler, Fritz Streletz, and Hans Albrecht—were sentenced to prison terms for their role in decisions of the National Defense Council to perpetuate the border regime, including shootings and the installation of minefields. Although the decision to use deadly force originated in the Politburo or the SED leadership—or, indeed, in the Soviet Union—the decisions of the National Defense Council were high in the chain of command in putting that decision into effect. According to the court, there was no statutory defense for these actions because the decisions were made before the passage of the GDR Border Law in 1982. Indeed, no statute ever authorized minefields and similar zones along the border. In July 1994, the convictions were upheld by the BGH which found the defendants principally guilty of manslaughter, instead of instigation and complicity—as had the Berlin court. 40 BGHSt 218 (1994); see FAZ, Sept. 19, 1994, at 14 col. 2.

This decision of the BGH opened the door to the prosecution of other high GDR officials for maintaining the deadly border regime. See, e.g., Winters, Justiz und

Zeitgeschichte, 1993 DA 273. Criminal actions have been filed against generals of the GDR Army and seven members of the SED Politburo, including Egon Krenz, Günter Schabowski, and Harry Tisch. See Wesel, Moralisch schuldig, Die Zeit (overseas ed.), Mar. 31, 1995, at 5 col. 4; FAZ, Nov. 10, 1995, at 4 col. 1; FAZ, Aug. 18, 1995, at 5 col. 4. Prosecutors also reinstated the action against Erich Mielke following his conviction for a murder committed in 1931, but the proceeding was effectively terminated because of Mielke's ill health. See FAZ, Sept. 5, 1994, at 7 col. 3; FAZ, Nov. 15, 1993, at 4 col. 4; FAZ, Nov. 4, 1994, at 2 col. 2. Erich Honecker died in Chile in May 1994, and Harry Tisch died in June 1995.

53. The summary trial and execution of the Ceausescus in Rumania at the end of 1989 is an extreme example. Cf. Symposium, 9 New York Law School Journal of Human Rights at 601–6 (remarks of Adrian Nitoiu).

54. One of the charges turned out not to be an offense under West German law—as required by the Unification Treaty—and Tisch was acquitted of the other charge. See Jacqueline Hénard, Geschichte vor Gericht: Die Ratlosigkeit der Justiz 13–18 (1993).

55. Wesel, Aristoteles, Markus Wolf und die Mauerschützen, in Marion Dönhoff et al., Weil das Land Versöhnung braucht 90–91 (1993). Tisch was later charged with offenses relating to his role in the fatal regime at the GDR border, but he died before the case could come to trial.

56. Id. at 100.

57. See Hénard at 36.

58. FAZ, Sept. 5, 1994, at 7 col. 3. The conviction and sentence were upheld by the Federal Supreme Court (BGH) in March 1995. The BGH found that the applicable statute of limitations for this 1931 offense had been suspended—in part, because Mielke had enjoyed legal immunity as a member of the GDR Volkskammer. See FAZ, Mar. 11, 1995, at 4 col. 3.

59. As a former member of the GDR Politburo, Mielke was also charged with complicity in the shootings at the Wall, but the octogenarian's declining health resulted in effective dismissal of the proceeding. FAZ, Sept. 5, 1994, at 7 col. 3; FAZ, Nov. 4, 1994, at 2 col. 2. Moreover, in September 1994 an investigation of Mielke's possible complicity in terrorist acts of the West German Red Army Faction was concluded without the filing of charges. FAZ, Sept. 17, 1994, at 4 col. 4. Having served the requisite portion of his sentence for the 1931 murders, Mielke was released from prison in August 1995. FAZ, Aug. 3, 1995, at 4 col. 3.

60. Hénard at 22–23; Konrad H. Jarausch, The Rush to German Unity 37–38 (1994). For a documentation from the ranks of the reformers, see Ralph Sköries et al., Wahlfall 89: Eine Dokumentation (mimeograph, 1989).

61. The overwhelming majorities routinely accumulated by SED candidates were, in substantial part, attributable to the method of voting. See, e.g., Timothy Garton Ash, The Uses of Adversity: Essays on the Fate of Central Europe 8 (1990): "In an East German polling station, a voter presents himself before a board of two or three officials, shows his ID card, and collects a ballot paper. To vote for the National Front [the official SED slate], he folds his ballot paper once and drops it, unmarked, into the box. To vote any other way, he has to walk across the room to mark his ballot paper in a voting booth, beside which sits a *Vopo*. A *Vopo* is a 'people's policeman.' The moment the voter steps toward the booth, his name is noted. One independent-minded voter described the few paces to the polling booth as 'the longest walk in my life.' The consequences may include demotion at work or, for a student, expulsion from the university."

62. References to the May election fraud were prominent, for example, in the great Alexanderplatz demonstration of November 4, 1989. See Ch. 3. In February 1990, the GDR Round Table considered a document urging the Council of State to declare the May election invalid and seeking to impose personal "responsibility" on members of the GDR leadership who had been involved in the falsification. See Helmut Herles & Ewald Rose (eds.), Vom Runden Tisch zum Parlament 148–49 (1990).

63. 39 BGHSt 54 (1992), affirming BG Dresden, Judgment of Feb. 7, 1992, 1992 NJ 363. Berghofer was convicted under the West German Criminal Code, because its election fraud provision was milder than the corresponding section of the GDR statute.

64. A screening panel of the Federal Constitutional Court rejected Berghofer's constitutional complaint on the ground that it was without merit. BVerfG (Chamber 2 of Second Senate), Judgment of Mar. 31, 1993, 1993 NJ 315.

65. See FAZ, Apr. 21, 1993, at 2 col. 2. The Bundestag lifted Modrow's constitutional immunity as a member of parliament so that he could be tried on these charges. See art. 46(2) GG; FAZ, Mar. 20, 1992, at 1 col. 2; see generally FAZ, Apr. 30, 1992, at 4 col. 6.

66. See Friedrich Schorlemmer, Freiheit als Einsicht 191–93 (1993). Similarly, Modrow's counsel argued that—unlike most GDR officials—Modrow did his best to resist or reform the SED hierarchy: "The young [western] prosecutors have certainly not themselves lived under a dictatorship. They have therefore had no occasion to test their own capacity for acts of political heroism. . . . Above all, you have not understood that sitting across from you at the defendant's table is the man who had become, for many people in the GDR, the essence of resistance against precisely that power structure that you are prosecuting him for being a part of." Dokumentation: Das Verfahren gegen H. Modrow u.a. wegen Wahlfälschung, 1993 NJ 493, 500. Modrow also argued that, by complying with the SED leadership on the falsification of the vote, he had preserved political stability which allowed him to choose the "right moment" to help return democratic rights to the people. FAZ, May 26, 1993, at 4 col. 3.

67. FAZ, Apr. 22, 1993, at 8 col. 1. Similarly, Modrow's lawyer argued that the prosecution was part of a campaign against a humane socialism: it was part of a struggle intended to extirpate "the recollection of a political alternative . . . which would have saved [people] from sad experiences with the blessings of capitalism." Dokumentation, 1993 NJ at 496.

68. FAZ, Apr. 22, 1993, at 8 col. 1; FAZ, May 25, 1993, at 4 col. 4; Dokumentation, 1993 NJ at 496–97.

69. Modrow was found guilty, but the conviction could be annulled if he did not commit another offense within a year. Modrow was also required to pay trial costs and contribute DM 20,000 to social institutions such as Amnesty International. LG Dresden, Judgment of May 27, 1993, 1993 NJ 493; see FR, May 28, 1993, at 1 col. 1.

70. LG Dresden, 1993 NJ at 495. See also FAZ, May 28, 1993, at 3 cols. 4 & 5; FR, May 28, 1993, at 1 col. 1. The court also found that SED members and officials were accustomed to years of observing party discipline and the leading role of the party, guaranteed in the constitution. LG Dresden, 1993 NJ at 494. In noting this point, the judge was perhaps responding to the following arguments of Modrow's counsel: "Party discipline was obviously a principle that determined the constitutional reality in the GDR beyond the boundaries of party membership. In light of the leading role of the SED set forth in article 1 of the GDR Constitution, [orders of the party leadership] were more strongly in the political and legal consciousness of election officials than the paper tiger of the Criminal Code." Dokumentation, 1993 NJ at 499.

71. LG Dresden, 1993 NJ at 495.

72. BGH, Judgment of Nov. 3, 1994, 1995 NJ 96, 98.

73. The Sun (Baltimore), Aug. 10, 1995, at 7A col. 4. Modrow's conviction will most likely not end the judicial testing of issues arising from the 1989 communal elections. Other members of the Politburo—including former party leader Egon Krenz, who was chair of the GDR Election Commission—have been charged with fraud or incitement in connection with those elections. Former local officials in the GDR have also been convicted on similar charges. FAZ, July 8, 1995, at 1 col. 2.

Indeed, Hans Modrow himself may have further tribulations before the criminal court in Dresden. In early 1994 he was charged with making false statements before a committee of the Saxon parliament concerning government meetings in Dresden in autumn 1989. FAZ, Mar. 12, 1994, at 1 col. 2.

74. FAZ, Apr. 22, 1993, at 8 col. 2.

75. See Limbach, Recht und Unrecht in der Justiz der DDR, 1992 ZRP 170.

76. Some of the extensive network of statutes penalizing speech and related activity are reprinted in Gilbert Furian, Der Richter und sein Lenker: Politische Justiz in der DDR 256–67 (1992).

77. See, e. g., Lüderssen at 65.

78. See Ch. 13.

79. See § 336 StGB; § 244 StGB-DDR. This contrast between German and Anglo-American law seems to reflect, among other things, the more independent role of the judiciary in the common law system.

80. FAZ, July 23, 1992, at 5 col. 1; see Limbach, 1992 ZRP at 171 n. 1. Many of these cases grew out of actions filed by eastern citizens for "rehabilitation" and the nullification of GDR criminal convictions. See Ch. 15; Rautenberg & Burges, Anfangsverdacht wegen Rechtsbeugung gegen Staatsanwälte und Richter der früheren DDR—ein Beitrag zum Meinungsstand in der Praxis, 1993 DtZ 71; Lüderssen at 120–21. An oppressive judicial decision that gave rise to rehabilitation of its victim might also result in prosecution of the judge for perversion of justice.

The extraordinary number of investigations for "perversion of justice" is unprecedented, either in Germany or elswhere. See Roggemann, Richterstrafbarkeit und Wechsel der Rechtsordnung, 1994 JZ 769. Indeed, before unification, the West German offense of perversion of justice was seldom used and seemed consigned to marginality. See Roggemann, Die Justiz auf dem Prüfstand der Justiz, in Im Namen des Volkes? Über die Justiz im Staat der SED (Wissenschaftlicher Begleitband zur Ausstellung des Bundesministeriums der Justiz) 285–86 (1994) (hereafter, Im Namen des Volkes).

81. Cf. Rautenberg & Burges, 1993 DtZ 71.

82. § 244 StGB-DDR.

83. See § 336 StGB.

84. Cf. Maiwald, Rechtsbeugung im SED-Staat, 1993 NJW 1881, 1882–84, 1888–89.

85. Rautenberg & Burges, 1993 DtZ at 75.

86. See Maiwald, 1993 NJW at 1886–87.

87. §§ 214, 220 StGB-DDR. See Maiwald, 1993 NJW at 1886–87 (arguing that the expressions were indeed beyond the coverage of the GDR statutes).

88. LG Dresden, Judgment of July 14, 1993, 1993 NJ 519. See Verf. DDR (1974) arts. 97–98.

89. LG Berlin, Judgment of Aug. 17, 1992, 1993 NJ 37.

90. 40 BGHSt 30 (1993).

91. For a bitter attack on this decision for its apparent leniency to the GDR judges and its willingness to accord some respect to the GDR judicial system, see Wolf, Rechtsbeugung durch DDR-Richter, 1994 NJW 1390. See also Bemmann, Zu aktuellen Problemen der Rechtsbeugung, 1995 JZ 123.

More recently, the BGH reaffirmed the principles of this decision by acquitting a judge who had presided in a case in which a protestor had been sentenced to prison; the protestor had appeared at a swearing-in ceremony for border troops and had displayed a poster criticizing the GDR's closed border regime. 40 BGHSt 272 (1994). In reaching its decision, the court noted that the judge was rooted in the values of "a different legal system" and had followed the interpretive guidelines of the GDR's highest court. This decision has been criticized—see Spendel, Rechtsbeugung und Justiz, 1995 JZ 375—but the BGH has continued to hold that "Rechtsbeugung" can be found only in the most extreme examples of political justice. BGH, Judgment of Sept. 15, 1995, 1995 NJW 3324.

Yet the BGH has not always found that an acquittal is required in these cases. The court came to a different conclusion, for example, in the case of two GDR military prosecutors who had failed to file charges against a Stasi officer. The prosecutors knew that the officer, while intoxicated, had shot and killed two unarmed civilians, but they knowingly accepted a falsified version of the facts indicating that the officer had acted in a justified manner. The BGH reiterated the general principle that the legality of a judge's or prosecutor's act must be determined in accordance with the prevailing norms and methods of the GDR, but it found that the knowing falsification of the facts was so extreme as to have been an "arbitrary act." The court concluded, therefore, that the prosecutors could be convicted of "perversion of justice"—although the case was remanded to a lower court, for retrial, on a procedural point. 40 BGHSt 169 (1994). In a more recent decision on "perversion of justice," the BGH has upheld a prison sentence of three years and nine months against a judge of the GDR's highest court who had participated in handing down death sentences in espionage cases. FAZ, Nov. 17, 1995, at 5 col. 4.

92. See generally, Archivmaterial zu den Waldheimer Prozessen, 1991 NJ 392; Wassermann, Zur Anwendung der sogenannten Radbruchschen Formel auf Unrechtsurteile der DDR-Justiz, 1992 NJW 878.

93. See Maiwald, 1993 NJW at 1885.

94. See Hénard 51–61; FAZ, Nov. 11, 1992, at 4 col. 4; FAZ, Nov. 13, 1992, at 5 col. 4; FAZ, Nov. 21, 1992, at 4 col. 4.

95. FAZ, Aug. 27, 1993, at 4 col. 2. The defendant had been one of a number of "people's judges" trained for the judiciary in an accelerated process during the Soviet occupation period. See generally Gängel, Die Volksrichterausbildung, in Im Namen des Volkes at 47.

96. FAZ, Sept. 2, 1993, at 1 col. 3.

97. In March 1994, for example, criminal actions were filed against two former officials of the GDR Justice Ministry—eighty-three and eighty-four years old, respectively—for incitement to murder and to perversion of justice in connection with orders issued relating to death sentences in the Waldheim trials. FAZ, Mar. 2, 1994, at 6 col. 4.

98. Yet, in some areas of Stasi activity, the courts have been notably reluctant to impose criminal liability. The Federal Supreme Court, for example, has found that Stasi officers cannot be penalized for such common practices as telephone surveillance

or government removal of money and other valuable items from the mails. The court found that these activities failed to satisfy the requisites for criminality under the law of the GDR or the Federal Republic. BGH, Judgment of Dec. 9, 1993, 1994 NJ 231; FAZ, Dec. 15, 1995, at 4 col. 1. The BGH has also been reluctant to impose criminal liability on those who injured others by giving information to the Stasi; the court, however, has left open the possibility of civil liability in some cases. See 40 BGHSt 125 (1994); Wassermann, Die DDR-Denunzianten und der Bundesgerichtshof, 1995 NJW 931.

99. Lippold, Die Strafbarkeit der DDR-Spionage und ihre Verfassungsmäßigkeit, 1992 NJW 18, 19. See §§ 5(4); 94, 99 StGB. Cf. also art. 315(4) EGStGB, in the version set forth in Unification Treaty, attachment I, ch. III (C), para. II (1)(b).

100. § 9(1) StGB.

101. See BGH, Judgment of May 29, 1991, 1991 NJW 2498; KG (Berlin), Referral Decision of July 22, 1991, 1991 NJW 2501, 2502.

102. See U.S. v. Noriega, 746 F.Supp. 1506 (S.D. Fla. 1990); Restatement (Third) of the Foreign Relations Law of the United States § 402(1)(c)(1987). Cf. 37 BGHSt 305, 310–12 (1991); BGH, 1991 NJW at 2498–99 (permissibility in international law).

Indeed the GDR criminal law of espionage also had extraterritorial application and would have penalized West German spies operating against the GDR from the Federal Republic. See generally Lippold, 1992 NJW at 19; KG (Berlin), 1991 NJW at 2502; Simma & Volk, Der Spion, der in die Kälte kam, 1991 NJW 871, 873.

103. See, e.g., Albrecht & Kadelbach, Zur strafrechtlichen Verfolgung von DDR-Außenspionage, 1992 NJ 137, 146–47.

104. KG (Berlin), 1991 NJW at 2503–4; see art. 100 GG. This was the case of Werner Großmann, who was the last chief of the HVA.

105. See Wolfgang Schäuble, Der Vertrag: Wie ich über die deutsche Einheit verhandelte 268–72 (1991).

106. See FAZ, May 5, 1993, at 7 col. 1. See also Spiegel-Gespräch (Interview with Markus Wolf), Der Spiegel, 18/1993, at 40.

107. § 94 StGB. Moreover, in his closing remarks at trial, Wolf declared: "My land"—that is, the GDR—"I have never betrayed." FAZ, Nov. 25, 1993, at 3 col. 3.

108. The danger of serious disadvantage to the external security of the Federal Republic must also be shown. § 94(1) StGB.

109. See FAZ, Nov. 25, 1993, at 3 col. 3.

110. Cf. BGH, Judgment of July 30, 1993, 1993 NJW at 3147, 3148.

111. See, e.g., Lippold, 1992 NJW at 20–22.

112. See Ch. 2. Cf. Lüderssen at 21.

113. See, e.g., BGH, 1991 NJW at 2500.

Finally, some jurists maintained that the prosecution of eastern espionage agents violated article 31 of the Hague Convention Respecting the Laws and Customs of War on Land. Under this provision spies for a losing side in a war, who are captured with the losing army, cannot be tried for espionage by the winning side. Although the Hague Convention is not explicitly applicable to a peaceful "accession," instead of a lost war, this provision might conceivably be applied by analogy. See KG (Berlin), 1991 NJW at 2504; Lüderssen at 19–20, 150.

114. By further coincidence, Wolf and Kinkel grew up in the same Swabian town, where their fathers were both physicians, although Wolf was some years older than Kinkel. In "Wessis in Weimar," Rolf Hochhuth devotes a gripping chapter to this relationship, including sharp criticism of the decision to prosecute Wolf. See Rolf

Hochhuth, Wessis in Weimar: Szenen aus einem besetzten Land 173–88 (1993): "But since he, Kinkel as Wessi, / stands on the side of the winners—like all of us Wessis, /without really deserving it / —he wants not only to disarm the loser / that is understandable / but also to criminalize him, to lock him up! / And he calls himself Justice Minister, / invokes the 'rule of law.' " Id. at 183.

115. FAZ, Dec. 7, 1993, at 4 col. 4. Wolf's father was the noted dramatist, Friedrich Wolf. As a Communist and a Jew, Friedrich Wolf had to flee the Nazis, and he and his family lived in the Soviet Union until the end of World War II. For glimpses of the young Markus ("Mischa") Wolf during this period and in Germany during the Soviet occupation period, see Wolfgang Leonhard, Die Revolution entläßt ihre Kinder 233, 576–78 (1990).

116. See Schäuble, Der Vertrag, at 268–72.

117. See Simma & Volk, 1991 NJW at 874–75; BGH, Judgment of Jan. 30, 1991, 1991 JZ 713, 716–17; cf. Classen, Anmerkung, 1991 JZ 717.

118. BVerfG (Second Senate), Judgment of May 15, 1995, 1995 NJ 363. This decision did not come in Wolf's case, however, but in the combined cases of his successor, Werner Großmann, and other agents. The BGH reversed Wolf's conviction in a later decision. See FAZ, Oct. 19, 1995, at 1 col. 2.

119. BVerfG, 1995 NJ at 364–66.

120. Id. at 366–69.

In a vigorous dissent, three judges complained that the Court's decision represented a partial amnesty—generally a legislative function. The majority had therefore stepped beyond constitutional law into the realm of politics. According to the dissenting judges, moreover, any reliance by eastern agents on perpetual immunity from prosecution was unreasonable: eastern agents should have known that the Basic Law required German unification—a goal endorsed by all western governments—and that no one could predict what espionage law would be applicable after unification. Id. at 369–72 (opinion of Judges Klein, Kirchhof, and Winter).

For early commentary on this decision, see Albrecht, Das Rechtsstaatsprinzip des Gesamtstaates, 1995 NJ 337; Widmaier, DDR-Spionage und Rechtsstaat, 1995 NJ 345; Currie, The Pains of Growing Together: The Case of the East-German Spies, 4 East European Constitutional Review, Summer 1995, at 66.

121. See, e.g., Fromme, Zwiespältiges aus Karlsruhe, FAZ, May 26, 1995, at 1 col. 5.

122. See, e.g., FAZ, Jan. 26, 1995, at 5 col. 4 (president of BGH advocates amnesty to further legal repose); see also Sendler, Unrechtsstaat und Amnestie, 1995 NJ 225; Schröder, Laßt sie auf ihren Ladenhütern sitzen!, FAZ, Mar. 21, 1995, at 38 col. 1 (amnesty is justified because the GDR had distorted the "legal consciousness" of its citizens); Eberan, Amnestie für Straftaten unter dem DDR-Regime, 1995 NJ 299, 300 (argument of prominent east German lawyer that amnesty is justified because GDR crimes were a product of the Cold War and their prosecution unduly burdens courts).

123. Eberan, 1995 NJ at 300 (remarks of Lutz Rathenow).

124. Id. at 300–301 (remarks of Bärbel Bohley).

125. From a very early point after unification, a number of prominent eastern reformers—fearing that the criminal law would yield only an incomplete "confrontation" with the GDR past—advocated the creation of "tribunals" that would investigate and pass judgment on instances of injustice in the GDR, without any sanction or penalty other than the tool of publicity. See, e.g., Wolfgang Thierse, Mit eigener Stimme sprechen 247–70 (1992); Friedrich Schorlemmer, Versöhnung in der Wahrheit 244–66

(1992); for criticism, see Lüderssen at 129–33. The purpose of these hearings would be to clarify aspects of the GDR past without the limitations of judicial process or restricted definitions of criminality, and they would be conducted by eastern citizens instead of the western judges who would of necessity preside at the criminal trials.

The call to create nonjudicial tribunals, as such, failed to attract widespread support. Perhaps as a substitute, however, the Bundestag voted in May 1992 to create a parliamentary Commission of Inquiry for the purpose of investigating aspects of the SED dictatorship in East Germany. Rainer Eppelmann, a veteran of the GDR reform movement and former defense minister under de Maizière, was appointed chair of the commission. After hearing hundreds of witnesses and conducting approximately forty open hearings, the commission issued its report on May 31, 1994, covering such areas as the structure of the SED state; law, justice, and the police in the GDR; the role of the church; and opposition activity and the peaceful revolution of 1989. See Bericht der Enquete-Kommission "Aufarbeitung von Geschichte und Folgen der SED-Diktatur in Deutschland," May 31, 1994, Bundestag Drucksache 12/7820. Moreover, the testimony of witnesses and experts has been published in a multi-volume set. The commission's mandate expired at the end of the parliamentary period in 1994, but the new parliament has established a second commission—also with Rainer Eppelmann as its chair—to continue the inquiry.

## Chapter 15
## Undoing the Past: "Rehabilitation" and Compensation

1. Erich Loest, Durch die Erde ein Riß: Ein Lebenslauf (1990).

2. Id. at 357–59. In 1990, during the period of the East German revolution, Loest's conviction was annulled in a decision of the GDR's highest court. See Oberstes Gericht (DDR), Judgment of Apr. 24, 1990, 1990 DtZ 285.

3. See FAZ, June 19, 1992, at 3 col. 1; see also FAZ, June 9, 1992, at 15 col. 1 (correspondence); Klaus Lüderssen, Der Staat geht unter—das Unrecht bleibt? Regierungskriminalität in der ehemaligen DDR 65 (1992).

4. FAZ, June 9, 1992, at 15 col. 1 (correspondence).

5. FAZ, June 19, 1992, at 3 col. 1. Thus an average of more than DM 100,000 was paid for each prisoner. Elizabeth Pond, Beyond the Wall: Germany's Road to Unification 293–94 (1993), citing Ludwig A. Rehlinger, Freikauf: Die Geschäfte der DDR mit politisch Verfolgten 1963–1989 (1991). See also Hirschman, Exit, Voice, and the Fate of the German Democratic Republic, 45 World Politics 173, 185 (1993).

6. See, e.g., Inga Markovits, Imperfect Justice: An East-West German Diary 6 (1995). See generally Sendler, Die DDR ein Unrechtsstaat—ja oder nein?, 1993 ZRP 1.

7. Analogous statutes of compensation and rehabilitation were enacted in a number of the states of the former east bloc as they turned away from the Stalinist past. Indeed, a rehabilitation statute enacted in Czechoslovakia in April 1990 was the second of its type. A similar statute had been enacted in the course of the "Prague Spring" in 1968, but it was rendered ineffective by the invasion of Warsaw Pact troops later that year. See Pfister, Zur "Rehabilitierung" von Opfern der DDR-Justiz, 1992 NJ 196, 197.

8. See, e.g., Buchholz, Wiedergutmachung von Unrecht, 1990 ZRP 466.

9. See Lüderssen at 120–21.

10. Buchholz, 1990 ZRP at 466–67. Originally the remedy of cassation could be issued not only in favor of a criminal defendant but also against the defendant, to

reverse an acquittal or increase a penalty. After the GDR Code of Criminal Procedure was liberalized in June 1990, as required by the first State Treaty, cassation could be issued in favor of the defendant only. Id. at 467 n. 9. See Ch. 7.

11. Cf. Martin Amelung et al., Rehabilitierung und Kassation: Beseitigung von Justizunrecht in der DDR 17–18 (1991).

12. GDR Code of Criminal Procedure § 311(2); see Buchholz, 1990 ZRP at 467.

13. Indeed, this development led to a "previously unthinkable dogmatic flowering" in criminal law in the last days of the GDR. Bruns, Schröder, & Tappert, Bereinigung von Justiz-Unrecht der DDR: Das neue Strafrechtliche Rehabilitierungsgesetz (Teil 1), 1992 NJ 394, 395.

14. Präsidium des Obersten Gerichts (DDR), Judgment of Jan. 5, 1990, 1990 DtZ 31.

15. See generally Der Prozeß gegen Walter Janka und andere: Eine Dokumentation (1990) (hereafter, Der Prozeß gegen Walter Janka). The "show trials against critical intellectuals" such as Janka—as well as the trial against the writer Erich Loest—were undertaken by Stasi chief Erich Mielke at the very beginning of his term of office. See Anne Worst, Das Ende eines Geheimdienstes 10 (1991).

16. Indeed, precisely that argument had been made—in vain—by Janka's lawyer before the GDR Supreme Court in 1957. See Walter Janka, Schwierigkeiten mit der Wahrheit 88 (1990). Janka's gripping memoir of his trial and imprisonment was first published in 1989 and itself became an important and acclaimed document of the East German revolution. Id.; see Pond at 10. In an irony not uncharacteristic of the post-unification period, Friedrich Wolff, the young lawyer who represented Janka in 1957, also represented Erich Honecker in his trial in Berlin in 1992–93. See Ch. 9.

17. Cf. Amelung et al. at 18.

18. Der Prozeß gegen Walter Janka at 150.

For other decisions granting cassation in 1990, see Oberstes Gericht (DDR), Judgment of Mar. 30, 1990, 1990 NJ 206 (reversing 1957 convictions of Dr. Wolfgang Harich and others for "Boykotthetze" under article 6 of the 1949 constitution in connection with the reform proposals also at issue in the Janka case); Oberstes Gericht (DDR), Judgment of June 15, 1990, 1990 NJ 287 (reversing 1978 conviction of philosopher Rudolf Bahro for illegal transfer of information and related offenses, in connection with his publication in the Federal Republic of a book discussing unsolved social and economic problems in the GDR); Oberstes Gericht (DDR), Judgment of May 29, 1990, 1990 NJ 289 (reversing 1988 conviction of reformer Vera Wollenberger for "attempted participation in mob action" for seeking with others to display a banner citing the free-speech guarantee of article 27 of the GDR Constitution at a memorial demonstration honoring Rosa Luxemburg and Karl Liebknecht).

Judges and a prosecutor who participated in Rudolf Bahro's 1978 conviction have recently been charged with the crimes of "perversion of justice" and "unlawful imprisonment" in connection with their actions in that case. FAZ, Mar. 6, 1995, at 4 col. 5.

19. Unification Treaty art. 18(2); id. attachment I, ch. III(A), para. III (14)(h). Because cassation had originally been a method to insure Communist Party control of the courts, prior law specified that only a prosecutor or a Supreme Court judge could file a petition for cassation.

The Unification Treaty afforded another method through which a decision of GDR courts could be called into question. If a GDR judicial decision still remained to be implemented, it would only be enforced if it conformed to the principles of the rule of law. Id. art. 18(1); id. attachment I, ch. III (A), para. III (14)(d). Similarly, administrative acts of the GDR would remain in effect, unless they were inconsistent with the Unification Treaty or "with principles of the rule of law." Id. art. 19.

20. The Unification Treaty also extended principles of the West German law on "prisoners assistance" to residents of eastern Germany. This law had provided some compensation for GDR political prisoners who had succeeded in reaching the territory of the Federal Republic. See Unification Treaty, attachment I, ch. II(D), para. II (2); Rüfner, Wiedergutmachung von DDR-Unrecht, in II(2) Klaus Stern (ed.), Deutsche Wiedervereinigung: Die Rechtseinheit 105 (1992) (hereafter, Deutsche Wiedervereinigung).

21. See Wolfgang Schäuble, Der Vertrag: Wie ich über die deutsche Einheit verhandelte 197–98 (1991). According to Schäuble, "the increasingly hectic 'end-spurt atmosphere'" of the GDR Volkskammer, as the date of accession approached, seemed "inappropriate for the resolution of such difficult and sensitive questions." Rather, the question of rehabilitation was to be resolved in the all-German parliament where all interests could be considered. Id. at 198.

22. Rehabilitierungsgesetz, of Sept. 6, 1990, GBl DDR I 1459 (hereafter, RehaG-DDR). Use of the term "rehabilitation" (*Rehabilitierung*), which was also employed in the Unification Treaty, has been subjected to criticism on the ground that it was derived from a concept used in the former east bloc systems. See Schroeder, "Rehabilitierung" von SED-Opfern?, 1992 ZRP 41. But others respond that use of the term extends back to the early nineteenth century. See Pfister, 1992 NJ at 197 n.7.

23. RehaG-DDR preamble, § 3.

24. Id. §§ 21–42.

25. Id. §§ 18–20.

26. Schäuble, Der Vertrag, at 197. Indeed, uncertainty over the financial implications had been the subject of "frequent comment" in the Volkskammer itself. Bruns, Schröder, & Tappert, 1992 NJ at 395 n. 11.

27. Vereinbarung zur Durchführung und Auslegung des Einigungsvertrags, of Sept. 18, 1990, BGBl II 1239, art. 3(6) (hereafter, Vereinbarung); cf. Unification Treaty art. 9(3). Sections providing rehabilitation for actions of the occupation regime were also deleted. On the other hand, the method of cassation was expanded to annul certain GDR judgments that were "inconsistent with the standards of the rule of law." Vereinbarung art. 4(2); see Amelung et al. at 32, 156–59. Thus the Unification Treaty as amended moved away from the principle that, to accord relief, the earlier judgment must have violated GDR law applicable at the time of conviction.

28. See Pfister, 1992 NJ at 198. Cf. Stefan Heym, Filz: Gedanken über das neueste Deutschland 7–16 (1992).

29. Erstes SED-Unrechtsbereinigungsgesetz, of Oct. 29, 1992, BGBl I 1814. The first article of the statute is separately referred to as the Law for Criminal Rehabilitation (StrRehaG). The urgency of achieving clarification on relevant points is indicated by reports that at the end of 1991—that is, before the new law was adopted—more than 70,000 petitions for rehabilitation or cassation had been filed in the courts of the five new Länder and Berlin. Bruns, Schröder, & Tappert, 1992 NJ at 395 n. 15. Work on the statute was accompanied by the Bundestag's passage of a "declaration of honor" for those who had been subject to oppression under the criminal justice system of the GDR.

30. See Keck, Schröder, & Tappert, Das strafrechtliche Rehabilitierungsgesetz im Überblick, 1993 DtZ 2, 5. See also Bruns, Schröder, & Tappert, 1992 NJ at 399.

31. StrRehaG § 1(1).

32. Id. § 1(1)(1)–(2). Oppressive measures imposed by criminal authorities without a judicial order will also give rise to rehabilitation and compensation. Id. § 1(5).

33. Schröder, Fahnenflucht als regelmäßiger Rehabilitierungsgrund?, 1993 NJ 350.

34. Bruns, Schröder, & Tappert, 1992 NJ at 396–97. Some offenses that were often employed for political repression were not specified in the statutory listing because they were also used for legitimate purposes. The offense of *Rowdytum* (rowdiness), for example, was frequently invoked to penalize political demonstrators, but it was also employed for routine breaches of the peace. With respect to petitions for rehabilitation from such convictions, the courts will have to determine whether the petitioner's individual case was or was not a case of political discrimination. See id. at 398–99; Schröder, 1993 NJ at 351. Yet some provisions of the Criminal Code were so often used for political oppression that their exclusion from the catalog may unnecessarily multiply the cases in which individual proof of political oppression must be offered. See Roth & Saathoff, Alternativvorschläge zur Rehabilitierung und Entschädigung von DDR-Unrecht, 1992 DA 405, 406.

35. See Ch. 14.

36. StrRehaG § 1(2).

37. See BG Dresden, Judgment of Oct. 28, 1991, 1992 NJ 69. In this case the court found that the "draconian" Waldheim judgments were issued by "special courts," employing concepts of collective guilt without individual findings, under massive pressure from the SED. Indeed, the Waldheim trials "were not seriously directed toward . . . the question of an individual defendant's guilt; rather they were misused by the SED . . . as an instrument to strengthen the party's position of power within the new and as yet unsecured state structure of the GDR." BG Dresden, 1992 NJ at 70. Yet, the court also noted that declaring the invalidity of the Waldheim judgments on these grounds did not necessarily indicate that the Waldheim defendants were innocent. These defendants might still be subject to retrial. For the Waldheim trials, see generally Archivmaterial zu den Waldheimer Prozessen, 1991 NJ 392. Some surviving judges and prosecutors in the Waldheim trials are currently being tried on charges of perversion of justice. See Ch. 14.

38. StrRehaG § 1(1)(1)(g).

39. Id. § 1(1)(1)(i). The organization in question is presumably NATO.

40. See Ch. 2.

41. See Bruns, Schröder, & Tappert, 1992 NJ at 398. See also Schäuble, Der Vertrag, at 197.

42. See Schröder, 1993 NJ 350.

43. Keck, Schröder, & Tappert, 1993 DtZ at 3; Bruns, Schröder, & Tappert, 1992 NJ at 395.

44. See Ch. 11.

45. StrRehaG § 25(2)(2); see Bruns, Schröder, & Tappert, Bereinigung von Justiz-Unrecht der DDR: Das neue Strafrechtliche Rehabilitierungsgesetz (Teil 3), 1992 NJ 485, 490. Moreover, persons who were convicted by Soviet occupation courts may apply to the Soviet (now Russian) Embassy or Foreign Ministry for the official annulment of such a conviction. Some of these applications have been successful. Interview, Brandenburg Ministry of Justice, May 24, 1993; see also FAZ, May 19, 1995, at 7 col. 3.

46. StrRehaG § 3(2). See Ch. 11.

47. StrRehaG § 6.

48. Id. § 17; Keck, Schröder, & Tappert, 1993 DtZ at 3.

49. See Bruns, Schröder, & Tappert, 1992 NJ at 488. Individuals who suffered particular economic damage or impairment of health, as a result of imprisonment pursuant to such a conviction, may receive additional financial assistance. StrRehaG §§ 18–21.

Payments will not be made, however, to any claimant who "violated the principles of humanity or the rule of law, or misused his position to his own advantage or to the disadvantage of another, in a serious manner." StrRehaG § 16(2). This provision excludes payments to individuals who, although they may have been imprisoned at one time or another under the GDR, rendered special services to the SED or to the state—such as SED functionaries, unofficial collaborators of the Stasi, and individuals who filed political denunciations against others. See Bruns, Schröder, & Tappert, 1992 NJ at 486–87.

50. See Isensee, Nachwort: Der deutsche Rechtsstaat vor seinem unrechtsstaatlichen Erbe, in Josef Isensee (ed.), Vergangenheitsbewältigung durch Recht 101 (1992). See generally FAZ, June 19, 1992, at 2 col. 5; FAZ, June 9, 1992, at 15 col. 1 (correspondence); FAZ, July 11, 1992, at 4 col. 4.

51. StrRehaG § 9; see Bruns, Schröder, & Tappert, Bereinigung von Justiz-Unrecht der DDR: Das neue Strafrechtliche Rehabilitierungsgesetz (Teil 2), 1992 NJ 436, 437–38.

52. For hair-raising accounts of imprisonment for political offenses in the GDR, see Loest, Durch die Erde ein Riß, at 354–91; Janka, Schwierigkeiten mit der Wahrheit, at 106–11. For a powerful fictional evocation of the life of a former political prisoner in the GDR, see Christoph Hein, Der Tangospieler (1989).

53. Interview with Katharina Doyé, Brandenburg Ministry of Education, Youth, and Sport, Potsdam, May 13, 1993.

Notwithstanding many problems, numerous claims for criminal rehabilitation have been filed under the first Statute for the Correction of SED Injustice. By mid-1995, for example, over 21,000 claims had been filed in Brandenburg alone, of which more than 12,000 were found to be fully or partially justified. Of this number, almost 7,300 claimants have been awarded a total of DM 60.5 million in rehabilitation payments. FAZ, Aug. 16, 1995, at 6 col. 1.

54. For these and other typical examples, see Bürger, Die Leistungen nach dem 2.SED-Unrechtsbereinigungsgesetz, 1995 DtZ 106.

55. See Unification Treaty art. 17.

56. Zweites SED-Unrechtsbereinigungsgesetz, of June 23, 1994, BGBl I 1311. The statute is divided into two components, the Administrative Rehabilitation Law (VwRehaG) and the Employment Rehabilitation Law (BerRehaG). See generally Leutheusser-Schnarrenberger, Das Zweite Gesetz zur Bereinigung von SED-Unrecht, 1993 DtZ 162.

For criticism of the statute, see Roth, Saathoff, & Vom Stein, Das Zweite SED-Unrechtsbereinigungsgesetz, 1994 DA 449; Roth & Saathoff, Auf dem Wege zu einem "2. SED-Unrechtsbereinigungsgesetz," 1994 ZRP 135. See also Kaschkat, Die Haftung für DDR-Unrecht und der Entwurf des 2. SED-Unrechtsbereinigungsgesetz, 1993 DA 598; Saathoff, Roth, & Vom Stein, Kritik am Entwurf der Bundesregierung für ein 2. SED-Unrechtsbereinigungsgesetz, 1993 DA 603.

For general criticism from the ranks of the GDR victims, see, e.g., FAZ, Aug. 19, 1995, at 8 col. 4 (correspondence): many former GDR police and prison officials have become *Beamte* in the Federal Republic, but the promise of adequate compensation for victims, contained in article 17 of the Unification Treaty, "has been broken."

57. VwRehaG § 1(1) (emphasis added).

58. Id. § 1(2). The federal justice minister has suggested—without any explicit basis in the text of the statute—that in the case of administrative decisions far in the past, only "crass" violations should trigger rehabilitation. Leutheusser-Schnarrenberger, 1993 DtZ at 164.

59. Roth, Saathoff, & Vom Stein, 1994 DA at 451; see Unification Treaty arts. 17–19.

60. See Roth, Saathoff, & Vom Stein, 1994 DA at 452.

In a special paragraph, however, the statute does specify one category of oppressive acts that will trigger rehabilitation: the forcible removal of individuals from the area of the East German border and the accompanying expropriation of their property. VwRehaG § 1(3); see Leutheusser-Schnarrenberger, 1993 DtZ at 164. These massive programs of removal were directed toward assuring that only "politically reliable" individuals resided near the intra-German border. The programs had been undertaken in May and June 1952, after the Federal Republic began its process of integration in the western military alliance, and in October 1961 shortly after the erection of the Berlin Wall. These expropriations had originally been excluded from rules for the return of property under the Property Statute. See Ch. 11; Bennewitz, Rehabilitierung und Entschädigung der Opfer von Zwangsaussiedlungen, 1994 DA 461. This section of the second rehabilitation law, however, did not cover expropriations of the "Wall property" under the Defense Statute of 1961. See Ch. 11; Roth, Saathoff, & Vom Stein, 1994 DA at 453; von Welck, Zweites SED-Unrechtsbereinigungsgesetz, 1994 DtZ 226, 227.

61. See Ch. 11. In contrast with the treatment of criminal convictions in the first rehabilitation law, oppressive administrative acts of the Soviet occupation regime are completely excluded from coverage under the second statute. See Roth, Saathoff, & Vom Stein, 1994 DA at 453.

62. See id. at 450–51.

63. The drafters apparently did consider a provision under which any oppressive administrative act could be challenged and annulled, with the remedy of compensation to be granted in serious cases only. But this approach was rejected as impractical. See Leutheusser-Schnarrenberger, 1993 DtZ at 164.

64. See id. at 165–66: "Causes for discrimination in employment were varied. For example: inadequate societal activity in general, contacts with the west, criticism of the prevailing system or its leaders, refusal to collaborate with an institution like the [Stasi], or [the filing of] an application to travel abroad."

65. BerRehaG § 1.

66. See Roth, Saathoff, & Vom Stein, 1994 DA at 456.

67. Leutheusser-Schnarrenberger, 1993 DtZ at 162–63.

68. Roth & Saathoff, Alternativvorschläge zur Rehabilitierung und Entschädigung von DDR-Unrecht, 1992 DA 405, 408.

69. 84 BVerfGE 90 (1991); see Ch. 11.

70. See Ch. 11.

71. Leutheusser-Schnarrenberger, 1993 DtZ at 163.

72. This terminology may also reflect the view that "equalization payments" need not be as high as "compensation." Cf. Ch. 11. Indeed, use of the term "social equalization payments" in the first rehabilitation statute was criticized precisely on this ground—and also on the related ground that article 17 of the Unification Treaty requires "an appropriate rule of compensation," and not "equalization payments."

Kaschkat & Schlip, Zum Entwurf des 1. SED-Unrechtsbereinigungsgesetzes, 1992 DA 123, 125–26.

73. Former owners of Bodenreform land, expropriated under the Soviet occupation regime in the period 1945–49, will be entitled to "equalization payments" at the same level as the compensation received by persons whose property was expropriated under the GDR. It should be noted, however, that under the federal compensation statute of 1994, former owners who do not recover their property may receive payments that are substantially less than market value. See Ch. 11.

74. It has also been argued that influential circles in the west have vigorously supported the rights of property claimants while evincing a relative lack of interest in issues of rehabilitation. See Roth & Saathoff, 1994 ZRP at 137: "While the former property owners receive comprehensive scholarly and journalistic support and help, the politically oppressed stand alone with no one to turn to. In Germany, the loss of a piece of meadow property still seems to weigh more heavily than imprisonment, exclusion from employment, and lifelong harassment by the apparatus of the state."

Indeed, the disparity between redress received by property claimants and that accorded to victims of less readily measurable oppressions is a general problem in all former east bloc countries. Some theorists argue that because of this inherent inequality, no restitution of expropriated property should be undertaken. See, e.g., Elster, On Doing What One Can, 1 East European Constitutional Review, Summer 1992, at 15–17; see also Bruce Ackerman, The Future of Liberal Revolution 89–92 (1992): "Property owners have no right to demand that the injustices they have suffered be singled out for special treatment while the more grievous injustices suffered by others are given a lesser priority."

## Chapter 16
## Confronting the Past: The Stasi Files

1. Joachim Gauck, Die Stasi-Akten 27 (1991). See also Konrad H. Jarausch, The Rush to German Unity 35 (1994) (109,000 employees); Anne Worst, Das Ende eines Geheimdienstes 17–18 (1991) (85,000 employees).

2. One authority puts the number of IMs at "up to 300,000," adding that "the dreaded Stasi employed about one of every twenty-five adults." Jarausch at 35. For an even higher estimate, see Worst at 18 (possibly 500,000 IMs).

3. David Gill & Ulrich Schröter, Das Ministerium für Staatssicherheit: Anatomie des Mielke-Imperiums 279 (1993) (quoting Stefan Heym).

4. Worst at 9.

5. Gauck, Stasi-Akten, at 11–12.

6. See, e.g., Klaus-Dietmar Henke (ed.), Wann bricht schon mal ein Staat zusammen! Die Debatte über die Stasi-Akten und die DDR-Geschichte auf dem 39. Historikertag 1992, at 90 (1993) (remarks of Professor Dietrich Grille) (hereafter, Wann bricht).

7. Remarks of Joachim Gauck, in Günter Gaus (ed.), Neue Porträts in Frage und Antwort 192 (1992).

8. Wann bricht at 107 (remarks of Hansjörg Geiger).

9. Wolfgang Schäuble, Der Vertrag: Wie ich über die deutsche Einheit verhandelte 273 (1991). Indeed, sometimes Schäuble thought about "whether all of [the files] couldn't be destroyed unread." Id. See also Interview with Peter-Michael Diestel, for-

mer interior minister under de Maizière, Potsdam, June 29, 1993; Bruce Ackerman, The Future of Liberal Revolution 81–82 (1992): "Burn [the files], I say. . . . Even the most perfect process will make lots of mistakes. . . . [Even on optimistic assumptions,] hundreds or thousands will be falsely identified as unofficial collaborators. Is this a morally acceptable outcome?"

10. See Ackerman, Liberal Revolution, at 83–87. In effect this argument also points toward destruction of the files because, given their vast extent, adequate safeguards would be impossible as a practical matter. Id. at 85–86. See generally Hans-Dieter Schütt, Peter-Michael Diestel: "Rebellion tut gut" 61 (1992).

11. In one famous case the opposition writer Vera Wollenberger discovered in her Stasi file that the chief secret informant against her over a period of years had been her own husband. See Wollenberger, Eine zweite Vergewaltigung, in Hans Joachim Schädlich (ed.), Aktenkundig 154 (1992) (hereafter, Aktenkundig).

12. See also Gauck, Stasi-Akten, at 21: "[Certain readers] had to overcome a literally physical disgust in order to read to the end. . . . Indeed, looking through a Stasi file brings little pleasure. . . . Friends reveal themselves as spies, long forgotten or suppressed events are again called to mind, intimate details or arguments from married life are meticulously recorded."

13. See Ch. 15.

14. See, e.g., Kunert, Meine Nachbarn, in Aktenkundig at 49: "Indeed, right here and now, I have to apologize to my neighbors, some of whom I thought to be [Stasi] informants—infected by the epidemic of general mistrust, as I was. . . . That is also a truth transmitted by the [Stasi] files—a reason why they are read and should be read. It's not just that they implicate fellow citizens; they also rehabilitate them." Cf. also Wann bricht at 110–11 (remarks of Isolde Stark).

In gripping remarks at the Haus der Demokratie in Berlin in 1993, the east German writer Klaus Schlesinger recounted that he had been suspected of collaboration with the Stasi and was only able to clear his name through the availability of the Stasi files. See generally Schlesinger, Die Akte, 1993 Neue deutsche Literatur 108.

15. But cf. Reich, Am DDReizehnten Grad östlicher Länge, Die Zeit (overseas ed.), Nov. 19, 1993, at 16 col. 1: "It is said that the East Germans are a population of spies [, but that ignores] that in contrast with the 150,000 informal collaborators [of the Stasi] there were three times that number of people who rejected such collaboration or somehow got out of it. The Gauck files are full of [examples]. . ." For a less enthusiastic assessment, however, see Gauck, Stasi-Akten, at 47–49.

16. See, e.g., Worst at 116–24; 139–54.

17. Gauck, Stasi-Akten, at 76.

For a dramatic account of the seizure of the Stasi headquarters in Leipzig by a citizens committee during the Monday evening demonstration of December 4, 1989, see Hartmut Zwahr, Ende einer Selbstzerstörung: Leipzig und die Revolution in der DDR 117–28 (1993); for an account of the same event from the viewpoint of a Stasi officer, see Ariane Riecker et al., Stasi intim: Gespräche mit ehemaligen MfS-Angehörigen 40, 47–50 (1990) (hereafter, Stasi intim). The Stasi building in Leipzig occupied a prominent position on the Leipzig Ring, the traditional route of the Monday evening demonstrations. Also on December 4, citizens committees occupied the Stasi headquarters in Rostok and Greifswald among other cities. Zwahr, Ende einer Selbstzerstörung, at 127–28; see also Gauck, Stasi-Akten, at 76–79; Worst at 25–26; Elizabeth Pond, Beyond the Wall: Germany's Road to Unification 142–43 (1993).

The occupation of the Stasi offices by citizens groups marked an important step in the East German revolution. Indeed, "for many of the participants, these actions were the real turning point. They deprived the [Communist] Party of its sword." Carstens, Staubpilz im Herbst, FAZ, Oct. 12, 1994, at 10 col. 2.

18. See, e.g., Gauck, Stasi-Akten, at 79–80; Worst at 32–42; for a general account, see Jarausch at 95–97.

19. See Gill & Schröter at 177–91; Links, Die Akteure der Auflösung, in Worst at 73–83.

20. Gill & Schröter at 285.

21. See Helmut Herles & Ewald Rose (eds.), Vom Runden Tisch zum Parlament 26, 35–36, 48–53, 55, 57–58, 60–62, 78–79, 82, 84–86, 104–5, 151–52 (1990); Worst at 28–32; Links in Worst at 67–73.

Under pressure to dissolve the Stasi, Modrow originally sought to convert the existing "Ministry for State Security" into an "Office for National Security" with little substantive change. According to Joachim Gauck, "it was unmistakable that [Modrow] felt more obligated to the [officials of the Stasi] than to the angry citizens" who sought its dissolution. Gauck, Stasi-Akten, at 81–82.

22. Worst at 58, 112–16; Gauck, Stasi-Akten, at 82.

23. Regierungserklärung des Ministerpräsidenten der DDR, Lothar de Maizière, Apr. 19, 1990, reprinted in Ingo von Münch (ed.), Dokumente der Wiedervereinigung Deutschlands 192 (1991).

24. Gill & Schröter at 257–63. The commission was established pursuant to a resolution (Beschluß) of the Council of Ministers, of May 16, 1990. For Janka's imprisonment under the GDR and his rehabilitation during the East German revolution, see Ch. 15.

25. See Links in Worst at 90–93.

26. Id. at 83–90; Gauck, Stasi-Akten, at 83.

27. See Worst at 43–48; Gauck, Stasi-Akten, at 83–84.

28. Worst at 48; Wolfgang Thierse, Mit eigener Stimme sprechen 41 (1992); Interview with Peter-Michael Diestel, June 29, 1993. Indeed, Diestel originally sought to place espionage leader Markus Wolf on the government commission proposed by de Maizière in his acceptance speech. After a storm of incredulous protest, however, Diestel was forced to drop this plan. See Links in Worst at 90.

29. Schütt at 107–8; Interview with Peter-Michael Diestel, June 29, 1993.

30. Gill & Schröter at 281–84; Links in Worst at 93–96; Gauck, Stasi-Akten, at 85–86.

31. Sabine Bergmann-Pohl, Abschied ohne Tränen: Rückblick auf das Jahr der Einheit 101–10 (1991).

32. Schäuble, Der Vertrag, at 273–74.

33. Gesetz über die Sicherung und Nützung der personenbezogenen Daten des ehemaligen Ministeriums für Staatssicherheit/Amtes für Nationale Sicherheit, of Aug. 24, 1990, GBl DDR I 1419; reconfirmed 30 Aug. 1990.

34. Kind, Umgang mit den Stasi-Akten, in II(2) Klaus Stern (ed.), Deutsche Wiedervereinigung: Die Rechtseinheit 67 (1992) (hereafter, Deutsche Wiedervereinigung). In this respect, the Volkskammer's action on the Stasi files paralleled its last-minute enactment of a statute on questions of rehabilitation and compensation for oppressive acts under the GDR. See Ch. 15. The Volkskammer's iniative ultimately met greater success in the case of the Stasi files than in the case of compensation upon rehabilitation—for which the western treasury would essentially be responsible.

35. See generally Schäuble, Der Vertrag, at 274–80.

36. Id. at 275–77.

37. This compromise plan was hammered out at the last possible moment—during the night before the Unification Treaty was to be signed. Hansjörg Geiger & Heinz Klinghardt, Stasi-Unterlagen-Gesetz mit Erläuterungen für die Praxis 10–11 (1993); Schäuble, Der Vertrag, at 276–77.

38. Unification Treaty, attachment I, ch. II(B), para. II (2), reprinted in Geiger & Klinghardt at 195–96.

39. Bergmann-Pohl at 111–15; Worst at 49–60; cf. Biermann, "Des Satans Spießgesellen," Der Spiegel, 49/1993, at 42, 45 ("[O]ur hunger strike against the planned deportation of the files into eternal darkness"). For contemporaneous protests in Leipzig and Dresden, see Zwahr, Ende einer Selbstzerstörung, at 201–2 n. 54. Western officials have vehemently denied any intention to move the files out of eastern Germany. Schäuble, Der Vertrag, at 274; Wann bricht at 114–15 (remarks of Tilman Koops, official of Federal Archive, Koblenz).

40. See II(2) Deutsche Wiedervereinigung at 99 (remarks of Bruno Schmidt-Bleibtreu).

41. Vereinbarung zur Durchführung und Auslegung des Einigungsvertrages, of Sept. 18, 1990, BGBl II 1239, art. 1. The supplemental agreement also contained new provisions relating to rehabilitation. See Ch. 15.

42. Gesetz über die Unterlagen des Staatssicherheitsdienstes der ehemaligen Deutschen Demokratischen Republik (Stasi-Unterlagen-Gesetz—StUG), of Dec. 20, 1991, BGBl I 2272. See generally Stoltenberg, Die historische Entscheidung für die Öffnung der Stasi-Akten—Anmerkungen zum Stasi-Unterlagen-Gesetz, 1992 DtZ 65.

43. See II(2) Deutsche Wiedervereinigung at 88–89 (remarks of Hansgeorg Kind).

44. StUG § 1(1); see generally Kind in II(2) Deutsche Wiedervereinigung at 63.

45. StUG § 1(1)(3); see also id. § 1(1)(4).

46. The draft of a separate statute supported by Bündnis 90/Greens is set forth in Gauck, Stasi-Akten (appendix).

47. See, e.g., Remarks of Ingrid Köppe (Bündnis 90/Greens) in Bundestag Debate of June 13, 1991, reprinted in Wann bricht at 140–44: the statute "places the security of the state and its secret services above the interests of the victims [of the Stasi]."

48. See generally StUG § 2; see also id. §§ 7–11, 35–41.

Reflecting the compromise reached in the supplemental agreement of September 18, 1990, the statute also allows the Länder to choose special state commissioners to advise the federal agency on local problems relating to the files. The state commissioners may also perform other special functions such as providing psychological counseling to readers of the files. StUG § 38(3); Interview with Martin Gutzeit, Berlin State Commissioner for the Stasi Files, Berlin, May 18, 1993.

49. See, e.g., FAZ, Aug. 9, 1994, at 4 col. 1. Ordinarily, administrative officials are anonymous figures in Germany, and it is almost unheard of for an administrative body to be known by the name of its chief—as is the case of the Gauck Agency. But Gauck as an individual has played a special symbolic role in the history of the Stasi files: "As a result of his life history, [he] personifies the demand—formulated by the citizens committees, emphatically underscored by the Volkskammer, and brought to fruition against much opposition from the west—that the files not be destroyed but rather systematically worked through." Simitis, Die "Gauck-Behörde": Drei Jahre danach, 1994 NJW 99.

50. StUG § 3.

51. Id. § 13.

52. Wolf Biermann, for example, reports that his Stasi file contains forty thousand pages. Der Spiegel, 49/1993, at 46. Sometimes, however, a reader may encounter a laconic notice that portions of the dossier have been destroyed. See, e.g., Rathenow, Teile zu keinem Bild oder das Puzzle von der geheimen Macht, in Aktenkundig at 67. Such discoveries may reflect questionable handling of the files in the last year of the GDR.

53. StUG § 13(4)–(5). "Third persons" have similar rights. § 13(7). Yet the definition of "third person" includes a number of peculiar anomalies, and in some instances the term may even cover certain officials of the SED regime. See Stoltenberg, 1992 DtZ at 66–67. Indeed, the entire statute has been sharply criticized for using western terminology that is unfamiliar in the east and may be of unclear application to the categories of Stasi activity. See Weichert, Von der rechtlichen und tatsächlichen Unmöglichkeit des Stasi-Unterlagengesetzes, 1992 ZRP 241, 242.

Here and elsewhere in the statute, Stasi collaborators who were under eighteen years of age receive special protections of anonymity. StUG § 13(6). This provision is important because the Stasi often enlisted young persons as "unofficial collaborators"—particularly in the years after the "Prague Spring" when a higher level of dissatisfaction and protest became evident among the young. See Gauck, Stasi-Akten, at 32–36.

54. StUG §§ 16, 17.

55. One category of material in the Stasi files, however, has been excluded from a general right of access—even for victims. Judicial and prosecutorial records of the GDR included in the Stasi files are subject to a much more restrictive regime. See StUG §§ 18, 24. These limitations have enraged Stasi victims, for whom court records, contained in the Stasi files, could form the basis of a claim for rehabilitation. Yet, despite sharp criticism, this odd provision remains in the statute. See Stoltenberg, 1992 DtZ at 69–70; see also Simitis, 1994 NJW at 101.

56. StUG § 14.

57. See Wann bricht at 84–85 (remarks of Wolfgang Mommsen).

58. Id. at 86–87 (remarks of Hansjörg Geiger).

59. StUG §§ 20, 21. These provisions are unclear, however, because they do not specify the government or corporate officials who are entitled to receive this information. See Weichert, 1992 ZRP at 242.

A person mentioned in the files as an unofficial collaborator has no right to prevent the transfer of this information, even if the accused individual claims that the information is inaccurate; rather, a notice of the claimed inaccuracy will be placed in the file and the reviewing agency can take that claim into account in making its decision. See VG Berlin, Judgment of Feb. 24, 1992, 1992 LKV 419; OVG Berlin, Judgment of May 27, 1992, 1992 LKV 417.

60. StUG § 23; § 5(1).

61. See id. at § 25; Kind in II(2) Deutsche Wiedervereinigung at 76–77; remarks of Ingrid Köppe (Bündnis 90/Greens) in Bundestag Debate of June 13, 1991, reprinted in Wann bricht at 141–42.

62. See generally Schuppert, Das Stasi-Unterlagen-Gesetz: ein Maulkorb für die Presse?, 1992 AfP 105.

63. FAZ, Nov. 12, 1993, at 6 col. 5.

64. See generally II(2) Deutsche Wiedervereinigung at 92 (remarks of Hansgeorg Kind).

65. StUG §§ 32, 34. The same rules for access and publication apply to "political and historical" researchers.

66. Id. §§ 32(1)(3), 33–34.

67. Id. § 44. See Stoltenberg, 1992 DtZ at 72.

68. On the problems of free speech and press that remained in the statute, see Schuppert, 1992 AfP 105; Gounalakis & Vollmann, Die pressespezifischen Vorschriften des Stasi-Unterlagen-Gesetzes im Lichte des Art. 5 GG, 1992 DtZ 76.

69. See BGH, Judgment of Oct. 11, 1994, 1995 NJW 256; Märker, Unrechtsbereinigung auf dem Zivilrechtsweg?, 1995 DtZ 37.

70. "The GDR had been a closed society, lacking a public sphere. . . . The opening of the files has suddenly brought the informal and private networks of oppositional and dissident activities into the open, including the most intimate features of people's lives." Lemke, Trials and Tribulations: The *Stasi* Legacy in Contemporary German Politics, German Politics and Society 43, 47 (Summer 1992).

71. See Deckname "Lyrik": Eine Dokumentation von Reiner Kunze (1990).

72. Id. at 32, 48, 56–58, 67–69. See also Worst at 110–11.

73. Deckname "Lyrik" at 97–98.

74. See, e.g., Stasi-Akte "Verräter" (Spiegel Spezial 1/1993) at 12–13; see generally Erich Loest, Die Stasi war mein Eckermann (1991).

Moreover, the agency sometimes circulated rumors that opposition figures were themselves Stasi collaborators—seeking to discredit them within their own circles—and secretly organized campaigns criticizing their work at their place of employment. "Many people in the old GDR were pure bundles of nerves, because they had to hold out against all of this and constantly confront an invisible opponent. . . . To be a target of the Stasi generally meant years of psychological pressure." Gauck, Stasi-Akten, at 24–26.

75. Quoted in Reiner Kunze, Am Sonnenhang: Tagebuch eines Jahres 138–39 (1993). See also Wollenberger in Aktenkundig at 157: "The files reveal a grotesque visage, in which there can be no human face—at most some humanitarian camouflage. We must ask ourselves what it was that—for the second time in little more than a half century—made us become victims, perpetrators, collaborators, profiteers, and tolerators of a dictatorial regime."

76. For the recollections of outraged reformers, who believed that their defense lawyer Schnur was vigorously defending their interests when he was actually telling all to the Stasi, see Klier, Aktion "Störenfried," in Aktenkundig at 91; Wollenberger in Aktenkundig at 154. After unification, Schnur was excluded from the bar, and ultimately prosecuted, as a result of these activities. See Ch. 13.

77. See FAZ, Sept. 13, 1991, at 1 col. 2; cf. Worst at 106–8.

78. FAZ, Apr. 13, 1992, at 1 cols. 2 & 5; id. at 3 cols. 1 & 4.

79. FAZ, Apr. 20, 1992, at 4 col. 3; for Stolpe's explanation, essentially along the same lines, see FAZ, May 14, 1992, at 4 col. 4. On the Stolpe case, see also FAZ, June 19, 1992, at 5 col. 4. For a comparison of the de Maizière and Stolpe cases, see FAZ, Feb. 27, 1992, at 14 col. 2.

80. Interestingly, the Stolpe affair has contributed to an apparent re-evaluation of the role of the Evangelical Church in the GDR. Previously the church had been viewed as a center of opposition to the regime, but disclosures of broad collaboration with the Stasi and other state agencies suggest that the role of the church may ultimately have been to pacify and neutralize opposition groups, thus in a sense actually supporting the regime. See Schröder, Die DDR einst—und jetzt?, APuZ, Oct. 2, 1992, at 3.

81. See, e.g., Lemke, German Politics and Society (Summer 1992), at 50–51.

82. According to Müller, these contacts with the Stasi were initiated in order to

improve relations between the theater and the SED bureaucracy. FAZ, Mar. 13, 1995, at 37 col. 3.

Although Müller was in a sense an official GDR dramatist, his critical spirit challenged the regime, and his memoirs record a succession of crises in which his dramas were faced with censorship. See Heiner Müller, Krieg ohne Schlacht: Leben in zwei Diktaturen (1992). A late work written in the final years of the GDR, Wolokolamsker Chausee V (Der Findling), is a bitter attack on the Stalinist system of the GDR and its practice of official and private "forgetting" of the terrors and atrocities for which the system was responsible. Müller reports that when he read this work aloud on the stage of the Deutsches Theater in Berlin in January 1988, "there was a breathless stillness in the over-filled auditorium. People still did not believe that it was possible . . . that such a thing could be read aloud." Müller, Krieg ohne Schlacht, at 351. For a parallel theme in Czech literture of the post-1968 period, see Milan Kundera, The Book of Laughter and Forgetting (1981). Heiner Müller died in late December 1995.

83. See Hermann Vinke (ed.), Akteneinsicht Christa Wolf: *Zerrspiegel und Dialog*: Eine Dokumentation (1993).

84. For Wolf's own reflections on the case of her Stasi file, see Porträts 5 (in conversation with Günter Gaus) 7–34 (1993). See also Christa Wolf, Was bleibt (1990).

Disclosures of collaboration with the Stasi have not been limited to eastern citizens. Recent articles have revealed, for example, that Dietrich Staritz, a highly respected western expert on the history of the GDR, was a Stasi collaborator from 1961 to 1972. During the same period, Staritz was apparently also delivering information to the West German intelligence service. Der Spiegel, 38/1994, at 95.

85. See, e.g., Ackerman, Liberal Revolution, at 81–89. A government employee could be dismissed on the basis of such an opinion from the Gauck Agency, perhaps also without a hearing. See Joachim Gauck, in Gaus, Neue Porträts in Frage und Antwort, at 214. Subsequent judicial review would, however, be available.

86. See Simitis, 1994 NJW at 100.

87. VG Berlin, Judgment of June 3, 1993, 1993 NJW 2548; see StUG §§ 37(1)(5); 32(3).

88. VG Berlin, 1993 NJW at 2550–51.

89. Id. at 2550.

90. LG Halle, Judgment of June 22, 1993, 1994 LKV 71. The judgment was ultimately upheld after a series of appeals. See 1995 LKV 304. In a similar case, another person named on the same list also received judicial protection of anonymity. OLG Naumburg, Judgment of Nov. 25, 1993, 1994 DtZ 73. In this case, an appellate court noted that the plaintiff had not occupied a prominent role in public life or in the Stasi. During the East German revolution of 1989–90, it might have been justifiable to reveal names of ordinary Stasi collaborators; but that need is no longer present because the political situation has been stabilized and much is now publicly known about the nature and extent of the Stasi's activities. This decision was affirmed in the Federal Supreme Court. See BGH, Judgment of July 12, 1994, 1995 JZ 253.

Additional legal actions have been brought by others mentioned in the purported list of collaborators in Halle. See Horch und Guck, 3/1993, at 32.

91. OLG Hamburg, Judgment of Oct. 10, 1991, 1992 DtZ 223.

92. OLG Hamburg, Judgment of May 6, 1993, 1993 DtZ 349.

93. See generally FAZ, Feb. 29, 1992, at 27 col. 1. For a proposal for the dissolution of the Gauck office, see FAZ, Apr. 24, 1992, at 5 col. 1.

94. Der Spiegel, 11/1992, at 32.

95. See FAZ, Mar. 19, 1992, at 1 col. 1.

96. FAZ, Apr. 29, 1992, at 1 col. 2.

97. FAZ, Nov. 20, 1993, at 4 col. 5.

98. FAZ, Nov. 15, 1993, at 4 col. 6; cf. Hans-Dieter Schütt, Regine Hildebrandt: "Bloß nicht aufgeben!" 102–5 (1992).

99. See Friedrich Schorlemmer, Zu seinem Wort stehen 55 (1994).

100. FAZ, Nov. 15, 1993, at 4 col. 6. Indeed, in a later speech Heitmann emphasized that "insistence on the opening of the [Stasi] files" was the "core" of the East German revolution of 1989–90. FAZ, Sept. 2, 1994, at 13 col. 1.

101. See Biermann, Der Spiegel, 49/1993, at 42.

102. Id. at 46.

103. FAZ, July 4, 1994, at 4 col. 5; FAZ, Nov. 24, 1993, at 4 col. 6. See Ch. 13.

104. StUG §§ 7–9. See Gounalakis & Vollmann, 1992 DtZ 77. These provisions, however, have not evoked a high level of compliance. See Simitis, 1994 NJW at 100.

105. StUG § 45.

106. FAZ, July 9, 1994, at 4 col. 4.

107. Id.; FAZ, Nov. 12, 1993, at 6 col. 5; FAZ, Apr. 15, 1994, at 5 col. 1. See generally Gounalakis & Vollmann, 1992 DtZ 77.

108. FAZ, July 9, 1994, at 4 col. 4.

109. And see the revealing debate between Regine Hildebrandt, social minister in the Stolpe cabinet, and Bärbel Bohley, a veteran of the East German civil rights movement, FR, Feb. 8, 1993, at 12 col. 1. For a good expression of the view of many GDR reformers, see also Weiss, "Wir müssen uns der Wahrheit stellen," Spiegel Spezial, 1/1993, at 6, 9: "No—contempt is not enough. We must hate. We cannot turn away from this destructive evil with pious maxims and mild forgiveness. We must take care that the victims receive justice and that the offenders are punished. There cannot be an amnesty without punishment and remorse—otherwise the evil will just spread. . . . All of those who have assaulted the body, life, and dignity of individuals must be called to account. It is a question of social hygiene. The thought that offenders can go scot-free is unbearable. Therefore, this chapter of German history will not be closed so quickly."

110. See Chs. 4 & 9.

111. "The few that exercised active opposition against the GDR regime are as much in favor of an unrestrained reckoning with cowards, collaborators, and fellow travelers, as strict anti-Communists." Jesse, "Entnazifizierung" und "Entstasifizierung" als politisches Problem: Die doppelte Vergangenheitsbewältigung, in Josef Isensee (ed.), Vergangenheitsbewältigung durch Recht 14 (1992).

112. Cf. Schuppert, 1992 AfP at 108–9.

## Chapter 17
## The European Context of Unification and the Reserved Rights of the World War II Allies

1. In an important sense, both goals were intimately related to basic constitutional themes of representative democracy and human rights: the unification of Germany would—it was hoped—remove the "other part" of Germany from the totalitarian sphere, and the unification of Europe would so embed Germany in democratic structures that a return to authoritarian and militaristic traditions of the past would be forever rendered impossible.

2. See, e.g., Stephen F. Szabo, The Diplomacy of German Unification 5 (1992): "Adenauer gave priority to integration with the West and close links to the United States and relegated national unification to a future in which a strong West was constructed. . . . He believed deeply in the desirability of a postnational Europe both as an end in itself and as a means of overcoming the dangers of German nationalism." Indeed, Adenauer saw the policy of western integration as "the most effective means—perhaps the only means—of protecting Germany from itself." Christian Hacke, Weltmacht wider Willen: Die Aussenpolitik der Bundesrepublik Deutschland 52 (1993) (quoting Paul Henri Spaak); see also id. at 47–53.

3. "[In Adenauer's view,] a politically democratic and economically stable Federal Republic, firmly integrated in the Atlantic Alliance, would radiate like a magnet toward the east and have an attracting effect." Hacke at 69.

4. Karl Kaiser, Deutschlands Vereinigung: Die internationalen Aspekte 165 (Document 13)(1991). See Ch. 3.

5. Kaiser, Deutschlands Vereinigung, at 197 (Document 27).

6. Cf., e.g., Kohl's remark in February 1990 that the "history of this century shows: nothing is more detrimental to the stability of Europe than a Germany that is wavering between two worlds, between West and East." Id. at 198.

7. Eduard Shevardnadze, Die Zukunft gehört der Freiheit 235, 241 (1993); see also Ulrich Albrecht, Die Abwicklung der DDR 154–76 (1992). See generally Ch. 22.

8. Report of the Crimea (Yalta) Conference, Feb. 11, 1945, reprinted in 3 Charles I. Bevans (ed.), Treaties and Other International Agreements of the United States of America 1776–1949, at 1007 (1969). The Yalta accord reflected an agreement on future occupation zones, entered into by Great Britain, the United States, and the Soviet Union in London in 1944. See Protocol on the Zones of Occupation in Germany and the Administration of "Greater Berlin," and amending agreement, Sept. 12 & Nov. 14, 1944, 5 U.S.T. 2078, T.I.A.S. No. 3071, 227 U.N.T.S. 279; see also Mosely, The Occupation of Germany: New Light on How the Zones Were Drawn, 28 Foreign Affairs 580 (1950). The Yalta Report contemplated that France, although not represented at the conference, would also administer an occupation zone. See generally J. P. Nettl, The Eastern Zone and Soviet Policy in Germany 1945–50, at 38–44 (1951); Edward R. Stettinius Jr., Roosevelt and the Russians: The Yalta Conference (1949); Richard F. Fenno Jr. (ed.), The Yalta Conference (1972). Because of these and other agreements concluded at the conference, Yalta became "the prevailing shorthand for the division of Europe"—although that division was actually the result of a longer historical process. Timothy Garton Ash, In Europe's Name: Germany and the Divided Continent 5–6 (1993).

9. Berlin Declaration of June 5, 1945, 60 Stat. 1649, T.I.A.S. No. 1520, 68 U.N.T.S. 189.

10. 60 Stat. at 1650.

11. Id.

12. Report on the Tripartite Conference of Berlin (Potsdam), Aug. 2, 1945, reprinted in 3 Bevans at 1224 (hereafter, Potsdam Report). For important memoirs of the Potsdam Conference, see Winston S. Churchill, The Second World War, vol. 6: Triumph and Tragedy 630–76 (1953); 1 Harry S. Truman, Memoirs: Year of Decisions 343–414 (1955). See also, e.g., Wolfgang Benz, Potsdam 1945 (1986).

13. Lucius D. Clay, Decision in Germany 37–43 (1950). But the precise status of the Potsdam accord was subject to dispute. Some German scholars argued that the accord

was not actually a treaty in international law and, in any case, could not bind Germany which was not a signatory. See, e.g., Otto Kimminich, Die Eigentumsgarantie im Prozeß der Wiedervereinigung 75 (1990); see also 5 BVerfGE 85, 113–25 (1956) (KPD case).

14. Potsdam Report at 1227.

15. Id. at 1228.

16. Id. The Allies did indeed move quickly to establish state governments. By September 1945, for example, the states of Bavaria, Württemberg-Baden, and Hesse had been created in the American zone. Elected assemblies drafted state constitutions which were adopted in plebiscites in 1946 after approval by the American military commander. See Clay at 84–90. Although states were also established in the British zone at an early point, these governments did not adopt constitutions before the Basic Law became effective in 1949. The British government favored greater centralization and was reluctant to accord independent authority to the German states. See generally Clay at 393–94.

This difference between the zones had a interesting result. The constitutions of the states in the American zone, which were adopted before 1949, were full constitutions containing their own series of basic rights, totally independent of the Basic Law. The constitutions of the states of the British zone, in contrast, were adopted after the effective date of the Basic Law and relied to a significant extent on the basic rights of the Basic Law, rather than including their own separate catalogs of rights. Cf. Starck, Verfassunggebung in den neuen Ländern, 1992 ZG 1, 1–2; Peter H. Merkl, The Origin of the West German Republic 8–15 (1963). For some contemporary implications of this distinction, see generally Ch. 9.

17. Potsdam Report at 1229. The accord also stated that "*for the time being* no central German government shall be established"—implying that a central German government would be created in the future. Id. (emphasis added); see also Nettl at 259, 260: "The conception of Potsdam was of a Germany undivided in principle, but administered in four parts. . . . Zonal frontiers were not intended primarily as frontiers for the Germans, but between the different Allies."

18. Byrnes, Restatement of U.S. Policy on Germany, reprinted in U.S. Department of State, Germany 1947–1949: The Story in Documents 6 (1950) (Secretary Byrnes's Stuttgart speech of Sept. 6, 1946).

19. See U.S. Department of State, Germany 1947–1949, at 57–67; see also Clay at 141–62.

20. See Clay at 163–84.

21. See id. at 343–57, 363.

The Allied Control Council enjoyed a brief revival in December 1989 when the Soviet Union—"concerned about the pace of events" in the crumbling GDR—called the council back into being for one final session. Szabo at 43. The meeting marked the first time in eighteen years that representatives of the four Allied powers had met in Berlin, and it left a "negative impression" because it suggested that "a revival of the anti-Hitler coalition of 50 years ago" could combat the growth of democracy in Germany and "endanger the establishment of new European structures, at the very outset." Kaiser, Deutschlands Vereinigung, at 53–54; see Richard Kiessler & Frank Elbe, Ein runder Tisch mit scharfen Ecken: Der diplomatische Weg zur deutschen Einheit 73–76 (1993).

22. Clay at 358–92; see generally Nettl at 107–9.

23. Frankfurt Documents, July 1, 1948; reprinted in 1 Ingo von Münch (ed.),

Dokumente des geteilten Deutschland 88–91 (1976) (hereafter, Dokumente).

The Frankfurt Documents were issued after six western allies, meeting at a conference in London, decided to proceed with the founding of a state in western Germany and established the basic principles of the constitution. See Merkl, Origin, at 19, 21; Clay at 394–409; Six-Power Communiqué, of June 2, 1948, reprinted in 1 Dokumente at 82–85. See generally U.S. Department of State, Germany 1947–1949, at 75–88.

24. 1 Dokumente at 90. Among other things, these powers included control over Germany's foreign relations, measures necessary for the security of the occupation forces, and the authority to ensure that the German government observed its own constitution.

25. Id.

26. Id. at 91.

27. See Merkl, Origin, at 50–54.

28. Similarly, the group that met to adopt the document was referred to as a "parliamentary council" rather than the more weighty term, "constituent assembly," that had been used in the Frankfurt Documents. Id at 53–54; see generally Clay at 409–11.

29. See Letter from the Three Western Military Governors to the President of the Parliamentary Council, May 12, 1949, reprinted in 1 Dokumente at 130.

30. Occupation Statute Defining the Powers to be Retained by the Occupation Authorities, Apr. 8, 1949, effective Sept. 21, 1949, 63 Stat. 2819, T.I.A.S. No. 2066, 140 U.N.T.S. 202.

31. Occupation Statute, 63 Stat. at 2819–20. The Allies also retained the power to cancel federal or state legislation, but they declared that they would not exercise this authority "unless in their opinion [the legislation] is inconsistent with the Basic Law, a Land Constitution, legislation or other directives of the occupation authorities themselves or the provisions of [the Occupation Statute], or unless it constitutes a grave threat to the basic purposes of the occupation." See Occupation Statute, 63 Stat. at 2820. See also Agreed Memorandum regarding the Principles Governing Exercise of Powers and Responsibilities of US-UK-French Governments Following Establishment of German Federal Republic, Apr. 8, 1949, 63 Stat. 2818, T.I.A.S. No. 2066, 140 U.N.T.S. 200. Moreover, under the Occupation Statute, any amendment of the Basic Law required "the express approval of the occupation authorities before becoming effective." 63 Stat. at 2820.

There was adverse reaction in Germany to the broad powers reserved by the Allies in the Occupation Statute. See Thomas Alan Schwartz, America's Germany: John J. McCloy and the Federal Republic of Germany 38–39 (1991). On the statute, see generally Clay at 412–18, 428–30.

32. See 1 Dokumente at 130; see also arts. 23, 144(2) GG.

33. Directive of the Supreme Commander of the Soviet Military Administration in Germany, Oct. 22, 1945, reprinted in 1 Dokumente at 294.

34. See Nettl at 96–97; see also Ch. 4.

35. See generally Nettl at 88–90; 97–106. Most experts hold that this merger was compelled by the Soviet authorities. See, e.g., Andrea Zieger & Gottfried Zieger, Die Verfassungsentwicklung in der Sowjetischen Besatzungszone Deutschlands/DDR von 1945 bis zum Sommer 1952, at 40–51 (1990); but for a somewhat different view, see Hans Mayer, Der Turm von Babel 18–39 (1991). In any case, the Social Democrats were soon rendered powerless within the SED, which was controlled by its Communist members at an early point. See Nettl at 107.

36. See H. W. Koch, A Constitutional History of Germany in the Nineteenth and Twentieth Centuries 345 (1984). This move substantially paralleled steps that had been taken earlier in 1949 by the western Allies before the adoption of the Basic Law. Id. at 343; see Message to the Bonn Parliamentary Council from the Foreign Ministers of the US, UK, and France, Apr. 8, 1949, 63 Stat. 2825, T.I.A.S. No. 2066, 140 U.N.T.S. 218. See also Nettl at 112–13.

37. Declaration of the Chairman of the Soviet Control Commission with Respect to the Transfer of Administrative Functions to German Officials, Nov. 11, 1949, reprinted in 1 Dokumente at 325–27.

38. This agreement was originally signed in 1952 but its ratification was delayed when a companion treaty on the European Defense Community was rejected by the French National Assembly. After modification, the treaty was signed again in 1954 and came into effect after ratification by the signatory parties. See Convention on Relations between the Three Powers and the Federal Republic of Germany, May 26, 1952, 6 U.S.T. 4251, T.I.A.S. No. 3425, as amended Oct. 23, 1954, 6 U.S.T. 4121, T.I.A.S. No. 3425 (hereafter, General Treaty).

39. See J.K. Sowden, The German Question 1945–1973, at 158–62 (1975); Stern, Der Staatsvertrag im völkerrechtlichen und verfassungsrechtlichen Kontext, in 1 Klaus Stern & Bruno Schmidt-Bleibtreu (eds.), Verträge und Rechtsakte zur Deutschen Einheit 12–14 (1990) (hereafter, Verträge und Rechtsakte).

40. General Treaty art. 1(2).

41. Id. art. 2.

42. See generally Rauschning, Deutschlands aktuelle Verfassungslage, 1990 DVBl 393, 397–98; von Goetze, Die Rechte der Alliierten auf Mitwirkung bei der deutschen Einigung, 1990 NJW 2161, 2165. The joint Allied responsibility for "matters affecting Germany as a whole" can be traced back to a three-power "Agreement on Control Machinery in Germany," signed by the United States, Great Britain, and the Soviet Union in November 1944. See 1 Dokumente at 29. See also Rauschning, 1990 DVBl at 397.

43. See General Treaty art. 3(1). This pledge accords with the preamble of the Basic Law, which envisions the Federal Republic as an "equal member of a united Europe."

44. See UN Charter art. 2(4) (no "threat or use of force against the territorial integrity or political independence of any state").

45. General Treaty art. 7(2).

46. See, e.g., Hailbronner, Völker- und europarechtliche Fragen der deutschen Wiedervereinigung, 1990 JZ 449, 450; Klein, An der Schwelle zur Wiedervereinigung Deutschlands, 1990 NJW 1065, 1067.

One other reservation in the General Treaty is worth noting. In order to ensure the safety of stationed troops, the western Allies—in very general language—reserved the right to employ secret electronic surveillance in the Federal Republic, until the German government obtained domestic legal authorization to undertake these measures itself. General Treaty art. 5(2). In response, the Basic Law was amended in 1968 to allow the government to undertake secret surveillance if the "free democratic basic order" would thus be protected and if parliamentary committees exercised a degree of review. See arts. 10(2), 19(4) GG; Note, Recent Emergency Legislation in West Germany, 82 Harvard Law Review 1704, 1707 n. 25 (1969).

The Constitutional Court upheld this amendment against claims that it was invalid as violating certain fundamental ideas of human dignity and principles of the rule of law. 30 BVerfGE 1 (1970) (Klass case); Donald P. Kommers, The Constitutional Jurisprudence of the Federal Republic of Germany 230–31 (1989). See arts. 1, 20, 79(3) GG. Before the *Bodenreform* case, discussed in Chapter 11, this was the only decision of the Constitutional Court that contained a significant discussion of constitutional limits on the amendment of the Basic Law.

47. Declaration of the Government of the USSR concerning the Granting of Sovereignty to the German Democratic Republic, Mar. 25, 1954; reprinted in 1 Dokumente at 329–31; see Stern in 1 Verträge und Rechsakte at 14.

48. 1 Dokumente at 330.

49. Id. at 330–31.

50. Additional statements confirming the Allied reserved rights can be found in the preamble of the Four-Power Treaty on Berlin (1971), discussed below, and in a four-power declaration concerning the applications of the Federal Republic and the GDR to join the United Nations. See Rauschning, 1990 DVBl at 395–96; Heberlein, Rechtliche Aspekte einer ständigen Mitgliedschaft Deutschlands im UN-Sicherheitsrat, 1994 ZRP 358, 363.

51. See, e.g., Rauschning, 1990 DVBl at 396; but see von Goetze, 1990 NJW at 2162–63 (arguing that all of the remaining reserved rights of the Allies are occupation rights).

52. See Hailbronner, 1990 JZ at 450–51.

53. See generally Stern, Grundfragen der Rechtslage Berlins, in Georg Brunner et al. (eds.), Sowjetsystem und Ostrecht, Festschrift für Boris Meissner zum 70. Geburtstag 793–803 (1985).

54. See generally 2 Ingo von Münch (ed.), Grundgesetz-Kommentar art. 23, Nos. 7–8 (1983).

55. Letter from the Three Western Military Governors to the President of the Parliamentary Council, May 12, 1949, reprinted in 1 Dokumente at 130 (emphasis added).

56. See Provisional Constitution for Greater Berlin, Aug. 13, 1946, reprinted in 1 Dokumente at 138, and accompanying Note of Allied Commanders, id. at 149.

The Allied Kommandatura was the highest legislative and executive organ of occupied Berlin, originally composed of one representative of each of the four Allied commanders in chief. In June 1948 at a time of increasing tensions—after the Soviet delegation had walked out of the Allied Control Council—the Soviet representative withdrew from the Allied Kommandatura, which continued to function with the three remaining representatives, exercising authority over the western part of Berlin only. See generally I. D. Hendry & M. C. Wood, The Legal Status of Berlin 57–59 (1987). Until the point of unification, the law of the Allied Kommandatura (and other Allied law) superseded German law in Berlin. Hendry & Wood at 83–90.

57. Clay at 377–79.

58. Declaration of the Allied Kommandatura of the City of Berlin concerning the Principles of the Relationship of the City of Greater Berlin to the Allied Kommandatura, May 14, 1949, reprinted in 1 Dokumente at 154. The 1950 constitution was partially based on a Berlin Constitution of 1948 which had been issued by the city council but never went into effect. See Ch. 9.

59. Note of the Allied Kommandatura of Berlin concerning the Approval of the Constitution of Berlin, Aug. 29, 1950, reprinted in 1 Dokumente at 172. The 1950 Constitution of Berlin is reprinted in id. at 158–71. See also Ch. 9.

60. Indeed, in the 1960s Berlin was the center of a dangerous three-sided game: the Federal Republic sought to cement closer relations with Berlin, and the Soviet Union sometimes responded with maneuvers and other military demonstrations. The western

Allies were obliged to intercede when the situation threatened to get out of hand. See Yuli A. Kvitsinsky, Vor dem Sturm: Erinnerungen eines Diplomaten 219–20 (1993).

61. See, e.g., 7 BVerfGE 1 (1957) (Berlin is a state of the Federal Republic); 19 BVerfGE 377 (1966) (Constitutional Court may decide certain cases arising in Berlin).

62. Note of the Allied Kommandatura of Berlin, May 24, 1967, concerning the Decision of the Federal Constitutional Court of Jan. 20, 1966, reprinted in 1 Dokumente at 200–201. The case that evoked this note can be found at 19 BVerfGE 377 (1966).

63. 1 Dokumente at 200–201.

64. See Quadripartite Agreement on Berlin, Sept. 3, 1971, 24 U.S.T. 283, T.I.A.S. No. 7551, 880 U.N.T.S. 115; the text of the treaty and accompanying documents are reprinted in Hendry & Wood at 335–50.

65. For tense negotiations over the status of Berlin, see, e.g., A. James McAdams, East Germany and Detente: Building Authority after the Wall 110–21 (1985).

66. Quadripartite Agreement on Berlin part II(B). See generally Schiedermair, Die Bindungen West-Berlins an die Bundesrepublik, 1982 NJW 2841. For comments from the Soviet perspective on the negotiation of this treaty, see Kvitsinsky at 237–51.

## Chapter 18
## The Oder-Neiße Line and the Map of Central Europe

1. For these territories, see the map of Germany at the outset of this volume.

2. Report of the Crimea (Yalta) Conference, Feb. 11, 1945, reprinted in 3 Charles I. Bevans (ed.), Treaties and Other International Agreements of the United States of America 1776–1949, at 1010–11 (1969). See Ch. 17.

The Curzon Line was a boundary that had been proposed by British negotiators in 1920, in the aftermath of the Treaty of Versailles, to mark a frontier between the newly re-created state of Poland and the Soviet Union. See James T. Shotwell & Max M. Laserson, Poland and Russia 1919–1945, at 5–16 (1945). In the Treaty of Riga in 1921, however, the final inter-war border was drawn considerably to the east of the Curzon Line, thus confirming Poland's seizure of territory from the weak Bolshevik regime in battles immediately following World War I. The Soviet Union regained this territory after the Hitler-Stalin pact and the invasion of Poland but lost it once again after Germany invaded Russia in 1941. The Soviet Union had always maintained that the territories east of the Curzon Line had been wrongfully taken from it by Poland, and it vigorously sought return of these lands. At Yalta—with the Soviet army firmly in control of the disputed territory—the western Allies in effect accepted these claims. See Edward R. Stettinius Jr., Roosevelt and the Russians: The Yalta Conference 301 (1949); see also J. K. Sowden, The German Question 1945–1973, at 228–51 (1975); Jean Laloy, Yalta: Yesterday, Today, Tomorrow 24–29 (1988); 2 Norman Davies, God's Playground: A History of Poland 488, 504–5 (1982).

3. Report on the Tripartite Conference of Berlin (Potsdam), Aug. 2, 1945, reprinted in 3 Bevans at 1234 (hereafter, Potsdam Report). See also Ch. 17.

4. See, e.g., Winston S. Churchill, The Second World War, vol. 6: Triumph and Tragedy 647–48 (1953).

5. See Stettinius at 123, 209–12, 259–61, 269–71. See also Roosevelt, Address to Congress on the Crimean Conference, Mar. 1, 1945, reprinted in B. D. Zevin (ed.), Nothing to Fear: The Selected Addresses of Franklin Delano Roosevelt 1932–1945, at

450 (1946); Byrnes, Restatement of U.S. Policy on Germany, reprinted in U.S. Department of State, Germany 1947–1949: The Story in Documents 8 (1950) (Secretary of State Byrnes's Stuttgart speech of Sept. 6, 1946).

6. Potsdam Report at 1232–33.

For contemporary criticism of the treatment of the Polish borders by the Allies, see Woolsey, Poland at Yalta and Dumbarton Oaks, 39 American Journal of International Law 295 (1945); Wright, Poland and the Crimea Conference, 39 American Journal of International Law 300 (1945). See also Fainsod, The Development of American Military Government Policy during World War II, in Carl J. Friedrich et al., American Experiences in Military Government in World War II, at 40 (1948): "The decision to compensate Poland with a slice of eastern Germany was made under Soviet pressure and involved Roosevelt and Churchill in an embarrassing repudiation of the principles [of self-determination] to which they had subscribed in the Atlantic Charter."

7. Although a peace conference with Germany never took place, the Allies did sign peace treaties with Italy, Rumania, Bulgaria, and Hungary (the four European nations allied with Germany in World War II) at the Paris Peace Conference in 1946. A treaty with Finland was signed at this conference as well. See, e.g., James F. Byrnes, Speaking Frankly 138–55 (1947).

8. Under Polish law, in contrast, the territory in question was apparently treated—from a very early point—as fully incorporated territory of Poland, and not merely as territory remaining under provisional administration. See 40 BVerfGE 141, 158–59 (1975). These territories were settled, in large part, by Polish-speaking persons transferred from the former Polish regions east of the Curzon Line which had been regained by the Soviet Union.

9. See Christian Hacke, Weltmacht wider Willen: Die Aussenpolitik der Bundesrepublik Deutschland 92, 129 (1993).

10. "In the early years of the Federal Republic, these refugees and expellees [from the Oder-Neiße lands and Czechoslovakia] made up nearly one fifth of the new state's population. They were a formidable constraint on Konrad Adenauer's freedom of action in relations with the East. At the beginning of the 1960s, the umbrella organisation of the different regional groups of refugees and expellees, the Federation of Expellees, claimed three million members. Thirty years later it would still claim some two million members (although some of these were in fact the children of refugees and expellees, who, in an extraordinary provision, formally inherited 'expellee' status). . . . [Expellee leaders] remained, even in the 1980s, a significant influence upon the policy of the Christian Democrats." Timothy Garton Ash, In Europe's Name: Germany and the Divided Continent 29–30 (1993).

Indeed, as late as September 1989 groups of expellees distributed leaflets at a CDU party congress, advocating a German state in the borders of 1937. The leaflets referred to the Oder-Neiße lands as "eastern provinces" of the "German Reich" that were under Polish and Soviet "administration." This incident enraged the top Soviet leadership. Richard Kiessler & Frank Elbe, Ein runder Tisch mit scharfen Ecken: Der diplomatische Weg zur deutschen Einheit 25–26 (1993).

11. See generally Elizabeth Pond, Beyond the Wall: Germany's Road to Unification 193 (1993).

12. See, e.g., New York Times, Feb. 27, 1990, at A8 col. 1; see also New York Times, Mar. 3, 1990, at A6 col. 3 (Kohl argues that German ratification of the Polish border should be accompanied by Poland's waiver of any rights to war reparations);

Horst Teltschik, 329 Tage: Innenansichten der Einigung 30, 163–76 (1991); Stephen F. Szabo, The Diplomacy of German Unification 72–76 (1992); Peter H. Merkl, German Unification in the European Context 339–43 (1993).

Moreover, the omission of a reference to the Polish border issue in Kohl's Ten-Point Plan of November 1989—see Ch. 3—"made the matter into an international issue and set off a torrent of declarations by various governments emphasizing the permanence of the border as a condition of German unification." Karl Kaiser, Deutschlands Vereinigung: Die internationalen Aspekte 91 (1991).

13. Cf., e.g., McCurdy, German Reunification: Historical and Legal Roots of Germany's Rapid Progress Towards Unity, 22 New York University Journal of International Law & Politics 253, 275–76 (1990); Teltschik at 14, 166.

14. See Teltschik 150–51 (views of French President Mitterrand), 187. Prime Minister Thatcher's reaction was particularly sharp: "[Kohl] was vague about the question of borders—too vague for my liking—arguing that the Oder-Neisse line, which marked the border with Poland, should not become a legal issue. He did not seem now or later to understand the Polish fears and sensitivities. . . . Chancellor Kohl had managed to convey the worst possible impression by his unwillingness to have a proper treaty to settle Germany's border with Poland." Margaret Thatcher, The Downing Street Years 797, 799 (1993).

15. Szabo at 76.

16. See, e.g., Teltschik at 163–64.

17. See Ch. 6.

18. See, e.g., Klein, An der Schwelle zur Wiedervereinigung Deutschlands, 1990 NJW 1065, 1072.

19. See, e.g., Heintschel von Heinegg, Der Beitritt "anderer Teile Deutschlands" zur Bundesrepublik nach Art. 23 Satz 2 GG, 1990 DÖV 425, 427–29.

20. Yet December 31, 1937, was *after* the 1936 reoccupation of the Rhineland by Hitler's military forces in violation of the Versailles Treaty—"an act which we now realize was the determining first step along the road that led to World War II." James Bryant Conant, Germany and Freedom: A Personal Appraisal 83 (1958).

21. Warsaw Declaration, of June 6, 1950, reprinted in 1 Ingo von Münch (ed.), Dokumente des geteilten Deutschland 496 (1976) (hereafter, Dokumente); Agreement concerning the Demarcation of the Established and Existing Polish-German State Frontier, July 6, 1950, 319 U.N.T.S. 93, reprinted in 1 Dokumente at 497–99.

East Germany's acceptance of the Polish border represented the reversal of an earlier position taken by the SED to the contrary. Indeed, the 1950 Warsaw Declaration was part of a process through which the GDR sought to overcome wartime hostilities and achieve greater integration—including increased trade—with the other countries of the eastern bloc. See J. P. Nettl, The Eastern Zone and Soviet Policy in Germany 1945–50, at 293–94 (1951).

22. See Declaration of Bundestag, June 13, 1950, reprinted in 1 Dokumente at 496–97.

23. See Sowden at 244–45.

24. See generally A. James McAdams, East Germany and Detente: Building Authority after the Wall 75–77, 98–106 (1985); Garton Ash, In Europe's Name, at 28–47.

25. Treaty between the Federal Republic of Germany and the USSR, Aug. 12, 1970, BGBl 1972 II 354, art. 3. See generally Hacke at 183–90.

26. Treaty between the Federal Republic of Germany and the Peoples Republic of

Poland concerning the Basis of the Normalization of Their Mutual Relations, Dec. 7, 1970, BGBl 1972 II 362. See generally Hacke at 190–95.

Along the same lines, the Helsinki Final Act, which was executed by both German states in 1975, committed the signatories to observe existing European borders including, of course, the Oder-Neiße line. See Kiessler & Elbe at 116.

27. This position seems to have been taken by the Brandt government, and may be implied by the Constitutional Court's discussion of this aspect of the treaties. See Sowden at 337–38; 40 BVerfGE 141, 171–75 (1975). See also Hailbronner, Völker- und europarechtliche Fragen der deutschen Wiedervereinigung, 1990 JZ 449, 451 (noting that the federal government made this point clearly in negotiations over its east bloc treaties, but that the GDR did not make similar reservations with respect to its treaties with Poland). On the other hand, the Soviet Union apparently took the position that the note transmitted by the Federal Republic at the signing of the Moscow Treaty was without legal effect.

That the problems of the Moscow and Warsaw treaties can still evoke passionate responses is demonstrated by newspaper correspondence at the time of unification. FAZ, Sept. 3, 1990, at 8 col. 1 (discussion of political background of treaties). See also Garton Ash, In Europe's Name, at 70: "[E]ven in the late 1980s any bold assertions of new 'revelations' about [the Moscow and Warsaw treaties] were certain to raise temperatures rapidly, as with an old fever in the bones."

28. See, e.g., Pond at 193–95.

29. See Klein, 1990 NJW at 1072.

30. See Klein, Wiedervereinigungsklauseln in Verträgen der Bundesrepublik Deutschland, in Georg Brunner et al. (eds.), Sowjetsystem und Ostrecht, Festschrift für Boris Meissner zum 70. Geburtstag 783–91 (1985).

31. In his speech supporting the first State Treaty in the Bundestag, Kohl strongly urged a vote for the resolution confirming the Oder-Neiße line. See Ch. 7. He had doubtless been educated by strong international criticism of his past ambiguity on this subject.

32. FR, July 18, 1990, at 1 col. 1. See Ch. 20.

33. See Ch. 21.

## Chapter 19
## NATO and the Pact System

1. Preamble GG.

2. See 68 BVerfGE 1 (1984) (Pershing Rockets case).

3. 90 BVerfGE 286 (1994) (Bundeswehr case). See Ch. 22.

4. For the political struggles surrounding West German rearmament, see, e.g., Thomas Alan Schwartz, America's Germany: John J. McCloy and the Federal Republic of Germany 145–55 (1991); James Bryant Conant, Germany and Freedom: A Personal Appraisal 71–77 (1958).

5. See Ch. 17. See generally Christian Hacke, Weltmacht wider Willen: Die Aussenpolitik der Bundesrepublik Deutschland 78–82 (1993).

6. "West German membership in NATO meant that the [Federal Republic] made considerable forces available to Western defense against a possible Soviet or Warsaw Pact attack. These forces, however, up to the highest command levels, were completely integrated into the multinational NATO structure so as to avoid leaving a German

army under German command to pursue German objectives—such as liberating East Germany or the Oder-Neisse area." Peter H. Merkl, German Unification in the European Context 354 (1993). At the same time the Federal Republic renounced nuclear, biological, and chemical weapons. Id. See also Hanrieder, The FRG and NATO: Between Security Dependence and Security Partnership, in Emil J. Kirchner & James Sperling (eds.), The Federal Republic of Germany and NATO: 40 Years After, at 200 (1992) (inclusion in the western military alliance was part of the price that the Federal Republic had to pay for sovereignty).

7. For an illuminating discussion of the historical background of NATO emphasizing these points, see Gregory F. Treverton, America, Germany, and the Future of Europe 38–91 (1992).

8. See Treaty of Friendship, Co-operation and Mutual Assistance, Signed at Warsaw, May 14, 1955, 219 U.N.T.S. 3. The preamble of the Warsaw Pact refers specifically to the rearming of West Germany and its inclusion in NATO. But the Warsaw Treaty had been preceded by a "series of defence pacts between the countries of the Eastern bloc" concerted as early as 1948. See J. P. Nettl, The Eastern Zone and Soviet Policy in Germany 1945–50, at 286 (1951).

9. With the publication of the "Harmel Report" in 1967, NATO may have offered a possible method of "cautious accommodation and cooperation" with the eastern bloc, but this opportunity—if it indeed was one—was not realized. Linnenkamp, The Security Policy of the New Germany, in Paul B. Stares (ed.), The New Germany and the New Europe 103 (1992).

10. See, e.g., FAZ, Apr. 10, 1995, at 5 col. 5.

11. See, e.g., FAZ, Sept. 13, 1990, at 4 col. 1 (Czechoslovak Army to cease participation in large-scale military exercises of Warsaw Pact).

12. See Hailbronner, Völker- und europarechtliche Fragen der deutschen Wiedervereinigung, 1990 JZ 449, 452.

13. New York Times, Sept. 25, 1990, at A10 col. 3. See Karl Kaiser, Deutschlands Vereinigung: Die internationalen Aspekte 280 (Document 55) (1991).

14. See New York Times, Apr. 1, 1991, at A9 col. 2; New York Times, Feb. 26, 1991, at A1 col. 1; Hacke at 315 (dissolution of Warsaw Pact military alliance).

15. Kaiser, Deutschlands Vereinigung, at 71–72.

16. Stephen F. Szabo, The Diplomacy of German Unification 42–44, 70, 79 (1992); Richard Kiessler & Frank Elbe, Ein runder Tisch mit scharfen Ecken: Der diplomatische Weg zur deutschen Einheit 59 (1993). In taking this position, President Bush was apparently responding to Chancellor Kohl's Ten-Point Plan, which foresaw steps toward unification but omitted any reference to NATO. Kiessler & Elbe at 55. See generally Ch. 3.

17. Kaiser, Deutschlands Vereinigung, at 70.

18. Szabo at 69; Artur Hajnicz, Polens Wende und Deutschlands Vereinigung 50–51 (1995).

19. See Hailbronner, 1990 JZ at 452. Perhaps such a significant change in the borders might have justified other states in leaving NATO, but no such action was taken or even considered. Id. For a different perspective on this issue, however, see Tomuschat, A United Germany within the European Community, 27 Common Market Law Review 415, 422 (1990).

20. See Horst Teltschik, 329 Tage: Innenansichten der Einigung 180–81 (1991); Ulrich Albrecht, Die Abwicklung der DDR 56 (1992); see also Yuli A. Kvitsinsky, Vor dem Sturm: Erinnerungen eines Diplomaten 21–24 (1993).

21. Kiessler & Elbe at 133.

22. Helmut Herles & Ewald Rose (eds.), Vom Runden Tisch zum Parlament 168 (1990). The Modrow government also took a similar position. Kiessler & Elbe at 134.

23. The Soviet leadership had to explain "not only to the opponents of perestroika, but also to the Soviet people—who had paid a high cost in blood during the Great Patriotic War—why [unified] Germany should belong to NATO, a military alliance that Soviet propaganda had portrayed for decades as the enemy. . . . From the Soviet point of view, the thought of a [united] Germany in NATO initially seemed [to indicate that] the results of World War II would be revised." Kiessler & Elbe at 133.

24. See generally Hailbronner, 1990 JZ at 453 (double membership for united Germany "would actually [have been] the dissolution of both pact systems through an all-European security system"); Albrecht at 57–58, 60–64.

25. See FAZ, Oct. 13, 1990, at 3 col. 3. Including family members of military personnel, a total of 600,000 Soviet citizens were stationed in the GDR. Id.

26. London Declaration on a Transformed North Atlantic Alliance, July 6, 1990, reprinted in Public Papers of the Presidents of the United States, George Bush (1990 Book II) at 964–67 (hereafter, Bush Papers [1990]). See generally Szabo at 88–93.

27. See, e.g., Teltschik at 195, 196. As a conciliatory document, the London Declaration had antecedents, for example, in "nine assurances" on Germany that the United States government furnished to President Gorbachev at a Washington summit in May 1990; President Bush struck a similar tone in a letter to the NATO allies immediately before the London meeting. Szabo at 86, 91. The way had also been paved by a conciliatory message extending "the hand of friendship to the Soviet Union and all other European lands," transmitted by the NATO foreign ministers at a meeting in Turnberry, Scotland, in June 1990. See Kiessler & Elbe at 153–54, 248; Kaiser, Deutschlands Vereinigung, at 225 (Document 38). An even earlier forerunner was NATO's conciliatory decision, in May 1989, to postpone "modernization" of its short-range nuclear missile system. Kiessler & Elbe at 22.

28. The Declaration emphasized the reduction of forces, and announced a new military strategy "moving away from 'forward defense'" and modifying the strategy of "flexible response" to de-emphasize nuclear weapons. The plan included a proposal for reciprocal removal of nuclear artillery shells from Europe. Bush Papers (1990) at 966.

29. Id. at 971. For the importance of the London Declaration to the Soviet government, see Kvitsinsky at 50. But for a more skeptical analysis of the document, see Albrecht at 89–94.

30. Meissner, Der XXVIII. Parteitag der KPdSU: Innen- und Außenpolitik, 1991 Aussenpolitik 38, 45. These attacks evoked ironic echoes of the debates over "who lost China" heard in the United States in the 1950s.

31. Id. at 46.

32. Id. at 48. See also Szabo at 95–97; Kiessler & Elbe 164–67.

33. This eight-point agreement was announced by Kohl and Gorbachev in a joint press conference at Schelesnowodsk in the Soviet Union on July 16, 1990. A transcript of this press conference is printed in Hans Klein, Es begann im Kaukasus 305–23 (1991) (hereafter, Es begann im Kaukasus); see also FAZ, July 17, 1990, at 1 col. 1; id. at 2 col. 2; FR, July 18, 1990, at 2 col. 4. For another important press conference on this subject, held by Kohl on July 17 after his return to Bonn, see Es begann im Kaukasus at 324–53.

In his remarks at Schelesnowodsk, President Gorbachev explicitly acknowledged the significant impact that the London Declaration had on his government's view of

NATO membership for united Germany. According to Gorbachev, "what took place in London was indeed something like the beginning of a new historical development." Es begann im Kaukasus at 310.

Although no transcript of the Caucasus conference is available, a record of the previous day's meeting between Kohl and Gorbachev in Moscow has been published by Gorbachev. See Mikhail S. Gorbachev, Gipfelgespräche: Geheime Protokolle aus meiner Amtszeit 161–77 (1993). According to this protocol, Kohl and Gorbachev agreed that they were well equipped to develop relations between Germany and the Soviet Union because both remembered World War II and the hardships of that time. Kohl congratulated Gorbachev on his success at the Communist Party Congress (id. at 164), and Gorbachev noted the geopolitical change worked by the London Declaration, which, in his words, "took a great step in the direction of releasing us from the chains of the past." Id. at 170. Gorbachev also remarked that "the presence of American troops in Europe is a stabilizing factor." Id. at 169. Kohl raised the idea of a comprehensive treaty between Germany and the Soviet Union, and both leaders exchanged notes on the possible content of such an agreement. The protocol breaks off with points relating to NATO resolved in principle, but with a detailed agreement awaiting the next day's discussions in the Caucasus. Anticipating the next day's meeting, Gorbachev concludes by stating that in "the clear mountain air one sees many things more clearly." Id. at 177. For descriptions of the Caucasus meeting by important participants, see Hans-Dietrich Genscher, Erinnerungen 833–41 (1995); Teltschik at 333–39. See generally Kvitsinsky at 47–49; Szabo at 98–102; Kiessler & Elbe at 168–79.

34. Es begann im Kaukasus at 306–7; FAZ, July 17, 1990, at 1 col. 1; id. at 2 col. 2. The German and Soviet governments were to enter into treaties regulating the details of withdrawal and also providing for significant German payments. Indeed, much of the cost of withdrawal was borne by Germany. See Ch. 21.

35. Es begann im Kaukasus at 307; FAZ, July 17, 1990, at 2 col. 2.

36. Es begann im Kaukasus at 307; FAZ, July 17, 1990, at 2 col. 2.

37. See Es begann im Kaukasus at 311, 321.

38. Id. at 307; FAZ, July 17, 1990, at 2 col. 2.

39. Es begann im Kaukasus at 307.

40. Albrecht at 87. See Ch. 3.

41. See Kiessler & Elbe at 178–79.

## CHAPTER 20
## THE TWO PLUS FOUR TREATY AND THE LEGAL STATUS OF GERMANY

1. Treaty on the Final Settlement with Respect to Germany, Sept. 12, 1990, S. Treaty Doc. No. 20, 101st Cong., 2d Sess., reprinted in 29 I.L.M. 1186 (1990) (hereafter, Two Plus Four Treaty).

2. For the American role, see, e.g., Kaiser, Germany's Unification, 70 Foreign Affairs (No. 1) 179, 190 (1990–91).

3. Stephen F. Szabo, The Diplomacy of German Unification 26–27 (1992); Richard Kiessler & Frank Elbe, Ein runder Tisch mit scharfen Ecken: Der diplomatische Weg zur deutschen Einheit 189–201 (1993); see generally Ulrich Albrecht, Die Abwicklung der DDR (1992). Accordingly, the views of the GDR reformers on foreign policy—generally pacifist in nature—played a negligible role in German unification. Karl Kaiser, Deutschlands Vereinigung: Die internationalen Aspekte 48 (1991). As one participant noted, the citizens of the GDR "started the ball rolling, but now at the negotiating

table they were unable to participate in determining its direction and speed." Kiessler & Elbe at 204 (quoting Wolfram von Fritsch).

4. See generally Szabo at 46–51; Kiessler & Elbe at 63–65.

5. Horst Teltschik, 329 Tage: Innenansichten der Einigung 147, 194 and passim (1991).

6. Yuli A. Kvitsinsky, Vor dem Sturm: Erinnerungen eines Diplomaten 20 (1993); Kiessler & Elbe at 108–10.

7. Gornig, Die vertragliche Regelung der mit der deutschen Vereinigung verbundenen auswärtigen Probleme, 1991 Aussenpolitik 3, 5.

8. The stage was set for negotiations by a declaration of the foreign ministers in Ottawa on February 13, 1990, only a few days after President Gorbachev had agreed in principle to German unification. See Ch. 3. The declaration made clear that the two German states would participate in the discussions, along with the World War II Allies. Formal negotiating meetings of the six foreign ministers took place in May (Bonn), June (Berlin), and July (Paris), before the concluding meeting in Moscow on September 12. The foreign minister of Poland participated in the meeting in Paris in July.

For accounts of these meetings, see 1. *Ottawa*: Teltschik at 147–48; Szabo at 64–65; Kiessler & Elbe at 99–105; Philip Zelikow & Condoleezza Rice, Germany Unified and Europe Transformed 191–95 (1995); Hans-Dietrich Genscher, Erinnerungen 724–31 (1995); 2. *Bonn*: Teltschik at 221–24; Szabo at 82–84; Kiessler & Elbe at 122–32; Zelikow & Rice at 244–50; Genscher at 768–85; 3. *Berlin*: Teltschik at 284–86; Szabo at 88; Kiessler & Elbe at 160–63; Zelikow & Rice at 294–303; Genscher at 823–26; 4. *Paris*: Teltschik at 344–45; Kiessler & Elbe at 180–81; Zelikow & Rice at 343; Genscher at 841–47.

9. Teltschik at 248; Kiessler & Elbe at 106–7. This emphasis on the CSCE accorded with Soviet wishes to increase the importance of the organization. See Ch. 22.

10. See Ch. 19.

11. Very sweeping positions were set forth, for example, in the first comprehensive negotiating draft of the Soviet Union, presented at the second Two Plus Four meeting in June 1990 in Berlin. This draft is reprinted in full in Kvitsinsky at 41–46; it is summarized with some commentary in Albrecht at 73–81. See also Eduard Shevardnadze, Die Zukunft gehört der Freiheit 248–49 (1993). Yet even at the time this draft was presented, Foreign Minister Shevardnadze seemed to concede that these positions could not be maintained. Indeed, this draft may have been advanced primarily to appease hard-line critics in Moscow. Cf., e.g., Teltschik at 286; Albrecht at 81; Szabo at 88.

12. See Kvitsinsky at 11–12.

13. Teltschik at 220–21, 226–28, 230–35, 243–44; Kvitsinsky at 24–31.

14. Kvitsinsky at 65–66.

15. The statement acclaiming European peace, while accurate at the time, has since been contradicted by bitter warfare accompanying the dissolution of Yugoslavia.

16. See Kiessler & Elbe at 218.

17. Two Plus Four Treaty art. 1(3). This language "corresponds with formulations in other peace treaties and also appears in the treaties of the Federal Republic with eastern states at the beginning of the 1970s." Gornig, 1991 Aussenpolitik at 9.

18. Two Plus Four Treaty art. 1(2). For the Border Treaty between Germany and Poland, see Ch. 21.

19. Two Plus Four Treaty art. 1(4). The Soviet Union originally proposed that contrary statements be annulled not only in the constitution of united Germany, but also in

"other legal determinations and rules." Kvitsinsky at 41. This proposal, which was not adopted, might have required that the jurisprudence of the Federal Constitutional Court somehow be amended to invalidate assertions that the German "Reich" within the borders of 1937 survived the German defeat in World War II.

20. Unification Treaty art. 4. See Ch. 10; Kiessler & Elbe at 181.

21. Yet, even these provisions did not go as far as the guarantees sought by Poland, to still its fears that a strong and united Germany might someday seek to recover the Oder-Neiße lands. Poland had suffered greatly from Germany's invasion and occupation in World War II, and Chancellor Kohl's pronounced reluctance to endorse the existing border in early 1990 had revived old anxieties. See Ch. 18. At various points during the Two Plus Four negotiations, therefore, the Polish government sought an Allied guarantee of the border, insisted that a Polish-German border treaty be signed before the Allies released their reserved rights over Germany, and argued—like the Soviet Union—that references to the German borders of 1937 be removed from all German legal rules and jurisprudence.

But at the third Two Plus Four meeting in Paris in July 1990, the Polish foreign minister had to accept a flat rejection of all such arguments. The Kohl-Gorbachev agreement had been reached the day before in the Caucasus, and none of the Allies was willing to interrupt the momentum so achieved. On these points, see Albrecht at 101–16; but for a somewhat different view of these events, see Kiessler & Elbe at 198–99.

In light of the argument that a treaty signed by separate German states could not bind the united Germany on territorial questions, the Two Plus Four Treaty required that its provisions be ratified by the all-German parliament after unification. Two Plus Four Treaty art. 8(1); see Ch. 18. This step was accomplished in October 1990.

22. This provision of the Two Plus Four Treaty, requiring that Germany observe the UN Charter, had a forerunner in article 3(1) of the General Treaty of 1954, entered into between the Federal Republic of Germany and the three western Allies. See Ch. 17.

23. Moreover, of course, Germany (and many other countries) have relinquished substantial "sovereign" rights by joining NATO and the European Union among other international organizations.

24. The Federal Republic had originally renounced those weapons in 1954 in order to calm European fears at the time of German rearmament and the integration of German forces in NATO. Cf. Rudolf Dolzer, The Path to German Unity: The Constitutional, Legal and International Framework 23 (1990); Gregory F. Treverton, America, Germany, and the Future of Europe 90 (1992).

25. See Treaty on the Non-Proliferation of Nuclear Weapons, July 1, 1968, 21 U.S.T. 483, T.I.A.S. No. 6839, 729 U.N.T.S. 161.

26. Kvitsinsky at 21, 54.

27. Id. at 42.

28. Two Plus Four Treaty art. 3(2). In this statement the German government also noted its expectation that other participants at Vienna would make a contribution to European security, by limiting the number of their own armed forces. Id. The German troop reduction had been agreed upon by Kohl and Gorbachev at the Caucasus meeting, but the obligation was officially recorded at the Vienna Conference—rather than in the Two Plus Four agreement—in order to avoid the appearance of discrimination against Germany in the treaty. Kiessler & Elbe at 141.

29. Linnenkamp, The Security Policy of the New Germany, in Paul B. Stares (ed.), The New Germany and the New Europe 95–97 (1992) (hereafter, The New Germany and the New Europe). Moreover, the Treaty on Conventional Forces in Europe, signed

shortly after unification, required that unified Germany make significant reductions in military equipment. Id. at 96–97.

30. Kiessler & Elbe at 176.

31. Gornig, 1991 Aussenpolitik at 7; see generally Szabo at 104–5; Kaiser, Deutschlands Vereinigung, at 79: "[T]he total military potential of a united Germany was particularly important for the Soviet Union, where the memory of the German attack of 1941 was still vivid." Moreover, the "reduction of German forces by forty percent and the pledge of a continuing non-nuclear status were intended to insure—in the eyes of the other European nations—that Germany would not be able to resume the position of a great military power, even under changed political circumstances." Id. at 79–80.

32. Teltschik at 251–52, 261–62.

33. See Ch. 19.

34. For the withdrawal of Soviet troops pursuant to these provisions, see Ch. 21.

35. FAZ, July 17, 1990, at 2 col. 2. See Ch. 19.

36. Two Plus Four Treaty art. 5(2).

37. See Treaty on the Final Settlement with Respect to Germany, Senate Executive Report No. 33, 101st Cong., 2d Sess. 28–54 (1990).

38. See Ch. 19.

39. Szabo at 54–62, 102–4; Kiessler & Elbe at 79–87, 111, 245–46. At the outset of negotiations, the western powers may also have assured the Soviet Union that no former east bloc nations would be admitted to NATO. Szabo at 65; see also FAZ, May 8, 1995, at 7 col. 1.

40. Kaiser, Deutschlands Vereinigung, at 75.

According to recent plans, 50,000 of Germany's total of 370,000 forces will be stationed in eastern Germany, and these 50,000 troops will not include "offensive forces." Linnenkamp in The New Germany and the New Europe at 102.

Even though the Two Plus Four Treaty prohibited the stationing or deployment of foreign NATO troops in eastern Germany, it was not clear whether foreign NATO troops might engage in relatively short maneuvers in that territory after the Soviet withdrawal: the issue rested on the meaning of the word "deployed." Apparently this issue was first raised on the day before the treaty was scheduled to be signed, when the British delegation announced its wish to preserve the possibility of joint NATO maneuvers in former GDR territory. See Blumenwitz, Der Vertrag vom 12.9. 1990 über die abschließende Regelung in Bezug auf Deutschland, 1990 NJW 3041, 3046; Kvitsinsky at 61–62; Genscher at 865–75. Some speculated that this last-minute imbroglio was British Prime Minister Thatcher's revenge for being excluded from the Kohl-Gorbachev meeting in the Caucasus. Albrecht at 135–37; but see Zelikow & Rice at 359–62 (the United States was as "adamant" on this point as Great Britain). The problem was ultimately resolved by a separate addendum providing that, should questions arise, the word "deployed" will be interpreted by the united German government "in a reasonable and responsible way taking into account the security interests" of the signatories of the agreement. See New York Times, Sept. 13, 1990, at A1 col. 3; Szabo at 111–12; Kiessler & Elbe 209–12.

41. But foreign forces might be permitted to bring nuclear weapons into eastern Germany during any maneuver that is interpreted not to constitute a "deployment" under article 5(3) of the treaty and the related addendum.

42. New York Times, Sept. 13, 1990, at A1 col. 3.

43. Two Plus Four Treaty art. 5(3). See Kiessler & Elbe at 208–9.

44. Interestingly, however, the provision does not specifically refer to NATO. The agreement therefore leaves open the possibility that Germany may, at some time in the future, enter an exclusively European alliance—"such as an altered [Western European Union]." Kaiser, Deutschlands Vereinigung, at 74.

45. Indeed, this point was of central importance to the western alliance. In February 1990, even before the Two Plus Four negotiations began, Chancellor Kohl and President Bush had agreed that articles 5 and 6 of the NATO Treaty would have to cover eastern Germany—regardless of whether NATO troops could ultimately be stationed there. See Kiessler & Elbe at 111–12.

46. See 3 Klaus Stern & Bruno Schmidt-Bleibtreu (eds.), Verträge und Rechtsakte zur deutschen Einheit 93–94 (1991); for an English translation, see Senate Executive Report No. 33, 101st Cong., 2d Sess. 21–22 (1990).

47. See Ch. 11.

48. The legal effect of this letter may not be entirely clear because it is not actually set forth as an obligation in the treaty. Yet it must have been intended by the parties to have some binding effect. Cf. Blumenwitz, 1990 NJW at 3048. Accordingly, when President Bush sent the Two Plus Four Treaty to the Senate, he specifically called attention to the letter and noted that it formally conveyed "additional assurances." See Senate Executive Report No. 33, 101st Cong., 2d Sess. 23 (1990).

The Soviet Union at first sought to have assurances on the status of the Bodenreform contained in the Two Plus Four Treaty itself, but finally agreed to have this point covered in a letter instead.

49. Treatment of war memorials and graves has been a long-standing concern of the Soviet government, reflected in other treaties entered into by the Soviet Union over the years. For example, a similar provision appears in the Soviet-German partnership treaty. See Ch. 21; Blumenwitz, 1990 NJW at 3048.

50. Letter from de Maizière and Genscher, as translated in Senate Executive Report No. 33, 101st Cong., 2d Sess. 21 (1990).

51. See Ch. 13.

52. Subsequently, of course, the Soviet Union banned its own Communist Party for a period.

53. Finally, the de Maizière-Genscher letter also incorporated the provision of the Unification Treaty that set forth principles governing the future validity of treaties of the GDR. See Ch. 10. The Soviet Union was particularly concerned about this issue because it feared that unification would terminate economically important commercial treaties with East Germany. Indeed as early as March 1990, Soviet Foreign Minister Shevardnadze had opposed unification under article 23 on the ground that "accession" would result in the cancellation of the GDR's treaty obligations. Teltschik at 170. See also id. at 185, 198, 200–201, 202–3.

54. Two Plus Four Treaty art. 7(1). The agreements and other decisions so canceled included such cornerstones of postwar foreign affairs as the Potsdam accord, the Berlin Declaration of June 5, 1945, and the Berlin Quadripartite Agreement of 1971. The provision also abolished the institutions of postwar occupation, such as the Allied Control Council and the Berlin Kommandatura. See Albrecht at 138–39 (quoting British Foreign Office document).

55. Two Plus Four Treaty art. 7(2).

56. See New York Times, Oct. 2, 1990, at A11 col. 1. The United States Senate approved the Two Plus Four Treaty by a unanimous vote on October 10, 1990. FAZ,

Oct. 26, 1990, at 1 col. 3. The Federal Republic completed its process of ratification on October 8. See Blumenwitz, 1990 NJW at 3041 n.3.

On March 4, 1991, the Soviet Union became the last of the parties to ratify the Two Plus Four Treaty. See New York Times, Mar. 5, 1991, at A3 col. 4. Certain related Soviet-German treaties were ratified or approved by the Soviet parliament on the same date. See Ch. 21; FAZ, Mar. 5, 1991, at 1 col. 1, and at 2 col. 4. Along with the instruments of ratification, the Soviet parliament issued a declaration stating that the parliament "proceeds from the proposition that human rights will be seriously observed in unified Germany and that, in particular, discrimination against citizens of the former GDR from political and other motives will be barred." FAZ, Mar. 9, 1991, at 4 col. 4; cf. FAZ, Mar. 19, 1991, at 5 col. 6. In this statement the parliament apparently sought to protect former members of the SED from exclusion from the public service and also, perhaps, to prevent criminal trials of former GDR officials. Apparently the delay in the Soviet Union's ratification of the Two Plus Four Treaty arose from the government's fear that the treaty might encounter resistance in the legislature. Smyser, U.S.S.R.-Germany: A Link Restored, 1991 Foreign Policy (No. 84) 125, 133.

57. Ullmann, Deutsche Einheit—aber was ist das?, in Bernd Guggenberger & Tine Stein (eds.), Die Verfassungsdiskussion im Jahr der deutschen Einheit 76–77 (1991).

## Chapter 21
## Sequels and Consequences of the Two Plus Four Treaty: Germany and the Structure of Central Europe

1. See Ch. 20.

2. Vertrag zwischen der Bundesrepublik Deutschland und der Republik Polen über die Bestätigung der zwischen Ihnen bestehenden Grenze, of Nov. 14, 1990, BGBl 1991 II 1329 (hereafter, Border Treaty), reprinted in 3 Klaus Stern & Bruno Schmidt-Bleibtreu (eds.), Verträge und Rechtsakte zur Deutschen Einheit 211 (1991) (hereafter, Verträge und Rechtsakte).

3. This provision had a forerunner in a statement, signed by Polish Prime Minister Mazowiecki in late 1989, expressing sadness and empathy for the German-speaking "expellees." See Lintner, Die Deutschen in Ostmitteleuropa im ersten nichtkommunistischen Jahr, 1991 DA 794, 796. In general, Polish statements of this kind were important to Chancellor Kohl's government, in order to "counter ultra-conservative pressures" from the far right wing. Rachwald, Poland and Germany: From Foes to Friends?, in Dirk Verheyen & Christian Søe (eds.), The Germans and Their Neighbors 239 (1993) (hereafter, Germans and Neighbors).

4. See Ch. 18.

5. Border Treaty arts. 1–3; see FAZ, Nov. 15, 1990, at 2 col. 4.

6. See Jansen, Grenzvertrag mit Polen, 1990 DA 1820; see also FAZ, Nov. 15, 1990, at 2 col. 2; FAZ, Nov. 16, 1990, at 2 col. 4.

7. See Vertrag zwischen der Bundesrepublik Deutschland und der Republik Polen über gute Nachbarschaft und freundschaftliche Zusammenarbeit, of June 17, 1991, BGBl II 1315 (hereafter, Friendship Treaty), reprinted in 3 Verträge und Rechtsakte at 213. An important forerunner of this agreement was the "Joint Declaration" issued by Chancellor Kohl and Polish Prime Minister Mazowiecki in November 1989, during the east European revolution. See FAZ, Nov. 14, 1994, at 7 col. 3; FAZ, Nov. 9,

1991, at 1 col. 1; FAZ, June 18, 1991, at 1 col. 2. See also 1992 NJW 3222 (screening committee of Constitutional Court rejects constitutional attack on the Border Treaty).

8. See Weydenthal, The Polish-German Reconciliation, Report on Eastern Europe, July 5, 1991, at 19, 20. Cf. Sabbat-Swidlicka, The Signing of the Polish-German Border Treaty, Report on Eastern Europe, Dec. 7, 1990, at 16, 18.

9. Friendship Treaty arts. 5–6.

10. Id. arts. 8–9.

11. Id. arts. 20–22; see Rachwald in Germans and Neighbors at 243. The "German minority" in Poland includes almost one million individuals. Lintner, 1991 DA at 796.

The "Polish minority" in Germany is also protected by the treaty, but this category excludes hundreds of thousands of guest workers and other Polish speakers who live in Germany but are not German citizens. Instead, in an accompanying letter, the German government stated that it would try "to create the possibility" for Polish citizens in Germany to receive protections similar to those of the treaty. See 3 Verträge und Rechtsakte at 225; Jansen, Nachbarschaft mit Polen, 1991 DA 787, 788.

12. See Friendship Treaty art. 25 (language teaching); art. 28 (cultural objects and historical places). In a reciprocal manner, these provisions protect Polish language, cultural objects and historic places in Germany as well.

13. Rachwald in Germans and Neighbors at 245.

14. See 3 Verträge und Rechtsakte at 225; Weydenthal in Report on Eastern Europe, July 5, 1991, at 19, 20. See also Peter H. Merkl, German Unification in the European Context 343–46 (1993).

15. Weitz, Pursuing Military Security in Eastern Europe, in Robert O. Keohane et al. (eds.), After the Cold War 354 (1993) (hereafter, After the Cold War).

16. FAZ, Apr. 29, 1995, at 6 col. 1.

17. FAZ, Nov. 14, 1994, at 7 col. 3.

Widespread fears of massive German land purchases in the Oder-Neiße territories also seem to have been overdrawn. Indeed, legal restrictions generally exclude land purchases of more than one hectare by non-Polish nationals. FAZ, May 17, 1993, at 8 col. 1; see also FAZ, Aug. 31, 1993, at 1 col. 1.

18. Ulrich Albrecht, Die Abwicklung der DDR 143–46 (1992). The Soviet Army had enjoyed a similar autonomous status in Poland during the Cold War. See FAZ, Sept. 17, 1993, at 6 col. 5.

19. Vertrag zwischen der Bundesrepublik Deutschland und der Union der Sozialistischen Sowjetrepubliken über die Bedingungen des befristeten Aufenthalts und die Modalitäten des planmäßigen Abzugs der sowjetischen Truppen aus dem Gebiet der Bundesrepublik Deutschland, of Oct. 12, 1990, BGBl 1991 II 258, reprinted in 3 Verträge und Rechtsakte at 139. See FAZ, Oct. 13, 1990, at 3 col. 3.

20. See Karl Kaiser, Deutschlands Vereinigung: Die internationalen Aspekte 76 (1991): "The Red Army, which had once conquered eastern Germany, had become accustomed to living there as an occupation force and had conducted itself accordingly, even after the establishment of the East German government. Now, overnight, it had to adjust itself to the fact that it was lingering—as the result of a freely negotiated treaty—on the territory of a completely sovereign state."

21. See Yuli Kvitsinsky, Vor dem Sturm: Erinnerungen eines Diplomaten 100 (1993).

22. In theory at least, subsidies for Soviet troops temporarily remaining in Germany

were designed to defray increased costs resulting from the introduction of the hard-currency Deutsche Mark into eastern Germany.

23. See Abkommen zwischen der Regierung der Bundesrepublik Deutschland und der Regierung der Union der Sozialistischen Sowjetrepubliken über einige überleitende Maßnahmen, of Oct. 9, 1990, BGBl II 1655, reprinted in 3 Verträge und Rechtsakte at 125. See generally Kvitsinsky at 95–96.

24. The departure of the western Allies was heralded by speeches and a solemn military ceremony at the Brandenburg Gate, featuring the Prussian "Great Tattoo" (großer Zapfenstreich), said to be a sign of respect. See FAZ, Sept. 9, 1994, at 1 col. 2; Hénard, Zapfenstreich: Die Bundeswehr verabschiedet ihre Alliierten, FAZ, Sept. 10, 1994, at 27 col. 4. Eastern Germany bade farewell to the Russian troops in a separate ceremony.

In contrast with their long residual sojourn in eastern Germany, Soviet troops departed from Czechoslovakia and Hungary in summer 1991. See Weitz in After the Cold War at 360; Wallander & Prokop, Soviet Security Strategies toward Europe, in After the Cold War at 74. Following "extremely difficult" negotiations, the former "Northern Group" of the Soviet Army left Poland in September 1993. FAZ, Sept. 17, 1993, at 6 col. 5. Some troops had remained to assist in transporting Russian forces from eastern Germany, through Poland, back to Russia. FAZ, Sept. 17, 1993, at 6 col. 5.

25. Vertrag über gute Nachbarschaft, Partnerschaft, und Zusammenarbeit zwischen der Bundesrepublik Deutschland und der Union der Sozialistischen Sowjetrepubliken, of Nov. 9, 1990, BGBl 1991 II 703 (hereafter, German-Soviet Partnership Treaty), reprinted in 3 Verträge und Rechtsakte at 95; see also Denkschrift zu dem deutsch-sowjetischen Partnerschaftsvertrag, reprinted in 3 Verträge und Rechtsakte at 105. See FAZ, Nov. 10, 1990, at 1 col. 2; FAZ, Sept. 14, 1990, at 7 col. 1. For an English translation of the text, see 30 I.L.M. 504 (1991).

26. See Horst Teltschik, 329 Tage: Innenansichten der Einigung 204–7, 219–21 (1991); Kvitsinsky at 19–20, 31, 94. The Partnership Treaty was initialed at the Moscow meeting in which the Two Plus Four Treaty was signed. Richard Kiessler & Frank Elbe, Ein runder Tisch mit scharfen Ecken: Der diplomatische Weg zur deutschen Einheit 202–6 (1993).

27. See, e.g., Stephen F. Szabo, The Diplomacy of German Unification 121 (1992): for the Soviet Union, the treaty "created a German-Soviet economic partnership that made Germany the most important external support of Gorbachev's economic reforms." See also Albrecht at 142.

28. Kaiser, Deutschlands Vereinigung, at 278 (Document 54). These new relations had an antecedent in a joint declaration seeking closer cooperation, issued on the occasion of Gorbachev's visit to Kohl in Germany in June 1989. Kiessler & Elbe at 24–25.

29. German-Soviet Partnership Treaty art. 15.

30. Id. art. 16. In the ratification debate in the Supreme Soviet, this provision was attacked by the Soviet minister of culture; it was defended by the Foreign Ministry, in part, on the ground that art objects seized by the Soviet Union in the war remain inaccessible to the public "and are often not even properly stored." Kvitsinsky at 97–98. Although this provision was repeated in a German-Russian Agreement on Cultural Cooperation in December 1992, no art objects had been returned to Germany by late 1994. See Ritter, Zum Schicksal deutscher Kulturgüter in Rußland, 1994 DA 1190, 1192–93. Indeed in early 1995, spectacular exhibitions in Moscow and St. Petersburg presented some of these masterpieces to the public for the first time in fifty years, while

negotiations for their return to Germany seemed to make little headway. See, e.g., New York Times, Feb. 28, 1995, at A1 col. 2.

31. Larrabee, Moscow and the German Question, in Germans and Neighbors at 221; German-Soviet Partnership Treaty arts. 2–3.

32. Larrabee in Germans and Neighbors at 228 n. 54; see also Blumenwitz, Der Vertrag vom 12.9.1990 über die abschließende Regelung in bezug auf Deutschland, 1990 NJW 3041, 3047 & nn. 67–68.

33. See Kvitsinsky at 59–60.

34. Vertrag zwischen der Bundesrepublik Deutschland und der Union der Sozialistischen Sowjetrepubliken über die Entwicklung einer umfassenden Zusammenarbeit auf dem Gebiet der Wirtschaft, Industrie, Wissenschaft und Technik, of Nov. 9, 1990, BGBl 1991 II 799, reprinted in 3 Verträge und Rechtsakte at 113.

35. Smyser, U.S.S.R.-Germany: A Link Restored, 1991 Foreign Policy (No. 84) 125, 130–31.

36. Id. at 125–27 and passim.

37. Szabo at 15.

38. See, e.g., Hans Klein, Es begann im Kaukasus 317–18, 338–40 (1991).

39. See generally Larrabee in Germans and Neighbors at 203; Schweisfurth, Rapallo Treaty (1922), in 4 Rudolf Bernhardt (ed.), Encyclopedia of Public International Law 163 (1982) (hereafter, Encyclopedia of Public International Law).

40. See Vertrag zwischen der Bundesrepublik Deutschland und der Tschechischen und Slowakischen Föderativen Republik über gute Nachbarschaft und freundschaftliche Zusammenarbeit, of Feb. 27, 1992, BGBl II 463 (hereafter, 1992 German-Czechoslovakian Friendship Treaty). For the initialing of the treaty, see FAZ, Oct. 8, 1991, at 1 col. 2; id. at 3 col. 4; for the signing of the treaty, see New York Times, Feb. 28, 1992, at A5 col. 1; FAZ, Feb. 28, 1992, at 1 col. 2.

41. The parties to the Munich accord were England, France, Germany, and Italy. Czechoslovakia was excluded. See generally Schieder, Munich Agreement (1938), in 3 Encyclopedia of Public International Law at 285.

42. See Hauner, The Czechs and the Germans: A One-Thousand-Year Relationship, in Germans and Neighbors at 268–69.

Early in his tenure as president of post-Communist Czechoslovakia, President Václav Havel "issued an unequivocal moral condemnation" of the Beneš expulsions of 1945, which a noted Czech historian had previously referred to as a "totalitarian" act. See id. at 252–53; Timothy Garton Ash, The Uses of Adversity: Essays on the Fate of Central Europe 186 (1990). It has been argued that the expulsions constituted "genocide" under international law, although the "orderly" transfer of the population was endorsed by the Potsdam accord. See Tomuschat, Sudetendeutsche Fragen, FAZ, May 8, 1992, at 11 col. 1 (reviewing Felix Ermacora, Die sudetendeutschen Fragen [1992]).

43. Vertrag über die gegenseitigen Beziehungen zwischen der Bundesrepublik Deutschland und der Tschechoslowakischen Sozialistischen Republik, of Dec. 11, 1973, 1974 BGBl II 989 (hereafter, 1973 German-Czechoslovakian Treaty); see 43 BVerfGE 203 (1977). This was the last of the bilateral eastern treaties of the Brandt period. See Christian Hacke, Weltmacht wider Willen: Die Aussenpolitik der Bundesrepublik Deutschland 216–17 (1993).

44. Schieder in 3 Encyclopedia of Public International Law at 287. The German government argued that it could legitimately represent the interests of the "Sudeten Germans" because—pursuant to the provisions of the Munich Treaty—they were Ger-

man citizens at the time of their expulsion from Czechoslovakia in 1945. These "expellees" would not have been German citizens in 1945 if the Munich agreement was void from the beginning, as argued by the Czech government. Moreover, if the "expellees" were not German citizens in 1945, their claim to the recovery of expropriated lands under international law could be seriously impaired.

45. 1973 German-Czechoslovakian Treaty preamble, art. 1; Dolzer, Das Münchener Abkommen von 1938, FAZ, Feb. 19, 1992, at 8 col. 5.

46. 1973 German-Czechoslovakian Treaty arts. 2, 4. Some "Sudeten Germans," whose property had been confiscated in the postwar expulsions, challenged the 1973 treaty in the Federal Constitutional Court on the grounds that it deprived complainants of their property as well as the right of free movement throughout the "German Reich." The Court rejected the complaint. 43 BVerfGE 203 (1977).

47. 1992 German-Czechoslovakian Friendship Treaty preamble (emphasis added).

48. See, e.g., FAZ, Feb. 19, 1992, at 8 col. 5; FAZ, Feb. 28, 1992, at 2 col. 2. For President Havel's conciliatory view of this provision, however, see Václav Havel, Summer Meditations 96 (1993): "[I]t was in our own interests to admit that the expulsion of the Germans, and especially the way it was carried out, was in every way an inappropriate response to the crimes of the Nazis and the Henleinians. Of course, such an admission is not to the detriment of our citizens, who cannot be held responsible for the decisions and actions of their predecessors. The point is that wrongs must never again be redressed by new wrongs."

The treaty's failure to include an explicit denial of "expellees" property claims also evoked outrage in Czechoslovakia.

49. 1992 German-Czechoslovakian Friendship Treaty preamble. On a related point, the preamble of the 1992 treaty did declare "that the Czechoslovakian State has never ceased to exist since 1918." But this well-intentioned statement evoked protests from another quarter, on the grounds that it rejected the "independent" Slovakia established by German occupiers during World War II. Slovakian "patriots" oddly wished to honor the memory of this fascist puppet state, as a forerunner of Slovakian independence. See Hauner in Germans and Neighbors at 271.

50. See Havel at 95–97. Indeed, it seems quite difficult to understand how a government of the democratic Federal Republic could possibly defend rights derived from one of Nazi Germany's most infamous pre-war acts—the dismemberment of Czechoslovakia through a treaty imposed upon that nation by threat of force.

51. 1992 German-Czechoslovakian Friendship Treaty arts. 20–21. Similar guarantees for "Czech" and "Slovak" minorities, however, may conceivably be implied by more general provisions of the treaty.

52. Id. art. 27. The joint historians commission, however, has later complained that its efforts have not been adequately supported. FAZ, Feb. 1, 1994, at 3 col. 3.

53. See BGBl 1992 II 472–73; cf. 1992 German-Czechoslovakian Friendship Treaty art. 10(2). Czechoslovakia, a member of the Council of Europe, entered into an association agreement with the European Union, see id. art. 10(1); Havel at 87–88, and the goal of becoming a full member "has been one of the principal aims of Czechoslovak foreign policy." Hauner in Germans and Neighbors at 271.

54. Indeed, this right would presumably be open in any event to all citizens of the member states of the European Union—including Germany—if Czechoslovakia or its successor states are granted membership.

55. BGBl 1992 II 472–73; see FAZ, Feb. 28, 1992, at 1 col. 2; Havel at 96.

56. FAZ, July 5, 1994, at 3 col. 1. In any case, the Bonn government has refused to

pay compensation to surviving Czech victims of the Nazi regime until the land claims of the "Sudeten Germans" are resolved. While the stalemate continues, the Prague government itself has decided to accord the Czech Nazi victims a small "symbolic" compensation. Der Spiegel, 2/1995, at 26, 28–30.

57. See New York Times, Feb. 2, 1992, Week in Review, at 6 col. 1; FAZ, Feb. 28, 1992, at 2 col. 5.

58. FAZ, Feb. 13, 1992, at 5 col. 4; see also FAZ, July 5, 1994, at 3 col. 1.

59. FAZ, May 21, 1992, at 1 col 2. See BGBl 1992 II 475 (Friendship Treaty with Hungary). In March 1992, the German and Rumanian governments initialed a friendship treaty. With the conclusion of this agreement, Germany has negotiated treaties with all of the European members of the former east bloc. The treaty provides for economic cooperation and protection of German-speaking groups in Rumania. FAZ, Mar. 13, 1992, at 1 col. 3.

60. See, e.g., Thumann, Starrer Riese, Die Zeit, Mar. 31, 1995, at 1 col. 1.

61. Indeed, on this ground, the state of Bavaria voted against the Czechoslovakian Friendship Treaty in the Bundesrat. See FAZ, July 5, 1994, at 3 col. 1.

62. FAZ, Feb. 21, 1994, at 3 col. 1. In a recent speech, Czech President Havel has also reiterated that, notwithstanding the dubious moral status of the Beneš decree, the postwar expropriations could not be undone. FAZ, Feb. 18, 1995, at 5 col. 1; see also Constitution Watch, 4 East European Constitutional Review, Spring 1995, at 10. Moreover, in March 1995 the Czech Constitutional Court upheld the Beneš decree and the expropriation of the "Sudeten Germans"—a decision that was attacked as a violation of international law by the Bavarian CSU. FAZ, Mar. 11, 1995, at 5 col. 1; Constitution Watch, 4 East European Constitutional Review, Spring 1995, at 9–10. But this decision has apparently not foreclosed more limited litigation, which deals with property claims of German-speaking Czech citizens rather than property claims of all of the "Sudenten Germans." The Czech courts are still considering this narrower issue. Constitution Watch, 4 East European Constitutional Review, Summer 1995, at 8.

63. On the issues discussed in this and the following paragraph, see Feldmeyer, Alle Verträge werden fortgesetzt, FAZ, Feb. 3, 1992, at 10 col. 2. See also Dieter Blumenwitz, This Is Germany: Germany's Legal Status after Unification 25–26 (1994).

64. These criteria included respect for the rule of law, democracy, human rights, and the protection of minorities, as well as observance of the UN charter, the Helsinki Final Act, the Charter of Paris, and relevant obligations of disarmament and nuclear nonproliferation. See Declaration on the "Guidelines on the Recognition of New States in Eastern Europe and in the Soviet Union," 31 I.L.M. 1486–87 (1992).

65. Agreement Establishing the Commonwealth of Independent States, of Dec. 8, 1991, 31 I.L.M. 143, 145 (1992); see also Declaration by the Heads of State of the Republic of Belarus, the RSFSR, and Ukraine, of Dec. 8, 1991, 31 I.L.M. 142 (1992).

66. But see Blumenwitz, Germany's Legal Status, at 28–29 (questioning continued validity of the treaty).

## Chapter 22
## United Germany and the Western Security System: The Future Role of German Armed Forces

1. Hans Schauer, Europa der Vernunft: Kritische Anmerkungen nach Maastricht 84 (1993).

2. Moreover, the official United States position has also been sharply contested within the American foreign policy establishment. See, e.g., Mandelbaum, Preserving

the New Peace: The Case against NATO Expansion, 74 Foreign Affairs (No. 3) 9 (1995); Talbott, Why NATO Should Grow, New York Review of Books, Aug. 10, 1995, at 27; Davies, Should NATO Grow?—A Dissent, New York Review of Books, Sept. 21, 1995, at 74.

3. Blackwill, Patterns of Partnership: The U.S.-German Security Relationship in the 1990s, in Steven Muller & Gebhard Schweigler (eds.), From Occupation to Cooperation: The United States and United Germany in a Changing World Order 127 (1992) (hereafter, From Occupation to Cooperation).

4. See, e.g., Treverton, The New Europe, 71 Foreign Affairs (No. 1) 94, 110–12 (1991–92); Blackwill in From Occupation to Cooperation at 134–35. The number of NATO nuclear weapons is also being reduced. Id. at 138 & n. 36.

5. See, e.g., FAZ, Apr. 22, 1993, at 12 col. 2.

6. Treverton, 71 Foreign Affairs (No. 1) at 111.

7. See, e.g., Schauer at 95.

8. See id. at 82–83. See also Christian Hacke, Weltmacht wider Willen: Die Aussenpolitik der Bundesrepublik Deutschland 525–26 (1993).

9. Schauer at 78.

10. Id. at 78–90. The Netherlands and the United Kingdom would even like to embed the WEU forces within NATO. Id. at 98.

11. See generally, e.g., Blackwill in From Occupation to Cooperation at 140–41.

12. See generally Kirchner & Sperling, From Instability to Stability, in Emil J. Kirchner & James Sperling (eds.), The Federal Republic of Germany and NATO: 40 Years After 20–23 (1992); Peter H. Merkl, German Unification in the European Context 374–80 (1993).

At the time of German unification, the CSCE was an organization of thirty-three European states (including the Soviet Union), along with the United States and Canada. Subsequently, its membership has been increased by the inclusion of a number of former Soviet republics, and its name has been changed to the Organization for Security and Cooperation in Europe (OSCE).

13. 14 I.L.M. 1292. The Helsinki Final Act contained provisions for peace, stability, and human rights in Europe. At the Helsinki conference, the western states had pushed for provisions that would extend human rights to the east, while the eastern governments sought to guarantee the legitimacy of postwar borders, including the border between East and West Germany as well as the Oder-Neiße line. See Hacke at 288–90. In the end, the document included both types of provisions.

14. 30 I.L.M. 190 (1991).

15. Id. at 193.

16. Id. at 198. The Charter of Paris also included a provision for "developing market economies"—a provision that was not possible in the Helsinki Final Act. Id. at 195.

17. See New York Times, Nov. 22, 1990, at A1 col. 3. On the other hand, at the same Paris Conference, the NATO and Warsaw Pact leaders signed a Treaty on Conventional Armed Forces in Europe, providing for substantial reductions of tanks, combat aircraft, and other military equipment stationed throughout Europe. The leaders also signed a declaration rejecting previous relations of hostility and pledging to "establish new relations of partnership and mutual friendship." New York Times, Nov. 20, 1990, at A1 col. 1.

18. See Ch. 20.

19. See Misha Glenny, The Fall of Yugoslavia: The Third Balkan War 238 (1994); see also Susan L. Woodward, Balkan Tragedy: Chaos and Dissolution after the Cold War 187–88 (1995).

20. The German foreign minister also noted that the right of self-determination occupied a central place in the CSCE Charter of Paris. See Hacke at 490.

21. Glenny at 163, 191; see also Hacke at 491.

22. Glenny at 191.

23. Id.; see also id. at 237.

24. "The death sentence for Bosnia-Hercegovina was passed in the middle of December 1991 when Germany announced that it would recognize Slovenia and Croatia unconditionally on 15 January 1992." Id. at 163. After considerable discussion, the other European Community leaders reluctantly decided to follow Germany in this move, rather than to take a divided position on this foreign policy matter. Hacke at 491–92.

25. Glenny at 163. The British diplomat, Lord Carrington, had also issued a similar warning. Hacke at 491; Woodward at 183–84; but see Hans-Dietrich Genscher, Erinnerungen 964–65 (1995).

26. For a former chancellor's criticism of the German recognition of Croatia and other assertive foreign policy moves of the post-unification period, see Helmut Schmidt, Handeln für Deutschland 203–6 (1994). According to Schmidt, an "unpleasant combination of inner weakness and a craving for importance vis-à-vis the outside world affords a foretaste of a development that is feared by many of our neighbors." Id. at 206. See also Woodward at 187: "the more assertive [the Germans] became [about Yugoslavia], the more fears they aroused that the old habits of *Gross Deutschland* had not died."

In contrast, however, former German Foreign Minister Genscher has sharply rejected such critical attacks. In his memoirs Genscher denies that Germany pressured other European states to recognize Croatia and argues, in addition, that recognition did not contribute to the war in Bosnia-Herzegovina. See Genscher at 927–68.

27. See Chs. 17 & 19.

28. Linnenkamp, The Security Policy of the New Germany, in Paul B. Stares (ed.), The New Germany and the New Europe 117 (1992) (hereafter, The New Germany and the New Europe); Müller, German Foreign Policy after Unification, in id. at 139. For a skeptical view of this argument, see Ruehl, Limits of Leadership: Germany, in From Occupation to Cooperation at 108–9.

29. See Müller in The New Germany and the New Europe at 136–37; Fach & Ringwald, Curing Germany, Saving Europe, Telos, Winter 1991–92, at 89, 95–96. In addition to these constitutional considerations, the German foreign minister also believed that military participation in the Gulf War could imperil Soviet ratification of the Two Plus Four Treaty, which was still pending in January 1991. See Genscher at 907–8.

30. See generally Hacke at 474–84.

31. See, e.g., Kriele, Nochmals: Auslandseinsätze der Bundeswehr, 1994 ZRP 103; Kaiser, Patterns of Partnership, in From Occupation to Cooperation at 170–71.

32. Kriele, 1994 ZRP at 103–4. Indeed, differences on the use of forces led to a sharp dispute between the FDP and CDU within the governing coalition. Hacke at 516.

33. See generally Müller in The New Germany and the New Europe at 139–42.

34. See Security Council Resolution 713, of Sept. 25, 1991; Resolution 724, of Dec. 15, 1991; and Resolution 757, of May 30, 1992. These resolutions were issued pursuant to Chapter VII of the UN Charter.

35. See generally 90 BVerfGE 286, 305–9 (1994). For the main points of the government's response in the Constitutional Court, see FAZ, Apr. 24, 1993, at 4 col. 4 (briefs of Professors Isensee and Randelzhofer).

36. Security Council Resolution 816, of Mar. 31, 1993. This resolution extended existing Security Council Resolution 781, of Oct. 9, 1992, which prohibited the flight of military aircraft only. See 88 BVerfGE 173, 174–75 (1993).

37. See 88 BVerfGE at 181. Accordingly, the UN secretary general placed great importance on the participation of German personnel in these measures.

38. 88 BVerfGE 173. Avoiding a decision on the merits, the Court decided that more immediate damage would be occasioned by withdrawing the AWACS troops than by leaving them there pending the outcome of the controversy.

39. See FAZ, Apr. 13, 1993, at 1 col. 2. At the same time at least two voices were heard from within the CDU and CSU, calling for the participation of German fighter planes in these measures as well. Id. at 2 col. 6.

40. In "UNOSOM II," the UN sought to distribute aid to a famine-stricken population in Somalia and to maintain appropriate conditions for the distribution. Authorized by Security Council Resolution 814, of Mar. 26, 1993, UNOSOM II followed earlier Security Council Resolutions 751 and 794, issued in 1992. See 89 BVerfGE 38, 39–40 (1993).

41. 89 BVerfGE at 40–41.

42. FAZ, Apr. 22, 1993, at 1 col. 2. See FAZ, June 8, 1993, at 1 col. 2.

43. FAZ, Apr. 22, 1993, at 3 col. 3.

44. 89 BVerfGE at 41.

45. According to the Court, if a later decision on the merits was to require parliamentary approval for the Somalia venture, the prior sending of the troops—without a parliamentary decision—would unfairly place the Bundestag under pressure to grant that approval. 89 BVerfGE at 45; see generally Riedel, Die Entscheidung über eine Beteiligung der Bundeswehr an militärischen Operationen der UNO, 1993 DÖV 994.

46. 90 BVerfGE at 313.

47. Article 87a GG was added to the Basic Law in a general revision of emergency provisions that took place in 1968. It replaced an earlier section that had been added in 1956. See Thalmair, Die Bundeswehr im Ausland—eine offene Verfassungsrechtsfrage?, 1993 ZRP 201, 203.

48. Art. 87a(2) GG (emphasis added). Article 87a(3)–(4) then provides express authorization for the use of troops within the Federal Republic in the case of certain emergencies, including the necessity of protecting the "free democratic basic order."

49. See generally, e.g., Bähr, Verfassungsmäßigkeit des Einsatzes der Bundeswehr im Rahmen der Vereinten Nationen, 1994 ZRP 97, 99–100; Fibich, Auslandseinsätze der Bundeswehr, 1993 ZRP 5, 6–7.

50. Cf., e.g., Bähr, 1994 ZRP at 100–101; Fibich, 1993 ZRP at 6.

51. See, e.g., Stein, Die verfassungsrechtliche Zulässigkeit einer Beteiligung der Bundesrepublik Deutschland an Friedenstruppen der Vereinten Nationen, in Joachim Abr. Frowein & Torsten Stein (eds.), Rechtliche Aspekte einer Beteiligung der Bundesrepublik Deutschland an Friedenstruppen der Vereinten Nationen 17 (1990).

52. See, e.g., Bähr, 1994 ZRP at 97–98.

53. 90 BVerfGE 286.

54. Art. 24(2) GG (emphasis added); see 90 BVerfGE at 345–55.

55. 90 BVerfGE at 349–51. In holding that NATO was a system of mutual collective security under article 24(2), the Court decided a question that it had left open in its Pershing Rockets decision of 1984. See 68 BVerfGE 1. In contrast, it has been vigorously argued that NATO was not intended to exercise the broad peace-keeping powers of a "collective *security* system" under article 24(2), but rather that it was authorized

only to exercise the narrower military powers of collective *self-defense*. See Lutz, Seit dem 12. Juli 1994 ist die NATO ein System kollektiver Sicherheit!, 1994 NJ 505.

56. 90 BVerfG at 357–72. The Court reached this specific conclusion by an evenly divided 4–4 vote; in such a case, the side favoring the constitutionality of a challenged measure prevails. The four judges opposing constitutionality argued that because the original idea of the NATO and WEU treaties was the defense of the members' territory, the recent actions outside of that territory—accompanied by numerous joint proclamations of the member states—represent such a significant change that new parliamentary approval of the policy was required under article 59(2) GG. See 90 BVerfGE at 372–78.

57. 90 BVerfGE at 378–81.

58. Id. at 355–57. For a critical view of this argument, see Bähr, 1994 ZRP at 102–3. See also Lutz, 1994 NJ 505 (suggesting that article 24[2] did not imply any authorization of the use of troops because when the Basic Law was adopted in 1949, West Germany had no armed forces and no provision for the military in its constitution).

59. 90 BVerfGE at 381–90. Legislative approval is not required, however, in the case of "assistance projects" abroad where German soldiers are not included in armed units. Id. at 388.

60. Id. at 382.

61. Id. at 387–88. The Court also suggested that the respective powers of the Bundestag and the executive in this area could be regulated in advance by general statute. Such an enactment could serve a function similar to that intended in the United States by the framers of the War Powers Act, 50 U.S.C. §§ 1541–1548, but—in light of the Court's opinion—with substantially more solid political and constitutional acceptance than the American War Powers Act has yet received.

62. FAZ, July 23, 1994, at 1 col. 2. The opposition SPD also supported the resolution approving these ventures.

63. But a period of tenuous parliamentary control did indeed follow the election of November 19, 1994. In the new Bundestag, the CDU/CSU/FDP coalition was able to re-elect Chancellor Kohl with only the most narrow of margins.

In more recent developments, however, the Bundestag voted by a substantial amount—including some SPD members—to approve a government plan to furnish "Tornado" fighter-bomber and reconnaissance aircraft and other assistance to a French-British "fast reaction force" in the former Yugoslavia. FAZ, July 1, 1995, at 1 col. 2. In accordance with this authorization, German aircraft flew reconnaissance flights over Bosnia in September 1995, "[r]isking combat for the first time since World War II." New York Times, Sept. 2, 1995, at 2 col. 3. In December 1995, moreover, the Bundestag overwhelmingly approved the deployment of 4,000 German ground troops to assist in supporting a peace agreement in Bosnia-Herzegovina. FAZ, Dec. 7, 1995, at 1 col. 2.

## Chapter 23
## The Unification of Germany and the Unification of Europe: European Community and European Union

1. These communities were then merged into a common structure in 1965. See Davidson, The Treaty on European Union or a Guided Tour of Maastricht, 5 Canterbury Law Review 102, 103–4 (1992). As discussed below, the European Union—a structure that includes the communities—was created by the Maastricht Treaty in 1992.

2. See Gregory F. Treverton, America, Germany, and the Future of Europe 92–118 (1992).

3. Id. As the Warsaw Pact was created in response to the formation of NATO, the east bloc formed a trading association (CMEA) in order to respond to western Marshall Plan aid. See Giegerich, The European Dimension of German Reunification: East Germany's Integration into the European Communities, 51 ZaöRV 384, 389–92 (1991). But because of its economic weakness, this eastern trading organization played a less important role in economic life than did the Warsaw Pact in the military sphere.

4. Hans Schauer, Europa der Vernunft: Kritische Anmerkungen nach Maastricht 26–27 (1993). See generally David P. Currie, The Constitution of the Federal Republic of Germany 92–94 (1994).

5. See, e.g., Helmut Schmidt, Handeln für Deutschland 192–93, 217 (1994). See generally Giegerich, 51 ZaöRV at 385–87; Eveling, Überlegungen zur Struktur der Europäischen Union und zum neuen Europa-Artikel des Grundgesetzes, 1993 DVBl 936, 937–38.

6. See, e.g., 2 Ingo von Münch (ed.), Grundgesetz-Kommentar art. 24, No. 2 (1983); Stern, Der Staatsvertrag im völkerrechtlichen und verfassungsrechtlichen Kontext, in 1 Klaus Stern & Bruno Schmidt-Bleibtreu (eds.), Verträge und Rechtsakte zur Deutschen Einheit 14–16 (1990).

7. Giegerich, 51 ZaöRV at 397; 73 BVerfGE 339 (1986).

8. See, e.g., Grabitz & von Bogdandy, Deutsche Einheit und europäische Integration, 1990 NJW 1073, 1076.

9. See Randelzhofer, Deutsche Einheit und europäische Integration, 49 VVDStRL 101, 112–13 (1990); cf. Sedemund, Deutsche Einheit und EG, 1990 EuZW 11, 12.

10. See Tomuschat, A United Germany within the European Community, 27 Common Market Law Review 415, 424–25 (1990).

11. Protokoll über den innerdeutschen Handel und die damit zusammenhängenden Fragen, of Mar. 25, 1957, BGBl II 984. For commentary, see Beise, Deutsche Einheit und Europäische Integration, in Thomas Oppermann & Erich-Wolfgang Moersch (eds.), Europa-Leitfaden: Ein Wegweiser zum Europäischen Binnenmarkt 1992, at 206–8 (1990).

12. See, e.g., Beise in Oppermann & Moersch at 213–14; Sedemund, 1990 EuZW at 11–12. The European Council decided on April 28, 1990 that German unification could occur without amendment of the EEC Treaty. Schmidt-Bleibtreu, Der Vertrag über die Schaffung einer Währungs-, Wirtschafts- und Sozialunion zwischen der Bundesrepublik Deutschland und der Deutschen Demokratischen Republik, 1990 DtZ 138, 141.

If German unification had occurred with the adoption of a new, all-German constitution under article 146 of the Basic Law, the problems might have been more difficult. Under those circumstances, the resulting entity may not have been viewed as the continuing Federal Republic but rather as a new all-German state. But see Ch. 6. In that case, perhaps, the new entity could have assumed the role of the Federal Republic in the EEC, under the doctrine of state "succession." If not, the new entity would presumably have had to apply for membership under article 237 of the EEC Treaty. See, e.g., Randelzhofer, 49 VVDStRL at 115–17.

In any case, EC members "were eager to avoid an accession treaty for the GDR or for a newly constituted German state, since either would have required a renegotiation of the Treaty of Rome in the midst of difficult ongoing talks over the implementation of the Single European Act, not to mention [economic and monetary union] and political union." Anderson & Goodman, Mars or Minerva? A United Germany in a Post-Cold War Europe, in Robert O. Keohane et al. (eds.), After the Cold War 31 (1993) (hereafter, After the Cold War).

13. See generally Tomuschat, 27 Common Market Law Review at 426–27 (European Parliament); McCurdy, German Reunification: Historical and Legal Roots of Germany's Rapid Progress towards Unity, 22 New York University Journal of International Law & Politics 253, 307 n. 299 (1990).

14. Accordingly, the number of German representatives in the European Parliament was increased from eighty-one to ninety-nine. At the same time, the number of representatives of France, Great Britain, and Italy in the European Parliament was increased from eighty-one to eighty-seven. See Official Journal of the European Communities, No L 33/15 (Feb. 1, 1993).

15. See generally Rengeling, Das vereinte Deutschland in der Europäischen Gemeinschaft: Grundlagen zur Geltung des Gemeinschaftsrechts, 1990 DVBl 1307, 1309–11.

16. Article 10 of the Unification Treaty outlines the legal relationship between unified Germany and the European Communities. Article 10(1) extends the treaties of the European Communities to the territory of the former GDR, but article 10(2) notes that other EC measures will extend to that territory only insofar as EC law itself has not instituted special exceptions. See Ch. 10.

17. Indeed, representatives of the EC were present at treaty negotiations between the two German governments. Schäuble, Der Einigungsvertrag—Vollendung der Einheit Deutschlands in Freiheit, 1990 ZG 289, 301. Moreover, EC Commission President Jacques Delors played a crucial role, behind the scenes, in speeding the process of unification. Christian Hacke, Weltmacht wider Willen: Die Aussenpolitik der Bundesrepublik Deutschland 447–48 (1993).

18. State Treaty preamble, art. 11(3); Joint Protocol accompanying State Treaty, part A, art. I(1); see Ch. 7. See also The Community and German Unification: Implications of the Staatsvertrag, reprinted in The European Community and German Unification 20 (Bulletin of the European Communities Supp. 4/90).

19. The Community and German Unification, Communication presented by the Commission to the European Council on Aug. 22, 1990, reprinted in The European Community and German Unification 38 (Bulletin of the European Communities Supp. 4/90).

20. For an analysis of measures proposed by the Commission, see Carl, Die Gemeinschaft und die deutsche Einigung, 1990 EuZW 561.

21. See Schäuble, 1990 ZG at 301.

22. See Priebe, Die Beschlüsse des Rates zur Eingliederung der neuen deutschen Bundesländer in die Europäischen Gemeinschaften, 1991 EuZW 113. These measures replaced certain provisional regulations that had been in effect since October 3, 1990. Id. at 114 & n. 10.

23. See Hailbronner, Das vereinte Deutschland in der Europäischen Gemeinschaft, 1991 DtZ 321, 325–27.

24. Cf. Priebe, 1991 EuZW at 113–15.

25. Anderson & Goodman in After the Cold War at 32.

26. FAZ, May 5, 1993, at 5 col. 1.

27. See generally Horst Teltschik, 329 Tage: Innenansichten der Einigung 200 (1991); Murray, Major Actors in European Union, 10 European Studies Journal (No. 1–2) 79, 87 (1993).

28. See, e.g., Cameron, The 1992 Initiative: Causes and Consequences, in Alberta M. Sbragia (ed.), Euro-Politics: Institutions and Policymaking in the "New" European Community 67–71 (1992) (hereafter, Euro-Politics).

Some saw a similar danger in the feared loosening of Community institutions in response to pressures for association or membership from the new democracies of eastern Europe. In this view, a strong western community was made possible by the somewhat artificial exclusion of the weaker eastern economies from Europe after World War II as a result of the Cold War. Accordingly, premature inclusion of these economies would impair the binding economic and political strength of the Community and ultimately risk dangers of an independent German economic and political role. Bertram, Visions of Leadership: Germany, in Steven Muller & Gebhard Schweigler (eds.), From Occupation to Cooperation: The United States and United Germany in a Changing World Order 48–69 (1992).

29. Oppermann & Classen, Die EG vor der Europäischen Union, 1993 NJW 5, 11.

30. These sweeping economic measures were accompanied by certain less dramatic institutional changes such as a modest increase in the power of the European Parliament. See generally, Cameron in Euro-Politics at 23–24.

31. Treaty on European Union, of Feb. 7, 1992, 31 I.L.M. 247 (1992), art. G (25) at art. 104c (hereafter, TEU).

32. See Ress, Die Europäische Union und die neue juristische Qualität der Beziehungen zu den Europäischen Gemeinschaften, 1992 JuS 985, 987–89.

33. See Oppermann & Classen, 1993 NJW at 10–11; see also Cameron in Euro-Politics at 71–74. Yet the limited provisions on the European Parliament and joint foreign and security policy fell far short of the much more substantial shift of power to the EU that had been advocated by Chancellor Kohl in the treaty negotiations. See Hans-Peter Schwarz, Die Zentralmacht Europas: Deutschlands Rückkehr auf die Weltbühne 32–33 (1994).

34. See FAZ, May 18, 1993, at 3 col. 3.

35. FAZ, Dec. 3, 1992, at 1 col. 2.

36. See FAZ, Dec. 3, 1992, at 2 col. 4.

37. FAZ, Dec. 3, 1992, at 1 col. 2.

This requirement of Bundestag approval lies beyond the provisions of the treaty and would apply even if the treaty's conditions for commencement of the third stage had all been met. Accordingly, it has attracted the ire of some supporters of the Maastricht accord. Indeed, a former German chancellor suggested that this special German requirement might reveal "a touch of Wilhelmine arrogance." Helmut Schmidt, Was wird aus Deutschland?: Helmut Schmidt im Gespräch mit Eberhard Jäckel und Edzard Reuter 35–36 (1994). See also Schmidt, Handeln für Deutschland, at 205–6.

38. FAZ, May 18, 1993, at 2 col. 1.

39. In order to secure British assent, a protocol to the treaty also gives Great Britain the option of remaining outside the monetary union. See Harden, The Constitution of the European Union, 1994 Public Law 609, 617.

40. See, e.g., Kurt H. Biedenkopf, Einheit und Erneuerung: Deutschland nach dem Umbruch in Europa 324–25 (1994).

41. See generally Scholz, Grundgesetz und europäische Einigung, 1992 NJW 2593. See Ch. 10.

42. One state official declared, for example, that these changes achieve "a new political-constitutional quality in the relationship between the central government and the

states." FAZ, Nov. 28, 1992, at 4 col. 2 (Gerster [SPD], chair of the conference of Europe Ministers of the Länder).

43. See, e.g., Oppermann & Classen, 1993 NJW at 11.

44. See Scholz, 1992 NJW at 2593–94; Scholz, Europäische Union und deutscher Bundesstaat, 1993 NVwZ 817, 818–19.

45. The new article 23 appropriately filled the space occupied by the former article 23, which had authorized the GDR's "accession" to the Federal Republic and which was deleted from the Basic Law upon unification. See Chs. 6 & 10. Thus a provision furthering European unification replaced the provision that had effected German unification.

46. See generally, e.g., Schauer at 26–34.

47. See, e.g., Ress, 1992 JuS at 988–89.

48. See Scholz, 1992 NJW at 2598. The Maastricht Treaty did indeed strengthen the European Parliament to some extent. See Oppermann & Classen, 1993 NJW at 7–8.

49. When powers are shared by the European Community and the member states, the Community can act "only if and in so far as the objectives of the proposed action cannot be sufficiently achieved by the Member States and can therefore, by reason of the scale or effects of the proposed action, be better achieved by the Community." TEU art. G (5). The principle of subsidiarity does not apply to powers that lie within the exclusive competence of the Community. See generally Oppermann & Classen, 1993 NJW at 8; Scholz, 1992 NJW at 2599.

50. Compare, e.g., Carter v. Carter Coal Co., 298 U.S. 238 (1936), with Wickard v. Filburn, 317 U.S. 111 (1942); compare National League of Cities v. Usery, 426 U.S. 833 (1976), with Garcia v. San Antonio Metropolitan Transit Authority, 469 U.S. 528 (1985). See Weber, Zur künftigen Verfassung der Europäischen Gemeinschaft, 1993 JZ 325, 328; cf. Schauer at 39–40; Ress, 1992 JuS at 990. For an exhaustive analysis of the concept of subsidiarity, with American comparisons, see Bermann, Taking Subsidiarity Seriously: Federalism in the European Commmunity and the United States, 94 Columbia Law Review 331 (1994).

51. See Oppermann & Classen, 1993 NJW at 8; Schauer at 38–39; Schmidt, Handeln für Deutschland, at 215.

52. See, e.g., Foster, The German Constitution and E.C. Membership, 1994 Public Law 392, 395–96; Currie, The Constitution of the Federal Republic of Germany, at 95–98.

53. 37 BVerfGE 271 (1974); see also 52 BVerfGE 187 (1979). The European Court of Justice is the highest judicial organ of the European Community.

54. 73 BVerfGE 339, 374–88 (1986) ("Solange II").

55. TEU art. F(2); see Ress, 1992 JuS at 990.

56. Art. 23(1) GG.

57. For a thorough discussion, see Scholz, 1993 NVwZ at 821–22.

58. See generally id. at 819; Biedenkopf at 204–8.

59. Art. 23(5) GG.

60. Scholz, 1992 NJW at 2597–98. But article 23(5) GG also requires that, in this process, "the federal responsibility for the country as a whole is to be preserved," and a new statute seeks to provide a method for resolving differences that may arise under this provision. See Scholz, 1993 NVwZ at 823. Moreover, if the measure could have financial consequences for the federation, the approval of the federal government must be obtained. Art. 23(5) GG.

61. Art. 23(6); see Scholz, 1993 NVwZ at 823–24.

62. Schauer at 23–24. For broad criticism of the new article 23 GG, arguing that it serves little function and will obscure political responsibility and create delay, see Oppermann & Classen, 1993 NJW at 12. For general analysis, see Scholz, 1992 NJW 2593; Scholz, 1993 NVwZ 817.

In addition to the provisions of article 23 GG, an amendment of article 24 GG also authorizes the Länder to transfer their sovereign powers over matters of state concern to regional institutions near their borders; the federal government must approve such a transfer. Art. 24(1a) GG. Other new provisions authorize the Bundestag and Bundesrat to establish committees for the purpose of carrying out their powers relating to the European Union. Arts. 45, 52(3a) GG. Moreover, the federal government must promptly inform the legislative bodies of its plans relating to the European Union—a provision that recalls similar requirements imposed on the executive in certain constitutions of the new eastern Länder. Art. 23 (2) GG; see Ch. 9. Because of the complexity of the 1992 amendments, the parliament has enacted two statutes for the purpose of clarifying the relationships between the government and the Bundestag and between the states and the federation under these provisions. See Scholz, 1993 NVwZ at 822.

63. See Le Gloannec, The Implications of German Unification for Western Europe, in Paul B. Stares (ed.), The New Germany and the New Europe at 256 (1992); Scholz, 1993 NVwZ at 820; Oppermann & Classen, 1993 NJW at 9. For the background of the Maastricht currency union in the looser European currency system created in 1979, see Oppermann & Classen, 1993 NJW at 9; Schmidt, Handeln für Deutschland, at 226–27, 229.

The requirements of economic stability that are imposed as a condition for the currency union represent an important political decision. As one commentator remarked: "It will be apparent from this that the [Maastricht Treaty] largely entrenches a conservative view of public finances, and it is arguable that the guiding hand of the Chicago School of economics might be discerned in the formulation of the monetary principles which underpin the Community's structure." Davidson, 5 Canterbury Law Review at 114.

64. Although naturalization by law is also possible, it is generally very difficult as a practical matter.

65. 83 BVerfGE 37 (1990); 83 BVerfGE 60 (1990).

On this aspect of German constitutional doctrine, see, e.g., Winkler, Rebuilding of a Nation: The Germans before and after Unification, 123 Daedalus (No. 1) 107, 122–23 (1994):

> "There is, however, a historical burden linked to the German idea of nation, from which the Federal Republic has not freed itself. As defined in ARTICLE 116 of the Basic Law, the nation is an evolutionary community based on descent. . . . The traditional German conception of ethnic origin is still invoked today by those who deny naturalization to foreigners who have lived in Germany for decades and to their children who were born there, and thus refuse to acknowledge that Germany has become a country of immigrants. Xenophobia is nourished all too often by that ethnic, if not *völkisch*, idea of nation which has characterized German nationalism since the early nineteenth century."

See also Quint, Constitution-Making by Treaty in German Unification: A Comment on Arato, Elster, Preuss, and Richards, 14 Cardozo Law Review 691 (1993).

66. Cf. TEU art. G (C). On the other hand the Joint Commission of the Bundestag and the Bundesrat considering constitutional amendments failed to adopt an SPD proposal that the Basic Law be amended to extend local voting rights to *all* non-citizens

with a permanent residence in Germany. A majority of the commission favored the proposal, but it failed to achieve the requisite two-thirds approval. See Bericht der Gemeinsamen Verfassungskommission, Nov. 5, 1993, Bundestag Drucksache 12/6000, at 97–98.

67. Der Spiegel, 21/1993, at 25.

68. See generally FAZ, May 24, 1993, at 4 col. 1.

The "constitutionalizing" of these international issues in Germany drew some tart commentary from experienced observers. See, e.g., Schmidt, Was wird aus Deutschland?, at 36:

> "The Maastricht Treaty evoked national concerns in various European nations. Understandably. Three nations submitted the issue to a plebiscite. The Danes first said 'no,' and then later 'yes.' The French said 'yes' although it was close. A single member state let its judges decide on the 'yes' or the 'no.' Unbelievable! In three mature and grown-up democracies of Europe, the decision was made by the highest tribunal—that is, the people themselves. In Germany the decision was made by judges in Karlsruhe."

Actually, the quasi-judicial Constitutional Council also played an important role in this process in France. The council found that the Maastricht Treaty would be invalid in the absence of certain amendments to the French Constitution, and the amendments were then adopted in response to this decision. See Tomlinson, Reception of Community Law in France, 1 Columbia Journal of European Law 183, 192–94 (1995).

69. Ingo Winkelmann (ed.), Das Maastricht-Urteil des Bundesverfassungsgerichts vom 12. Oktober 1993, at 129–42 (1994) (brief of complainant in Constitutional Court). For discussion, see, e.g., Peter M. Huber, Maastricht—ein Staatsstreich? 22 (1993). See also Penski, Bestand nationaler Staatlichkeit als Bestandteil der Änderungsgrenzen in Art. 79 III GG, 1994 ZRP 192.

70. 89 BVerfGE 155 (1993).

71. Meessen, Maastricht nach Karlsruhe, 1994 NJW 549, 553–54.

72. As a preliminary matter, the Court found that the complainant—a German voter—could permissibly bring the action because the right to vote protected by article 38 GG includes protection of "the basic democratic content of this right." Moreover, the Basic Law prohibits a constitutional amendment that would so "empty out" the reality of democratic control of government that the democratic principle of article 20 GG—protected from amendment by article 79(3) GG—would be unduly infringed. 89 BVerfGE at 171–73. See, e.g., Meessen, 1994 NJW at 550–51.

73. 89 BVerfGE at 182–84.

74. Id. at 184.

75. Id. at 185.

76. Id. at 185–86.

77. Id. at 186.

78. Id.

79. Id. at 187.

80. Id. at 188.

In this passage, therefore, the Court "reserved the right to review legal instruments issued by the European Union with a view to determining whether or not they were compatible with the powers transferred. In other words the Community legal order is subject to the approval of the [Federal Constitutional Court]." Foster, 1994 Public Law at 404. This "watchman's role . . . as protector of the German Constitution even against measures of European law [sets] a completely new tone in the Court's jurisprudence on

European questions." Rupp, Maastricht und Karlsruhe, in Manfred Brunner (ed.), Kartenhaus Europa? 112–13 (1994).

This new doctrine reserving supreme authority in the German Constitutional Court has drawn criticism on the ground that it might impair the system of European law if the German court came to conclusions different from those reached by the European Court of Justice. See Meessen, 1994 NJW at 552–53. This doctrine could also "create the potential for a breach of Treaty obligations by the [Federal Constitutional Court] and thus Germany." Foster, 1994 Public Law at 408 (footnote omitted).

81. 89 BVerfGE at 189–91.

82. Id. at 191–207.

83. Id. at 192–93.

84. Id. at 194–99.

85. Id. at 202–4.

86. Id. at 204–5.

87. It is true that the European Central Bank will be insulated from parliamentary control, but that provision—permitted by article 88 GG—is an allowable restriction of democracy in order to protect a stable currency. 89 BVerfGE at 207–8.

88. 89 BVerfGE at 209–10.

89. Id. at 210–12.

90. Id. at 212.

91. 90 BVerfGE 286 (1994). See Ch. 22.

# GLOSSARY OF FREQUENTLY USED TERMS

| | |
|---|---|
| Bundesrat | House of parliament of the Federal Republic of Germany, representing the governments of the Länder. |
| Bundestag | Popularly elected house of parliament of the Federal Republic of Germany. |
| Bündnis 90 | Alliance of reform parties that led the 1989–90 revolution in the GDR. |
| CDU | Christlich Demokratische Union (Christian Democratic Union). The leading party in the coalition currently governing the Federal Republic of Germany. |
| CSCE | See OSCE. |
| CSU | Christlich Soziale Union (Christian Social Union). A counterpart and ally of the CDU, active only in Bavaria. |
| DSU | Deutsche Soziale Union (German Social Union). Conservative East German party allied with the CSU. |
| FDP | Freie Demokratische Partei (Free Democratic Party). Currently a coalition partner of the CDU/CSU. Though a relatively small party, the Free Democrats have for many years held the balance of power between the CDU and the SPD. |
| Greens | German political party which concentrated originally on ecological issues but has expanded its interests to cover all areas of politics. |
| Länder | The German states. Länder is the plural form; Land is the singular. |
| OSCE | Organization for Security and Cooperation in Europe (previously known as Conference on Security and Cooperation in Europe [CSCE]). |
| PDS | Partei des Demokratischen Sozialismus (Party of Democratic Socialism). Successor of the SED. |
| Round Table | Council of GDR parties and other groups that exercised a measure of control over the SED government in late 1989 and early 1990. |
| SED | Sozialistische Einheitspartei Deutschlands (Socialist Unity Party of Germany). The Communist Party of East Germany. In the course of the revolutionary events of 1989–90, it changed its name to SED-PDS (Party of Democratic Socialism) and then dropped the initials SED entirely. |
| SPD | Sozialdemokratische Partei Deutschlands (Social Democratic Party of Germany). Currently the main opposition party in Germany. |
| Stasi | Ministerium für Staatssicherheit (Ministry for State Security). The secret police of the GDR. |
| Volkskammer | Single-house parliament of the GDR. |

# LIST OF ABBREVIATIONS

Legal Sources

| | |
|---|---|
| BAG | Bundesarbeitsgericht (Federal Labor Court) |
| BAGE | Entscheidungen des Bundesarbeitsgerichts (Decisions of the Federal Labor Court) |
| BGBl | Bundesgesetzblatt (compilation of the laws of the Federal Republic of Germany) |
| BGH | Bundesgerichtshof (Federal Supreme Court) |
| BGHSt | Entscheidungen des Bundesgerichtshofes in Strafsachen (Decisions of the Federal Supreme Court in Criminal Matters) |
| BGHZ | Entscheidungen des Bundesgerichtshofes in Zivilsachen (Decisions of the Federal Supreme Court in Civil Matters) |
| BVerfGE | Entscheidungen des Bundesverfassungsgerichts (Decisions of the Federal Constitutional Court) |
| BVerwGE | Entscheidungen des Bundesverwaltungsgerichts (Decisions of the Federal Administrative Court) |
| EGBGB | Einführungsgesetz zum Bürgerlichen Gesetzbuche (Introductory Law for the Federal Civil Code) |
| EGStGB | Einführungsgesetz zum Strafgesetzbuch (Introductory Law for the Federal Criminal Code) |
| GBl DDR | Gesetzblatt der Deutschen Demokratischen Republik (compilation of the laws of the GDR) |
| GG | Grundgesetz für die Bundesrepublik Deutschland (Basic Law [Constitution] of the Federal Republic of Germany) |
| LAG | Landesarbeitsgericht (appellate court in labor matters) |
| LG | Landgericht (court of first instance in civil and criminal matters) |
| OLG | Oberlandesgericht (appellate court in civil and criminal matters) |
| OVG | Oberverwaltungsgericht (appellate court in administrative matters) |
| RT-Entwurf | Arbeitsgruppe "Neue Verfassung der DDR" des Runden Tisches, Verfassungsentwurf für die DDR (Round Table draft of a new constitution for the GDR) |
| StGB | Strafgesetzbuch (Criminal Code) of the Federal Republic of Germany |
| StGB-DDR | Strafgesetzbuch (Criminal Code) of the GDR |
| T.I.A.S. | Treaties and Other International Acts Series |
| U.N.T.S. | United Nations Treaty Series |
| U.S.T. | United States Treaties and Other International Agreements |
| Verf. Berlin | Verfassung von Berlin (Constitution of Berlin) |
| Verf. Berlin (Ost) | Verfassung von Berlin (Ost) (Constitution of East Berlin) |
| Verf. Br. | Verfassung des Landes Brandenburg (Constitution of Brandenburg) |
| Verf. DDR | Verfassung der DDR (Constitution of the GDR) |
| Verf. Hessen | Verfassung des Landes Hessen (Constitution of Hesse) |

| | |
|---|---|
| Verf. Meckl.-Vorp. | Verfassung des Landes Mecklenburg-Vorpommern (Constitution of Mecklenburg-Vorpommern) |
| Verf. Sachs. | Verfassung des Freistaates Sachsen (Constitution of Saxony) |
| Verf. Sachs.-Anh. | Verfassung des Landes Sachsen-Anhalt (Constitution of Saxony-Anhalt) |
| Verf. Schles.-Holst. | Verfassung des Landes Schleswig-Holstein (Constitution of Schleswig-Holstein) |
| Verf. Thür. | Verfassung des Freistaates Thüringen (Constitution of Thuringia) |
| VG | Verwaltungsgericht (court of first instance in administrative matters) |
| WRV | Verfassung des Deutschen Reichs (Weimarer Reichsverfassung; the Weimar Constitution) |

PERIODICALS

| | |
|---|---|
| AfP | Archiv für Presserecht |
| AöR | Archiv des öffentlichen Rechts |
| APuZ | Aus Politik und Zeitgeschichte (supplement to the weekly journal Das Parlament) |
| BB | Der Betriebs-Berater |
| DA | Deutschland-Archiv |
| DÖV | Die Öffentliche Verwaltung |
| DtZ | Deutsch-Deutsche Rechts-Zeitschrift |
| DVBl | Deutsches Verwaltungsblatt |
| EuGRZ | Europäische Grundrechte-Zeitschrift |
| EuZW | Europäische Zeitschrift für Wirtschaftsrecht |
| FAZ | Frankfurter Allgemeine Zeitung |
| FR | Frankfurter Rundschau |
| I.L.M. | International Legal Materials |
| JöR | Jahrbuch des öffentlichen Rechts der Gegenwart |
| JuS | Juristische Schulung |
| JZ | Juristenzeitung |
| KJ | Kritische Justiz |
| LKV | Landes- und Kommunalverwaltung |
| NJ | Neue Justiz |
| NJW | Neue Juristische Wochenschrift |
| NVwZ | Neue Zeitschrift für Verwaltungsrecht |
| RdA | Recht der Arbeit |
| RuP | Recht und Politik |
| StV | Strafverteidiger |
| ThürVBl | Thüringer Verwaltungsblätter |
| VBlBW | Verwaltungsblätter für Baden-Württemberg |
| VerwArch | Verwaltungsarchiv |
| VIZ | Zeitschrift für Vermögens- und Investitionsrecht |
| VVDStRL | Veröffentlichungen der Vereinigung der Deutschen Staatsrechtslehrer |
| ZaöRV | Zeitschrift für ausländisches öffentliches Recht und Völkerrecht |
| ZG | Zeitschrift für Gesetzgebung |
| ZRP | Zeitschrift für Rechtspolitik |

## *SELECT BIBLIOGRAPHY*


Ackerman, Bruce. 1992. The Future of Liberal Revolution. New Haven: Yale University Press.

Albrecht, Ulrich. 1992. Die Abwicklung der DDR. Opladen: Westdeutscher Verlag.

Alexy, Robert. 1993. Mauerschützen: Zum Verhältnis von Recht, Moral und Strafbarkeit. Göttingen: Vandenhoeck & Ruprecht.

Amelung, Martin, et al. 1991. Rehabilitierung und Kassation: Beseitigung von Justizunrecht in der DDR. Munich: C. H. Beck.

Bergmann-Pohl, Sabine. 1991. Abschied ohne Tränen: Rückblick auf das Jahr der Einheit. Berlin: Ullstein.

Bevans, Charles I. (ed.). 1969. Treaties and Other International Agreements of the United States of America, 1776–1949. Vol. 3. Department of State Publication 8484, Washington, D.C.

Biedenkopf, Kurt H. 1994. Einheit und Erneuerung: Deutschland nach dem Umbruch in Europa. Stuttgart: Deutsche Verlags-Anstalt.

Brouër, Dirk, Trimbach, Herbert, et al. 1995. Offene Vermögensfragen—ein Ratgeber. Reinbek bei Hamburg: Rowohlt Taschenbuch Verlag.

Brunner, Georg, et al. (eds.). 1985. Sowjetsystem und Ostrecht. Festschrift für Boris Meissner zum 70. Geburtstag. Berlin: Duncker & Humblot.

Childs, David. 1988. The GDR: Moscow's German Ally. 2d ed. London: Unwin Hyman.

Christ, Peter, & Neubauer, Ralf. 1991. Kolonie im eigenen Land. Berlin: Rowohlt Berlin.

Clay, Lucius D. 1950. Decision in Germany. Garden City, N.Y.: Doubleday.

Currie, David P. 1994. The Constitution of the Federal Republic of Germany. Chicago: University of Chicago Press.

Dahrendorf, Ralf. 1992. Betrachtungen über die Revolution in Europa. Bergisch Gladbach: Bastei Lübbe.

Flug, Martin. 1992. Treuhand-Poker: Die Mechanismen des Ausverkaufs. Berlin: Ch. Links Verlag.

Försterling, Wolfram. 1993. Recht der offenen Vermögensfragen. Munich: C. H. Beck.

Furian, Gilbert. 1992. Der Richter und sein Lenker: Politische Justiz in der DDR. Berlin: Verlag Das Neue Berlin.

Garton Ash, Timothy. 1990. The Uses of Adversity: Essays on the Fate of Central Europe. New York: Vintage Books.

———. 1993. In Europe's Name: Germany and the Divided Continent. New York: Random House.

Gauck, Joachim. 1991. Die Stasi-Akten. Reinbek bei Hamburg: Rowohlt Taschenbuch Verlag.

Gaus, Günter. 1990. Deutsche Zwischentöne: Gesprächs-Porträts aus der DDR. Hamburg: Hoffmann und Campe.

Genscher, Hans-Dietrich. 1995. Erinnerungen. Berlin: Siedler Verlag.

Gill, David, & Schröter, Ulrich. 1993. Das Ministerium für Staatssicherheit: Anatomie des Mielke-Imperiums. Reinbek bei Hamburg: Rowohlt Taschenbuch Verlag.

Glaeßner, Gert-Joachim (ed.). 1993. Der lange Weg zur Einheit. Berlin: Dietz Verlag.

Glenny, Mischa. 1994. The Fall of Yugoslavia: The Third Balkan War. Rev. ed. New York: Penguin Books.

Guggenberger, Bernd, & Stein, Tine (eds.). 1991. Die Verfassungsdiskussion im Jahr der deutschen Einheit. Munich: Carl Hanser Verlag.

Hacke, Christian. 1993. Weltmacht wider Willen: Die Aussenpolitik der Bundesrepublik Deutschland. Rev. ed. Frankfurt am Main: Ullstein.

Hankel, Wilhelm. 1993. Die sieben Todsünden der Vereinigung. Berlin: Siedler Verlag.

Hardtwig, Wolfgang, & Winkler, Heinrich A. (eds.). 1994. Deutsche Entfremdung: Zum Befinden in Ost und West. Munich: C. H. Beck.

Havel, Václav. 1993. Summer Meditations. Translated by Paul Wilson. New York: Vintage Books.

Hénard, Jacqueline. 1993. Geschichte vor Gericht: Die Ratlosigkeit der Justiz. Berlin: Corso bei Siedler.

Henke, Klaus-Dietmar (ed.). 1993. Wann bricht schon mal ein Staat zusammen! Die Debatte über die Stasi-Akten auf dem 39. Historikertag 1992. Munich: Deutscher Taschenbuch Verlag.

Herles, Helmut, & Rose, Ewald (eds.). 1990. Vom Runden Tisch zum Parlament. Bonn: Bouvier Verlag.

Heym, Stefan. 1992. Filz: Gedanken über das neueste Deutschland. Munich: C. Bertelsmann Verlag.

Hickel, Rudolf, & Priewe, Jan. 1994. Nach dem Fehlstart: Ökonomische Perspektiven der deutschen Einigung. Frankfurt am Main: S. Fischer Verlag.

Hochhuth, Rolf. 1993. Wessis in Weimar: Szenen aus einem besetzten Land. Berlin: Verlag Volk & Welt.

Isensee, Josef (ed.). 1992. Vergangenheitsbewältigung durch Recht. Berlin: Duncker & Humblot.

James, Harold. 1994. A German Identity. London: Phoenix.

Jarausch, Konrad H. 1994. The Rush to German Unity. New York: Oxford University Press.

Kaiser, Karl. 1991. Deutschlands Vereinigung: Die internationalen Aspekte. Bergisch Gladbach: Bastei Lübbe.

Kampe, Dieter. 1993. Wer uns kennenlernt, gewinnt uns lieb: Nachruf auf die Treuhand. Berlin: Rotbuch Verlag.

Keohane, Robert O., et al. (eds.). 1993. After the Cold War. Cambridge, Mass.: Harvard University Press.

Kiessler, Richard, & Elbe, Frank. 1993. Ein runder Tisch mit scharfen Ecken: Der diplomatische Weg zur deutschen Einheit. Baden-Baden: Nomos.

Kimminich, Otto. 1990. Die Eigentumsgarantie im Prozeß der Wiedervereinigung. Frankfurt am Main: Landwirtschaftliche Rentenbank.

Kirchner, Emil J., & Sperling, James (eds.). 1992. The Federal Republic of Germany and NATO: 40 Years After. New York: St. Martin's Press.

Klein, Hans. 1991. Es begann im Kaukasus. Berlin: Ullstein.

Kohl, Helmut. 1992. Die deutsche Einheit: Reden und Gespräche. Bergisch Gladbach: Gustav Lübbe Verlag.

Kommers, Donald P. 1976. Judicial Politics in West Germany: A Study of the Federal Constitutional Court. Beverly Hills: Sage Publications.

———. 1989. The Constitutional Jurisprudence of the Federal Republic of Germany. Durham, N.C.: Duke University Press.

Kruse, Joachim von (ed.). 1988. Weißbuch über die "Demokratische Bodenreform" in der Sowjetischen Besatzungszone Deutschlands. Rev. ed. Munich: Verlag Ernst Vögel.

Kvitsinsky, Yuli A. 1993. Vor dem Sturm: Erinnerungen eines Diplomaten. Translated by Hilde Ettinger and Helmut Ettinger. Berlin: Siedler Verlag.

Leonhard, Wolfgang. 1990. Die Revolution entläßt ihre Kinder. Cologne: Kiepenheuer & Witsch.

Liebert, Ulrike, & Merkel, Wolfgang (eds.). 1991. Die Politik zur deutschen Einheit. Opladen: Leske + Budrich.

Liedtke, Rüdiger (ed.). 1993. Die Treuhand und die zweite Enteignung der Ostdeutschen. Munich: Edition Spangenberg.

Lüderssen, Klaus. 1992. Der Staat geht unter—das Unrecht bleibt? Regierungskriminalität in der ehemaligen DDR. Frankfurt am Main: Suhrkamp Verlag.

Luft, Christa. 1992. Zwischen WEnde und Ende. 2d ed. Berlin: Aufbau Taschenbuch Verlag.

Maaz, Hans Joachim. 1991. Das gestürzte Volk oder die verunglückte Einheit. Berlin: Argon Verlag.

Maleck, Bernhard. 1991. Wolfgang Ullmann: "Ich werde nicht schweigen." Berlin: Dietz Verlag.

Mampel, Siegfried. 1982. Die sozialistische Verfassung der Deutschen Demokratischen Republik. Frankfurt am Main: Alfred Metzner Verlag.

Mangoldt, Hans von. 1993. Die Verfassungen der neuen Bundesländer. Berlin: Duncker & Humblot.

Markovits, Inga. 1993. Die Abwicklung: Ein Tagebuch zum Ende der DDR-Justiz. Munich: C. H. Beck.

———. 1995. Imperfect Justice: An East-West German Diary. Oxford: Clarendon Press.

Mathiopoulos, Margarita. 1993. Das Ende der Bonner Republik. Stuttgart: Deutsche Verlags-Anstalt.

McAdams, A. James. 1985. East Germany and Detente: Building Authority after the Wall. Cambridge: Cambridge University Press.

McCauley, Martin. 1983. The German Democratic Republic since 1945. New York: St. Martin's Press.

Merkl, Peter H. 1963. The Origin of the West German Republic. New York: Oxford University Press.

———. 1993. German Unification in the European Context. University Park: Pennsylvania State University Press.

Modrow, Hans. 1991. Aufbruch und Ende. Hamburg: Konkret Literatur Verlag.

Müller, Michael, & Thierse, Wolfgang (eds.). 1992. Deutsche Ansichten: Die Republik im Übergang. Bonn: Dietz.

Muller, Steven, & Schweigler, Gebhard (eds.). 1992. From Occupation to Cooperation: The United States and United Germany in a Changing World Order. New York: W. W. Norton.

Münch, Ingo von (ed.). 1976. Dokumente des geteilten Deutschland. Vol. 1. Stuttgart: Alfred Kröner Verlag.

———. 1983. Grundgesetz-Kommentar. 2d ed. Vols. 2–3. Munich: C. H. Beck.

———. 1991. Dokumente der Wiedervereinigung Deutschlands. Stuttgart: Alfred Kröner Verlag.

Muszynski, Bernhard (ed.). 1993. Wissenschaftstransfer in Deutschland. Opladen: Leske + Budrich.

Nettl, J. P. 1951. The Eastern Zone and Soviet Policy in Germany 1945–50. London: Oxford University Press.

Pond, Elizabeth. 1993. Beyond the Wall: Germany's Road to Unification. Washington, D.C.: Brookings Institution.

Priewe, Jan, & Hickel, Rudolf. 1991. Der Preis der Einheit. Frankfurt am Main: Fischer Taschenbuch Verlag.

Reich, Jens. 1991. Rückkehr nach Europa: Zur neuen Lage der deutschen Nation. Munich: Carl Hanser Verlag.

Riecker, Ariane, et al. 1990. Stasi intim: Gespräche mit ehemaligen MfS-Angehörigen. Leipzig: Forum Verlag.

Ringer, Fritz K. 1990. The Decline of the German Mandarins: The German Academic Community, 1890–1933. Reprint ed. Hanover, N.H.: University Press of New England.

Roggemann, Herwig. 1989. Die DDR-Verfassungen: Einführung in das Verfassungsrecht der DDR. 4th ed. Berlin: Berlin Verlag Arno Spitz.

Sbragia, Alberta M. (ed.). 1992. Euro-Politics: Institutions and Policymaking in the "New" European Community. Washington, D.C.: Brookings Institution.

Schädlich, Hans Joachim (ed.). 1992. Aktenkundig. Berlin: Rowohlt Berlin Verlag.

Schäuble, Wolfgang. 1991. Der Vertrag: Wie ich über die deutsche Einheit verhandelte. Stuttgart: Deutsche Verlags-Anstalt.

Schauer, Hans. 1993. Europa der Vernunft: Kritische Anmerkungen nach Maastricht. Munich: Bonn Aktuelle.

Schmidt, Helmut. 1994. Handeln für Deutschland. Reinbek bei Hamburg: Rowohlt Taschenbuch Verlag.

———. 1994. Was wird aus Deutschland?: Helmut Schmidt im Gespräch mit Eberhard Jäckel und Edzard Reuter. Stuttgart: Deutsche Verlags-Anstalt.

Schorlemmer, Friedrich. 1992. Versöhnung in der Wahrheit. Munich: Knaur.

———. 1993. Bis alle Mauern fallen. Munich: Knaur.

———. 1993. Freiheit als Einsicht. Munich: Knaur.

———. 1994. Zu seinem Wort stehen. Munich: Kindler Verlag.

Schramm, Hilde (ed.). 1993. Hochschule im Umbruch. Berlin: BasisDruck Verlag.

Schröder, Richard. 1993. Deutschland schwierig Vaterland. Freiburg im Breisgau: Verlag Herder.

Shevardnadze, Eduard. 1993. Die Zukunft gehört der Freiheit. Translated by Informationsagentur Nowosti. Reinbek bei Hamburg: Rowohlt Taschenbuch Verlag.

Shklar, Judith N. 1964. Legalism: Law, Morals, and Political Trials. Cambridge, Mass.: Harvard University Press.

Sinn, Gerlinde, & Sinn, Hans-Werner. 1992. Jumpstart: The Economic Unification of Germany. Cambridge, Mass.: MIT Press.

Sowden, J. K. 1975. The German Question 1945–1973. New York: St. Martin's Press.

Stares, Paul B. (ed.). 1992. The New Germany and the New Europe. Washington, D.C.: Brookings Institution.

Stern, Klaus (ed.). 1991–93. Deutsche Wiedervereinigung: Die Rechtseinheit. Vols. I-IV. Cologne: Carl Heymanns Verlag.

Stern, Klaus, & Schmidt-Bleibtreu, Bruno (eds.). 1990–91. Verträge und Rechtsakte zur Deutschen Einheit. Vols. 1–3. Munich: C. H. Beck.

Süssmuth, Rita, & Schubert, Helga. 1992. Bezahlen die Frauen die Wiedervereinigung? Munich: Piper.

Szabo, Stephen F. 1992. The Diplomacy of German Unification. New York: St. Martin's Press.

Teltschik, Horst. 1991. 329 Tage: Innenansichten der Einigung. Berlin: Siedler Verlag.

Thaysen, Uwe. 1990. Der Runde Tisch. Oder: Wo blieb das Volk? Opladen: Westdeutscher Verlag

Thierse, Wolfgang. 1992. Mit eigener Stimme sprechen. Munich: Piper.

Treverton, Gregory F. 1992. America, Germany, and the Future of Europe. Princeton: Princeton University Press.

Turner, Henry Ashby, Jr. 1992. Germany from Partition to Reunification. New Haven: Yale University Press.

Ullmann, Wolfgang. 1992. Verfassung und Parlament. Berlin: Dietz Verlag.

Verheyen, Dirk, & Søe, Christian (eds.). 1993. The Germans and Their Neighbors. Boulder, Colo.: Westview Press.

Weber, Hermann. 1985. Geschichte der DDR. Munich: Deutscher Taschenbuch Verlag.

———. 1991. DDR: Grundriß der Geschichte. Hannover: Fackelträger.

Weizsäcker, Richard von. 1993. Von Deutschland nach Europa. Berlin: Goldmann Verlag.

Wesel, Uwe. 1994. Der Honecker-Prozeß: Ein Staat vor Gericht. Frankfurt am Main: Eichborn.

Woodward, Susan L. 1995. Balkan Tragedy: Chaos and Dissolution after the Cold War. Washington, D.C.: Brookings Institution.

Worst, Anne. 1991. Das Ende eines Geheimdienstes. Berlin: LinksDruck Verlag.

Zelikow, Philip, & Rice, Condoleezza. 1995. Germany Unified and Europe Transformed. Cambridge, Mass.: Harvard University Press.

Zwahr, Hartmut. 1993. Ende einer Selbstzerstörung: Leipzig und die Revolution in der DDR. Göttingen: Vandenhoeck & Ruprecht.

# *I N D E X*

About the author

PETER E. QUINT is Jacob A. France Professor of Constitutional Law at the University of Maryland School of Law.

3 5282 00425 6841